EARLY MEDIEVAL MONETARY HISTORY

Studies in Early Medieval Britain and Ireland

Series editors:

Joanna E. Story, University of Leicester, UK,
Roy Flechner, University College Dublin, Ireland

Studies in Early Medieval Britain and Ireland illuminates the history of Britain and Ireland from the start of the fifth century to the establishment of French-speaking aristocracies in the eleventh and twelfth centuries, for historians, archaeologists, philologists and literary and cultural scholars. It explores the origins of British society, of communities, and political, administrative and ecclesiastical institutions. It was in the early middle ages that the English, Welsh, Scots and Irish defined and distinguished themselves in language, customs and territory and the successive conquests and settlements lent distinctive Anglo-Saxon, Scandinavian and Norman elements to the British ethnic mix. Royal dynasties were established and the landscape took a form that can still be recognised today; it was then too that Christian churches were established with lasting results for our cultural, moral, legal and intellectual horizons.

Studies in Early Medieval Britain and Ireland reveals these roots and makes them accessible to a wide readership of scholars, students and lay people.

Other titles in the series

Bede and the Future
Edited by Peter Darby and Faith Wallis

Heaven and Earth in Anglo-Saxon England
Theology and Society in an Age of Faith
Helen Foxhall Forbes

Bede and the End of Time
Peter Darby

Women's Names in Old English
Elisabeth Okasha

Early Medieval Monetary History

Studies in Memory of Mark Blackburn

Edited by

RORY NAISMITH
University of Cambridge, UK

MARTIN ALLEN
Fitzwilliam Museum, Cambridge

ELINA SCREEN
University of Oxford, UK

Routledge
Taylor & Francis Group

LONDON AND NEW YORK

First published 2014 by Ashgate Publishing

2 Park Square, Milton Park, Abingdon, Oxfordshire OX14 4RN
52 Vanderbilt Avenue, New York, NY 10017

Routledge is an imprint of the Taylor & Francis Group, an informa business

First issued in paperback 2020

British Library Cataloguing in Publication Data
A catalogue record for this book is available from the British Library

The Library of Congress has cataloged the printed edition as follows:
Early Medieval Monetary History: Studies in Memory of Mark Blackburn /
    edited by Rory Naismith, Martin Allen and Elina Screen.
        pages   cm. – (Studies in Early Medieval Britain and Ireland)
    Includes index.
    Festschrift for Dr Mark Blackburn.
    1. Money – Europe – History – To 1500. 2. Economic history – Medieval, 500-1500.
    3. Commerce – History – Medieval, 500-1500. I. Naismith, Rory, compiler of edition.
    II. Allen, Martin (Martin R.) compiler of edition. III. Screen, Elina, compiler of edition.
    HG243.E27 2014
    332.4'940902–dc23   2014013555

ISBN 13: 978-1-4094-5668-1 (hbk)
ISBN 13: 978-0-367-59999-7 (pbk)

Contents

List of Colour Plates

The colour plates fall between pages 382 and 383

List of Figures

Unless otherwise stated, all coins are illustrated at life size except for the *sceattas* in chapter 7, which are illustrated at 1.5 times life size.

List of Tables

Abbreviations

AASS	*Acta sanctorum quotquot in orbe coluntur*, ed. J. Bolland et al. (67 vols, Antwerp and Brussels, 1643–)
Adelson	H.L. Adelson, *Light Weight Solidi and Byzantine Trade during the Sixth and Seventh Centuries*, ANS Numismatic Notes and Monographs, 138 (New York, 1957)
Allen	M. Allen, *Mints and Money in Medieval England* (Cambridge, 2012), Appendix E
ANS	American Numismatic Society
ASC	*Anglo-Saxon Chronicle*
ASE	*Anglo-Saxon England*
ASFN	*Annuaire de la Société française de numismatique*
ASMH	M. Blackburn (ed.), *Anglo-Saxon Monetary History: Essays in Memory of Michael Dolley* (Leicester, 1986)
ASSAH	*Anglo-Saxon Studies in Archaeology and History*
A&W	R.A. Abdy and G. Williams, 'A catalogue of hoards and single finds from the British Isles *c.* AD 410–675', in *Coinage and History in the North Sea World, c. AD 500–1250: Essays in Honour of Marion Archibald*, ed. B. Cook and G. Williams (Leiden, 2006), 11–74
BAR	British Archaeological Reports
BCEN	*Bulletin du Centre d'Études numismatiques* (Brussels)
BEH	B.E. Hildebrand, *Anglosachsiska mynt i Svenska Kongliga Myntkabinett: funna i Sveriges jord*, 2nd edn (Stockholm, 1881)
Biddle	M. Biddle (ed.), *The Winchester Mint, and Coins and Related Finds from the Excavations of 1961–71*, Winchester Studies, 8 (Oxford, 2012)

B&L	R. Bland and R.X. Loriot, *Roman and Early Byzantine Gold Coins found in Britain and Ireland, with an Appendix on Coin Finds from Gaul*, RNS Special Publication, 46 (London, 2010)
BMC	C.F. Keary and H.A. Grueber, *A Catalogue of English Coins in the British Museum: Anglo-Saxon Series* (2 vols, London, 1887–93) G.C. Brooke, *A Catalogue of English Coins in the British Museum. The Norman Kings*, 2 vols (London, 1916)
BNC	C. Morrisson, *Catalogue des monnaies byzantines de la Bibliothèque nationale* (2 vols, Paris, 1970)
BNJ	*British Numismatic Journal*
BNS	British Numismatic Society
Brooke	G.C. Brooke, *A Catalogue of English Coins in the British Museum. The Norman Kings*, 2 vols (London, 1916)
BSFN	*Bulletin de la société française de numismatique*
CBA	Council for British Archaeology
CGB	Compagnie générale de bourse
Checklist	M. Blackburn and H. Pagan, 'A revised checklist of coin hoards from the British Isles *c*.500–1100', in *ASMH*, 291–313; an updated version is maintained at <www.fitzmuseum. cam.ac.uk/dept/coins/projects/hoards/>
CNI	V.E. Di Savoia et al., *Corpus Nummorum Italicorum* (20 vols, Rome, 1910–43)
CNS	*Corpus nummorum saeculorum IX–XI qui in Suecia reperti sunt. Catalogue of Coins from the Viking Age Found in Sweden* (9 vols, Stockholm, 1975–2010)
Comm. 1	*Commentationes de nummis saeculorum IX–XI in Suecia repertis, 1.* Kungl. Vitterhets Historie och Antikvitets Akademiens Handlingar. Antikvariska serien, 9 (Stockholm, 1961)
2	*Commentationes de nummis saeculorum IX–XI in Suecia repertis, 2.* Kungl. Vitterhets Historie och Antikvitets Akademiens Handlingar. Antikvariska serien, 19 (Stockholm, 1968)

n.s.	*Commentationes de nummis saeculorum IX–XI in Suecia repertis, nova series*
CR	Coin Register (printed annually in *BNJ* since 1987)
CTCE	C.E. Blunt, B.H.I.H. Stewart and C.S.S. Lyon, *Coinage in Tenth-Century England, from Edward the Elder to Edgar's Reform* (Oxford, 1989)
Dbg	H. Dannenberg, *Die deutschen Münzen der sächsischen und fränkischen Kaiserzeit*, 4 vols (Berlin, 1876–1905)
EcHR	*Economic History Review*
EHD 1	*English Historical Documents, vol. 1: c. 500–1042*, ed. D. Whitelock (2nd edn, London, 1979)
EHR	*English Historical Review*
EMC	Corpus of Early Medieval Coin Finds (Fitzwilliam Museum, Cambridge: <www.fitzmuseum.cam.ac.uk/coins/emc/>)
EME	*Early Medieval Europe*
GDR	*gratia Dei rex*
Hbg	P. Hauberg, *Myntforhold og udmyntninger i Danmark indtil 1146* (Copenhagen, 1900)
Inventory	J.D.A. Thompson, *Inventory of British Coin Hoards, AD 600–1500*, RNS Special Publication 1 (London, 1956)
JMP	*Jaarboek voor Munt- en Penningkunde*
Laf-M	J. Lafaurie and C. Morrisson, 'La pénétration des monnaies byzantines en Gaule mérovingienne et visigotique du VIe au VIIIe siècle', *RN, 6th series, 29* (1987), 38–98
Malmer	B. Malmer, *The Anglo-Scandinavian Coinage, c. 995–1020*, Comm. n.s. 9 (Stockholm, 1997)
MEC 1	P. Grierson and M. Blackburn, *Medieval European Coinage, with a Catalogue of the Coins in the Fitzwilliam Museum, Cambridge, vol. 1: the Early Middle Ages (5th–10th Centuries)* (Cambridge, 1986)

	6	M. Crusafont, A.M. Balaguer and P. Grierson, *Medieval European Coinage, with a Catalogue of the Coins in the Fitzwilliam Museum, Cambridge,* vol. 6: *the Iberian Peninsula* (Cambridge, 2013)
MG		K.F. Morrison and H. Grunthal, *Carolingian Coinage*, ANS Numismatic Notes and Monographs, 158 (New York, 1967)
MGH		Monumenta Germaniae Historica
	Capit.	Capitularia regum Francorum
	DD Kar.	Diplomata Karolinorum
	SS	Scriptores
	SSRG	Scriptores rerum Germanicarum separatim editi
MIB		W. Hahn, *Moneta Imperii Byzantini: Rekonstruktion des Prägeaufbaues auf Synoptisch-Tabellarischer Grundlage,* vol. 3: *von Heraclius bis Leo III* (Vienna, 1981)
MIBE		W. Hahn and M.A. Metlich, *Money of the Incipient Byzantine Empire: Anastasius I– Justinian I (491–565)* (Vienna, 2000)
MIBEC		W. Hahn and M.A. Metlich, *Money of the Incipient Byzantine Empire Continued: Justin II–Revolt of the Heraclii, 565–610* (Vienna, 2009)
Mossop		H.R. Mossop. *The Lincoln Mint c. 890–1279* (Newcastle upon Tyne, 1970)
N		J.J. North, *English Hammered Coinage,* vol. I: *Early Anglo-Saxon to Henry III c. 600–1272,* 3rd ed. (London, 1994)
NC		*Numismatic Chronicle*
NCirc		(Spink's) *Numismatic Circular*
NMI		National Museum of Ireland, Dublin
NNÅ		*Nordisk Numismatisk Årskrift*
NNF-Nytt		*Norsk Numismatisk Tidsskrift – Nytt*
NNUM		*Nordisk Numismatisk Unions Medlemsblad*
NUMIS		Numismatic Information System, Geldmuseum, Utrecht (<www.numis.geldmuseum.nl/nl/zoek/numis>)

ODNB	H.C.G. Matthew and B. Harrison (ed.), *Oxford Dictionary of National Biography, from the Earliest Times to the Year 2000*, 61 vols (Oxford, 2004)
Pagan	H. Pagan, 'The *Pacx* type of Edward the Confessor', *BNJ, 81* (2011), 9–106
PAS	Portable Antiquities Scheme ()
PL	*Patrologiae cursus completus: series (latina) prima*, ed. J.P. Migne (221 vols, Paris, 1844–64)
RBN	*Revue belge de numismatique*
RN	*Revue numismatique*
RNS	Royal Numismatic Society
S	P.H. Sawyer, *Anglo-Saxon Charters: an Annotated List and Bibliography*, Royal Historical Society Guides and Handbooks, 8 (London, 1968)
SCBI	*Sylloge of Coins of the British Isles*
t.a.q.	*terminus ante quem*
Thompson	J.D.A. Thompson, *Inventory of British Coin Hoards A.D. 600–1500*, Royal Numismatic Society Special Publication 1 (London, 1956)
t.p.q.	*terminus post quem*
TRHS	*Transactions of the Royal Historical Society*
T&S	D.M. Metcalf, *Thrymsas and Sceattas in the Ashmolean Museum, Oxford*, RNS Special Publication 27 (3 vols, London, 1993–4)
VCCBI	M. Blackburn, *Viking Coinage and Currency in the British Isles*, ed. E. Screen and R. Naismith, BNS Special Publication, 7 (London, 2011)

Foreword

This book is the second to appear under the new series title, *Studies in Early Medieval Britain and Ireland* (*SEMBI*). This evolution of our title reflects an early medieval reality, since the cultural, intellectual, and political histories of the islands of Britain and Ireland between the fifth and twelfth centuries were closely linked. It also reflects the vibrance of contemporary, twenty first-century scholarship on the early middle ages; the augmented series title offers a new publishing opportunity for academic books that focus on early medieval Ireland as well as those that explore the lives and ideas of the peoples who lived in the island of Britain in the medieval centuries before AD 1100, and the connections of all these people and places with the wider world. The move to *Studies in Early Medieval Britain and Ireland* was enthusiastically welcomed by Professor Nicholas Brooks, the founding editor of the series, who always intended it to be a vehicle for the publication of ground-breaking scholarship – both monographs and edited collections – by new scholars as well as those with established academic reputations. He was keen for it to embrace all disciplines (including history, archaeology, numismatics, language, literature) that contribute to our knowledge of Britain in the long period between the collapse of Roman imperial authority and the establishment of French-speaking aristocracies in different areas in the eleventh and twelfth centuries, and for the focal length of published studies to extend beyond the boundaries of Anglo-Saxon England. The new series title gives the current editors an opportunity to extend his vision and to welcome proposals from scholars, old and new, for *Studies in Early Medieval Britain and Ireland*.

The book that follows is a tribute to one of the most influential scholars of early medieval Britain in recent decades. Mark Blackburn's contribution to the field of numismatics was profound, not least because he made his subject accessible, and in doing so introduced many non-numismatists to its significance. This was true not only for students of history and archaeology, who understood with his help that coins could reveal so much more than a date, but also for the general public who encountered coins through metal detecting and chance finds. Mark realised the potential of data from single finds recovered by metal detectorists to change the quality and quantity of the material record; over time this new class of information has revolutionised our knowledge and understanding of the monetary economies of early medieval Britain, and it paved the way for the development of other nationwide schemes to garner evidence from chance finds of metal artefacts and to share this new knowledge with the public.

Thirty scholars have contributed essays to this collection, which reflect the geographical and chronological range of Mark Blackburn's scholarship on early medieval monetary history. The essays gathered here centre on evidence from Anglo-Saxon and Anglo-Scandinavian England located firmly within its wider European setting, reaching out to Carolingian Francia, Viking Age Scandinavia, Ireland, Byzantium, Visigothic and Arab Spain. As such, the book exemplifies not only the goals of this series but also the gratitude of so many scholars of early medieval Europe for Mark's life and work.

JOANNA STORY
The University of Leicester

ROY FLECHNER
University College, Dublin

September 2014

Acknowledgement

The editors are grateful to the Department of Anglo-Saxon, Norse and Celtic in the University of Cambridge, and the Fitzwilliam Museum, Cambridge, for support towards the publication of this volume.

List of Contributors

Martin Allen is Senior Assistant Keeper in the Department of Coins and Medals at the Fitzwilliam Museum, Cambridge.

Marion M. Archibald is a former Assistant Keeper of early medieval coins in the Department of Coins and Medals at the British Museum.

Martin Biddle is Emeritus Professor of Archaeology at the University of Oxford, and Emeritus Fellow of Hertford College, Oxford, and an honorary Fellow of Pembroke College, Cambridge.

Kristin Bornholdt Collins has published extensively on the numismatic history of the Isle of Man.

Simon Coupland is a vicar in Kingston upon Thames, and has written extensively on Carolingian coinage and history.

Michael Cowell is a former researcher in the Department of Conservation and Scientific Research at the British Museum.

Allison Fox is Curator of Archaeology at Manx National Heritage.

Anna Gannon is an Affiliated Lecturer in History of Art at the University of Cambridge and Fellow of St Edmund's College, Cambridge.

Megan Gooch is a Collections Curator and Learning Producer at Historic Royal Palaces, at the Tower of London.

James Graham-Campbell is Emeritus Professor of Medieval Archaeology at UCL.

Svein H. Gullbekk is Professor in the Department of Numismatics and Classical Archaeology of the Museum of Cultural History at the University of Oslo.

Jonathan Jarrett is Interim Coin Curator, the Barber Institute of Fine Arts, University of Birmingham.

Kenneth Jonsson is Professor of Numismatics and Monetary History at the University of Stockholm.

Mauri Kiudsoo is Keeper of Coins at the Institute of History, Tallinn University.

Joe Leighton is an optometrist, and has conducted extensive research on Irish Sea coinages of the tenth and eleventh centuries.

Ivar Leimus is Senior Researcher at the Estonian History Museum and the Institute of History, Tallinn University.

Stewart Lyon is a retired actuary, and has written extensively on Anglo-Saxon numismatics.

D. M. Metcalf is Emeritus Professor of Numismatics at the University of Oxford, and former Keeper of Coins and Medals at the Ashmolean Museum, Oxford.

Jens Christian Moesgaard is a Senior Researcher at the National Museum, Copenhagen.

Cécile Morrisson is Director of Research Emerita at the Centre National de la Recherche Scientifique, Paris, and Adviser for Byzantine Numismatics at the Dumbarton Oaks Research Library and Collection, Washington DC.

Rory Naismith is a Leverhulme Early Career Research Fellow at the University of Cambridge, and a Fellow of Clare College, Cambridge.

Hugh Pagan is an antiquarian bookseller, and has written extensively on Anglo-Saxon numismatics.

Elina Screen is a Departmental Lecturer in Early Medieval History at the University of Oxford, and College Lecturer at Trinity College, Oxford.

David Symons is Curator of Archaeology and Numismatics at Birmingham Museums and Art Gallery.

Tuukka Talvio is Keeper of Coins at the National Museum, Helsinki.

Ülle Tamla is Head of Office in the Department of Archaeology, Institute of History, Tallinn University.

Gareth Williams is Assistant Keeper of early medieval coins in the Department of Coins and Medals at the British Museum.

Andrew R. Woods is Curator of Numismatics at Yorkshire Museums Trust.

Mark Blackburn in the Grierson Room, Department of Coins and Medals,
Fitzwilliam Museum, Cambridge (photograph by Dan White).

Chapter 1

Introduction: Mark Blackburn and Early Medieval Monetary History

Rory Naismith, Martin Allen and Elina Screen

In 1985, when writing a characteristically self-effacing preface to a volume of memorial essays for Professor Michael Dolley (1925–83), Mark Blackburn emphasised the vitality of the field in which he was working:

> Anglo-Saxon studies have flourished during the last 35 years, not least in the field of coinage and monetary history. The growing awareness among historians of the need to pursue all forms of primary evidence inspired a post-war generation of numismatists to reassess their material critically and to look for its wider relevance. Significant and rapid advances were made, initially in terms of recording, classification, and chronology, tasks which are fundamental to all numismatic research. This work continues, but building upon it new techniques of analysis and new lines of enquiry have been developed ... [T]hey indicate the rich potential which lies in the coinage as a source of evidence for the Anglo-Saxon period.[1]

What he did not address was his own major role in this story. Mark had already been very much a part of it for more than a decade, and would be a central figure in realising the 'rich potential' to which he referred up to his untimely death on 1 September 2011. He worked during a crucial transitional phase in numismatics, beginning in the early 1970s. No small credit is due to Mark for the secure and respected place that numismatics now holds within early medieval studies more widely. The subject stands in a stronger position than ever. It was for this reason that the editors gathered together the chapters contained in the present volume: to survey the methods, achievements and challenges of early medieval numismatics and monetary history after two generations of fast-paced change, and above all to pay tribute to a dear friend, colleague and mentor whose work has left a profound academic impact. Indeed, *Early Medieval Monetary History* was selected as a title not only to pay tribute to one of Mark's own books – that same collection of essays in memory of Michael Dolley he assembled in the

---

[1] M. Blackburn, 'Preface', in *ASMH*, v–vi, at v.

mid-1980s[2] – but also to highlight the breadth of the book's contents. While Mark's volume, focused on the work of Michael Dolley, concentrated very much on Anglo-Saxon topics, this collection, inspired by Mark himself, takes a broader view that extends beyond the boundaries of England, and also beyond the strict remit of numismatics. Mark knew well the value of collaboration with colleagues elsewhere in Europe and in related disciplines, as well as the importance of carving a niche for numismatics and monetary history alongside the fields of history and archaeology. For this reason the editors have chosen to stress a range of the areas in early medieval studies on which Mark's work touched, and invited contributions which exemplify the advantages to be gained by interpreting coins in their wider geographical and disciplinary context. It is a measure of Mark's standing that the editors could easily have filled a second volume, and unfortunately constraints of space mean that many other good friends and colleagues of Mark's are not represented here.

Mark Blackburn was born on 5 January 1953 in Camberley, Surrey. He grew up there and in Tonbridge Wells, Kent, where he attended the Skinners' School. In 1971 he went up to St Edmund Hall, Oxford, reading chemistry and later jurisprudence. His studies paved the way for a career in the law, and in September 1975 he was called to the bar at Middle Temple. After three years, Mark left the law and took up a position with the merchant banking firm Kleinwort Benson Ltd, where he remained until 1982. In that year he made an important decision: to pursue professionally what had previously been an abiding personal interest in numismatics. Mark had had an interest in coins and their interpretation since his school days, but a more academic approach was prompted by Stewart Lyon's 1970 presidential review in the *British Numismatic Journal*, where he lamented the shortage of researchers on the series.[3] Mark responded to this appeal, and published his first scholarly work on Anglo-Saxon and Norman coinage while still an undergraduate in Oxford.[4] By the early 1980s he was an established authority among the small fraternity of numismatists who had turned their attention to Anglo-Saxon and related coinages in the decades since the Second World War. Professor Michael Dolley and Dr Stewart Lyon in particular encouraged Mark's numismatic studies, and soon became close friends as well as respected colleagues.

The immediate cause for Mark's departure from his job in the City in 1982 was an offer to work in Cambridge as a research assistant with Professor Philip Grierson (1910–2006), doyen of early medieval European numismatics. Philip had decided to prepare for publication his great collection of medieval coins, and sought an assistant whose expertise lay in the field of British coinage. This

---

[2]   *ASMH*.

[3]   C.S.S. Lyon, 'The President's Review of the Year', *BNJ, 39* (1970), 205–10, at 207.

[4]   For a full list of Mark's publications (beginning in 1973) see *VCCBI*, 391–403.

invitation shows the esteem in which Mark was held; the fact that he accepted, and gave up his prospects in London for a far less secure academic position, reflects his passion for the discipline.

Mark and Philip together wrote the first volume of the series Medieval European Coinage, published in 1986,[5] and in the years thereafter began to prepare others. Working in the Fitzwilliam Museum, Mark was ideally placed to take up the Keepership of the Department of Coins and Medals when it fell vacant in 1991. He was to hold the post for the next 20 years. During this time he saw the department go from strength to strength, and become one of the most outstanding numismatic collections and research centres in the world.[6]

In addition to his work as Keeper and latterly as a Lecturer and Reader in the Department of Anglo-Saxon, Norse and Celtic at the University of Cambridge, Mark pursued research into early medieval coinage throughout his career. Overall he published more than 200 academic books and papers.[7] In subject matter these extended from Visigothic Spain to thirteenth-century Flanders, but the heart of his research was always the British Isles, Scandinavia and their neighbours in the early Middle Ages. Within this area his work was notable for both its variety and depth. He dedicated his presidential addresses to the British Numismatic Society to the Anglo-Viking coinages of the late ninth and tenth centuries. These lectures presented the culmination of two decades of research into the coinages of Viking England, all now published in a volume of collected papers.[8] In addition, Mark devoted much attention to the contemporary Anglo-Saxon coinages of Alfred and his successors, showing especially well how these issues could inform (and offer opportunities for collaboration with) historians and archaeologists.[9] Late Anglo-Saxon coinage and its impact in Ireland and Scandinavia provided another rich avenue of research. Mark's involvement began towards the end of a crucial period of work on the coinages of England between about 973 and 1066. Since the late 1950s, Michael Dolley, Christopher Blunt (1904–87) and others had shown how much could be gained by cultivating closer ties with professional historians and by devoting minute attention to the rich collections preserved in Scandinavian museums. Mark was a major figure in the next stage of this research, which was focused on the processes which took English coins across the North and Irish Seas, and on how they were used

---

5   *MEC* 1.

6   R. Naismith, 'Obituary: Mark Blackburn, LittD, FSA (1953–2011)', *BNJ, 81* (2011), 300–303.

7   Listed in *VCCBI*, 391–403.

8   Ibid.

9   See, for example, *Kings, Currency and Alliances: History and Coinage of Southern England in the Ninth Century*, ed. M.A.S. Blackburn and D.N. Dumville (Woodbridge, 1998); M. Blackburn, 'Mints, burhs and the Grately Code cap. 14.2', in *The Defence of Wessex: the Burghal Hidage and Anglo-Saxon Fortifications*, ed. D. Hill and A. Rumble (Manchester, 1996), 160–75.

and imitated by local authorities. Many of the coinages inspired by late Anglo-Saxon models, issued from Dublin to Sigtuna, benefited from Mark's sensitive and patient analysis. These series are among the more challenging in medieval numismatics. The lack of meaningful inscriptions poses a serious obstacle, and date and attribution can be difficult to determine. As a consequence, die- and hoard-studies assume special importance, and yield precious information about how imitative coinages and the manufacturing systems behind them could be structured. Mark excelled at combining these demanding techniques, and as a result was able to turn these difficult coinages into models of numismatic methodology.[10]

Some of these approaches were also used in Mark's analysis of Anglo-Norman coins and of the *sceattas*: early Anglo-Saxon silver coins of diverse appearance, very few of which carry significant inscriptions naming mint or maker. The chronology of these coins, which spanned some 75 years (*c.*675–750), was brilliantly elucidated by Mark on the basis of hoard contents, metallurgy and other criteria. His scheme for dating them remains authoritative.[11] Anglo-Norman coins offer more detail in the form of inscriptions naming mint, moneyer and ruler, yet still present thorny problems of chronology and historical interpretation. In his major papers on the coinages of Henry I (1100–35) and Stephen (1135–54), Mark combined critical assessment of historical sources with traditional numismatic analysis, and also undertook an important comparison of hoards with single-finds. Critically, he noted that some coin-types appeared to be common simply because of the fortuitous discovery of a large hoard from the relevant period. Single-finds, Mark found, present a much surer guide to the nature of the monetary economy, for each one is likely to represent a random loss.

Consideration of single-finds had by this stage become a hallmark of his writing. In the early 1980s Mark (with Mike Bonser and others) was instrumental in gathering and publishing finds brought to light by metal-detector users in England.[12] He also played a central role in the establishment of the Coin Register of the *British Numismatic Journal*, and later the digital Corpus of

---

[10] See (*inter alia*) M. Blackburn, 'An imitative workshop active during Æthelræd II's *Long Cross* Issue', in *Studies in Northern Coinages of the Eleventh Century*, ed. C.J. Becker (Copenhagen, 1981), 29–88; M. Blackburn, 'English dies used in the Scandinavian imitative coinages', *Hikuin, 11* (1985), 101–24.

[11] M. Blackburn, 'A chronology for the sceattas', in *Sceattas in England and on the Continent*, ed. D. Hill and D.M. Metcalf, BAR British Series, 128 (Oxford, 1984), 165–74; *MEC* 1, 164–89.

[12] M. Blackburn and M. Bonser, 'Single finds of Anglo-Saxon and Norman coins – 1', *BNJ, 54* (1984), 63–72; M. Blackburn and M. Bonser, 'Single finds of Anglo-Saxon and Norman coins – 2', *BNJ, 55* (1985), 55–78; M. Blackburn and M. Bonser, 'Single finds of Anglo-Saxon and Norman coins – 3', *BNJ, 56* (1986), 64–101.

Early Medieval Coin Finds of the Fitzwilliam Museum (which was founded in 1997).[13] By the time of writing in winter 2012, nearly 10,000 single-finds had been recorded on the Corpus. Ways of interpreting these finds are legion. Mark himself was particularly successful in using them to unveil details of the early medieval monetary economy. He was among the first to draw attention to the phenomenon of the 'productive site': a location which produces a concentration of individual coin finds.[14] These sites are found mostly in eastern England in what are now quiet rural areas, yet it seems likely that they served an important purpose in the Anglo-Saxon economy. The precise nature of most 'productive sites' remains obscure, given the rarity of archaeological or historical context, though one example investigated in detail by Mark shows how effectively the numismatic record can be married up with the written record. The 'productive site' at Torksey in Lincolnshire has produced several hundred coins, including the largest group of dirham fragments from anywhere in the British Isles, as well as more than a thousand other metallic artefacts. Combining a survey of this material with the statement of the Anglo-Saxon Chronicle that in 872/3 the Viking great army wintered at *Tureces iege* (Torksey) led Mark to the conclusion that the Torksey site was where the Great Army and its followers had stayed that winter.[15]

On a more general level, the geographical and chronological distribution of single-finds – both at individual sites and across England – enabled Mark to reconsider the shape of the monetary economy in Anglo-Saxon England. He was able to show the extraordinary effervescence of the early eighth century, when the *sceattas* expanded to become the best represented silver coinage among single-finds from England between the Romans and the thirteenth century.[16] He was able to apply some of the methods he had developed in work on English material to other areas, for instance the single-finds of dirhams from the important trading site of Kaupang in Norway. Through detailed comparison of hoards and other Scandinavian 'productive sites', Mark constructed a method of dating and contextualising these losses. He thereby showed that Kaupang enjoyed a period of rich activity late in the ninth century but declined swiftly in the tenth.[17]

These points cover only a selection of Mark's interests as a scholar of early medieval monetary history. They serve to highlight features of his legacy: how

---

[13]   See <www.fitzmuseum.cam.ac.uk/emc/>.

[14]   M. Blackburn, '"Productive" sites and the pattern of coin loss in England, 600–1180', in *Markets in Early Medieval Europe: Trading and 'Productive' Sites, 650–850*, ed. T. Pestell and K. Ulmschneider (Macclesfield, 2003), 20–36.

[15]   M. Blackburn, 'The Viking winter camp at Torksey, 872–3', in *VCCBI*, 221–64.

[16]   Blackburn, '"Productive" sites'.

[17]   M. Blackburn, 'The coin finds from Kaupang', in *Kaupang – the Means of Exchange*, ed. D. Skre (Aarhus and Oslo, 2008), 29–74.

he has affected the field, and how it might develop in light of his contribution. Mark's rigorous and incisive methods determined so much about some coinages that his conclusions are unlikely to be superseded, at least until significant new finds come to light. His interpretation of the coinage of Alfred still stands firm, for example, whereas Anglo-Viking numismatics has already been moved forward by several new hoards.[18] One strongly suspects, however, that Mark himself would have wholeheartedly approved, for an abiding feature of his work was readiness to confront new material head on, and to follow its implications through to the full – a principle which must be maintained as new finds continue to emerge on an almost daily basis. He applied the rigour and dynamism of the generation of scholars associated with Michael Dolley to the new challenges offered by proliferating single-finds. It behoves current and future scholars to continue this tradition: to apply new techniques to the rich material now available from England, and to embark on comparative work with other parts of Europe, as has already begun.[19] It is also necessary for scholars to bear in mind other specialisations. Mark reached out to scholars in related fields – historians, archaeologists, philologists and others – through publications in broader collections of essays and close collaboration with colleagues. Dialogue between numismatists and monetary historians and those in related disciplines can and should continue, especially as readings of the early medieval economy tend more towards integration across geographical and disciplinary boundaries.[20]

***

The editors have arranged this volume to reflect four intersecting themes inspired by Mark's research. These are the development and position of the field in general; interdisciplinary approaches to numismatics; the use and circulation of coin; and the interpretation of specific coins and coin finds. The first section embraces chapters on aspects of English coinage, which always remained central to Mark's work. Together, they reflect the healthy state in which he left the field, in large part thanks to his own efforts. These surveys comprise Gareth Williams on the Anglo-Viking coinage, Rory Naismith on England in the tenth century and Martin Allen addressing the coinage of early Norman England – all areas where the benefits of numerous recent finds and collaboration with historians and philologists shine through very clearly.

---

[18]   See Gareth Williams's chapter in this volume (Chapter 2).

[19]   Rich records of single-finds are also available from Denmark and Netherlands. For 'productive sites' and their significance in the Carolingian empire see S. Coupland, 'Carolingian single finds and the economy of the early ninth century', *NC, 170* (2010), 287–319.

[20]   As in, for example, C. Wickham, *Framing the Early Middle Ages: Europe and the Mediterranean 400–800* (Oxford, 2005).

The interdisciplinary element of Mark's work is present to some extent in many of the chapters in this volume, but is showcased particularly prominently in the section comprising the contributions of Martin Biddle, Simon Coupland, Anna Gannon, Tuukka Talvio and Jonathan Jarrett. The first two of these delve into the archaeological and art-historical background of coins from western Europe: Biddle argues that the building shown on the XPICTIANA RELIGIO reverse of Charlemagne's portrait deniers is a representation of the Tomb of Christ in the Church of the Holy Sepulchre in Jerusalem (with an important check-list of all known examples of Charlemagne's portrait coinage by Simon Coupland), while Gannon considers the links between certain Anglo-Saxon *sceattas* and Christian artefacts representing the Lamb of God. They complement one another in stressing the integration of numismatic iconography into religious life at a profound level. Tuukka Talvio looks at the coinage of Edward the Confessor with a similar aim in mind, showing how centralised and coherent the stylistic structure – and by extension the distribution of dies – generally was in this king's reign. Jonathan Jarrett also demonstrates what can be gained through disciplinary integration, in his case focusing on monetary terminology in the complex transactions carried out in tenth- and eleventh-century Spain, in which cows, sheep and pigs featured in the same terms as coins of silver or gold. He shows how flexible the notion of a standard price for these animals could be, and how cautiously one must deal with attestations (and historiography) concerning them. All of the chapters in this section, therefore, demonstrate ways in which coins can be made to divulge important information about the cultural milieu in which they were produced and used.

From these readings of coins as a source for the broader economic and cultural background the volume moves to the third group of chapters, which focuses on the use of coin in early medieval society. These studies discuss different geographical areas, yet touch several times on similar themes and methodologies. In an important review of early Byzantine coin finds from Britain and their interpretation, Cécile Morrisson argues for a more optimistic reading of their role as artefacts of early medieval circulation rather than souvenirs of modern travellers. The coins she considers are comparatively few and may often have been used in a non-monetary context. Michael Metcalf, on the other hand, addresses an altogether different problem, and offers a characteristically dynamic survey of the full economic ramifications of the *sceattas* which circulated in late seventh- and early eighth-century England, based on the voluminous corpus of single-finds now known. Simon Coupland reaches a broadly similar conclusion about the vibrancy of the ninth-century monetary economy of the Carolingian empire, but he is forced to do so with very different tools. Single-finds are numerous but unevenly reported across the vast territory once ruled by Charlemagne (768–814) and Louis the Pious (814–40); however, a few particularly rich sites together with a relatively extensive written body of material on coin-use opens up the possibility of a new approach to the subject. Andrew Woods contends with still greater difficulties in the case of Irish material. Single-finds are scarce, and documents rarer still – but this in itself is argued to be an important point, partly reflecting modern legal policy as well as a genuine difference in the nature of the monetary economy in and around Dublin. No Norwegian documents at all are available to Svein H. Gullbekk, who picks up on Mark's important study of the coins from Kaupang to consider the Viking-Age monetary economy of the region around Oslo, and particularly a major new 'productive site' comparable in many respects to that at Kaupang. These significant sites allow Gullbekk to shed important new light on the use of silver coin within the complex monetary setting of ninth- and tenth-century Norway. Somewhat different is the subject matter of Elina Screen, who looks at the piercing of Anglo-Saxon and related coins as a potential window onto the religious and symbolic meaning and changing use of coins in conversion-period Norway. Her judicious analysis hints at the multifarious ways in which users viewed coins: some treated them simply as conveniently round pieces of bullion; others may have seen the cross-motifs on English coins as a way to demonstrate their faith. Another interesting case of coins crossing boundaries between religions as well as kingdoms is discussed by Marion Archibald. Her study of Spanish Islamic gold pieces circulating in Norman and Plantagenet England elegantly combines coin finds with documentary records to highlight the important part these coins played in high-value exchange.

The last and largest group of chapters considers particular coins or coin finds, and in a sense represents the specific application of the wider points developed in the previous sections. Work such as this is the bedrock of numismatics, especially in the era of the metal-detector: it is telling that virtually all of these chapters include at least some specimens brought to light in this way. Five specific hoards from as far afield as the Baltic and Ireland are considered by Kristin Bornholdt Collins, Allison Fox, James Graham-Campbell, Hugh Pagan, David Symons, Kenneth Jonsson, and Ivar Leimus, Mauri Kiudsoo and Ülle Tamla. These present quite diverse problems. Those broached by Jonsson, and Leimus, Kiudsoo and Tamla belong to the later Viking Age, when the quantity of English coins entering Scandinavia and the Baltic had begun to decline: both hoards provide important new evidence for how and why this occurred. Bornholdt Collins, Fox and Graham-Campbell integrate an important new hoard from the Isle of Man (deposited in the eleventh century) into the broader setting of the island's bullion economy, while Symons highlights a small but significant English hoard from the ninth century, containing particularly rare and debatable coins of Burgred, king of the Mercians (852–74). The tenth-century Port Glasgow hoard discussed by Pagan differs in its very early date of discovery (1699): reconstruction of its contents hence requires delicate analysis of antiquarian documents, as well as of surviving coins. Other approaches to individual coins or groups of coins are taken by the remaining chapters in this section, which again serve to highlight the range of knowledge and methodologies required for full appreciation of surviving coins. Like Marion Archibald's analysis of the few but important finds of high-value coins, Stewart Lyon examines a coin of exceptional worth and importance – one of the very rare early Anglo-Saxon *solidi*. Drawing on metallurgical analyses, he concludes that the coin was indeed die-struck, but like most other related specimens it seems to have been mounted for display early in its life. Display and prestige seem to have been at least as central to its function as any monetary role. Jens-Christian Moesgaard, Megan Gooch and Andrew Woods and Joe Leighton consider further groups of historically associated coins. Each concentrates on a particularly complex segment of coinage – respectively, ninth-century Rouen, Viking York and the Irish Sea area of the eleventh century. All three chapters demonstrate how finely detailed numismatic techniques – such as die-studies leading to quantitative estimates of production, careful attention to hoard distribution and sophisticated stylistic analysis – can lead to persuasive conclusions of significance to all scholars working on the period: an appropriate result for any collection associated with Mark's achievement.

Rich and varied though they are, the studies in this volume can only give a flavour of Mark's own tastes and achievements in research. As curator of oriental as well as early medieval coins, for example, he devoted much time to the study of Indian, Japanese and Korean coins, and cultivated close relationships with colleagues working in those areas. Neither are even all of his early medieval interests broached here, such was the extent of his activity. Yet the goal of *Early Medieval Monetary History* is not, strictly speaking, to touch on all of the material on which Mark worked over his prolific career. The aim of this book is, rather, to celebrate Mark's work by showing how it has impacted on his colleagues, friends and pupils. All of the authors shared some connection with Mark, and through his scholarship and also his personal kindness and warmth Mark has left an indelible impression on all their outlooks and, by extension, on the subject more broadly. Moving forward, there can be no doubt that his legacy as a world-class numismatist is secure.

PART I
Progress in Early Medieval Monetary History

PART I

Chapter 2

Coins and Currency in Viking England, AD 865–954

Gareth Williams

Introduction

Mark Blackburn had a prolific output across many areas of numismatics, but one in which he made a particularly important contribution was that of Viking coins and currency. This was a subject that he had addressed throughout his career, and especially the final decade or so of his life.[1] His detailed work on Anglo-Scandinavian coinage began with the 1984 hoard from Ashdon, Essex, and continued with studies of the hoard from Thurcaston, Leicestershire, and the important productive site of the Viking winter camp at Torksey, Lincolnshire. These were followed by surveys of Anglo-Scandinavian coinage both north and south of the Humber, and Mark chose the subject of *Currency under the Vikings* for the series of five Presidential Addresses which he delivered to the British Numismatic Society in 2004–8. *Viking Coinage and Currency in the British Isles* was also the subject of his final book, which reprinted the Presidential Addresses and eight other articles, with added comments and updates where appropriate, together with a major new article on the major Viking site at Torksey.[2] This might suggest that there is little value in reviewing the state of the subject again so soon. However, a number of factors contribute to a developing understanding of the subject.

The first is a wider development in the study and interpretation of coinage and silver economies across the Viking world. In December 2008 the University of Aarhus hosted a symposium on *Silver Economies, Monetisation and Society in Scandinavia, c.800–1100*. The speakers included both archaeologists and numismatists, and reflected the healthy state of research in this field. Although the focus was on Scandinavia rather than the British Isles, the symposium and the

---

[1]   M.A.S Blackburn, 'Bibliography of Mark Blackburn's publications', in *VCCBI*, 391–403; G. Williams, 'Mark Blackburn: an appreciation', in *Silver Economies, Monetisation and Society in Scandinavia, 800–1100*, ed. J.A. Graham-Campbell, S.M. Sindbæk and G. Williams (Aarhus, 2011), 25–7.

[2]   *VCCBI.*

resulting publication presented both new finds and conceptual frameworks for the studies of coinage and exchange which can be applied to Viking Britain and Ireland.[3] The symposium followed the publication in 2007 of another volume of conference papers on related topics, and in 2008 of an edited volume on *Means of Exchange* published as part of the Kaupang research project, in which the various contributors engaged in a stimulating debate on the methodology of studying silver economies, and particularly of comparing the evidence of hoards, site finds and stray finds of diverse coins and bullion objects in societies with limited systematic control of silver circulation.[4]

Secondly, the body of evidence is increasing at an unprecedented rate. Single-finds have been multiplying since the 1970s as a result of metal detecting, and have been published systematically since the 1980s in the Coin Register of the *British Numismatic Journal*, and more recently through the online databases of the *Corpus of Early Medieval Coin Finds* (EMC) maintained by the Fitzwilliam Museum, and of the Portable Antiquities Scheme (PAS), maintained by the British Museum.[5] A growing corpus of coins with identified find-spots permits more detailed study of the distribution of individual coin types, which is particularly important in the Anglo-Scandinavian series, given that many of the types within this series lack mint signatures, while some do not even clearly indicate the issuing authority. Furthermore, the Portable Antiquities Scheme is not limited to numismatic material, so there is a growing corpus of single-finds of Viking weights, hack-silver and ingots, all of which contribute to an understanding of the bullion economy which flourished alongside the use of coins in Viking England in the late ninth and early tenth centuries.[6]

In addition to single-finds, there has been a massive increase in the number of Viking hoards discovered in recent years (Colour Plate 2.1). Interpretation of the chronology and attribution of the Anglo-Scandinavian coinage has to a great extent been derived from the combinations of different types within a few major hoards, most notably Cuerdale and Bossall/Flaxton. While some of the new hoards discovered in the last 15 years have merely reinforced the evidence of existing hoards, others have included entirely new types, or have

---

[3]   J.A. Graham-Campbell, S.M. Sindbæk and G. Williams (eds), *Silver Economies, Monetisation and Society in Scandinavia, 800–1100* (Aarhus, 2011).

[4]   J.A. Graham-Campbell and G. Williams (eds), *Silver Economy in the Viking Age* (Walnut Creek, CA, 2007); and D. Skre (ed.), *Means of Exchange: Dealing with Silver in the Viking Age*, Kaupang Excavation Project Publication Series, 2, Norske Oldfunn, XXIII (Oslo, 2008).

[5]   The databases, which are updated frequently, are available at <www-cm.fitzmuseum.cam.ac.uk/emc> and <www.finds.org.uk> respectively.

[6]   Viking-Age single-finds of a monetary character are currently the subject of a postdoctoral research project being undertaken by Dr Jane Kershaw of UCL.

changed the distribution patterns of existing types.[7] Thus, Mark Blackburn's 2011 reprint of his 2005 Presidential Address included an update to his corpus of Anglo-Scandinavian Sword types of the 920s, reflecting their presence in the Flusco Pike (2) hoard (2005) and the Vale of York hoard (2007), but since then a further parcel has emerged in the 'Near York' hoard discovered in 2012, while other important recent hoards include Furness, Cumbria (2011), Silverdale, Lancashire (2011) and Bedale, North Yorkshire (2012).[8] Between them, the Viking hoards discovered in the last decade span the period from the first Viking settlements of the 870s to the aftermath of the fall of Viking Northumbria in the 950s, and thus impact on our understanding of the entire sequence of coinage and currency in Viking England.

Metal detecting has also revealed two important new sites of the 870s, at the very beginning of the settlement period. An association between the deposition of hoards and the movements of the *micel here* ('great raiding band') in the 860s and 870s was noted as long ago as 1966 by Michael Dolley, and explored in more detail by Nicholas Brooks and James Graham-Campbell, but the assemblage of detected finds from Torksey in Lincolnshire, historically documented as the winter camp of the *micel here* in 872–873, is the first such assemblage from a site of this kind.[9] The Torksey assemblage casts new light on exchange and currency

---

[7]   G. Williams, 'RORIVA CASTR: a new Danelaw mint of the 920s', in *Scripta varia numismatico Tuukka Talvio sexagenario dedicate*, ed. O. Järvinen, Suomen Numismaattisen Yhdistyksen julkaisuja, 6 (Helsinki, 2008), 41–7; G. Williams, 'The Coins from the Vale of York Viking hoard: preliminary report', *BNJ, 78* (2008), 227–34; G. Williams, 'Hoards from the northern Danelaw from Cuerdale to the Vale of York', in *The Huxley Viking Hoard: Scandinavian Settlement in the North West*, ed. J.A. Graham-Campbell and R.A. Philpott (National Museums Liverpool, 2009), 73–83; G. Williams, 'Coinage and monetary circulation in the northern Danelaw in the 920s in the light of the Vale of York hoard', in *Studies in Early Medieval Coinage, vol. 2: New Perspectives*, ed. T. Abramson (Woodbridge, 2011), 146–55; G. Williams, 'A new coin type (and a new king?) from Viking Northumbria', *Yorkshire Numismatist* 4 (2012), 261–76; G. Williams, 'The Northern hoards revisited: hoards and silver economy in the northern Danelaw in the early tenth century', in *Early Medieval Art and Archaeology in the Northern World: Studies in Honour of James Graham-Campbell*, ed. A. Reynolds and L. Webster (Leiden, 2013), 459–86; G. Williams and B. Ager, *The Vale of York Hoard* (London, 2010).

[8]   Williams, 'Northern hoards revisited'; M.A.S. Blackburn, 'Supplements to the articles 2011', in *VCCBI*, 371–90, at 376–84; D. Boughton, G. Williams and B. Ager, 'Viking hoards: buried wealth of the Norse North-West', *Current Archaeology, 264* (March 2012), 26–31; G. Williams, 'Viking Hoards from Yorkshire, *c.*866–954: A survey', in *A Riverine Site Near York: a Possible Viking Camp, and Other Related Papers*, ed. G. Williams (in preparation); Treasure cases 2005 T471 (Flusco Pike 2), 2007 T2 (Vale of York), 2011 T283 (Furness), 2011 T259 (Silverdale), 2012 T341 ('Near York') and 2012 T373 (Bedale).

[9]   R.H.M. Dolley, 'Provisional listing of Viking-Age hoards from Great Britain and Ireland', in his *SCBI 8: The Hiberno-Norse Coins in the British Museum* (London, 1966), 47–91; N.P. Brooks and J.A. Graham-Campbell, 'Reflections on the Viking-Age silver hoard from Croydon,

in the 870s (see below), and the Torksey evidence is reinforced by a smaller but directly comparable detected assemblage from a riverine site in North Yorkshire which, unlike Torksey, is not historically recorded in the late ninth century. Both sites have produced a combination of coins (of different types), weights, hack-silver and hack-gold, providing a broader range of evidence concerning forms of exchange than any of the hoards of the early settlement period (Colour Plate 2.2).[10]

The third major factor which has the potential to influence our interpretation of the Anglo-Viking coinage is the broader interpretation of the history of Viking England in the late ninth to mid-tenth centuries. The few surviving contemporary historical sources from England from this period tend to focus on Wessex and southern Mercia, so coverage of the different areas of Viking settlement is very incomplete. Anglo-Saxon sources can be complemented by contemporary references from Ireland and the Continent, as well as by material recorded by later English chroniclers and (debatably) derived from now lost contemporary accounts, and by later sagas and related Latin texts from Scandinavia. The different types of evidence raise different problems of source criticism, and there are also numerous conflicts and contradictions, not just between different types of evidence but between, for example, different texts of the *Anglo-Saxon Chronicle*. Although an important synthetic narrative history of the Viking settlements of northern England has been available since the 1970s in the work of Alfred Smyth,[11] Smyth's interpretations have not been universally accepted. Since the mid-1990s, a number of historians have discussed and re-evaluated the history of Viking Northumbria in this period and, although there is still no consensus on a single definitive narrative, understanding of the historical framework within which the coins functioned is certainly more nuanced than was the case up to the 1990s. Reinterpretations vary between relatively minor adjustments to the accepted chronology, and more radical positions, including the suggestion that the conventional use of

---

Surrey', in *ASMH,* 91–110 (repr. and updated in N.P. Brooks, *Communities and Warfare 700–1400* (London, 2000), 69–92). M.A.S. Blackburn, 'Finds from the Anglo-Scandinavian site of Torksey, Lincolnshire', in *Moneta Mediævalis. Studia numizmatyczne i historyczne ofiarowane Profesorowi Stanisławowi Suchodolskiemu w 65. rocznicę urodzin,* ed. B. Paszkiewicz (Warsaw, 2002), 89–101 (*VCCBI,* 207–20); M.A.S. Blackburn, 'The Viking winter camp at Torksey, 872–3', in *VCCBI,* 221–64; G. Williams, 'Silver economies, monetisation and society: an overview', in *Silver Economies, monetisation and society,* ed. Graham-Campbell, Sindbæk and Williams, 337–72; G. Williams, 'Viking camps and the means of exchange in Britain and Ireland in the ninth century', in *Before and after the Battle of Clontarf: The Vikings in Ireland and Beyond,* ed. H.B. Clarke and R. Johnson (Dublin, forthcoming).

[10]   R. Hall and G. Williams, with B. Ager and N. Rogers, 'A riverine site near York', in *Riverine Site Near York,* ed. Williams (in preparation); Williams, 'Viking camps'.

[11]   A.P. Smyth, *Scandinavian York and Dublin: the History and Archaeology of Two Related Viking Kingdoms,* 2 vols (Dublin, 1975–9).

terms such as 'the Danelaw', 'the Five Boroughs', and 'the Kingdom of York' is based on misconceptions and may fundamentally distort our understanding of the political landscape of late ninth- and tenth-century England.[12] One area on which there now seems to be agreement is that, even taken as a whole, the historical sources have significant gaps, and that the coins cannot simply be mapped onto an accepted text-based chronology; but also that the coins in many cases fill what would otherwise be gaps, and are themselves amongst the most important surviving contemporary historical sources for the period. As noted by Peter Sawyer, detailed consideration of the numismatic evidence may yet offer a solution to the conflicting chronologies offered by different texts.[13] However, while coins have formed part of the discussion in most if not all of the works cited above, most historians in recent years have considered the numismatic evidence without seriously questioning the established numismatic chronology, while recent numismatic work, although acknowledging the existence of a wider historical debate over aspects of the chronology, has largely followed the established chronology derived from the *Anglo-Saxon Chronicle*. This leads to the unfortunate situation that, taken separately, both history and numismatics can find justification from the other in maintaining the *status quo*, despite the wealth of important work that has taken place in both disciplines in recent years. A more integrated approach is needed to take our understanding of coins and currency in Viking England to the next stage.

The idea of taking an integrated approach to history and numismatics in order to understand the Anglo-Scandinavian coinage, while at the same time recognising that coins may in some cases fill gaps in the historical record, can be traced back to the beginnings of the serious study of this coinage. Daniel Haigh, in a series of articles in the *Numismatic Chronicle* and elsewhere, considered the coinage of both East Anglia and Northumbria.[14] He provided a detailed

---

[12]   P.H. Sawyer, 'The last Scandinavian kings of York', *Northern History*, 31 (1995), 39–44; A. Woolf, 'Erik Bloodaxe revisited', *Northern History*, 34 (1998), 189–93; A. Woolf, 'Amlaíb Cuaran and the Gael', in *Medieval Dublin* III, ed. S. Duffy (Dublin, 2002), 34–42; D. Rollason, *Northumbria, 500–1100: Creation and Destruction of a Kingdom* (Cambridge, 2003); C.E. Downham, 'The chronology of the last Scandinavian Kings of York', *Northern History*, 40 (2003), 25–51; C.E. Downham, 'Eric Bloodaxe – axed? The mystery of the last Viking king of York', *Mediaeval Scandinavia*, 14 (2004), 51–77; C.E. Downham, *Viking Kings of Britain and Ireland: the Dynasty of Ívarr to AD 1014* (Edinburgh, 2007); G. Williams, *Eirik Bloodaxe* (Kernavik, 2011); G. Williams, 'Towns and Identities in Viking England', in *Everyday Life in Viking Towns: Social Approaches to Viking Age Towns in Ireland and England c. 850–1100*, ed. D.M. Hadley and L. Ten Harkel (Oxford, 2013), 14–34.

[13]   Sawyer, 'Last Scandinavian kings', 44.

[14]   D. Haigh, 'On the pennies of Regnald', *NC*, 2 (1839–40), 7–11; D. Haigh, 'On the coins of the Cuerdale find, with the names of "Siefredus", "Cunnetti", and "Ebraice"', *NC*, 5 (1843), 105–17; D. Haigh, *Essay on the Numismatic History of the Ancient Kingdom of the East Angles*

discussion of the problems of reconciling the different groups of historical sources mentioned above before using this historical framework as background to a suggested attribution and dating for the Northumbrian series. Many of his detailed conclusions have since been superseded, but his approach laid the foundations for all subsequent study of the subject, including the attribution of the Cuerdale phase of Northumbrian coins to York, the recognition of the importance of both Christian and specifically Frankish influence on the development of the Anglo-Scandinavian coinage, and the need to look beyond contemporary Anglo-Saxon documentary sources alone to provide a satisfactory chronology for the attribution of the coinage.

Anglo-Scandinavian coinage continued to attract attention from historians and numismatists throughout the late nineteenth and early twentieth centuries, although with mixed effect. However, it was from the 1950s onwards that a series of major studies appeared which between them have led to the currently accepted classification and interpretation of the coinage. A full discussion of the numismatic literature in this field lies beyond the scope of this chapter, but a number of contributions have been particularly important. Michael Dolley established a clear distinction between those coinages which pre-dated Athelstan's assumption of authority over Northumbria in 927, and those which dated from the period between Athelstan's death in 939 and the more lasting integration of Northumbria into a single kingdom of England from 954.[15] Equally important was the classification of the Northumbrian coins of the Cuerdale phase by Stewart Lyon and Ian Stewart, who together with Christopher Blunt also refined the chronology and attribution of much of the post-Cuerdale coinage.[16] Blunt provided the first detailed study of the St Edmund Memorial coinage (later refined in the light of more recent hoard evidence by Mark Blackburn and Hugh

---

(Leeds, 1845); and D. Haigh, 'The coins of the Danish kings of Northumberland', *Archaeologia Æliana*, 2nd series, 7 (1876), 21–77.

[15] R.H.M. Dolley, 'The post-Brunanburh Viking coinage of York', *Nordisk Numismatisk Årsskrift* 1957–8, 13–88.

[16] C.S.S. Lyon, and B.H.I.H. Stewart, 'The Northumbrian Viking coins in the Cuerdale hoard', in *Anglo-Saxon Coins: Studies Presented to F. M. Stenton on the Occasion of His 80th Birthday*, ed. R.H.M. Dolley (London, 1961), 96–121; I. Stewart and S. Lyon, 'Chronology of the St Peter coinage', *Yorkshire Numismatist*, 2 (1992), 45–73; B.H.I.H. Stewart, 'The St Martin coinage of Lincoln', *BNJ*, 36 (1967), 46–54; B.H.I.H. Stewart, 'The anonymous Anglo-Viking issue with sword and hammer types and the coinage of Sihtric I', *BNJ*, 52 (1982), 108–16; B.H.I.H. Stewart, 'CVNNETTI reconsidered', in *Coinage in Ninth-Century Northumbria: the Tenth Oxford Symposium on Coinage and Monetary History*, ed. D.M. Metcalf, BAR British Series 180 (Oxford, 1987), 345–54; B.H.I.H. Stewart, 'On the date of the Bossall hoard', *NC, 151* (1991), 175–82; C.E. Blunt and B.H.I.H. Stewart, 'The coinage of Regnald I of York and the Bossall Hoard', *NC, 143* (1983), 146–63; and *CTCE*, 97–107 and 211–34.

Pagan).[17] Blunt also reconstructed elements of the Cuerdale hoard which were abstracted from the hoard before it was properly recorded, or which were not properly identified by early commentators, and established to the satisfaction of most scholars the attribution of the coins of the Cuerdale phase in the name of ALVVALDVS to Æthelwold, the exiled nephew of Alfred the Great.[18] Veronica Smart has added to our understanding of the origins of the moneyers within the St Edmund Memorial coinage, as many of the moneyers have Continental Germanic names, indicating the likely use of imported Frankish moneyers to develop the coinage.[19] Marion Archibald's detailed study of the composition of the Cuerdale hoard established that it could not realistically have been deposited before *c.*905, which impacts not only on the historical context in which the hoard was deposited, but also on the chronology of the Cuerdale and post-Cuerdale phases of the Anglo-Scandinavian coinage.[20] She has also examined the secondary testing of coins as evidence for use within a bullion economy, with specific reference to the Cuerdale hoard, but also in other Viking hoards of the late ninth and early tenth centuries from England and elsewhere, and this has clarified the dating of the development of the bullion economy in Viking England in the late ninth and early tenth centuries.[21] Archibald's work on testing feeds into the broader topic of a 'dual economy' of bullion currency alongside local minting in areas of Viking settlement, which has also been considered by Mark Blackburn and James Graham-Campbell, and the relationship between different types of silver economy and the composition of Viking hoards has been considered in the light of a number of recent hoards.[22] Recent discussions have

---

[17]   C.E. Blunt, 'The St Edmund Memorial coinage', *Proceedings of the Suffolk Institute of Archaeology, 31* (1969), 234–55; M. Blackburn and H. Pagan, 'The St Edmund coinage in the light of a parcel from a hoard of St Edmund pennies', *BNJ, 72* (2002), 1–14.

[18]   C.E. Blunt, 'The composition of the Cuerdale hoard', *BNJ* 53 (1983), 1–6; and C.E. Blunt, 'Northumbrian coins in the name of Alwaldus', *BNJ, 55* (1985), 192–4.

[19]   V. Smart, 'The moneyers of St Edmund', *Hikuin, 11* (1985), 83–90; and V. Smart, 'Scandinavians, Celts and Germans in Anglo-Saxon England: the evidence of moneyers' names', in *ASMH*, 171–84.

[20]   M.M. Archibald, 'Dating Cuerdale: the evidence of the coins', in *Viking Treasure from the North West: the Cuerdale Hoard in its Context*, ed. J. Graham-Campbell, National Museums and Galleries on Merseyside Occasional Papers 5 (Liverpool, 1992), 15–20.

[21]   M.M. Archibald, 'Pecking and bending: the evidence of British finds', in *Sigtuna Papers: Proceedings of the Sigtuna Symposium on Viking-Age Coinage 1–4 June 1989*, ed. K. Jonsson and B. Malmer, Commentationes de nummis saeculorum IX–XI in Suecia repertis, Nova series 6 (Stockholm, 1990), 11–24; M.M. Archibald, 'Testing', in *The Cuerdale Hoard and Related Viking-Age Silver and Gold, from Britain and Ireland, in the British Museum*, ed. J. Graham-Campbell, British Museum Research Publication 185 (London, 2011), 51–64.

[22]   M.A.S Blackburn, 'Expansion and control: aspects of Anglo-Scandinavian minting south of the Humber', in *Vikings and the Danelaw: Select Papers from the Proceedings of the Thirteenth Viking Congress*, ed. J. Graham-Campbell, R. Hall, J. Jesch and D.N. Parsons (Oxford, 2001),

also moved beyond 'dual economies' to 'multiple economies', including social as well as monetary and or quasi-monetary exchange, while finds of imitative gold coins, gold ingots and hack-gold point to the monetary use of gold as well as silver. There may also be evidence for the monetary use of copper alloy in the late ninth century, although this has yet to be considered in detail.[23] The iconography of the Anglo-Scandinavian coinage, and particularly the relationship between coinage, Christianity and royal authority, has been considered, with varying conclusions, by Mark Blackburn, Megan Gooch and myself,[24] and Gooch has also contributed in this volume a detailed study of the *Swordless St Peter* type, the one substantive Anglo-Scandinavian series which had not previously received detailed attention.[25] The remaining Anglo-Scandinavian series have all been surveyed in some detail in recent years by Blackburn, while I have suggested some further refinements of chronology and attribution in certain series in the light of recent hoards, and in the discussion of the coins in Graham-Campbell's recent catalogue of the Cuerdale hoard.[26]

125–42; J.A. Graham-Campbell, 'The Dual economy of the Danelaw. The Howard Linecar memorial lecture 2001', *BNJ*, 71 (2001), 49–59; J.A. Graham-Campbell, 'The Northern hoards; from Cuerdale to Bossall/Flaxton', in *Edward the Elder, 899–924*, ed. N.J. Higham and D.H. Hill (London, 2001), 212–29; G. Williams, 'Kingship, Christianity and coinage: monetary and political perspectives on silver economy in the Viking Age', in *Silver Economy*, ed. Graham-Campbell and Williams, 177–214; Williams, 'Hoards from the northern Danelaw'; Williams, 'Coinage and monetary circulation in the northern Danelaw'; and Williams, 'Northern Hoards revisited'.

[23]   G. Williams, 'Silver economies, monetisation and society', 354; Blackburn, 'Viking winter camp', 236; Hall and Williams, 'Riverine Site Near York'.

[24]   M.A.S. Blackburn, 'Crosses and conversion: the iconography of the coinage of Viking York *ca* 900', in *Cross and Culture in Anglo-Saxon England: Studies in Honor of George Hardin Brown*, ed. K.L. Jolly, C.E. Karkov and S.L. Keefer, Medieval European Studies IX (Morganstown WV, 2008), 172–200 (*VCCBI*, 308–36); Williams, 'Kingship, Christianity and coinage', 198–9; M. Gooch, 'Viking kings, political power and monetisation', in *Studies in Early Medieval Coinage 2*, ed. Abramson, 111–20; M. Gooch, 'Money and power in the Viking kingdom of York' (Unpublished PhD thesis, University of Durham, 2012).

[25]   See Chapter 21, this volume.

[26]   M.A.S. Blackburn, 'The coinage of Scandinavian York', in *Aspects of Scandinavian York*, ed. R. Hall, Archaeology of York: Anglo-Scandinavian York 8.4 (York, 2004), 325–49 (*VCCBI*, 281–307); M.A.S. Blackburn, 'Presidential address 2004. Currency under the Vikings. Part 1: Guthrum and the earliest Danelaw coinages', *BNJ*, 75 (2005), 18–43 (*VCCBI*, 2–31); M.A.S. Blackburn, 'Presidential address 2005. Currency under the Vikings. Part 2: the two Scandinavian kingdoms of the Danelaw, c. 895–954', *BNJ*, 76 (2006), 204–26 (*VCCBI*, 32–57); Williams, 'Coinage and monetary circulation in the northern Danelaw'; G. Williams, 'The Cuerdale coins', with a contribution by M.M. Archibald, in *Cuerdale Hoard*, ed. Graham-Campbell, 39–71.

The Current State of Research

Between them, the various works cited in the previous section have created a much more comprehensive picture of coinage and currency in Viking England than was available hitherto, while at the same time raising a number of questions which can only be answered by further research. The remainder of this chapter will attempt to summarise the current state of our knowledge, while identifying some of the key questions which remain to be answered. Since the period saw a number of changes in the character of coinage and other forms of exchange, which to some extent reflect wider developments within Anglo-Scandinavian society, this section has been divided into a number of distinct phases.

Phase 1, 865–c.880

Although the *micel here* arrived in East Anglia in 865, and conquered Northumbria the following year, it was not until 874 that Scandinavian settlement rather than campaigning was recorded in Northumbria, East Anglia and eastern Mercia. The section of the *micel here* normally said to have settled East Anglia under Anund, Guthrum and Oscytel reverted to its previous role as a raiding force, however, until Guthrum's submission to Alfred of Wessex at Wedmore in 878 following his defeat by Alfred at the battle of Edington. This period saw the deposition of a number of hoards, some of which can be associated with specific historical events, and pre-Viking coinage continued to be used for much of the period, in addition to/alongside a bullion economy.[27] The bullion economy was predominantly based on silver, but hack-gold is present at both Torksey and the North Yorkshire productive site, indicating the use of gold bullion. This is reinforced by single-finds of hack-gold and ingots, but these cannot be precisely dated.[28] In contrast with the precious metal (including imported dirhams) used as bullion, the coins in circulation in England before the Viking conquests did not in most cases have particularly high precious metal content. The Lunettes coinage of Mercia and Wessex was made of debased silver, while the Northumbrian *stycas* were made of copper alloy, with a minimal silver content. Nevertheless, these coins are found in Viking contexts and apparently functioned as coinage, possibly with a nominal value in excess of their bullion value. What appears to be a lead trial-piece for an imitative Lunettes penny has

---

[27] Brooks and Graham-Campbell, 'Reflections on the Viking-Age silver hoard'; Blackburn, 'Viking winter camp'.

[28] M.A.S. Blackburn, 'Gold in England during the "Age of silver" (eighth–eleventh centuries)', in *Silver Economy in the Viking Age*, ed. Graham-Campbell and Williams, 55–98; Blackburn, 'Viking winter camp', 233–5; Hall and Williams, *Riverine Site near* York; J.F. Kershaw, 'Metals and exchange in Viking-Age Yorkshire: the contribution of single finds', in *Riverine Site Near York*, ed. Williams (in preparation).

been found at Torksey (as well as a trial-piece for an imitative gold solidus), and this suggests that Viking imitations of Lunettes were produced before the end of the Lunettes coinage, *c.*874–75, although no such imitations have yet been discovered.[29] The presence at both Torksey and the riverine site in North Yorkshire of Northumbrian *stycas* suggests that these may also have continued in circulation after the fall of Northumbria in 866. The established chronology for *stycas* is based on the assumption that minting ceased with the Viking conquest of Northumbria, but the presence of coins of this type in assemblages of the 870s raises the question of whether minting may have continued, especially as the last phase of the *styca* coinage was dominated by coins with blundered inscriptions. These also appear in hoards with no obvious Viking characteristics, but which also include *stycas* in the name of Osberht, the last Anglo-Saxon king of Northumbria, who was killed in 866, although some blundered issues appear in hoards which appear to terminate rather earlier. On this basis, it is possible that some, although not necessarily all, of the late blundered *stycas* may be Viking imitations rather than pre-Viking issues, but this theory has yet to be tested in detail, and a comprehensive review of the late *stycas* is much needed. Such a review would need to consider a range of permutations, including seeing the *stycas* as purely pre-Viking issues; seeing some of them as imitative issues under Viking rule; and also considering the possibility of some sort of continuity of native rule, as in East Anglia (see below).[30]

This phase also saw the reform of the silver content of Southumbrian coinage, with the introduction of the *Cross and Lozenge* type (and related issues) in both Mercia and Wessex, lasting from *c.*874–75 to *c.*880.[31] As yet, no Viking imitations are recorded of this type, although this may partly reflect the current absence of any major hoards of the late 870s, and even the official issues are comparatively rare. Marion Archibald has plausibly suggested that the introduction of the characteristic Viking method of testing coins known as pecking may date from this period, as such testing would make sense against the background of the transition from the base silver Lunettes to the purer *Cross and Lozenge* type. Pecking is not visible in hoards of the early to mid-870s, and is

[29] Blackburn, 'Finds from the Anglo-Scandinavian Site at Torksey', 93–4; Blackburn, 'Viking winter camp', 225 and 228.

[30] Blackburn 'Finds from the Anglo-Scandinavian Site at Torksey', 91–2; Hall and Williams, *Riverine Site near York*. For evidence in later chronicles of 'puppet' kings in Northumbria in the transition to Viking rule, see Downham, *Viking Kings*, 69; S. McLeod, *The Beginning of Scandinavian Settlement in England: the Viking 'Great Army' and Early Settlers, c. 865–900* (Turnhout, 2014), 173–203.

[31] M.A.S. Blackburn and S.D. Keynes, 'A Corpus of the Cross-and-Lozenge and Related Coinages of Alfred, Ceolwulf II and Archbishop Æthelred', in *Kings, Currency and Alliances: History and Coinage of Southern England in the Ninth Century*, ed. M.A.S. Blackburn and D.N. Dumville (Woodbridge, 1998), 125–50.

present from the mid-890s onward but, as Archibald notes, the gap in the hoard evidence between these two phases leaves a question as to exactly when in the intervening period pecking began.[32]

A final feature of this phase of coinage is the transition from pre-Viking to Anglo-Viking coinage in East Anglia. The last historically recorded Anglo-Saxon king of East Anglia was Edmund, killed in 869 and later venerated as a saint. However, rare issues of East Anglian type survive in the names of the otherwise unknown Æthelred and Oswald.[33] It is unclear whether these should be seen as purely East Anglian claimants, attempting to fill the vacuum in power between the death of Edmund and the eventual Viking settlement of East Anglia, or whether they should be seen as 'puppet' rulers, governing East Anglia on behalf of their Viking masters, although one may note that the paradigm for Viking puppet kings provided by West Saxon accounts of Ceolwulf II of Mercia is called into question by the reassessment of Ceolwulf II by Simon Keynes and Mark Blackburn.[34] In addition to the coins in the names of Æthelred and Oswald, a literate lead striking of an East Anglian Temple type with the name EÐELSTAN REX was discovered at Hoxne in Suffolk *c.*1996. Together with two badly blundered imitations of the same type from the Cuerdale hoard which can plausibly read as derived from an EÐELSTAN REX prototype, it has been identified as an issue of Guthrum, the Viking leader defeated by Alfred of Wessex at Edington in 878, who subsequently accepted baptism with the name Athelstan, and ruled East Anglia under a peace treaty (if not an active alliance) with Alfred.[35] Coins of Athelstan II/Guthrum of East Anglia imitating Alfred's *Two Line* coinage have been recognised since the discovery of the Cuerdale hoard and are discussed in more detail in the next section, but the possibility that the blundered *Temple* types from Cuerdale might also belong to this ruler was only recognised in the light of the recent literate example. Other illiterate *Temple* imitations may be derived from any of the three rulers, or directly from Frankish prototypes.

It seems most obvious to place Æthelred and Oswald in the period immediately following the death of Edmund in 869, but before Athelstan II/Guthrum was permanently established in East Anglia in *c.*879–80. Blackburn suggests that the Athelstan II *Temple* type was issued after his baptism in 878 and probably after 879–80, with the blundered issues following even later, providing continuity within the type, and giving a total duration for the *Temple* issues of 10–15 years

---

[32] Archibald, 'Testing', 62–4.

[33] M. Dolley, *Viking Coins of the Danelaw and Dublin* (London, 1965), 16; Blackburn, 'Guthrum and the earliest Danelaw coinages', 23–5.

[34] S.D. Keynes, 'King Alfred and the Mercians', in *Kings, Currency and Alliances*, ed. Blackburn and Dumville, 1–46, at 12–19; Blackburn and Keynes, 'Corpus of Cross-and-Lozenge', passim.

[35] Blackburn, 'Guthrum and the earliest Danelaw coinages', 26–7.

after the death of Edmund.[36] This is a plausible reading of the evidence, but it is not the only one, as it is uncertain whether there was direct continuity from the *Temple* issues of Æthelred and Oswald to those of Athelstan II, and also whether Athelstan II's *Temple* type pre-dates or post-dates his *Two Line* issue, which must date from at least the early 880s (see below). An earlier date would imply a degree of assimilation and possibly even Christianisation before the battle of Edington, while a reversion to an East Anglian design after the West Saxon-derived *Two Line* type might point to a distancing from Alfred which is not otherwise recorded, but which would prefigure the St Edmund coinage (see below). The dangers of relying on a purely West Saxon historical narrative have already been noted, and the extent of Athelstan/Guthrum's authority and assimilation in East Anglia between his arrival there in 876 and his attack on Wessex over the winter of 877–78 remains unclear, and is likely to remain so unless resolved by fresh numismatic evidence. Athelstan/Guthrum's relations with Alfred in the years following the Treaty of Wedmore are also obscure, and would bear further consideration, especially in the light of the re-dating of Alfred's taking control of London to *c*.878–80,[37] as this has implications for the dating of the surviving treaty between Alfred and Guthrum.

Phase 2, c.880–895

This period is characterised by the production and circulation of Anglo-Scandinavian coinage alongside a mixed bullion economy, within which intact ornaments, ingots, hack-silver, imported and locally issued coin all circulated as forms of currency within a bullion economy. The ultimate value of precious metal within this economy probably derived from the role of gold and silver in various forms of social exchange, which lie beyond the scope of this chapter. Nevertheless, the recognition that gold and silver might have a social rather than purely economic value is a warning that one should think in terms of multiple economies rather than simply the dual economy discussed in some of the literature.[38]

---

[36]　Ibid., 28–30.

[37]　M.M. Archibald, 'Coins', in *The Making of England: Anglo-Saxon Art and Culture, AD 600–900*, ed. L. Webster and J. Backhouse (London, 1991), 284–9, at 286; Keynes, 'King Alfred and the Mercians', 19–24; M. Blackburn, 'The London mint in the reign of Alfred', in *Kings, Currency and Alliances*, ed. Blackburn and Dumville, 105–23.

[38]　R. Samson, 'Fighting with silver: rethinking trading, raiding and hoarding', in *Social Approaches to Viking Studies*, ed. R. Samson (Glasgow, 1991), 123–33; M. Gaimster, 'Viking economies: evidence from the silver hoards', in *Silver Economies*, ed. Graham-Campbell and Williams, 123–33; S.M. Sindbæk, 'Silver economies and social ties: long-distance interaction, long-term investments – and why the Viking Age happened', in *Silver Economies, Monetisation*

The Anglo-Scandinavian coinage of this phase exclusively takes the form of imitative issues, although these are divided between those which imitate the designs of Anglo-Saxon or Frankish issues, but with distinct literate inscriptions relating to Anglo-Scandinavian rulers, and anonymous imitations on which not only the designs but the inscriptions were copied, with varying degrees of literacy. The former group contains coins in the names of four, or perhaps six, rulers. Of these, the most extensive coinage is that of Athelstan II (Guthrum) of East Anglia, imitating the *Two Line* type of Alfred of Wessex. Here the numismatic evidence largely supports the narrative provided by contemporary or near-contemporary West Saxon sources. The Viking leader Guthrum was defeated by Alfred at the battle of Edington in 878; by the terms of the peace subsequently agreed in the Treaty of Wedmore, he accepted Christianity, with Alfred as his godfather, and took the baptismal name of Athelstan, whereupon he was accepted as ruler of East Anglia by Alfred. This is reflected in a coinage bearing versions of EDELSTAN REX, with a distribution suggesting a Viking origin, and clearly imitating the *Two Line* type of Alfred (introduced *c.*880), and apparently sharing some moneyers with Alfred. Such issues point to the relationship between Alfred and Athelstan/Guthrum, as well as a wider correlation between minting and an ideal of Romanised Christian kingship.[39] As discussed in the previous section, there are also rare issues of Athelstan/Guthrum imitating a Carolingian *Temple* type, but the relative chronology of these and the more common *Two Line* type is unclear, and they sit less comfortably with the West Saxon narrative.

Imitative issues can be identified by weight, as well as by style. As noted by Blackburn, Anglo-Viking coinage maintained the weight standard of *c.*1.35 grams found in all the Southumbrian English coinage prior to *c.*880, whereas Alfred's reforms at that time raised the West Saxon coinage to a weight standard of *c.*1.5 grams.[40] This choice to maintain the pre-reform standard rather than imitating the weight as well as the designs of Alfred's new coinage now appears more explicable if there was continuity across the period in East Anglia, as suggested above. The weight standards were not very precisely applied, so the distinction on weight alone is not always clear cut, with the heaviest Anglo-Viking coins outweighing the lightest official West Saxon issues.

Imitations exist of several of Alfred's later types, including the *Two Line* and *London Monogram* types as well as the rarer OHSNAFORDA type from

and Society, ed. Graham-Campbell, Sindbæk and Williams, 41–66; Williams, 'Silver Economies, Monetisation and Society', passim.

[39] Blackburn, 'Guthrum and the earliest Danelaw coinages', 30–34; Williams, 'Kingship, Christianity and coinage', 180 and 206–7.

[40] Blackburn, 'Expansion and control', 128–32; M.A.S. Blackburn, 'Alfred's coinage reforms in context', in *Alfred the Great. Papers from the Eleventh-Centenary Conferences*, ed. T. Reuter (Aldershot, 2003), 199–218; Blackburn, 'Guthrum and the earliest Danelaw coinages', 20–23.

Oxford, imitated by the Vikings with the form ORSNAFORDA. Most of these Alfredian imitations are anonymous, and cannot be precisely attributed, although there are varieties with literate mint signatures for Lincoln and Leicester. As noted, a literate coinage in the name of Athelstan/Guthrum was minted in East Anglia, but that does not preclude the minting of anonymous coinage there as well. Anonymous coinage may well also have been issued in this phase in Northumbria, as well as in the Midlands, and while the attributions of the various anonymous types were considered by Blackburn in his paper to the 1997 Viking Congress, more detailed analysis is still required.[41]

In addition to Athelstan/Guthrum, there are three other named rulers in this phase of the coinage, all known from rare or unique examples. Coinage in the name of Sihtric Comes, or Earl Sihtric was struck at SCELDFOR (probably Great or Little Shelford in Cambridgeshire, rather than Shelford in Nottinghamshire, which raises questions about the relationship between Sihtric and the rulers of East Anglia, and the extent of Sihtric's authority, especially as this is the only coinage in Britain or Scandinavia to be struck in the name of a *jarl*, or earl, rather than a king, despite the importance of other individuals with the same title.[42]

A solitary, and incomplete example of a *Two Line* imitation with the partial inscription XGV DE F[ ] RE survives in the Ashdon hoard. This has been interpreted as signifying Guthfrith, a Viking ruler of Northumbria who died in 895, and was buried in York Minster, although Blackburn argued on stylistic grounds that this coin is likely to have been struck south of the Humber, based on its similarity to imitative issues with a Lincoln monogram, as well as to some of the less securely attributed anonymous imitations.[43] This would also be consistent with Viking rulers of Northumbria in the tenth century who appear to have exercised authority south of the Humber (see below), and while a single fragment is insufficient to provide a secure attribution, there is nothing inherently implausible about the attribution to Guthfrith, which seems likely to stand unless other examples are found in contexts which suggest an alternative.

The final coins considered within this phase carry versions of the name ALFDENE or HALFDENE, representing anglicised forms of the Scandinavian name Halfdan. This name appears on a unique coin combining the reverses of Alfred's *London Monogram* and *Two Emperors* issues, as well as on two imitations of Alfred's *Two Line* type. While on current evidence an imitation of the *Two*

---

[41]   Blackburn, 'Expansion and control', 130–32; Williams, 'The Cuerdale coins', 48–9 and 68.

[42]   C. Hart, 'The *Aldewerke* and minster at Shelford, Cambridgeshire', *ASSAH, 8* (1995), 43–68; Blackburn, 'Expansion and Control', 132; Williams, 'Kingship, Christianity and coinage', 200–1

[43]   M.A.S. Blackburn, 'The Ashdon (Essex) hoard and the currency of the southern Danelaw in the late ninth century', *BNJ, 59* (1989), 13–38, at 18–20 (*VCCBI*, 177–205, at 182–4).

Emperors type could conceivably be associated with the Halfdan who led the settlement of Northumbria in 876 but was killed the following year, both the *London Monogram* and *Two Line* types postdate his death, and are unlikely to relate to this individual. Another Halfdan (possibly based in Northumbria, north-west Mercia, or around the Irish Sea), was killed at the battle of Tettenhall in 910. This would be consistent with the presence of two Halfdan coins in the Cuerdale hoard, but the name is not particularly unusual, and Alfredian imitations might fit better with another unrecorded ruler of that name active in the 880s or 890s.[44]

A number of outstanding questions remain for this phase. From a numismatic perspective, the largest and most important of these is the classification and attribution of the various anonymous imitations. Do these indeed represent a single group, and were they all minted in the same region, or would more detailed analysis reveal different stylistic groupings, as in various Anglo-Saxon series, which point to different mint-places/die-cutting centres despite a shared design? This could probably be attempted at least in part on the basis of the current evidence, but would also benefit from new recorded finds, whatever the find circumstances. From an historical perspective, the more interesting questions relate to the regal coins. With so few examples, further evidence is also needed for the coins attributed to Guthfrith and Halfdan. While the attribution to Guthfrith seems likely with only a partial inscription of the name, a complete example is needed to secure the attribution to that ruler, while the place(s) and dates of minting of both Guthfrith's and Halfdan's coins remain to be determined. These are questions on which recorded stray finds are likely to have only limited impact, but which might be answered by hoards and finds from secure archaeological contexts.

Phase 3, c.895–910

This is the most extensive phase of the Anglo-Viking coinage, at least in terms of the number of surviving examples, if not necessarily the original scale of minting. Here our understanding of the coinage is necessarily dominated by the Cuerdale hoard, in which both the East Anglian and Northumbrian series are heavily represented. The East Anglian series takes the form of a single type, imitating the design and obverse inscription of the final coinage before the Viking Conquest, that of King Edmund (d. 869). Edmund came to be venerated as a saint and martyr, and the earliest evidence for this comes from coins which carry the name EADMVND REX prefaced by SC or SCE with a contraction mark, indicating *sancte*. This coinage was minted on a large scale, by at least 70 moneyers, several

---

[44] Williams, 'Cuerdale coins', 47–8.

of whom, to judge by their names, were of Frankish origin.[45] Blackburn has argued, partly on the basis of distribution and partly through the identification of St Edmund moneyers with moneyers of the same names in other types, that minting in this type extended beyond the pre-Viking boundaries of East Anglia into eastern Mercia. Judging from the hoard evidence, the type began to be issued *c.*895, and seems to have been well regulated, successfully excluding other coin types (and to some extent the bullion economy) from East Anglia during its period of circulation. A previous interpretation of a division into an early 'heavy' phase and a later 'light' phase was rejected by Blackburn, following the discovery of the so-called 'Baldwin parcel' from an undeclared hoard, although an internal chronology can still be argued on the basis of style and the literacy of the legends, and of different levels of pecking on coins of different styles within the type.[46] The absence of other information concerning the political history of East Anglia in this period means that the precise circumstances under which this coinage was struck are a mystery, and seems likely to remain so. The design suggests a conscious resurgence of East Anglian identity, and perhaps a corresponding rejection of West Saxon influence, and in addition demonstrates the development of the cult of St Edmund within a generation or so of his death, and therefore of a strong Christian identity. This points to the survival of some ecclesiastical authorities within East Anglia under Viking rule, but both the scale of the coinage and the apparent control of currency circulation suggest strong political authority as well. It therefore seems unlikely that this is a purely ecclesiastical coinage, even if any secular authorities behind the coinage are entirely anonymous. Given that place-name evidence suggests that Viking settlement was less intense in this region than further north one may question quite what the balance of 'Anglo' and 'Scandinavian' was in the case of this particular coinage. While the historical context for this coinage remains opaque, the coinage itself is now well understood numismatically; and although a full corpus and die-study might refine recent interpretations, it seems unlikely to produce major changes in our understanding unless new varieties are discovered.

Around the same time, an extensive coinage was minted in Northumbria, very possibly exclusively in York. The bulk of this coinage appears to be in the name of two rulers, Sigeferth and Cnut, assuming that the forms *Sifredus* and *Sievert*, both of which appear within the coinage, are alternative forms of the same name. Sigeferth is recorded as a 'pirate' from Northumbria in 893, although not as a king, and Cnut is otherwise unrecorded in contemporary historical sources, although later (and unreliable) Scandinavian tradition places a Cnut in Northumbria at this time.[47] There are coins which combine the names

[45]   Smart, 'Moneyers of St Edmund'.
[46]   Blackburn, 'Expansion and Control', 132–4; Blackburn, 'Scandinavian kingdoms', 206–7.
[47]   Smyth, *Scandinavian York and Dublin*, 1, 47–52.

of both rulers, and both names are also combined with a York mint signature, normally in the form EBRAICE. There are also religious inscriptions, including MIRABILIA FECIT and various contractions of *Dominus Deus* (*omnipotens*) *rex*. The Christian message of these inscriptions is reinforced by the use of a central cross on both obverse and reverse, while the majority of the coins of Cnut arrange the letters of his name around the cross in the form of signation (making the sign of the cross), repeating the process with the title REX and a small cross. The different inscriptions appear in various permutations, while the inscription CNVT REX is also found in combination with an enigmatic inscription CVNNETTI.[48] Three other inscriptions within the series will be discussed separately below.

Since the death of Guthfrith is recorded in 895, the assumption has been that Sigeferth succeeded him, while the joint issues of Sigeferth and Cnut, and the sole issues of Cnut appear to be slightly later, *c*.900. The various permutations within this series were considered in detail by Lyon and Stewart, who established a complete typology and relative chronology for the series. This lacks a full die corpus, based as it was on a large but not complete sample of the series, but otherwise remains the definitive work on the subject, with only minor modifications since.

The internal chronology of the series has largely been confirmed by Archibald's study of test marks, based on the number of pecks typically found on different coin types represented in the Cuerdale hoard.[49] A small number of coins within the series carry the name ALVVALDVS, and Blunt plausibly argued that this should be identified with Æthelwold, nephew of Alfred of Wessex, who failed to enforce his claims to Wessex on the death of Alfred in 899 and fled to Northumbria, where he was accepted as a king by the Vikings. This interpretation has generally been accepted.[50] There is an elongated cross-on-steps on some of the coins of Sigeferth, and while the cross-on-steps is a design found on Byzantine coins (indeed, one such coin was found in the Cuerdale hoard), Blackburn proposed that this elongated form was not derived from Byzantine coins, but from the tall stone cross sculptures of Northumbria, although this interpretation is not accepted by all scholars.[51]

Some coins with crude versions of the CNVT REX inscription were combined with a Quentovic mint signature, in good style. Especially since the CNVT REX inscription was not immediately deciphered, owing to the unusual arrangement of the letters, the presence of the Quentovic inscription initially

---

[48]   Lyon and Stewart, 'Northumbrian Viking coins', passim; Stewart, 'Cunnetti reconsidered', passim; Blackburn, 'Coinage of Scandinavian York', 286–7; Williams, 'Cuerdale coins', 43–5.

[49]   Archibald, 'Testing', 60.

[50]   Blunt, 'Alwaldus', passim; Williams, 'Cuerdale coins', 45.

[51]   Blackburn, 'Crosses and conversion', 326–9.

led to the view that the whole series was of Frankish origin. Even after the series as a whole was reinterpreted as Northumbrian, the Quentovic mint signature was not satisfactorily explained until Philip Grierson and Mark Blackburn argued that the Quentovic inscriptions were produced with unofficial dies, and could thus be considered as Viking imitations. However, the CNVT REX inscriptions combined with the Quentovic inscriptions are much more crudely cut than other coins of the same type, and are unlikely to have been produced by the same die-cutters, so it seems likely that the coins with this combination should be seen as a separate imitative group, rather than as part of the main Northumbrian series.[52]

A final addition to this series was provided by the discovery of a new hoard near Silverdale in Lancashire in 2011. Both coins and non-numismatic material indicate that the hoard was deposited around the same time as Cuerdale, and the hoard also contained coins from the Northumbrian series, including a new type. One side carries the inscription D[OMI]N[V]S REX, with the two words crossing at right angles to form the sign of the cross. The other side includes the inscription ΛIRDE CONVT, or possibly CONVT ΛIRDE. Within the context of a largely literate coinage, it seems likely that this represents a name of some sort, although the continued enigma of the meaning of CVNNETTI means that one must be wary of assuming that all inscriptions can necessarily be decoded. I have suggested that this could be an attempt to represent the name Harthacnut, but on current evidence this cannot be regarded as more than a possibility.[53]

Within this phase, coinage clearly circulated within a bullion economy, as hoards typically contain a mixture of coins and non-numismatic material.[54] However, Archibald's work on test marks demonstrates that the later Northumbrian coins within Cuerdale show little or no evidence of testing, suggesting that they may have been accepted at face value, at least in some areas,[55] and it is possible that different monetary systems may have prevailed in York itself, and more widely in Northumbria and other areas of Viking settlement (see also Phase 5 below). The fact that York has produced so few Viking weights compared with Dublin, and with the ninth-century assemblages from Torksey, the riverine site in North Yorkshire and Woodstown, may indicate the presence of a more regulated coin-based economy within York than elsewhere, although the presence of several mixed hoards found within a few miles of York suggests

---

[52]　*MEC* 1, 322; Stewart, 'CVNNETTI reconsidered', 346; Williams, 'Cuerdale coins', 49.

[53]　Williams, 'New coin type'.

[54]　Williams, 'Cuerdale coins', 68–71; Williams, 'Northern hoards reconsidered', 475–81; Boughton, Williams and Ager, 'Viking hoards'.

[55]　Archibald, 'Testing', 60–61.

that firm regulation of monetary circulation may not have extended beyond the city itself.[56]

The number of surviving examples of both the St Edmund Memorial type and the Northumbrian series means that both are comparatively well understood. Complete die-studies of either series might add slightly to our understanding, but would be unlikely to cause fundamental changes to the existing classifications and relative chronology, although the new dating of Cuerdale to 905–10 rather than the former *c.*905 may necessitate minor adjustments to the exact chronology of this and the following phase. New hoards of this phase from York itself and, for example, from rural Yorkshire, might help to determine whether there were regional distinctions in monetary systems, while the outstanding questions regarding interpretation of CVNNETTI and ΛIRDE CONVT are only likely to be conclusively resolved if more transparent variant inscriptions are discovered.

Phase 4, c.910–c.919

There is only one distinct new series in the phase immediately following the Cuerdale phase. This is the *Swordless St Peter* coinage, which carries the inscription S[AN]C[T]I PETRI MO[NETA], or 'money of St Peter', combined with a York mint signature. This coinage is treated in detail by Megan Gooch elsewhere in this volume, so only a brief discussion is given here.[57] The inscription in the name of St Peter rather than a ruler is interesting, since it follows directly from a regal coinage, although that coinage also contained some varieties with religious inscriptions (see above). The absence of a regal inscription led David Rollason to propose that these coins were issued by the archbishops of York rather than by Viking rulers.[58] While this interpretation is not impossible, it is difficult to reconcile either with the strength of royal authority implicit in the previous coinage, or with broader patterns of minting authority in both Anglo-Saxon and Anglo-Scandinavian coinage.[59] It is possible that the inscription simply follows the example of the St Edmund type. The lack of written accounts of Northumbria in this period means that this point is unlikely to be resolved. The end of the St Edmund type (introduced in the previous phase) overlapped with the beginning of the St Peter type. The exact dates are uncertain, but the St Edmund type certainly came to an end at some point in the second decade of the tenth century, probably following the conquest of East Anglia and the adjoining

---

[56] Williams, 'Viking hoards from Yorkshire'.

[57] See Chapter 21, this volume.

[58] Rollason, *Northumbria*, 313–14.

[59] Blackburn, 'Aspects of minting', 159–60; Blackburn, 'Coinage of Scandinavian York', 333.

areas in *c.*917.[60] It is also possible that the inscription may have been influenced by the mint names on some Frankish coins, although the absence of moneyer's names on this and the preceding phase in the Northumbrian coinage means that it is impossible to be certain whether Frankish moneyers were imported to develop the coinage, as is known to be the case in East Anglia.

Otherwise, two important points emerge from Gooch's study of the coinage. Firstly, while the total number of surviving coins in this coinage is not large compared with the previous phase, the previous phase only appears to be so much larger because it was so well represented in the Cuerdale hoard, which is quite exceptional by the standards of the late ninth and tenth centuries, and is otherwise comparatively rare. However, the number of dies represented within the *Swordless St Peter* type relative to the number of surviving coins indicates that this must also have been minted on a large scale (if perhaps not quite so large as the Cuerdale phase) and it is only the absence of a major hoard from this phase which means that the corpus is not larger. Secondly, it was formerly argued that there were two distinct sub-phases within the series, distinguished by 'heavy' and 'light' sub-types.[61] Gooch, developing earlier work by Stewart and Lyon, argues convincingly that this distinction was caused by failing to account for the condition of the coins, and thus by counting damaged coins as a distinct lighter weight standard.[62] There is probably little further to be done with this coinage at present, but additional hoards from the beginning and end of the phase might help to clarify the chronology of the transitions between phases.

In addition to the *Swordless St Peter* coinage, this phase also saw the continuation of anonymous imitations of Anglo-Saxon issues. These have been studied in the context of Edward the Elder's coinage.[63] However, following significant growth in the number of known coins in the name of Edward the Elder (including imitations) as a result of recent hoards, both Edward's official coinage and the imitations would bear a detailed re-examination.

Phase 5, c.919–27

Anonymous imitations continued in this phase, which also saw the resurgence of explicitly regal coins, together with new varieties in the name of St Peter from York, and a similar issue from Lincoln in the name of St Martin. Stray St Edmund coins still appear in some later hoards, but minting in this type appears to have stopped in the previous phase. A coinage in the name of Regnald of

---

[60]   Blackburn, 'Aspects of minting', 156; Blackburn, 'Scandinavian kingdoms', 34–5.

[61]   R.H.M. Dolley, 'The Anglo-Danish and Anglo-Norse coinages of York', in *Viking Age York and the North*, ed. R.A. Hall, CBA Research Report 27 (London, 1978), 27.

[62]   See pp. 461–2.

[63]   *CTCE*, 81 and 207–8.

Northumbria (*c*.919–21) is comparatively rare today, but extremely varied, suggesting that the coinage was more substantial than the surviving number of examples would initially suggest. The majority of Regnald's issues imitate Frankish and/or Anglo-Saxon types, but two designs are distinctive. One shows what appears to be a bow and arrow, unparalleled on any other coinage of the period, but possibly originally inspired by the stylised ships on some Carolingian coins of Dorestad and Quentovic, with the ship turned through ninety degrees so that the mast becomes the arrow in the new design. This would be consistent with the clear Carolingian influence of the KAROLVS monogram on other coins of Regnald. More interesting in some ways is the appearance of a T-shaped design, which has generally been interpreted as representing Thor's hammer, although it may conceivably represent a tau cross.[64]

The Thor's hammer is also a feature of the *Sword* series which followed Regnald's coinage. This series has several types and sub-types, all characterised by the use of a sword as the main obverse design. The two main types are an issue in the name of St Peter, with a York mint signature, and an issue in the name of Sihtric, mostly without mint signature, and including several examples with blundered inscriptions. Each of these has three main sub-types: one with a hammer like that on the coins of Regnald on the reverse; a second with a more unambiguous hammer with voided head and handle (usually described as a 'mallet' to distinguish it from the previous sub-type); and a cross on the third. In the case of the 'cross' variety, the St Peter type incorporates the 'mallet' design on the obverse, making the I of PETRI the handle of a miniaturised mallet. I have argued elsewhere that this may have been a tool of the conversion process, linking Thor with St Peter in a form of religious syncretism.[65] The Sihtric named on the corresponding types must be Sihtric I Caoch, recorded as king of Northumbria (921–26/7), but only one known example in his name has a York mint signature, and Blackburn argued, primarily on the basis of distribution, that these were minted south of the Humber.[66] While coins in the name of Sihtric have subsequently been found in three hoards north of the Humber, they have been outnumbered in each case by the *Sword St Peter* type, and Blackburn's interpretation in my opinion still holds. This was also based in part on the existence of a related type in the name of St Martin with a Lincoln mint signature.[67] What appears to be another mint name appears on one of the Sihtric types, with the inscription EORT CASTRA, or CASTRA EORT, which cannot be closely identified, but which clearly represents a place-name,[68] and which may

---

[64]   Blunt and Stewart, 'Coinage of Regnald I of York', passim; *CTCE*, 105–6; Blackburn, 'Coinage of Scandinavian York', 332–5.

[65]   Williams, 'Kingship, Christianity and coinage', 198.

[66]   Blackburn, 'Scandinavian kingdoms', 212.

[67]   Stewart, 'St Martin Coinage', passim; Blackburn, 'Scandinavian kingdoms', 210–15.

[68]   Blackburn, 'Scandinavian kingdoms', 215.

be a Latinisation of Old English *eorþbyrig,* or 'earthern fortification' a known name form, if not one which permits attribution to a specific mint.[69] A further mint appears to be identified on a currently unique Sword type discovered in the Vale of York hoard with an inscription which appears to read rORIVACASTR, or possibly hORIVACASTR which I have tentatively linked to Rocester in Staffordshire, or possibly to Castor near Peterborough. This coin type appears to be derived from the Cross sub-type of *Sword St Peter,* including the insertion of a miniaturised Thor's hammer in the obverse design.[70] A final *Sword* variety, typically with blundered inscriptions, has been known as the *Anonymous Sword* type, but a recent single-find of this type from near Newark, Nottinghamshire, carries a slightly blundered Sihtric inscription, so this variety can also either be attributed to Sihtric, or interpreted as an imitation derived from Sihtric's issues, while the Nottinghamshire provenance reinforces the attribution to the Midlands of the coinage in the name of Sihtric.[71] Blackburn's die catalogue of the majority of the Sword series includes all the known examples with the exception of a few finds from recent hoards.[72]

The fact that all of the recent hoards (including two certainly dating from the reign of Athelstan) contain only the *Cross* sub-type of the *Sword St Peter type* suggests, first, that this was the latest of the three sub-types, and secondly that there may have been a relatively controlled circulation of coinage within York itself (and therefore that the coinage obtainable directly from York was relatively homogeneous), although outside the town a number of hoards demonstrate a continued mixed bullion economy even within a few miles of York into the mid- and late 920s. On the basis of the extent of die duplication within the known corpus, it seems likely that this phase saw minting on a substantially smaller scale than in the Cuerdale phase (phase 3 above), but here the evidence may be distorted by the fact that Cuerdale alone provides a much larger sample than all of the hoards of the 920s combined. Initial comparison of the new finds with Blackburn's corpus suggests that the majority of dies within the series have been recorded, but this could easily be altered by the discovery of another major hoard.

---

[69] Williams, 'Towns and identities', 30.

[70] Williams, 'RORIVACASTR', passim.

[71] *VCCBI,* 377–9.

[72] A corpus of examples known in 2005 was published in Blackburn, 'Two Scandinavian kingdoms', supplemented in *VCCBI,* 376–84, with more recent finds of all of the Sword types thought to be minted south of the Humber. This means that the combined corpus currently lacks the Sword St Peter issues from the Vale of York and Flusco Pike hoards, and the various Sword types in the 2012 'near York' hoard. The monograph in preparation for the Vale of York and related hoards, which will include all three hoards, will present a further supplement to Blackburn's corpus incorporating these and any additional finds which may appear in the interim.

The attribution of Sihtric's coins to a mint or mints south of the Humber upsets the established chronology for the conquest of the Midlands by the West Saxon dynasty, based on the *Anglo-Saxon Chronicle*. According to this, Edward the Elder already had control of everything south of the Humber by 920, and there is no mention of this territory being lost again before Athelstan gained control of Northumbria as well in 927, although there were brief incursions from Viking Northumbria into the Midlands in the reign of Athelstan's younger brother Edmund. However, if the Midlands were in the hands of Sihtric from some time in the early 920s until his death, this would make sense of a meeting between Athelstan and Sihtric in Tamworth in 926, as Tamworth probably represented Athelstan's northern frontier at the time. If Athelstan had to conquer the Midlands as well as Northumbria, this would furthermore make sense of a coin type in the name of Athelstan which shows a building, and which includes both mint-signed coins from York and a number of coins without mint signatures but which carry the name of moneyers who can be linked in various ways with Midland towns. According to this interpretation, the type was a short-lived issue celebrating Athelstan's assumption of authority across Sihtric's former kingdom before the type was replaced by types giving him the title *Rex totius Britanniae* in the wake of his meeting with various northern kings on his new northern frontier at Eamont Bridge near Penrith on 12 July 927. The previously rare type was well represented by comparatively freshly struck coins in the Vale of York hoard, which spanned Athelstan's conquest of 927, and is also well represented in both parcels of the slightly later hoard (or hoards) from 'near York'.

Phase 6, c. 939–954

The Anglo-Scandinavian coinage was interrupted by the unification of England under Athelstan in 927, and resumed with the re-emergence of an independent Northumbria following his death in 939, although as in Phase 5 some of these Anglo-Scandinavian coins appear to have been issued south of the Humber. This final phase is perhaps the richest from an iconographic perspective, since it contains a number of innovative designs as well as a variety of imitations of Anglo-Saxon and earlier Anglo-Viking types. At the same time, it is probably the least well understood phase of the Anglo-Viking coinage, because of the problems of associating it with the historical context. Unlike Phase 3, which was issued in a historical vacuum, the period 939–54 is recorded in a number of historical sources, which show numerous shifts in power between members of the West Saxon dynasty, two different branches of Uí Ímair (the dynasty which had previously ruled York and now ruled Dublin) and *Yric Haroldssunu* (Eric son of Harold), who is normally identified with the Norwegian Eric Bloodaxe, but who may conceivably have represented another branch of Uí Ímair. Unfortunately the different historical sources conflict on the chronology of political change, and there is continued debate on which sources should be privileged (even different versions of the *Anglo-Saxon Chronicle* disagree) and whether some sources such as later chronicles and sagas should be considered as admissible evidence at all. There is also a lack of consensus as to whether the different branches of Uí Ímair should be seen as allies or rivals (or both at different times).[73] Matters are further complicated by the existence of several types issued by a king or kings called Anlaf (the standard rendering in Old English of the name Óláfr), when two rulers of this name are documented. There are also coins in the name of Sihtric, who does not appear in any contemporary historical account but may be recalled in the later account of Adam of Bremen, although there are difficulties with Adam's chronology.[74] In addition, individual moneyers struck coins for several different rulers in the space of a few years, while the political instability meant that rulers had no choice but to accept this situation. As a result, it is possible to arrange various permutations of type sequence, all of which provide continuity of minting by individual moneyers. At the same time most types are too rare for the absence of a particular moneyer from any given type to be significant. Together, these factors mean that it is not practical to use the careers of individual moneyers to construct a clear sequence for the coinage as a whole, as one might hope.

Against this background, a clear chronology is impossible on the basis of current evidence. The existing sequence and attributions are based on an important study by Michael Dolley, refined by subsequent work by Stewart and Blackburn,[75] but this is based on a normalised chronology of the *Anglo-Saxon Chronicle*, pre-dating the historical debate on this subject, and which can no longer be regarded as in any way certain. Again, single-finds (except in very large numbers) are unlikely to provide illumination. However, given the political instability of the time, the period is remarkably lacking in hoards, and there must be a reasonable hope that new hoards from this phase of the coinage will be discovered. Hoards have the potential to provide both a larger sample of different types, which may improve our understanding of the careers of individual moneyers, and a fuller view of combinations of types within such hoards, which might help to illuminate their sequence. One may note, however, that coins of this phase are also relatively rare even as single-finds, and are found

---

[73] Woolf, 'Erik Bloodaxe revisited'; Downham, 'Eric Bloodaxe – axed?'; Williams, *Eirik Bloodaxe*.

[74] Adam of Bremen, *Gesta Hamburgensis ecclesiae pontificum* ii.22 (MGH SS rer. Germ. 2 (Hannover and Leipzig, 1917), 79–81; *Adam of Bremen: History of the Archbishops of Hamburg-Bremen*, trans. with an introduction by F.J. Tschan, with a new introduction by T. Reuter (New York, 2002), 70–1).

[75] Dolley, 'Post-Brunanburh coinage'; *CTCE*, 211–34; Blackburn, 'Coinage of Scandinavian York', 340–44; Blackburn, 'Two Scandinavian kingdoms', 218–20.

only in small numbers in Viking hoards from elsewhere in Britain, Ireland and Scandinavia, suggesting that they never made up more than a small proportion of the total coin stock available in the period. Nevertheless, die estimates suggest that minting during this phase may have been on a more substantial scale than the low numbers of surviving examples alone would suggest.[76]

Conclusions

All parts of the Anglo-Viking coinage have benefited from repeated and extensive study. Recent finds have shown that we can continue to expect new discoveries within any of the phases. However, while some phases have scope for major reassessment if the right new material appears, others seem unlikely to change very much. A hoard of the 880s could help to bridge the current gap in our knowledge between the settlement phase of the 870s and the hoards of the 890s (Phases 1 and 2), by which time the St Edmund coinage had already begun. The lack of chronological fixed points and the danger of circular arguments mean that new hoards would be unlikely to offer firm dates within this period, or indeed in subsequent phases up to the accession of Regnald in Northumbria in *c.*919. However, they might help to clarify the relative chronology of different coinages in Northumbria, East Anglia and in the Midlands, as well as the question of when pecking was introduced. New provenanced finds, whether single-finds, hoards or site assemblages, could also help with the attribution of the various types imitating coins of Alfred, including both the anonymous imitations and the various rare issues in the names of individual rulers. The Cuerdale phase (Phase 3), and now the *Swordless St Peter* phase (Phase 4), are probably sufficiently well understood numismatically on the one hand, and lacking a clear historical context on the other, that new finds are likely to add only minor details, although new hoards at either end of the *Swordless St Peter* phase might help our understanding of the transitions between phases. Certainly a properly documented hoard from the reign of Regnald has considerable potential to aid the interpretation of a coinage which on current evidence is still comparatively rare, but which is sufficiently varied to hint at minting on a considerable scale. With a concentration now of hoards apparently dating from the mid- to late 920s, a hoard from Northumbria or the Midlands from the early 920s could either confirm or challenge the internal dating of the *Sword* types suggested by recent hoards, while a hoard from the Midlands in particular (preferably supported by a number of single-finds from the same region) could either confirm or challenge the assumption that most if not all of the *Sword* types except for those with York mint signatures were minted south of

---

[76] Blackburn, 'Two Scandinavian kingdoms', 215–16.

the Humber. Finally, while single-finds may add details to our knowledge of the coinage between 939 and 954 (Phase 6), a series of hoards spanning the period is probably the only way to establish a more conclusive relative chronology for the many different coin types. Such a chronology could have a major impact for the historical interpretation of a complicated but significant period in the transition from regional independence north of the Humber under the rule or leadership of Anglo-Scandinavian or Hiberno-Scandinavian kings, to the integration of Northumbria into an emerging kingdom of England, and the end both of separate Anglo-Scandinavian rule and of the distinct Anglo-Scandinavian coinage and currency systems.

Chapter 3

Prelude to Reform: Tenth-Century English Coinage in Perspective[1]

Rory Naismith

The year 973 was an *annus mirabilis* for the kingdom of the English. It has been taken as the apogee of Edgar's reign, itself viewed as a pivotal period in the emergence of England as a coherent political entity approximating its modern counterpart in geographical extent.[2] In the course of this year King Edgar 'the Peaceable' (king of the Mercians 957–59; king of the English 959–75) was crowned at Bath in a ceremony redolent with regal and imperial associations, woven from a blend of Roman, Carolingian and West Saxon tradition.[3] Shortly thereafter Edgar journeyed north to Chester. In this strategically important stronghold near the Welsh border,[4] his status as overlord not only within England but across all Britain was cemented with the submission of several other northern and western kings, who allegedly rowed him along the Dee.[5] The achievements of the West Saxon dynasty were thus celebrated with suitable

[1]   Acknowledgements: This chapter originated as a paper given at the Research Seminar of the Department of Anglo-Saxon, Norse and Celtic in the University of Cambridge in November 2009. Mark Blackburn was instrumental in its development. I am also grateful to others who offered comments or questions subsequently, especially to Simon Keynes, Stewart Lyon, George Molyneaux, Hugh Pagan and Levi Roach.

[2]   S. Keynes, 'Edgar, *rex admirabilis*', in *Edgar, King of the English, 959–975: New Interpretations*, ed. D. Scragg (Woodbridge, 2008), 3–59; G. Molyneaux 'The formation of the English kingdom, *c.* 871–*c.*1016' (DPhil thesis, University of Oxford, 2010).

[3]   J. Nelson, 'Inauguration rituals', in her *Politics and Ritual in Early Medieval Europe* (London, 1986), 283–307, at 296–303; A. Jones, 'The significance of the regal consecration of Edgar in 973', *Journal of Ecclesiastical History, 33* (1982), 375–90.

[4]   S. Matthews, 'King Edgar, Wales and Chester: the Welsh dimension in the ceremony of 973', *Northern History, 44* (2010), 9–26, esp. 22–4.

[5]   Keynes, 'Edgar', 48–51. For a range of alternative views see J. Barrow, 'Chester's earliest regatta? Edgar's Dee-rowing revisited', *EME, 10* (2001), 81–93; A. Williams, 'An outing on the Dee: King Edgar at Chester, A.D. 973', *Mediaeval Scandinavia, 14* (2004), 229–43; S. Jayakumar 'Some reflections on the "foreign policies" of Edgar "the Peaceable"', *Haskins Society Journal, 10* (2001), 17–37; G. Molyneaux, 'Why were some tenth-century English kings presented as rulers of Britain?', *TRHS, 6th series, 21* (2011), 59–91, at 66–8.

pomp and circumstance, and made a deep impression on contemporary and subsequent commentators.[6]

Numismatists have also claimed 973 as a significant date, attributing to it a major reform of the English currency. Justification for doing so is insecure at best. Roger of Wendover (d. 1236), in his *Flores historiarum*, mentioned a reform of the coinage under Edgar, which he placed in 975. However, this annal was not very chronologically specific, and Roger dated the coin reform to the same year as the submission of Cináed/Kenneth II, king of Alba (971–95), to Edgar, which is very probably identical with the Chester ceremony of 973.[7] Whatever its exact date, no doubt exists that a major change in the coinage did occur towards the end of Edgar's reign. The old currency was swept away, and a new, highly unified coinage appeared at 44 mints from York to Exeter, carrying the royal name, title and bust on the obverse, and (on the reverse) the name of the mint and moneyer (Figure 3.1).[8] Most dies were initially distributed from the same source, and new, higher standards for weight and fineness were asserted. In early medieval terms, this was the gold standard of currency systems. It is all the more impressive because essentially the same system persisted in England for over a century and a half thereafter, with nation-wide recoinages every few years.[9]

English numismatists therefore have good reason to take pride in the late Anglo-Saxon currency, and in the quality of research which scholars have devoted to it in the last 60 years. Edgar's coinage reform, the event which brought the new system into being, has been hailed as 'a true revolution,'[10] and one of the most prominent legacies of the late Anglo-Saxon kingdom. Assessments of

---

[6]   D.E. Thornton, 'Edgar and the eight kings, A.D. 973: *textus et dramatis personae*', *EME*, *10* (2001), 49–79. For an adulatory account see Byrhtferth of Ramsey, *Vita S. Oswaldi* iv.6–7, (*Byrhtferth of Ramsey: Lives of St Oswald and St Ecgwine*, ed. M. Lapidge (Oxford, 2009), 104–11).

[7]   Roger of Wendover, *Flores historiarum* s.a. 975 (*Rogeri de Wendover Chronica; sive, Flores historiarum*, ed. H.O. Coxe (5 vols., London, 1841–4), 1, 415–16); M. Dolley, 'Roger of Wendover's date for Eadgar's coinage reform', *BNJ, 49* (1979), 1–11. More critical readings include I. Stewart, 'Coinage and recoinage after Edgar's reform', in *Studies in Late Anglo-Saxon Coinage in Memory of Bror Emil Hildebrand*, ed. K. Jonsson (Stockholm, 1990), 456–85, at 461–2; J. Brand, *Periodic Change of Type in the Anglo-Saxon and Norman Periods* (Rochester, 1984), 9–17; K. Jonsson, *The New Era: the Reformation of the Late Anglo-Saxon Coinage* (Stockholm, 1987), 83–5.

[8]   M. Allen, *Mints and Money in Medieval England* (Cambridge, 2012), 16.

[9]   M. Dolley and D.M. Metcalf, 'The reform of the English coinage under Eadgar', in *Anglo-Saxon Coins: Studies Presented to F. M. Stenton on the Occasion of His 80th Birthday*, ed. M. Dolley (London, 1961), 136–68; Jonsson, *New Era*.

[10]   H.R. Loyn, *Anglo-Saxon England and the Norman Conquest*, 2nd edn (London, 1991), 125.

Figure 3.1   *Reform* penny of Edgar, Stamford mint, moneyer Æscman (Fitzwilliam Museum, Cambridge).

the coinage extending from *c.*973 to 1086/7, 1135 or even 1158 are numerous.[11] Here, however, the emphasis will be on the approach to this famous point of departure – on Edgar's recoinage as the culmination of what had come before. The new coinage was a product of contemporary institutional and ideological developments, but also of more than a century of gradual military conquest and monetary sophistication, most notably in the period after *c.*880, though also extending back to the general establishment of a visible degree of royal control over minting in the eighth century.[12] The term 'royal control' is used here advisedly, for kings' engagement with the coinage was and always had been a grey area of ups, downs and shifting priorities.[13] It was not simply an on-off process. Change, especially on a large scale, required substantial commitment if it was to take hold; maintenance of an established but perhaps less ambitious system was often more feasible. One must also think 'bottom-up' as well as 'top-down', and consider the viewpoint of lower-level minting agencies in addition to that of the king, agencies such as the moneyers who had played a major role well before the reform of *c.*973, and would continue to do so long afterwards.

The importance of the coinage for knowledge of the tenth century goes far beyond the confines of numismatics and monetary history. Coins have the virtue of comparatively plentiful and consistent survival, and the now large body of recorded single-finds provides an especially piercing insight into the changing form of the monetary economy.[14] Coins were also a product of royal government in action: an important manifestation of control and rulership which can be

---

[11]   I. Stewart, 'The English and Norman mints, *c.*600–1158', in *A New History of the Royal Mint*, ed. C.E. Challis (Cambridge, 1992), 1–82; D.M. Metcalf, *An Atlas of Anglo-Saxon and Norman Coin Finds, c. 973–1086* (London, 1998); F.M. Stenton, *Preparatory to Anglo-Saxon England* (Oxford, 1970), 374.

[12]   M. Dolley, *The Norman Conquest and the English Coinage* (London, 1966), 8; S. Keynes, 'England, 900–1016', in *The New Cambridge Medieval History, vol. 3: c.900–c.1024*, ed. T. Reuter (Cambridge, 1999), 456–84, at 459; Keynes, 'Edgar', 23–4.

[13]   See especially below, pp. 42–6.

[14]   Metcalf, *Atlas*; R. Naismith, 'The English monetary economy, *c.*973–1100: the contribution of single finds', *EcHR*, 66 (2013), 198–225; M. Blackburn, 'Coin finds as primary historical evidence for medieval Europe', in *Dynamism in Coinage: Europe, China and Japan.*

used as a gauge for political aspirations.[15] Study of the coins spanning the tenth century is therefore nothing less than study of the nature of late Anglo-Saxon government and all that goes with it: the evolution of the 'late Anglo-Saxon state' itself.[16]

The English Coinage *c.*880–973: 'a Maximum View'[17]

Even in the able hands of modern numismatists, the coinage as it was on the eve of Edgar's reform is far from as pliable a source as its successor.[18] Pennies were not normally mint-signed, and several types were produced simultaneously. But it is misleading to focus solely on the obstacles accentuated by comparison with the reform issue. A more positive view of the coinage issued *c.*880–973 is entirely possible. Central to this are two important constants: the names of the king and of the moneyer. The former in particular represents a strand of continuity which cut across designs, regions and even kingdoms. Anglo-Saxon kings from the time of Eadberht of Northumbria (737–58) and Offa of Mercia (757–96) exercised close control over the coinage, which was symbolised by the imposition of the current king's name and title.[19] Similar privileges were only rarely extended to

Comparative Viewpoints. Proceedings of the 12th Conference of the Coin Finds Research Group Held in Fukuoka 2005, ed. S. Sakuraki (Fukuoka, 2005), 7–50.

[15] I. Garipzanov, *The Symbolic Language of Authority in the Carolingian World (c.751–877)* (Leiden and Boston, MA, 2008), 1–41.

[16] See, above all, J. Campbell, *The Anglo-Saxon State* (London, 2000), esp. 32. Selected further discussion includes R. Davies, 'The medieval state: the tyranny of a concept', *Journal of Historical Sociology, 16* (2003), 280–300, at 286–9; S. Keynes, 'Re-reading King Æthelred the Unready', in *Writing Medieval Biography 750–1250: Essays in Honour of Professor Frank Barlow*, ed. D. Bates, J. Crick and S. Hamilton (Woodbridge, 2006), 77–97, at 82–7; C. Wickham, *The Inheritance of Rome. A History of Europe from 400 to 1000* (London, 2009), 463–6; S. Baxter, 'The limits of the late Anglo-Saxon state', in *Der frühmittelalterliche Staat – europäische Perspektiven*, ed. W. Pohl and V. Wieser (Vienna, 2009), 503–13; S. Foot, 'The historiography of the Anglo-Saxon "nation-state"', in *Power and the Nation in European History*, ed. L. Scales and O. Zimmer (Cambridge, 2005), 125–42; T. Reuter, 'The making of England and Germany, 850–1050: points of comparison and difference', in *Medieval Europeans: Studies in Ethnic Identity and National Perspectives in Medieval Europe*, ed. A. Smyth (London, 1998), 53–70.

[17] Cf. Campbell, *Anglo-Saxon State*, 1–30.

[18] The key studies are C. Blunt 'The coinage of Athelstan, 924–939', *BNJ, 42* (1974), 35–160; M. Archibald and C. Blunt, *SCBI 34: British Museum. Anglo-Saxon Coins V: Athelstan to the Reform of Edgar, 924–c. 973* (London, 1986); *CTCE*. For a survey see I. Stewart, 'English coinage from Athelstan to Edgar', *NC, 149* (1988), 192–214; new developments for Edgar's coinage are addressed in H. Pagan, 'The pre-reform coinage of Edgar', in *Edgar*, ed. Scragg, 192–207.

[19] R. Naismith, 'Kings, crisis and coinage reforms in the mid-eighth century', *EME, 20* (2012), 291–332.

other rulers. After the 820s no sub-kings are known to have issued coins in their own name, including Æthelred (d. 911) and Æthelflæd (d. 918) of the Mercians. Even when the kingdom of the English was temporarily split between Eadwig and Edgar in 957, there is no evidence that mints in Edgar's territory north of the Thames ceased to recognise Eadwig.[20] Occasionally therefore *de facto* supervision over minting lay outside the over-king's control, as one aspect of local administration which fell within the purview of the local ruler.[21] But only rarely was this recognised in the inscription, even though a greater measure of either open or covert control could easily have been granted to or seized by local rulers, as happened with increasing frequency in the Carolingian empire and its successors in the late ninth and tenth centuries.[22] A strong inclination towards recognition of the overlords of the West Saxon dynasty seems to have prevailed from the reign of Alfred onwards. Very few English magnates issued coinage in their own name before the twelfth century, with just a few exceptions. Coins bearing the name *Alvaldus* can probably be attributed to the West Saxon pretender Æthelwold (d. 902), but these were struck outside the English kingdom at Viking York.[23] Archbishops of Canterbury, on the other hand, placed their name on the pennies issued by certain moneyers in Canterbury from the late eighth century onwards. But these were phased out with the death of Archbishop Plegmund (890–923). The other exception is a unique surviving penny apparently in the name of Hywel Dda, king of Deheubarth (d. 950), struck around the 940s by a moneyer associated with Chester.[24] Otherwise, the West Saxon king was the sole ruler named on coins struck in the growing kingdom of England. In a very real sense the pre-reform coinage of the tenth century was a unified entity, in that the current king was always recognised at every mint under his authority from Exeter to York – a point which should not be underestimated, especially in the wider European context of the tenth century.

Crucial to the king's involvement with the coinage was a close and long-standing relationship with the moneyers across the kingdom. Coinage in southern England had been based on a flexible but generally effective collaboration between these two agencies since at least the middle of the eighth century. From the 850s

---

[20] *CTCE*, 278–80; Jonsson, *New Era*, 68–70.

[21] See below, pp. 78–9.

[22] F. Dumas, 'La monnaie au Xe siècle', *Settimane di studio del Centro italiano di studi sull'alto medioevo, 38* (1991), 565–609; Reuter, 'Making'; Molyneaux, 'Formation', 246–62. See also below, n. 175.

[23] C. Blunt, 'Northumbrian coins in the name of Alwaldus', *BNJ*, 55 (1985), 192–4; R. Lavelle, 'The politics of rebellion: the *Ætheling* Æthelwold and West Saxon royal succession, 899–902', in *Challenging the Boundaries of Medieval History: the Legacy of Timothy Reuter*, ed. P. Skinner (Turnhout, 2009), 51–80.

[24] *CTCE*, 138; C. Blunt, 'The cabinet of the marquess of Ailesbury and the penny of Hywel Dda', *BNJ, 52* (1982), 117–22.

in Wessex there had been a noticeable swing in favour of royal direction,[25] but it was under Alfred, in the *Cross and Lozenge* and especially *Horizontal* coinages beginning *c.*875 and *c.*880 respectively, that a number of important features in the moneyers' role emerged which would become hallmarks of the later English currency.[26] Above all, minting became one of the roles associated with the numerous fortress-towns known as *byrg* (sing. *burh*). These figured prominently in the military campaigns of the late ninth and early tenth centuries, and many were set up on the direct orders of Alfred, Edward, Æthelred or Æthelflæd.[27] They were a vital component of English military success, and shared a principal common purpose, at least by the early tenth century, as fortified redoubts for securing territory.[28] Their fundamentally military role was signalled by the core meaning of *burh*, which was 'fortification';[29] other functions – such as providing a sheltered and well-located focus for a permanent population and commerce – were not forgotten, but were decidedly secondary to military and associated

---

[25]   R. Naismith, *Money and Power in Anglo-Saxon England: the Southern English Kingdoms 757–865* (Cambridge, 2012), 109–12.

[26]   M. Blackburn, 'The London mint in the reign of Alfred', in *Kings, Currency and Alliances: History and Coinage of Southern England in the Ninth Century*, ed. M. Blackburn and D. Dumville (Woodbridge, 1998), 105–23, at 106–8.

[27]   E.g. *ASC* 907, 910 BCD, 912, 913, 914, 918 (= 915) ABCD, 919 (= 916) A, 920 (= 917), 921 (= 918) ABCD, 922 (= 919) and 923 (= 920) A (all references to the *ASC* are taken from *Two of the Saxon Chronicles Parallel, with Supplementary Extracts from the Others*, ed. C. Plummer (2 vols., Oxford, 1892); and *The Anglo-Saxon Chronicle: a Revised Translation*, trans. D. Whitelock, D. Douglas and S. Tucker (London, 1961)). Also of note is Asser, *Vita Ælfredi regis*, ch. 91 (*Asser's Life of King Alfred together with the Annals of Saint Neots Erroneously Ascribed to Asser*, ed. W.H. Stevenson, with foreword by D. Whitelock (Oxford, 1959), 76–9; *Alfred the Great. Asser's Life of King Alfred and Other Contemporary Sources*, trans. S. Keynes and M. Lapidge (London, 1983), 101–2).

[28]   D. Hill and A. Rumble (ed.), *The Defence of Wessex: the Burghal Hidage and Anglo-Saxon Fortifications* (Manchester, 1996).

[29]   A.H. Smith, *English Place-Name Elements*, English Place-Name Society 25–6 (2 vols., Cambridge, 1956), 1, 58–62; D.N. Parsons and T. Styles, *The Vocabulary of English Place Names (BRACE–CÆSTER)* (Nottingham, 2000), 74–85; S. Draper, 'The significance of Old English *Burh* in Anglo-Saxon England', *ASSAH*, 15 (2008), 240–53; J. Baker and S. Brookes, *Beyond the Burghal Hidage: Anglo-Saxon Civil Defence in the Viking Age* (Leiden, 2013), 90–106. *Port* was often preferred in non-military contexts such as trade and minting (Smith, *English Place-Name Elements*, 2, 70–1). In Latin terminology, size and function seem not to have been the main factors in the classification of towns for Anglo-Saxon observers: more important was the presence or absence of Roman remains. The coinage of Athelstan (Blunt, 'Athelstan', 45) famously denotes Roman cities as *civitas*, while non-Roman and/or *de novo* foundations like Lewes, Oxford and Southampton are labelled *urbes*. This echoes the general custom of Bede's day: J. Campbell, *Essays in Anglo-Saxon History* (London, 1986), 99–119.

administrative needs, and might or might not blossom over time.[30] The *byrg* were not created according to a standard blueprint: they had diverse origins, and met diverse fates in later periods.[31] But while not every *burh* was to play a substantial urban role, all minting was strictly confined to these fortress-towns.[32] In the words of the famous monetary passage of the law-code II Athelstan, 'nan mon ne mynetige buton on port'.[33]

The expansion of the *byrg* was underpinned by an important change in royal policy towards minting. Beginning on a modest scale in the late 870s, moneyers emerged at a number of new locations in English Mercia as well as Wessex. A decision to expand beyond the very few mint-towns active *c.*875 must have found support in both kingdoms, although it is likely to have been driven by Alfred the Great and subsequently Edward the Elder.[34] Following the progress of the new mints is problematic due to the rarity of mint-names at this time. But in addition to the long-established mint-towns of London and Canterbury, mints at Oxford, Gloucester, Exeter, Winchester and Bath were named on coins produced *c.*875– 905, and there were certainly several others which went unnamed. By the time mint-signatures became widespread for the first time under Athelstan in the late 920s, approximately 37 mints were active: these constituted the large majority of

---

[30] R. Holt, 'The urban transformation in England, 900–1100', *Anglo-Norman Studies, 32* (2009), 57–78; A. Vince, 'Saxon urban economies: an archaeological perspective', in *Environment and Economy in Anglo-Saxon England*, ed. R. Rackham, CBA Research Report 89 (York, 1994), 108–19; M. Carver, *The Birth of a Borough: an Archaeological Study of Anglo-Saxon Stafford* (Woodbridge, 2010), 138–43.

[31] The formative statement is M. Biddle and D. Hill, 'Late Saxon planned towns', *Antiquaries Journal, 51* (1971), 70–85; elaborated in M. Biddle, 'Towns', in *The Archaeology of Anglo-Saxon England*, ed. D.M. Wilson (Cambridge), 99–150, at 124–41. The diverse origins of the *byrg* are stressed in J. Blair, *The Church in Anglo-Saxon Society* (Oxford), 330–7; Holt, 'Urban transformation'; Carver, *Birth*, 127–45. Recent case-studies include N. Christie et al., '"Have you found anything interesting?" Exploring late-Saxon and medieval urbanisation at Wallingford: sources, results and questions', *Oxoniensia, 75* (2010), 35–47; S. Bassett, 'The middle and late Anglo-Saxon defences of western Mercian towns', *ASSAH, 15* (2008), 180–239; D. Griffiths, 'The north-western Mercian burhs: a reappraisal', *ASSAH, 8* (1995), 75–86. For an alternative interpretation of the genesis of the burghal network see J. Haslam, 'King Alfred and the Vikings: strategies and tactics, 876–886 AD', *ASSAH, 13* (2005), 122–54.

[32] M. Blackburn, 'Mints, burhs and the Grateley code, cap. 14.2', in *Defence*, ed. Hill and Rumble, 160–75, esp. 165; G. Williams, 'Military and non-military functions of the Anglo-Saxon *burh, c.* 878–978', in *Landscapes of Defence in Early Medieval Europe*, ed. J. Baker, S. Brookes and A. Reynolds (Turnhout, 2013), 129–64, esp. 135–40. For the case that many 'urban' developments post-date the Burghal Hidage see D. Hill, 'Athelstan's urban reforms', *ASSAH, 11* (2000), 173–85.

[33] 'No-one is to mint money except in a fortress-town'. II Athelstan, ch. 14 (*Die Gesetze der Angelsachsen*, ed. F. Liebermann (3 vols., Halle, 1903–16), 1, 158; *EHD* 1, 420 (no. 35)).

[34] M. Blackburn, 'Alfred's coinage reforms in context', in *Alfred the Great. Papers from the Eleventh-Centenary Conferences*, ed. T. Reuter (Aldershot, 2003), 199–218, at 207–8.

those Edgar drew on in *c.*973.[35] In the eastern parts of England during the reign of Edward the Elder, these new mints often came in the wake of conquering armies; many were set up in the same location, or even using the same personnel, as earlier Anglo-Viking mint-places.[36] The presumption is that the moneyers' presence in these new centres fulfilled a combination of economic and especially administrative needs.[37] A conscious development of *byrg* which shared some functions of older substantial, defended settlements (including minting), was surely part of this process, as was a wish to replace the coinage in newly won areas.[38] Expanding the mint network without compromising the outward royal monopoly over minting was a powerful manifestation of coinage's place very much within the remit of royal government, especially in the half-century after *c.*875.

Universal recognition of the king did not of course mean standardisation in every respect. On the contrary, prior to Edgar's reform many important features of the coinage were seemingly quite varied. This is not the place to embark on a detailed chronological survey of the tenth-century Anglo-Saxon coinage, but enough is known to show that its diversity often followed some internal logic, and that the coinage should not be judged solely by the benchmark of the reformed issue of Edgar. It was out of this earlier currency, warts and all, that the reformed coinage developed,[39] and there were also important common characteristics which spanned the entire period from Alfred to the eleventh century. A selection of these features – typology, the spread of English minting, circulation, physical features and administrative organisation – will be discussed further below.

Typology

It is in typology, and associated matters of die-distribution, that the disunity of the tenth century is most marked.[40] Several designs were current simultaneously in different parts of the country, and were not changed as frequently or as systematically as would later be the case. Mint-names were given only

---

[35]   Blackburn, 'Mints'.

[36]   *CTCE*, 52–4. See also below, pp. 53–6.

[37]   P. Stafford, *Unification and Conquest. A Political and Social History of England in the Tenth and Eleventh Centuries* (London, 1989), 141.

[38]   See below, pp. 78–9.

[39]   See below, pp. 81–3.

[40]   K. Jonsson, *New Era*, 65–78; K. Jonsson, 'The pre-reform coinage of Edgar – the legacy of the Anglo-Saxon kingdoms', in *Coinage and History in the North Sea World c. 500–1250: Essays in Honour of Marion Archibald*, ed. B. Cook and G. Williams (Leiden and Boston, 2006), 325–46; Stewart, 'English Coinage'.

sporadically, meaning that many coins can only be assigned to a region.[41] But although diverse in comparison with the later coinage, the variation of the earlier tenth century should not be exaggerated (Figure 3.2). The number of groups and types was relatively small. The oldest and most widespread is known as the *Horizontal* type: a simple design which places the king's name on the obverse around an inner circle containing a small cross. The reverse carries the moneyer's name in two lines ornamented with crosses, pellets or other devices.

The institution of this type was a turning point for the English coinage.[42] From *c*.880 it soon spread across Wessex and English Mercia.[43] To a significant extent the thrust of military and monetary expansion *c*.880–925 went hand in hand with the *Horizontal* coinage, which came to be the prevalent currency associated with the growing kingdom of Alfred and Edward the Elder (Figure 3.2a).[44] It was issued on a substantial scale down to the 970s, and was the dominant coin-type of the whole kingdom until the late 920s. Several local variants can be identified, even in the years immediately after the type's emergence. The most interesting of these belongs to the west Midlands, and dispenses with the basic reverse design during the middle part of Edward the Elder's reign, replacing it with a range of attractive pictorial types. The obverse of these types remained unchanged. It is probable that this pictorial coinage comes from the northern part of English Mercia between 911 (or earlier) and 918, when it lay under the control of Æthelflæd, Edward the Elder's sister and Æthelred's widow, implying a rare and limited numismatic recognition of political distinction.[45]

Other significant variants under Edward included a small but possibly widespread type bearing a bust, and a series from East Anglia struck to a light weight standard and with garbled legends.[46] Two other principal types emerged in the reign of Athelstan: the *Circumscription* coinage, which differed in arranging the moneyer's name in circumscription rather than in two lines (Figure 3.2b); and the *Bust Crowned* type, which placed a bust of the king on the obverse, usually with a *Circumscription*-type reverse (Figure 3.2c).[47] At any one

---

[41]   Known attributions are listed in *CTCE*, 281–312.

[42]   Cf. D.M. Metcalf, 'The monetary history of England in the tenth century viewed in the perspective of the eleventh century', in *ASMH*, 133–57, at 142.

[43]   M. Blackburn 'The Ashdon (Essex) hoard and the currency of the southern Danelaw in the late ninth century', *BNJ*, 59 (1989), 13–38, at 16–18 (*VCCBI*, 177–205); M. Blackburn, 'The earliest Anglo-Viking coinage of the southern Danelaw (late 9th century)', in *Proceedings of the 10th International Congress of Numismatics, London 1986* (London, 1989), 341–8, at 342–3 (*VCCBI*, 167–75, at 168–9).

[44]   See below, pp. 50 and 63.

[45]   *CTCE*, 34–43; S. Lyon, 'The coinage of Edward the Elder', in *Edward the Elder, 899–924*, ed. N. Higham and D. Hill (London, 2001), 67–78, at 72–3.

[46]   For the latter see below, p. 54.

[47]   Blunt, 'Athelstan', 46–51.

Figure 3.2   *Horizontal-Trefoil* penny of Edmund, moneyer Wigheard (left); *Circumscription Cross* penny of Athelstan, Chester mint, moneyer Mældomen (centre); *Bust Crowned* penny of Edgar, London mint, moneyer Ælfnoth (right) (all Fitzwilliam Museum, Cambridge).

time, therefore, even the divergent coinages of England usually shared a similar design on at least one face. Dies used to manufacture these coinages were made and distributed on a regional basis, and stylistic groups suggest that by the last decades of the ninth century there were centres of die-production associated with London, Canterbury and Winchester, though only the last of these survived to the end of the reign. There was also a smaller group of moneyers whose work can be associated with English Mercia.[48]

Tracing these regional groupings in die-cutting and design is complex, and reveals that few areas remained static in their affiliations (cf. Figure 3.3).[49] 'English Mercia' (effectively the modern west Midlands), for example, switched back to regular *Horizontal* and associated types around the time of Æthelflæd's death in 918. After about 930 the most characteristic regional feature of this area was avoidance of the *Bust Crowned* type, and use of rosettes in place of crosses on coins of *Horizontal* and *Circumscription* types.[50] Variations on this level are significant for the numismatist, and doubtless carried meaning for the makers of coins and dies, yet prompt the question of how far they constituted a different type in the view of contemporary rulers and users. Detailed modern classification sometimes risks obscuring the wood with the trees. Moreover, the area of the *Rosettes* types probably did not cover all of English Mercia: only its northern part, and there were typological variations even within this territory. What happened at mints in the southern part of English Mercia over much of the tenth century is unclear.[51] Moneyers based there under Athelstan sometimes also operated at Shrewsbury (which was normally associated monetarily with Chester), but typologically there were links with both north and south.[52]

More substantial differences prevailed in eastern England. East Anglia displayed a strong tendency towards *Bust Crowned* designs from the time of

---

[48]   Blackburn, 'Earliest Anglo-Viking coinage', 342–3 (*VCCBI*, 168–9); Blackburn, 'Ashdon', 16–18 (*VCCBI*, 180–2); *CTCE*, 25–32.

[49]   The overall divisions are succinctly outlined in Stewart, 'English coinage', 195–206.

[50]   Pagan, 'Pre-reform', 199–205; Blunt, 'Athelstan', 97–103; *CTCE*, 109, 120–22, 134–7, 148–52, 162–4 and 176–8.

[51]   H. Pagan, 'Pre-reform', 197; H. Pagan, 'Mints and moneyers in the west Midlands and at Derby in the reign of Eadmund (939–46)', *NC, 155* (1995), 139–61, at 151–2; Blunt, 'Athelstan', 103–4.

[52]   One moneyer at Hereford struck characteristically northern Rosette types under Athelstan and Edmund, but *Horizontal Trefoil* pennies associated with southern England under Eadred, while another moneyer at Gloucester produced 'southern' *Circumscription Cross* and *Bust Crowned* pennies under Athelstan (the latter generally eschewed in English Mercia: Blunt, 'Athelstan', 123), but a 'Mercian' ornamental type under Edmund. Cf. *CTCE*, 287, 293, 299 and 302.

Athelstan until the 970s.[53] Yet the East Anglian moneyers may have switched temporarily to a *Horizontal* coinage under Eadwig,[54] while under Eadred there were marked stylistic similarities between the *Bust Crowned* type of East Anglia and that of the 'north-eastern' region. This was another area which often went its own way. Under Athelstan and Edgar it consistently resisted the imposition of 'national' coinages. On the other hand, it frequently shared designs and even dies with York, which again often followed its own course. The extent and influence of the north-eastern region – which had its heartland in the northern east Midlands, in the area of Lincoln and Stamford – seem to have fluctuated: towns such as Nottingham and Leicester may have looked both to suppliers of 'north-eastern'-style dies and to Derby, which was numismatically aligned with Chester and English Mercia.[55] To the south, 'north-eastern' dies were often employed at Northampton and Bedford, and sometimes entered use as far afield as Hertford and Maldon.[56] Southern England – which, for monetary purposes, encompassed Wessex, most of Essex and south-east England, as well as parts of what had been English Mercia such as London, Oxford and Buckingham[57] – may have been more coherent on the whole, though since the bulk of surviving hoard material comes from the north, the coinage of this part of the country is substantially more obscure.[58]

This sketch of geographical trends is no more than cursory, but it must be reiterated that the typological breakdown of the kingdom into five principal regions (the south, English Mercia, East Anglia, the 'north-east' (*viz.* the east Midlands) and Northumbria) was by no means stable. Neither should this fluidity be surprising given the piecemeal nature of English conquest over the tenth century, which saw a number of counterattacks and other setbacks along the way. The impact of this process of conquest will be further explored below,[59] but there were times when some or all these divisions were overcome. Alfred and Edward the Elder's coinages, for example, were broadly coherent in their dominance by the *Horizontal* type. The most impressive step towards unity in type came in the late 920s when Athelstan instituted the *Circumscription Cross*

---

[53] Blunt, 'Athelstan', 191–6. For an alternative regional division see D.M. Metcalf, 'The Rome (Forum) Hoard of 1883', *BNJ, 62* (1992), 63–96, at 66–9.

[54] Blunt, 'Athelstan', 194–5. The coins of the moneyers Bruning and Folcard are suggestive. Both are known for East Anglian-style *Bust Crowned* pennies under Edgar, but only for *Horizontal Trefoil* pennies under Eadwig (the former of 'northeastern' style) (ibid., 289 and 295).

[55] Blunt, 'Athelstan', 93–7; Pagan, 'Mints', 153–4.

[56] Blunt, 'Athelstan', 82; *CTCE*, 112 and 266.

[57] On the takeover of these Mercian territories see D.N. Dumville, *Wessex and England from Alfred to Edgar: Six Essays on Political, Cultural, and Ecclesiastical Revival* (Woodbridge, 1992), 8–13 and 24–7.

[58] Pagan, 'Pre-reform', 193–7.

[59] See below, pp. 53–6.

design at all mints from York to Exeter and Canterbury, with the sole exception of the 'north-east'. This coinage was also marked by adoption of an innovative royal style, mirrored in contemporary charters and other texts, which honoured Athelstan as *rex totius Britanniae* ('king of all Britain').[60] Also of widespread but somewhat less general distribution was the immediately succeeding *Bust Crowned* type, which was the first in the Anglo-Saxon coinage to feature a contemporary form of crown.[61] The two decades after Athelstan's death were the most marked by regional tendencies in the typology of the coinage, but there was a return to relative unity in the earlier part of Edgar's reign. Behind this was a conscious attempt to imitate the coinage of Athelstan, the clearest demonstration of which was a revival of *Circumscription Cross* (or, in the northern part of English Mercia, *Circumscription Rosette*), sometimes even extending to re-use of the title *rex totius Britanniae*; *rex Anglorum* was more widespread, however, and both titles find parallels in contemporary documents.[62] To a limited extent the *Bust Crowned* type also returned to prominence outside East Anglia.[63] At London another reference to past coinages came with halfpennies which used the *Lundonia* monogram known from Alfred's reign.[64] It must be stressed that the understanding of these coinages depends on a relatively small body of material, because of the absence of substantial hoard material covering southern England: new mints and moneyers continue to be discovered.[65]

---

[60] On this, see now Molyneaux, 'Why'; S. Foot, *Æthelstan: the First King of England* (New Haven, CT, and London, 2011), 212–26. Avoidance of the title in East Anglia and the 'northeast' is noted in Blunt, 'Athelstan', 115, though does not necessarily carry political significance. For other specific sources, S. Keynes, 'King Athelstan's books', in *Learning and Literature in Anglo-Saxon England*, ed. M. Lapidge and H. Gneuss (Cambridge, 1985), 143–201, at 149–51 (on the inscription of London, British Library, MS Cotton Tiberius A.II, fol. 15v); M. Lapidge, *Anglo-Latin Literature 900–1066* (London, 1993), 71–81 and 86 (on the poem *Carta dirige gressus*); S. Foot, 'Where English becomes British: rethinking contexts for *Brunanburh*', in *Myth, Rulership, Church and Charters: Essays in Honour of Nicholas Brooks*, ed. J. Barrow and A. Wareham (Aldershot, 2008), 127–44, at 140–41; C. Karkov, *The Ruler Portraits of Anglo-Saxon England* (Woodbridge, 2004), 79–83.

[61] Karkov, *Portraits*, 66–7; Foot, *Æthelstan*, 216–23.

[62] *CTCE*, 172–81; Pagan, 'Pre-reform', esp. 193–5; Keynes, 'Edgar', 25; E. John, *Orbis Britanniae and Other Studies* (Leicester, 1966), 55–6. Under Edgar the title *rex totius Britanniae* was most characteristic of mints in western Mercia, though was also found occasionally elsewhere.

[63] *CTCE*, 195–7.

[64] *CTCE*, 203–4; C. Blunt, 'Tenth-century halfpennies and C. Roach Smith's plate of coins found in London', *BNJ, 31* (1962), 44–8.

[65] Pagan, 'Pre-reform', esp. 193–5. Significant new finds include M. Lessen, 'A presumed "Hampshire" hoard of Eadgar CC type', *NCirc, 111* (2003), 61–2; S. Lyon, 'The earliest signed penny of Cricklade: a local find of Edgar's "Circumscription Cross" issue', in *Studies in Early Medieval Coinage, vol. 2: New Perspectives*, ed. T. Abramson (Woodbridge, 2011), 181–2; R. Naismith, 'An additional moneyer for Winchester in Edgar's Circumscription Cross coinage', in

In several ways, Edgar's reign was thus marked by tentative steps towards widespread renovation of the coinage even before the famous reform of his last years. The internal chronology remains obscure. In the south *Bust Crowned* and (perhaps slightly later) *Circumscription Cross* were probably dominant throughout the reign, while in the north of English Mercia *Circumscription Rosette* pennies were produced from the beginning of Edgar's reign but gave way shortly before the reform to a mint-signed variant of the *Horizontal* type.[66] At York *Circumscription* types were probably adopted only later in the reign, while in the 'north-east' *Circumscription* was introduced on a very restricted level, again seemingly late in the reign.[67] These limitations reveal similar fault lines to those of Athelstan's coinage, which affected the expanded Anglo-Saxon kingdom throughout the tenth century: the 'north-west' (meaning the northern part of English Mercia) differed slightly but noticeably and persistently from Wessex; York was sometimes slow to accept new developments from the south; and the separateness of the 'north-east' and East Anglia in particular was a *Leitmotiv*.

Chronologically as well as geographically, there were thus major variations in the degree of regionalisation which prevailed over the tenth century. Monetary divisions were never completely static, and although there was undeniably some link to the divisions of Wessex, English Mercia and the three principal segments of the Danelaw, they did not map perfectly onto the political and ethnic geography as deduced by modern scholars;[68] neither did they always stand up to periodic attempts to enforce greater typological coherence. In the period of Alfred and Edward the Elder there had (with a few notable exceptions) been a measure of numismatic unity in the expanding kingdom founded on the dominance of the *Horizontal* type. Under Athelstan and Edgar in particular there were stronger if not lasting or complete efforts to create a typologically unified coinage for the kingdom. The creation of this system is in itself an impressive demonstration of both the aims and the achievements of the growing English currency of the tenth century.

The Winchester Mint and Coins and Related Finds from the Excavations of 1961–71, ed. M. Biddle, Winchester Studies 8 (Oxford, 2012), 55.

[66]   Pagan, 'Pre-reform', 200–2.

[67]   *CTCE*, 172–81; Pagan, 'Pre-reform', 195–6 and 203. The 'Galli Tassi' hoard provides tentative evidence that the *Circumscription* coinage of southern England was significant by 964, if the hoard is correctly associated with Otto I's descent on Lucca: A. Saccocci, 'Il ripostiglio dall'area "Galli Tassi" di Lucca e la cronologia delle emissioni pavesi e lucchesi di X secolo', *Bollettino di numismatica*, 36–9 (2002), 167–204.

[68]   See below, p. 79.

Conquest and Conformity: the Establishment of the English Currency

The genesis of the regional currency of the tenth-century English kingdom did not lie in any active decision to institute a diversified system. Rather, the shape of the coinage emerged gradually and organically, first as Wessex and Mercia came together, and subsequently – and most significantly – as the rulers of these areas conquered their Viking neighbours. Edward the Elder and Æthelflæd found in their new territories an already distinct and sophisticated range of monetary systems.[69] These underwent diverse transitions to the English pattern of coinage, which serve to illustrate the strengths and weaknesses of the developing kingdom's infrastructure.

Pennies imitating English issues had been produced in Viking territory from the 880s onwards, graduating by the turn of the tenth century into new native designs.[70] The two principal Anglo-Viking series were the St Edmund Memorial coinage associated with East Anglia and some parts of the east Midlands, and the various types minted at Scandinavian York, alongside which there was probably some ongoing imitation at Midland mints of English types.[71] Together these issues dominated the coinage of the Danelaw as a whole, but did not enjoy a monopoly as contemporary English coins generally did within Anglo-Saxon territory. Viking pennies circulated alongside an element of foreign coins and hack-silver.[72] English and Carolingian coins were based on different weight systems, so could only circulate together if they were being accepted solely by virtue of their silver content. As a rule this diversity came to an end with English

---

[69] *VCCBI.*

[70] M. Blackburn, 'Currency under the Vikings. Part 1: Guthrum and the earliest Danelaw coinages', *BNJ, 75* (2005), 18–43 (*VCCBI*, 2–31); M. Blackburn, 'Expansion and control: aspects of Anglo-Scandinavian minting south of the Humber', in *Vikings and the Danelaw: Selected Papers from the Proceedings of the Thirteenth Viking Congress, Nottingham and York, 21–30 August 1997*, ed. J. Graham-Campbell et al. (Oxford, 2001), 125–42 (*VCCBI*, 149–66).

[71] C. Blunt, 'The St Edmund memorial coinage', *Proceedings of the Suffolk Institute of Archaeology and History, 31* (1967–9), 234–55; *MEC* 1, 319–20; *CTCE*, 100–2; M. Blackburn and H. Pagan, 'The St Edmund coinage in the light of a parcel from a hoard of St Edmund pennies', *BNJ, 72* (2002), 1–14 (*VCCBI*, 265–80). On York, see M. Blackburn, 'The coinage of Scandinavian York', in *Aspects of Scandinavian York*, ed. R. Hall et al., Archaeology of York 8.4 (York, 2004), 325–49 (*VCCBI*, 281–307). For ongoing imitation in the 'Five Boroughs' region, see M. Blackburn, 'Currency under the Vikings. Part 2: the two Scandinavian kingdoms of the Danelaw, *c.* 895–954', *BNJ, 76* (2006), 204–26, at 215 (*VCCBI*, 32–57, at 43).

[72] J. Graham-Campbell, 'The dual economy of the Danelaw', *BNJ, 71* (2001), 49–59; G. Williams, 'The "northern hoards" revisited: hoards and silver economy in the northern Danelaw in the early tenth century', in *Early Medieval Art and Archaeology in the Northern World: Studies in Honour of James Graham-Campbell*, ed. A. Reynolds and L. Webster (Leiden, 2013), 459–86; R. Naismith, 'Islamic coins from early medieval England', *NC, 165* (2005), 193–222.

conquest.[73] In East Anglia the transition is vividly demonstrated by the contents of the geographically and chronologically close Manningtree and Brantham hoards,[74] the former consisting largely of St Edmund Memorial pennies, the latter entirely made up of *Horizontal* pennies by moneyers associated with the east Midlands. However, the Morley St Peter and Framingham Earl hoards from Norfolk suggest that late in Edward's reign moneyers within East Anglia were minting imitations of Edward the Elder's *Bust* and *Horizontal* types which used the weight standard of earlier Viking issues.[75] A more regular issue in the name of the West Saxon king did not emerge until the reign of Athelstan.[76] In monetary terms, therefore, East Anglia remained under patchy and peripheral English control for several years.[77]

The situation in the east Midlands was still more complicated. The *Anglo-Saxon Chronicle* states that Edward the Elder took Northampton in 917 and Stamford in 918, to which region a substantial late coinage in his name can be attributed, following the regular weight standard and *Horizontal* design of the English coinage (although, as in East Anglia, there was some coinage of poor literacy).[78] By 920 Edward held Nottingham and Bakewell, and the assumption has often been that this phase of campaigning brought all territory south of the Humber under English control.[79] Yet into the 920s Lincoln continued to produce a coinage modelled on that of York which used the traditional Viking weight standard and in no way recognised Edward the Elder's suzerainty.[80] In terms of circulation there are hints that other parts of the east Midlands did not immediately abandon the mixed currency of earlier times. The Thurcaston, Leicestershire, hoard datable to *c.*925 comprised a mix of Anglo-Saxon pennies from southern England, Viking pennies from York and Lincoln and also some

---

[73]   Blackburn, 'Expansion', 137–8 (*VCCBI*, 161–2).

[74]   Checklist, no. 98b (Manningtree); A. Gannon, 'Brantham, Suffolk 2003', *NC, 164* (2004), 279; Blackburn, 'Scandinavian kingdoms', 206–7 (Brantham) (*VCCBI*, 34–5).

[75]   Checklist, nos 105a and 107. Cf. Blackburn, 'Scandinavian kingdoms', 205–8 (*VCCBI*, 33–6); *CTCE*, 52–3.

[76]   Blunt, 'Athelstan', 80–81.

[77]   Blackburn, 'Scandinavian kingdoms', 208 (*VCCBI*, 36). For political and administrative developments see L. Marten, 'The shiring of East Anglia: an alternative hypothesis', *Historical Research, 81* (2008), 1–27.

[78]   *CTCE*, 52–4; Blackburn, 'Expansion', 138 (*VCCBI*, 162).

[79]   E.g., F.M. Stenton, *Anglo-Saxon England*, 3rd edn (Oxford, 1971), 331. The view of Sarah Foot (*Æthelstan*, 14–16) is that all the region was conquered, as seems to be inferred by the ASC entry for 918, but that Viking control was subsequently reasserted over Lincoln.

[80]   I. Stewart, 'The anonymous Anglo-Viking issue with Sword and Hammer types and the coinage of Sihtric I', *BNJ, 52* (1982), 108–16; Blackburn, 'Scandinavian kingdoms', 209–15 (*VCCBI*, 37–43).

cut fragments of Arabic dirhams.[81] It indicates that at least some inhabitants of the Danelaw continued to use Viking coins and Viking ways of handling silver after the English takeover.

For the moneyers at York, English conquest in 927 brought in a new design naming Athelstan and showing a church, based on a weight standard intermediate between the old Viking one (*c.*1.30 g) and that of the rest of England (*c.*1.60 g). Additional moneyers may have been drafted in from the east and west Midlands to assist in producing this type. Before long York's mint-output began to conform more closely to that of the rest of the kingdom: it began issuing *Circumscription Cross* pennies of regular weight, and also eventually *Bust Crowned* pennies.[82] Circulation in Northumbria around this time has recently been illuminated by the Vale of York hoard.[83] Dating to very shortly after Athelstan's takeover of the kingdom of Northumbria in 927, it sheds valuable light upon a currency in transition, and illustrates the encroachment of pennies in the name of Edward and Athelstan, although a significant 'Viking' component of York pennies, dirhams and hack-silver still remained.[84] Other hoards suggest that a similar mixture of local and foreign coins and uncoined silver was current across Northumbria, at least down to *c.*930.[85] But after the conquest of York by Viking rulers from Dublin in 939, who ruled over the city intermittently until 954, there was no general reversion to the earlier mixed currency.[86] Indeed, after a brief return to the old, lower Viking weight standard, the moneyers of Viking York in the 940s and 950s moved gradually to the weight standard prevalent at English mints.[87] Other aspects of the Viking minting establishment at York proved more persistent. Unlike in the south, there was no proliferation of new mint-locations north of the Humber: York apparently remained the sole mint until after 1066. Also, a distinct focus on a single unusually productive moneyer emerged after the initial *Church* type of Athelstan, possibly reflecting the background of production in earlier times. In terms of organisation, therefore, the Vikings left a strong mark on the coinage of York.

---

[81]   Checklist, no. 109a; M. Blackburn, 'A Viking hoard from Thurcaston, Leics.: preliminary report', *NC, 161* (2001), 349–52.

[82]   Blunt, 'Athelstan', 88–93; Blackburn, 'Scandinavian York', 335–6 and 340 (*VCCBI*, 291–2 and 296).

[83]   B. Ager and G. Williams, 'The Vale of York Viking hoard: preliminary catalogue', in *New Perspectives*, ed. Abramson, 146–55.

[84]   G. Williams, 'Coinage and monetary circulation in the northern Danelaw in the 920s in the light of the Vale of York hoard', in *Studies*, ed. Abramson, 148–57, at 153–7.

[85]   G. Williams, 'Hoards from the northern Danelaw from Cuerdale to the Vale of York', in *The Huxley Viking Hoard: Scandinavian Settlement in the North West*, ed. J. Graham-Campbell and R. Philpott (Liverpool, 2009), 73–84, at 78–82.

[86]   *CTCE*, 211–34; Blackburn, 'Scandinavian York', 335–8 (*VCCBI*, 291–4).

[87]   *CTCE*, 241; Blackburn, 'Scandinavian York', 339–40 (*VCCBI*, 295–6).

By 927 Athelstan had vanquished the Viking rulers of northern England, and extended the borders of his kingdom to approximately those of all former Anglo-Saxon territories: in the words of one contemporary poet, conquest of Northumbria rendered Athelstan ruler of 'ista perfecta Saxonia'.[88] There and elsewhere, change to the currency came swiftly after English conquest. It took the form of recognition of the English king and, often, the adoption of widely used types. Local coinages and extensive use of a bullion-based economy retreated. In general there seems to have been a strong sense that English conquest meant acceptance of English currency, albeit with some concessions to local custom. Parts of East Anglia for several years used effectively illiterate coins modelled on Edward's issues but based on Viking weight standards, and while York and the 'north-east' switched to generally mainstream English currency shortly after conquest, they remained out of perfect step with the southern and western parts of the kingdom.[89] In these newly won areas a compromise was struck, resulting in quick expansion of English coinage at the expense of detailed regularisation. The experience of conquest hence proved to be integral to the emergence of late Anglo-Saxon currency: it was forged from cold, hard steel as much as from silver.

One Kingdom, One Coinage?

The most famous written statement on English coinage in the tenth century is a group of clauses contained in the law-code associated with a royal meeting at Grately, Hampshire, under Athelstan. Prominent among these is the command that 'an mynet sy ofer eall ðæs cynges onweald'.[90] When Edgar's law-code governing both ecclesiastical and secular matters (II/III Edgar) was promulgated some three decades later, it included a virtual repetition of the command of II Athelstan, that 'ga an mynet ofer ealne ðæs cynges anweald', with the important qualification that 'þane nan man ne forsace'.[91] By this time, it seems, Edgar's – and, one suspects, Athelstan's – precept was understood as applying to unity of circulation rather than unity of design as such.

The acid test of how far the coinage of tenth-century England really did or did not constitute *an mynet* is therefore the degree to which it made up a coherent and interchangeable whole in the eyes of contemporary coin-users. What features qualified a coin to be part of the sanctioned circulating medium are not stated in any law-code, and so only recourse to actual finds can show

---

[88]   'This England (now) made whole'. *Anglo-Latin Literature*, ed. Lapidge, 75–7.

[89]   See further below, pp. 61 and 67.

[90]   'There should be one coinage throughout the king's realm'. II Athelstan, ch. 14 (ed. Liebermann, *Gesetze*, 1, 158; trans. *EHD* 1, 420).

[91]   'One coinage should be current throughout the king's dominion, and no man is to reject it'. II/III Edgar, ch. 8 (ed. Liebermann, *Gesetze*, 1, 204; trans. *EHD* 1, 433).

how far users would have accepted one coin for another within the English kingdom. 'English kingdom' is here used to mean territories which were, or can reasonably be assumed to have been, inherited or conquered by Alfred and his heirs. However, as in the case of Lincoln in the 920s, there is reason to be cautious of delineating the borders of the kingdom too sharply. There may well have been other areas, particularly in the north Midlands, where patterns of control were more complex, while in the 940s and early 950s there were times when Northumbria and parts of the eastern Danelaw were temporarily retaken by Viking rulers.[92] But on the whole the pattern is clear. Areas of contention are rare, and have provided relatively few coin finds. In general it is possible to be quite confident in speaking of where English and Viking territory lay in the tenth century.

Analysis of circulation within the kingdom is in the first place based on the presumption that there was a secure and widely disseminated view of what was *not* acceptable English currency. The best demonstration of this is that 'foreign' coins – meaning issues from continental Europe and the Viking kingdoms within Britain – were effectively excluded from circulation.[93] Virtually no coins from the former Carolingian realms of the tenth century, or from other parts of contemporary continental Europe, have been found in territory that was controlled by the West Saxon dynasty. Indeed, one surviving example of a *denarius* from Cologne re-struck in the name of Athelstan hints at the likely fate which awaited most incoming foreign coin.[94] Only a few stragglers of European currency survived in large hoards from England itself, and as a whole the record reflects effective removal of coin coming in from outside the British Isles.[95]

Viking coinages minted within Britain were more problematic, but as a rule enjoyed limited circulation in English-held areas. In Wessex and western Mercia

---

[92]   P. Sidebottom, 'The north-western frontier of Viking Mercia: the evidence from stone monuments', *West Midlands Archaeology*, 39 (1996), 3–15; P. Stafford, *The East Midlands in the Early Middle Ages* (Leicester, 1985), 135–43. Another possible challenge to the accepted narrative has recently been offered by a coin from the Vale of York hoard, associated with the Sword coinage of York in the 920s, with an inscription naming a previously unknown mint (RORIVA/ HORIVA CASTR), tentatively identified as Rocester, Staffordshire by Gareth Williams ('*Roriva Castr*: a new Danelaw mint of the 920s', in *Scripta varia numismatico Tuukka Talvio sexagenario dedicata*, ed. O. Järvinen (Helsinki, 2008), 41–7).

[93]   B. Cook, 'Foreign coins in medieval England', in *Moneta locale, moneta straniera: Italia ed Europa XI–XV secolo: the Second Cambridge Numismatic Symposium*, ed. L. Travaini (Milan, 1999), 231–84, at 232–7.

[94]   C. Blunt, 'A penny of the English King Athelstan overstruck on a Cologne denier', in *Lagom. Festschrift für Peter Berghaus zum 60. Geburtstag am 20. November 1979*, ed. T. Fischer and P. Ilisch (Münster, 1981), 119–21.

[95]   These include (for example) three Carolingian *denarii* in the Chester (1950) hoard of *c*.965 (Checklist, no. 144).

– territories which had never been effectively under Scandinavian control – they were particularly scarce. Ten Viking coins minted across the period *c.*880–954 can be traced as single-finds from probably English-held areas, found in locations from Kent and Cambridgeshire to Gloucestershire.[96] In hoards they were also generally few.[97] Yorkshire and Lincolnshire (which lay to the immediate south of the Humber and had a long tradition of monetary interaction with regions to the north) were a somewhat special case. Lincolnshire probably lay under Viking control until some time in the 920s, so finds of Viking coins produced before *c.*927 should not necessarily be treated as 'foreign' finds. There are also five known single-finds of post-939 Viking pennies from Lincolnshire, at least one of them minted (and very possibly lost) during a period when this territory was again under Viking control.[98] As for Northumbria, Viking pennies found there must be treated as 'local' finds, though it is of course entirely possible that some of the six known single-finds were lost when the area answered to a West Saxon king.

By and large, therefore, Anglo-Saxon conquest was associated with effective acceptance of English coinage to the exclusion of others. The crux of the matter is how far circulation within this expanding kingdom reflects general acceptability of English coinage: could any penny in the name of an English king be used in any part of the kingdom?

Hoards and single-finds are the two primary sources needed to reach a conclusion. As noted above, the hoard record for the tenth century is limited in its regional representation.[99] Hoards within England dating to *c.*900–980 are predominantly from the north. Issues from the 'north-west', the 'north-east' and York are also a major element in the several hoards of this period from Ireland,

---

[96]   EMC 2008.0409 (Coberley, Gloucestershire), 2001.0964 (Romney Marsh, Kent), 1999.0149 (North Waltham, Hampshire), 2001.0972 (Stowting, Kent), 1893.0002 (Long Wittenham, Oxfordshire), 1893.0003 (Cholsey, Oxfordshire), 2006.0086 (Leckhampstead, Buckinghamshire), 2001.1175 (Burton upon Trent, Staffordshire), 1983.9940 (Lincoln, Lincolnshire), 2001.0912 (Belton, Lincolnshire), 2007.0059 (Lincolnshire), 1981.5007 (Wells, Somerset), 2000.0048 (Grendon, Northamptonshire), 1986.7271 (Kirtling, Cambridgeshire).

[97]   Viking coins occurred in hoards probably or certainly deposited in English territory in eight cases: these included the Vale of York hoard as well as a small Thames hoard from London (Checklist, no. 93b), the St John's, Chester hoard of *c.*917 (Checklist, no. 99), Morley St Peter, Norfolk hoard of *c.*925 (Checklist, no. 107), the Bossall/Flaxton, North Yorkshire hoard of *c.*927 (Checklist, no. 108), the Kirtling, Cambridgeshire hoard of *c.*955 (Checklist, no. 137), the Tetney, Lincolnshire hoard of *c.*965 (Checklist, no. 141) and the Chester (1950) hoard of *c.*965 (Checklist, no. 144).

[98]   EMC 1996.0194 (Lincolnshire).

[99]   The difficulties are laid out in *CTCE*, 248–54.

Scotland and Wales.[100] Southern coins are better represented in some of the tenth-century hoards which have been found in France and Italy. Yet these foreign finds must be excluded from consideration of the English currency itself, leaving a total of some 34 hoards deposited in English territory *c.*900–973.[101] In blunt terms, the majority of these hoards can be characterised as regional, in that 50 per cent or more of their content is made up of the local variety of English coins. But it must be stressed that they do not constitute an overwhelming majority, and there is some chronological variation: while twelve of the hoards deposited *c.*925–73 were more than 50 per cent local, eight were not. Eight of the hoards from before *c.*925 were mostly local, and six were not. These figures should be taken with a pinch of salt, as they mask the fact that some hoards are so small – just two or three coins – that it is misleading to work solely from percentages, while in all cases there are nuances within the headings of local and non-local. Some hoards may represent travellers' purses, and in the case of hoards deposited on the periphery of one area or another it can be difficult to judge what the local type ought to have been, as with those from Hertfordshire, which lay on the borderland between East Anglian, 'north-eastern' and southern influences.[102] There is also some simplification involved in pinning down regions. For these purposes, I have used the five-fold division that can broadly be applied to typology: Northumbria, the 'north-east' (east Midlands), East Anglia, southern England and the 'north-west' (English Mercia, the west Midlands) (see Figure 3.3). It is usually possible to attribute an English coin to one of these regions by style or type, and sometimes to a more specific location or area within them. For the sake of convenience these regions are mapped according to modern (pre-1974) county borders (Figure 3.3).

---

[100] K.A. Bornholdt-Collins, 'Viking-Age coin finds from the Isle of Man: a study of coin circulation, production and concepts of wealth', (PhD thesis, University of Cambridge, 2003), 265–74.

[101] Details are given in Checklist, nos. 89, 93b, 99, 100, 102, 104, 105a, 107, 108, 109, 109a (the aberrant Thurcaston, Leicestershire hoard: see above, n. 80), 112, 113, 117a, 118, 120, 121 (though possibly deposited under Viking rule), 126, 133, 140, 141, 144, 148, 151, 153, 171a and 171b. Not included in Checklist are the Vale of York hoard (see above, n. 82), the poorly-known hoard of *Circumscription* pennies probably found in Hampshire *c.*1993 (see above, n. 64) and four hoards from Sussex: one from Lewes deposited during the reign of Edward the Elder (T. Clifford and G. Williams, 'Lewes, East Sussex, 2006', *NC, 168* (2008), 413); another from Berwick, again dating to the time of Edward the Elder (L. Burnett and G. Williams, 'Berwick, East Sussex 2007', *NC, 169* (2009), 352); one from Plumpton, probably deposited under Edmund (G. Thomas (with M. Archibald), 'A casket fit for a West Saxon courtier? The Plumpton hoard and its place in the minor arts of late Saxon England', in *Early Medieval Art and Archaeology*, ed. Reynolds and Webster, 425–58, at 428–34); and one from Up Marden, probably deposited under Eadred (G. Williams, 'Up Marden, West Sussex, 2006', *NC, 170* (2010), 432).

[102] Blackburn, 'Coin finds', 11–17.

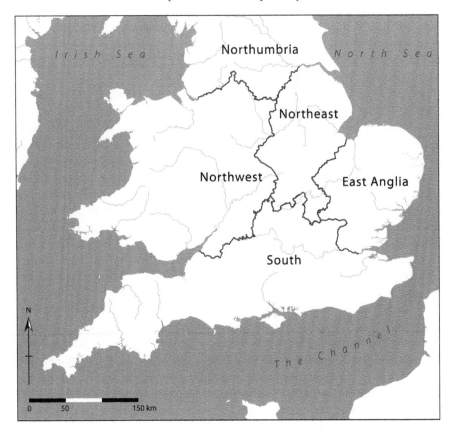

Figure 3.3   Regional divisions used in interpretation of coin finds.

Despite their shortcomings, the hoards of tenth-century England hint at important underlying trends in the movement of the coinage. East Anglian coins are rare outside East Anglian hoards, and the largest non-local elements in the latter are issues from southern England (especially until about the 930s), with an increasingly important element of coins from the 'north-eastern' regions that mirrors the typological connection between the two areas. The southern English hoards, few and often small, present a very mixed selection. On the one hand there are a few hoards like those from Cannon Street station in London, Amesbury and 'Hampshire' which are wholly or almost wholly comprised of southern issues; indeed, in the case of the poorly recorded 'Hampshire' hoard of Edgar's reign the large majority were in fact issues from Winchester and Southampton, and there was perhaps only one coin from York. On the other there are hoards mostly or entirely made up of non-local coins. One small hoard allegedly found in Threadneedle Street in London included only two southern coins alongside two from the 'north-east' and one from English Mercia. The Kintbury hoard from

Berkshire is known from ten coins, none of them southern: four came from the north-west and six from the 'north-east'. A hoard of similar non-local makeup was found at Bath in 1755.[103] Ideally one would enter into greater detail about which southern coins come from Kent, London, Winchester, Wessex or elsewhere, and the 'Hampshire' hoard suggests that more localised circulation could sometimes prevail, but at present further elaboration is not possible.

Clearly there was a strong tradition of coins from northern England passing into use further south, which can be observed in hoards from across this period. The opposite was also true, though to a lesser degree, and movement across the Pennines and the Humber was more pronounced. The large Tetney hoard from Lincolnshire in the 960s was, not unexpectedly, mostly made up of 'north-eastern' issues, with a substantial contribution from Northumbria but none from the south, East Anglia or English Mercia. Hoards from north of the Humber tend to be fairly evenly composed of Northumbrian issues from York and 'north-eastern' issues. The situation in the 'north-west' is more complicated, partly because the evidence is richer. No fewer than four hoards were deposited in or near Chester over the course of this period, one of them containing over 500 coins.[104] Another small hoard was found at Shrewsbury, dating to about 910. Within these hoards, pennies of local origin are often dominant, though not to the same extent as the local issues of the 'north-east' and Northumbria are in their areas of origin. The Shrewsbury hoard consisted entirely of southern coins, while the earliest of the four Chester hoards included a selection of local coins alongside a slightly higher number of Viking pieces. The 546 coins of the Chester (1950) hoard deposited around 970 were a heterogeneous collection in which local issues were the largest single element, but with substantial contributions from both southern England and the 'north-east', and smatterings from Northumbria and East Anglia. The date-range of this hoard was remarkably wide, with some coins from as far back as the reign of Alfred the Great. But geographical diversity was not restricted to the older coins: even the recent part of the hoard had a significant proportion of southern and 'north-eastern' specimens. Thus, although large hoards such as this perhaps stand a higher chance of representing savings rather than a random sample of the currency, whoever put the Chester (1950) together had enjoyed sustained and regular contact with coins from all over the kingdom. It differs from the other mid-tenth-century hoards from Chester and its environs, which are significantly smaller and are almost completely composed of local, 'north-western' coins, with only one 'north-eastern' intruder in the Chester (1857) hoard of about 80 coins.

---

[103] C. Blunt and H. Pagan, 'Three tenth-century hoards: Bath (1755), Kintbury (1761), Threadneedle Street (before 1924)', *BNJ*, 45 (1975), 19–32, at 32.

[104] H. Pagan, *SCBI 64: Grosvenor Museum, Chester, Part II: Anglo-Saxon Coins and Post-Conquest Coins to 1180* (Oxford, 2012).

Single-finds of the tenth century remain scarce in comparison with those of the eighth or even ninth century.[105] However, more than three decades of metal-detecting activity has produced over 475 single-finds of this period (including Viking issues).[106] If anything these are even more valuable as a source than the hoards. Single-finds are believed to represent random losses, and therefore constitute a very valuable window onto the makeup of the currency.[107] Their interpretation is hardly straightforward, however: not all finds are reported, and the local distribution is affected by modern land-use and searching patterns as well as actual distribution of medieval material.[108]

For present purposes the single-finds of the period *c.*880–973 have been divided into two groups: those dating to the reigns of Alfred and Edward the Elder (*c.*880–924/5) and those from the beginning of Athelstan's reign to Edgar's reform of *c.*973. This division of the period into approximately equal halves allows for some possibility of tracing long-term developments, whereas breaking down the finds into individual reigns does not result in a sufficient sample to reach any sound conclusions. Splitting them at the accession of Athelstan is somewhat arbitrary, but it does permit a secure chronological cut-off (at least in date of production) and takes account of the territorial expansion which occurred early in Athelstan's reign. It must also be recognised that this was not a period of regular renewal of the currency, and issues from before 924 continued to circulate right down to the 970s. There is normally no way to determine when a single-find was lost, but if the wastage rates of tenth-century hoards as assessed by Michael Metcalf are any guide, the currency had a half-life

---

[105] M. Blackburn, '"Productive sites" and the pattern of coin loss in England, 600–1180', in *Markets in Early Medieval Europe: Trading and 'Productive' Sites, 650–850*, ed. T. Pestell and K. Ulmschneider (Macclesfield, 2003), 20–36.

[106] This total consists of the material on the Early Medieval Corpus of Coin Finds (<www-cm.fitzmuseum.cam.ac.uk/dept/coins/emc/>) and the Portable Antiquities Scheme (<www.finds.org.uk/>) as of May 2012. Some additional finds are listed in Jonsson, *New Era*. Five further single-finds include: a *Two Line* penny of Alfred (moneyer Tirwald) found in excavations at Hereford (R. Shoesmith et al., *Hereford City Excavations* (4 vols., London, 1980–2002), 3, 33); a *Circumscription Cross* penny of Athelstan, Chester mint, moneyer Eadmund, found at Oswestry, Shropshire, 1999 (*SCBI 64*, 113); a *Bust Crowned* penny of Athelstan, Winchester mint, moneyer Amelric found in the nave of Canterbury cathedral (Y. Harvey, 'A penny of Æthelstan', in *Canterbury Cathedral Nave: Archaeology, History and Architecture*, ed. K. Blockley, M. Sparks and T. Tatton-Brown (Canterbury, 1997), 95); a *Two Line* penny of Athelstan (moneyer Weard, assigned to the NE II group) from Castle Cary in Somerset, now in the Fitzwilliam Museum; a *Horizontal Rosettes* penny of Eadred, moneyer Boga (probably minted at Derby) found near the amphitheatre in Chester before 1955 (*SCBI 64*, 270).

[107] Blackburn, 'Coin finds', 17–22.

[108] J. Richards, J. Naylor and C. Holas-Clarke, 'Anglo-Saxon landscape and economy: using portable antiquities to study Anglo-Saxon and Viking England', *Internet Archaeology, 25* (<www.intarch.ac.uk/>) (2009).

of 10 to 15 years; in other words, circulation long after production was generally small in scale.[109]

Table 3.1   Regional distribution of single-finds of pennies minted *c.*880–924.

Region	No. of finds	Origin of finds									
		Mercia		North-east		East Anglia		South		Uncertain	
		No.	%	No.	%	No.	%	No.	%	No.	%
North-east	11	1	9	3	27	0	0	6	55	1	9
Mercia	3	0	0	0	0	0	0	2	67	1	33
East Anglia	28	4	14	6	21	3	11	9	32	6	21
Wessex	19	2	11	0	0	0	0	11	58	6	32
South-east	22	2	9	0	0	0	0	20	91	0	0

Despite these caveats, the single-finds of *c.*880–973 provide a crucial insight into the shape of the circulating currency. The key feature of the currency under Alfred and Edward is the dominance exerted by the southern English mints (Table 3.1). These can be grouped stylistically, but attributing coins to individual mints is generally not possible.[110] In all areas, pennies from southern England were the largest segment of single-finds, most conspicuously in south-east England. Many of these finds from East Anglia and the 'north-east' could, of course, have been used and lost before the West Saxon conquest.

Assessing the circulation of coinages struck in Mercia and the newly conquered Danelaw during the reigns of Alfred and Edward is particularly problematic. At present, one can only note emerging trends which may or may not be substantiated as further evidence emerges. Coins from English Mercia, like their counterparts from the south, circulated widely, implying a measure of integration with the rest of the kingdom and a continuation of developments from earlier in the ninth century.[111] Circulation within Mercia has, however, left barely a trace among single-finds. The products of the newly taken 'north-eastern' mints were used heavily in East Anglia, supporting the evidence of

---

[109] Metcalf, 'Monetary history', 146–50.

[110] See above, p. 61.

[111] Naismith, *Money and Power*, 209–18.

the Brantham hoard and establishing a tradition that would persist into later decades. The native East Anglian coinage from Edward's last years, on the other hand, seems to have enjoyed fairly limited circulation, and its rarity among the relatively numerous single-finds from East Anglia leads to the suspicion that it may not have been a substantial coinage, despite its fortuitous representation in hoards.

In their overall regional distribution, the single-finds of *c.*925–73 provide a valuable corrective to the strong northern bias presented by the hoards, which at first glance suggest that the coinage was dominated by the issues of these mints. In contrast, coins from southern England and especially East Anglia are substantially better represented proportionally among single-finds than they are in surviving hoards (see Table 3.2). A thorough die-study is needed to confirm how this information relates to the actual scale of production at various locations; but it is likely to emerge as an effective lesson in the distortion which restricted hoard evidence can create.

Table 3.2   Total   numbers   of   single-finds   of   English   pennies minted *c.*924/5–73.

Region of origin	No. of single-finds	% of total
East Anglia	52	29
North-east	50	28
South	43	24
North-west	17	10
Northumbria	16	9
Total	178	100

Table 3.3   Regional distribution of single-finds of pennies minted *c.*924/5–73.

Region	No. of English finds	Origins of finds											
		North-west		North-east		Northumbria		East Anglia		South		Uncertain	
		No.	%	No.	%	No.	%	No.	%	No.	%	No.	%
North-umbria	13	0	0	3	23	7	54	0	0	1	8	2	15
Lincoln-shire	16	0	0	9	56	5	31	1	6	0	0	1	6
East Midlands	19	1	5	7	37	2	11	2	11	3	16	4	21
North-west	13	9	69	2	15	0	0	0	0	1	8	1	8
East Anglia	81	2	2	17	21	2	2	43	53	2	2	15	18
Wessex	34	3	9	6	18	0	0	0	0	19	56	6	18
South-east	33	2	6	6	18	0	0	6	18	14	42	5	15

The picture of circulation offered by the single-finds to a large extent supports that of the hoards (see Table 3.3). Coin circulation after *c.*925 remained substantially localised, but always with a significant admixture of finds from elsewhere in England: enough to suggest that there was no active policy of excluding non-local coins from circulation such as applied to Viking and Continental European currency. The proportion of local coins among finds in each region during the period from after *c.*925 is 40–70 per cent. The exact makeup of the currency varies considerably from region to region. Northumbria and the 'north-east' each contributed a substantial proportion of currency to the other, alongside about 55 per cent local coin in circulation. English Mercia is poorly represented by single-finds, but also shows the strongest concentration of local issues, at 70 per cent of the total. By way of contrast, East Anglia is by far the richest source of tenth-century single-finds, with over 80 from the period *c.*925–73. This partly reflects the population and wealth of the region, and partly the strong tradition of collaboration between detectorists and archaeologists in Norfolk.[112] Among these numerous finds local pennies are most prominent,

---

[112]   Richards, Naylor and Holas-Clarke, 'Anglo-Saxon landscape and economy', §§ 2.4.1 and 2.4.2.4; M. Chester-Kadwell, *Early Anglo-Saxon Communities in the Landscape of Norfolk*, BAR

accounting for 53 per cent, with a substantial contribution (21 per cent) from the east Midlands. In the south there was some contrast between the south-east and Wessex. Both are known from approximately the same number of single-finds, and it is not normally possible to distinguish coins made in Wessex from those minted in the south-east. Yet southern coins are noticeably more dominant in Wessex (58 per cent of all finds) than in the south-east (42 per cent of all finds). The south-east produced a relatively high proportion of East Anglian coins (20 per cent), whereas no East Anglian pennies have occurred as single-finds in Wessex. Doubtless this is in large part a facet of proximity, as well as of trade and other relations.

Regional differences in the content of the currency did therefore exist, some areas being more dominated by local issues than others, but not enough to suggest systematic exclusion of other English pennies. Importantly, this basic pattern persisted after Edgar's reform. The period *c.*973–1066 was marked overall by a more vibrant pattern of circulation, delineated effectively by Michael Metcalf.[113] Coins regularly travelled far and wide across England, with only Northumbria standing somewhat apart. But just as it is in some respects misleading to examine the coinage of *c.*880–973 as a single unit, so it is dangerous to look at the century after *c.*973 as a whole.[114] Breaking it down type by type – which is now a viable option thanks to the volume of single-finds – shows that the dynamic monetary economy of late-tenth- and eleventh-century England was not established overnight with Edgar's new coinage. This is made most apparent by focusing on the Reform type itself. Some 89 single-finds of the Reform-type coinage are now known, and in many particulars these perpetuate the patterns seen earlier in the tenth century (Table 3.4).

British Series 481 (Oxford, 2009), esp. 62–90.

[113] D.M. Metcalf, 'Continuity and change in English monetary history, *c.* 973–1086. Part 1', *BNJ, 50* (1980), 20–49, at 24–31, *Atlas.*

[114] Jonsson, *New Era*, 100–14 (though many new single-finds have occurred subsequently).

Table 3.4   Regional distribution of single-finds of Reform-type pennies of Edgar, Edward the Martyr and Æthelred II.

Region	Total	North-umbria		North-east		North-west		East Anglia		South-east		Wessex		Uncertain	
		No.	%	No.	%	No.	%	No.	%	No.	%	No.	%	No.	%
North-umbria	14	9	64	2	14	0	0	0	0	1	7	0	0	2	14
North-east	12	1	8	7	58	0	0	1	12	1	8	0	0	2	17
North-west	7	3	43	3	43	0	0	0	0	0	0	0	0	1	14
East Anglia	27	4	15	10	37	3	11	3	20	5	19	1	4	1	4
South-east	18	2	11	4	22	0	0	1	6	10	56	1	6	0	0
Wessex	11	0	0	1	9	0	0	0	0	4	36	6	55	0	0

From this table it can be seen, for instance, that 9 of 14 finds from north of the Humber came from York (64 per cent), with 2 from mints in the 'north-east' (14 per cent). In the latter region, local mints accounted for 7 out of 12 finds (58 per cent), and more than half the recorded contents of a hoard from the period of this type found at Oakham in 1749 came from 'north-eastern' mints.[115] Wessex and the south-east were also dominated by finds from local mints. There were some significant shifts, particularly in English Mercia and East Anglia. In both these regions the representation of local mints among single-finds was slight: no single-finds from local mints of this period are known from the 'north-west', and a hoard from Chester deposited around 980 contained only 20 local coins out of 121;[116] and while East Anglia remains the most productive region in overall number of finds, during the currency of the Reform type only 3 out of 27 finds (20 per cent) came from local mints. The 'north-east', in contrast, provided 10 of the East Anglian finds (37 per cent). This downturn of localised circulation in both areas can be put down to changes in the pattern of minting

---

[115] Checklist, no. 175.
[116] Checklist, no. 174.

as well as of circulation.[117] Chester in particular saw a marked decline around the time of Edgar's reform, which surely left a significant void in the surrounding hinterland.[118] No such dramatic change is apparent in East Anglia, though it should be noted that there was relative discontinuity in the moneyers working at the various mints: just one continued across the reform at Cambridge and one or two at Norwich,[119] and none at Thetford or Ipswich. Yet for the most part Edgar's reform did not fundamentally alter the pattern of circulation in England as a whole: as far as can be seen, there had indeed been *an mynet* in England long before *c.*973.

Metrology and Fineness

There was considerable if gradual deterioration in the maintenance of both weight and metal quality in England, especially after *c.*940.[120] The full details of how various regions, mints and types diverged remain unclear, although preliminary analyses of metrology (Table 3.5) suggest that by the time of Edgar there could be some differences by mint, and by type within a mint, as well as quite strong similarities embracing large areas of the country.

Table 3.5   Metrology of selected pre-reform mints and types under Edgar.

	Chester	London		Winchester	East Anglia	York			'North-east'
	CR	HR3	(BC)	(CC)	(BC)	CC	HT etc.		HT etc.
No. of undamaged coins in sample	12	28	11	25	12	73	59		174
Mean weight	1.47	1.33	1.47	1.43	1.44	1.28	1.25		1.20
Median weight	1.49	1.34	1.47	1.42	1.46	1.38	1.23		1.23

---

[117] Cf. Metcalf, *Atlas*, 39–42.

[118] Jonsson, *New Era*, 128–30; D. M. Metcalf, 'The monetary economy of the Irish Sea province', in *Viking Treasure from the North West: the Cuerdale Hoard in its Context*, ed. J. Graham-Campbell (Liverpool, 1992), 89–106, at 90–91 and 102.

[119] A second moneyer, Swerting, may have survived at Norwich though he is not known for pennies struck before Æthelred II's Second Hand type (cf. EMC 2008.0472).

[120] *CTCE*, 235–45. Cf. Metcalf, 'Rome (Forum) hoard', 89–92.

At Chester, for example, it appears that the various *Circumscription* types of Edgar were struck to a heavier standard than the mint-signed *Horizontal* pennies.[121] Some other mints striking coins of *Circumscription* and *Bust Crowned* type seem to have been working to a standard close to that of the *Circumscription* pennies from Chester, including London, Winchester and even the generally idiosyncratic East Anglian issues. York and the 'north-east', however, present a contrast: the *Circumscription* issues (not always mint-signed, though here only coins of the moneyers Fastolf, Herolf and Durand – confidently associated with York – have been included) and especially the *Horizontal* issues are significantly lighter. A lower average weight for York coins may be a hangover from Viking issues, which were struck to a standard of *c.*1.40 grams. The low weight of Northumbrian coinage was mirrored in the 'north-east'.

It would be folly to assert any very coherent metrological pattern in the years before Edgar's reform based on this small selection of data. Many mints and types are too poorly known to be considered in detail. Nevertheless, there was a general trend in the revived *Circumscription* coinage and some others of Edgar's reign towards a higher and more consistent weight than had been the case in earlier coinages. There is a temptation to associate this with the statement in the law-code II/III Edgar that a single weight was to be current, based on that used at London and Winchester – although if so, it clearly did not attain universal acceptance.[122] Significant variations in weight by mint and region persisted: the south and East Anglia, as well as (in the case of *Circumscription* coins) English Mercia, shared comparable weight standards and distributions, with the 'north-east' and York being marked out by noticeably lighter coinage.[123] Everywhere the reform of Edgar's last years brought a general increase in weight, but not to the same standard. Local peculiarities persisted, and mints in the 'north-eastern' area – above all Stamford – tended towards lighter-weight coins, just as had been the case in earlier issues.[124]

The fineness of the tenth-century coinage is still more obscure than its metrology. Given current data, the story is basically one of relatively high silver content of 85–95 per cent persisting down to Edgar's reign, with only a small proportion of less fine coins known for Eadred and Eadwig. Under Edgar a substantial proportion of coins continued to be struck in silver of 85 per cent pure or more, although the majority were debased to a greater or lesser extent. But there are significant qualifications to this outline. A relatively limited selection of analyses is available, dominated by the

---

[121] All these figures are based on undamaged coins.

[122] II/III Edgar, ch. 8.1 (ed. Liebermann, *Gesetze*, 1, 204; trans. *EHD I*, 433). The date of this law-code is uncertain, but it is apparently the earlier law-code mentioned in IV Edgar, suggesting that it probably belongs before the more famous reform associated with *c.*973: P. Wormald, *The Making of English Law. King Alfred to the Twelfth Century, vol. 1: Legislation and Its Limits* (Oxford, 1999), 313–17 and 441–2; Keynes, 'Edgar', 11–12.

[123] Cf. Blunt, 'Athelstan', 59.

[124] Cf. Jonsson, *New Era*, 95–100; Metcalf, *Atlas*, 66–9.

plentiful 'north-western', 'north-eastern' and York issues in the Edinburgh collection; from the reign of Edgar, for example, only three pennies from southern England (all from London) were analysed. The same pattern is repeated for earlier rulers. As a result, understanding of metal standards in the tenth century is badly skewed in favour of the north, and a new round of analyses is required to shed further light on the topic.[125]

The Minting Establishment from *c.*880

There are thus a number of significant points on which the regionalised character of the English coinage from *c.*880 to 973 can be challenged. The West Saxon monarch's name and the moneyer's name were constant features; hoards and single-finds suggest a currency that was never completely regionalised; and fluctuations in typology and occasional essays at a 'national' type indicate a system which was flexible and which could, when driven by a determined effort, give way to something similar to Edgar's new coinage of the 970s. In sum, the tenth-century English coinage evolved into a complex entity which married central and royal concerns with those of moneyers, die-cutters and others across the kingdom.

One might well ask how this coinage meshed with other aspects of contemporary government. Unfortunately, the mechanisms of men, communications and ideals which lay behind it are to a great extent lost from view. Aside from the coins themselves, the key sources for understanding the coinage are the brief numismatic passages in Anglo-Saxon law-codes. The earliest and most detailed of these is a section of the code known as II Athelstan, which discusses coinage in relation to trading regulations. This confirms many of the basic axioms of minting organisation discernible from contemporary coins. Thus the numismatic section of II Athelstan begins by asserting the unity of the coinage, and that all minting is to be done in a *burh*.[126] Fraudulent moneyers are condemned, and harsh punishments laid down for them. There follows a list of 12 locations where two or more moneyers are, or may be, based, concluding with the statement 'to þam oðrum burgum an'.[127] This important list is laid out in detail below (Table 3.6), along with data on the total numbers of named mints and their moneyers known in and either side of the reign of Athelstan.

---

[125]   H. McKerrell and R. Stevenson, 'Some analyses of Anglo-Saxon and associated oriental silver coinage', in *Methods of Chemical and Metallurgical Investigation of Ancient Coinage*, ed. E.T. Hall and D.M. Metcalf (London, 1972), 195–209. The reliability of these results has been queried in Metcalf, 'Monetary History', 145.

[126]   For references see above, pp. 43–6.

[127]   'Otherwise in the other boroughs one'. Hastings is permitted one moneyer, although this is immediately followed by *oþer to Cysseceastre* ('the other for Chichester'), which may indicate that two moneyers were shared between these two mints: Blackburn, 'Mints', 170.

Table 3.6   II Athelstan mint-locations and other named mints active under Athelstan.

	Mint	No. of moneyers in II Ath	No. of moneyers occurring under Edward	No. of moneyers occurring in early Athelstan	No. of moneyers named in Athelstan CC etc.	Change	No. of moneyers named in Athelstan BC etc.	No. of moneyers occurring under later rulers
(a) Mints named in II Athelstan (in order of appearance)								
1	Canterbury	7	4	3	5	-1	4	3
	– king	(4)						
	– archbishop	(2)						
	– abbot	(1)						
2	Rochester	3	0	1	1	-1	0	0
	– king	(2)						
	– bishop	(1)						
3	Winchester	6	4	5	4	-2; +4	6	4
4	London	8	11	11	11	-4; +3	10	9
5	Lewes	2	0	1	1	-	1	1
6	Hastings	1	0	0	0	-	0	0
7	Chichester	1	1	1	1	-1	0	1
8	Southampton	2	2	2	2	-2	0	1
9	Wareham	2	2	2	2	-1	1	1
10	Dorchester [a]	1	0	0	0	-	0	0
11	Exeter	2	1	1	2	-2	0	2
12	Shaftesbury	2	1	1	2	-2	0	1
(b) Mints named on coins of Athelstan but not in II Athelstan								
13	Bath	-	1(?)	0	2	-2	0	2(?)
14	Bridport/Bredy [b]	-	0	1	1	-1	0	0

	Mint	No. of moneyers in II Ath	No. of moneyers occurring under Edward	No. of moneyers occurring in early Athelstan	No. of moneyers named in Athelstan CC etc.	Change	No. of moneyers named in Athelstan BC etc.	No. of moneyers occurring under later rulers
15	Chester	-	10	14	25		NA	12
16	Darent [c]	-	1(?)	0	1	-1	0	1(?)
17	Derby	-	0	1	9		NA	2
18	Dover	-	0	1	1	-	0	0
19	Gloucester	-	0	0	1		NA	1(?)
20	Hereford	-	1	2(?)	2	-	NA	2(?)
21	Hertford	-	0	1	1		1	0
22	Leicester	-	0	0	1		NA	0
23	Langport	-	1(?)	1(?)	2	-1	1	2
24	Lymne	-	1	1	1	-1	0	0
25	Maldon	-	0	1	1	-	1	1
26	Norwich	-	0	0	NA		7	6
27	Nottingham	-	0	1	4		NA	1
28	Oxford	-	1	3(?)	4	-3; +3	4	2
29	Shrewsbury	-	5	5	7		NA	5
30	Smrierl [d]	-	0	0	0	-	1	0
31	Stafford	-	1	2	2		NA	1(?)
32	Tamworth	-	0	1	2		NA	1(?)
33	Thelwall(?) [e]	-	1(?)	1(?)	1		NA	1(?)
34	Wallingford	-	1	1	1	+2	3	2
35	Warwick	-	0	0	1		NA	1
36	Weardburh [f]	-	1(?)	0	1		NA	1(?)
37	York	-	1	1	1 [g]	+1	2	1

Notes: The italicised columns count only earlier and later occurrences of moneyers who issued mint-signed coins under Athelstan. NA here signifies 'not applicable'.

(a) Dorchester is mentioned only in the Latin *Quadripartitus* version of II Athelstan.

(b) The reading on the relevant coins is *Bridian* or similar, and it is presumably identical with the *Brydie* mentioned in the Burghal Hidage.[128]

(c) This probably refers to a location on the River Dart, perhaps Totnes itself.[129]

(d) The location of this mint is uncertain. On stylistic grounds it probably lay somewhere in southern England or East Anglia.[130]

(e) This mint is also uncertain, the attribution being based on the presence of an Ð as a probable mint signature.[131]

(f) This *burh* of uncertain location was established by Æthelflæd in 915. Numismatic affiliations under Athelstan suggest a location in the general vicinity of Gloucester, Hereford and Shrewsbury.[132]

(g) It is possible that a number of York moneyers did not in fact sign their dies at this time: Blunt, 'Athelstan', 88–93.

The composition of such a list might be thought of as the natural counterpart to the appearance of mint-names on coins for the first time in the late 920s, but its contents do not match up with the mints and moneyers under Athelstan: as can be seen from Table 3.6, some contained substantially more moneyers than they were permitted, like London, while others, such as Rochester and Canterbury, never reached their full allowance. No moneyers are known to have worked at Dorchester or Hastings at all until the 980s. The list's layout of the mints is broadly east to west, like the near-contemporary Burghal Hidage, though the first four places are an exception. These include the largest and oldest mints in the country. But, with the conspicuous exception of London, no mints north of the Thames are named – not even Oxford, which had struck coins for Alfred from the 880s and which formally came into the hands of Edward the Elder (along with London) in 911, or Chester, which housed the most moneyers

---

[128] There is some uncertainty, however, over whether these coins were minted at Bridport or in the vicinity of one of several nearby places named Bredy, or somewhere along the river Brit in Dorset: see J. Carroll and D.N. Parsons, *Anglo-Saxon Mint-Names, vol. I. Axbridge–Hythe* (Nottingham, 2007), 36–42.

[129] Blunt 'Athelstan', 75–6.

[130] Ibid., 78–9.

[131] Ibid., 101–2.

[132] Ibid., 101–2; see also F. Elmore Jones and C. Blunt, 'The tenth-century mint "æt Weardbyrig"', *BNJ*, 28 (1955–7), 494–8; R. Coates, 'Æthelflæd's fortification of *Weardburh*', *Notes and Queries*, 45 (1998), 8–12; J. Carroll, 'Coins and the Chronicle: mint-signatures, history, and language', in *Reading the Anglo-Saxon Chronicle: Language, Literature, History*, ed. A. Jorgensen (Turnhout, 2010), 243–74, at 251–4.

of any English mint in the early tenth century. South of the Thames there are also significant gaps, including mints in Berkshire (Wallingford), Kent (Dover and Lymne) and Somerset (Bath and Langport). Bath's absence is especially striking, as it was active already at the turn of the tenth century, and had two moneyers when mint-signatures were used there under Athelstan.

Some of these omissions can be put down to the patchiness of the corpus, and it is naïve to assume that surviving pennies offer complete representation of the mints and moneyers active in tenth-century England. One might also invoke the final tantalising clause of the mint-list, that all other *byrg* were permitted a moneyer. Yet some single-moneyer mints (Chichester, Dorchester and Hastings) were already named, and it is by no means certain that all the southern mints active by Athelstan's reign but missing from the list had always been home to only one moneyer: the vagaries of attribution of the many unassigned moneyers of the earlier tenth century are too great to inspire confidence in any such conclusion.

Given these difficulties, it is simply not possible to see the mint-list of II Athelstan as a blueprint for Athelstan's mint-signed coinage. Rather, the formulation of the whole numismatic section indicates that it constituted part of a separately numbered document on trading and towns subsumed into II Athelstan. This has been recognised for over a century, but the date of the earlier document is not known for certain.[133] The mint-list itself can be dated approximately, since several of the locations it names probably only emerged as *byrg* in the early tenth century, and hence in its final form the list cannot pre-date the reign of Edward the Elder.[134] However, it is possible that the list was added to in several stages over a long period without alteration to previously established complements (despite possible changes in practice). The first named mints in particular – Canterbury, Rochester, London and Winchester – may belong to a substantially older stratum originating in the ninth century. Moneyer complements at some of the mints during this period match the Grately totals very well.[135] Canterbury had been home to between six and eight moneyers consistently between the 790s and the 840s, including two archiepiscopal moneyers. Much greater fluctuation prevailed in subsequent decades.[136] From the 820s until the 840s Rochester had been home to three

---

[133] II Athelstan, ch. 13–18 (ed. Liebermann, *Gesetze* 1, 158–9; trans. Whitelock 1979, 420). For the first proposal of an earlier text see Liebermann, *Gesetze* 3, 100.

[134] Blackburn, 'Mints', 172. For a reading which favours a date in the 910s, see Molyneaux, 'Formation', 111–25.

[135] Naismith, *Money and Power*, 132–42.

[136] Up to 50 were active *c.*864, but towards the end of Alfred's reign the activity of Canterbury declined dramatically: *CTCE*, 21. Eighteen moneyers struck mint-signed and/or archiepiscopal coins at Canterbury in the last coinage of Alfred (Blackburn, 'Earliest Anglo-Viking coinage', 343 (*VCCBI*, 169)); there is, however, no way of knowing how many of them operated simultaneously.

moneyers, and also produced a series of coin-types which have been plausibly attributed to the bishop. These ecclesiastical issues were all minted during the tenure of Beornmod (803×805–842×844), possibly indicating an *ad hominem* concession.[137] Besides these coins and the reference in II Athelstan, there is no documentary or numismatic evidence for the bishop of Rochester ever holding rights to or profits from minting.[138] Moreover, Rochester's moneyers apparently ceased minting altogether in the 860s, following a period of greater fluctuation in complement; Rochester cannot be shown to have operated again until Athelstan's reign. London and Winchester fit less closely with the early ninth century. The former had boasted a complement of between six and ten moneyers from the 790s to approximately the 820s; it varied substantially thereafter, and was apparently home to only one moneyer by the time it fell into West Saxon control for a brief period in 829–30, whereas a dozen were named there in the coinage of Berhtwulf (*c.*845–51) and a higher but very uncertain and variable number from the time of Burgred onwards. Winchester may have been the location of the early West Saxon mint which opened under Beorhtric (786–802), and although its output at that time was small it apparently housed a substantial number of moneyers: eight were named there in the reign of Ecgberht (802–39).[139] On the other hand, Southampton also has a strong case for being home to the early West Saxon mint, and either way Winchester most clearly took off as a mint during and after its substantial urban redevelopment in the late ninth century.[140] It may be that London and Winchester represent an intermediary stage of the text, added after Canterbury and Rochester but at some time later in the ninth century when the number of mints remained small and all of them had passed into West Saxon hands.

Even if there are multiple layers within the mint-list which assumed its final form under Edward the Elder or early in the reign of Athelstan, it still remains perplexing why the new material covered only a limited selection of the mints south of the Thames. No obvious explanation presents itself, although the list may have followed some now-lost administrative logic, or perhaps be incomplete.[141] A more productive approach is to consider not only the murky origins of what may have been a composite document, but also where it ended up: in a widely circulated law-code emanating from the royal presence. Athelstan's ambitious legislation provides a valuable window onto the inner workings of written legal

[137] Naismith, *Money and Power*, 121–3.

[138] Cf. C. Blunt, 'Ecclesiastical coinage in England. 2: after the Norman conquest', *NC, 7th series, 1* (1961), i–xxi, at v.

[139] M. Dolley, 'The location of the pre-Ælfredian mint(s) of Wessex', *Proceedings of the Hampshire Field Club and Archaeology Society, 27* (1970), 57–61.

[140] M. Biddle, 'The study of Winchester: archaeology and history', in *British Academy Papers on Anglo-Saxon England*, ed. E.G. Stanley (Oxford, 1990), 299–341, at 325–32.

[141] Blackburn, 'Mints, 171; Molyneaux, 'Formation', 111–25.

practice, in that several of the 'law-codes' designated I–VI Athelstan represent local responses to royal commands, such as those preserved in the Grately code. Three of these other codes refer to clauses in the passage of II Athelstan concerned with towns and trade.[142] These references show that for tenth-century readers, there was no question of this part of the law-code being anything other than the king's will. Of course, not all the measures laid down in II Athelstan were fully enforced, as the king himself complained;[143] but as a statement of principle rather than of specific practice, the mint-list of II Athelstan fits well into Athelstan's reign, when the association between moneyers and increasingly numerous mint-places was first made explicit on the coins.[144]

If the mint-list of II Athelstan is understood as a model for the general notion of moneyers being more closely associated with their mint-places, then it follows that the distribution of the mints need not have any implications for the other sections of the law-code concerned with coinage. In particular, the *cynges onweald* over which a single coinage was to be current may have been significantly larger than the area covered by the mints. *Onweald* is usually translated as 'authority' or 'dominion', and was only partially synonymous with a kingdom as such; indeed, *onweald* was sometimes said to be necessary to rule a *rice* ('kingdom'), and it could be used to gloss the Latin words *potestas/potentia* and more occasionally *monarchia*, *imperium* and *virtus*.[145] Later law-codes which call on the same terminology indicate that a single king's *onweald* was entirely compatible with a mixture of national and local regulations, as seen with the coinage. One might compare the provisions of IV Edgar, which famously conceded that the Danes

---

[142] III Athelstan, ch. 8 (ed. Liebermann, *Gesetze*, 1, 170); IV Athelstan, ch. 2 (ed. Liebermann, *Gesetze*, 1, 171); VI Athelstan, ch. 10 (ed. Liebermann, *Gesetze*, 1, 180).

[143] V Athelstan, prologue (ed. Liebermann, *Gesetze*, 1, 166–7).

[144] On Athelstan's legislation see Wormald, *Making*, 290–308; S. Keynes, 'Royal government and the written word in late Anglo-Saxon England', in *The Uses of Literacy in Early Mediaeval Europe*, ed. R. McKitterick (Cambridge, 1990), 226–57, at 237–41; D. Pratt, 'Written law and the communication of authority in tenth-century England', in *England and the Continent in the Tenth Century: Studies in Honour of Wilhelm Levison (1876–1947)*, ed. R. Rollason, C. Leyser and H. Williams (Turnhout, 2010), 331–50; L. Roach, 'Law codes and legal norms in later Anglo-Saxon England', *Historical Research*, 86 (2013), 465–86; E. Screen, 'Anglo-Saxon law and numismatics: a reassessment in the light of Patrick Wormald's *The Making of English Law*', *BNJ*, 77 (2007), 150–72.

[145] W.A. Kretzschmar, 'Adaptation and *anweald* in the Old English Orosius', *ASE, 16* (1987), 127–45, at 138–44; M. Godden, 'Money, power and morality in late Anglo-Saxon England', *ASE, 19* (1990), 41–65, at 45–6; D. Pratt, *The Political Thought of King Alfred the Great* (Cambridge, 2007), 289–92. The different meanings are particularly well illustrated in the tract known as 'Edgar's Establishment of Monasteries': *Councils and Synods, with Other Documents Relating to the English Church 871–1204*, ed. D. Whitelock, C. Brooke and M. Brett (2 vols., Oxford, 1981), 1, 142–54; trans. *EHD I*, 920–3 (no. 238). For the Latin glosses, see the University of Toronto's *Dictionary of Old English* (<www.doe.utoronto.ca/>).

should determine their own secular laws. This is contrasted with other measures which were to affect *eallum leodscipe, ægðer ge Anglum ge Denum ge Bryttum, on ælce endum mines anwealdes.*[146] Indeed, this entire tract was promulgated as a reaction to pestilence *wide gynd his anweald*, and includes another stipulation which *sy us eallum gemæne, þe on þissum iglandum wuniað.*[147] Different minting organisations within one *onweald* thus did not invalidate the coherence of a ruler's coinage, just as legal or administrative peculiarities did not offset the unity of a king's dominion as a whole.[148]

The emphasis II Athelstan places on the moneyers' relationship with the king is also striking. The entire numismatic section is headed *be myneterum* ('on moneyers'), and is exclusively concerned with the links between the king and the moneyers (save for the mention of moneyers answerable to abbots and bishops at Rochester and Canterbury). Other figures – reeves, ealdormen and bishops – are not part of the equation. The same is true of other Anglo-Saxon law-codes which discuss coinage: the document known as IV Æthelred, for example, enjoins the help of ealdormen and bishops only in relation to vigilance against forgery.[149] It is of course dangerous to argue from what is *not* contained in Anglo-Saxon legislation. All Anglo-Saxon law-codes as they survive now have been heavily filtered both by contemporary concerns, and by complex subsequent transmission. Nevertheless, the emphasis on the role of the moneyer rather than on any higher-level supervisory authority is surely significant, and accords well with what can be seen from the coins themselves. As stressed above, there are no known coins in the names of ealdormen or (after *c.*923) archbishops. Moreover, the patterns of die-distribution and regional style bear

---

[146] 'All the nation, whether Englishmen, Danes or Britons, in every province of my dominion'.

[147] 'Far and wide throughout [Edgar's] dominion'; 'should be common to all of us who inhabit these islands'. IV Edgar, preface and ch. 2.2 and 14.2 (ed. Liebermann, *Gesetze*, 1, 206–15; trans. *EHD I*, 434–6).

[148] This was especially true of the complex realm over which English kings of the tenth century presided: S. Keynes, 'King Alfred and the Mercians', in *Kings*, ed. Blackburn and Dumville, 1–45, at 19–45; Keynes, 'England', 460–6. The emergence of this kingdom was not a foregone conclusion, and different views can be traced, above all in English Mercia: P. Stafford, '"The annals of Æthelflæd": annals, history and politics in early tenth-century England', in *Myth*, ed. Barrow and Wareham, 101–16; P. Stafford, 'Political women in Mercia, eighth to early tenth centuries', in *Mercia: an Anglo-Saxon Kingdom in Europe*, ed. M.P. Brown and C.A. Farr (London), 35–49, at 45–7; P. Stafford, 'Succession and inheritance: a gendered perspective on Alfred's family history', in *Alfred*, ed. Reuter, 251–64, at 259–61; N. Cumberledge, 'Reading between the lines: the place of Mercia within an expanding Wessex', *Midland History*, 27 (2002), 1–15.

[149] IV Æthelred, ch. 8 (ed. Liebermann, *Gesetze*, 1, 238). This section of the document is problematic, however, and it may be substantially later than the association with Æthelred II suggests: Wormald, *Making*, 325–6; M.K. Lawson, *Cnut: England's Viking King*, 2nd edn (Stroud, 2004), 186–7; D. Keene, 'Text, visualisation and politics: London, 1150–1250', *TRHS, 6th series, 18* (2008), 69–99, at 93–4.

little relation to the known ealdormanries of England.[150] Tracing the number
and boundaries of the latter is deeply problematic, though it is generally clear
that ealdormanries shifted and fluctuated in number more frequently than the
structure of the coinage changed.[151] Neither did the organisation of the coinage
bear an obvious connection to bishoprics or even to shires:[152] different mints
in the same shire sometimes followed divergent practices, and areas of die-
distribution, circulation and moneyer movement were not notably affected by
shire boundaries.[153]

Existing legal, administrative and ethnic divisions of newly conquered
eastern England certainly affected its subsequent monetary development.[154]
Conquest of the entire area from Northampton to the Welland and East Anglia
by Edward the Elder in 917 did not result in a single unified coinage within this
area. Neither did Lincoln's probable escape from English control into the 920s
prevent its subsequent close association with Stamford, which fell to Edward in
918. Links like these can only be explained as a result of earlier divisions within
conquered territory, which could be preserved for decades thereafter. But there
were also revealing exceptions in which these local ties seem to have been cast
aside. One might, for example, draw a connection between the generally distinct
'north-eastern' mints and the Danelaw, the inhabitants of which were allowed
special dispensation by Edgar in matters of *woruldgeriht* ('secular law').[155] But

---

[150]   *Pace* P. Stafford, 'Historical implications of the regional production of dies under Æthelred
II', *BNJ, 48* (1978), 35–51; Jonsson, *New Era*, 67–8 and 185–8; Jonsson, 'Pre-reform'. Cf. D.M.
Metcalf, 'Were ealdormen exercising independent control over the coinage in mid-tenth-century
England?', *BNJ, 57* (1987), 24–33.

[151]   N. Banton, 'Ealdormen and earls in England from the reign of King Alfred to the reign of
King Æthelred II' (DPhil thesis, University of Oxford, 1981); H.M. Chadwick, *Studies in Anglo-
Saxon Institutions* (Cambridge, 1905), 161–97; Stafford, *Unification*, 37–9 and 150–61. For
specific individuals and families, see A. Williams, '*Princeps Merciorum Gentis*: the family, career
and connections of Ælfhere, ealdorman of Mercia, 956–83', *ASE, 10* (1982), 143–72; C.R. Hart,
The Danelaw (London, 1992), 115–40 and 569–604; A. Wareham, *Lords and Communities in
Early Medieval East Anglia* (Woodbridge, 2005).

[152]   F. Barlow, *The English Church 1000–1066*, 2nd edn (London, 1979), 162–83. Shires were
of diverse origins, and in Mercia and the former Viking territories their status during the tenth
century remains debatable: see Stenton, *Anglo-Saxon England*, 292–3 and 337–8; A. Williams,
Kingship and Government in Pre-Conquest England c. 500–c. 1066 (Basingstoke, 1999), 88–9;
Chadwick, *Studies*, 202–27; Marten, 'Shiring'; D. Hinton, 'The fortifications and their shires',
in *Defence*, ed. Hill and Rumble, 151–9; D. Hill, 'The shiring of Mercia – again', in *Edward*, ed.
Higham and Hill, 144–59.

[153]   Jonsson, *New Era*, 95; Metcalf, *Atlas*, 60–62.

[154]   On the internal divisions of the Danelaw (which seem to have emphasised specific *byrg*
and associated armies, with East Anglia forming a separate large unit) see Hart, *Danelaw*, 3–24.

[155]   IV Edgar, ch. 2.1 (ed. Liebermann, *Gesetze*, 1, 210; trans. *EHD I*, 435).

it is not clear how far earlier kings had condoned such special treatment,[156] and the Danelaw was defined by more than the presence of Scandinavian settlers.[157] There were also large parts of the Danelaw – most notably Derby, Newark and (probably) Leicester and Nottingham – which numismatically were linked to northern English Mercia (dominated by Chester).[158] In this case, the origins of the division probably go back to the circumstances of conquest: Derby and Leicester were both taken by Æthelflæd, who approached from the western territories of English Mercia.[159]

In short, the currency seems to have been governed by its own systems of interaction and distribution.[160] While the coinage was subject to the will of the king, and malefactors would face justice from local authorities including the ealdorman and the town-reeve,[161] the system of mint-towns and moneyers formed its own sphere of government. Many elements of it have been closely studied in the context of the post-973 coinage: key features include the number of moneyers at various mints; movements of moneyers between mints; fluctuating regional and national levels of die-distribution; and occasional movements of dies between mints.[162] All of these can be paralleled well before 973. The rarity of mint-signatures imposes certain limits on what can be known, but in the mint-signed coinage of Athelstan there was already inter-mint die-

---

[156] For the case of IV Edgar's provisions, see N. Lund, 'King Edgar and the Danelaw', *Mediaeval Scandinavia, 9* (1976), 181–95.

[157] For selected views, see D. Hadley, 'Viking and native: re-thinking identity in the Danelaw', *EME, 11* (2002), 45–70; L. Abrams 'King Edgar and the men of the Danelaw', in *Edgar*, ed. Scragg, 171–91, at 176–85; J. Kershaw, 'Culture and gender in the Danelaw: Scandinavian and Anglo-Scandinavian brooches', *Viking and Medieval Scandinavia, 5* (2009), 295–325; Hart, *Danelaw*, 3–24. On the problem of definition, see L. Abrams, 'Edward the Elder's Danelaw', in *Edward*, ed. Higham and Hill, 128–43; Graham-Campbell et al. (eds.), *Vikings*.

[158] Pagan, 'Mints' and 'Pre-Reform', 199–203 (building on *CTCE*, 275) stresses the complexity of the relationship between Derby and the north Mercian mint-towns (especially Chester), though at no time do Derby moneyers appear to have received coins of 'northeastern' style.

[159] *ASC* 917 and 918 BCD. The conquest of Nottingham is not mentioned, although it was apparently under English control by 920, when Edward visited and ordered the construction of a second *burh*.

[160] Campbell, *Anglo-Saxon State*, 201–27.

[161] Cf. II Athelstan, ch. 25 (ed. Liebermann, *Gesetze*, 1, 164; trans. *EHD I*, p. 421). C. Cubitt, '"As the lawbook teaches": reeves, lawbooks and urban life in the anonymous Old English legend of the Seven Sleepers', *EHR, 124* (2009), 1021–49.

[162] Late Anglo-Saxon inter-mint die-links have been listed by Stewart Lyon and Bill Lean for publication in a forthcoming article.

linking, moneyers who worked at multiple centres, and often large fluctuations in die-distribution.[163]

Edgar utilised this complex network of moneyers, mint-towns and die-cutters to implement his reform of *c.*973. In doing so he built on an already well-established basis of organisation and expertise which stood the English coinage in good stead down to the Norman conquest and beyond. Edgar's famous reform and the system which it established were thus only possible thanks to what had come before: they owed a major debt to Athelstan's precedent, to earlier reforms in Edgar's own reign and above all to the minting system of tenth-century England.

Conclusion: the Impact of Edgar's Reform

On any view, Edgar's reform of *c.*973 was a major and successful enterprise. It also fits into the historical developments of its day. Uncertainty surrounding the exact date and context of the reform precludes any definitive association with a specific moment in the reign, but it fits the overall tone of Edgar's later years extremely well. At its heart were determined efforts to strengthen the cohesion of the kingdom in matters both secular and spiritual.[164] A prominent part in advancing this agenda of improvement and renewal was played by Edgar's advisers, among them St Æthelwold, bishop of Winchester (963–84). In the tract he composed as a preface to the Old English Benedictine *regula*, Æthelwold lauded the young king as one who 'þæs rices twislunge eft to annysse brohte'.[165] Similarly, in the *Regularis concordia* – the famous rule drawn up to standardise practice among the newly reformed Benedictine houses across England – Æthelwold stated that the unity imposed by its precepts was 'ne impar ac varius unius regulae ac unius patriae usus probrose vituperium sanctae conversationi irrogaret'.[166]

---

[163] *CTCE*, 110 (for an inter-mint die-link under Athelstan). For die-distribution see Metcalf, 'Rome (Forum) hoard', 83–9. There are many moneyers who worked at multiple mints, often crossing shire boundaries: Baldric worked at Bedford and Northampton under Edgar, Æthelmund at Oxford and Wallingford under Athelstan, Abenel at Hertford and Maldon under Athelstan and possibly Ælfsige at Winchester and Wilton under Edgar (ibid., 282, 284 and 286).

[164] Keynes, 'England', 481–2; Keynes, 'Edgar', 45; John, *Orbis Britanniae*, 56–61; R. Deshman, *The Benedictional of Æthelwold* (Princeton, NJ, 1995), esp. 198–200 and 212–14; R. Deshman, '*Benedictus monarcha et monarchus.* Early medieval ruler theology and the Anglo-Saxon reform', *Frühmittelalterliche Studien*, 22 (1988), 204–40, esp. 219–28.

[165] 'Brought back to unity the divisions of the kingdom'. Ed. Whitelock, Brooke and Brett, 1, 146–7.

[166] 'Lest differing ways of observing the customs of one Rule and one country should bring the holy custom [of the monasteries] into disrepute'. *Regularis concordia*, prologue ch. 4 (*Consuetudinum saeculi X/XI/XII monumenta non-Cluniacensia*, ed. T. Symons, rev. S. Spath, M.

On a number of fronts the 16 years of Edgar's sole reign were taken as a fresh start, and saw moves to restore the perceived glories of the kingdom.[167] Monastic leaders sought out sites for new foundations which were laden with historical meaning, such as those mentioned in the writings of the venerable Bede.[168] Meanwhile, Edgar's charters show memories of the reign of Athelstan being rekindled. Edgar was the first king since Athelstan regularly to be styled *rex totius Britanniae* ('king of all Britain').[169] The symbolic rowing trip on the Dee when Edgar was joined by other kings of Britain demonstrated the reality of this bold claim.[170]

Athelstan's regime also provided a touchstone for the coinage. Edgar revived the *Circumscription* type using the same grandiose royal style as appeared in the charters, just as in the late 920s and 930s. The *Bust Crowned* coins of Athelstan likewise provided a model, if a less direct one, for the post-reform pennies of Edgar.[171] Ideologically Edgar's reform therefore did not spring *ex nihilo*: it was

---

Wegener and K. Hallinger, Corpus Consuetudinum Monasticarum 7.3 (Siegburg, 1984), 71). The date of this document within the period 966×975 remains debated: Keynes, 'Edgar', 45; J. Barrow, 'The chronology of the Benedictine "Reform"', in *Edgar*, ed. Scragg, 211–23.

[167] Cf. T.A. Bredehoft, *Textual Histories: Readings in the Anglo-Saxon Chronicle* (Toronto, 2001), 103–10; M. Salvador-Bello, 'The Edgar panegyrics in the *Anglo-Saxon Chronicle*', in *Edgar*, ed. Scragg, 252–72 for the historial use of poetry in the late tenth century.

[168] A. Gransden, 'Traditionalism and continuity during the last century of Anglo-Saxon monasticism', *Journal of Ecclesiastical History*, 40 (1989), 159–207; P. Wormald, 'Æthelwold and his continental counterparts: contact, comparison, contrast', in *Bishop Æthelwold: his Career and Influence*, ed. B. Yorke (Woodbridge, 1988), 13–42, at 38–41. This was not the sole driving force behind royal or ecclesiastical policy: J. Barrow, 'The ideology of the tenth-century English Benedictine "reform"', in *Challenging*, ed. Skinner, 141–54; C.A. Jones, 'Ælfric and the limits of "Benedictine reform"', in *A Companion to Ælfric*, ed. H. Magennis and M. Swan (Leiden and Boston, MA, 2009), 67–108.

[169] Keynes, 'Edgar', 24–5 and 48–51; Stafford, *Unification*, 55–6; Y. Coz, *Rome en Angleterre. L'image de la Rome antique dans l'Angleterre anglo-saxonne, du VIIe siècle à 1066* (Paris, 2011), 342. Titles asserting overlordship of *totius Britanniae/Albionis* had not vanished in the period 939–59; variations on the theme persisted in certain contexts, not least the 'Dunstan B' charters of the 950s: S. Keynes, 'The "Dunstan B" charters', *ASE*, 23 (1994), 165–93, at 180. In contrast, the 'alliterative' charters of the 940s and 950s, probably associated with Coenwald, bishop of Worcester (928×929–957/8), favoured variants of the style *rex Angulsæxna et Northanhumbrorum imperator, paganorum gubernator, Breotumque propugnator*: Keynes, 'Books', 156–9; Hart, *Danelaw*, 436–45.

[170] On the Chester 'regatta', see above, pp. 39–40.

[171] It may be significant that Winchester and occasionally other mints had, under Athelstan, issued *Bust Crowned* pennies which enclosed the bust with an inner circle and a longer legend (*rex to[tius] Brit[anniae]*), and combined this with the small cross and circumscription reverse later selected for Edgar's reform issue: Blunt, 'Athelstan', 66 and nos. 299, 301, 303, 305 (Winchester), 308–9 (York) and 323 (uncertain mint, possibly Oxford).

grounded in contemporary developments in other areas and in a wider effort to emulate the successes of esteemed predecessors, including the best features of earlier English coinage. In implementation, however, Edgar went well beyond earlier monetary policies. Athelstan's coinage had fallen short of complete or lasting standardisation, and so the minting organisation slipped back into a more regionalised pattern. Edgar's reformed coinage set a new benchmark for unity and regularisation: never before had a single coin-type been securely established at all 40 or so mint-places in the kingdom. Still more impressive were two other facets of the reform. One was its durability. A common type was maintained across broadly the same network of mints down to the twelfth century. The other main lasting effect of Edgar's reform was on the circulating medium. Athelstan never undertook what monetary historians have called a *renovatio monetae*: foreign coins were generally excluded from circulation, but there was no systematic recoinage of the native currency for nearly a century after *c*.880. Edgar's recoinage swept away the older currency, and ushered in a period (beginning in the 980s) when recoinages were enacted on a relatively frequent basis. These may or may not have been part of Edgar's plan; much or all of the credit for their development should be assigned to Æthelred II and his advisers.[172] Inspiration for this important new step must have come from long-established (possibly written) West Saxon or Carolingian precedent, for it had not been the regular custom in England or the Frankish kingdoms within living memory by the 970s.[173] Even if Edgar and his contemporaries could not necessarily have predicted its full impact, the recoinage of *c*.973 was, in the long run, nothing short of revolutionary.

Yet Edgar's reform was a change of tune and conductor rather than orchestra, and important components of the earlier regime persisted. Many moneyers remained in place either side of the reform. More importantly, the number and distribution of mint-towns also remained largely stable.[174] Their establishment should be counted as one of the key achievements of the earlier tenth century. In circulation, too, there was much continuity across the reform, implying that the underlying currents of the monetary economy stayed intact and already

---

[172]	Classic accounts of these changes of type include Dolley and Metcalf, 'Reform'; M. Dolley, 'An introduction to the coinage of Ethelred II', in *Ethelred the Unready: Papers from the Millenary Conference*, ed. D. Hill, BAR British Series 59 (Oxford, 1978), 115–33. More nuanced views include Brand, *Periodic Change*; Stewart, 'Coinage and recoinage'; P. Grierson, 'Numismatics and the historian', *NC, 7th series, 2* (1962), i–xiv, at viii–xiv; S. Keynes and R. Naismith, 'The *Agnus Dei* pennies of King Æthelred the Unready', *ASE, 40* (2012), 175–223.

[173]	M. Dolley, 'Ælfred the Great's abandonment of the concept of periodic recoinage', in *Studies in Numismatic Method Presented to Philip Grierson*, ed. C.N.L. Brooke (Cambridge, 1983), 153–60.

[174]	Allen, *Mints*, 16; *CTCE*, 255–63.

embraced the whole kingdom. The organisation of minting after the reform likewise showed glimmers of the old order.

Edgar's reform of *c.*973 should therefore be seen not only as a major event but as part of an ongoing process, and the royal control it demonstrates as a high-point in a continuum which had seen kings play a substantial role in English minting for over two centuries. Whatever else it was, the coinage of *c.*880–973 was a universally royal entity naming the kings of the West Saxon dynasty, even in newly conquered territories. It was the first English coinage recognising a single king ever to be issued on so large a geographical scale. The reasons for its variation were fundamentally different from those which affected the Carolingian empire from the mid-ninth century onwards, as formerly unified kingdoms and their coinages broke apart.[175] Rather, the English coinage's gradual advancement was bound to the military expansion of the West Saxon dynasty: the pattern of conquest left tangible marks for decades. The English coinage of this period must be taken on its own terms, and measured against what it replaced as well as what it preceded. Gone was the pattern of a small number of mints concentrated in the east; gone too, after West Saxon and Mercian conquest, was minting or substantial circulation of coin in the name of any ruler other than the West Saxon overlord. In terms of circulation, organisation and royal recognition a revolutionary currency was already beginning to emerge even in the later years of the ninth century.

---

[175] S. Coupland, *Carolingian Coinage and the Vikings: Studies on Power and Trade in the 9th Century* (Ashgate, 2007). See also *MEC I*, 218–59; J. Lafaurie, 'Numismatique: des Carolingiens aux Capétiens', *Cahiers de civilisation médiévale, 13* (1970), 117–37; F. Dumas, 'Le début de l'époque féodale en France d'après les monnaies', *Bulletin du Cercle d'études numismatiques* 1973, 65–77.

Chapter 4

Coinage and Currency Under William I and William II

Martin Allen

In the 1990s Mark Blackburn published two magisterial surveys of the English coinage and currency under Henry I (1100–35) and in the reign of Stephen (1135–54), which have served as a foundation of all subsequent work in the subject.[1] The coinage of the first two Norman kings, William I (1066–87) and William II (1087–1100), received attention in Michael Dolley's brief book on *The Norman Conquest and the English Coinage* in 1966, and in the work of Philip Grierson and Michael Metcalf on Domesday Book and the *Paxs* type in the 1980s, but the study of the English monetary system under William I and William II is still heavily dependent upon George Brooke's *British Museum Catalogue* (*BMC*) of the Anglo-Norman coinage, published as long ago as 1916.[2] It is the aim of this chapter to attempt to emulate Mark Blackburn's two survey papers with an up-to-date review of the English coinage in its historical context between 1066 and 1100.

Dolley's central argument in 1966 was that the English coinage was relatively little affected by the Norman Conquest, at least to begin with.[3] By 1066 Anglo-Saxon England had a well-established monetary system of silver pennies of uniform national designs and good metal produced by large numbers of moneyers in dozens of towns and cities throughout the kingdom, with

---

[1]   M. Blackburn, 'Coinage and currency under Henry I: a review', *Anglo-Norman Studies, 13* (1990), 49–81; M. Blackburn, 'Coinage and currency', in *The Anarchy of King Stephen's Reign*, ed. E. King (Oxford, 1994), 145–205.

[2]   M. Dolley, *The Norman Conquest and the English Coinage* (London, 1966); P. Grierson, 'Domesday Book, the geld *de moneta* and *monetagium*: a forgotten minting reform', *BNJ, 55* (1985), 84–94; P. Grierson, 'The monetary system under William I', in *Domesday Book Studies*, ed. A. Williams and R.W.H. Erskine (London, 1987), 75–9; D.M. Metcalf, 'The taxation of moneyers under Edward the Confessor and in 1086', in *Domesday Studies. Papers Read at the Novocentenary Conference of the Royal Historical Society and the Institute of British Geographers, Winchester, 1986*, ed. J.C. Holt (Woodbridge, 1987), 279–93; D.M. Metcalf, 'Notes on the "PAXS" type of William I', *Yorkshire Numismatist, 1* (1988), 13–26; G.C. Brooke, *A Catalogue of English Coins in the British Museum. The Norman Kings* (2 vols., London,1916).

[3]   Dolley, *The Norman Conquest*, 11–15.

recoinages at frequent intervals, and this continued after 1066. The duchy of Normandy had a radically different coinage of debased silver *deniers*, but there was no attempt to impose elements of the Norman system in England.[4] The English penny served the Norman kings very well as a medium of revenue and expenditure. There was some short-term disruption of mint organisation in the early years of the conquest, with 16 of Harold II's mints being at present unknown in the first coinage type of William I, but 15 of these mints reappear later in the reign of William I (the single exception being Droitwich), and there was no new mint until the appearance of Pevensey in William I's type 5 in the late 1070s or early 1080s. Only 48 (32 per cent) of the 149 known moneyers of Harold II are recorded at present in William I's first type (1066–*c.*1068), rising to 74 (nearly 50 per cent) in type 2 (*c.*1068–70), but other men with predominantly Anglo-Saxon or Anglo-Scandinavian names took their places.[5] A more fundamental change than the temporary closure of mints or the loss of some of the moneyers was the introduction of a new system of revenue from the coinage, replacing small regular payments from the moneyers with a much heavier tax imposed upon local communities. This change, which is amply documented in Domesday Book, did not survive after the sudden death of William II in 1100.

Domesday Book and the Coinage

Domesday Book must have a leading role in any discussion of the English coinage under the first two Norman kings. The Domesday Book record is very selective, providing evidence of the existence of only 13 mints under Edward the Confessor (1042–66) and 20 at the time of the Domesday survey in 1086 (a minority of the mints in operation in each case), but it is very revealing about many aspects of the monetary system.[6] In the time of Edward the Confessor moneyers paid an annual farm from their profits, usually of one mark (two-thirds of a pound) of silver, and also a tax of 20s. when the type of the coinage was changed, which occurred at intervals of no more than a few years between Edgar's reform of the coinage in about 973 and the mint reorganisation after the Assize of Moneyers of 1124–25. At some of the mints of Edward the Confessor the local earl had a one-third share or third-penny (*tertius denarius*) of the mint revenues, as was the case in Chester, Huntingdon and Lewes, and the operation of ecclesiastical minting rights is shown by the bishop of Hereford's right to the

---

[4]   J.C. Moesgaard, 'La monnaie au temps de Guillaume le Conquérant', in *La Tapisserie de Bayeux: une chronique des temps vikings? Actes du colloque international de Bayeux 29 et 30 mars 2007*, ed. S. Lemagen (Bonsecours, 2009), 89–99.

[5]   M. Allen, 'Mints and moneyers of England and Wales, 1066–1158', *BNJ, 82* (2012), 54–120.

[6]   The evidence is summarised by Grierson, 'Domesday Book'; idem, 'The monetary system'.

20s. recoinage dues paid by one of the seven Hereford moneyers.[7] The Hereford entry is exceptionally informative, revealing that the moneyers struck as many coins as was required from the king's silver when he came to the city, that they were obliged to go with the local reeve when he took an army into Wales under penalty of a payment of 40s., and that the king had a relief of 20s. when a moneyer died or the moneyer's whole estate if he died intestate.[8] The Hereford moneyers were the king's men in many respects (apart from the bishop's moneyer), but these arrangements may not have been typical of England as a whole, because Hereford was subject to the unusual conditions of border warfare. The Hereford moneyers each paid 18s. for their new dies in addition to the usual 20s. when the coinage was changed, and the entry for Worcester records the payment of the 20s. at London to receive dies (*ad Londoniam pro cuneis monetae accipiendis*).[9] The production of dies had become centralised in London during the reign of Cnut, with a few notable exceptions, and used dies of Cnut, William I, Henry I and Stephen (from the Norwich, Wareham, Southwark and Northampton mints) found in spoil from the Thames Exchange site on London's northern waterfront in 1989–90 seem to have been returned to the London die workshop after use.[10] Otto the Goldsmith, who farmed royal manors in Essex and Suffolk in Domesday Book and worked on the tomb of William I, was the die-cutter in

---

[7]   Domesday Book I, 26, 179, 203, 262b; G.C. Brooke, 'Notes on the reign of William I', *NC, 4th ser. 11* (1911), 268–90, at 281–2; G.C. Brooke, *A Catalogue*, 1, cxxxv, clxii; G.C. Brooke, 'Quando moneta vertebatur: the change of coin-types in the eleventh century; its bearing on mules and overstrikes', *BNJ, 20* (1929–30), 105–16, at 105; Grierson, 'Domesday Book', 85–9; Metcalf, 'The taxation of moneyers', 286–9; M. Allen, *Mints and Money in Medieval England* (Cambridge, 2012), 182–3.

[8]   Domesday Book I, 179; Brooke, *A Catalogue*, 1, cxlii; Grierson, 'Domesday Book', 85–6, 88; Metcalf, 'The taxation of moneyers' 286.

[9]   Domesday Book I, 172; Brooke, 'Notes', 281–2; Brooke, *A Catalogue*, 1, cxxxv; Brooke, 'Quando moneta vertebatur', 106–8.

[10]   M.M. Archibald, J.R.S. Lang and G. Milne, 'Four early medieval coin dies from the London waterfront', *NC, 155* (1995), 165–200; Allen, *Mints and Money*, 108–9, 116; S. Lyon, 'Minting in Winchester: an introduction and statistical analysis', in *The Winchester Mint and Coins and Related Finds from the Excavations of 1961–71*, ed. M. Biddle, Winchester Studies, 8 (Oxford, 2012), 3–54, at 11–12. Brooke, 'Notes', 283, discusses the use of local dies at Lincoln and Norwich in William I type 2, Winchester in type 3, Lincoln, Stamford and York in type 4, and St Davids in type 8 (*Paxs*). In addition, a pair of local dies was used at York in type 3 (C.E. Blunt and M. Dolley, with F. Elmore Jones and C.S.S. Lyon, *SCBI 11: Reading University, Anglo-Saxon and Norman Coins; Royal Coin Cabinet, Stockholm, Part VI: Anglo-Norman Pennies* (Oxford, 1969), (Stockholm) no. 14; A.J.H. Gunstone, *SCBI 27: Lincolnshire Collections. Coins from Lincolnshire Mints, and Ancient British and Later Coins to 1272* (Oxford, 1981), no. 1773), and the use of the local dies in Wales in type 8 was not restricted to St Davids (see below, p. 93).

London by the time of his death in 1098, and the office became hereditary in his family until the fourteenth century.[11]

Domesday Book is our only source of evidence for the radical change in the system of mint revenue under William I. At the time of the survey in 1086 the moneyers' payments of a mark or 20s. at various times had been superseded by an annual tax levied from the borough (or, in the case of Oxford, from the shire), which varied very widely from 50s. at Taunton to £75 at Lincoln.[12] Grierson attempted to draw a distinction between a geld *de moneta* paid instead of the moneyers' annual payments and any unrecorded additional payments of profits that may have occurred under Edward the Confessor, and a new *monetagium* tax to cover the profits of recoinage, but a much simpler and more effective interpretation of the evidence is that there was just one annual mint tax given a variety of names.[13] A customary third-share of this new tax was paid to the local earl at Ipswich and to the sheriff (Hugh de Grandmesnil) at Leicester, but William de Warenne had half of the tax at Lewes.[14] The bishop of Thetford had the profits of one moneyer at Norwich if he wished.[15] At Wallingford a moneyer had a house free of dues for as long as he worked at the mint, and the Oxford moneyer Suetman also had a free house.[16] Metcalf has estimated that the introduction of the new tax could have increased the total annual revenue from the mints from some £200–£250 to at least £750 and possibly over £1,000, but that this may have been more than the working profits of the mints could sustain.[17] The annual payment of £20 from Ipswich fell into arrears of £27 over a period of four years, which implies that the new system was introduced no later than 1082.[18] Henry I's coronation charter of 5 August 1100 abolished a tax called the *monetagium commune* collected by the boroughs and shires, because it was not levied under Edward the Confessor, and there is good reason to believe

---

[11]   A.E. Packe, 'The coinage of the Norman kings', *NC*, 3rd ser., *13* (1893), 129–45, at 140; Brooke, *A Catalogue*, 1, cxxxiii; Archibald, Lang and Milne, 'Four early medieval coin dies', 195–7; Allen, *Mints and Money*, 117–20.

[12]   Grierson, 'Domesday Book', 85–7, 89–90; Grierson, 'The monetary system', 77; Metcalf, 'The taxation of moneyers', 281–2, 291–2; Allen, *Mints and Money*, 183–4. It may be reasonable to assume that the old fees of one mark and 20s. were subsumed in the new tax, but the absence of any mention of them in 1086 is not definitive proof of this.

[13]   Grierson, 'Domesday Book', 84, 90–91.

[14]   Domesday Book I, 26, 230, II, 290b; Brooke, *A Catalogue*, 1, cxlii.

[15]   Domesday Book II, 117b; Brooke, *A Catalogue*, 1, cxlii.

[16]   Domesday Book I, 56, 154; Brooke, *A Catalogue*, 1, cxli.

[17]   Metcalf, 'The taxation of moneyers', 290, 292–3.

[18]   Domesday Book II, 290b; Grierson, 'Domesday Book', 92–3; Grierson, 'The monetary system', 77, noting that the Colchester and Maldon entry also seems to imply that the new system was introduced at least four years before 1086.

that this can be identified with the new mint tax of Domesday Book.[19] After this abolition something like the old system was restored, as shown by a survey of the estates and revenues of Peterborough Abbey in the 1120s, which records a payment of 20s. by the moneyers of Stamford every year at Easter, and a further 20s. at a change of type.[20]

In the 1980s Grierson and Metcalf both argued that the introduction of the new mint tax seen in Domesday Book could be associated with an apparent increase in the weight of the English penny in William I's type 6, in the 1070s or early 1080s, which seemed to be indicated by Brooke's summary of the weights of the coins in his *BMC*.[21] The assumption that there was a general increase in weight standard in William I's type 6 has however been undermined by Metcalf's observation that there was variation in weight standards between mints until type 8 (*Pax*), when a single standard weight of *c*.1.37–1.38 g for the penny was finally achieved.[22] Stewart Lyon has suggested that payments in multiples of 254½d. in Domesday Book may relate to the number of pennies struck from each pound of silver, with a standard weight of about 1.37 g.[23] There has never been any suggestion that the high standard of fineness of the English coinage was altered by William I or William II, but the traditional assumption that the modern sterling standard of 92.5 per cent fine silver applied in the eleventh century will not stand up to critical examination. John Brand's work on the documentary evidence, supported by modern analyses of Anglo-Saxon and Anglo-Norman coins, indicates that the actual standard was more than 93 per cent fine, and that the modern standard of 92.5 per cent fine only evolved in the fourteenth century.[24]

---

[19] W. Stubbs (ed.), *Select Charters and other Documents Illustrative of English Constitutional History*, 9th ed., ed. H.W.C. Davis (Oxford, 1921), 118 (cap. 5); Brooke, *A Catalogue*, 1, lxx, cxlii–iii; Grierson, 'Domesday Book', 84; Allen, *Mints and Money*, 184–5.

[20] *Chronicon Petroburgense*, ed. T. Stapleton, Camden Series 47 (London, 1849), 166; Allen, *Mints and Money*, 3, 185.

[21] Grierson, 'Domesday Book', 90–94; Grierson, 'The monetary system', 77; Metcalf, 'The taxation of moneyers', 281–2.

[22] D.M. Metcalf, *An Atlas of Anglo-Saxon and Norman Coin Finds, c. 973–1086*, RNS Special Publication, 32 (London, 1998), 178–9, 181–2, 184–7, 189–90; Allen, *Mints and Money*, 137–8.

[23] S. Lyon, 'Silver weight and minted weight in England *c*.1000–1320, with a discussion of Domesday terminology, Edwardian farthings and the origin of English troy', *BNJ*, 76 (2006), 227–41, at 232–5.

[24] J.D. Brand, *The English Coinage 1180–1247: Money, Mints and Exchanges*, BNS Special Publication, 1 (London, 1994), 73–5; Allen, *Mints and Money*, 157–62.

Chronology

In the early years of the twentieth century P.W.P. Carlyon-Britton argued that the English *monetagium* was directly derived from the tax of that name in Normandy, which was levied once in every three years in return for a promise not to change the coinage by debasement, and that consequently it could be assumed that the types of the English coinage were changed at exactly three-year intervals, at Michaelmas (29 September), with perhaps three months allowed to change the old money.[25] These bold assumptions became the basis of the first published chronology of the thirteen coinage types bearing the name of a King William between 1066 and 1100 (see Table 4.1). Carlyon-Britton's theories were very effectively demolished by Brooke, who argued that there was no true relation between the *monetagium* in Henry I's coronation charter and the tax of that name in Normandy, because the English and Norman currencies were fundamentally different (with no debasement in England), and that there was no reason to believe that the English *monetagium* was triennial, or that changes of type were triennial.[26] Brooke also argued that there was no definitive evidence for the allocation of eight types to William I and five to William II, and he would go no further than observing that it may have been normal for a type to last for two or three years.[27] He deliberately avoided suggesting any chronology for the coinages of William I and William II in his *BMC*, and there the matter rested until 1966, when Dolley returned to the triennial theory of Carlyon-Britton, modifying it in an attempt to make it fit his construction of the facts. Dolley proposed a reduction in the lengths of William I's types 1, 2, 3 and 4 from three years to two only, so that William I's type 8 (*Paxs*) could be given a full three years (1083–66) and not just one (1086–87), as in Carlyon-Britton's chronology. The Scaldwell hoard (ending in William I's type 5) could now be associated with the revolt of 1075, an increase in mint activity in the *Paxs* type would coincide with the payment of a particularly heavy (6s. per hide of land) geld in 1083–84, and it could be proposed that the burying of the Beauworth hoard (which predominantly consisted of the *Paxs* type) might have been caused by the fears of a Danish invasion in 1085.[28] When Metcalf reviewed the evidence in his analysis of the *Paxs* type in the 1980s he supported the alternative suggestion that the Beauworth hoard may have been part of the bequests of alms distributed from

[25]   P.W.P. Carlyon-Britton, 'On the coins of William I and II and the sequence of the types', *NC, 4th ser., 2* (1902), 208–23, at 209–11; P.W.P. Carlyon-Britton, 'A numismatic history of the reigns of William I and II (1066–1100). First part', *BNJ, 2* (1905), 87–184, at 92–4.

[26]   G.C. Brooke, 'Monetagium', *NC, 4th ser., 12* (1912), 98–106; Brooke, *A Catalogue*, 1, lxix–lxx.

[27]   Brooke, 'Monetagium', 103–4; Brooke, *A Catalogue*, 1, lxviii–lxxi; Brooke, 'Quando moneta vertebatur', 106, 113.

[28]   Dolley, *The Norman Conquest*, 15–18, 20–21, 39–40.

William I's treasury after his death in September 1087, but Brooke and Robin Eaglen have argued against this assumption.[29] Marion Archibald has considered the possibility that the *Paxs* type may actually have been the first type of William II in 1087 as an accession coinage, because versions of the word *Pax* on the first type of Edward the Confessor, the coinage of Harold II in 1066 and the *Paxs* type itself may refer to the king's peace, which died with the king and was renewed at his successor's coronation.[30] Archibald's suggestion has been favourably received by the author and by Eaglen, who used it in his proposed chronology for the coinages of 1066–1100.[31] Eaglen assumed a triennial change of type between 1066 and 1093, and a biennial change thereafter, but it can be argued that there is no more reason to assume such regularity than there was when Brooke rejected Carlyon-Britton's triennial chronology nearly a century ago.

Table 4.1   Chronologies of the English coinage, 1066–1100.

Reign	Type	Carlyon-Britton [a]	Dolley [b]	Eaglen [c]	Allen
William I	1	1066–68	1066–68	1066–69	1066–c.1068
	2	1068–71	1068–70	1069–72	c.1068–early 1070s
	3	1071–74	1070–72	1072–75	early/mid-1070s
	4	1074–77	1072–74	1075–78	mid-/late 1070s

---

[29]   Metcalf, 'Notes on the "PAXS" type', 13–14; Brooke, *A Catalogue*, 1, xxii; R.J. Eaglen, *The Abbey and Mint of Bury St Edmunds to 1279*, BNS Special Publication 4 (London, 2006), 57. W.J. Andrew, 'Buried treasure: some traditions, records and facts', *BNJ, 1* (1903–4), 9–59, at 27–9, assumed that the Beauworth hoard constituted the bequest of six marks of gold or 8,640 silver pennies (£36) to Winchester Cathedral, but Brooke noted that E. Hawkins, *The Silver Coins of England* (London, 1841), 75, estimated the total number of coins as 'scarcely less than 12,000 [£50]'.

[30]   M.M. Archibald, 'Coins', in *English Romanesque Art 1066–1200*, ed. G. Zarnecki (London, 1984), 320–41, at 324, 328. Packe, 'The coinage of the Norman kings', 135, 143, suggested that the *Paxs* type was introduced in 1087 specifically for the payment of William I's bequests. S. Keynes, 'An interpretation of the *Pacx, Pax* and *Paxs* pennies', *ASE, 7* (1978), 165–73, discusses the possible symbolic significance of *pax* on the coinage.

[31]   M. Allen, 'The Durham mint before Boldon Book', in *Anglo-Norman Durham 1093–1193*, ed. D. Rollason, M. Harvey and M. Prestwich (Woodbridge, 1994), 381–98, at 385; Eaglen, *The Abbey and Mint*, 56–7 (offering the alternative suggestion that the *Paxs* type might refer to a prayer for the peace of William I's soul); Allen, *Mints and Money*, 25–6. Blackburn, 'Coinage and currency under Henry I', 57–8, 61–2, argues that the significance of the *Pax* types remains uncertain and demonstrates that Henry I's *Pax* type was probably the third and certainly not the first type of his reign.

Reign	Type	Carlyon-Britton [a]	Dolley [b]	Eaglen [c]	Allen
	5	1077–80	1074–77	1078–81	late 1070s–early 1080s
	6	1080–83	1077–80	1081–84	early/mid-1080s
	7	1083–86	1080–83	1084–87	mid-1080s–?1087
	8	1086–87	1083–86	1087–90	1087(?)–*c.*1090
William II	1	1087–90	1086–89	1090–93	early 1090s
	2	1090–93	1089–92	1093–95	early/mid-1090s
	3	1093–96	1092–95	1095–97	mid-1090s
	4	1096–99	1095–98	1095–99	mid-/late 1090s
	5	1099–1100	1098–1100	1099–1100	late 1090s–1100

(a) Carlyon-Britton, 'On the coins of William I and II', 208–15; Carlyon-Britton, 'A numismatic history ... First part', 92–4, 130–83 passim.

(b) Dolley, *The Norman Conquest*, 15–18, 20–21.

(c) Eaglen, *The Abbey and Mint*, 55–8.

Table 4.1 includes the author's suggested tentative chronology for the coinages of William I and William II. This does not differ radically from Eaglen's chronology, apart from a rejection of the assumption of regular triennial or biennial changes of type, for which there is no historical evidence. A change from the first type of William I to his second in about 1068 would certainly be consistent with the number of moneyers recorded at York, which declines from eleven in type 2 to only one moneyer (Outhgrim) in type 3.[32] Dolley was surely right to connect this decline and the exceptional number of Yorkshire hoards ending in the early types of William I with the northern rebellions of 1068–69 and William's extremely destructive 'harrying of the north' in 1069–70.[33] Much less convincing is Dolley's attempt to connect eight hoards ending in various types from 3 to 6 or uncertain types of William I with the rebellion of Hereward

---

[32] Blunt and Dolley, *SCBI 11* (Stockholm), no. 14; Gunstone, *SCBI 27*, no. 1773: two die-duplicates from irregular, local dies. Brooke, *A Catalogue*, 1, cxxxviii–cxxxix, notes that irregular dies were used at Lincoln in William I type 2, and at Lincoln, Stamford and York in type 4.

[33] Dolley, *The Norman Conquest*, 13, 15, 39. Allen, *Mints and Money*, 457–8 (nos 74–80), lists seven Yorkshire hoards that definitely or probably ended with William I's type 2.

the Wake in 1070–71 and later episodes of discontent culminating on the Revolt of the Earls in 1075.[34] Dolley also suggested that the rebellion of 1075 caused a reduction in the number of Lincoln moneyers from eight to two,[35] but the numbers of moneyers now recorded at Lincoln show a later and more gradual fall from seven in William I's type 5 to four in types 6 and 7 in the 1080s, and finally to two in the *Paxs* type. The proposed dating of type 6 to the early/mid-1080s might be thought to receive some support from a damaged and partly illegible coin of this type from local dies excavated at Cardiff Castle, which has been attributed to a mint in Cardiff and associated with the foundation of the castle (which is probably to be dated to 1081), but the surviving portion of the mint signature ([...]*eri*) does not unambiguously indicate Cardiff.[36] George Boon's attribution of some Welsh copies of the *Paxs* type to a mint in Abergavenny, which was founded by Hamelin de Ballon (d. 1106) soon after the accession of William II in 1087, may provide limited support for the suggestion that *Paxs* was the first type of William II, but again the mint identification is far from certain.[37] The attribution of *Paxs* coins to a mint in Rhuddlan, which is not in doubt, might seem to indicate that *Paxs* was current in 1086, because Domesday Book records the rights of Robert of Rhuddlan (d. 1088) and the earl of Chester to share various revenues in and around Rhuddlan, including the profits of a mint, but it is possible that the right to have a mint had not yet been implemented in 1086.[38] One further piece of evidence provided by Domesday Book is the Oxford moneyer Suetman's free house rated at 40d., and his payment of 3s. per annum for two houses.[39] This might be thought to indicate that the *Paxs* type was current at the time of the Domesday survey in 1086, because it is the only type in which coins of this moneyer have yet been recorded, but it is worth

---

[34]   Dolley, *The Norman Conquest*, 39.

[35]   Dolley, *The Norman Conquest*, 13–14.

[36]   G.C. Boon, *Welsh Hoards 1979–1981* (Cardiff, 1986), 40, 46; G.C. Boon, *Coins of the Anarchy 1135–54* (Cardiff, 1988), 13, 16; Allen, *Mints and Money*, 23. Boon and Dolley also attributed a William I type 7 fragment in the Royal Coin Cabinet at Stockholm to Cardiff (Boon, *Welsh Hoards*, 46, 66 n. 36), but Blackburn, 'Coinage and currency under Henry I', 57, noted that this is actually a missing part of a published coin of London (Blunt and Dolley, *SCBI 11* (Stockholm), no. 55).

[37]   Boon, *Welsh Hoards*, 67; E. Besly, 'Few and far between: mints and coins in Wales to the Middle of the thirteenth century', in *Coinage and History in the North Sea World, c. AD 500–1200. Essays in Honour of Marion Archibald*, ed. B. Cook and G. Williams (Leiden and Boston, 2006), 701–19, at 707–8; Allen, *Mints and Money*, 25.

[38]   P.W.P. Carlyon-Britton, 'The Saxon, Norman and Plantagenet coinage of Wales', *BNJ*, 2 (1905), 31–56, at 41–3; F. Elmore Jones, 'Thoughts on the Norman coinage of Wales in the light of two additions to the series', *BNJ*, 28 (1955–7), 191–5; Besly, 'Few and far between', 708; Allen, *Mints and Money*, 25–6; Domesday Book I, 269.

[39]   Domesday Book I, 154; Brooke, *A Catalogue*, 1, cxli.

observing that the record of moneyers in the previous type (William I's type 7) is probably relatively incomplete. The only recorded examples of type 7 in English or Welsh hoards are eleven coins in the Beauworth hoard, two coins in the Abergavenny area hoard, and possibly a further two coins from Bradenham in Suffolk, which might be unrelated single-finds.[40] In contrast, the Beauworth hoard is known to have contained at least 6,493 coins of the *Paxs* type, including 67 pennies of Suetman (Sw(w)etman on his coins).[41] There is no good evidence for the dating of any the five types conventionally attributed to William II, although a penny of William II's type 2 from irregular dies has been associated with William FitzBaldwin's occupation of Rhyd-y-Gors (Carmarthenshire) in *c.*1093–96.[42] If this is not simply an English contemporary forgery it might be a coin of Rhuddlan.[43]

Hoards, Single-Finds and the Money Supply

The Appendix summarises the contents of 40 English and Welsh hoards that are known to have included coins of William I or William II.[44] For three of these hoards there is no information about the types represented, but 24 of the remaining 37 hoards certainly or probably contained coins of only one or two types, providing some support for the assumption that the coinage in circulation predominantly consisted of the current type, with a rapidly diminishing residue of the previous type not yet converted by recoinage. Some of the hoards representing a greater range of types may be evidence of the hoarding of obsolete types as savings, avoiding the costs of recoinage until it was necessary to spend the old money hoarded. The Denge Marsh hoard seems to have consisted of some coins of Harold II with a large number of die-duplicate William I type 1 pennies of the Romney moneyer Wulfmær,

---

[40] See the summary of hoards in the Appendix, and Allen, *Mints and Money*, 521.

[41] E. Hawkins, 'Description of a large collection of coins of William the Conqueror discovered at Beaworth, in Hampshire; with an attempt at a chronological arrangement of the coins of William I. and II.', *Archaeologia*, 26 (1836), 1–25, repr. in R. Ruding, *Annals of the Coinage of Great Britain and its Dependencies from the Earliest Period of Authentic History to the Reign of Victoria*, 3rd ed. (3 vols., London, 1840), 1, 151–61.

[42] P.W.P. Carlyon-Britton, 'A penny of Llywelyn, son of Cadwygan, of the type of the second issue of William Rufus', *BNJ*, 8 (1911), 83–6; Boon, *Welsh Hoards*, 65; Besly, 'Few and far between', 708.

[43] Dolley, *The Norman Conquest*, 33; Allen, *Mints and Money*, 26; Allen, 'Mints and moneyers', 79 n. 189.

[44] The figures in the Appendix are based upon Allen, *Mints and Money*, 520–21, with amendments and the addition of three hoards containing coins of unknown types: Bury St Edmunds (Mill Lane), Colsterworth (or 'near Grantham'), and Sutton.

apparently fresh from the process of recoinage at the mint nearest to the place where the hoard was deposited.[45] Some other hoards also have a pronounced local bias in the latest coins represented. The Tibberton (Gloucestershire) hoard consisted of four William I type 4 pennies of Gloucester, including three die-duplicates, and the ten coins definitely attributed to a mint in the Norwich (Garlands) hoard included six of Norwich (with two pairs of die-duplicates) and three coins of the other Norfolk mint, Thetford.[46] York coins prominently feature in York hoards probably associated with the troubles of 1068–70, the Corringham (Lincolnshire) hoard has a Lincoln bias in William I's types 1 and 2, and 24 of the 264 coins of William I's type 5 (including one type 4/5 mule) in the Scaldwell (Northamptonshire) hoard were of the Northampton moneyer Sæwine.[47] The Beauworth (Hampshire) hoard had a bias towards the nearest place of minting, Winchester, which might not have been caused by it being money from the king's treasury at Winchester, as has been suggested.[48] Other hoards do not show any clear evidence of a bias towards local mints, suggesting that the coins of all mints became fairly thoroughly dispersed in circulation, at least towards the end of a type. The 6,551 pennies and eighteen cut halfpennies listed by Edward Hawkins from the Beauworth hoard include coins of 64 of the 65 known mints of the *Paxs* type (the sole exception being Guildford), and all but 11 of the type's 178 recorded moneyers.[49] Some of the missing moneyers may well have been represented in the unrecorded portion of the hoard, which when it was complete might have consisted of 100 marks (£66 13s. 4d. or 16,000d.) in

[45] D.M. Metcalf, 'Find-records of medieval coins from Gough's Camden's *Britannia*', *NC*, 6th ser., *17* (1957), 181–207, at 186–90; P.B. Purefoy, 'Fifty pence from Romney', *NCirc, 104* (1996), 367–8; Metcalf, *Atlas*, 178–9.

[46] Information on the Tibberton hoard from Dr Gareth Williams; T.H.McK. Clough, 'A small hoard of William I type I pennies from Norwich', *BNJ, 43* (1973), 142–3; Metcalf, *Atlas*, 178.

[47] E.J.E. Pirie, *SCBI 21: Coins in Yorkshire Collections. The Yorkshire Museum York. The City Museum, Leeds. The University of Leeds* (London, 1975), xxxv–vi; M.M. Archibald, 'Corringham, Lincolnshire, 1994', *NC, 156* (1996), 291–2 (Coin Hoards 1996, no. 131); R.C. Carlyon-Britton, 'A hoard of coins of William the Conqueror found in a trench in the War Area', *BNJ, 12* (1916), 15–32; Metcalf, *Atlas*, 32–3, 182, 185.

[48] See above, pp. 90–1, for this interpretation of the Beauworth hoard. Winchester supplied 1,606 (24.8 per cent) of the 6,484 coins of the *Paxs* type in the Beauworth attributed to a mint, but Metcalf, 'Notes on the 'PAXS' type', 24, estimates that Winchester had only some 15 per cent of total national output in the type.

[49] Hawkins, 'Description'. The 11 moneyers not in Hawkins's list of the hoard are: [ ]ric at Cambridge, Wulfward or Wulfword at Colchester, Seric at Guildford, Ælfric at Huntingdon, Seword at Malmesbury, [ ]ivan at Rhuddlan, Coc at Romney, Ifliwine at St Davids, Godesbrand at Shrewsbury, Godric at Stafford and Bran at Wareham.

cash, or more than 16,000 coins (including cut halfpennies).[50] Even without its unrecorded coins the Beauworth hoard dominates the aggregate figures in the Appendix, with 6,569 coins in all (83.0 per cent of the minimum total of about 7,913–7,914 coins from all hoards combined).

Mark Blackburn showed in his surveys of finds of coins of the reigns of Henry I and Stephen that hoard aggregates can be less satisfactory than single-finds as a source of evidence for patterns of monetary activity, because hoard data tend to be biased by individual hoards of great size (such as Beauworth) or by a relatively large number of hoards in one part of the period under consideration.[51] Consequently it is fortunate that numbers of single-finds have increased substantially in recent years, with the growth in the use of metal detectors, and that online databases have been established to record them. In 1998 Metcalf knew of only 588 single-finds of English coins attributed to a type and mint from Edgar's reform of the English coinage (*c.*973) to the *Paxs* type, but Rory Naismith's new analysis of finds over a slightly longer period from the reform to 1100 is based upon 1,852 coins, from the Corpus of Early Medieval Coin Finds (EMC) and the Portable Antiquities Scheme (PAS).[52] Numbers of coins of William I and William II recorded by EMC have increased from 184 in 2001 to 233 in 2004 and 339 at the end of 2011, as shown in Table 4.2.[53] The total number of finds in EMC for the period from 1042 to 1158 has more than doubled in the decade from 2001 to 2011, but the chronological trend in the numbers of finds per annum has remained essentially unaltered, with a fall to about half of the level of 1042–66 and 1135–58 between 1066 and 1135, which is consistent with Peter Spufford's suggestion that a decline in silver production at the Rammelsberg mines in the Harz mountains caused a contraction in European supplies of coinage in the mid-eleventh century.[54]

---

[50]   The capacity of the lead containers of the Beauworth hoard and the 1902 and 1969 Colchester hoards is discussed by M.M. Archibald and B.J. Cook, *English Medieval Coin Hoards: I. Cross and Crosslets, Short Cross and Long Cross Hoards*, British Museum Occasional Paper, 87 (London, 2001), 91–4.

[51]   Blackburn, 'Coinage and currency under Henry I', 52–5; Blackburn, 'Coinage and currency', 148–50.

[52]   Metcalf, *Atlas*; R. Naismith, 'The English monetary economy *c.*973–1100: the contribution of single-finds', *EcHR, 66* (2013), 198–225; EMC; PAS.

[53]   M. Allen, *The Durham Mint*, BNS Special Publication 4 (London, 2003), 67 (EMC data current on 31 March 2001); M. Allen, 'The volume of the English currency, *c.*973–1158', in *Coinage and History in the North Sea World*, ed. Cook and Williams, 487–523, at 499–500, 502 (EMC on 1 April 2004); EMC online on 31 December 2011. Blackburn, 'Coinage and currency under Henry I', 54–5, 79, summarises 104 finds for the reign of Henry I (1100–35); Blackburn, 'Coinage and currency', 148–50, has 108 finds for 1135–58.

[54]   P. Spufford, *Money and its Use in Medieval Europe* (Cambridge, 1988), 95–7; Blackburn, Coinage and currency under Henry I', 73.

Table 4.2   Single-finds in EMC, 1042–1158.

Period	2001		2004		2011	
	Finds	p. a.	Finds	p. a.	Finds	p. a.
1042–66	251	10.5	321	13.4	463	19.3
1066–1100	184	5.4	233	6.9	339	10.0
1100–35	195	5.6	247	7.1	419	12.0
1135–58	239	10.4	329	14.3	523	22.7
Total	869		1,130		1,744	

Table 4.3 compares the 2011 figures for single-finds of each type of William I and William II in EMC with numbers of mints and moneyers recorded from all sources, to investigate trends between 1066 and 1100.[55] The continuing discovery of new mints or moneyers in various types indicates that the record is incomplete, and in an attempt to take account of this factor the table includes adjusted figures for mints and moneyers, which assume that a moneyer was active in a type in which he is not yet known if he has been recorded in the adjacent types.[56] There is an early peak in the single-finds in William I's type 2 (*c.*1068–70) and higher peaks in types 5, 7 and 8 in (probably) the late 1070s and the 1080s, followed by a decline to a generally lower level in William II's types 1–5. Numbers of mints and moneyers also peak in William I's types 2, 5 and 8 (but not in type 7), only showing a clear decline in William II's types 4 and 5, in the last years of the eleventh century. William II's type 3 has only 14 single-finds, which is one of the lowest figures in the table, but its numbers of mints and moneyers are amongst the highest. A tentative interpretation of all of the figures combined might be that mint output was relatively high in William I's types 2, 5, 7 and 8, due to heavy demand for new coins to pay taxes, high levels of silver supplies through foreign trade or a longer than normal duration of type, or a combination of these factors, and that a recession in output in the 1090s caused a closure of mints as a delayed reaction. The number of mints known in each type remains at a low level in the early years of the twelfth century, never exceeding 33 until Henry I's type 10 (*c.*1117–19).[57]

---

[55] The EMC data in Table 4.3 exclude eight coins attributed to William I of uncertain type.
[56] Allen, 'Mints and moneyers', 60–65.
[57] Allen, 'Mints and moneyers', 61–2, 65–6.

Table 4.3   Single-finds, mints and moneyers, 1066–1100.

Reign	Type	EMC	Mints	Mints (adjusted)	Moneyers	Moneyers (adjusted)
William I	1	18	37	45	94	120
	2	34	44	46	136	141
	3	17	37	41	96	115
	4	27	42	44	107	116
	5	55	56	56	127–29	131–33
	6	16	36	43	82	98
	7	42	42	48	89	107
	8	46	65	65	178	181
William II	1	11	51	54	108–109	128–29
	2	29	56	56	154	158
	3	14	52	54	134–36	141–43
	4	8	33	37	72	87
	5	14	35–37	35–37	68–70	72–74

Single-finds can provide some indication of the relative output of the mints. In the 2011 EMC data, 268 of the 339 recorded finds are attributed to a mint, providing the figures in Table 4.4. London is in a clear first place, as might be expected, and the remainder of the top ten in the table largely consists of eastern commercial and administrative centres from Canterbury and Southwark in the south to York in the north, broadly confirming the trends found by Metcalf in his analysis of Anglo-Saxon coins of c.973–1066 in Scandinavian museums and English single-finds from c.973 to the *Paxs* type. This supports the assumption that imports of silver from England's trade with continental Europe predominantly entered through eastern and south-eastern ports.[58] Most of the English mints made no more than a negligible contribution to total money supply, as far as that is manifested in the single-finds: 38 mints contribute only about one-third of the finds between them, and 18 of the English mints active between 1066 and 1100 are completely unrepresented in the EMC data.

---

[58]   D.M. Metcalf, 'Continuity and change in English monetary history, c.973–1086. Part 1', *BNJ, 50* (1980), 20–49, at 31–5, 49; D.M. Metcalf, 'Continuity and change in English monetary history, c.973–1086. Part 2', *BNJ, 51* (1981), 68–85; Metcalf, *Atlas*, 18–21.

Table 4.4   Mints in EMC data, 1066–1100.

Mint	Finds	%
1. London	53	19.8
2. Thetford	29	10.8
3. Lincoln	22	8.2
4. Norwich	15	5.6
5. Canterbury	13	4.9
6. York	12	4.5
7. Wallingford	11	4.1
8=. Colchester	8	3.0
8=. Ipswich	8	3.0
8=. Southwark	8	3.0
Other mints (38 mints)	89	33.2
Total	268	

Table 4.5 Numbers of moneyers in the *Paxs* type.

Probable no. of moneyers	Mints
8	London
7	Norwich
6	Canterbury, Thetford, Winchester
4	Chester, Dover, Hereford, Ipswich, Southwark, Worcester, York
3	Bath, Bristol, Colchester, Exeter, Lewes, Oxford, Romney, Sandwich, Shaftesbury, Shrewsbury, Stamford, Warwick, Wilton
2	Bedford, Cambridge,* Cardiff, Chichester, Derby, Dorchester, Gloucester, Hastings, Hertford, Huntingdon, Lincoln, Maldon, Nottingham, Rhuddlan, Rochester, Salisbury, Stafford, Tamworth, Wallingford, Wareham
1	Abergavenny(?), Barnstaple, Bridport, Cricklade, Durham, Guildford, Hythe, Ilchester, Launceston, Leicester, Malmesbury, Marlborough, Northampton, Pevensey, St Davids, Steyning, Sudbury, Taunton, Watchet, Winchcombe

*The Beauworth hoard had coins of only one Cambridge moneyer in the *Paxs* type (Ulfcil), but a recent single find (EMC 2012.0004) has provided a second moneyer, [ ]ric.

Table 4.5 summarises the probable numbers of moneyers at the 65 mints in the *Paxs* type, with London again heading the list, followed by three places prominent in the single find data for 1066–1100 (Norwich, Canterbury and Thetford) and also Winchester, which is the best-represented mint in the

Beauworth hoard, with 1,606 coins of the *Paxs* type (24.8 per cent of the total).[59] The *Paxs* type can be analysed in much greater depth than any of the other types of William I or William II, thanks to the Beauworth hoard. The preliminary work for Brooke's *BMC* included some groundbreaking die analysis of the coins attributed to William I in the British Museum and other collections, which he published in 1911, finding extensive die-linking (with shared use of obverse dies) between moneyers and mints in *Paxs*.[60] Brooke found die-links between moneyers at 20 mints, showing that the sharing of obverse dies was common practice, although the documentary evidence from Winchester suggests that moneyers usually had their own separate workshops.[61] He also discovered evidence of transfers of dies between nine pairs of mints, which were usually in the same part of the country.[62] Dies were expensive, as Domesday Book shows, and evidently it was worthwhile to borrow them in time of need.

Metcalf has used data from Brooke's *BMC* to estimate that the *Paxs* type was produced from a total of about 550–1100 reverse dies, with 600–880 as a 'best guess'.[63] He has also estimated that the total mint output and size of the currency in *Paxs* was £35,000–£40,000 or c.£36,000, if 880 dies struck an average of 10,000 coins each.[64] Dolley had estimated an output of £25,000 or £37,500 from 600 reverse dies, at 10,000 or 15,000 coins per die.[65] There is a large element of guesswork in these estimates, because they were not based upon

---

[59]   Allen, *Mints and Money*, 399–402. The figures for numbers of moneyers differ in some respects from those of Grierson, 'The monetary system', 78; Metcalf, 'Notes on the 'PAXS' type', 20–23.

[60]   Brooke, 'Notes', 274–80; Brooke, *A Catalogue*, 1, cxxxix–cxl.

[61]   M. Biddle, et al., *Winchester in the Early Middle Ages. An Edition and Discussion of the Winton Domesday*, Winchester Studies, 1 (Oxford, 1976), 36, 397–403, 405, 407, 409–10, 421–2, 443–4; Allen, *Mints and Money*, 6–8. Metcalf, 'Notes on the "PAXS" type', 14–16, investigates the die-links between the four York moneyers of the *Paxs* type.

[62]   The pairs of mints are: Barnstaple and Exeter, Canterbury and Hythe, Chichester and Guildford, London and Southwark, London and Ipswich, Marlborough and Salisbury, Salisbury and Wilton, Cricklade and Wilton, and finally Shrewsbury and St Davids. Carlyon-Britton, 'A numismatic history ... First part', 50–52, had already noted the die link between Shrewsbury and St Davids, but Brooke, *A Catalogue*, 1, clxxx, suggested that the relatively crude reverse die in the name of the Shrewsbury moneyer Godesbrand involved in the die-link may have been made in St Davids. Brooke, 'Notes', 278, also records die-links between London, Thetford and the probably fictitious mint 'MAINT' in William I's type 2, and between London and Exeter in type 3.

[63]   Metcalf, 'Continuity and change ... Part 2', 55, 84–5; idem, 'Notes on the "PAXS" type', 20–23; idem, *Atlas*, 188–9. Metcalf used *BMC* data for 28 mints.

[64]   Metcalf, 'The taxation of moneyers', 285; D.M. Metcalf, 'Large Danegelds in relation to war and kingship: their implications for monetary history, and some numismatic evidence', in *Weapons and Warfare in Anglo-Saxon England*, ed. S.C. Hawkes, Oxford University Committee for Archaeology Monograph, 21 (Oxford, 1989), 179–89, at 186–7.

[65]   Dolley, *The Norman Conquest*, 14.

a comprehensive die study of the *Paxs* type and we have no evidence for the output of dies in English mints before the mid-thirteenth century. Metcalf's best guess of 600–880 reverse dies and a relatively wide estimate of 10,000–20,000 coins per die has been used as the basis of a tentative alternative figure of about £30,000–£70,000 for total mint output and the currency in *Paxs*.[66]

Dolley's rather questionably precise estimate of £37,500 for mint output in the *Paxs* type has served as a figure for money supply in 1086 in Nicholas Mayhew's models of the English economy based upon the Quantity Theory of Money.[67] Mayhew has been more cautious about his estimate of England's GDP in 1086, tentatively suggesting that it was about £300,000–£400,000, and his conclusion that relatively high figures for income velocity (V) in 1086 imply a society obliged to stretch an inadequate money supply by non-monetary expedients (such as deferred payments, barter and payments in kind) is convincing.[68] The shortage of cash would have been made more acute by the diversion of large amounts of money into the king's treasury and presumably into other reserves of cash, some traces of which have been glimpsed in the coin hoards discovered. Henry of Huntingdon, writing in the 1130s, believed that when William II took possession of the treasury at Winchester after his father's death in 1087 it contained 60,000 pounds in silver, as well as gold and other precious objects, and the treasury was certainly capable of providing 5,000 pounds in silver for William I's youngest son Henry, as well as numerous other bequests.[69] The English currency was also being depleted by exports of coins at around the time of William I's death. Finds of English coins in Scandinavian hoards decline to a relatively low level in the mid-eleventh century, but there is a modest revival in the 1080s and 1090s, with Swedish hoards including relatively large numbers

---

[66]   Allen, 'The volume', 494, 500–501; Allen, *Mints and Money*, 320–21.

[67]   N.J. Mayhew, 'Modelling medieval monetisation', and 'The calculation of GDP from Domesday', in *A Commercialising Economy: England 1086 to c.1300*, eds. R.H. Britnell and B.M.S. Campbell (Manchester, 1995), 55–77, at 60–62, 68, 71–4, 195–6; N.J. Mayhew, 'Coinage and money in England, 1086–c.1500', in *Medieval Money Matters*, ed. D. Wood (Oxford, 2004), 72–86, at 74–6, 79–80.

[68]   G.D. Snooks, 'The dynamic role of the market in the Anglo-Norman economy and beyond, 1086–1300', in *A Commercialising Economy*, ed. Britnell and Campbell, 27–54, at 33; J. McDonald and G.D. Snooks, *Domesday Economy. A New Approach to Anglo-Norman History* (Oxford, 1986), 117–24, proposed a much lower estimate for GDP in 1086 of about £137,000. Mayhew's estimate does not conflict with the new figure (£342,472) calculated by J.T. Walker, 'National income in Domesday England', Henley Business School, University of Reading, Discussion Paper 067 (Reading, 2009).

[69]   Henry of Huntingdon, *Historia Anglorum*, VI: *Historia Anglorum (History of the English People)*, ed. and trans. D. Greenway (Oxford, 1996), 406–7; Orderic Vitalis, *Historia ecclesiastica*, VII.12: *The Ecclesiastical History of Orderic Vitalis*, ed. and trans. M. Chibnall (6 vols., Oxford, 1969–80), 4, 94–7; F. Barlow, *William Rufus* (Yale, 1983), 64.

of English coins from William I's type 7 to William II's type 3, peaking in *Paxs*, and Dolley suggested that this is evidence of large exports of English coins to the Baltic from *c.*1085 to *c.*1095, possibly connected with payments to mercenaries in the emergency of 1085 and subsequent undocumented political payments in addition to trade.[70] The summary of coins of William I and II in Continental hoards in Table 4.6 shows that this brief boom in the supply of English coinage also reached Estonia.[71]

Table 4.6   Coins of William I and William II in Continental hoards.

	William I BMC types									William II BMC types						William I or II	Total
	1	2	3	4	5	6	7	8	?	1	2	3	4	5	?		
Normandy (3 hoards)								7		1							8
France (excluding Normandy) (1 hoard)										1							1
Germany (2 hoards)		1		1													2
Denmark (6 hoards)	3	1	2		6	1	3	10		1	2	1	2				32

---

[70]   M. Blackburn and K. Jonsson, 'The Anglo-Saxon and Anglo-Norman element of North European coin finds', in *Viking-Age Coinage in the Northern Lands. The Sixth Oxford Symposium on Coinage and Monetary History*, ed. M.A.S. Blackburn and D.M. Metcalf, BAR International Series 122 (2 vols., Oxford, 1981), 1, 147–255, at 184; Blunt and Dolley, *SCBI 11*, 46–7; M. Blackburn and K. Jonsson, *SCBI 54B: Royal Coin Cabinet, Stockholm. Supplement to Part VI. Anglo-Norman Coins, 1066–1180* (London, 2007), 179–80.

[71]   Table 4.6 is based upon A. Molvõgin, 'Normannische Fundmünzen in Estland und anderen Ostseeländern', in *Sigtuna Papers. Proceedings of the Sigtuna Symposium on Viking-Age Coinage 1–4 June 1989*, ed. K. Jonnson and B. Malmer (Stockholm, 1990), 241–9, at 242–3, 245 (Tables 1–3), with four additional Estonian hoards from I. Leimus and A. Molvõgin, *SCBI 51: Estonian Collections. Anglo-Saxon, Anglo-Norman and later British Coins* (Oxford, 2001), 32–3, 41–2, 45–6; data for Normandy from J.C. Moesgaard, 'Two finds from Normandy of English coins of the Norman kings', *NC, 154* (1994), 209–13, and one French hoard (from St-Germain-en-Laye): M.A.S. Blackburn, 'Les monnaies de Beauvais dans un trésor découvert aux environs de Paris vers 1987 (la soi-disant "trouvaille de Beauvais")', *BSFN, 46* (1991), 110–16. There were no recorded coins of William I or William II in any of the French hoards listed by J. Duplessy, *Les trésors monétaires médiévaux et modernes découverts en France, vol. 1: 751–1223* (Paris, 1985), or in the Belgian hoards listed by J.-L. Dengis, *Trouvailles et trésors monétaires en Belgique* (19 vols., Wetteren, 2009–).

	William I BMC types									William II BMC types						William I or II	Total
	1	2	3	4	5	6	7	8	?	1	2	3	4	5	?		
Sweden (excluding Gotland) (8 hoards)	5	1			2	3	5				4					1	21
Gotland (25 hoards)	1	3	1	3	3	6	27	50	37–38	23	33	13		3		24	227–8
Finland (4 hoards)				2	1	2				1							6
Estonia (24 hoards)	1			2			13	24		11	26	17	1			3	98
Latvia (2 hoards)						1				1							2
Poland (1 hoard)								1							1		2
Total	10	6	3	3	12	11	48	99	37–38	36	65	33	1	6	1	28	399–400

There were exports of English coins to the duchy of Normandy, but there is relatively little evidence of this from coin finds. Jens Christian Moesgaard has published two small hoards of English pennies from Normandy: 'several' coins of William II found at Lillebonne no later than 1840 (including a William II type 3 penny), and a hoard of coins attributed to William I (including two *Paxs* pennies) from Louviers in 1877.[72] The enigmatic 'Lower Normandy' find, which probably consisted of parts of more than one hoard, included five coins of the *Paxs* type.[73] Two *Paxs* pennies were found in excavations at Sébécourt, and a penny attributed to William I was excavated at Thaon, but most single-finds of this period in Normandy are local coins.[74] Although written sources begin to refer to English currency in Normandy shortly after the conquest of England many of the coins concerned may have been recycled into local currency before

---

[72] Moesgaard, 'Two finds from Normandy', 209–10, 212–13; Moesgaard, 'La monnaie au temps de Guillaume le Conquérant', 97.

[73] J. Béranger, 'Une trouvaille de monnaies anglo-normandes', *Bulletin de Numismatique*, *12* (1905), 67–72; R.H.M. Dolley, 'The continental hoard-evidence for the chronology of the Anglo-Irish pence of John', *NCirc, 74* (1966), 30–32, at 30–31; J. Yvon, 'Esterlins à la croix courte dans les trésors Français de la fin du XIIe et de la première moitié du XIIIe siècle', *BNJ, 39* (1970), 24–60, at 49–50 (no. 21); Duplessy, *Les trésors monétaires*, 1, 140 (no. 397); Moesgaard, 'Two finds from Normandy', 211.

[74] J. Pilet-Lemière, 'Catalogue de monnaies', in J. Decaens, 'L'enceinte fortifiée de Sébécourt (Eure)', *Chateau-Gaillard, 7* (1975), 49–65, at 63 (nos 2–3); F. Delahaye and C. Niel, 'Les résultats des campagnes 2000–2003', *Nouvelles de la vieille église de Thaon, 4* (March 2004), 4–5; Moesgaard, 'Two finds from Normandy', 211; Moesgaard, 'La monnaie, 97.

they could be spent.[75] Orderic Vitalis (writing in the 1130s) refers to three gifts of English sterlings to the abbey of St Evroul's at Ouche, in or shortly before 1079, between 1077 and 1089, and in 1081, and Archbishop Lanfranc gave 44 pounds in English money to the abbey in 1077.[76] An undated charter of 1087×1095 from the Norman abbey of Les Préaux also refers to English money, and in another charter of this abbey dated to 1085, 1104 (most probably) or 1123 a certain Richard acknowledges that he has mortgaged some land to the monks in return for 8s. of sterlings, paid to him by the monk Warin of England, who may have brought the coins concerned to Normandy.[77] The king himself probably exported much greater sums of English currency to Normandy, for example in 1086, when the *Anglo-Saxon Chronicle* records that he obtained a large amount of money from his men, and then immediately left for the duchy, as he had done on other occasions, and Norman magnates may also have exported large sums from their English estates, but the circulation of English money in Normandy was evidently very limited.[78] The relatively small numbers of finds of coins of William I and William II, particularly outside the Baltic region, clearly indicate that English sterlings had not yet attained the role of an international currency they were to achieve later.

Conclusion

If one of Harold II's moneyers could have been transported from his pre-Conquest world of 1066 to England in 1100, after Henry I abolished William I's innovation of *monetagium*, there would have been much that he would have recognised in the monetary system, although so much else had changed. Moneyers in dozens of towns and cities still made the English silver penny, which had not diminished in quality, from dies with nationally uniform types changed

---

[75]   L. Musset, 'Y eut-il une aristocratie d'affaires commune aux grandes villes de Normandie et d'Angleterre entre 1066 et 1204?', *Etudes normandes, 35.3* (1986), 7–19, at 16; L. Musset, 'Réflexions sur les moyens de paiement en Normandie aux XIe et XIIe siècles', *Aspects de la société et de l'économie dans la Normandie médiévale*, Cahiers des Annales de Normandie, 22 (Caen, 1988), 65–89, at 87–8; Moesgaard, 'Two finds from Normandy', 212.

[76]   Orderic Vitalis, *Historia ecclesiastica*, III.18: *Ecclesiastical History*, ed. and trans. Chibnall Chibnall, III, 12; VI, 5; D. Bates (ed.), *Regesta regum Anglo-Normanorrum: the Acta of William I (1066–1087)* (Oxford, 1998), 722 (no. 255); P. Grierson, 'Sterling', in *Anglo-Saxon Coins. Studies Presented to F.M. Stenton on the Occasion of his 80th Birthday 17 May 1960*, ed. R.H.M. Dolley (London, 1961), 266–83, at 267–8.

[77]   J.H. Round (ed.), *Calendar of Documents preserved in France Illustrative of the History of Great Britain and Ireland* (London, 1899), 110–12 (nos. 321, 327); Grierson, 'Sterling', 267–8, 279 n.11.

[78]   *The Anglo-Saxon Chronicle*, ed. and trans. M.J. Swanton (London, 1996), 217.

at regular intervals. Hoard evidence suggests that the recoinages at changes of type were usually relatively complete, and that the coins of England's numerous mints became fairly well dispersed throughout the country during the issue of a type. The chronology of the thirteen types of William I and William II remains elusive, as does the exact size of the currency in any of the types, but single-finds and numbers of mints and moneyers suggest that there was a recession in the money supply during the late eleventh century, which reached a low point in the last decade of the century. The English mints were heavily dependent upon imports of silver at east coast ports, which were vulnerable to a general European decline in silver supplies. The available currency was never sufficient to support a fully monetised economy, and the role of the English penny as a major international currency was far in the future, but the coinage amply served the needs of the first two Norman kings as a stable medium of revenue and expenditure.

Appendix

English and Welsh Hoards Containing Coins of William I and William II

	Anglo-Saxon	William I BMC types									William II BMC types					Henry I or later
		1	2	3	4	5	6	7	8	?	1	2	3	4	5	
1. Denge Marsh, Kent, 1739	×	×															
2. Norwich (Garlands), 1972	-	11/12															
3. Rotherham, 1939	30+	2+															
4. Soberton, Hants., c.1850	237	22															
5. York Minster, 1970–71	-	3															
6. Uncertain location, before 1853	c.16+	2+															
7. Salisbury Plain, Wilts., in or before 1855	-	1+															
8. Middleham, N. Yorks., before 1848	-	-	3+														
9. Oulton, Staffs., 1795	15+	1+	4+														
10. York (Baile Hill), 1802	-	-	3+														

	Anglo-Saxon	William I BMC types									William II BMC types					Henry I or later
		1	2	3	4	5	6	7	8	?	1	2	3	4	5	
11. York (Bishophill, no. 2), 1882	-	5+	42+														
12. York (High Ousegate), 1704	-	×	×														
13. York (Jubbergate, no. 1), 1845	1+	1+	166+														
14. Wallingford, Oxon, 1894	-	-	2														
15. Corringham, Lincs., 1994	76	12	11	1													
16. Whitchurch, Oxon, before 1900	1+	-	2+	2+													
17. London (City/Queen Victoria Street/Walbrook), 1872	2,358+	-	2+	-	2+												
18. London (St Mary at Hill), 1774	59+	1+	1+	16+	2+												
19. Malmesbury, Wilts., 1828	-	-	1+	-	10+												
20. Stogumber, Somerset, 2012	-	-	-	-	4?												
21. Tibberton, Glos., 2008–9	-	-	-	-	4												
22. Beddington Park, Sutton, 1978	-	-	-	-	4												

	Anglo-Saxon	William I BMC types									William II BMC types					Henry I or later
		1	2	3	4	5	6	7	8	?	1	2	3	4	5	
23. Cranwich, Norfolk, 1993–4	-	-	-	-	2											
24. Maltby Springs, N. Lincs., 1999	-	-	-	-	1	4										
25. Scaldwell ('War Area'), Northants., 1914	-	-	-	-	-	264										
26. Tiverton, Cheshire, 2000	-	-	-	-	-	6										
27. Abergavenny area, Monmouthshire, 2002	130	-	1	-	-	62	4	2								
28. York (Monkgate), 1851	-	-	-	-	1+	42+	30+									
29. Winchester (Cathedral Green), Hants, 1964	-	-	-	-	-	-	2									
30. Bradenham, Norfolk, 1994	-	-	-	-	-	-	-	2								
31. Beauworth, Hants, 1833	-	-	-	-	-	31+	34+	11+	6,493+							
32. Louth area, Lincs, 1992	-	-	-	-	-	-	-	-	2							
33. York (Jubbergate, no. 2 or Peterlane), 1847	-	-	-	-	-	-	-	-	8+							

	Anglo-Saxon	William I BMC types									William II BMC types					Henry I or later
		1	2	3	4	5	6	7	8	?	1	2	3	4	5	
34. Bury St Edmunds (Mill Lane), Suffolk, 1851	-	-	-	-	-	-	-	-	-	×						
35. Colsterworth (or 'near Grantham'), Lincs., before 1735	-	-	-	-	-	-	-	-	-	×						
36. Sutton, Cambs., 1694	-	-	-	-	-	-	-	-	-	c.100						
37. Stalbridge, Dorset, 2005	-	-	-	-	-	-	-	-	-	-	1+	1+	-	-	-	
38. Tamworth, Staffs., 1877	-	-	-	-	-	-	-	-	30+	-	97+	167+	-	-	-	
39. Bermondsey, Southwark, c.1820	5	-	-	-	-	-	-	-	-	-	-	3	-	5	-	5
40. Shillington, Beds., 1871	-	-	-	-	-	-	-	-	-	-	32+	52+	62+	16+	-	21+
Total coins	61/62+	238+	19+	c.30+	411+	70+	15+	6,533+	c.100+		130+	223+	62+	21+	0	[c.7,913–14]

Notes to the Appendix

These notes give the principal modern publications for each find, from which further details may be found. An indication of the *terminus post quem* is included in the entries for Continental hoards.

1. D.M. Metcalf, 'Find-records of medieval coins from Gough's Camden's *Britannia*', *NC, 6th ser., 17* (1957), 181–207, at 186–90; P.B. Purefoy, 'Fifty pence from Romney', *NCirc, 104* (1996), 367–8; Allen no. 66.

2. T.H.McK. Clough, 'A small hoard of William I type I pennies from Norwich', *BNJ, 43* (1973), 142–3. Allen no. 67.

3. D. Allen, 'Treasure trove, 1933–9. 1. Rotherham, Yorks, 1939', *BNJ, 23* (1938–41), 269–74; Thompson no. 316; Allen no. 68.

4. Brooke, 1, xvii–xviii; Thompson no. 334; Allen no. 69.

5. E.J.E. Pirie with M.M. Archibald, 'Post-Roman coins', in D. Phillips and B. Heywood, *Excavations at York Minster. Vol. 1. From Roman Fortress to Norman Cathedral. Part 2. The Finds*, ed. M.O.H. Carver (London, 1995), 527–30, at 530; Allen no. 70.

6. C.E. Blunt, 'Grangerized copies of Ruding's Annals', *NCirc, 84* (1976), 226–7, at 227; Allen no. 71.

7. R.H.M. Dolley, 'En penning fra Magnus den Gode fundet i England', *NNUM* 1957, 253–6; Allen no. 72.

8. W.J. Davis, *The Nineteenth-Century Token Coinage* (London, 1904), plate opposite 167; Allen no. 80.

9. P.H. Robinson, 'The Stafford (1800) and Oulton (1795) hoards', *BNJ, 38* (1969), 22–30, at 24–30; P.H. Robinson, 'A further small parcel of coins from the Oulton hoard (1795)', *BNJ, 49* (1979), 125–7; Allen no. 73.

10. G. Benson, 'Coins; especially those relating to York', *Annual Report of the Yorkshire Philosophical Society* 1913, 1–104, at 97; Allen no. 74.

11. M. Dolley, 'The mythical Norman element in the 1882 Bishophill (York) find of Anglo-Saxon coins', *Annual Report of the Yorkshire Philosophical Society* 1971, 88–101; E.J.E. Pirie, 'Early Norman coins in the Yorkshire Museum', *Annual Report of the Yorkshire Philosophical Society* 1972, 33–8; Thompson no. 386; Allen no. 75.

12. R. Thoresby, *Ducatus Leodiensis*, ed. T.D. Whitaker, 2nd ed. (Leeds, 1816), 60–1; Thompson no. 387; Allen no. 76.

13. *Antiquaries Journal, 2* (1845), Proceedings, 384; Thompson no. 388; Allen no. 77.

14. CR 1987, no. 170; Allen no. 81; possibly unrelated single-finds.

15. *NC, 156* (1996), Coin Hoards 1996, no. 131; Allen no. 82.

16. P.W.P. Carlyon-Britton, 'A numismatic history ... First part', 115–16; Thompson no. 376; Allen no. 83.

17. E.H. Willett, 'On a hoard of Saxon pennies found in the City of London in 1872', *NC, 2nd ser., 16* (1876), 323–94; J. Evans, 'On a hoard of Saxon pennies found in the City of London in 1872.– Appendix', *NC, 3rd ser., 5* (1885), 254–73; Thompson no. 255; Allen no. 86.

18. G. Griffith, 'Account of coins, &c. found in digging the foundations of some old houses near the Church of St. Mary's Hill, London, 1774', *Archaeologia, 4* (1777), 356–63; Thompson no. 250; Allen no. 87.

19. C.W. Loscombe, 'Pennies of William the Conqueror', *Numismatic Journal, 2* (1837), 106; Thompson no. 264; Allen no. 89.

20. Information from Dr Gareth Williams (fused pile of four coins, only two of which can be attributed to a type).

21. Information from Dr Gareth Williams; Allen no. 88.

22. *Coin Hoards, 5* (1979), no. 278; Allen no. 84.

23. CR 1994, nos. 237–8; Allen no. 85.

24. A. Gannon and G. Williams, 'Two small hoards of William I', *BNJ, 71* (2001), 162–4; Allen no. 90.

25. Carlyon-Britton, 'A hoard of coins of William the Conqueror found in a trench in the War Area'; R.H.M. Dolley, 'The find-spot of the "War Area" hoard of pence of William I', *BNJ, 28* (1955–7), 650–51; Thompson no. 323; Allen no. 92.

26. Gannon and Williams, 'Two small hoards of William I'; Allen no. 92; H. Pagan, *SCBI 64: Grosvenor Museum, Chester. Part II: Anglo-Saxon Coins and Post-Conquest Coins to 1180* (Oxford, 2012), 32–3.

27. *Treasure Annual Report 2002*, 139–40, no. 217.

28. Pirie, *SCBI 21*, xxxvi (no. 18); Thompson no. 390; Allen no. 94.

29. C.E. Blunt and M. Dolley, 'Coins from the Winchester excavations 1961–1973', *BNJ, 47* (1977), 135–8, at 137 (nos. 15–16); Allen no. 93.

30. CR 1994, nos. 240, 242; Allen no. 95.

31. Hawkins, 'Description'; Thompson no. 37; Allen no. 96.

32. CR 1998, no. 155; Allen no. 97.

33. Pirie, *SCBI 21*, xxxvii (no. 19); Allen no. 98.

34. *Proceedings of the Bury & West Suffolk Archaeological Institute, 1* (1849–53), 309; Thompson no. 62; Allen no. 99.

35. *Journal of the British Archaeological Institute, 2nd ser., 5* (1899), 148; Allen no. 100.

36. R.A. Smith, 'The Beeston Tor hoard', *Antiquaries Journal, 5* (1925), 135–40, at p. 138; Thompson no. 346; Allen no. 101.

37. *NC, 168* (2008), Coin Hoards 2008, no. 54; Allen no. 102.

38. I. Stewart, 'Coins of William II from the Shillington hoard', *NC, 152* (1992), 111–32, at 129–32; Thompson no. 350; Allen no. 103.

39. E. Hawkins, 'Discovery of English pennies at Bermondsey', *NC, 1st ser., 8* (1845–6), 170; Thompson no. 42; Allen no. 105.

40. Stewart, 'Coins of William II from the Shillington hoard'; Thompson no. 330; Allen no. 108.

PART II
Interdisciplinary Perspectives

Chapter 5
XPICTIANA RELIGIO and the Tomb of Christ

Martin Biddle*

Charles the emperor, later Charlemagne, Karl der Grosse, died on 28 January 814. During the last months of his reign he issued new coins which are among the glories of early European coinage.[1] The obverse bears a bust of the emperor, reflecting

* As an archaeologist, I am honoured to be able to contribute this chapter on the intersections between architecture, archaeology and numismatics in memory of Mark Blackburn, who did so much to encourage the production of *The Winchester Mint, and Coins and Related Finds from the Excavations of 1961–71,* Winchester Studies, 8 (Oxford, 2012), and the work at Repton of myself and my late wife, Birthe Kjølbye-Biddle. Her contributions to our joint investigation of the Tomb of Christ in Jerusalem played a fundamental role in the thinking behind this chapter. I am most grateful to Simon Coupland for steering me through the Carolingian coinage of which he is the master, and for constant encouragement and much needed correction. I owe special debts to Bjørn Ambrosiani, Kenneth Jonsson, Erik van der Kam, Bernd Kluge and Jan Pelsdonk for information about some of the coins and for new images for study and reproduction. Steven Ashley, Simon Hayfield and Francis Morris have provided and processed the figures. The editors of the volume have been tireless in their patience, encouragement, and invaluable handling of the text.

[1] The principal discussions are: H.H. Völckers, 'Die Christiana Religio-Gepräge. Ein Beitrag zur Karolingerforschung', *Hamburger Beiträge zur Numismatik, 6–7* (1952/53), 9–54; P. Grierson, 'Money and coinage under Charlemagne', in *Karl der Grosse: Persönlichkeit und Geschichte*, ed. H. Beumann (Düsseldorf, 1965), 501–36, at 518–27; P. Grierson, 'Symbolism in early medieval charters and coins', *Settimane di studio del Centro italiano di studi sull'alto medioevo, 23* (1976), 601–40; J. Lafaurie, 'Les monnaies impériales de Charlemagne', *Comptes-rendus des séances de l'Académie des inscriptions et Belles-Lettres, 122* (1978), 154–76; R. Schumacher-Wolfgarten, 'XPICTIANA RELIGIO. Zu einer Münzprägung Karls des Grossen', *Jahrbuch für Antike und Christentum, 37* (1994), 122–41; B. Kluge, 'Die Bildnispfennige Karls des Grossen', in *Moneta Mediævalis: studia numizmatyczne i historyczne ofiarowane Profesorowi Stanisławowi Suchodolskiemu w 65 rocznicę urodzin*, ed. R. Kiersnowski et al. (Warsaw, 2002), 367–77, 554–7; S. Coupland, 'Charlemagne's coinage: ideology and economy', in *Charlemagne: Empire and Society*, ed. J. Story (Manchester, 2005), 211–29 (reprinted in his *Carolingian Coinage and the Vikings. Studies on Power and Trade in the 9th Century* (Aldershot, 2007)). The 44 or 45 known examples of Charlemagne's Portrait coinage are referred to in the text and figures in this article by the numbers given them in Simon Coupland's list, this volume Chapter 6. For the date, see

c

Figure 5.1   Charlemagne's Portrait coinage with the *XPICTIANA RELIGIO*
reverse: the three obverse legends (x 2). (a) Legend 1: *DN KARLVS*
IMP AVG REX F ET L, Coupland 1; reverse, double pediment
Type 1 (Staatliche Museen, Berlin); (b) Legend 2: *KARLVS IMP*
AVG, Coupland 21; reverse, single pediment Type 2 (Künker);
(c) Legend 3: *KAROLVS IMP AVG*, Coupland 25; reverse, single
pediment Type 2 (Staatliche Museen, Berlin).

Lafaurie, 'Monnaies impériales', 166–8; P.-H. Martin, 'Eine Goldmünze Karls des Grossen',
Numismatisches Nachrichtenblatt, 46/8 (August 1997), 351–5, at 353; Kluge, 'Bildnispfennige',
374–5.

a   b

Figure 5.2   Charlemagne's *XPICTIANA RELIGIO* reverse: Type 1, building with double pediment (x 3). (a) Coupland 1; (b) Coupland 13 (both Staatliche Museen, Berlin).

a   b

Figure 5.3   Charlemagne's *XPICTIANA RELIGIO* reverse: Type 2, building with single pediment (x 3). (a) Coupland 16 (Kungliga Myntakabinettet, Stockholm); (b) Coupland 29 (Geld-museum, Utrecht).

imperial Roman prototypes but so sensitively detailed that it is clearly a portrait 'von wunderbarer Feinheit und hoher künstlerische Qualität' (Figure 5.1, a–c).[2] The reverse of the majority of these Portrait coins bears the image of a classical building,

2   Völckers, 'Christiana Religio', 14; Grierson, 'Symbolism', 621.

a   b

Figure 5.4   Charlemagne's *XPICTIANA RELIGIO* reverse: Type 2,
               building with single pediment (x 3). (a) Coupland 21 (Künker);
               (b) Coupland 25 (Staatliche Museen, Berlin).

a   b

Figure 5.5   Charlemagne's *XPICTIANA RELIGIO* reverse, 'linear' versions
               (x 3). (a) Type 1, building with double pediment, Coupland 12
               (Elsen); (b) Type 2, building with single pediment, Coupland 15
               (Bibliothèque royale de Belgique, Brussels).

minutely detailed, the depiction of which is 'in Proportion und in Schlichtheit ... wirkungsvoll und künstlerischer fein behandelt',[3] the interpretation of which has been intensively but inconclusively debated (Figs. 5.2–5.5).

Some 45 coins of Charlemagne's Portrait type are now known, 31 or 32 of which (cf. Appendix 1, Tables 5.1–5.2) carry on the reverse this image of a pedimented building surrounded by the legend *XPICTIANA RELIGIO*, 'The Christian Faith' (Figs. 5.2–5.5).[4] The first four letters are in Greek capitals (*chi, rho, iota, sigma*, the latter in the so-called 'lunate' form of *C* rather than *Σ*). The next four letters could be Greek (*tau, iota, alpha, nu*) or Roman capitals. The final letter is not Greek but the feminine singular ending -*A* of the Latin adjective *christiana* which in Greek from the second century AD onwards would have been χριστιανή, requiring *H*, the capital of *eta*. The use of the Greek *XP*, in the form of the Christogram 'Chi-Rho', as an abbreviation for the name of Christ (Χριστός), was used on Roman coins from the time of Constantine and was still known in the West, even in the early ninth century,[5] but the adjectival form was not. This is needed here to qualify the Latin noun *RELIGIO*, 'faith', 'religion', for which the Greek feminine noun πίστις, 'faith', 'belief', would probably have been the original. In capitals as ΠΙΣΤΙΣ or even ΠΙΣΤΙΣ this would have given a possible reconstructed legend *XPICTIANH ΠICTIΣ*. These words contain too many Greek letters to have been readily intelligible in the ninth-century West, hence perhaps their partial conversion into more readily comprehensible Roman letters.

The possible source of these words is dealt with at the end of this chapter but their function is the same as that of the obverse legends, to identify and set out the significance of the image portrayed, '[This is] Charles, Emperor, Augustus', '[This is] the Christian faith'.

The legend surrounds a building of classical type (Figs. 5.2–5.5). A pediment enclosing a triangular tympanum rests on a horizontal entablature supported by pairs of columns set on a podium approached by two steps. The whole composition, from the apex of the pediment to the underside of the lower step, averages in height about

---

3   Völckers, 'Christiana Religio', 14.

4   For Simon Coupland's list of the currently (September 2013) known coins, see below, Chapter 6. Coin 12b reported in his postscript (p. 154) was identified too late to be included here, except in Tables 1, 2, and 4, in Appendix 1, and as a find-spot on Figure 5.12. Since both articles went to press however, Dr Coupland has shown that coins 9 and 11 are probably the same. The number of known coins of Charlemagne's *XPICTIANA RELIGIO* type is now therefore 31 or 32.

5   A. Grabar, *Christian Iconography: a Study of its Origins* (London, 1980), 38–40. For the use of *XP* on Carolingian royal seals, see G. Kornbluth, *Engraved Gems of the Carolingian Empire* (University Park, PA, 1995), 58–63 (No. 6: seal of Lothar II (855–69)?, Aachen?), 109–13 (No. 20: seal of Louis II (855–75)?, Italy?). For further commentary on the legend, see the discussion between C.A. Mastrelli and Grierson at Spoleto: Grierson, 'Symbolism', 636–40. Knowledge of Greek was still limited in the West: even in the mid-ninth century 'the *nomen sacrum* χω *Christo* seemed to [John Scottus] to require interpretation, while χρε *Christe* did not': W. Berschin, *Greek Letters and the Latin Middle Ages* (Washington D.C., 1988), 120–21, with 312 (n. 74).

11.7 mm and in width across the entablature 9.4 mm, considerably smaller than the bust of Charles on the obverse, which averages in height about 14.5 mm.[6]

This tiny icon of a building comprises both consistent features and considerable variation in detail. The image is of two types, depending on whether the pediment is double (Type 1, Figure 5.2) or single (Type 2, Figs. 5.3 and 5.4). Both types also sometimes appear in a 'spindly' or 'linear' form (Figure 5.5).

Certain elements are common to both types (Table 5.3): a pedimented structure, supported by four columns in two pairs, each column with a capital and a base, the whole approached by two steps, and enhanced by two expanding-arm crosses, one inside the building, between the two pairs of columns, the other on the apex of the pediment.

A number of tiny details also appear on some coins of both types. These comprise a ball supporting the cross on the apex of the pediment; acroteria (roof ornaments) projecting vertically from the outer ends of the entablature; decorative elements on the tympanum within the pediment; and an elongation of the foot of the inner cross. Table 5.3 shows that these details appear on images of both Type 1 and Type 2 (that is, with the single or double pediment, respectively), and are not restricted to one type or the other. The fact that these details can appear on both types of a basically identical image suggests that they derive from the copying of a common original.

Leaving aside for the moment the question of the nature and identity of the original structure, it is useful to enquire how the images were produced. The appearance of the two types, one with a double (Type 1) the other with a single (Type 2) pediment, suggests that two schemes were drawn up to guide the production of the image to appear on the coins. Whether such drawn schemes, if that is what they were, were produced by one or by different artists, the lesser details defined on Table 5.3 are to some degree shared by both schemes. How then to account for the variations shown on the coins? Since two of the reverses represented among the 31 or 32 known coins can now be shown to have struck multiple coins (coins 3 and 7, and coins 4 and 9/11), a minimum of 28 dies must have been cut, presumably by several die-cutters rather than by one.[7] Without strict product control, the die-cutter presumably adapted whichever of the two schemes he was following, omitting or including details according to his skill, preference or the practicality of actually cutting the tiny details involved. The skill of the die-cutters fully justifies the comment by Völckers quoted in the first paragraph of this essay.

---

[6]   The figures given here are averaged over the seven coins for which measurements are quoted in the various entries. The scale of many images, whether supposedly full-size or enlarged, does not appear to be sufficiently accurate for direct measurement from published images.

[7]   Of the 31 or 32 coins, no reverse image is available for Coupland 22, lost since 1937 or before from the binding of the Morienval Gospels (see Appendix 2); and there seems to be no modern image for Coupland 28. Coupland 12b came to light too late to be included in this comparison.

The striking feature, therefore, of these reverse images on Charlemagne's deniers is that they are of the two types, with double or single gables, share a variety of sometimes complex details, and can be remarkably fine (e.g. Figs. 5.2 and 5.3). Images of the *XPICTIANA RELIGIO* type on the reverses of Charlemagne's successors follow a generally simpler design. Although almost without exception of Type 1, they are increasingly crude.[8] They show the double-gabled pediment on two pairs of columns approached by steps, but rarely have a ball beneath the upper cross, omit the acroteria and ignore the decorative elements in the tympanum. The cross between the columns, usually equal-armed, can vary greatly; images of the 'spindly' kind (cf. Figure 5.5) rarely occur. The virtual suppression of the single gable (Type 2) suggests a decision to keep to the double gables as a more accurate representation of the original.[9]

What then was this original? Sometimes described as a 'temple' or a 'church', the image has sometimes been thought to derive from one or other of the Roman coin-types showing a pedimented classical temple.[10] This derivation supposes that the Christian crosses – one on the apex of the pediment, the other between the central columns of the portico – indicate that the pagan prototype has been converted to Christian use. If this is the case, the implied message can only be a general statement of the triumph of Christianity over paganism, made explicit by the part-Greek, part-Latin legend, 'the Christian religion'.[11] Other suggestions have seen the pedimented

---

[8]   For images, see Simon Coupland's comprehensive sequence of studies: 'Money and coinage under Louis the Pious', *Francia* 17/1 (1990), 23–54; 'The coinages of Pippin I and Pippin II of Aquitaine', *RN, 6th ser., 31* (1989), 194–222; 'The coinage of Lothar I (840–855)', *NC, 161* (2001), 157–98; and 'The early coinage of Charles the Bald, 840–864', *NC, 151* (1991), 121–58. These four papers are reprinted in Coupland, *Carolingian Coinage.*

[9]   Counting the reverse images in the four papers listed in n. 8, of the 37 images of the coins of Louis the Pious, none has a single gable; of the seven images of coins of Pippin I and Pippin II, one has a single gable and is of the 'spindly' type (Coupland, 'Pippin I and Pippin II', pl. XX, 1), and a second may have a single gable (ibid., pl. XX, 9); of the 67 images of coins of Lothar I, only one (Coupland, 'Lothar I', pl. 35, 1) has a single gable; and of the 47 images of such coins of Charles the Bald only one has a single gable (Coupland, 'Charles the Bald', pl. 22, 25).

[10]   Grierson, 'Money and coinage', 519; M. Matzke, 'Antikenrezeption am Beispiel der Münzen Karls des Grossen', *Geldgeschichtliche Nachrichten, 31/n. 176* (November 1996), 264–73, at 271–2 (an extreme view). For a useful discussion of the problems of showing details of temple architecture on Roman coins and the methods adopted by the die-cutters, see D.F. Brown, *Temples of Rome as Coin Types*, ANS Numismatic Notes and Monographs, 90 (New York, 1940), 13–30. Of the four methods he describes, Method 1, 'the simple frontal style' (20, cf. 36), with some of the extra devotion to detail characteristic of Method 2, 'the frontal ornate style' (22–5), is closest to that adopted by Charlemagne's die-cutters.

[11]   K. Lange, *Münzkunst des Mittelalters* (Leipzig, 1942), 54; Grierson, 'Money and coinage', 519, an idea described by V.H. Elbern, 'Frühmittelalterliche Zierkunst im Lichte der "Renovatio"', *Settimane di studio del Centro italiano di studi sull'alto medioevo, 22* (1975), 865–97, at 894–5, as 'sehr literarisch'; cf. Grierson, 'Symbolism', 628. Kluge has strongly restated the case for this interpretation; B. Kluge, 'Nomen imperatoris und Christiana Religio', in *799 Kunst und Kultur*

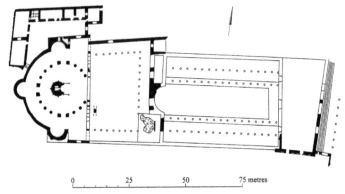

0　　　　　25　　　　　50　　　　　75 metres

Figure 5.6　　Constantine's Church of the Holy Sepulchre in Jerusalem, dedicated 335, as it was in the time of Charlemagne, showing the edicule at the centre of the Rotunda of the Resurrection (the Anastasis). (Drawn by Steven Ashley).

building as Constantine's Church of the Holy Sepulchre in Jerusalem,[12] as St Peter's in Rome,[13] as the entrance to Charlemagne's palace-chapel church in Aachen[14] or as the Fountain of Life.[15]

---

der Karolingerzeit: Karl der Grosse und Papst Leo III. in Paderborn. Katalog der Ausstellung, Paderborn 1999, ed. C. Stiegemann and M. Wemhoff (3 vols., Mainz 1999), 1, 82–90, at 83.

[12] That is, Constantine's vast basilican church known as the *martyrium* (Figure 5.6) as distinct from the adjacent 'edicule' which housed the remains of the rock-cut tomb supposed to be that in which the body of Jesus was laid after the crucifixion, but whether it is precisely the *martyrium* church to which Grierson ('Symbolism', 634) was referring in discussion is unclear. Schumacher-Wolfgarten, 'XPICTIANA RELIGIO', 125, points out that a 'weniger imposanten Gattung' than a temple or church facade must lie behind the image on the coins.

[13] M. Prou, *Les monnaies carolingiennes* (Paris, 1896), xi. Prou's suggestion has found no support: Völckers, 'Christiana Religio', 14 ('eine offene Frage'); Grierson, 'Money and coinage', 519 ('extremely unlikely'); cf. Grierson, 'Symbolism', 628; Kluge, 'Nomen imperatoris', 83.

[14] H.C. Fallon, *Imperial Symbolism on Two Carolingian Coins*, ANS Museum Notes, 8 (New York, 1958), 119–31, at 122, etc.; Grierson, 'Money and coinage', 519; Grierson, 'Symbolism', 629, and V.H. Elbern's comment and Grierson's reply in the discussion of Grierson's paper, ibid., 632–4. Their discussion may well have been influenced by the colonnaded portico at the entrance to the Aachen chapel in Leo Hugot's model shown at the Karl der Grosse exhibition in Aachen (*Karl der Grosse: Werk und Wirkung*, Exhibition Catalogue (Aachen 1965), 395–400, esp. 398 (entry 567(9)), Abb. 119–21 and just visible in Abb. 120. But the portico appears to be unsubstantiated and is not shown on later plans and reconstructions.

[15] P. Underwood, 'The Fountain of Life in manuscripts of the gospels', *Dumbarton Oaks Papers*, 5 (1950), 41–138, at 91–7, 101–5, 117–18, discusses the very complex relationship between representations of the tomb and of 'fountains of life', but does not mention the coins. E. Robert, J.-L. Desnier, and J. Belaubre, 'La Fontaine de Vie et la propagation de la véritable religion chrétienne', *RBN, 134* (1988), 89–106, identify the image on the *XPICTIANA RELIGIO* coins

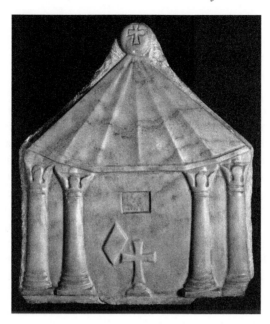

Figure 5.7   Marble plaque, perhaps from Syria, apparently showing the east front of the Constantinian edicule. Sixth century? (Dumbarton Oaks, Washington D.C., Byzantine Collection, Acc. no. 38.56).

Until now only two writers have addressed the possibility that the building on the coins represents the one structure which might be thought to encompass the essence of Christianity, the place of Christ's Resurrection: Constantine's edicule enclosing the rock-cut Tomb of Christ at the centre of the Rotunda of the Resurrection in the Church of the Holy Sepulchre in Jerusalem (Figure 5.6). The first appears to have been V.H. Elbern at the Spoleto Conference in 1974 where he made a direct comparison between the 'Tempelfront' reverse of a Carolingian *XPICTIANA RELIGIO* denier and a Byzantine marble plaque of possible Syrian origin now in Dumbarton Oaks (here Figure 5.7).[16] The plaque shows what is evidently a relatively small building with a pointed roof supported by pairs of columns to either side, with a cross engraved on a ball on the point of the roof and a second cross standing between the columns. The essential similarity to the building on the reverse of the Carolingian denier is immediately convincing. In publishing the plaque in 1950, Paul Underwood concluded that

---

as a representation of the fountain of life; they do not mention the tomb of Christ. I owe this reference to the kindness of Cécile Morrisson.

[16]   Elbern, 'Frühmittelalterliche Zierkunst', 894–5, with Abb. 30 (the Carolingian denier) facing Abb. 31 (the Dumbarton Oaks plaque).

the image on the plaque was 'a composite of the two most popular images ... the Crucifixion as symbolized by the representation of the "life-giving tree" of the cross; and the Resurrection, indicated by the scene of the Marys and the angel at the Holy Sepulcher in Jerusalem'.[17]

There was apparently no discussion following Elbern's Spoleto presentation of 1974, but at the next year's Spoleto Conference Elbern himself contributed to the discussion following a paper by Grierson, who had restricted himself to suggesting that the building on Charlemagne's coins might perhaps be intended to represent the entrance to the atrium of the palace chapel at Aachen.[18] Elbern, speaking in English in the discussion, recalled his own paper of the previous year, emphasising that both the plaque and the coin should be interpreted in the same way as representing 'the lifegiving sepulchre of Christ, the very centre of Christianity'.[19] Grierson in his reply was cautious, agreeing only 'that there is a strong likeness of the reverse coin-type to symbolic representations of the church at Jerusalem, and of course we know that Charlemagne was protector of the Holy Sepulchre [and that] aspects of the problem that should certainly be looked into'.

There the matter seems to have rested for two decades, neither Elbern's proposition of 1974 nor his strongly worded repetition of 1975 having apparently attracted numismatic comment. It was not until 1994 that a second writer came independently to the view that the image on Charlemagne's coins represented the sepulchre of Christ in Jerusalem. Although Renate Schumacher-Wolfgarten did not refer to the Dumbarton Oaks plaque or to the discussion between Elbern and Grierson in Spoleto in 1975, she put forward her views on the basis of a wide-ranging review of the literary, art-historical, and iconographical evidence as it was then known, including a range of images preserved in written descriptions and on contemporary objects such as Palestinian pilgrim flasks, incense-burners, and other objects.[20] After reviewing previous views, she came to the conclusion that the evidence indicated that the Tomb of Christ in Jerusalem was of the form we find on the *XPICTIANA RELIGIO* coins 'als Kürsel' and in particular that the coins showed the entrance or eastern face.[21] Her article was not up-to-date in numismatic terms nor in relation to developing knowledge of

---

[17] Underwood, 'Fountain of Life', 91–3, with Figures 39–40.

[18] See above, n. 14.

[19] Grierson, 'Symbolism', printed discussion on 632–4, with Grierson's response.

[20] As above, n. 1. She notes on 141, in a postscript to n. 109, that V.H. Elbern told her, after completion of her article, that he had already come to the same thought ('Vermutung') that the 'Tempelfront' on coins of Louis the Pious showed the 'Hl. Grab', the Tomb of Christ, in Jerusalem, noting that Grierson in the Spoleto discussion of 1975 had not turned the idea down.

[21] Ibid. 129, 131. See further, Ildar H. Garipzanov, 'The image of authority in Carolingian coinage: the *image* of a ruler and Roman imperial tradition', *EME*, 8 (1999), 197–218, at 203–4, not least for his comment on 204 that 'the temple was originally the sign of the *palatina moneta*'.

the probable actual structure and appearance of the tomb, as we shall see, but it was a remarkable advance on previous work. It was nevertheless greeted with severe comments which its thoroughness and importance did not deserve: 'sehr unwahrscheinlich',[22] 'ebenso unwahrscheinlich ist die Deutung als Abbreviatur für Kalvarienberg und Grabeskirche in Jerusalem'.[23]

None of these writers, neither those who had made more general suggestions in earlier studies, nor Elbern in 1974–75 or Schumacher-Wolfgarten in 1994, had attempted to use the architectural and archaeological evidence for the Tomb of Christ, from which it is possible to reconstruct the form and appearance of the structure (now commonly known as the 'edicule') which Constantine had erected around the rock-cut Tomb of Christ before the dedication of his new complex in 336 (Figure 5.6). A start on this journey was made by Robert Willis of Cambridge as long ago as 1849 in his *Architectural History of the Church of the Holy Sepulchre at Jerusalem*, a work of exemplary scholarship, still in some ways unmatched; an achievement all the more remarkable as he had never visited Jerusalem.[24] Willis's plan of the Church of the Holy Sepulchre, based on a survey made by J.J. Scoles in 1825, includes as an inset Willis's reconstruction of the plan of Constantine's edicule, together with two further insets showing the plan of the edicule as it was before and after the fire which badly damaged the church in 1808.[25] Willis's reconstruction is more important for the approach adopted than for its verisimilitude, for it heralded the start of a new approach to the study of the church as a whole and of the edicule in particular, using not only the elements of the structure as reflected in the present plan and scale of the edicule, but also the many written accounts and representations of at least 13 different kinds.[26]

Publication by Lauffray in 1962 of the Narbonne model provided the next major advance in understanding the edicule (Figure 5.8, cf. Figure 5.9, D and E).[27] This three-dimensional model, possibly dating from the fifth century and carved of Pyrenaen marble (therefore produced locally rather than in Palestine), was found broken and reused as building stone in the medieval defences of the city.

[22] Matzke, 'Antikenrezeption', 272.

[23] Kluge, 'Nomen imperatoris', 83, cf. 90, in 'Literatur', 'ebensowenig überzeugend'.

[24] Originally published in G. Williams, *The Holy City. Historical, Topographical, and Antiquarian Notices of Jerusalem*, 2nd ed. (2 vols., London, 1849), 2, 129–293, published separately at the same time from the same type but with its own pagination under the title quoted above.

[25] Reproduced and discussed in M. Biddle, *The Tomb of Christ* (Stroud, 1999), 15–19 and Figure 14.

[26] Reviewed and illustrated ibid. 20–52.

[27] J. Lauffray, 'La *Memoria Sancti Sepuchri* du Musée de Narbonne et le Temple Rond de Baalbek: essai de restitution du Saint Sépulchre constantienne', *Mélanges de l'Université Saint Joseph, 38* (1962), 199–217.

Figure 5.8   The Narbonne model of the Tomb of Christ, Pyrenean marble.
              ?Fifth century. (Photograph by John Crook).

There can be no doubt that it represents the edicule in the Church of the Holy
Sepulchre, as the burial couch in the inner chamber powerfully demonstrates.[28]
At a surviving height of 1.24 metres to the apex of the rotunda, the Narbonne
model is about one-seventh of the scale of the original Constantinian structure.

First to apply this new evidence to reconstructing the edicule itself
was John Wilkinson in 1972, who produced not only scale drawings but a
three-dimensional model.[29] As I wrote in 1999, Wilkinson's reconstruction
'is as close as we are likely to get to the original form of the structure unless
new representations are found or until new evidence for its precise plan and
dimensions are recovered in the restoration of the present structure'.[30]

The stone-by-stone examination and survey of the edicule undertaken
between 1989 and 1999 by myself and my wife, the late Birthe Kjølbye-Biddle,
from Hertford College, Oxford, in collaboration with Michael Cooper and

---

[28]   Biddle, 'Tomb of Christ', 110–11, Figure 76.
[29]   J. Wilkinson, 'The tomb of Christ: an outline of its structural history', *Levant, 4* (1972),
83–97, pl. X.
[30]   Biddle, *Tomb of Christ*, 21.

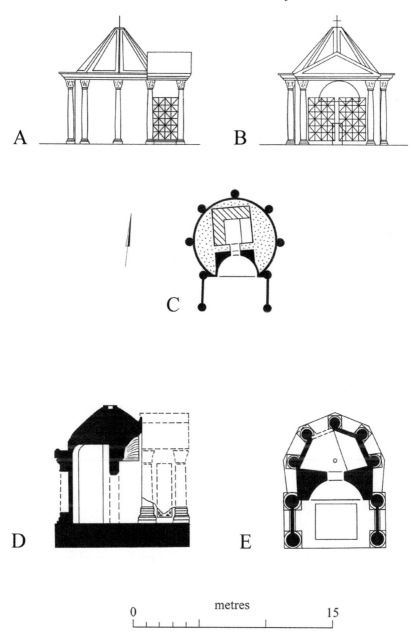

Figure 5.9   Constantine's edicule containing the rock-cut Tomb of Christ, dedicated 335 (A, south elevation; B, east (front) elevation; C, plan); Narbonne model (D, section, west-east; E, plan). (Reconstructions drawn by Steven Ashley).

Stuart Robson of City University, London, provided for the first time a three-dimensional computer-based model of the entire structure, together with a stone-by-stone architectural record and analysis of its many details.[31] As a result of this work, it was possible to present a series of reconstructed plans and sections of the edicule at each of the four major stages in its structural development: Constantinian (325/6–335), Byzantine and medieval (*c.* 1012–40), Renaissance (1555), and as rebuilt following the fire of 1808.[32] The reconstructed south elevation and plan of the Constantinian edicule as published in 1999 are reproduced here (Figure 5.9 A and C). Because we were not then thinking about Charlemagne's *XPICTIANA RELIGIO* coins, we did not produce a reconstruction of the east or entrance façade. This is now included here in a new drawing by Steven Ashley which derives strictly from the already published south elevation and plan, with the addition only of the grilles and the arched niche opening into the tomb chamber behind (Figure 5.9 B).

It can be seen that this reconstruction provides a good match for and explanation of the image on the reverse of Charlemagne's coins (cf. Figs 5.1–5). The smaller inner pediment and the inner columns define the porch, the outer pediment indicates the (somewhat depressed) cone of the roof, and the outer columns represent, as the plan demonstrates, the easternmost pair of the five columns set around the rotunda containing the tomb chamber.

Close inspection of the images on the coins, more clearly seen when enlarged (Figs. 5.2–5.5), shows the presence on some specimens of both Type 1 (double pediment) and Type 2 (single pediment) of a number of lesser features, especially on the entablature and within the tympanum of the pediment (Table 5.3). Attention was called to these 'Akrotere' on the entablature and 'schmückende Aufsätze in der Mitte' (i.e., in the tympanum) by Schumacher-Wolfgarten, who also pointed out that the edicule represented on the coins was probably that restored by Abbot Modestus after the Persian attack of 614 rather than the Constantinian structure in its original state.[33]

Figure 5.10 provides a schematic idea, based on the analysis in Table 5.3, of how the image copied/produced for those cutting the coin dies may have looked. The 'acroteria' to either side appear to sit on the projecting entablature of the rotunda (and if so presumably continued round above all five columns), while the nature of the elements within the tympanum (usually shown as three) cannot be identified. The relatively heavy equal-armed cross above is a consistent feature, as is the cross with an elongated lower arm which appears

---

31   For a full account, see ibid., *passim.*

32   Ibid., Figures 64, 66.

33   Schumacher-Wolfgarten, 'XPICTIANA RELIGIO', 124, 127. It certainly appears, for example, that the elaborate grilles seen on earlier representations of the edicule (e.g. Biddle, *Tomb of Christ*, Figures 17–19, and as a fragment of grill-like carving on the 'south' face of the Narbonne model) do not appear in later images.

Figure 5.10   Reconstruction of the front of a model of the Tomb of Christ, drawn for copying by those cutting the dies for the reverse of coins of Charlemagne's *XPICTIANA RELIGIO* type. (Drawn by Steven Ashley).

between the columns. The lower cross often appears to be floating (but possibly hanging?) and seems usually to be regarded as symbolic. On a silver dish now in the Hermitage, however, one of the three medallions shows the Virgin Mary and Mary Magdalene at the Sepulchre with an elegant cross set between the columns on what appears to be a tall rectangular base.[34] For three reasons that is the solution adopted on Figure 5.10: first, because a rectangular cut and fixing

---

[34]   R. Cormack and M. Vassilaki (eds), *Byzantium 330–1453* (London, 2008), 329, 452–3 (no. 286: 'Central Asia, ninth or tenth century'). Also in J.P.C. Kent and K.S. Painter (eds), *Wealth of the Roman World* (London, 1977), 90 (no. 153: ?Syrian, 'seventh century'). On the Dumbarton Oaks plaque (Figure 5.7) the inner cross is shown standing somewhat unsteadily on a three-lobed base which may be intended to indicate Golgotha. There is no other evidence for this feature which is perhaps symbolic, like the displaced lozenge-shaped feature perhaps indicating the stone rolled away from the entrance to the tomb.

holes in the floor of the portico of the Narbonne model show that something was once set there (Figure 5.8); second because early pictures of the interior of the porch almost always show a raised element there, usually identified as a relic of the 'Rolling Stone';[35] and third, because there is ample room for the visitor to move through to either side of the present 'Altar of the Rolling Stone' which stands in exactly this position.[36]

What then was being copied for reproduction by the die-cutters of Charlemagne's coins? And where in particular may it have been? The Narbonne model provides some indications. At 1.24 metres (4 feet 1 inch) in height and carved from Pyrenean marble, the model can only have been produced locally. Accurate handling of the three-dimensional complexity of the structure and the precision of reproduction of the surviving architectural detail, seen especially in the carving of the shell-niche (Figure 5.8), implies information from Jerusalem in the form of drawings or a model. Although easiest to transport, drawings of the kind required (a scale plan or plans, sections and elevations) are unlikely to have been available by the sixth century. A wooden model, perhaps dismountable, seems much more likely, and probably one that was quite large, perhaps of the same size as the marble copy. Although there is no survivor, the making of the Narbonne marble is unthinkable without such a guide to follow.

The image on Charlemagne's coins might derive from drawings of the front of the edicule which had reached his court from Jerusalem, but it seems more likely that here too the source was a model from which, as suggested above, one or more drawings might have been made to guide the engravers of the dies.[37]

At his coronation on Christmas Day 800 in Rome, Charlemagne was presented with gifts brought from Jerusalem: 'claves sepulchri Dominici ac loci calvariae, claves etiam civitatis et montis cum vexillo'.[38] Charlemagne's deepening interest in the Holy Land in the years which followed was reflected in the production of a 'breue commemoratorii de illis casis Dei uel monasteriis qui sunt in sancta ciuitate Hierusalem uel in circuitu eius'.[39] This not only

---

[35] Biddle, *Tomb of Christ*, e.g. figs. 9, 15, 35, 52.

[36] Ibid., figs. 85, 91, 93, 100.

[37] See above, p. 120.

[38] 'The keys of the Lord's tomb and of the place of Calvary, the keys too of the City and of the Mount, with a banner'. *Annales regni Francorum*, s.a. 800: MGH SSRG, 6 ed. F. Kurze (Hanover, 1895), 112. The significance and nature of the gifts has been much discussed: see M. Borgolte, *Der Gesandtenaustausch der Karolinger mit den Abbasiden und mit den Patriarchen von Jerusalem*, Münchener Beiträge, 25 (Munich, 1976), 67–76. For the *vexillum*, 'banner', as 'eine Metapher für das Heilige Kreuz', i.e. a piece of the True Cross, see ibid., 72–3 with further references.

[39] 'An inventory memorandum of God's houses and monasteries that are in the holy city of Jerusalem and its environs'. The *Breue commemoratorii de illius casis Dei*, is now reproduced, critically edited, translated, and fully discussed by M. McCormick, *Charlemagne's Survey of the Holy Land: Wealth, Personnel, and Buildings of a Mediterranean Church between Antiquity and*

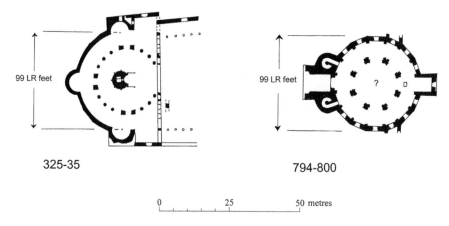

99 LR feet

325-35

99 LR feet

794-800

0   25   50 metres

Figure 5.11   Constantine's Rotunda of the Resurrection (to the left), surrounding the edicule, the Tomb of Christ, compared with Charlemagne's chapel at Aachen (to the right) completed *c*.800. The '?' at the centre of the Aachen rotunda indicates the suggested possible location of a model of the Tomb of Christ. (Drawn by Steven Ashley).

described in detail and enumerated their personnel and expenditures, but also set out the measurements of some of the buildings, including *sancto sepulchro Domini* ('the church of the Sepulchre of the Lord'), which here clearly means the Rotunda of the Resurrection, the Anastasis. The *Breue commemoratorii* seems to have been composed before the autumn of 810, possibly in 808.[40] A few years later, in 812, in response to an embassy to Constantinople in 811 led by Abbot Heito of Reichenau, Greek ambassadors came to Aachen. They provoked great admiration with their *organa*, which Charlemagne immediately ordered to be copied and built. The Greek legate sang the antiphons on the octave of epiphany, and offered *laudes* in Greek, calling Charlemagne emperor and *basileus*.[41]

It may have been in the course of these events that a model of the edicule in Jerusalem was obtained by or presented to Charlemagne. If so, the likeliest place in which it might have been set is at the centre of his octagonal chapel in Aachen (Figure 5.11). Whether this model was one actually brought from Jerusalem or possibly a new and perhaps larger version made specially to be placed in the church, we shall probably never know, and no trace has been

---

the Middle Ages (Washington, D.C., 2011), quotation at 200–201, and including discussion of Charlemagne's Portrait coinage and of the *XPICTIANA RELIGIO* type in particular at 187–91.

⁴⁰   Ibid., 177.

⁴¹   Berschin, *Greek Letters*, 114–17.

found of the foundation on which such a model might have been set.[42] The skill to make models (albeit on a small scale) in strict adherence to the canons of Vitruvian architecture is however demonstrated by the remains of a shrine with ivory columns, arguably made by Einhard himself, perhaps in the 820s, for his monastery at Seligenstadt.[43]

If the existence of such an architectural model at the centre of the Aachen chapel were to be thought a wild surmise, one should perhaps recall the long tradition of making full-sized copies of the edicule which still survive, or are known from documentary evidence to have existed, in churches throughout Europe.[44] None survive which are certainly earlier than the twelfth century, but the wear which has eroded the opening between the portico and the tomb chamber of the ?fifth-century Narbonne model shows that it served for several centuries as a focus for the devotion of caressing fingers reaching in towards the tomb (Figure 5.8). A model of the edicule, whether large or small, in Charlemagne's church at Aachen would not be out of place in such a sequence.

Such a model of whatever kind or size might be the source of the words *XPICTIANA RELIGIO* written on the entablature of its portico, whether in Greek or in the mixed form preserved on the coins. Although the phrase *christiana religio* 'appears in Christian Latin right from the start, since Tertullian (fl. *c.*200)' and was used frequently by Augustine and also by Bede,[45] and after Charlemagne's death by Einhard,[46] it is on the coins that the phrase appears for the first time in the form *XPICTIANA RELIGIO*.

The distribution of those coins of the *XPICTIANA RELIGIO* type whose find-spots are known is distinctive, being limited to the great rivers and to a few far-flung trading places reachable in a short time by sea (Appendix 1, Figure

---

[42]　I am grateful to Dr Sebastian Ristow of the University of Cologne for confirming that no trace of such a feature has been recorded. It is not clear however whether a foundation would have been needed for a model set on a plinth or directly on the flagged stone floor, and in any case the marble flooring installed in 1907–13 now in the centre of the chapel would have removed any traces there may have been.

[43]　R. Büchler and H. Zeilinger, 'Reste einer karolingischen Elfenbeinarbeit in Seligenstadt', *Kunst in Hessen und am Mittelrhein*, 11 (1971), 19–31.

[44]　The literature is immense, but a small part of the evidence is reviewed with illustrations and further references in Biddle, *Tomb of Christ*, 28–52.

[45]　McCormick, *Charlemagne's Survey*, 190–91, 195.

[46]　Einhard, *Vita Karoli*, ch. 26: '[Charlemagne] religionem christianam ... sanctissime et cum summa pietate coluit, ac proper hoc plurimae pulchritudinis basilicam Aquisgrani exstruxit auroque et argento ... adornavit' ('practised the Christian religion with great devotion and piety ... This explains why he built a cathedral of such beauty at Aachen, decorating it with gold and silver'): MGH SSRG, 25, ed. G.H. Pertz and G. Waitz (Hanover and Leipzig, 1911), 30; *Einhard and Notker the Stammerer: Two Lives of Charlemagne*, trans. L. Thorpe (Harmondsworth, 1969), 79.

5.12 and Table 5.4). The minting places of the seven coins with a letter beneath Charlemagne's bust (e.g. Figure 5.1c; Table 5.1–5.2) are likewise all, if correctly identified, on the great rivers. This tight distribution and the rarity of the coins argues for a limited issue over a short period of time, a view which supports the suggestion that the coins were minted in the last year of Charlemagne's reign.[47] The majority of the coins (23 out of 31 or 32) carry no mint-mark. They are in that sense anonymous, but it has reasonably been conjectured that the dies were cut at the palace in Aachen.[48] The reverse image, its proposed origin, and the possible location in Aachen of the structure of which the image (with its readily identifiable legend) may have been the immediate copy, suggest that no specific indication of the mint was needed. The distribution of the known finds supports the view that they were minted at Aachen.

The portrait on Charlemagne's coins proclaims a personal devotion to the Christian faith, made explicit on the reverse by his motto *XPICTIANA RELIGIO* surrounding a building he ardently believed to the place of Jesus' burial and Resurrection. From the time of his coronation in Rome on Christmas Day 800, when he was presented with the keys of the sepulchre and of the city, Charlemagne's feeling of personal responsibility for the holiest city of the Christian faith had been growing. Sometime towards the end of the decade he received a report on the location, physical and financial condition, and size of the religious communities in the Holy Land. What his intentions would have been had he lived we can never know. His coins provide the last known expression of the personal pilgrimage on which his mind, and with him the mind of his people, was to be set.

---

[47] See above, p. 115.
[48] Coupland, 'Charlemagne's coinage', 226.

Appendix 1

Portrait Coins of Charlemagne with the XPICTIANA RELIGIO Reverse

The purpose of this appendix and of Figure 5.12 is to emphasise the location of the mints and find-spots of deniers of this type. For the identification of the mints based on the letters placed below the bust on seven of the coins (Coupland **23–9**), see Table 5.2. For the find-spots of the coins, see the individual entries under the numbers assigned to the coins by Simon Coupland (printed here in bold) in his catalogue of the known examples of Charlemagne's Portrait deniers on pp. 147–54, where full details of each coin will be found, together with references to the most available illustrations. I am most grateful to Dr Coupland for making his catalogue available to me in advance of publication and for much helpful correspondence. For the denier from a cover of the Morienval gospel book (**22**), see Appendix 2.

Deniers of the *XPICTIANA RELIGIO* type illustrated in the present article are marked on Table 5.4 with an asterisk (*).

Table 5.1   The *XPICTIANA RELIGIO* reverse of Charlemagne's Portrait coins: analysis of the elements appearing in images of Types 1 and 2. The collection and/or find-spot, where known, are given in brackets after the Coupland catalogue number for each coin.

Reverse Type 1 double gable	*Obv. legend*	*Reverse Type 2 single gable*	*Obv. legend*
1 (Berlin)	1	**3**? (Berlin)	1
2 (Berlin, ?Trier)	1	**5** (Paris)	1
4 (Berlin, Dorestad)	1	**7**? (Bib. Municipale, Rouen)	1
6 (Banque de France)	1	**10** (Tiel)	1
8 (Vitenskapsmuseet, Trondheim)	1	**12b** (Amay, Arch. Hutoise, Huy)	1
9 (Cahn)	1	**14** (Paris)	2
11 (University of Zimbabwe)	1	**15** (Brussels, Dorestad)	2
12 (Elsen)	1	**16** (SHM, Birka)	2
13 (Berlin)	2 (*S* for *C* in *XPISTIANA*)	**17** (M&M Basel)	2
30 (Oosterbierum)	3, no letter?	**18** (Geldmus. Utrecht, ?Dorestad)	2
		19 (Elsen, Dodewaard)	2
Plus probably:		**20**? ('in France')	2

Reverse Type 1 double gable	*Obv. legend*	*Reverse Type 2 single gable*	*Obv. legend*
22 (Morienval)	2 (*S* for *C*; cf. **13**, above)	**21** (Künker)	2
		23 (Berlin)	3, letter C
		24 (Bank Leu)	3, letter C
		25 (Berlin)	3, letter F
		26 (Paris)	3, letter M
		27 (Berlin)	3, letter V
		28 (van der Chijs 36, ?Dorestad)	3, letter V
		29 (Geldmus. Utrecht, Minnertsga)	3, letter V
		31 (Market Weighton)	3, no letter?
Total: 10 coins (supposing **9** = **11**)	Total with Legend 1: 7 Total with Legend 2: 2 Total with Legend 3: 1 Total with obv. mint-letter: 0	Total: 21 coins	Total with Legend 1: 5 Total with Legend 2: 8 Total with Legend 3: 8 6 (possibly 7 or 8) with an obverse mint-letter

Table 5.2   *XPICTIANA RELIGIO* deniers by obverse inscription and probable mint (cf. Figure 5.1).

Obverse inscription	Mint-mark (under bust)	Mint	Coupland number
DN KARLVS IMP AVG REX F ET L	None	?Aachen (Lat. *Aquae Granni*; 9th cent. *Aquaegrani*)	**1–12b**
KARLVS IMP AVG	None	?Aachen	**13–22**
KAROLVS IMP AVG	C	Cologne (Lat. *Colonia Aggripinensis*; 9th cent. *Colonia*) or ?Coblenz (Lat. *Ad Confluentes*; 9th cent. *Confluentes*)	**23–4**
	F	?Frankfurt *Franconofurt* (794) or *Franconofurd* (see Figure 5.1c)	**25**
	M	?Mainz (Lat. *Mogontiacum*)	**26**
	V	?Worms (*Vormantia* since 6th cent.), *Wormantia* 8th/9th cent.	**27–8**
	B	?Bonn (Lat. *Bonna*) or ?Bingen am Rhein (Lat. *Bingium*; 9th cent. *Bingia*) or no letter	**29**
	No letter recognisable	-	**30–1**

Table 5.3   The *XPICTIANA RELIGIO* reverse of Charlemagne's Portrait coins: analysis of the elements appearing in images of Types 1 and 2 (31/2 examples, 29 available for study; for coin numbers, see Coupland, Chapter 6).

Elements common to both types:

- Horizontal entablature
- Four columns in two pairs, each column with a capital and base

- Podium approached by two steps
- Expanding-armed crosses on the apex and between the columns

Elements present/absent in Types 1 and 2 (coin numbers only given where the evidence is clear or possible):

Element (numbers refer to coins illustrated in Figs. 5.1–5)	Type 1 (double pediment)		Type 2 (single pediment)	
	Present	*Absent*	*Present*	*Absent*
Ball below cross on apex (e.g. **1, 13**)	1?, **2**, **4**, **8**, 9?, 11?, **13**	**6, 12**	**3**, 7?, **10**	14–18, 21, 23, 24?, 25–6, 27?, 28–9, 31
Acroteria vertical (e.g. **1, 7, 16, 21**)	**1, 2, 6**	**4, 8, 9, 11–13**	3?, 5?, **7, 14, 16–17, 21**	10?, **15, 18–19, 23–9, 31**
Decorative element(s) in tympanum (e.g. **16, 21**)	**2, 6, 12**	**1, 4, 8–9, 11, 13, 30**	**3, 7, 10, 14, 16,** 18?, 20?, **21**	5?, **15, 17–19,** 23?, **24–9, 31**
Elongated lower arm of inner cross (e.g. **1, 13**)	**1, 2, 4, 12, 13**	6?, 8?, 9?, **11, 30**	**5, 10, 14, 27**	**3, 7, 15–21, 25–6, 28–9, 31**

Table 5.4   List of known find-spots of *XPICTIANA RELIGIO* deniers, arranged by modern country (with date of find); numbers refer to entries in Simon Coupland's list, Chapter 6, pp. 147–54.

Belgium		
	Huy, prov. Liège (1991)	**12b**
France		
	Morienval abbey, dép. Oise (1868 or before), from the binding of a gospel book probably written at Rheims	**22*** (cf. Appendix 2)
	Uncertain location (*c.*2010)	**20**
Germany		
	Trier (Römerbrücke), Rheinland-Pfalz (*c.* 1963)	**2**
Netherlands		
	Dodewaard, prov. Gelderland (2008 or before)	**19**
	Minnertsga, prov. Friesland (1991)	**29***
	Oosterbierum, prov. Friesland (1998)	**30**

	Tiel, prov. Gelderland (1995)	**10**
	Wijk bij Duurstede (Hoard I), prov. Utrecht (1845/6)	**15***
	Wijk bij Duursetede (Dorestad), prov. Utrecht (1866 or before)	**4, 18, 28**
Norway		
	Moksnes, Frosta, Nord-Trondelag (grave find, 1838)†	**8**
Sweden		
	Birka (grave 66), Ekerö (1875)	**16***
UK		
	Market Weighton, East Yorkshire (before 2005)	**31**

Note: * denotes coins illustrated in this chapter. † I am indebted to Ildar H. Garipzanov for information on the correct find-spot: see his 'Karl den Stores kejsermønter i Norge og Sverige', *NNUM*, 5 (2005), 140–3.

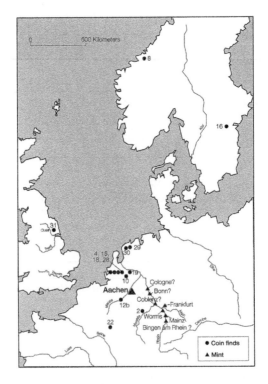

Figure 5.12   Distribution map showing the possible mints and find-spots (where known) of coins of Charlemagne's *XPICTIANA RELIGIO* type. (Drawn by Simon Hayfield).

Appendix 2

Carolingian Coins from the Binding of the Morienval Gospel Book

The ninth-century covers of the gospel book from Morienval Abbey in Picardy (formerly in the treasury of Noyon cathedral but now exhibited in the Hôtel de Ville) are among the finest to survive from the European early Middle Ages.[49]

Decorated with ivory plaques and borders, cast copper-alloy, and other materials, and set with relics and with two coins, they were first described by L'Abbé Eugène Müller in 1868 in an address to the Comité archéologique de Noyon marking the acquisition of the book by the cathedral that year.[50] Four years later he published a longer account, concerned principally with the manuscript itself, with a few pages devoted to the binding and including a lithograph (his pl. VI) showing the obverses of the two coins visible in position in copper capsules on the front cover.[51] These were placed one above, the other below, a central ivory plaque showing Christ in Glory handing a key to St Peter and a scroll to St. Paul (the *traditio legis*), and separated from it by two lesser plaques of ivory with the symbols of the evangelists, Matthew above and John below (then already missing). Müller drew on the numismatic knowledge of Dr Alexandre Colson, president of the Noyon archaeological committee, to confirm the identity of the coins as deniers of Charlemagne and Lothar with reverses showing a '*temple* avec la légende *christiana religio*'.[52]

In 1895 the gospel book was published again by Émile Molinier with superb heliogravure plates of both covers by Paul Dujardin of Paris.[53] His pl. XXVII, (reproduced here as Figure 5.13, with the coin enlarged in Figure 5.14) shows

---

[49] Noyon, cathedral library, s.n. Probably removed from Morienval Abbey during the Revolution, by 1832 the gospel book was in the possession of L'Abbé Santerre (E. Müller, 'Évangéliaire de la Cathédral de Noyon', *Comptes rendus et mémoires lus aux séances, Comité archéologique de Noyon, 1* (1872), 309–33, at 332 n. 3).

[50] E. Müller, *Quelques mots sur l'Évangéliaire de la Cathédrale de Noyon* (Noyon, 1868), esp. 9–12.

[51] Müller, 'Évangéliaire'; the binding is described at 327–33, the coins at 329. There is disagreement on which is the front and which is the back cover. I follow Müller and the overwhelming majority of modern scholars (Table 5.5) in regarding the cover with the ivory of Christ in Glory and the coins above and below as the front cover.

[52] Colson was a well-known numismatist, a founding member of the Société française de numismatique, whose collection included four Carolingian coins, two of which may be identifiable with nos. 25 and 44 in Simon Coupland's list (pp. 150, 153): A. Colson, 'Quatre deniers carlovingiens', *Annuaire de la Société française de numismatique et d'archéologie, 1* (1866), 478–80, pl. XL, 2 and 3.

[53] É. Molinier, 'L'Évangéliaire de l'Abbaye de Morienval conservé à la Cathédrale de Noyon', *Monuments et mémoires de la Fondation Eugène Piot, 2.2* (1895), 215–26, pls. XXVI, XXVII.

Figure 5.13 The later ninth-century upper cover of the Morienval Gospels as photographed in 1895 showing the obverse faces of silver deniers of Charlemagne and Lothar I, both of the *XPICTIANA RELIGIO* type, both still in position. The upper coin, a denier of Charlemagne, has been missing since at least 1937. (Molinier, 'Évangéliaire' (n. 53), planche XXVII).

Figure 5.14   Enlargement (rotated 180°) of the denier of Charlemagne from Figure 5.13.

the two coins still in position, with their obverse faces visible. Molinier was able to have the coins identified by his friend Maurice Prou (1861–1930), the leading French numismatist of their generation, who had long been working in the Cabinet des médailles of the Bibliothèque nationale and who was to produce a catalogue of its Carolingian coins the following year.[54] The Morienval coins were both detachable in 1895, for Prou was able to read their reverses,[55] and must already have been loose by 1868 when both faces were also seen.[56]

Both covers of the Morienval gospels were photographed at least five times before World War I, in 1872, 1886×1896, 1895, 1900, and 1914 (Table 5.5).[57] Both coins were still in place in the front cover in these photographs, but their orientation changes and the crimping of their copper-alloy mounts, already buckled in the lithograph published by Müller in 1872, differs in subsequent images.[58] The implication seems clear: the coins had been taken out and replaced already by 1872 and were taken out again on at least one subsequent occasion, when they were identified in 1895, then replaced again before 1900 and perhaps subsequently.

---

[54]   J.M. Prou, *Les monnaies carolingiennes: catalogue des monnaies françaises de la Bibliothèque nationale* (Paris, 1896).

[55]   Molinier, 'Évangéliaire', 219–20, acknowledging his debt for the identifications to 'mon excellent confrère et ami Maurice Prou, du Cabinet des Médailles'.

[56]   Müller, *Quelques mots*, 10, described the reverse of the coins as 'semblable', and confirmed this in 'Évangéliaire', 329.

[57]   1872: Müller, as n. 49; 1886×1896: *Album archéologique*, Société des Antiquaires de Picardie, fasc. 1–11 (Amiens), exact date and fasc. not ascertainable; 1895: Molinier, as n. 53; 1900: *Catalogue officiel illustré de L'Exposition Rétrospective de l'Art Français des Origines à 1800* (Paris, 1900), no. 24; 1914: Goldschmidt, as n. 60.

[58]   The head of Charlemagne on the upper coin is as follows: 1872: 12 o'clock; 1886×1896: 12 o'clock; 1895: 6 o'clock; 1900: 12 o'clock; 1914: 12 o'clock. The head of Lothar on the lower coin is as follows: 1872: 10.30 o'clock; 1886×1896: 7.30 o'clock; 1895: 3 o'clock; 1900: 1 o'clock; 1914: 1 o'clock; 1956 (Masson, as n. 62): 11 o'clock; 1965 (Steenbock, as n. 69): 11 o'clock; 1987 (Inventaire, as n. 64): 10 o'clock.

Table 5.5   Identifications of front and back cover of the Morienval Gospels.

Traditio legis (with two coins, one only by 1937, possibly by 1932) as front cover	Crucifixion (with relics) as front cover
Müller 1868	*Molinier 1895
*Müller 1872	Boinet 1906
*Album 1886×1896	
*Paris Expo. 1900 (?) (*see note*)	
*Goldschmidt 1914	
London exhibition 1932	
Paris 1937	
Paris 1954	
*Masson 1956	
*Steenbock 1965	
*Vision 1987	
*Inventaire 1987	
Total: 12	*Total:* 2

Note: * designates publications with covers illustrated. Full references to works cited are in notes 49, 50, 53, 57, 59–62, 64, 69, 73 and 75. In the *Catalogue officiel* of the 1900 Paris exposition, the covers were photographed as one, laid out flat, 'Crucifixion' to left, *traditio legis* to right, the latter therefore the upper.

Although both coins were still in position when Boinet wrote in 1905,[59] and are still there in the photograph published by Goldschmidt in 1914,[60] the denier of Charlemagne was subsequently lost. The catalogue entry for the London exhibition of 1932 refers to two coins, but the entry may have been written and printed on the basis of Goldschmidt's catalogue, and the coin only found to be missing on the arrival of the book in London.[61] It was certainly missing by the Paris exhibition of 1937,[62] and when Jean Lafaurie wrote his article

---

[59]   A. Boinet, 'L'Évangéliaire de Morienval à la Cathédrale de Noyon', *Congrès archéologique de France, 72* (1906), 637–50, at 639.

[60]   A. Goldschmidt, *Die Elfenbeinskulpturen* (4 vols., Berlin, 1914–26), 1, 59 (no. 119, Taf. LII).

[61]   *Commemorative Catalogue of the Exhibition of French Art, 1200–1900, Royal Academy of Arts, London, 1932* (London, 1933), 220 (no. 1032), where the coins are described as 'gold'. Molinier, 'Évangéliaire', 219, described them as as 'portant des traces de dorure'.

[62]   *Chefs d'Œuvre de l'Art Français, Palais National des Arts* (Paris, 1937), 566 (no. 1249); *Les manuscrits à peintures en France du VIIe au XIIe siècle*, Bibliothèque nationale (Paris, 1954), no.

on Charlemagne's Portrait coinage in 1978.[63] It was still missing and even its copper capsule had been removed by the time the covers were inventoried and photographed in 1987, when the lower coin, the denier of Lothar, was still in position, although differently oriented.[64]

The upper coin was a Portrait denier of Charlemagne with the obverse legend *KARLVS IMP AVG* (Figure 5.14) and with a 'temple' on the reverse surrounded by the legend *XPISTIANA RELIGIO*. The letter 'S' in the reverse legend appears (unless it is an error in transcription) to have been Prou's reading.[65] Grierson noted a denier of Charlemagne of this type with the spelling *XPISTIANA* in his seminal article of 1965 (illustrated here as Figure 5.2b).[66] Any gilded denier of Charlemagne of this type appearing on the market should be carefully checked against records of this lost specimen.

The lower coin was also a Portrait denier with the obverse legend *LOTARIVS IMP AVG* (Figure 5.13) and on the reverse 'le même attribut et la même légende que sur la pièce précédente': in other words, a denier of Lothar I (840–55) with the letter 'S' instead of a Greek 'C' in the reverse legend.[67]

When and where was the Morienval gospel book written and the cover provided, if indeed they are of the same date? Bernhard Bischoff's considered view, published posthumously in 1998, was that the manuscript was written in the third quarter of the ninth century.[68] Frauke Steenbock in her survey of early medieval bindings published in 1965 concluded that the binding was to be dated to the tenth century, although believing that the manuscript was earlier, of the second half of the ninth century.[69] Peter Lasko in his revised edition of *Ars Sacra*, published in 1994, thought that the binding dated 'from the late ninth

---

49 (pp. 25–6); A. Masson, *La Bibliothèque du Chapitre de Noyon et L'Évangéliaire de Morienval* (Noyon, 1956).

    [63]   J. Lafaurie, 'Les monnaies impériales de Charlemagne', *Comptes-rendus des séances de l'Académie des Inscriptions et Belles-Lettres, 122e année, 1* (1978), 154–76, at 171 (no. 27).

    [64]   http://inventaire.picardie.fr/docs/PALISSYIM60000321.html (accessed 1 May 2013); and cf. n. 58. See also, C. Dupont-Logié, 'La reliure de l'évangéliaire de Morienval', in *La Ville de Noyon: catalogue de l'exposition 'Noyon, mille ans d'art et d'architecture'*, Cahiers de l'Inventaire, 10 (Noyon, 1987), 172, figs. 180–81 (photographs of the front and back covers by Vision à Noyon).

    [65]   Molinier, 'Évangéliaire', 219–20.

    [66]   Grierson, 'Money and coinage', 522.

    [67]   Coupland, 'Lothar I', discusses Lothar's Portrait coinage on 160–64, concluding that it was most probably issued to mark his coronation by the pope in Italy in 823 (164).

    [68]   B. Bischoff (B. Ebersperger (ed.)), *Katalog der festländischen Handschriften des neunten Jahrhunderts* (2 vols., Wiesbaden, 2004), 2, no. 3637.

    [69]   Reproduced in F. Steenbock, *Der Kirchliche Prachteinband im frühen Mittelalter: von den Anfängen biz zum Beginn der Gotik* (Berlin, 1965), no. 37, Abb. 55.

or early tenth century.[70] The evidence of the coins does not seem to have been given much weight. The coin of Lothar I provides only a *terminus post quem* of 823 if Coupland's dating is correct, and would easily fit Bischoff's dating of the manuscript to 850–75. Perhaps that is where the matter should stand, pending a technical examination of the relationship between the binding and the written leaves it holds.

Where was the binding produced? Lasko thought 'probably… in Lotharingia'.[71] The view of French scholarship is clear: 'sans doute exécuté à Reims au 9e siècle'.[72] Wherever the binding was made, the coins were probably no longer still in circulation. The place of production of the binding is therefore equivalent to an archaeological find-spot. The coin of Charlemagne from the binding, now no. **22** in Simon Coupland's list (see below, Chapter 6), is therefore shown on Figure 5.12 in the region of Reims/Metz.

Why include these coins in the binding? It has been suggested that they might have been caps for relics placed below them in the copper capsules provided in the binding.[73] Inscriptions on the back binding claim that it contained relics of the Wood of Paradise (the True Cross), of the Holy Sepulchre, and of Calvary, as well as of five saints. The answer may lie in the argument of the main part of this chapter: that the temple-like building surrounded by the legend *XPICTIANA RELIGIO* on the reverse of both these coins may be a depiction of the Tomb of Christ in Jerusalem. If the coins were originally set to display their reverses, with the gilded image of the tomb, the Holy Sepulchre, rather than the heads of the Carolingian emperors, the coins themselves would in a sense be relics.[74]

---

[70] P. Lasko, *Ars Sacra 800–1200*, 2nd ed. (New Haven CT and London, 1994), 89–90.

[71] Ibid.

[72] Ministère de la culture, Région Picardie – Inventaire générale: link as in n. 64.

[73] Müller, 'Évangélaire', 329; cf. the questions raised by Molinier, 'Évangéliaire', 219.

[74] In 1956 André Masson (*Bibliothèque du Chapitre de Noyon*, 24 n.) suggested that a 'planche hors texte' in an unspecified article by Müller indicated that it may have been the reverses of the coins which were originally displayed in the binding. It has not so far proved possible to identify this image which might be an insert into a copy of Müller in a Noyon library. Such an image would support the view that the coins were probably included as 'relics' because they carried an image of the tomb of Christ, a fragment of the rock of which was included among the relics in the back cover.

Chapter 6

The Portrait Coinage of Charlemagne

Simon Coupland

The Portrait coins minted by Charlemagne at the end of his reign are the most exhaustively studied and most frequently reproduced of all Carolingian coinage types, undoubtedly because of the quality of their portraiture and the iconic power of the imperial image. Philip Grierson provided an important overview of the coinage in his contribution to the magisterial survey of Charlemagne and his reign which appeared alongside the Aachen exhibition of 1965.[1] In 1978 Lafaurie provided the first catalogue of all known finds, listing 29 specimens, of which he illustrated 14 (one by a line drawing),[2] and in 2002 Bernd Kluge was able to add another six coins to this list, four of them finds from the Netherlands and the other two recent acquisitions by the Münzkabinett in Berlin (omitting one coin in Lafaurie's list which was lost: no. 22 below).[3] In the meantime a unique coin of Rouen listed by all three authors but purportedly lost and even judged of doubtful authenticity had been rediscovered and published by Jacqueline Delaporte.[4] Since then a combination of detector-finds, auctions, and detective work in coin collections and numismatic literature has uncovered another ten coins, bringing the total of known specimens available for study to 45. The list below includes all coins known to me up to July 2014.

In the nineteenth century these coins were attributed to several different rulers, but there is now general agreement that they were all struck by Charlemagne at the end of his reign. There has been much discussion about the dating of the type, with Lafaurie's suggestion that they were produced from 812 evidently winning over Grierson, to judge from *MEC* 1, 209 and 524. In

---

[1] P. Grierson, 'Money and coinage under Charlemagne', in *Karl der Grosse, Lebenswerk und Nachleben*, ed. W. Braunfels (4 vols, Düsseldorf, 1965), 1, 501–36 (repr. in his *Dark Age Numismatics* (London, 1979), no. XVIII).

[2] J. Lafaurie, 'Les monnaies impériales de Charlemagne', *Comptes-rendus de l'académie des inscriptions et belles-lettres, 122.1* (1978), 154–76.

[3] B. Kluge, 'Die Bildnispfennige Karls des Großen', in *Moneta Mediævalis. Studia numizmatyczne i historyczne ofiarowane Profesorowi Stanisławowi Suchodolskiemu w 65. rocznicę urodzin*, ed. R. Kiersnowski, S.K. Kuczyński, M. Męclewska, M. Mielczarek and B. Paszkiewicz (Warsaw, 2002), 367–77, pl. 19–20.

[4] J. Delaporte, 'Un denier de Charlemagne frappé à Rouen', in *La Neustrie. Les pays au nord de la Loire de 650 à 850*, ed. H. Atsma (2 vols., Sigmaringen, 1989), 2, 41–3.

2002 Kluge suggested that production began in 800/801, with specimens struck over several years as memorial or ceremonial coins.[5] The number of single-finds is, however, considerably higher than that of other such token coinages, and Kluge has recently proposed that production took place to mark his son Louis's coronation as co-emperor in September 813.[6] This has more historical basis than the similar suggestion of Garipzanov that Charlemagne's chancery adopted a new imperial title in the summer of 813, when the Portrait coinage was introduced.[7] Both theories would account for the remarkably small number known: this figure of 45 coins compares with a current total of some 275 deniers and 43 oboles for the Portrait coinage of Louis the Pious, which appears to have been minted only between 814 and 816.[8]

Deniers illustrated in Martin Biddle's chapter (pp. 115–44 above) are asterisked (*). Nos. 12, 13, 15, 18, 21, 35, 37 and 40 are illustrated here as Figure 6.1a–g. Where known, at least one (sometimes more than one) illustration published elsewhere is listed at the end of each other entry. No attempt has been made to provide a complete list of the available images. Confusingly, the numbers on almost all the published illustrations are peculiar to the illustrations themselves and do not correspond with the numbers given to the coins in the accompanying lists or articles.

Finally, mention should also be made of a remarkable gold coin of Arles found during excavations at the Carolingian palace of Ingelheim in 1996.[9] Although the coin was not struck from any of the dies known to have been used to produce the silver coinage, it is of the same style as the latter and was evidently struck rather than cast, so it should almost certainly be regarded as a 'coin struck in gold from dies normally employed to strike silver pennies', in the words of *MEC*.[10] In this it is very different from the other gold Portrait 'coin' of Charlemagne, from Dorestad, whose date and significance have been much discussed and much disputed.[11] It is unlikely that any of these gold coins (others are known from Charlemagne's reign without a portrait) were intended

---

[5]   Kluge, 'Die Bildnispfennige Karls des Großen', 375

[6]   B. Kluge, 'Bildnisdenar Karls des Großen', in *Karl der Große / Charlemagne: Orte der Macht. Katalog*, ed. F. Pohle (Aachen, 2014), 150-1.

[7]   I.H. Garipzanov, 'Karl den Stores kejsermønter i Norge og Sverige – Forslag til nydatering', *NNUM* 2005; S. Coupland, 'Carolingian single finds and the economy of the early ninth century', *NC, 170* (2010), 287–319, at 297–8.

[8]   Coupland, 'Carolingian single finds', 298–300.

[9]   P.-H. Martin, 'Eine Goldmünze Karls des Großen', *Numismatisches Nachrichtenblatt, 46* (August 1997), 351–5.

[10]   *MEC* 1, 327.

[11]   *MEC* 1, 328.

to have any economic function; more probable is that they served some kind of ceremonial purpose.[12]

Expansion of obverse legends: D[ominus] N[oster] KARLVS IMP[erator] AVG[ustus] REX F[rancorum] ET L[angobardorum] ('Our lord Charles, emperor augustus, king of the Franks and of the Lombards'); and KARLVS IMP[erator] AVG[ustus] ('Charles, emperor augustus').

Christiana religio

Obv. D N KARLVS IMP AVG REX F ET L. Rev. XPICTIANA RELIGIO, church (traditionally referred to as a temple). MG no. 314; Depeyrot 2008, no. 1171.

*1. Berlin, Staatliche Museen 18202746, 1.68g (Kluge: from the collection of H. Dannenberg). Grierson 1965, nos 21 and 38; Lafaurie 1978, no. 1; Kluge 2002, no. 1. Illus. Grierson 1965, Pl. I, 21, Pl. IV, 38 (x2); MG, Pl. X, 314. *Same O die as nos. 4 and 9 (11).*

2. Berlin, Staatliche Museen, 1.64g (Kluge: from the collection of F. Stefan). Kluge 2002, no. 2. Illus. Kluge 2002, Taf. 19, Abb. II.1. *It seems highly likely that this is the coin found near the Römerbrücke at Trier, Rheinland-Pfalz, Germany, c. 1963, whose subsequent whereabouts were unknown: Gilles 1985, 46, no. 29. Same O die as no. 6.*

3. Berlin, Staatliche Museen, 1.52g. Lafaurie 1978, no. 7; Kluge 2002, no. 3. Illus. Lafaurie 1978, Pl. II, 24; Kluge 2002, Taf. 19, Abb II, 2. *There is a mystery surrounding this coin, in that it was acquired by the Münzkabinett in Berlin from the collection of F. Stefan in 1993, and is still in the Berlin collection (confirmed by Prof. Kluge 6 June 2013). However, an identical coin (in wear and damage as well as a die identity) was offered for sale by Münzen und Medaillen Deutschland in their auction 8 in Stuttgart on 10 May 2001 (lot 538), then sold by the same firm in their auction 19 on 16 May 2006 (lot 1424). Both these catalogues and Kluge list the coin as having been previously sold by Münzen und Medaillen AG Basel in auction 7, December 1948, lot 158. It is very likely the coin with the same weight from the Rousseau collection: de Longpérier 586. The fact that the coin(s) is/are struck from the same reverse die (but not the same obverse) as no. 7 guarantees the authenticity of at least one of them. Only further examination and ideally analysis of both specimens could permit a definite judgement.*

4. Berlin, Staatliche Museen, 1.24g, chipped; found at Wijk bij Duurstede, Utrecht, Netherlands: van der Chijs 1866, pl. XII, 38 (identified on 133 as owned by Balfoort, all of whose coins were found at the site of Dorestad);

---

[12] Cf. *MEC* 1, 329.

Gariel 1883–84, pl. XII, 170; H. Meyer sale (Rollin and Feuardent, 26 May–14 June 1902), lot 103. Lafaurie 1978, no. 5; Kluge 2002, no. 4. Illus. Kluge 2002, Taf. 20, Abb. 7. *Although the Berlin coin has an internal roof line absent from the drawings in van der Chijs and Gariel, the appearance of the coin is otherwise comparable, and the Meyer sale catalogue explicitly states that this is the coin illustrated by Gariel, which is the van der Chijs specimen. The congruence of the weights also supports this identification. Same O die as no. 1, same O and R dies as no. 9 (11).*

5. Paris, Bibliothèque Nationale, 1.42g, broken. Gariel 1883–84, pl. XII, 169; Grierson 1965, no. 39; Prou 1892, no. 982; Lafaurie 1978, no. 2; Kluge 2002, no. 5. Illus. Grierson 1965, Pl. IV, 39 (x2).

6. Paris, Banque de France (Lafaurie: ex E. Bourgey, 2 December 1964, lot 26). Lafaurie 1978, no. 8; Kluge 2002, no. 6. Illus. Lafaurie 1978, Pl. II, 23. *Same O die as no. 2.*

7. Rouen, Bibliothèque Municipale, damaged (Lafaurie: from the collection of B. Lecarpentier). Lafaurie 1978, no. 3; Kluge 2002, no. 7. Illus. Lafaurie 1978, Pl. II, 21, Pl. IV, 21 (x3). *Same R die as no. 3.*

8. Trondheim, Vitenskapsmuseet, 1.69g; found in a grave at Moksnes, Norway, 1838. Lafaurie 1978, no. 4; Kluge 2002, no. 8. Illus. Kluge 2002, Abb. 8; *NNUM* 2005, 141 (x3).

9. Location unknown, 1.6g. Cahn auction 59, 14 March 1928, lot 145. Lafaurie 1978, no. 6; Kluge 2002, no. 9. Illus. Lafaurie 1978, Pl. II, 22. *Same O die as no. 1; same O and R dies as no. 4; almost certainly the coin listed as no. 11 below: see note there.*

10. Location unknown, 1.60g; found at Tiel, Gelderland, Netherlands 1995: NUMIS 1029304. Kluge 2002, no. 10. Illus. Kluge 2002, Taf. 19, Abb. II, 3.

11. Harare, University of Zimbabwe, Courtauld collection; reportedly ex Naylor collection (Spink 5 May 1928) *(Spink were unfortunately unable to provide any corroboration of this information).* Coupland 2005, no. 1. Illus. Coupland 2005, Figure 9.1. *Comparison of the photographs and the correspondence of the sale/purchase dates strongly suggest that this is the coin also listed as no. 9 above.*

*12. Location unknown, 1.37g. J. Elsen auction 60, 11 December 1999, lot 1045. *My thanks to Guido Cornelissens for information about this coin.* Illus. Elsen auction catalogue 60, lot 1045.

Obv. KARLVS IMP AVG. MG no. 317 (incorrect legend); Depeyrot 2008, no. 1166 (incorrect legend).

*13. Berlin, Staatliche Museen 18238797, 1.37g; ex Gariel-Ferrari 1911. Lafaurie 1978, no. 24; Kluge 2002, no. 11. Illus. MG, Pl. X, 317.

14. Paris, Bibliothèque Nationale, 1.71 g. Gariel 1883–84, pl. XLV, 57; Prou 1892, no. 983; Grierson 1965, nos 20 and 25; Lafaurie 1978, no. 22; Kluge 2002, no. 12. Illus. Grierson 1965, Pl. I, 20, Pls. II and III, 25 (x2); Lafaurie 1978, Pl. III, 34; Coupland 2005, Figure 9.7; MG, Pl. X, 318 [sic].

*15. Brussels, Bibliothèque royale de Belgique, 1.56g, damaged; Wijk bij Duurstede I hoard 1845/46, Utrecht, Netherlands (1.65g when found): *RBN* 1857, pl. V, 4, Völckers 1965, no. III, 90. Gariel 1883–84, pl. XLV, 59; Lafaurie 1978, no. 23; Kluge 2002, no. 13. Illus. *RBN* 1857, Pl. V, 4.

*16. Stockholm, Kungliga Myntkabinettet, looped; found at Birka, Ekerö, Sweden, grave 66. Grierson 1965, no. 26; Lafaurie 1978, no. 25; Kluge 2002, no. 14. Illus. Grierson 1965, Pls. II and III, 26 (x2); *NNUM* 2005, 141 (x3).

17. Location unknown; Münzen und Medaillen Basel auction IX, 21–22 June 1951, lot 368; Crédit de la Bourse auction, 26–28 April 1993, lot 66. Lafaurie 1978, no. 26; Kluge 2002, no. 15. Illus. Lafaurie 1978, Pl. III, 33.

18. Utrecht, Geldmuseum HNM 03121, 1.45g; probably found at Wijk bij Duurstede, Utrecht, Netherlands. Illus. van der Chijs 1866, pl. XII, 37.

19. Private collection, 1.66g; found at Dodewaard, Gelderland, Netherlands (*pers. comm.*). J. Elsen auction 97, 13 September 2008, lot 599. Illus. Coupland 2010, 297 (x1.5).

20. Location unknown, 2.2g, gilded, looped; found in France *c.* 2010 (<www.la-detection.com/dp/message-105741.htm>). No known illustration.

*21. Location unknown, 1.53g. Künker auction 205, 12–13 March 2012, lot 1405. Illus. Künker auction catalogue 205, lot 1405; <www.mcsearch.info/record.html?id=717122> (accessed 29 April 2013).

22. Location unknown. Formerly mounted in a book cover in Morienval Abbey, Picardy, France (Noyon, cathedral treasury, s. ix³/⁴; Bischoff 1998, no. 3637); gilded on one or both faces; had disappeared by 1965 (see Martin Biddle's chapter, Appendix II, pp. 139–44). Lafaurie 1978, no. 27; cf. Kluge 2002, 370, n. 3. Illus. Molinier 1895, 219, Pl. XXVII.

Obv. KAROLVS IMP AVG.

With C under bust: MG no. 315 (incorrect legends), Depeyrot 2008, no. 1167.

23. Berlin, Staatliche Museen 18202749, 1.55g (Kluge: ex Dannenberg 1892). Grierson 1965, no. 27; Lafaurie 1978, no. 17; Kluge 2002, no. 16. Illus. Grierson 1965, Pls. II and III, 27 (x2). *Probable die duplicate of no. 24: see the comments there.*

24. Location unknown; Bank Leu list 17, January 1978, no. 17. Lafaurie 1978, no. 18; Kluge 2002, no. 17. Illus. Lafaurie 1978, Pl. III, 31. *It is impossible*

to be categorical given the poor state of both the image and the coin, but this appears to be a die duplicate of no. 23.

With F under bust: MG no. 319; Depeyrot 2008, no. 1168.

* 25. Berlin, Staatliche Museen 18202748, 1.71g; ex Gariel-Ferrari 1911. Gariel 1883–84, pl. XLV, 55; Grierson 1965, no. 28; Lafaurie 1978, no. 19; Kluge 2002, no. 18. Illus. Grierson 1965, Pls. II and III, 28 (x2), MG, Pl. X, 319.

With M under bust: MG no. 318; Depeyrot 2008, no. 1169.

26. Paris, Bibliothèque Nationale, 1.60g, chipped; ex Rousseau collection: de Longpérier 245. Gariel 1883–84, pl. XLV, 56; Prou 1892, no. 981; Grierson 1965, nos 19 and 29; Lafaurie 1978, no. 20; Kluge 2002, no. 19. Illus. Grierson 1965, Pl. I, 19, Pls. II and III, 29 (x2); Lafaurie 1978, Pl. III, 30, Pl. IV, 30 (x4); Coupland 2005, Figure 9.3 (x 3), 9.4.

With V under bust: MG no. 316; Depeyrot 2008, no. 1170.

27. Berlin, Staatliche Museen, 1.18 g, damaged; ex Gariel-Ferrari 1911. Grierson 1965, no. 30; Lafaurie 1978, no. 21; Kluge 2002, no. 20. Illus. Grierson 1965, Pls. II and III, 30 (x3).
28. Location unknown, 1.35g; found at Wijk bij Duurstede, Utrecht, Netherlands (van der Chijs 1866, 132: 'Balfoort collection': see no. 4 above). Illus. van der Chijs 1866, pl. XII, 36. *Although only a drawing exists of this coin, the illustrations in van der Chijs are clear and reliable enough to determine that it is not the same coin as no. 27.*

With B under bust, or no letter.

* 29. Utrecht, Geldmuseum 1995–1005, 1.39g; found at Minnertsga, Friesland, Netherlands 1991: NUMIS 1020635. Kluge 2002, no. 22 ('no letter'). Illus. Kluge 2002, Taf. 20, Abb. 5; Coupland 2005, Figure 9. 5.

With no recognisable letter under bust.

30. Location unknown, 1.37g; found at Oosterbierum, Friesland, Netherlands 1998: NUMIS 1022081. Kluge 2002, no. 21. Illus. Kluge 2002, Taf. 20, Abb. 4.
31. Location unknown; found at Market Weighton, East Yorkshire, UK. Coupland 2005, 6. Illus. Coupland 2005, Figure 9.6.

Arles

Obv. D N KARLVS IMP AVG REX F ET L. Rev. +ARELATO, with points in legend, town gate. MG no. 198; Depeyrot 2008, no. 58.

32. Berlin, Staatliche Museen 18202750, 1.65g, gilded and made into a brooch; ex Gariel-Ferrari 1911. Gariel 1883–84, pl. V, 9; Grierson 1965, no. 37; Lafaurie 1978, no. 9; Kluge 2002, no. 23. Illus. Grierson 1965, Pl. IV, 37 (x2). *Contra Kluge, it is unlikely that this is the coin found at Dorestad and recorded by de Coster in RBN 1852, 390, since Gariel records that he had acquired it from M. Charvet, who had in turn acquired it from the Comte de Vesvrotte: Gariel 1883–84, vol. 2, 98.*

33. Lyon, Musée des Beaux-Arts, 1.75g; probably found at Wijk bij Duurstede, Utrecht, Netherlands. Grierson 1965, no. 36; Lafaurie 1978, no. 10; Kluge 2002, no. 24. Illus. Grierson 1965, Pls. II–III, 36 (x2); Lafaurie 1978, Pl. II, 25. *By contrast, this is quite probably the single find from Wijk bij Duurstede mentioned by de Coster (Völckers 1965, no. III, 87), given that other coins of Charlemagne minted in Lyon were passed on by him to M. Morin of Lyon (see RBN 1852, 375 and RBN 1855, 19) and at least one of these – no. 34 below – subsequently found its way into the collection of the Musée des Beaux-Arts.*

Obv. KAROLVS IMP AVG.

34. Lyon, Musée des Beaux-Arts, 1.50g; ex M. Morin, ex L. de Coster: see *RBN* 1855, 19 and pl. I, 5. Grierson 1965, no. 34; Lafaurie 1978, no. 11; Kluge 2002, no. 25. Illus. Grierson 1965, Pls. II–III, 34 (x2); Lafaurie 1978, Pl. II, 26.

Obv. CARLVS IMP AVG. Depeyrot 2008, no. 58B.

35. Cambridge, Fitzwilliam Museum, *MEC* 1, no. 748, 0.84g, damaged and badly corroded; found at Mainz, Germany 1980: see C. Stoess, 'Die Münzen', in *Die frühmittelalterlichen Lesefunde aus der Löhrstrasse (Baustelle Hilton II) in Mainz*, ed. E. Wamers (Mainz, 1994), 177–90, at 180 (no. 34); cf. Haertle 1997, no. 660/002. Ex Vecchi-Schwer auction 1, 13 May 1983, lot 633; Busso Peus auction 16, 18 March 1982, lot 606. Kluge 2002, no. 26. Illus. *MEC* 1.748.

Dorestad

Obv. KAROLVS IMP AVG. Rev. DORESTADO, ship. MG no. 105; Depeyrot 2008, no. 412.

36. Brussels, Bibliothèque royale de Belgique, 1.48g. Found at Wijk bij Duurstede, Utrecht, Netherlands: van der Chijs 1866, 134, pl. XXII, 5; Völckers 1965, no. III, 88. Gariel 1883–84, pl. VI, 43; Grierson 1965, no. 31; Lafaurie 1978, no. 15; Kluge 2002, no. 27. Illus. Grierson 1965, Pls. II–III, 31 (x2); Lafaurie 1978, Pl. III, 28; Coupland 2005, Figure 9.8.
37. Private collection, unpublished, damaged and badly corroded; found in the Netherlands 2013: *pers. comm.* Guido Cornelissens. No published illustration.

Lyon

Obv. KAROLVS IMP AVG. Rev. LVGDVNVM, town gate. MG no. 167; Depeyrot 2008, no. 522.

38. Berlin, Staatliche Museen 18202759, 1.91g; found at Achlum, Friesland, Netherlands 1852: Gariel 1883–84, pl. XXIV, 90. Grierson 1965, nos 22 and 35; Lafaurie 1978, no. 12; Kluge 2002, no. 28 ('Posthume Prägung unter Ludwig dem Frommen'). Grierson 1965, Pls. I.22 and II–III, 35 (x2); Lafaurie 1978, Pl. III, 28.

Melle

Obv. KAROLVS IMP AVG. Rev. METALL GERMAN, coin dies and hammers. MG no. 313 ('indeterminate'), Depeyrot 2008, no. 638.

39. Paris, Bibliothèque Nationale, 1.52g. Gariel 1883–84, pl. IX, 97; Prou 1892, no. 972 ('Charles le Gros'); Grierson 1965, no. 24; Lafaurie 1978, no. 28; Kluge 2002, no. 32. Illus. Grierson 1965, Pl. I.24; Lafaurie 1978, Pl. III, 32. *Die duplicate of no. 40.*
40. Utrecht, Geldmuseum HNM 03120, 1.4g; found at Wijk bij Duurstede, Utrecht, Netherlands: see *RBN* 1855, 20; Völckers 1965, no. III, 89 ('Verbleib?', 'Karl der Dicke?'). Lafaurie 1978, no. 29; Kluge 2002, no. 33. Illus. *RBN* 1855, pl. I, 6; van der Chijs 1866, pl. XII, 35. *Die duplicate of no. 39.*

Obv. D N KARLVS IMP AVG REX F ET L

41. Leiden, Rijksmuseum van Oudheden, 1.05g; found at Wijk bij Duurstede, Utrecht, Netherlands 1969: NUMIS 1033478. Kluge 2002, no. 34 ('Privatbesitz'). Illus. Kluge 2002, Taf. 20, Abb. 6 (x2); Coupland 2005, Figure 9.2; Coupland 2010, 308 (x1.5).

Quentovic

Obv. KAROLVS IMP AVG. Rev. QVENTVVV ..., ship. MG no. 121a; Depeyrot 2008, no. 800.

42. Cambridge, Fitzwilliam Museum, *MEC* 1, no. 749, 1.65g. Grierson 1965, nos 23 and 32; Lafaurie 1978, no. 16; Kluge 2002, no. 29. Illus. Grierson 1965, Pls. I.23 and II–III, 32 (x2); Lafaurie 1978, Pl. III, 29; *MEC* 1.749 (x2); Coupland 2005, Figure 9.9.

Rouen

Obv. KAROLVS IMP AVG. Rev. +RODOMAGVM, town gate. MG no. 142; Depeyrot 2008, no. 875B (previously 881).

43. Rouen, Bibliothèque municipale, 1.60g (Delaporte: from the collection of B. Lecarpentier). Gariel 1883–84, pl. XXIV, 92 (reproducing an earlier line drawing); Lafaurie 1978, no. 13; Kluge 2002, no. 30 ('Standort nicht nachweisbar'). Illus. Delaporte 1989, 41 (x1.5).

Trier

Obv. KAROLVS I ... VG. Rev. TREVER ..., town gate. MG no. 116; Depeyrot 2008, no. 1064.

44. Berlin, Staatliche Museen 18202757, 1.76g (NB MG and Depeyrot both give '1.96g'), mounted, damaged. Grierson 1965, no. 33; Lafaurie 1978, no. 14; Kluge 2002, no. 31. Illus. Grierson 1965, Pls. II–III, 33 (x2); Lafaurie 1978, Pl. III, 27.

Postscript:

Following the completion of this list a further coin has come to light:

12b. Amay, Archéologie Hutoise; found during excavations in Huy, Belgium. Willems 1990–91, 28, 42–3 (mistakenly described as a coin of Louis the Pious). Illus. Willems 1990–91, 42. *My thanks to Wolfram Giertz for bringing this coin to my attention.*

References

Bischoff 1998: B. Bischoff, *Katalog der festländischen Handschriften des neunten Jahrhunderts* (2 vols, Wiesbaden, 1998).
Coupland 2005: S. Coupland, 'Charlemagne's coinage: ideology and economy', in *Charlemagne: Empire and Society*, ed. J. Story (Manchester, 2005), 211–29.
Coupland 2010: S. Coupland, 'Carolingian single finds and the economy of the early ninth century', *NC, 170* (2010), 287–319.
Delaporte 1989: J. Delaporte, 'Un denier de Charlemagne frappé à Rouen', in *La Neustrie. Les pays au nord de la Loire de 650 à 850*, ed. H. Atsma (2 vols, Sigmaringen), 2, 41–3.
De Longpérier: A. de Longpérier, *Notice des monnaies françaises de M. Jean Rousseau* (Paris, 1847).
Depeyrot 2008: G. Depeyrot, *Le numéraire carolingien: corpus des monnaies*, 3rd ed. (Wetteren, 2008).
Gariel 1883–84: E. Gariel, *Les monnaies royales de France sous la race carolingienne* (2 vols, Strasbourg, 1883–84).
Gilles 1985: K.J. Gilles, 'Fundmünzen der sächsischen Kaiserzeit aus dem Trierer Land', *Funde und Ausgrabungen im Bezirk Trier, 17* (1985), 40–47.
Grierson 1965: P. Grierson, 'Money and coinage under Charlemagne', in *Karl der Grosse, Lebenswerk und Nachleben*, ed. W. Braunfels (4 vols., Düsseldorf, 1965), 1, 501–36 (repr. in his *Dark Age Numismatics* (London, 1979), no. XVIII).
Haertle: C.M. Haertle, *Karolingische Münzfunde aus dem 9. Jahrhundert* (2 vols, Cologne, 1997).
Kluge 2002: B. Kluge, 'Die Bildnispfennige Karls des Großen', in *Moneta Mediævalis. Studia numizmatyczne i historyczne ofiarowane Profesorowi Stanisławowi Suchodolskiemu w 65. rocznicę urodzin*, ed. R. Kiersnowski, S.K. Kuczyński, M. Męclewska, M. Mielczarek and B. Paszkiewicz (Warsaw, 2002), 367–77, pl. 19–20.
Lafaurie 1978: J. Lafaurie, 'Les monnaies impériales de Charlemagne', *Comptes-rendus de l'académie des inscriptions et belles-lettres, 122.1* (1978), 154–76.

MG: K.F. Morrison and H. Grunthal, *Carolingian Coinage*, ANS Numismatic Notes and Monographs, 158 (New York, 1967).

Molinier 1895: E. Molinier, 'L'évangéliaire de l'abbaye de Morienval, conservé à la Cathédrale de Noyon', *Monuments et mémoires de la Fondation Eugène Piot*, 2.2 (1895), 215–26.

Prou 1892: M. Prou, *Catalogue des monnaies françaises de la Bibliothèque Nationale: les monnaies carolingiennes* (Paris, 1892).

Van der Chijs 1866: P.O. van der Chijs, *De munten der frankische en duitsch-nederlandsche vorsten* (Haarlem, 1866).

Völckers 1965: H.H. Völckers, *Karolingische Münzfunde der Frühzeit (751–800)*, Abhandlungen der Akademie der Wissenschaften in Göttingen, philologisch-historische Klasse, III.61 (Göttingen, 1965).

Willems 1990–91: J. Willems, 'L'occupation carolingienne au quartier d'Outre-Meuse à Huy. La fouille de la rue d'Amérique en 1991 (deuxième partie)', *Vie archéologique*, 37 (1990–91), 21–43.

Figure 6.1   Coins listed above, not illustrated in previous articles, by rows: (a) 12 (Elsen), (b) 13 (Staatliche Museen, Berlin); (c) 15 (Bibliothèque royale de Belgique, Brussels), (d) 18 (Geldmuseum, Utrecht); (e) 21 (Künker), (f) 35 (Fitzwilliam Museum, Cambridge); (g) 37 (Guido Cornelissens), (h) 40 (Geldmuseum, Utrecht).

Chapter 7

M for Mark: The Iconography of Series M, Variants and the *Agnus Dei*

Anna Gannon*

One of my most cherished memories of Mark, and of his pleasure in the quirky designs of Anglo-Saxon silver pennies, is the occasion when he proudly showed me his latest acquisition for the Fitzwilliam Museum: an interesting variant of Series M (Figure 7.1). I must confess equal delight, and not a little pride, at being able to immediately point out to him a similar specimen, albeit much worn, in the collection of the Ashmolean Museum: *T&S* 367 (Figure 7.2).[1] A stimulating conversation on the appeal of Anglo-Saxon pennies followed, and how new specimens contribute new perspectives and add to our long list of intriguing question marks. It seems therefore fitting to choose precisely these variants of Series M as an appropriate tribute to his memory, and in gratitude for all his guidance and encouragement.

Figure 7.1   *Sceat* of Series M from the Fitzwilliam Museum (CM.20–2009).

Figure 7.2   *Sceat* of Series M from the Ashmolean Museum (*T&S*, no. 367).

Series M (*BMC* Type 45) is understood to belong to the mid-secondary phase of the silver coinage, and to date to *c*.720.[2] Recorded find-spots include those of eight specimens from Kent (of which four are from Reculver), three

---

*   Note that all *sceattas* illustrated in this chapter are 1.5 times actual size.

[1]   *T&S*, 3, pl. 21, no. 367, ex Bodleian Library, old collection.

[2]   A. Gannon, *SCBI 63: British Museum Anglo-Saxon Coins I, Early Anglo-Saxon Gold and Anglo-Saxon and Continental Silver Coinage of the North Sea Area, c. 600–760* (London, 2013), 125.

from sites along the Thames in London, five from the south and south-west (one each from Southampton, Swindon and Walbury Camp hill fort in Berkshire, and two from Oxfordshire), plus three finds east and north of the Thames: one in Cambridgeshire, one from the productive site near Royston, Hertfordshire,[3] and one from the Woodham Walter hoard, Essex. Although some new finds can now be added to the map, the tentative attribution to east Kent put forward by Professor Michael Metcalf in 1994 would still appear to stand.[4]

The design of Series M is distinctive on account of its reverse which features a coiled vine-scroll with berries, whilst on its obverse there is a variety of forward-facing quadrupeds in various poses: generally leaping forward, but sometimes shown with paws tucked under the belly, and often with exaggerated curling tongue and tail. As is to be expected in the context of early Anglo-Saxon coinage, there are several departures from the basic designs,[5] so much so that in his seminal volumes of *T&S* Metcalf subdivided the Series into as many as seven sub-varieties, basically according to the variations in pose and direction presented by the quadrupeds on the obverse.[6] He also noted details that find echoes in other Series, such as the tucked-in foreleg of some of the quadrupeds of Series N and X, the curly tail seen on Series O and on some eclectic types, and the scattering of pellets in the field typical of Series Q. In addition, Metcalf records variants in the design of the vine-scroll and its berries, but concedes that in spite of the rougher rendering on some dies, the image remains legible.[7]

Surprisingly, in such a detailed survey of the Series, Metcalf makes no mention at all of a variant known from a rather attractive specimen, though chipped and with a badly defaced reverse, derived from the old collection of the Bodleian Library, of which only the obverse is illustrated along with the coins of Series M, as *T&S* 367.[8] The coiled vine-scroll faintly discernible on the reverse leaves no doubt as to its association with Series M; however, the delicately rendered quadruped is completely different from those that make up the bulk of the Series. Here we have an accurately observed animal, with a realistically rendered

---

[3]   The information on coin finds derives from <www-cm.fitzmuseum.cam.ac.uk/coins/emc/>, consulted on 7 February 2013.

[4]   *T&S*, 453–4. In addition, see the uniface specimen from Whitchurch, Buckinghamshire, ibid., 458; D.M. Metcalf, 'Twenty-five notes on sceatta finds', in *Sceattas in England and on the Continent*, eds D.H. Hill and D.M. Metcalf, BAR British Series, 128 (Oxford, 1984), 193–205, no. 17 at pp. 198–9, and see pl. 10, 14 (EMC 1984.0111). The coin is said to be imitative, and is in poor condition. The animal featured is related to those of Series M, with feet tucked below its body, but rather clumsy.

[5]   For a very useful illustrated tabulation of the variations in Series M, see T. Abramson, *Sceatta List* (Leeds, 2012), 151–2.

[6]   *T&S*, 453–4.

[7]   *T&S*, 454–6.

[8]   But see additional references below, n. 14.

body, well-planted on its four legs and standing in front of a plant. Interestingly, the metal analyses carried out on the coins in the Ashmolean Museum show that whilst the average silver standard for Series M appears to be well in excess of 50 per cent, our variant *T&S* 367 measures a very high (74 per cent) 'silver' content.[9]

This Ashmolean coin *T&S* 367, therefore, is very much the odd-one-out in the Series, and has always intrigued me, not only because of its unique iconography, but because, whilst leafing through a brief introduction to Celtic coinage in Britain, I had been struck by the similarities between this specimen and an ancient Carthaginian (or Siculo-Punic)[10] bronze coin found in Kent,[11] showing on its reverse a horse standing in front of a palm-tree in a stance which very much reminded me of the Oxford coin (Figure 7.3).[12] Whilst the correspondence is striking, I must make it very clear that I am not suggesting that these bronzes served as the direct prototypes for our coin; rather, I think it is intriguing to consider how much of the rich and varied heritage of ancient and classical imagery seems one way or the other to have inspired the iconography of the early Anglo-Saxon silver coinage.[13]

Figure 7.3   Bronze Siculo-Punic bronze coin (Fitzwilliam Museum).

A discussion of the iconography of this little Anglo-Saxon animal, which has remained so memorable for me as an art historian, will therefore form the main part of this short contribution. However, because since the publication of *T&S*

---

[9]   EPMA analyses by Dr J.P. Northover, in *T&S*, 672–3.

[10]   R. Calciati, *Corpus Nummorum Siculorum 3: la moneta di bronzo* (Novara, 1987).

[11]   P. de Jersey, *Celtic Coinage in Britain*, Shire Archaeology, 72 (Princes Risborough, 1996), 15, Figure 10. According to de Jersey these coins, dated to the fourth or third centuries BC and often associated with British Celtic coins, are principally found in Kent. David Holman (*pers. comm.*) has records of 19 specimens from the east Kent area, all from sites which produce both Celtic IA and Roman coins.

[12]   Comparable imagery is to be found on several North African mosaic floors where pairs of horses are confronted across a palm tree: see K.M.D. Dunbabin, *The Mosaics of Roman North Africa: Studies in Iconography and Patronage* (Oxford, 1978), 101.

[13]   Gannon, *Iconography*, 184–6.

in 1993–94 two more specimens have been found thanks to metal-detector users, and one more related coin has been added to the Ashmolean collection, the list which follows is also the first to present these coins together as a small sub-type.

Corpus of Series M Variant

Obverse: within a double frame, pelleted on the inside and linear on the outside, a quadruped standing right in front of tilted bush with bunches of berries and long symmetrical branches developing on either side; lower trunk of bush visible in front of the animal; groups of pellets in the field between the legs.

Reverse: within a single frame of pellets, a vine-scroll developing from the border of the coin with short opposed spurs bearing bunches of berries, coiling clockwise towards the centre and culminating in a bunch of berries.

1. Ashmolean Museum *T&S* 367: weight 0.55 g (chipped); ex Bodleian, old collection (Figure 7.2).[14]
2. Fitzwilliam Museum CM.20–2009 (= EMC 2008.0464; CR 2009, 184): weight 0.94 g; found at the productive site near Royston, Hertfordshire, 2008 (Figure 7.1).
3. Abramson Collection, M400 (= EMC 2010.0015; CR 2010, 111): weight 0.89 g; found Benson, Oxfordshire, by 2009 (Figure 7.4).

Figure 7.4   *Sceat* of Series M variant from the Abramson collection (no. M400).

The coins from the Fitzwilliam and the Abramson collections seem to share the same obverse die.

---

[14] This coin, although unprovenanced, can be traced to a manuscript catalogue of 1894. It has a defaced reverse, discussed in Metcalf, 'Twenty-five notes', 199, and see pl. 10, 15 as a parallel to the specimen from Whitchurch (see above, n. 4), which is similarly defaced. The Ashmolean coin was classified in P.V. Hill, 'Uncatalogued *sceattas* in the national and other collections', *NC, 6th series, 13* (1953), 92–114 as Type 42 Var. (see 108 and pl. VI, 35).

In addition, mention must be made of a further specimen, a variant of the variant as we might call it, acquired by the Ashmolean Museum after the publication of *T&S*. The quadruped on the obverse is clearly related to those described above, hence it is included in the discussion; however, the reverse shows a bird-in-vine motif akin to that of Series U. Here too there is a double frame, but this time the one with pellets is on the outside.

Obverse: quadruped, but stockier-bodied and with longer, rounder muzzle; large eye and oval ear; shorter legs and prominent feet, standing in front of tilted bush, as above.

Reverse: within a single frame of pellets, bird, r., nestled in vine-scroll with berries; large head and open beak pecking at leaves; splayed-out legs; tail as 'spatula'; 'hooked' upright wing.

    4. Ashmolean Museum, similar to *T&S* 367 (var.): weight 0.89; ex Patrick Finn List 17 (September 1999), no. 38 (Figure 7.5).[15]

Figure 7.5   *Sceat* of Series M variant from the Ashmolean Museum, Oxford (cf. *T&S* 367).

The Iconography

In discussing the iconography of the quadruped, Metcalf wondered if *T&S* 367 was 'the only Anglo-Saxon coin depicting a horse',[16] whilst Tony Abramson, intrigued by what appears to be a contour line tracing the back, neck and head of the animal, suggested it might in fact be '(a pair of ?) horse-like animals'.[17] Patrick Finn, more improbably, described it as a tapir, probably on account of the rounded and elongated muzzle.[18] Far more helpful is the entry for what is now Ashmolean *T&S* 367 (var.) in the tabulation of Finn's lists published by Abramson: there Abramson described that animal as a hound, noting similarities

---

[15]   Finn classified it as a K42/U mule.

[16]   Metcalf, 'Twenty-five notes', 199; cf. *T&S*, pl. 21, no. 367 (Horse?).

[17]   Abramson, *Sceatta List*, 152.

[18]   P. Finn List 17 (September 1999), 6.

with those of Series K, Type 42, and classified the coin as 'K,42/U mule'.[19] Indeed the slanted bush behind the quadruped very much resembles those vegetation motifs featured on the reverses of coins of this Series (Figure 7.6).

Figure 7.6   *Sceat*   of   Series   K   Type   42   from   the   Fitzwilliam Museum (CM.1806–2007).

I have already discussed the iconography of Series K, Type 42 in relation to that of Roman gems depicting Bacchus's panthers leaping in front of a *thyrsus*, as in the find from Ham Hill, Somerset, dating to the first century AD (Figure 7.7). That animal, whilst still wearing the collar which is a traditional accessory in classical representations of the god's panther, carried no pagan overtones, but can in fact be understood in a totally Christian context: feeding in a vine-scroll, a familiar motif in many contemporary artistic representations.[20] Trees or vegetation motifs were conventionally used in classical art to suggest that the scene was located outdoors,[21] and they were also an artistic device against which animals were conventionally represented, as seen on the ancient bronzes mentioned above, or on the Roman long-handled spoon with a panther from the Thetford treasure (Figure 7.8),[22] but also on early Christian catacomb paintings representing the Good Shepherd,[23] or monuments such as a sixth-century sarcophagus in S. Apollinare in Classe, Ravenna (Figure 7.9).

---

[19]   T. Abramson, 'The Patrick Finn *sceatta* index and analysis: a collector's perspective', in *Two Decades of Discovery: Studies in Early Medieval Coinage, 1*, ed. T. Abramson (Woodbridge, 2008), 155–96. The coin is tabulated at 164 and reproduced at 192.

[20]   Gannon, *Iconography*, 133–4, Figure 4.37a–b, and cf. 68.

[21]   I. Henderson, '*Primus inter pares*', in *The St Andrews Sarcophagus*, ed. S.M. Foster (Dublin 1998), 97–167, at 100. One may compare and contrast the use of the motif for the various episodes of the life of Christ represented on the Sarcophagus of Junius Bassus, fourth century AD (Museum of Saint Peter's Basilica, Vatican City).

[22]   British Museum, Prehistory and Europe: 1981,0201.66. See C. Johns and T. Potter, *The Thetford Treasure: Roman Jewellery and Silver* (London, 1983), 120, Figure 34.

[23]   For instance, in the catacombs of Priscilla and Domitilla, in Rome.

Figure 7.7   Roman engraved gemstone from Ham Hill, Somerset. First century AD (TTNCM A.1776) (© Somerset County Council Heritage Service).

Figure 7.8   Roman long-handled panther spoon, Thetford Treasure, Norfolk. Fourth century AD (Prehistory and Europe: 1981,0201.66) (© Trustees of the British Museum).

Figure 7.9   Sixth-century sarcophagus, S. Apollinare in Classe, Ravenna (author's photograph).

Although the designs on the obverses of Series M variant are not particularly well-preserved near the head of the animal on surviving specimens, it is apparent that on all of them the bush behind the quadruped is tilted just as on Series K, Type 42; but whilst the bushes on the latter sprout short and stiff lateral twigs with berries, the boughs on our coins grow long and bend gracefully under their own weight and that of their fruit. On Abramson M400 this is particularly clear: the branch on the left-hand side ends in a leaf, and its trunk sprouts a shorter stem ending in a bunch of berries. One can assume that, given the other bunch of berries just visible to the right, the design, which is worn, was intended to be symmetrical, but this side of the design comes too close to the border of pellets framing the motif for it to be so. There are other such boughs in the design, as well as berries, and I would interpret the contour round the back of the animal as vegetation, suggesting a close relationship between the two.

The design of Ashmolean *T&S* 367 (var.) is much crisper: the animal here has a large eye and a round ear, and the muzzle, far from that of a tapir, is more suggestive of a lamb. The creatures of Series K, Type 42, as well as the many birds in vines among the silver pennies are all depicted eagerly feeding on the berries. As in much contemporary Anglo-Saxon art, the motif of the bushy vine heavy with fruit can be read allegorically as an allusion to the True Vine,[24] and to the Eucharist.[25] Interestingly, the animals on our coins, although intimately connected with the vine behind, are not shown feeding on it: indeed on *T&S* 367 (var.) a stem ending in a bunch of berries appears to be issuing from its mouth.[26] This detail would suggest a special status of the animal, as being itself the source of salvation: I would argue that the quadruped represented on this coin is in fact a lamb, and that this might indeed be a representation of the *Agnus Dei*, symbolic of Christ, and make a claim for this as its first use among the Anglo-Saxon coinage.

Friends of Mark will certainly be aware of his great interest in the silver pennies of King Æthelred II the Unready (978–1016) with the *Agnus Dei* motif, dated to the year 1009, which have recently been reassessed by Simon Keynes and Rory Naismith in a work aptly dedicated to his memory.[27] Whilst the iconographical significance of the coins and their socio-political connotations at that troubled

---

[24]   John, XV.

[25]   Gannon, *Iconography*, 117–20, 133–4.

[26]   Cf. Gannon, *SCBI 63*, no. 548; and G.W. de Wit, *The de Wit Collection of Medieval Coins – Part V: the Sceattas (now part of the Fitzwilliam Museum Collection, Cambridge)* (Osnabrück, 2008), 55, no. S206. Both reverses show curled-up animals with long tongues ending in pellets. See Gannon, *Iconography*, 140.

[27]   S. Keynes and R. Naismith, 'The *Agnus Dei* pennies of King Æthelred the Unready', *ASE*, 40 (2011), 175–223.

time have been persuasively discussed in their work,[28] I am of course on far more difficult ground with the eighth-century and earlier pennies, owing to the lack of any inscription which might allow us to place the coins either geographically or chronologically, as well as the absence of historical sources and the scarcity of any *comparanda*.

It is undeniable that there are great iconographical differences between the *Agnus Dei* on Æthelred's pennies and what I argue are also representations of the Holy Lamb on our eighth-century coins. The former, *cruciger*, follows a convention that goes back to the fifth century AD, as witnessed by Paulinus of Nola's descriptions of the apse mosaics in the basilica of St Felix at Cimitile, where the inscription proclaims 'sanctam fatentur crux et agnus victimam'.[29] The *Agnus cruciger* continued in use, as for instance on the central clypeus on the *Crux gemmata* given by Justin II between 565 and 578 to the city of Rome,[30] and on sixth-century sarcophagi in Ravenna, till in 692 the deliberations of Canon 82 of the Council of Constantinople (the Quinisext or Trullan Council) questioned such symbolic representations.[31] The Roman response was robust, appealing to ancient Roman tradition, and culminated with Pope Gregory III's synods of 731 and 732, which rejected iconoclasm.[32] As Ó Carragáin has argued, theological explorations can be seen in the introduction of the *Agnus Dei* chant by Pope Sergius I (687–701), and the programme of apse mosaics in various Roman basilicas. In particular, in the vault of the basilica of Saints Cosmas and Damian, commissioned by Pope Felix IV (526–30) and renovated by Sergius we observe the juxtaposing of the human figure of Christ in glory with the symbolic *Agnus Dei* standing on a paradisiacal hillock from which flow four rivers, with two groups of six sheep processing towards Him. In addition, in the arch above the apse, there is also a representation of the enthroned apocalyptic Lamb.[33] Mention can also be made of the representation of a backward-looking Lamb

---

[28]   The iconography of the *Agnus Dei* is discussed in Keynes and Naismith, 'The *Agnus Dei* pennies', 180–81, n. 13–14.

[29]   'The lamb and the cross proclaim [*Christ*] the sacred victim'. F. Cabrol and H. Leclercq (eds), *Dictionnaire de l'archéologie chrétienne et de la liturgie* (15 vols., Paris, 1907–53), 1, col. 895 for the reference to Paulinus of Nola. These words are found in his letter XXXII.10 (*Paulinus von Nola: Briefe/Epistolae*, ed. M. Skeb, Fontes Christianae, 25.1–3 (3 vols., Freiburg, 1998), 2, 770–71), in which Paulinus describes and transcribes the *tituli* added to the wall paintings and mosaics in the basilica of St Felix at Cimitile. See also F. Stella, 'Poesia e teologia. L'occidente latino tra IV e VIII secolo', in *Figure del pensiero medievale*, ed. I. Biffi and C. Marabella (Milan, 1999), 471–564, at 512.

[30]   D. Rezza (ed.), *La Crux Vaticana o Croce di Giustino II* (Vatican City, 2009).

[31]   G. Nedungatt and M. Featherstone (eds), *The Council in Trullo Revisited* (Rome, 1995); H. Belting, *Likeness and Presence* (Chicago, 1994), 155.

[32]   É. Ó Carragáin, *Ritual and the Rood* (Toronto, 2005), 247–59.

[33]   Ó Carragáin, *Ritual and the Rood*, 254, and see figs 47–48 and pl. 12.

standing on a roll with seven apocalyptic seals, next to an inscription reading *ECCE AGNVS DI ECCE QVI TOLIS PECCATA MVNDI* in the centre of the aedicula of the recently discovered frescos from the sacristy of Santa Susanna, thought to be dating to *c.*700, part of the restoration work of Pope Sergius I mentioned in the *Liber Pontificalis*.[34]

Whilst undoubtedly the shock-waves of such controversies were felt throughout Christendom, away from the centre we witness the continuation of certain iconographies from the past, sometimes of eastern derivation and based on the Apocrypha,[35] at other times based on idiosyncratic local developments.[36] The development of the *Agnus Dei* in Anglo-Saxon art is one such case. Among the most interesting Anglo-Saxon examples of this creative approach is the eighth-century Wirksworth slab (Derbyshire),[37] one of the scenes on which shows a crouched lamb at the centre of an equal-armed cross (Figure 7.10). Whilst at one level the image can be read as a symbolic crucifixion,[38] the presence of the four Evangelists' symbols around the cross suggests complex apocalyptic overtones. Bailey has argued that this representation has simultaneous multiple meanings and that it 'embodies concepts of Crucifixion, Glory, Judgement and Eucharist'.[39]

I shall come back to the Lamb at Wirksworth later, in connection with some other Anglo-Saxon coins, but first, turning again to the iconography of Series M variants, in addition to the classical convention of combining trees

---

[34]   A number of articles exploring the discoveries are published in E. Russo (ed.), *1983–1993, dieci anni di archeologia cristiana in Italia: atti del VII Congresso nazionale di archeologia cristiana; Cassino, 20–24 settembre 1993* (Cassino 2003).

[35]   R. Cramp, 'Schools of Mercian Sculpture', in *Mercian Studies*, ed. A. Dornier (Leicester, 1977), 191–233, at 244.

[36]   See for instance the representation in the *Sacramentarium Gelasianum*, Biblioteca Apostolica, Vatican City, Vat. Reg. lat. 316, f.3v (north-east France, *c.*750). Here the Lamb *cruciger* is in the centre of the cross carrying Alpha and Omega *pendilia*; on the arch above it there is a representation of Christ between two animals. For an illustration, see J. Hubert, J. Porcher and W.F. Volbach, *Europe of the Invasions* (New York, 1967), 165, Figure 175; A. Dumas and J. Deshusses (eds), *Liber sacramentorum Gellonensis*, Corpus Christianorum Series Latina (CCSL 159A) (Turnhout 1981).

[37]   J. Hawkes, 'The Wirksworth slab: an iconography of Humilitas', *Peritia, 9* (1995), 246–89.

[38]   B. Kurth, 'The Iconography of the Wirksworth Slab', *Burlington Magazine for Connoisseurs, 86* (1945), 114–21, at 118, cites the fifth-century example from the Syrian-Palestinian tabernacle of St Mark's, Venice (Plate II, c). The iconography of the Lamb on Cross goes back to the fifth and sixth centuries: see also Cabrol and Leclercq, *Dictionnaire*, 1, col. 895. The association between Lamb and Cross recalls the *Agnus Dei* Roman chant and has Eucharistic connotations (Ó Carragáin, *Ritual*, 163–4).

[39]   R.N. Bailey, *The Meaning of Mercian Sculpture*, 6th Brixworth Lecture 1988 (Brixworth, 1990), 13. See also Hawkes, 'Wirksworth', 264–5.

Figure 7.10
Detail from the Wirksworth
slab, Derbyshire
(© Jane Hawkes).

with animals discussed above, I should like to mention the so-called desk of Saint Radegund (518–87).[40] The four corners are marked by the symbols of the Evangelists, connected vertically by two panels with crosses and horizontally by two panels showing a Chi-Rho monogram and a cross, both in wreaths and flanked by birds. The central panel presents the Lamb framed by vegetation motifs, possibly palms, symbolic of Paradise, typical of early Christian art. And a verdant Paradise is indeed the context to which I believe ultimately our Series M variants also make reference: the Lamb of God teamed with the Eucharistic vine promising salvation. Both their reverses – whether the fruitful coiled vine-scrolls or the bird-in-vine – are equally allusive to Eucharistic themes, and reinforce the message.[41]

If this is indeed the correct reading of the iconography of these variants of Series M, what about those we assume form the core of Series M? As we have seen, these are divided by Metcalf into seven sub-varieties,[42] and we may wonder, bearing in mind (in addition to the iconographic considerations) the metrology of the coins,[43] if we should perhaps put the variants at the head of the mainstream Series. In particular Ashmolean *T&S* 367 (var.) actually shows a convincing and coherent design prototype, which may subsequently have been reproduced and misunderstood on the others. Whilst we note that all sub-varieties present extended tongues (which, as I have argued, on Ashmolean *T&S* 367 (var.) is a fruiting branch), it is conceivable that the curly tails and indeed the 'wings' of

---

[40] Musée du Baptistere Saint-Jean, Poitiers, France. For an illustration, see Hubert, Porcher and Volbach, *Europe of the Invasions*, 21, Figure 23. This object is now described as a headrest.

[41] Gannon, *Iconography*, 163 and 117–20.

[42] See above, n. 6.

[43] *T&S*, pl. 21, no. 367 measures 74 per cent 'silver' (see n. 9 above).

sub-variety (a) might be rationalisations of a misunderstood design. One can only hope that subsequent finds might help us clarify the matter.[44]

Figure 7.11   *Sceat*   of   Series   QIID   from   the   Fitzwilliam Museum (CM.1894–2007).

A further question that one might legitimately ask is whether the iconography of the *Agnus Dei* is unique to these variants of Series M. Considering the importance of the symbol in Christian art, but the relative rarity of surviving *comparanda* at the time of our coins,[45] I have always been keen to consider the possibility, but reluctant to proffer suggestions. However, I would venture to propose that the slim-legged creatures of Series Q, Types QII and QIIIA (Figure 7.11),[46] with a long tail variously interlaced, or indeed 'crossed' might be obvious and hopefully uncontested candidates for classification as Lambs. The *Agnus Dei* is traditionally represented with a long, undocked tail, which would lend itself to playful, but always meaningful, renderings in Anglo-Saxon hands.

In addition to models for the more or less static representations of the Lamb standing which were discussed above, we must postulate the availability of some prototypes for the crouching Lamb, in addition to the rather clumsy example which remains at Wirksworth (see Figure 7.10). As we read in Bede's *Lives of the Abbots of Wearmouth and Jarrow*, from his fourth journey to Rome (dated 679/80) Benedict Biscop brought back, among many pictures, scenes from St. John's vision of the apocalypse.[47] Whilst I do not want to propose that any complex theological message of the type seen in the mosaics of Saints Cosmas and Damian would have coloured the decision to represent a lamb (standing or crouched) on coins, Bede's words are further confirmation that images of apocalyptic lambs, most probably crouched, were known in Anglo-Saxon

---

[44]   See discussion of EMC 2003.0206, a Series K coin from Maidstone, Kent, in A. Gannon, 'Series K: eclecticism and entente cordiale', in *Two Decades*, ed. Abramson, 45–52, at 47–9.

[45]   In addition to the Wirksworth slab, there are representations of St John and the Lamb on the Bewcastle and Ruthwell crosses.

[46]   I differentiate between the blithe animals of Type QIIIA, and the heavier ones, with leonine tripartite tails of Type QIII B (Gannon, *Iconography*, 126).

[47]   Bede, *Historia Abbatum*, 6 (*Baedae Opera Historica*, ed. C. Plummer (2 vols., Oxford, 1896), 1, 369–70).

England.[48] Coins may again help us test this proposition. I would like to put forward for consideration a very fine and rare specimen which teams a complex double cross-crosslet with a backward-looking animal, crouched in a fruiting vine-scroll (Figure 7.12).[49]

Figure 7.12   *Sceat* muling Series N and W (reproduced by kind permission of William MacKay).

The composition of this design is very elegant and almost calligraphic. The animal's extended tongue crosses one of the vine branches in an outspread X-shape, suggestive of the Greek letter 'chi' (*christos*), which is counterbalanced by an equally expansive one below the animal, this time formed by a forelimb intersected by another branch. Whilst it is impossible to prove beyond doubt that this is indeed the Holy Lamb, the fine design, and its being combined with a cross seem to support this suggestion.

I would venture to suggest that it may be appropriate to reconsider a number of coin designs with animals, and in particular those that are typically classified as 'monsters': crouched, backward-looking animals, with a tail curled over the body and a lappet (misunderstood ear?) at the back of their head. Although some elements, not unsurprisingly, are taken from traditional Germanic art,[50] it is my contention that these animals too might be ultimately derived from some early representations of the Holy Lamb enthroned, as postulated to have been behind the one seen at Wirksworth.

---

[48]   Mention might also be made of the three diagrams in the *Codex Amiatinus*, written in Monkwearmouth/Jarrow, early 8th century (Florence, Biblioteca Medicea-Laurenziana, fols. VIr, VIIr and VIIIr), which portray the division of the Bible according to Hilary, Jerome and Augustine. Each schema is surmounted by a medallion, respectively representing a bust, a standing lamb and a dove, perhaps a Trinitarian allusion: see the discussion in L. Nees, 'Problems of form and function in early medieval illustrated Bibles from Northwest Europe', in *Imaging the Early Medieval Bible*, ed. J. Williams, (University Park, PA, 1999), 121–76, at 161–72.

[49]   W. MacKay, 'A new early secondary *sceattas* type linking Series W and Series N', *NCirc, 164* (June 2004), 159–60. The coin, which is in the MacKay collection, has been classified as a mule of Series W and N; however the cross composition is far more ornate than any of those of Series W. Two specimens are known: the second one is in the Abramson Collection. See Abramson, *Sceattas*, 235, Series W/N mule.

[50]   Gannon, *Iconography*, 148–51.

It is beyond the scope of the present work to test this hypothesis by presenting an exhaustive tabulation of what kind of images are combined with the backward-looking animals, but possible examples include the twinned cross-bearers of Series N, the single figure with cross and vine (K/N), the facing head of Christ (Series X and QIG).[51] If this interpretation is correct, it would contribute greatly towards a thematic classification of the coinage. It would not only help us to see beyond our traditional, cluttered classification in Series and Types,[52] but also dispose at last of some unhelpful labels, such as that of 'Wodan/ Monster' given to coins of Series X (Type 31), which may instead be recognised as depicting a very Christian iconography with 'Head of Christ/Lamb of God', although perhaps unwittingly in pagan Denmark, where they may well have been understood as part of a quite different local pantheon (Figure 7.13).[53]

Figure 7.13   *Sceat* of Series X from the Fitzwilliam Museum (CM.1761–2007).

This survey of the variants of coins of Series M has, I hope, enabled us to recognise an important image in the repertoire of the silver pennies: the Lamb of God, which could be rendered either standing or crouching. Although early Christian mosaics and other models offered two distinct liturgical contexts originally associated with these representations (one of victory over death and one of Judgement), the fruiting vine-scrolls associated with the possible lambs on the coins considered here appear to point primarily to a Eucharistic context. In accordance with early Christian liturgy, this image looks forward to Christ's Second Coming with joyous anticipation:[54] it is at once comforting, salvific and paradisiacal. An equally optimistic iconography is shared by the imagery to be found across other Anglo-Saxon coins,[55] within which (in addition to a variety of crosses and fruitful vines) we can recognise a core vocabulary, familiar from

---

[51]   Often the animal is represented within complex, multiple borders. Particularly fine examples are the English varieties of Series X (e.g. Gannon, *SCBI 63*, no. 457).

[52]   See comments in Gannon, *Iconography*, 185.

[53]   Gannon, 'The contribution of art history to the study of early-medieval coinage: Series X and its international framework' (forthcoming).

[54]   É. Ó Carragáin, 'Conversion, justice, and mercy at the Parousia; liturgical apocalypses from eighth-century Northumbria, on the Ruthwell and Bewcastle crosses', *Literature and Theology, 26* (2012), 367–83, at 380.

[55]   Gannon, *Iconography*, 185.

early Christian art, of birds, doves, eagles, peacocks, stags, lions and snakes, as well as representations of the Virgin Mary and of Christ:[56] the Lamb of God is an appropriate addition to these. This religious iconography forms the nucleus of the so-called eclectic coinage, the bane of numismatic systematisation, where motifs responded to one another and were paired across Series and regional boundaries. However, these unruly coins are also the most attractive and thought-provoking of the early Anglo-Saxon period, and the ones that most delighted Mark. It is appropriate therefore that my offering in his memory should be concerned with the *Agnus Dei*.

---

[56] Gannon, *Iconography*; A. Gannon, 'Coins, images and tales from the holy land: questions of theology and orthodoxy', in *New Perspectives. Studies in Early Medieval Coinage 2*, ed. T. Abramson (Woodbridge, 2011), 88–103.

Chapter 8

The Stylistic Structure of Edward the Confessor's Coinage

Tuukka Talvio*

Several late Anglo-Saxon coin types are remarkably uniform when it comes to the visual appearance of the coins, while some of them offer much more diversity. The *Last Small Cross* type of Æthelred II is an example of the latter kind. Coins of this type, the last of Æthelred's types, are especially common in Scandinavian finds, and this probably was why Michael Dolley used them as the material for his 1958 study of engraving styles. He cited Sir Frank Stenton as the motivation for his research: 'More work is needed on the conditions under which the dies of this period were produced, and in particular on the extent to which the business of die-cutting was centralized in London'.[1]

According to Dolley, the *Last Small Cross* type can be divided into nine 'styles', which presumably were produced by nine different engravers or ateliers. Most subsequent studies of the late Anglo-Saxon engraving styles have been influenced by his paper. Like Dolley, their authors have usually concentrated on only one coin type at a time.[2] An attempt to survey all the ten types of Edward the Confessor in one short chapter naturally cannot be as exhaustive as the earlier studies, but the possibility of gaining an overview is tempting, especially as there would be little point in studying all the individual types separately but only from a stylistic point of view.

The potential significance of the 'styles' had been noted long before Dolley. In 1904, for example, Frederick Spicer wrote in his study of the coinages of William I and II that it 'would be interesting to attempt to trace who was

* I wish to thank Rory Naismith, Elina Screen and Martin Allen for their help with the editing of my text, finding the illustrations, and for correcting my English. I am, however, even more indebted to Mark Blackburn for inviting me to Cambridge, where I could study the collection of late Anglo-Saxon coins in the Fitzwilliam Museum as a Robinson Fellow for a month in 2003, staying at Wolfson College and enjoying the hospitality of Mark and his colleagues. The illustrations are reproduced from *SCBI* 1 (Fitzwilliam Museum, Cambridge) and *SCBI* 54A (Royal Coin Cabinet, Stockholm), by kind permission.

[1] F.M. Stenton, *The Latin Charters of the Anglo-Saxon Period* (Oxford, 1955), 24.
[2] R.H.M. Dolley, *Some Reflections on Hildebrand Type A of Æthelræd II* (Stockholm, 1958). For later studies see note 9.

responsible for engraving the dies during the latter part of Edward's reign and the short interregnum of Harold, for the style of the work on both is so similar to William's first coinages that we must conclude that the designs were executed by the same hand'.[3] At that time, photographic illustrations were still used sparingly, and Spicer simply could not know the material as well as the numismatists of later times. After all, the first volume of the *SCBI* was only published in 1958, the same year that Dolley's paper on the *Last Small Cross* came out.

Spicer did not present any detailed observations upon the similarities between the coins of Edward, Harold II and William I. Instead he was interested in the goldsmiths mentioned in the Domesday Book, and he singled out two of them, Theoderic and Otto, stressing that Theoderic had been active already under the Confessor.[4] Later writers have been more interested in Otto, because more is known of him, or at least of his descendants. According to G.C. Brooke, 'An *aurifaber*, or goldsmith, was probably employed for the designs of the coinage and perhaps controlled the engraving of the dies; a function which seems to have been hereditary in the family of the goldsmith Otto from the time of the Domesday, and apparently developed at a later date into the post of the Cuneator or Engraver of the dies … '.[5]

Studying the Styles

This chapter is based mainly on the coins published in *SCBI* 1–54. It is clearly a major disadvantage that I have not been able, in this connection, to consult the British Museum collection, which now contains some 3,000 coins of Edward the Confessor.[6] There are, however, nearly 4,700 coins of this reign published in the *SCBI*, and they should offer enough material for a survey of this kind. Despite Spicer's optimism there is very little hope that we can name any person who was responsible for engraving the dies during Edward's reign. Whether the goldsmith Theoderic actually was involved in minting, we do not know, and there seems to be no evidence of Otto's involvement before Norman times. It has been thought that the changes that took place in the design of Edward's coins in the 1050s could be connected with Theoderic's supposedly German origins,[7]

---

[3]   F. Spicer, 'The coinage of William I and William II' (part I), *NC, 4th series, 4* (1904), 144–79, at 148.

[4]   Spicer, 'William I and William II', 148–9.

[5]   G.C. Brooke, *A Catalogue of English Coins in the British Museum. The Norman Kings* (2 vols, London, 1916), 1, cxxxiii; E.A. Packe, 'The coinage of the Norman kings', *NC, 3rd series, 14* (1893), 129–45, at 145.

[6]   Information kindly provided by Gareth Williams.

[7]   M. Dolley, *Anglo-Saxon Pennies* (London, 1964), 29; I. Stewart, 'The English and Norman mints, c. 600–1158', in *A New History of the Royal Mint*, ed. C.E. Challis (Cambridge, 1992), 1–82, at 54.

but in that respect, too, we have no evidence. In this situation an analysis of the engraving styles of the coins can perhaps shed some light on the situation, even if the engravers themselves, as well as the persons responsible for designing the coins and controlling the making of the dies, will remain anonymous.

The 'style' of a coin can generally be defined as a complex of features that distinguish the products of one die-cutter or workshop from those of others. The definition of a style should be based on objective and, if possible, verbally defined criteria, but it is self-evident that questions of style cannot be discussed without illustrations. It is generally more realistic to think in terms of workshops than individual engravers, for master engravers are likely to have been helped by apprentices.

The features that we see as important for the defining of a style are not always as unambiguous as one should wish. It is therefore best to look for a combination of several features. Normally it is, however, the modelling of the portrait that is crucial, for the reverses tend to have much less variety. Epigraphic details, like letter-forms (barred or unbarred 'A's, etc.), may also be significant, but they have not been observed in this study.

There were both 'national' and local or regional styles. The former were mainly associated with the major 'die-centres' of southern England, while the latter are mostly found in northern England where it seems to have been an accepted custom to use locally engraved dies together with those provided by the die-cutting centres of the south. These coins are usually easy to recognise by their unconventional features and blundered inscriptions, but sometimes they imitate the metropolitan styles so convincingly that one cannot easily distinguish them from coins struck with 'official' dies. Sometimes we also meet atypical, odd pieces that cannot be connected with any style.

Since the publication of Michael Dolley's pioneering study in 1958, several late Anglo-Saxon coin types have been analysed.[8] Dolley could identify nine *Last Small Cross* styles, but the dies of the following type, Cnut's *Quatrefoil*, were,

---

[8]   R.H.M. Dolley, *Some Reflections on Hildebrand Type A of Æthelræd II* (Stockholm, 1958); see also R.H.M. Dolley and J. Ingold, 'Some thoughts on the engraving of the dies for the English coinage *c*. 1025', Comm. 1, 187–222; M. Dolley and T. Talvio, 'The regional pattern of die-cutting exhibited by the *First Hand* pennies of Æthelræd II preserved in the British Museum', *BNJ, 47* (1977), 53–65; M. Blackburn and S. Lyon, 'Regional die-production in Cnut's *Quatrefoil* issue', in *ASMH*, 223–72; K. Jonsson, *The New Era. The Reformation of the Late Anglo-Saxon Coinage*, Comm. n.s., 1 (Stockholm, 1987), 86–7; T. Talvio, 'Stylistic analyses in Anglo-Saxon numismatics: some observations on the *Long Cross* type of Æthelræd II', in *Sigtuna Papers: Proceedings of the Sigtuna Symposium on Viking-Age Coinage, 1–4 June 1989*, ed. K. Jonsson and B. Malmer, Comm. n.s. (Stockholm, 1990), 6, 327–30; T. Talvio, 'Harold I and Harthacnut's *Jewel Cross* type reconsidered', in *ASMH*, 273–90; S. Lyon, 'Die-cutting styles in the *Last Small Cross* issue of *c*. 1009–1017 and some problematic East Anglian dies and die-links', *BNJ, 68* (1998), 21–41; H. Pagan, 'The *PACX* type of Edward the Confessor', *BNJ, 81* (2011), 9–106.

according to Mark Blackburn and Stewart Lyon, produced by as many as 19 die-cutting centres.[9] It is apparent, however, that when Cnut had consolidated his power, the number of die-cutting centres was radically reduced: in the *Pointed Helmet* type Dolley and Joan Ingold identified only four different styles, and two of them accounted for 'more than four coins in every five'.[10] The same trend towards a centralisation of the die production continued during the following reigns.

The Coins of the Confessor

Relatively little was written on the coins of Edward the Confessor before the 1980s, and it was mostly about the type sequence and chronology.[11] The mints and moneyers of the reign were surveyed by Anthony Freeman in 1985.[12] The moneyers' names and the order of the coin types have been discussed by Fran Colman,[13] who in 2007 also published the second largest (after the British Museum) single collection of Edward's coins, the 1,280 pennies in the Royal Coin Cabinet in Stockholm.[14] Hugh Pagan has recently published a comprehensive study and die corpus of Edward's first type, the *Pacx*.[15] In a somewhat similar paper, published in 1990, he has also presented the coins of Harold II.[16]

No fewer than ten coin types were issued during Edward's reign, between the death of Harthacnut in June 1042 and Edward's own death in January 1066. According to the chronology constructed by Dolley, based on his theory of periodical type changes, the duration of Edward's coin types was at first two years and from 1051 three years.[17] It was in 1051 that the *heregeld* was abolished. There is no concrete evidence for the exact dating of any of the coin types, but thanks to 'mules' between successive types their order is not in doubt.

---

[9] Blackburn and Lyon, '*Quatrefoil* issue', 226.

[10] Dolley and Ingold, 'Some thoughts', 197.

[11] See e.g. R.H. Thompson, 'Published writings of Michael Dolley', in *ASMH*, 315–60, at 354.

[12] A. Freeman, *The Moneyer and the Mint in the Reign of Edward the Confessor, 1042–1066*, BAR British Series, 145 (2 vols, Oxford, 1985).

[13] F. Colman, *Money Talks. Reconstructing Old English* (Berlin and New York, 1992), 71–151, 231–358. The coin-types have also been commented in T. Talvio, 'The designs of Edward the Confessor's coins', in *Studies in Late Anglo-Saxon Coinage*, ed. K. Jonsson, Numismatiska Meddelanden, XXXV (Stockholm, 1990), 487–99.

[14] *SCBI* 54A.

[15] Pagan, '*PACX* type'.

[16] H. Pagan, 'The coinage of Harold II', in *Studies in Late Anglo-Saxon Coinage*, ed. Jonsson, 177–205.

[17] E.g. Dolley, *Anglo-Saxon Pennies*, 28–9.

All Anglo-Saxon coin types since Cnut's *Pointed Helmet* had diademed busts until a second *Pointed Helmet* type was introduced *c*.1053, followed by the *Sovereign/Eagles* type showing a crowned king on his throne. Then followed three other types with crowned portraits, and this tradition lived on under Harold II and the Norman kings.

Apart from the possible influence from foreign craftsmen, changes can also be connected with the ending of the *heregeld* in 1051. If the numismatic chronology is correct, this happened during the currency period of the *Expanding Cross* type (*c*.1050–53), when both the weight and diameter were increased. On the whole, the coins of Edward's five last types, from *Pointed Helmet* onwards, look so uniform that it seems natural to think that most of the dies were indeed produced by a single centre which presumably was London.[18] So Spicer seems to have been right – or almost right, for even the earlier coins were probably mostly engraved in London. The difference between Edward's early and late coin types has also been noted by more recent writers.[19] Obviously there were during his reign a series of innovations, whether initiated by the goldsmith Theoderic or not, and it is interesting to follow the situation from type to type.

Figure 8.1   Edward the Confessor, *Pacx* type, by row. Above: (a) Style A (*SCBI* 1, 820); (b) Style B (*SCBI* 1, 821); (c) Local style with large portrait (*SCBI* 54, 85). Below: (d) Local style, York mint (*SCBI* 54, 320A).

Pacx (1042–c.1044)

As already mentioned, Edward's first type has recently been the subject of a detailed study by Hugh Pagan, and his analysis also includes an examination of the styles. The bust of this type does not differ much from Harthacnut's last type, while the reverse – with letters forming a kind of motto in the cross angles

---

[18]   Stewart, 'English and Norman mints', 78.

[19]   E.g. M.M. Archibald, 'Anglo-Saxon coinage, Alfred to the Conquest', in *The Golden Age of Anglo-Saxon Art 966–1066*, ed. J. Backhouse et al. (London, 1984), 170–91, at 184–5.

– has a predecessor in the *Crux* type of Æthelred II. Basing his analysis on both portrait busts and inscriptions, Pagan identifies three main styles, all of them 'national'. In style 'A' the diadem is formed of a single band (Figure 8.1a), in style 'B' it is formed of two parallel bands (Figure 8.1b). Style 'C' is said to look like a crude variety of 'A'; it is mainly found in the north. Pagan also refers to the use of locally made dies, e.g. at Winchester.[20] The three 'national' styles he attributes to engravers working in London.[21]

It is, however, difficult to see the 'C' coins as a national style. In the light of what is known of the mints of Lincoln and York, the coins of which have been published extensively,[22] it would be more natural to consider them as two different local styles, one with poorly engraved, often large portraits (Figure 8.1c), mainly found at Lincoln, Stamford, Norwich and Thetford,[23] and another showing the portrait with a curious, almost turban-like headdress (Figure 8.1d), found at York.[24] They are less common than coins of the 'national' styles, and we may see them as products of local engravers who supplemented the 'official' dies.

Figure 8.2 Edward the Confessor, *Radiate/Small Cross* type. (a) Style A (*SCBI* 54, 584) (left); (b) Style B (*SCBI* 54, 509) (right).

Radiate/Small Cross (c.1044–46)

In or around 1044, *Pacx* was replaced by *Radiate/Small Cross*. The elements of the design are again familiar, though not from the immediate past: a similar 'spiky' diadem had made its appearance with the *Helmet* type of Æthelred II, based on a Roman prototype, and the 'small cross' reverse had been a recurrent motif during the tenth century and again at the end of Æthelred's reign. Can we still discern the stylistic features of the previous type? At first it must be noted that single-band diadems are now very rare – two bands being an essential feature of the design – and the exceptions are too few to be considered a 'style'. In

---

[20] Pagan, '*PACX* type', 22.

[21] Ibid., 20–23.

[22] H.R. Mossop, *The Lincoln Mint c. 890–1279* (Newcastle upon Tyne, 1970); for the coins of York see *SCBI* 21.

[23] E.g. Pagan, '*PACX* type', nos. 139, 141 (Lincoln), 402, 410 (Stamford), 361, 363 (Norwich), 435. 442 (Thetford).

[24] E.g. Pagan, '*PACX* type', nos. 517, 529. See also nos. 157 (Lincoln) and 370 (Nottingham).

general the busts are more or less uniform, although crude or otherwise unusual pieces can be found in the north.[25] It is, however, again possible to identify two different engraving styles, both of them 'national', and they are here named 'A' and 'B' – but no continuity from the 'A' and 'B' styles of the previous type is indicated. The difference between them is not always clear. Generally the style 'A' (Figure 8.2a) has short hair over the forehead (before the diadem) while in style 'B' (Figure 8.2b) the coiffure looks like a helmet with a prominent forepart. At the risk of being naïve, one could say that the portraits of style 'A' look 'nicer'; but the problem is that both styles are probably of southern origin and the coins of style 'B' can perhaps be seen as inferior copies of style 'A'.

Figure 8.3   Edward the Confessor, *Trefoil Quadrilateral* type. Style B (*SCBI* 54, 782).

Trefoil Quadrilateral (c.1046–48)

In this type the 'B' style described above is wholly dominant, even though the coiffure often looks like a peaked cap rather than a helmet (Figure 8.3). Not only is the design a rehash of features used before, but the overall impression is curiously motley and second-rate, even in London. Aesthetic judgements aside, these coins are generally a far cry from the clear and balanced designs that had been traditional in the late Anglo-Saxon coinage. The work of the local engravers in the north can also often be identified.[26]

Figure 8.4   Edward the Confessor, *Small Flan* type. From left to right: (a) 'A' style, similar to Figure 8.2a (*SCBI* 1, 850); (b) 'B' style, similar to Figure 8.2b and c (*SCBI* 1, 845); (c) Expressive bust (*SCBI* 1, 844).

---

[25]   E.g. *SCBI* 54, nos. 399 (Derby), 461 (Lincoln), 644, 675, 679 (York).

[26]   E.g. *SCBI* 54, nos. 719 (Derby), 752ff. (Lincoln), 825 (Norwich), 881, 886 (York).

Small Flan (c.1048–50)

The name of the type obviously refers to its diameter, which was only 14–15 mm, although it was a full-weight penny. Since the time of Alfred, the diameter of pennies had normally been *c.*20 mm or more, until it had sunk to 17–18 mm during the reign of Cnut. Except for the small diameter the design was typical: one more combination of a diademed bust and a 'long cross' reverse. Interestingly the quality of the engraving now seems to have been under better control, even though some of the coins can be compared with the 'B' style of the two preceding types (Figure 8.4b). Most coins have busts with two-band diadems, and there is a style, sometimes with single-band diadem, which has a rather expressive bust (Figure 8.4c), while a few coins resemble the 'A' type of the *Radiate/Small Cross* (Figure 8.4a). Both styles are mainly found at southern mints. Examples of recognisable 'northern' workmanship are not wholly absent,[27] but they seem to have been relatively rare.

Figure 8.5   Edward the Confessor, Expanding Cross type. From left to right: (a) Bust based on *Jewel Cross type*; (b) Bust based on double-diadem *Pacx* type (*SCBI* 1, 864); (c) Dominant style of the heavy series (*SCBI* 1, 866).

Expanding Cross (c.1050–53)

Although the overall impression is different, the *Expanding Cross* has affinities with the *Jewel Cross* type of the 1030s on both obverse and reverse. The bust normally has a diadem formed of a single band. In the early, lighter series we also find, however, busts that are based on either the original *Jewel Cross* (Figure 8.5a) or the *Pacx* type with double-band diadem (Figure 8.5b). Most of them are found in the north: at Lincoln and York they are the dominant variety in the light series.[28] As noted by Marion Archibald, the portraits on the lighter coins can be 'contrasted with the different style of effigy of the later, heavier group of the *Expanding Cross* type'.[29] Some of the 'heavy' coins of northern mints have

---

[27]   See Mossop, *Lincoln Mint*, pl. LXXII: 4.

[28]   E.g. Mossop, *Lincoln Mint*, pl. LXXII–III (Lincoln); *SCBI* 29, 749–69 (York).

[29]   Archibald, 'Alfred to the Conquest', 184.

in fact exaggerated features that indicate local work,[30] but generally the style is, with few exceptions, notably homogeneous (Figure 8.5c). The hairdo can be compared with the 'B' style described above in connection with *Radiate/Small Cross*. The increased weight of the coins was marked by an increased diameter (*c.*20 mm), which makes stylistic comparisons with the *Small Flan* type less easy.

Figure 8.6   Edward the Confessor, *Pointed Helmet* type. (a) Dominant style (*SCBI* 1, 875) (left); (b) 'Northern' style (*SCBI* 54, 1194) (right).

Pointed Helmet (c.1053–56)

Owing perhaps to a good engraver, the *Pointed Helmet* type makes a fresh impression (Figure 8.6a), even though the helmet with its pointed form, the arm-and-sceptre motif and the cross on the reverse are familiar from earlier types. Even a beard had already appeared in the Roman-inspired *Helmet* type of Æthelred II, although it had not been very noticeable. This time the beard was apparently a realistic detail,[31] although the coins of contemporary German kings and emperors may have influenced the design. The coin portraits are, of course, not realistic in the present meaning of the word, but this likeness of Edward seems more credible than the earlier ones – at least if the Bayeux Tapestry is used as a measure.

It is likely that a single atelier produced most of the dies, but examples of 'northern' work are evident from mints like Lincoln (Figure 8.6b) and York, and there are unusual pieces from other mints.[32]

Sovereign/Eagles (c.1056–59)

The obverse of this type is entirely new, showing the king enthroned (Figure 8.7a). The model for this presentation is supposed to have been the female personification of Constantinople, as seen on certain late Roman and Byzantine

---

[30]   E.g. Mossop, *Lincoln Mint*, pl. LXXV: 4 (Lincoln); *SCBI 21*, nos. 277, 280 (York).

[31]   F. Barlow, *Edward the Confessor*, 2nd ed. (London, 1997), 254.

[32]   E.g. *SCBI* 42, nos. 1253 (Chester), 1312–13 (Taunton), 1320 (Warwick).

gold coins,[33] but originally the motif must have been inspired by the king's new seal. The king, unlike the personification of Constantinople, is shown crowned. The details concerning the new royal seal and crown, both of them probably commissioned around 1050, are not well documented (one would hardly expect them to be), and the making of the crown seems to have met with difficulties.[34]

On the reverse there is a bird in the angles of the cross instead of a single geometric motif. The early antiquarians identified it as a martlet (martin) and believed it to be the heraldic emblem of Edward the Confessor. Heraldry as we know it did not, however, exist before the twelfth century and, as shown by Dolley and Elmore Jones, the bird is apparently an eagle, which is also seen on Edward's seal on top of his sceptre.[35] Some of the seemingly geometric motifs placed in the cross angles of late Anglo-Saxon reverse types can also be interpreted as sceptre heads (see *Trefoil-Quadrilateral* discussed above).

The minuscule details of the sitting full-length figure caused difficulties for the engravers. We can nevertheless see that even now most of the dies were produced by a single atelier. Local work can be identified at least at York, where the arms of the sitting figure sometimes are depicted in an exaggerated form.[36]

Figure 8.7   (a) Edward the Confessor, *Sovereign/Eagles* type (*SCBI* 1, 894) (left); (b) *Hammer Cross* type (*SCBI* 1, 908) (right).

Hammer Cross (c.1059–62)

Compared with the *Sovereign/Eagles*, and even with the *Helmet* type, the *Hammer Cross* has a simple design, with the new crown for the first time prominently displayed, but apparently in a simplified form (Figure 8.7b). As mentioned above, the reverses of late Anglo-Saxon coins often repeat some significant detail of the obverse, like a sceptre head, and this time the 'hammers'

---

[33]   P.D. Whitting, 'The Byzantine Empire and the coinage of the Anglo-Saxons', in *Anglo-Saxon Coins: Studies Presented to F.M. Stenton on the Occasion of His 80th Birthday*, ed. R.H.M. Dolley (London, 1961), 23–38, at 35; Archibald, 'Alfred to the Conquest', 185.

[34]   Barlow, *Edward the Confessor*, 106; F. Barlow, *The English Church 1000–1066* (London, 1963), 463–4; Lord Twining, *European regalia* (London, 1967), 35.

[35]   R.H.M. Dolley and F. Elmore Jones, 'A new suggestion concerning the so-called "martlets" in the "Arms of St Edward"', in *Anglo-Saxon Coins*, ed. Dolley, 215–26.

[36]   E.g. *SCBI* 21, nos. 357, 376, 389.

may have been inspired by the arches of the crown. (Arched crowns were considered more prestigious than open ones, having imperial associations.[37]) The obverse busts of this type look in general very similar to those of the *Pointed Helmet* type, and the style is similarly homogeneous. Certain coins of the northern mints, like Lincoln and York, can, however, again be recognised as local work by their exaggerated features.[38]

Bust Facing/Small Cross (c.1062–65)

Again a novel design, except for the reverse. A facing bust had not been seen on English coins since the ecclesiastical issues of the ninth century (Figure 8.8a). This time the nearest parallels are found in Germany, where coins with facing busts were common. Especially during the reign of Emperor Henry III (1039–56) the pendants of the crown were often shown in the same way as on Edward's coins.[39] The mints of Lincoln and York again offer peculiar varieties.[40]

Figure 8.8   (a) Edward the Confessor, *Bust Facing/Small Cross* type (*SCBI* 1, 953) (left); (b) *Pyramids* type (*SCBI* 1, 968) (right).

Pyramids (c.1065–66)

Edward's curiously named last type shows the king in profile with pendants hanging from the crown in a way that looks slightly awkward, but it is a detail that helps to make the representation seem more realistic (Figure 8.8b). The crown is still depicted with four arches, three of them visible, but their form seems to be pointed, like a wedge, and the same wedge is seen in the cross angles of the reverse. The style is still as a rule homogeneous, though there are some untypical pieces from London and, as usual, from York.[41]

---

[37]   Twining, *European regalia*, 35.

[38]   E.g. Mossop, *Lincoln Mint*, pl. LXXVII: 26 (Lincoln); *SCBI* 21, nos. 481–3 (York).

[39]   B. Kluge, *Deutsche Münzgeschichte von der späten Karolingerzeit bis zum ende der Salier* (Sigmaringen, 1991), 164–76. For the German imperial crown see Twining, *European Regalia*, 87–8.

[40]   E.g. Mossop, *Lincoln Mint*, pl. LXXIX (Lincoln); *SCBI* 21, nos. 604–11 (York).

[41]   *SCBI* 42, nos. 1658–9 (London); *SCBI* 21, nos. 664, 682.

Conclusion

As we have seen, there is evidence of continuing local die production, especially in the north and occasionally elsewhere, but even the northern mints mainly used dies acquired from the south. We may suppose that local dies were needed because of difficulties with communications, but further studies are still needed to confirm this, and die-cutting patterns could be complex also for political and other reasons.[42] That most of the dies during Edward's reign were produced by a southern centre, presumably London, need not be doubted. The differences in style and quality, when they occur, can at least partly be attributed to the system of master engravers letting their apprentices or assistants do a part of the work. As already noted, local dies are sometimes easy to recognise but they could also imitate the metropolitan styles so convincingly that they can be difficult or impossible to distinguish from 'official' dies. This phenomenon of engravers imitating each others' work makes any attempt to classify engraving styles within a short survey rather unrewarding.

Finally, as has been pointed out,[43] the system of several die-centres must have depended more on various practical reasons than on questions of capacity. When experimenting with medieval minting techniques, David Sellwood was able 'with next to no previous practice' to produce an obverse die imitating Edward the Confessor's *Bust Facing/Small Cross* type in 25 minutes and a reverse die in 15 minutes.[44] My 1986 study of the *Jewel Cross* type was based on some 500 obverse dies.[45] With Sellwood's method they would have taken about 200 hours to cut. A master engraver working with apprentices would have needed less time. This means that a single die-cutting centre could in principle have produced all the dies needed in the country.

Figure 8.9   Harold II, *Pax* type with crown of similar style to that of Edward's *Pyramids* type (*SCBI* 1, 969).

---

[42]   See P. Stafford, 'Historical implications of the regional production of dies under Æthelred II', *BNJ, 48* (1978), 35–51.

[43]   Stewart, 'English and Norman mints', 78.

[44]   D. Sellwood, 'Medieval minting techniques', *BNJ, 31* (1962), 57–65.

[45]   Talvio, '*Jewel Cross* type reconsidered'.

The use of crowned portraits, introduced in the 1050s, continued during Edward the Confessor's successors. Hugh Pagan has divided the obverses of Harold II's sole type, named after the word *Pax* on the reverse, into four categories,[46] two of which (C and D) have the same type of crown as Edward's last type, except that the dangling pendants have been transferred to the back of the head (Figure 8.9). These were presumably early varieties. On the more common A and B categories the crown is depicted in the same way as on most of the early Norman coin types. However, even in the case of the Norman coinage, most of the research has focused on the problems of chronology and the order of the types, rather than questions of iconography and engraving styles.

---

[46]   Pagan, 'Coinage of Harold II', 181–3.

Chapter 9

Bovo Soldare: A Sacred Cow of Spanish Economic History Re-evaluated[1]

Jonathan Jarrett

Introducing the *Bovo Soldare*

The *bovo soldare* is an entity that appears, in both masculine and feminine genders and a variety of spellings characteristic of the time, in transactional documents of northern Christian Spain from Galicia to Castile in the ninth and tenth centuries.[2] It almost invariably appears as a price: that is, it was given in exchange for goods of some other kind. In the records that survive, which ineluctably deal with durable property or they would hardly have been kept, these goods were almost always land. The term appears, simply enough, to mean an ox, or a cow, worth a *solidus*. The complication immediately arises, however, that this was not an area and period where coinage is known to have been struck: none had been struck since at latest the early eighth century, in fact, and neither would it be again until, at earliest, the mid-eleventh.[3] In any case, the usage, while persistent (attested from 796 to 1010 at least), is nonetheless

---

[1]   I must thank Drs Rory Naismith, Elina Screen and Martin Allen for the invitation to contribute to this volume and their suggestions with the text, and Professor Wendy Davies and Dr Anna Balaguer for helpful discussion of the subject. I would also like to thank Dr Mark Blackburn for discussions we had on this topic, but of course I cannot, now, and so I hope that he would have been amused by my returning to this subject and pleased with the results. No-one but myself can be blamed for my omissions and mistakes, however, or indeed my conclusions.

[2]   *Tumbos del Monasterio de Sobrado de los Monjes*, ed. P. Loscertales de G. de Valdeavellano (Madrid, 1976), doc. no. 67: *bove soldale*; *O Tombo de Celanova: estudio introductorio, edición e índices (ss. IX–XII)*, ed. J. Andrade (2 vols, Santiago de Compostela, 1995), doc. [hereafter Celanova] no. 504: *id est XVIII boves solidares*; Celanova no. 176: *vacca soldare*.

[3]   New discussion of such matters is now available in *MEC* 6, 203–9; a standard account is O. Gil Farres, *Historia de la moneda española* (Madrid, 1959), 189–91, but see now the more scientific terminological evaluation of J. Mínguez Martínez, 'Moneda medieval en el reino de León: análisis de terminus monetários en la documentación medieval de la Catedral de León (711–1252)', *Ab Initio, Número extraordinária, 1* (2011), 11–67, esp. 60–62, which does not, however, consider the *bovo soldare*. For that question, W. Davies, 'Sale, price and valuation in Galicia and Castile-Leon in the tenth century', *EME, 11* (2002), 149–74 is essential background, and its review of the evidence is the basic underpinning of my thinking here.

extremely rare.[4] Certainty about the meaning and value of these cattle is therefore at best some deductive distance away from a simple reading of the documents. This chapter takes new stock of this apparent monetary referent and suggests some implications of the system it supposedly demonstrates.

Numerous attempts have been made to elicit how this 'standard cow' made up for the lack of a monetary economy in these areas.[5] To the modern reader, especially if that reader has ever been near a cattle market, the idea that cows should have a standard value is itself somewhat unlikely.[6] The animals vary, in weight, in size, in milk yield, in fertility, in condition and health and in personality, though not all of these factors affect their valuation. Moreover, it is clear, as is shown below, that quite considerable variation was experienced in the prices paid for livestock in the period and area under study. Even if one wished to argue that the documents were the preserve of monastic elites comfortably isolated from the realities of the farmyard (an unlikely belief at the

---

[4]   I adduce 49 relevant documents below from the period 796–1010; this is from a wider preservation of some 2,000 charters from the period.

[5]   The historiography is discussed in detail below, but it effectively began with C. Sánchez-Albornoz, *Estampas de la vida en León hace mil años* (Madrid, 1926), here citing from 4th ed. under new title *Una ciudad hispano-cristiana hace un milenio: estampas de la vida en León* (Buenos Aires, 1947), where see 30–51, now in 11th ed. (Madrid, 1985); other works frequently cited in what follows are Sánchez-Albornoz, 'La primitiva organización monetaria de León y Castilla', *Anuario de Historia del Derecho Español*, 5 (1928), 301–41, repr. in his *Estudios sobre las instituciones medievales españolas* (México, 1965), 441–82, and his *Viejos y nuevos estudios sobre las instituciones medievales españolas* (3 vols, Madrid, 1976–83), 885–928; Sánchez-Albornoz, 'El precio de le vida en el reino astur-leonés hace mil años', *Logos, 6* (1944), 225–64, repr. in his *Estudios sobre instituciones*, 362–410, which edition cited hereafter, and his *Viejos y nuevos estudios*, 809–52; 'Moneda de cambio y moneda de cuenta en el reino asturleonés', *Cuadernos de Historia de España, 31–2* (1960), 5–32, repr. in *Moneta e scambi nell'alto medioevo* (= *Settimane di Studio del Centro Italiano di Studi sull'Alto Medioevo, 8* (1961)), 171–202, in Sánchez-Albornoz, *Estudios sobre instituciones*, 411–39, which edition cited hereafter, and his *Viejos y nuevos estudios*, 853–83; M. García Álvarez, 'Moneda y precios del ganado en la Galicia altomedieval', *Cuadernos de Estudios Gallegos, 24* (1969), 363–94. Almost all documentary references in what follows were initially gathered from: Sánchez-Albornoz, 'Precio de la vida', 397–410; M. del Pilar Laguzzi, 'El precio de la vida en Portugal durante los siglos X y XI', *Cuadernos de Historia de España, 5* (1946), 140–77, at 143–77; E. Sáez, 'Nuevos datos sobre el coste de la vida en Galicia durante la alta edad media', *Anuario de Historia del Derecho Español, 17* (1946), 865–88, at 871–88; or García Álvarez, 'Moneda y precios', 382–94. I have, however, checked their references against the most recent editions of the documents wherever possible, and cite their references only when more complete ones have not been possible to obtain.

[6]   This is not to contend that cattle could not, all the same, be used as currency, as they plainly were so being in these documents, or even that things could be valued in cattle, as the Irish laws of a slightly earlier period make clear, though even these must have been heavily adapted to reality to work in practice: see F. Kelly, *Early Irish Farming : A Study Based Mainly on the Law-Texts of the 7th and 8th Centuries AD* (Dublin, 1997), 587–99; cf. C. Wickham, *Framing the Early Middle Ages: Europe and the Mediterranean 400–800* (Oxford, 2005), 354–63.

best of times but especially so for the documents of this place and time), and our cows therefore largely formulaic, the writers of those documents would have been as aware as we are of Biblical stories involving cows of different quality, if not more so.[7]

Factors such as these, and the experience of checking some of the classic citations used in support of the standard idea in newer editions of the documents,[8] meant that my initial reaction to the idea was also one of scepticism, and Mark Blackburn was indeed one of the first people to hear this reaction when I found it in a work I was copy-editing for the Department of Coins and Medals in the Fitzwilliam Museum in 2010.[9] When invited to contribute to a volume in Mark's memory, therefore, it seemed that the best thing that I could offer would be a proper study of the phenomenon in an effort to get the documents to yield more sense on the subject than they have previously been made to do.

As may be deduced from the above, more thorough investigation reveals what might have been expected, that the *bovo soldare* is not so easily to be shooed away. For a start, it has companions. Although restricted entirely to records from the Galician monastery of Celanova, there was also a 'modial sheep', *ovelia modiale*, presumably worth a *modius* of grain, although what grain is never specified in this expression and several sorts can be found in use for payments, any of which would presumably have had a rather different value from the wheat that is usually assumed.[10] Though

---

[7]   On the character of monasticism in the area, see A. Linage Conde, *Los orígenes del monacato benedictino en la Península ibérica* (3 vols, León, 1973); A. Isla Frez, *La sociedad gallega en la alta edad media*, Biblioteca de Historia, 12 (Madrid, 1992), 105–28; W. Davies, *Acts of Giving: Individual, Community and Church in Tenth-century Christian Spain* (Oxford, 2007), 36–64 and *passim*; on the relation of formulae and reality see A. Rio, 'Charters, law codes and formulae: the Franks between theory and practice', in *Frankland: the Franks and the World of the Early Middle Ages. Essays in Honour of Dame Jinty Nelson*, ed. P. Fouracre and D. Ganz (Manchester, 2008), 7–27; C. West, 'Meaning and context: Moringus the lay scribe and charter formulation in late-Carolingian Burgundy' and J. Jarrett, 'Comparing the earliest documentary culture in Carolingian Catalonia', both in *Problems and Possibilities of Early Medieval Charters*, ed. J. Jarrett and A. Scott McKinley, International Medieval Research, 19 (Turnhout, 2013), 71–87 and 89–126 respectively. The Bible story is of course Genesis 41:17–21.

[8]   See nn. 39 and 46 below.

[9]   This reference occurred only in a draft version of the work in question, and so cannot be cited here.

[10]   Sheep, see Celanova nos 397, 403: both *ovelia modiale* (as part of much more complex prices. cf. Celanova no. 390, quoted below); Celanova no. 192: *oves IIas modiales*. For *modios* of different goods, see *Colección diplomática del monasterio de Sahagún (siglos IX y X)*, ed. J.M. Mínguez Fernández, Fuentes y Estudios de Historia Leonesa, 17 (León, 1976), doc. [hereafter Sahagún] no. 125: *trigo et ordeo modios IIII de civaria, stante ipse civaria in solidos XVI*; Celanova no. 390: *triigo [sic] uno modio, centeno modios III, milio quartarios VI et vino sestarios IIIIor et linteo tremisale ovelia modiale sub uno modios XIIII*. A brief new analysis of the use of *modios* as units of exchange is given in Mínguez, 'Moneda medieval', 28–9.

its appearances are few, there are also mentions of a *porco tremisale*, presumably a pig worth a *tremissis*, from the same area.[11]

A value hierarchy of cow = *solidus*, pig = *tremissis* and sheep = *modius* is therefore implied, which has an internal consistency that makes it somewhat harder to dismiss, even though these animals never appear together and the *modius* is at root a measure of volume, not value, and its value would as said vary depending on what grain was being measured.[12] It might have been possible to argue that to relate the *bovo soldare* to the *solidus* is a mistranslation, and that the adjective is more correctly an early Romance form of another meaning of the word, solid, reliable, dependable, since this sense would before long emerge in oaths of homage in the neighbouring Catalan counties; it might even be possible to stretch *modiale* to *mediale* and argue that the sheep was somehow a middling one, an average sheep, especially since middling cows, *vacas medias*, are also attested; but the pig worth a *tremissis* will not be removed by any such tricks of philology that I can think of, and in any case the feat gets less plausible with each species attempted.[13] It must be admitted, however, that after the year 1000, again, the pig appears to have suffered something of a demotion and become a *porco modial* [*sic*].[14] Despite this, though, it seems that we have to consider the likelihood that these standard animals existed in people's minds, and to try and extract from the records how they were envisaged and what use was made of them.

Bovine Historiography

The historian who made this cow do the most work for his theories was unquestionably Claudio Sánchez-Albornoz, a name still uttered with wary reverence among his successors.[15] Don Claudio, whose interests were broad but which had at their core a determination to uncover the origins of the social and economic institutions of the earliest Christian Spanish kingdoms in the era of

---

[11]   Celanova no. 409: *porcos duos, uno tremisale et alio de VI quartarios*.

[12]   Cf. the Leonese hierarchy of *solidus – arienzo – modius* detected by Mínguez, 'Moneda medieval', 27–8.

[13]   For solid homage, see P. Bonnassie, *La Catalogne du milieu du Xe à la fin du XIe siècle: croissance et mutation d'une société* (2 vols, Toulouse, 1975–6), 2, 741–6; García Álvarez, 'Moneda y precios', 388, citing Arquivo Distrital e Biblioteca Pública de Braga, *Liber Fidei Sanctae Bracarensis Ecclesiae*, no. 67: *una vaca media cum sua filia*. I have not been able to obtain *Liber Fidei Sanctae Bracarensis Ecclesiae*, ed. A. de Jesus da Costa (Braga, 1965–), in which this document is presumably printed.

[14]   Garcia Alvarez, 'Moneda y precios', 388, citing *Liber Fidei*, no. 76: *I marrano modial*, and no. 43: *Io porco modial*.

[15]   Since shortly before Don Claudio's death there has existed a Fundación Sánchez Albornoz in Ávila, whose webpages provide a convenient biography of him at <http://www.fsanchez-albornoz.com/index.php?datosbiograficos>, consulted on 27 September 2012.

the Reconquista (as he saw it), had a consequent interest in the details of the economy and of everyday life for society at all levels which made prices highly informative for him, and his early focus on such matters is not surprising to the reader of his work.[16] He was also, however, a fervent Republican who was thus forced in the 1930s to leave Spain for Argentina, where he would eventually become the President of the Republic of Spain in Exile. There he also established himself as the head of a school, in the broadest sense, in the Universidad de Buenos Aires and founded what is still one of the foremost journals of Spanish history, *Cuadernos de Historia de España*.[17] This allowed him to direct and support scholarship which was unpopular or discouraged in what had become Franco's Spain, but it also gave him as editor something like carte blanche to lambast and scorn his scholarly opponents in elevatedly sarcastic terms.[18] The exile also, and perhaps more importantly, separated him from the documents that he had made his own in his early work, so that for most of his career his opinions had to be founded on a slowly increasing corpus of editions and such photographs as he had managed to obtain of the charters before his departure.[19] It was, therefore, possible for him to be wrong, but few cared to tell him so and his later work demonstrates a tendency to regard what he had initially stated as a possibility, with due care and cavils, to have acquired the cast-iron character of fact if it had stood unchallenged for sufficiently long.[20] All of this is not to deny his considerable insight and perception and his sensitivity to minor matters,

---

[16] For his relevant works see n. 4 above.

[17] (Buenos Aires, 1944–).

[18] E.g. a diatribe directed at Évariste Lévi-Provençal under the title, 'La saña celosa d'un arabista', *Cuadernos de Historia de España*, 27 (1958), 3–42, of which 15–23 and 35–42 rev. under the less offensive title, 'En defensa de viejas teorías' in Sánchez-Albornoz, *Investigaciones sobre historiografía hispana medieval (siglos VIII al XII)* (Buenos Aires, 1979), 402–17; or the beautifully pitched but horrible demonstration of the errors of his scholarly enemy Justo Pérez de Urbel in Sánchez-Albornoz, 'De nuevo sobre la Crónica de Alfonso III y sobre la llamada Historia Silense' in *Cuadernos de Historia de España*, 37–8 (1963), 292–317, repr. in his *Investigaciones sobre historiografía*, 235–63.

[19] Sánchez-Albornoz, 'Precio de la vida', 395 of the reprint, n. 80, expresses confidence that his materials are adequate. Later editions of them did not weaken this belief, as witness his *Ciudad hispano-cristiana*, 209: 'No se han hallado empero nuevos fondos diplomáticos que yo no conociera y que pudiesen obligarme a cambiar estas *Estampas*, lo que me permite sentirme orgulloso de lo detenido de mis busquedas'.

[20] One can observe this process in the progress from his 'La redacción original de la crónica de Alfonso III', *Spanische Forschungen der Görresgesellschaft*, 2 (1930), 47–66, repr. in his *Investigaciones sobre historiografía*, 19–43, and his 'La crónica de Albelda y la de Alfonso III', *Bulletin Hispanique*, 32 (1930), 305–25, repr. in his *Investigaciones sobre historiografía*, 44–65, to his 'Alfonso III y el particularismo castellano', *Cuadernos de Historia de España*, 13 (1950), 19–100 at 90–100, and finally the revision of that last section as his 'Otra vez sobre la crónica de Alfonso III' in his *Investigaciones sobre historiografía*, 97–108.

or his intelligent determination to perceive systems and generalities that could explain what he saw as the 'historical enigma' of the development of Spain, but it does at least mean that it is worth seeing how well his arguments still hold up.[21]

For Sánchez-Albornoz, it was unlikely to the extreme, given the lack of finds, that the northern kingdoms had any coinage of local manufacture circulating in this period. He was, however, prepared to envisage a considerable residue of older money, Visigothic *tremisses*, Suevic *solidi* and perhaps even a certain amount of Roman coin still being available (though the one document that seems to say this last – in 952! – is extremely hard to interpret), and slowly replaced by silver coin imported from the Muslim south and the Carolingian east.[22] There seem also to have been pieces of silver bullion called *argencios* or *arienzos* in use, which Sánchez-Albornoz, like all after him, interpreted as hack-silver cut to a regular weight, although a similar documentary usage in Catalonia has usually been assumed to have implied ingots.[23] Of course, these disparate coinages could not make a coherent system of value, even if they were at all widely available. This made a more universal referent desirable, and for Sánchez-Albornoz, this was the sheep or the *modius* of wheat, both reckoned as equivalents to a *solidus*.[24] He assembled lengthy tables of prices and values in support of these ideas, and showed to his satisfaction that cows, however *soldare* they might be, almost always retailed at a much higher price.[25] Later additions to his lists, made by

---

[21]   Sánchez-Albornoz, *España: un enigma histórico* (2 vols, Buenos Aires, 1967, 10th ed. Barcelona, 1985). For a defence of the continuing value of Sánchez-Albornoz's work, see J.J. Larrea, 'Villa Matanza' in *Les sociétés méridionales à l'âge féodal (l'Espagne, Italie et sud de France Xe–XIIIe s.). Hommage à Pierre Bonnassie*, ed. H. Débax, Méridiennes, 8 (Toulouse, 1999), 223–28. On this subject, however, his work has not even been supplanted: witness F. Rodamilans Ramos, 'La moneda y la sistema monetária en la Castilla medieval', *Ab Initio, 1* (2010), 22–83, at 25–6; or Mínguez, 'Moneda medieval', 17 n. 6: 'Baste con citar aquí a Sánchez Albornoz, del que toman esta aseveración numerosos autores en trabajos posteriores'.

[22]   *Portugaliae monumenta historica a saeculo octavo post Christum usque ad quintumdecimum*, ed. A. Herculano de Corvalho e Araujo and J. da Silva Mendes Leal (Olispone, 1867–73), *Diplomata et chartae*, doc. [hereafter *PMH*] no. 64: *XXVIII solidos romanos usum terre nostra*, discussed Sánchez-Albornoz, 'Organización monetária', 308 of the original, and his 'Moneda de cambio', 417–18.

[23]   See Mínguez, 'Moneda medieval', 26–8; cf. J. Pellicer, 'Metrologia comtal: homenatge a Joaquim Botet i Sisó' in *Symposium Numismàtic de Barcelona*, ed. J.M. Gurt and A. Balaguer (2 vols, Barcelona, 1979), 1, 261–311 at 268–9; J. Jarrett, 'Currency Change in Pre-millennial Catalonia: coinage, counts and economics', *NC, 169* (2009), 217–43 at 226–7; on bullion economies elsewhere one might mention not least M. Blackburn, 'Currency under the Vikings, Part 5: The Scandinavian achievement and legacy', Presidential Lecture, *BNJ, 79* (2009), 43–71, at 48–51 (*VCCBI*, 119–47, at 124–7).

[24]   Sánchez-Albornoz, *Ciudad hispano-cristiana*, 36–9; Sánchez-Albornoz, 'Precio de la vida', *passim*; cf. now Mínguez, 'Moneda medieval', 28–30.

[25]   'Precio de la vida', 376–82, with tables 397–409, animals specifically 404–8.

those with access to the actual documents, were mostly of similar enough an order, and presented with sufficiently extensive flattery of his earlier work, that he could endorse them as 'fortificación'.[26]

The apparent contradiction set up by this system in which a sheep worth a *modius* worth a *solidus* would have to have the same value as a 'solidary' cow was resolved, for Sánchez-Albornoz, by invoking two separate *solidi*, the gold *solidus* of Roman origin used by the Sueves and Visigoths (albeit at different standards, as he found argued in the contemporary work of Wilhelm Reinhart), and the new silver standard of the Carolingian empire.[27] He had even earlier demonstrated the likelihood of a shift from one system to the other in the kingdom of Asturias-León, and with his prices assembled argued that all instances of cows with such low values, whether called *soldare* or just bought at that sort of price, must be reckoned on the gold standard, whereas the *modius* that a sheep was worth, which was also worth a *solidus*, must have been reckoned in notional silver, although he did not precisely link the two things, and in his later work preferred to see the shift of standard as later, more ragged and more market-driven than he had when young (when he had loyally blamed King Alfonso II).[28]

This set of developing arguments, when fully assembled, had the potential to resolve some of the problems, but by no means all. For a start, as Sánchez-Albornoz had recognised from the outset, these usages were extremely regionalised.[29] While *boves soldares* might be encountered in documents from most of the Spanish north, *ovelias modiales* are almost restricted to Galicia and Portugal, with some rare outliers in León, and *porcos tremisales* lack even these wider appearances. This may not be as representative as one would wish,

[26] 'Moneda de cambio', 422 n. 39; with reference to Sáez, 'Nuevos datos', of which a full half of the article text is taken up with gratulatory recapitulation of the work, 'magistral como todos los suyos', of the 'ilustre profesor' (865, 869), presumably because the point of his article was to point out things that Sánchez-Albornoz had missed; the older historian was of course the editor of Laguzzi, 'Precio de la vida'. García Álvarez, 'Moneda y precios', was not so respectful. As Chris Wickham observes of Spanish scholarship of the period more widely, 'post-Visigothic Spanish scholarship is stimulating, but not exactly eirenic' (*Framing the Early Middle Ages*, 231).

[27] Sánchez-Albornoz, 'Precio de la vida', 383–4, revised in 'Moneda de cambio', 424–30; his reference W. Reinhart, 'Los sueldos "gallecanas": monedas gallegas', *Cuadernos de Estudios Gallegos*, 2 (1944), 177–84.

[28] 'Organización monetária', 303–6; 'Precio de la vida', 383–4. On Alfonso II's Carolingian connections see R. Collins, 'Spain: the Northern Kingdoms and the Basques, 711–910', in *The New Cambridge Medieval History Vol. II: c. 700–c. 900*, ed. R. McKitterick (Cambridge, 1995), 272–89, at 279–80; J. Escalona, 'Family Memories: inventing Alfonso I of Asturias' in *Building Legitimacy: political discourses and forms of legitimacy in medieval societies*, ed. I. Alfonso, H. Kennedy and J. Escalona, The Medieval Mediterranean: peoples, economies and cultures 400–1500, 53 (Leiden, 2004), 223–62.

[29] 'Precio de la vida', 378–82; his tables are organised by province to make the differences clear.

since their occurrences are so very sparse in the first place, but Galicia's general preponderance of payments in produce and livestock makes it somewhat more likely that this is a genuine reflection of different sorts of economy.[30] Payment in *argenteos* was considerably more usual around the southern city (and after 914, capital) of León than anywhere else, and in certain areas livestock and grain, or other rarer products, were the sole means of payment. These regional variations have lately been given their full flavour in a study by Wendy Davies, but their unevenness is discomfiting for anyone after a systematic view, even if predominant agricultural practices as determined by local geography probably have a lot to do with it.[31]

There is also variation over time. Sánchez-Albornoz had also considered this, and indeed this was his major conclusion from his first assembly of prices, that, even allowing for regional differences, prices seemed to have taken definite leaps in the mid-to-late ninth and late-tenth centuries. The first of these he attributed to the change of value standard disrupting prices and causing devaluation and the second to damage to the economy caused by the raids of the armies of the Muslim *ḥājīb* al-Mansur. Thereafter, however, he detected a steady price rise.[32] This makes his use of relatively late evidence in the construction of his equivalence of sheep and *solidi* via the *modius* problematic, to say the least; when such an equivalence is to be established by two documents, from the same nunnery but from 950 and 1001, we must at least worry that this may not be like compared with like.[33]

So, there is room for considerably more variation over space and time in these systems than Sánchez-Albornoz, who was fundamentally looking for systems and social structures and believed that he had found them, was necessarily interested to display. This view was first expressed in an article by Sánchez-Albornoz's 'discipulo' Luis de Valdeavellano, once safely established in a chair in Barcelona, and seized upon by later opponents of Valdeavellano's 'cuidado maestro', but in fact the variant valuation that Valdeavellano had spotted is rather late, and his

---

[30]   Albeit that difference might be best seen as one of degree rather than of kind; see L. de Valdeavellano, 'Economía natural y monetária en León y Castilla durante los siglos IX, X y XI (notas para le historia económica de España en la edad media)', *Moneda y crédito, 10* (1944), 28–46.

[31]   Davies, 'Sale, price and valuation'.

[32]   'Precio de la vida', 383–7.

[33]   First used in his *Estampas de la vida*, p. 27 n. 46, the evidence registered again in 'Precio de la vida', 408; the documents to which he referred are now printed as *Colección diplomática de Santa María de Otero de las Dueñas (León) (854–1037)*, ed. G. del Ser Quijano, Textos Medievales, 20 (Salamanca, 1994), doc. [hereafter Otero] nos 8 of 961, which has a price in which the sheep must be worth a *modius* (*modios III et ovigula, sub uno modios IIIIor*) and 61 of 1008, in which half of a price of 200 *solidi* is paid with 100 sheep (*kaballo I, apreciato in solidos C, et obiculas C, adpreciatas in solidos C*).

article was concerned much more with a theoretical debate, largely between German scholars, about classifications of economic systems.[34]

More serious questions were therefore raised first by the French historian Jean Gautier Dalché, who in a 1969 article presented his own long lists of tables of prices indicating some of this variation, and suggesting that rather than being a value standard as such, these nominal beasts should be taken to have been average animals that happened to fit the notional value, which might explain the rarity with which they occurred.[35] This resolves, or at least acknowledges, some of the wrinkles in the evidence, but leads us back ineluctably to the picture of a northern Spain across which a Galician sheep and a Leonese cow might both be worth a *solidus* as contemporaries envisioned that quantity, from which Sánchez-Albornoz's more constructed paradigm had escaped.

At more or less the same time, the Galician historian M. Rubén García Álvarez published an article in which he demonstrated, without much more than lip-service to Sánchez-Albornoz's researches, that there were rather more charters containing such references than the older historian had been able to find before he left Spain, and that they necessitated (in García Álvarez's view) revision of Sánchez-Albornoz's date for the change from gold to silver standards, at least for Galicia, which was the only area in which García Álvarez was interested. For him, the various value systems found in use in 'la nuestra terra' continued in use into the early eleventh century, along with the legacy coinages to which they referred, while Sánchez-Albornoz had thought that the old gold currencies, even if still circulating, could not long have outlasted the new influx of silver that he saw in (eventually) the tenth century.[36] He also maintained that the variation in prices detectable in the records precluded any idea of a standard livestock referent, and critiqued Sánchez-Albornoz's explanations of those price changes over time by stressing that both parts of any valuation, the currency and the cereals or the livestock, might increase or decrease in value independently, with consequent

---

[34]   Valdeavellano, 'Economía natural y monetária', 36; cit. by García Álvarez, 'Moneda y precios', 370–71, apparently without having seen more than the report of it in Sáez, 'Nuevos datos', and criticising Sánchez-Albornoz for ignoring these contrary findings, which in fact he had not; they are engaged in Sánchez-Albornoz, 'Moneda de cambio', 422 n. 41 where he made the same objections as I do above. Sánchez-Albornoz cited the article of Valdeavellano ('mi discípulo') with approval elsewhere ('Moneda de cambio', 412 n. 2) and obviously thought the correction bearable. The document that Valdeavellano cited was *PMH* no. 779, of 1092.

[35]   J. Gautier Dalché, 'L'histoire monétaire de l'Espagne septentrionale et centrale du XI.ᵉ au XII.ᵉ siècles: quelques reflexions sur divers problèmes', *Anuario de Estudios Medievales*, 6 (1969), 43–95, at 49–51; it is a great pity that Gautier Dalché's tables only enumerated such valuations without citing or quoting them, as they are considerably more complete than any of Sánchez-Albornoz's or his successors'.

[36]   García Alvarez, 'Moneda y precios', 365–8, noticing but not integrating Sánchez-Albornoz's revision of his chronology (see n. 28 above), 364 and n. 5.

effect on valuations using both.[37] García Álvarez had indubitably found more charters than had Sánchez-Albornoz, and his economic explanations have more subtlety than the older historian's essentially political ones, but his arithmetic in decoding the often complex arrays of goods used to pay large amounts in Galicia, bent on disproving the existence of a silver standard in Galicia or any standard valuations in terms other than gold *solidi*, can sometimes reasonably be corrected.

For numismatists, also, there was considerable dispute to be had with Sánchez-Albornoz over his belief in the long survival of old money, and by extension even more so with García Álvarez's, based largely it seems on pride in Galician conservatism. Both held to this conclusion because of documents that appear to record payments in such coin. It has justly been argued, however, that such references are ambiguous, not least because of the non-existence of actual silver *solidi* such as they imply. García Álvarez thought that these would have been paid in *denarii*, which have at least been found in the area in hoards of this period, unlike almost every other coin so far mentioned, but the question still remains why the documents would say otherwise, especially since a very few do record payments in the smaller coins.[38] With each payment valued in *solidi* one finds that was explicitly fulfilled in bullion, grain, wine, cloth or other goods, however, it becomes less necessary to assume that any of them need have involved coin. Less disputable instances of payment in coin are recognisable in documents from contemporary Catalonia, where a negligible local coinage appears to have been in circulation, or indeed from later on in this area, once minting had certainly been resumed; such lack of ambiguity is significantly missing from the documents under review, however.[39]

---

[37]   García Alvarez, 'Moneda y precios', 374–80.

[38]   García Alvarez, 'Moneda y precios', 392, citing *Liber Fidei*, no. 28: *porco de VIII denars*. Sánchez-Albornoz, 'Moneda de cambio', 431–2, noted finds of Carolingian deniers in the ruins of the earliest church of Santiago de Compostela, citing M. Chamosa Lamas, 'Excavaciones arqueológicas en la catedral de Santiago (tercera fase)', *Compostellanum*, 2 (1957), 221–330, at 270–71. These finds do not appear to have passed into the numismatic literature.

[39]   For Catalonia, see G. Feliu Montfort, 'Las ventas con pago en moneda en el condado de Barcelona hasta el año 1010', *Cuadernos de historia economica de Cataluña*, 5 (1971), 9–41; now Jarrett, 'Currency'; the clearest reference is *Catalunya Carolíngia IV: els comtats d'Osona i Manresa*, Memòries de la Secció històrico-arqueològica 53 (3 vols, Barcelona, 1999), doc. no. 1172: *moneta propria publica ausonensis*, referring to money of the mint at Vic d'Osona. Valdeavellano ('Economía natural y monetária', 38) cited a document of 1099 from our area with a price given as *La solidos denariorum monete*, but it is not at his cited location (*PMH* p. 532). Other references to money payments from that era are however easy enough to find, e.g. *PMH* nos 741, 762 (*moneta domno adefonsi regis*, on which see *MEC* 6, 424–5; the document is now better printed as *Livro Preto, cartulário da Sé de Coimbra: texto integral*, ed. M.A. Rodrigues (Coimbra, 1999), doc. 26) or 809 (where *denarius*).

A *solidus*, or indeed a *tremissis*, need not therefore imply the actual coins of those names, therefore, even if specified in such detail as *XVm solidos gallecarios usui terre nostre* ('Galician *solidi* as are customary in our land'); a weight or a unit of account must probably be preferred.[40] This means that we are dealing, when these coinages come up, with objects just as imaginary as the Platonic cow implied by our *bovo soldare*. In its rare appearances, however, and indeed in the much larger numbers of payments made in some areas of northern Spain with livestock of unspecified values, we are dealing with animals that presumably did exist, unlike the coins. Something about the quality and value of the animals called *bovos soldares* apparently appealed to imaginary concepts, all the same. Can we therefore say with more care what these characteristics were?

Characterising the Data

The documents can, in fact, be quite forthcoming about cows. They are not infrequently distinguished by colour, black, white, dark, pale, red, maroon, chestnut or brindled; they are of course always distinguished by gender, *bove* or *vaca* (to use contemporary spellings) or sometimes both together; sometimes they came with calves, and sometimes would do shortly; sometimes they came in pairs, as a plough-team; one came with a cart and harness, thus making estimation of its sole value impossible.[41] They also evidently varied in value, or at least in quality; we have already mentioned the 'middling' cow, *vaca media*, but a 965 payment of three *boves obtimos*, for the value of 12 *solidi*, thus 4 *solidi* a head, suggests that a *bove soldare* ought to have been a somewhat poorer beast.[42] In this instance, we are unlikely to be comparing like with like, but it is clear that

---

[40]   *PMH* no. 29; I have not been able to obtain *Livro de Mumadona: Cartulário medievo existente no Arquivo Nacional da Torre do Tombo* (Lisbon, 1973), where this document should be better edited.

[41]   *Cartulario de Santo Toribio de Liébana*, ed. L. Sánchez Belda (Madrid 1948), doc. no. 4: *bove colore nigro*; *Libro de Regla, o, Cartulario de la antigua abadía de Santillana del Mar*, ed. E. Jusué (Madrid, 1912), doc. no. 47: *bobe albo*; del Ser, *Otero*, doc. no. 59: *bove per zolore forzo*, which Sánchez-Albornoz ('Precio de la vida', p. 407) read: *bove colore fosgo*; Celanova 452: *vaca soldare colore laurea*; 'Cartulario de la iglesia de Santa María del Puerto (Santoña) [I]', ed. M. Serrano y Sanz, *Boletín de la Real Academia de la Historia*, 73 (1918), 420–42, doc. no. 5: *I baca rubia*; Lugo, 929: *vaca colore maura*; *Colección documental del Archivo de la Catedral de León (775–1230): II (953–985)*, ed. E. Sáez and C. Sáez, Fuentes y Estudios de Historia Leonesa, 42 (León, 1990), doc. no. 478: *vobe pro colore castanio in V solidos, et bacca nigra per colore in alios V solidos, et tapete polemdo in VIII solidos, et XIII solidos arenzeos, quod est sub uno pretio conpletu apput nos XXXIII solidos*; Sánchez, *Liébana*, doc. no. 2: *baca vitulata*.

[42]   Sahagún 229: *IIIes boves obtimos apreciatos in XIIm solidos*.

the people using these concepts were also aware of the reality of variation in their supposed currency, as was suggested above that they must have been.

Making a good estimation of the value of that means of payment from these documents is, however, not simple. The number of transactions in which animals are used in payment of a stated price is not large; that where the price can clearly be mapped to the animals is smaller still. One document from the nunnery of Sobrado in which a price was set at, 'four *solidi* and a *tremiss*, made up of an ox [there follows a gap on the parchment fit for perhaps thirteen characters] some woollen clothing and 12 cheeses', is especially impressive in its irreducibility, but many others could be quoted, including combinations of horse and tack with cattle that leave no way to assign separate values to their components.[43] Without having repeated the lengthy trawl through the documents, published and unpublished, that would be needed to better the collective efforts of the historians so far mentioned, I reckon the number of documents in which the price of cattle is either clearly stated, or arithmetically reducible to a sum per head, to be a mere 36 from the period 796–1010 (a cut-off point chosen because it avoids any possibility of new coinage having been struck in the area, and because at that point many of the records from Celanova become temporarily hard to date).[44] Of these instances, 22 come from the uplands of Asturias, Galicia and what is now Portugal (Asturias being evident only early on, which is a mirror of its documentary preservation generally); the other 14 come from León, and to a lesser extent, Castile. The totals for other animals are far poorer: eight prices for sheep, all in *modios* and all but two from Galicia or the future Portugal, and three for pigs, all from that area.[45]

Presenting these figures then raises further issues. One naturally wants to try and gauge the mean price per year of the cows, but this means smoothing out considerable variation. A brief burst of sales containing useful data from León of 980, for example, gives three prices in which there feature a cow of 20 *solidi* and a bull and a cow of 5 *solidi* each. The cow is not said to be *obtima* but something obviously convinced the seller that she was worth the land concerned. We must remember that no actual coinage was involved here: the price thus implies only that both parties were happy to place a high value on what they exchanged, not that this value was necessarily real.[46] The mean price of 10 *solidi* a head for 980

---

[43]   Respectively Sobrado 18: *Precio id est bove colore marceno, manto laneo vilado et chomacio, kaseos XII [ ] et est ipso precio in aderado solidos IIIIor et I tremese*, and Celanova 204: *Equa una poldrada, bove I, solido inter panem et vinum, pelle una, flomazo pallio I, linteos VIII.*

[44]   Arguments can be made that minting was resumed under Fernando I; see Sánchez-Albornoz, 'Organización monetária', 315–41; *MEC 6*, 209–12.

[45]   The former of these figures could probably be increased, as García Álvarez, who found many other instances for cattle and swine that previous researchers did not, did not look for sheep.

[46]   The two 5-*solidi* beasts are in Sáez and Sáez, *León II*, doc. no. 478, quoted n. 41 above; the 20-*solidi* one is not at the location given by Sánchez-Albornoz, 'Precio de la vida', 407, which

fits Figure 9.2 below very well, in fact, but one cannot but feel that it is missing some important detail.

There is also the issue of different standards. This is more than a possibility: the values of cattle in the upland zone I have distinguished were far lower than in lowland León and Castile, and the question is merely why: all the scholars who have worked over these prices have seen the same separation.[47] The two graphs below (Figures 9.1 and 9.2) therefore repeat it, and by doing so hopefully make obvious the regional differences.

As will immediately be seen, prices in León and Castile simply did get higher than those further north and west in this period, although the picture is much more alike when one omits the highest and lowest figures in each case. It is also clear that Galicia was much more produce-based than the more urban lowlands: the absence of prices in *modios* from the second graph is not accidental, there are none recorded (at least, none that can be matched to a known quantity of livestock). The datapoints are few, but they do also seem to indicate a rise in prices towards the end of the tenth century; whereas a normal cow in León might have retailed for about five *solidi* in 925 (and in fact did, if the three in question were normal), by 990 ten *solidi* would be a more normal price. In Galicia, however, while late on 10 *modios* of grain might seem a fair price (which is encouraging for the equivalence of that measure to a *solidus*), prices in money were usually at the one-*solidus* mark until very late, with a sudden jump at the year 1000, but still not to Leonese levels. This may be the point at which we should look for the shift from gold to silver reckoning in this conservative area, but this has its own implication, to wit that the *bovo soldare* must have been worth a gold *solidus*, not a silver one, as indeed Sánchez-Albornoz seems to have come to suppose.[48] The conversion value, taking contemporary instances from the two zones, of roughly one to five, is much lower than any of the historians working on these matters would have supposed, but this is not least due to a late document that helpfully tells us that a *solidus* of gold was worth 15 of silver, something that no contemporary Andalusi trader, at least, would have given for it.[49] Since, of course, the actual coins were unlikely to have been at issue, such

---

appears to be scrambled. On social factors' effect on land prices, cf. C. Wickham, 'Vendite di terra i mercato della terra in Toscana nel secolo XI', *Quaderni Storici*, 65 (1987), 355–77, transl. and rev. as 'Land Sales and Land Market in Tuscany in the Eleventh Century', in Wickham, *Land and Power: studies in Italian and European social history, 400–1200* (London, 1994), 257–74; C. Wickham, *The Mountains and the City: the Tuscan Apennines in the early Middle Ages* (Oxford, 1988), 252–54.

[47]   See nn. 27 and 36 above.

[48]   'Moneda de cambio', 432–8.

[49]   Sánchez-Albornoz's source was late manuscripts of the Visigothic Law, arguably not a good index of contemporary practice even if updated; he gave a text at 'Moneda de Cambio', 436,

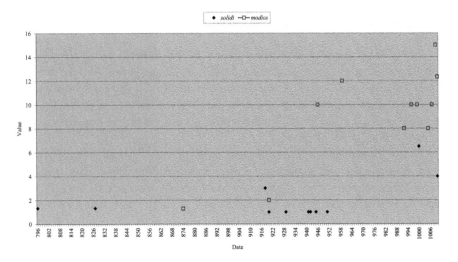

Figure 9.1 Prices of cattle in Asturias, Galicia and Portugal 796–1010. (Diamonds indicate prices in *solidi*, squares those in *modii*.)

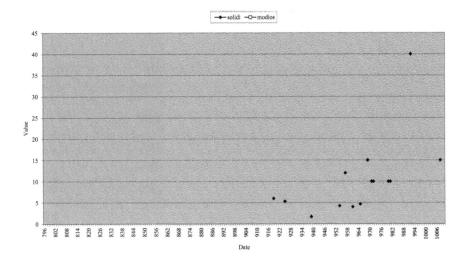

Figure 9.2 Cattle prices in León and Castile 796–1010.

arithmetic cannot be rigorous, but the idea of two different regional standards seems pretty irrefutable once the data are examined.

Giving the prices for sheep and pigs, few as they are, does not seem to require a plot; I present them below as tables (Tables 9.1 and 9.2).

Table 9.1   Prices of sheep (including *oveliae modiales*) in Northern Spain 796–1010.

Date	Province	Mean price in modios	Text
861	Asturias	0.75	*karnario unum in tria quartaria* [a]
942	Galicia	1	*cabra modiale* [b]
961	Galicia	0.25	*ovelia quartario* I [c]
961	Galicia	1	*ovelia modiale* [d]
962	Galicia	1	*ovelia modiale* [e]
964	Galicia	1	*ovelia modiale* [f]
1001	León	1	*cabra in modio* [g]
1008	León	1	*ovigula* [h]
1010	Galicia	2	*oves IIas* [i]

Notes: (a) Sahagún no. 3; (b) Celanova no. 451; (c) Celanova no. 406; (d) Celanova no. 390 (see n. 10 above); (e) Celanova no. 397; (f) Celanova no. 403; (g) Otero no. 42; (h) Otero no. 61(see n. 33 above); (i) Celanova no. 197.

Table 9.2   Prices of pigs in Northern Spain (including *porcos tremisales*) 796–1010.

Date	Province	Mean price in solidi	Mean price in modios
975 [a]	Portugal		2
990 [b]	Galicia	0.33 (*tremisale*)	
999 [c]	Portugal	0.67 (8 *denarii*)	

Notes: (a) García Álvarez, 'Moneda y precios', 392, citing Archivo de la Catedral de Lugo, est. 64, lg. 4, no. 12, of which there is as yet no edition; (b) Celanova no. 409 (see n. 11 above); (c) Sánchez-Albornoz, 'Precio de la vida', 408, Laguzzi, 'Precio de la vida', 146 (where given as 8 *solidi*), García Álvarez, 'Moneda y precios', 392, all citing *Liber fidei*, no. 28.

From these results it is very hard to get much at all. So many of the sheep were *ovelias modiales* that saying that sheep were commonly worth a *modius* is merely to adopt the presumption of the sources, and the value of pigs can hardly be assessed from so nugatory a sample. All that can be said is that other instances

---

citing *Leges Visigothorum*, ed. K. Zeumer, MGH Leges Nationum Germanicum 1 (Hannover, 1902), 33–456, at V.15.

can be adduced that make the Galician *solidus* come out at six *modios*, as the first pig here would imply if it were *tremisale*.[50]

Such tinkering, which García Álvarez carried out mainly to demonstrate the frailty of Sánchez-Albornoz's similar calculations, can certainly be done in a way that brings the more complex equivalencies into line with some of these results. An instance that he cites of a price composed of 4 *modios* paid with a *modius* of rye and a new and *tremisale* shirt, which seems to require that a *tremissis* be worth three *solidi*, is only as ridiculous as he supposed if one reckons that the equivalence of a *modius* and a *solidus* was to be calculated on the gold standard; but clearly no-one was so calculating, or the 'modial' sheep would have been as *solidare* as their more expensive bovine companions.[51] As long as the *modius* = *solidus* equivalence is only required to have operated with imaginary silver *solidi*, not imaginary gold ones, the shirt's price was impressive but consistent. On the other hand, some of the instances García Álvarez dragged up make less sense. Making a fixed system out of all of this is a game for madmen, and supposes a level of coordination between very different and separated communities that is frankly implausible. The standards that we are seeing may have varied from place to place, certainly did from time to time, and the transactors' estimations of the goods that were fitted to them can only ever have been subjective.

What we can say, however, is that relatively few cows seem to have been worth a (gold) *solidus*, although this is hard to reckon for places beyond the gold standard without a clear conversion figure, of course. While most of the sheep to which we can put a price were *modiale*, others were not, and the matter is complicated by the rise in prices one might expect over this period. Pigs, meanwhile, do not seem to have conformed to their notional value well either, though this is hard to judge within this period. The idea that such 'standard' animals could have formed a currency is beyond plausibility: obtaining a beast that everyone could agree was the right value, despite the obviously short-term relevance of any comparable exemplar beasts, would have placed a premium on such animals that would have immediately made them more expensive.[52] Finding a Suevic *tremissis* might even have been easier, although it seems more likely that the Galician documents that refer to an *usus nostri terra* mean the gold standard as a whole, set against the Leonese preference for silver, as opposed to a specifically Suevic one surviving through a century of Visigothic minting; this might also accommodate the one reference to 'Roman' *solidi* mentioned above.

---

[50]   Cf. Sahagún no. 125, quoted n. 10 above.

[51]   Celanova no. 192: *id est cibaria modios I, saia nova tremissale I, sub uno pretio modios IIIIor.*

[52]   A Cambridge instance of the same phenomenon could for a while be seen at the kiosk in the recently-built toilet block on Parker's Piece, which would happily sell one of the 20-pence coins that the toilets required to operate, for 35 pence each.

The *bovo soldare*, therefore, could not genuinely operate as a referent, and it seems clear that by and large it did not. Nonetheless it remained conceptually available, much as when someone wealthy nowadays is asked what bread costs in the supermarket. This is also a question with no single answer but the idea that it represents still has power. The *bove soldare* was, it seems, such an item: a gold *solidus*, itself only a remembered value, was what a Platonic, a notional cow, was worth, more or less, and now and then one turned up that was of that sort of value, but the occurrence was rarer than not and certainly not required for any given transaction. We should almost certainly assume the same of the sheep and the pig whose notional values fitted into the conceptual framework so neatly. Even if a given set of transactors could agree that the value of a cow, sheep or pig satisfied this expectation, we should not expect that the next time that animal were sold the same agreement on its value would be reached, even if it had changed not at all in the interim.

Conclusions and Speculations

Thus, the value standard implied by the *bovo soldare* obviously existed (just as did that implied by prices in *solidi* despite their even more thorough absence), but beasts' conformity to that standard was subjective, and very far from necessary. As a concept, it existed more strongly in Galicia than elsewhere, partly because of the greater density of transactions in livestock and produce there, and partly because the old currency system within which the valuation made sense seems to have hung on in people's heads there longest. The idea of what a cow should be worth was, however, transmitted more widely, including into areas less mountainous and (as Sánchez-Albornoz would have had it) more hazardous, and the system as variously applied seems broadly consistent, albeit with price changes that are best left to other historians to dispute.

Some further, more hypothetical observations may also be worthwhile. If we are to see the set of three animals with notional values as a coherently imagined system, which it may not have been, one notable feature of the system is that it is based both on coin and on produce, which implies that the economy that generated it was operating on a basis of only partial monetisation. To imagine this occurring in an economy in which coin was not, in fact, being produced, seems almost more likely than to find it in the Visigothic one, in which copper coins were struck that do not feature in the scheme. Coin was obviously remembered at this point, however, as *tremisses* had actually existed and may occasionally have been found in our period. The three-level standard would seem, therefore, necessarily to be post-Visigothic, but perhaps only narrowly so. All the same, when our first documents invoke it in 796 (when the cows in question were already over-valued) it cannot have been very old, either, and it may be that the creation of such a system, by whatever authority or consensus, was in fact provoked by the exposure to the Carolingian silver coinage now being struck in the north-west of the Peninsula.[53] These would have been too rarely available to make a standard by themselves, but they may have necessitated the imagination of a referent against which they could be reckoned, a referent which however affected more usual transactions in these areas very little. Thus to see the *bovo soldare* as a cow of anti-Carolingian reaction thinking is almost certainly going too far, but it may not be the oddest thing that has been imagined of the poor beast, and perhaps with this survey we have built a better home for the cow to come back to.

---

[53]   On this see Jarrett, 'Currency change', 218–21; *MEC 6*, 70–74.

PART III
Use and Circulation of Currency

Chapter 10
Byzantine Coins in Early Medieval Britain: A Byzantinist's Assessment

Cécile Morrisson

Λέγουσιν οὖν τὰς τῶν ἀποβιούντων ἀνθρώπων ψυχὰς ἐς τοῦτο ἀεὶ διακομίζεσθαι τὸ χωρίον [Βριττία Ὠκεανοῦ νῆσος]

('They say that the souls of men who die are always conveyed to this place [the island of *Brittia*]')

Procopius, Wars VIII.xx.48
(Procopius: Works, ed. and trans. H.B. Dewing, (7 vols, London 1914–40), 5, 267)

The story about ghostly Breton fishermen, who receive departed souls at night in mysterious boats and after an hour of rowing put in at *Brittia*, is one 'which bears a very close resemblance to mythology', and 'did not indeed seem to me at all trustworthy', just as it did to Procopius when he recorded it in the fourth book of the *Gothic War*.[1] But it seems an appropriate epigraph to celebrate the memory of Mark Blackburn, friend and colleague of more than three decades, outstanding figure of British early medieval monetary history and developer of the online Corpus of Early Medieval Coin Finds (EMC).

The pages devoted by Procopius to *Brittia*/Britannia and Thule have aroused learned discussions for centuries, and many British scholars have expressed scepticism over the reality and extent of the relations between Britain and the Byzantine Empire. In 1980 no less a scholar than Edward A. Thompson wrote: 'it must not be supposed that there is archaeological evidence for much intercourse between Britain and the Mediterranean at this date'.[2] On the same lines of thought, the tradition of Britain's 'splendid isolation' may have inspired John Kent's 1991 essay about its 'resistance to common money' over the *longue durée*, at a time when the mainstream was more optimistic about the future

---

[1]   Procopius, *Wars* VIII.xx.48 (trans. Dewing, 5, 267).

[2]   E.A. Thompson, 'Procopius on *Brittia* and *Britannia*', *Classical Quarterly, 30* (1980), 498–507, at 505, n. 32.

of the forthcoming euro, than it is in the present crisis of 2008 and after.[3] To go back to early medieval England, credit should be given to Robert Lopez's programmatic 1948 article which proclaimed:

> il n'y a pas, à *l'heure actuelle* [my italics], de preuves incontestables et explicites de l'existence de relations directes entre l'Angleterre et Byzance au haut Moyen Âge, mais un certain nombre d'indices suggèrent la possibilité de pareils rapports ... il faudrait que des spécialistes des différentes branches de l'histoire byzantine et anglo-saxonne réunissent leurs efforts, et qu'ils ne se contentent pas du point de vue que tout contact doit avoir été indirect et accidentel ... mais qu'ils gardent constamment à l'esprit la possibilité d'échanges économiques, politiques et culturels directs.[4]

This far-sighted wish has now been fulfilled insofar as the dramatic progress of British early medieval archaeology and numismatics – and notably the development of PAS that started in 1997[5] – has considerably enlarged the documentation concerning finds of Byzantine coins within the wider stock of contemporaneous issues, whether Merovingian, German, Frisian or early Anglo-Saxon ones found on British soil. It has completely overhauled our perspective upon the early period and the vitality of its monetary circulation in the 'Conversion' period. In 1961, Philip Whitting regretted that 'the finds of Byzantine coins in Britain are meagre and ill-recorded'. Referring to the list of 'ninety coins' then being assembled by George Boon, Whitting insisted that, apart from the two finds of gold coins from Ilchester that 'appear to be impeccably genuine', 'the rest do not look like genuine hoards or ancient losses at all, though some of them conceivably may be'.[6] He had seen the list that George

---

[3]   J.P.C. Kent, 'Facteurs de résistance à une monnaie commune', in *Une monnaie pour l'Europe/One Money for Europe*, ed. M. Alram (Brussels, 1991), 147–50.

[4]   'At present, there is no incontrovertible and explicit evidence for the existence of direct relations between England and Byzantium in the early Middle Ages, but several indications suggest the possibility of such relations ... it is necessary that specialists in different branches of Byzantine and Anglo-Saxon history combine their efforts, and not restrict themselves to the view that all contact must have been indirect and accidental ... rather, they should always bear in mind the possibility of direct economic, political and cultural exchange'. R.S. Lopez, 'Le problème des relations anglo-byzantines du septième au dixième siècle', *Byzantion, 18* (1946–8), 139–62, at 140 (repr. in his *Byzantium and the World around it: Economic and Institutional Relations* (London, 1978), no. IV).

[5]   R. Bland, 'Le *Treasure Act* et le *Portable Antiquities Scheme* en Angleterre et au Pays de Galles', *BSFN, 66* (2010), 270–76 offers a general assessment with impressive figures and examples.

[6]   P.D. Whitting, 'The Byzantine Empire and the coinage of the Anglo-Saxons', in *Studies presented to F.M. Stenton on the Occasion of his 80th Birthday*, ed. R.H.M. Dolley (London, 1961), 23–38, at 26.

Boon assembled from 1958 till 1988, which amounted to 140 items when he gave his statistics and rating of the finds, unfortunately without any details, in the 1991 volume about Exeter.[7]

A first synthetic detailed survey of gold finds was drawn up by Stuart Rigold in 1975 to provide comparanda for his epoch-making study of Sutton Hoo.[8] It included 23 imperial gold coins from Anastasius I to Leo III among a total of 140 fifth- to early eighth-century recorded specimens (some 16 per cent of the total and 18 per cent if one adds the three fifth-century coins of Leo I and Julius Nepos, nos. 21, 22, 24). In 1987, drawing on Rigold's and earlier publications, Jean Lafaurie surprisingly recorded only twelve gold and three copper finds.[9] In 2006, after a nearly a decade of intense PAS and EMC recording, the time was ripe for evaluating its impact on this particular topic. Richard Abdy and Gareth Williams updated the list of hoards and single finds of the fifth to seventh centuries on the same all-inclusive lines as Rigold, but added copper coins as well as the many Scottish finds recorded by Ann Robertson, Donal Bateson and Nicholas Holmes. Out of a total of 379 coins including five pre-410 pieces and 19 dating to 410–91, their register comprises 57 Byzantine items (37 gold, 20 copper) of the period 491–721 that I consider here: four gold coins re-used as ornaments, 28 other gold coins and 20 copper coins. It also included a few imperial coins from various hoards: the Italian *tremissis* of Justin II in the Canterbury St. Martin's hoard, the Ravennate *solidus* from the Crondall hoard and three of the four coins from the Horndean 'hoard'.[10] In 2010, Roger Bland and the late Xavier Loriot included in their massive reference work the same total of 37 Byzantine gold coins of the period 491–721.[11] In the same year

---

[7]   G.C. Boon, 'Byzantine and other exotic ancient bronze coins from Exeter', in *Roman Finds from Exeter*, ed. N. Holbrook and P.T. Bidwell (Exeter, 1991), 38–45.

[8]   S.E. Rigold, 'The Sutton Hoo coins in the light of the contemporary background of coinage in England', in *The Sutton Hoo Ship Burial, vol. 1: Excavations, Background, the Ship, Dating and Inventory*, ed. R.L.S Bruce-Mitford (London, 1975), 653–77, with 'Finds of Gold Coins in England other than Sutton Hoo and Crondall' at 665–77.

[9]   J. Lafaurie and C. Morrisson, 'La pénétration des monnaies byzantines en Gaule mérovingienne et visigotique du VIe au VIIIe siècle', *RN, 6th series*, 29 (1987), 38–98, at 93–4. The Heraclius light-weight *solidus* referred to as from 'Ickworth' is due to mistaken information from J. Casey, who confused the Ixworth brooch with the Wilton Cross (J. Casey, 'Roman coinage of the fourth century from Scotland', in *Between and Beyond the Walls. Essays on the Prehistory and History of North Britain, in Honour of George Jobey*, ed. R. Miket and C. Burgess (Edinburgh, 1984), 295–304).

[10]   R.A. Abdy and G. Williams, 'A catalogue of hoards and single finds from the British Isles *c.* AD 410–675', in *Coinage and History in the North Sea World, c. AD 500–1250: Essays in Honour of Marion Archibald*, ed. B. Cook and G. Williams (Leiden, 2006), 11–74.

[11]   R. Bland and X. Loriot, *Roman and Early Byzantine Gold Coins found in Britain and Ireland, with an Appendix on Coin Finds from Gaul*, RNS Special Publication, 46 (London, 2010).

Gareth Williams considered the question of Byzantine imports in the first of three articles considering the transition from Roman to Anglo-Saxon coinage with an updated list of finds including all Bland and Loriot's entries plus two additions and offering some comments on geographical distribution.[12] Since many of the recorded coins are illustrated in Bland and Loriot's volume, it is possible to check their mint attribution, and a few of them can be corrected.[13]

Low-value copper-alloy finds of the sixth century included by Richard Abdy and Gareth Williams in their catalogue were not commented upon in the 2006 volume, in which Abdy concentrated on fifth-century (post-410) finds and Williams focused on the function and use of coinage as a whole, and in fact implicitly on gold and silver.[14] The only general comments and lists concerning specifically Byzantine copper coin finds were offered by George Boon in 1991,[15] Michael Metcalf in 1995[16] and Sam Moorhead in 2009.[17] Michael Metcalf's hypercritical approach, on the lines previously sustained by George Boon, dismissed most of the finds of Byzantine bronzes ('at least 90% of the evidence is worthless'), notably those from Exeter and Caerwent, but did not close the door on them completely when he concluded that one should 'not let go entirely of the possibility that a few Byzantine coppers may have reached the southern and

---

[12]   G. Williams, 'Anglo-Saxon gold coinage, Part I: The transition from Roman to Anglo-Saxon gold coinage', *BNJ* 80 (2010), 51–75. I am grateful to the editors for having drawn my attention to this important study.

[13]   Bland and Loriot, *Roman and Early Byzantine Gold Coins*, no. 836: this *solidus* of Maurice from Dorchester-on-Thames is not *MIBE* 6 but *MIBE* 14, a lightweight solidus with OBXX exergue. I have omitted three coins from their list: no. 787 since this *tremissis* of Justin I is not a Byzantine coin but a Frankish one; no. 807, since this *solidus* of Justin I or Justin II is also not Byzantine (*pace* Lafaurie and Morrisson, 'Pénétration des monnaies byzantines'; Rigold, 'Sutton Hoo coins', 2; Abdy and Williams, 'Catalogue', no. 69 – the exergue legend given in the original publication by C. Roach Smith, 'Roman coins found at Richborough', *Archaeologia Cantiana, 18* (1889), 72–7, at 73 has a pellet in the centre of the CONOB exergue that is not attested in Constantinople); and no. 883, a coin of Anastasius I from Little Burstead, Essex that does not look imperial.

[14]   R.A. Abdy, 'After Patching: imported and recycled coinage in fifth- and sixth century Britain', in *Coinage and History*, ed. Cook and Williams, 75–98. Despite its title, this paper hardly deals with Byzantine sixth-century finds. See also G. Williams, 'The circulation and function of coinage in Conversion-period England, *c.* AD 580–673', in *Coinage and History*, ed. Cook and Williams, 145–92.

[15]   Boon, 'Byzantine'.

[16]   D.M. Metcalf, 'Byzantine coins from Exeter', *Byzantinische Forschungen, 21* (1995), 253–61.

[17]   S. Moorhead, 'Early Byzantine copper coins found in Britain. A review in light of new finds recorded with the Portable Antiquities Scheme', in *Ancient History, Numismatics and Epigraphy in the Mediterranean World. Studies in Memory of Clemens E. Bosch and Sabahat Atlan and in honour of Nezahat Baydur*, ed. O. Tekin and E. Atalay (Istanbul, 2009), 263–74.

western shores of Britain'.[18] *A propos* the Caerwent finds, Abdy and Williams remarked that

> Byzantine *folles*, being large and relatively common ancient coins, make attractive modern keepsakes, e.g. brought back from the Middle East by British servicemen. Those found in Britain are thus most likely to have been discarded curiosities. Most ... should be treated with caution (but note the more convincing discoveries from Southampton, Alderney, Richborough, Thelnetham and Meols).[19]

Sam Moorhead provided an extremely useful corpus of 31 coins that added 16 PAS or CR recorded finds to those from previous literature. He 'decided not to include a number of the finds, notably those from Scotland' and eliminated four of the 20 copper recorded in the PAS since 1998. But, considering for instance the concentration of several stray finds in the area of Meols, where an ampulla of St. Menas has also been recorded, it appeared to him, against the doubts that many had expressed, that at least 'some of them were imported in the early medieval period' and, on the whole, he took the view that many of these finds may not be modern losses, as was previously believed. Recently the subject has been taken up again in the publication of the Winchester coin finds of the period by Eurydice Georganteli, who also concludes that 'the recurrent pattern in the geographical distribution of sixth-century byzantine copper coins in Britain ... could not be accidental or the result of modern imports'.[20] Her approach is supported by the excavator, Martin Biddle: he, too, considers their 'skewed distribution difficult to explain on such an assumption [of modern losses]'.[21]

Relying on this documentation, I have compiled a list of early medieval finds of Byzantine coins from Great Britain minted between 491 and the early eighth century. The date of the issues is of course not necessarily that of their deposit. In the very few instances with known stratigraphy or context, there can be a more or less important gap: the Justinian I Carthage *dekanoummion* from Southampton 'came from a middle layer in a rubbish pit, dating from not earlier than 750'.[22]

---

[18]   Metcalf, 'Byzantine coins', 260.

[19]   Abdy and Williams, 'Catalogue', 34.

[20]   E.S. Georganteli, 'Byzantine Coins', in *The Winchester Mint: and Coins and Related Finds from the Excavations of 1961–71*, ed. M. Biddle, Winchester Studies, 8 (Oxford, 2012), 669–78. I am grateful to John Casey for bringing this publication to my attention.

[21]   M. Biddle, 'Byzantine and Eastern finds from Winchester: chronology, stratification and social context', in *Winchester Mint*, ed. Biddle, 665–8, at 665: 'although often dismissed as modern losses ... their skewed distribution is difficult to explain on such assumption'. Thanks are due to Martin Biddle for kindly sending a copy of the chapters referring to coins and seals.

[22]   D.M. Metcalf, 'Byzantine coins', 256, citing his original publication: 'The Coins', in *Southampton Finds, vol. 1: the Coins and Pottery from Hamwic, Southampton Finds*, ed. P. Andrews

The time-span between issue and deposition is even greater in the case of the hexagram of Heraclius of the 620s which found its way into the *c.*7,500 Anglo-Saxon, Carolingian and Arabic coins of the Cuerdale hoard, buried in the first decade of the tenth century, probably brought from the Danubian regions to the Baltic area by way of the river routes between the Elbe and Oder.[23] This table follows an all-inclusive, maximal approach (see Appendix). Two marginal groups that were left aside in some previous gazetteers have been included: namely Scottish finds and those that had been discarded in the past as 'modern losses', the two most famous being the finds from Exeter and those from Caerwent.

The Exeter finds began to come to light in the early nineteenth century and their long historiography as well as their context have been extensively and accurately discussed by George Boon.[24] He examined the surviving examples together with no less an expert than Martin Price for the Greek series, and concluded that 'the material was typical of coins brought back from the Eastern Mediterranean' and could be dismissed entirely. This 'brilliant forensic rebuttal' pointing out all the inconsistencies and the unreliable character of the whole group of finds was endorsed four years later by Michael Metcalf.[25] I have however included them in the present table, since, as Richard Goodchild observed of the Byzantine coins, contrary to other ancient exotica in the various Exeter batches: '[with regards to the Byzantine coins], there is nothing exceptional in the Exeter record'.[26]

(Southampton, 1988), 17–59, at 25 and 56 (no. 187).

[23]   The context is clearly a secondary one and G. Williams ('The Cuerdale coins', in *The Cuerdale Hoard and Related Viking-Age Silver and Gold from Britain and Ireland in the British Museum*, ed. J. Graham-Campbell (London, 2011), 39–71, at 51) suggests 'it represents Scandinavian trading links through the Russian river system to the Black Sea'. However hexagram finds are not documented in Scandinavia or in central Russia. Seventh-century finds of hexagrams in this area are concentrated in southern Ukraine and in the Caucasus (see P. Yannopoulos, *L'hexagramme: un monnayage en argent du VIIe siècle* (Louvain-la-Neuve, 1978). They are very rare in western or central Europe: apart from the famous Slovakian hoard of Zemiansky Vrbovok (16 ceremonial coins – *miliaresia* – and one hexagram of Constans II and one hexagram of Constantine IV), one is attested in a grave in Linz (J. Drauschke, 'Byzantinische Münzen des ausgehenden 5. bis beginnenden 8. Jahrhunderts in den östlichen Regionen des Merowingerreiches', in *Byzantine Coins in Central Europe between the 5th and 10th Century*, ed. M. Wołoszyn (Kraków, 2009), 279–323, at 315 (no. 165)); and another one in Szadzko, near Szczecin (Stettin) (M. Wołoszyn, 'Byzantinische Münzen aus dem 6.–7. Jh. in Polen', in *Byzantine Coins*, ed. Wołoszyn, 473–530, at 505 (no. 18)). I would favour seeing the latter specimen as tenuous evidence for the western river routes between the Elbe and the Oder. I am grateful to Marcin Wołoszyn for sharing his differing view on this topic.

[24]   Boon, 'Byzantine'.

[25]   Metcalf, 'Byzantine coins', 258.

[26]   R.G. Goodchild and J.G. Milne, 'The Greek coins from Exeter reconsidered', *NC, 5th series, 17* (1937), 124–34; cited by Boon, 'Byzantine', 39.

In spite of Boon's caveats,[27] the coins 'said to have been found at Caerwent' have been also included in this table, in accordance with their presence in Abdy and Williams's register. It is true that John Casey found in the 1990s that they came to the Museum Collection in the 1920s, not from excavations, but as a donation from Lord Tredegar, a local collector, who resided in Caerwent; and that they should be definitely discarded from the record of possible Byzantine finds, being indeed in this respect 'from Caerwent' but not a local find.[28] I have kept them in the table, however, not only for the record but also to give them a sort of 'last chance' given the possibility that Lord Tredegar might have found them on his estate, and also because the appearance of Byzantine coins of the sixth to ninth century from Sicily in Britain is not as implausible as was once believed.[29]

In fact the combination of ancient and modern finds – a few from excavations or graves, most of them from metal detecting – listed in the Appendix, gives a picture which is, in my opinion, more historically meaningful than was considered before. The chronological distribution shows a limited presence of pre-527 coins, the expected peak under Justinian I, with a continued representation of his successors through Constans II, and very sporadic finds for a few of his successors, including Constantine IV, Justinian II, Tiberius III and Leo III (Table 10.1).

---

[27]   G.C. Boon, 'Note on the Byzantine AE Coins said to have been found at Caerwent', *Bulletin of the Board of Celtic Studies, 17* (1958), 316–19.

[28]   I am grateful to John Casey for this information.

[29]   C. Morrisson, 'La Sicile byzantine: une lueur dans les siècles obscurs', *Numismatica e antichità classiche, 27* (1998), 307–34.

Table 10.1 Chronological distribution of finds according to Byzantine emperors.

Mints	Cple		The	Nic	Cyz	Ant	Ale	Car		Cat	Syr		Rav	Uncertain		TOTAL		
Emperors	AV	Æ	Æ	Æ	Æ	Æ	Æ	AV	Æ	Æ	AV	Æ	AV	AV	Æ	AV	Æ	AV+AE
Anastasius I	5	2												1	1	6	3	9
Justin I	7	4		2											2	7	8	15
Justinian I	4	9	1	2	1	3			2					2	1	6	19	25
Justin II	1	1	1		1								1		2	2	5	7
Tiberius	2	1														2	1	3
Maurice	4	1			1	1	1	1		1						5	5	10
Phocas	2			1			1		1				1			3	3	6
Heraclius	3	2		1					2			1		1		4	6	10
Constans II	1	2							4			1			3	1	10	11
Constantine IV	1	1														1	1	2
Justinian II												1					1	1
Tiberius III	1															1		1
Leo III											1					1		1
TOTAL	31	23	2	6	3	4	2	1	9	1	1	3	2	4	9	39	62	101

Note: In this and successive figures, the mint abbreviations Cple (Constantinople), The (Thessalonica), Nic (Nicomedia), Cyz (Cyzicus), Ant (Antioch), Ale (Alexandria), Car (Carthage), Cat (Catania), Syr (Syracuse) and Rav (Ravenna) are used.

The distribution of coins between Byzantine mints (identified for 88 out of 101 specimens) shows a constant predominance of Eastern mints (81 per cent) over the Western provincial ones (Carthage, Ravenna and Sicily) (19 per cent). But when split between the sixth and the seventh centuries, the pattern changes: the share of the East recedes from 92 per cent to 57 per cent and that of the West goes up from a modest 8 per cent to 42 per cent (Figures 10.1 and 10.2).

In the case of the sixth century, this conforms with the general pattern analysed by Michael Fulford, who advocated direct contacts with the East until at least the 550s.[30] The fact that seventh-century coin finds are half as numerous as those of the sixth century parallels the general downsizing of Byzantine trade in the seventh century, the protracted diffusion of Eastern ceramics that had reached the 'limits of the inhabited world (*oikoumene*)' in the Justinianic period, and the relative resilience in the diffusion of North African wares, now mostly perhaps through the Gallic/Frankish intermediary.[31]

It cannot be denied that the sample considered is small, and some of the individual finds liable to suspicion. However the geographical pattern which emerges from mapping these finds (Figure 10.3) confirms the concentration of gold finds in Kent, notably east Kent, and East Anglia,[32] secondarily in Northumbria, especially in the surroundings of York or within miles from the city; all regions known for their early greater monetisation, and closer contacts with the Frankish world, the key mediator of Byzantine precious metal.

Copper coins are not entirely absent from the Eastern regions, but they are the only ones attested in Wales, Scotland, south-west England (Wessex) and the western parts of Mercia and Northumbria. Most of the finds, whether gold or copper, are stray losses, and the majority of them have been found on the coast or on the network of Roman roads, a fact which points – if we believe in their ancient context at all – to casual losses by travellers, rather than to tokens of diplomatic exchange.

There is some similarity with the pattern of ceramic finds in which 71 per cent of the Mediterranean imports consist of Phocaean Red Slip tableware and LR1, LR2 and LR3 amphorae, while the North African wares amount to only 19 per cent.[33] But this general similarity with the geographical distribution

---

[30]   M. Fulford, 'Byzantium and Britain: a Mediterranean perspective on Post-Roman Mediterranean imports in western Britain and Ireland', *Medieval Archaeology, 33* (1989), 1–6.

[31]   See A.E. Laiou and C. Morrisson, *The Byzantine Economy* (Cambridge, 2007), ch. 2; D. Pieri, *Le commerce du vin oriental à l'époque byzantine,Ve–VIIe siècles: Le témoignage des amphores en Gaule*, Bibliothèque archéologique et historique, 174 (Beirut, 2005).

[32]   As underlined for all gold finds of the period in D.M. Metcalf, 'The availability and uses of gold coinage in England, *c.* 580–*c.* 670: Kentish primacy reconsidered', *Numismatiska Meddelanden, 37* (1989), (Festskrift till L. O. Lagerqvist), 267–74.

[33]   E. Campbell and C. Bowles, 'Byzantine trade to the edge of the world', in *Byzantine Trade, 4th–12th Centuries: the Archaeology of Local, Regional and International Exchange*, ed. M. Mundell Mango (Aldershot, 2009), 297–313, at 298–300.

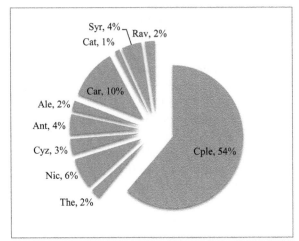

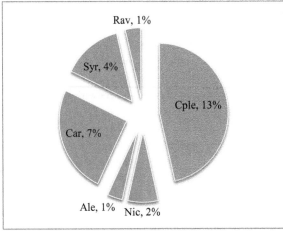

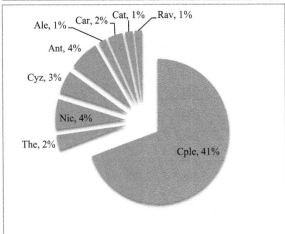

Figure 10.1 Mint distribution of Byzantine coin finds in Great Britain (all excluding coins of uncertain attribution). From top to bottom: (a) sixth–seventh centuries; (b) sixth century; (c) seventh century.

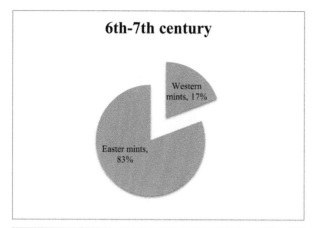

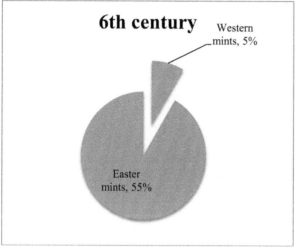

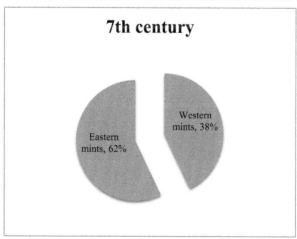

Figure 10.2
East-West mint
distribution of
Byzantine coin
finds in Great
Britain. From
top to bottom:
(a) sixth–seventh
centuries;
(b) sixth century;
(c) seventh century.

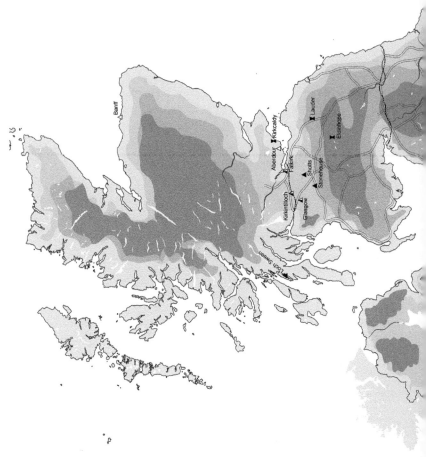

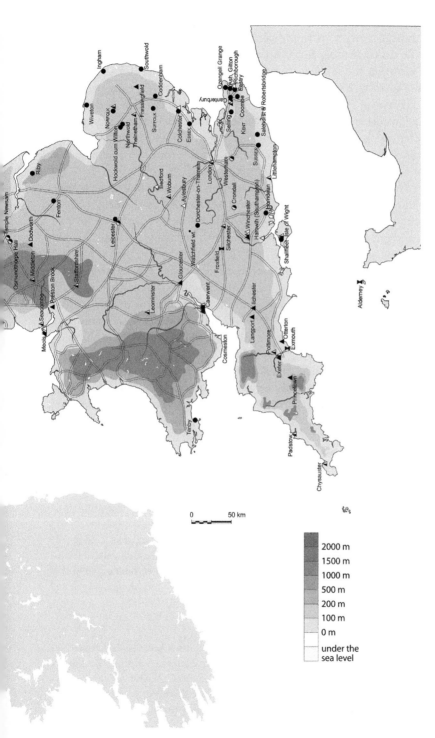

Figure 10.3   Byzantine coin finds in Great Britain (© C.Morrison and A. Ter-Markosyan 2013).

of Mediterranean pottery in south-west England, traditionally and plausibly related to the tin trade, does not overlap with the general location of coins of all metals. However the south-western copper coin finds do coincide with the tin and other metal rich areas.[34] Rare cases of close or relatively close proximity exist, such as between ceramics at Dinas Powys and the Heraclius half-*follis* from Carthage in Cosmeston or between the sherds at Cadbury Castle, Somerset and nearby Exeter, or those at Tintagel and the slightly more southern Justinian *dekanoummion* from Padstow. They provide tenuous, but still valuable, evidence in favour of the ancient presence of Byzantine coins in Britain.

A closer association between coins and weights at least on one and the same site, if not in the same archaeological context, is provided by the Anglo-Saxon grave at Gilton, Kent which yielded two Byzantine coin weights: one for two *nomismata* and one for a *tremissis*, from a site on which were also found a *solidus* of Avitus and one of Julius Nepos, both with loops, and more recently a *tremissis* of Justinian.[35] In Ozengell, near Ramsgate, the evidence of a grave with balances is now supplemented by the find of a Constantinople solidus of Justinian I.[36] Finally one should mention the third British occurrence of a sixth-century *tremissis* weight in the Watchfield (Somerset) grave together with a complete set of balances with two pans and worn Roman coins not later than the early fourth century.[37]

The survey of this material from a Byzantinist's perspective thus leads to an acceptable scheme of chronological and geographical distribution with a dual structure, opposing a richer eastern, and particularly south-eastern England to a less monetised but Atlantic-oriented Western part. The plausible pattern that can be derived from this base leads to a reversal of the burden of proof, which now falls on those who take the finds to be largely modern losses.[38] This challenge from an outsider is offered here as a tribute to the artisans behind the

---

[34] Compare the present map with figure 20.5 in Campbell and Bowles, 'Byzantine trade', 309.

[35] C. Scull, 'Scales and weights in Anglo-Saxon England', *Archaeological Journal, 147* (1990), 183–215, at 185 and 191–2. I am grateful to Simon Bendall for having reminded me of this find, cited and illustrated in his *Byzantine Weights. An Introduction* (London, 1996), 12. I could not access the earlier article of C. Scull, 'A sixth-century grave containing a balance and weights from Watchfield, Oxfordshire, England', *Germania, 65* (1986), 105–38.

[36] Bland and Loriot, *Roman and Early Byzantine Gold Coins*, no. 808.

[37] Scull, 'Scales and weights', 194, ill. 201.

[38] It is worth mentioning in this context that Inger Zachrisson has recently defended the authenticity of the few finds of Roman and Byzantine bronze coins in Sweden: I. Zachrisson, 'Vittnesbörd om pälshandel? Ett arkeologiskt perspektiv på romerska bronsmynt funna i norra Sverige' (Evidence for fur trade? An archaeological perspective on Roman bronze coins found in northern Sweden), *Fornvännen, 105* (2010), 197–202. I am grateful to Florent Audy who brought this article to my attention.

PAS, the EMC and other projects, in the hope that further collaboration may bring new discoveries along with a better understanding of Britain's relations with far-distant Byzantium in the early Anglo-Saxon period. They did not leave many traces but they were not a dream in northern mists.

Appendix: List of Recorded Finds of Byzantine Coins (491–721) in Great Britain

References

Archibald 2013: M.M. Archibald, 'The Wilton cross coin pendant: numismatic aspects and implications', in *Early Medieval Art and Archaeology in the Northern World: Studies in Honour of James Graham-Campbell*, ed. A. Reynolds and L. Webster (Leiden, 2013), 51–71

A&W (as in n. 10)

Bateson 1989: D. Bateson, 'Roman and medieval coins found in Scotland, to 1987', *Proceedings of the Society of Antiquaries of Scotland, 119* (1989), 165–88

Bateson & Holmes 1997: J.D. Bateson and N.M. McQ. Holmes, 'Roman and medieval coins found in Scotland, 1988–1995', *Proceedings of the Society of Antiquaries of Scotland, 127* (1997), 527–61

B&L (as in n. 11)

BNC: C. Morrisson, *Catalogue des monnaies byzantines de la Bibliothèque nationale* (2 vols, Paris, 1970)

Boon 1958 (as in n. 27)

Boon 1959: G.C. Boon, 'The latest objects from Silchester, Hants', *Medieval Archaeology, 3* (1959), 79–88

Boon 1991 (as in n. 7)

Georganteli 2012 (as in n. 20)

Harris 2003: A. Harris, *Byzantium, Britain and the West: the Archaeology of Cultural Identity, AD 500–650* (Stroud, 2003)

Metcalf 1988 (as in n. 22)

Moorhead 2009 (as in n. 17)

Rigold 1975 (as in n. 8)

Roach Smith 1848–80: C. Roach Smith, 'Anglo-Saxon remains discovered at Ozingell, Kent', in his *Collectanea Antiqua: Etchings and Notices of Ancient Remains, Illustrative of the Habits, Customs, and History of the Past Ages* (7 vols, London, 1848–80), 3, 1–18

Robertson 1949–50: A.S. Robertson, 'Roman coins found in Scotland, 1949–50', *Proceedings of the Society of Antiquaries of Scotland, 84* (1949–50), 137–69

Robertson 1960–1: A.S. Robertson, 'Roman coins found in Scotland, 1951–66', *Proceedings of the Society of Antiquaries of Scotland, 94* (1960–61), 133–83

Robertson 1983: A.S. Robertson, 'Roman coins found in Scotland, 1971–82', *Proceedings of the Society of Antiquaries of Scotland, 113* (1983), 405–48

Sutherland 1948: C.H.V. Sutherland, *Anglo-Saxon Gold Coinage in the Light of the Crondall Hoard* (Oxford, 1948)

Note: Unless otherwise stated, references are to numbers in the relevant publications, not to pages.

No.	Emperor	Mint	Metal	Denomination	Coin ref	Find location	Find details	Find references
1	Anastasius I	Constantinople	Au	*solidus*	*MIBE* 4a	Horndean, Hampshire	Detector find; ?grave good? (cf. Bland, p. 331) found with solidi of Honorius, Constans II and Constantine IV; site of an Anglo-Saxon cemetery	B&L 859; *NC* 1998, 298
2	Anastasius I	Constantinople	Au	*solidus*		Leicester (near), Leicestershire	Stray find before 1776; 'unexpected find from this area' (Bland, p. 73)	B&L 820
3	Anastasius I	Constantinople	Au	*solidus*		Eastry, Kent	Stray find	B&L 796; EMC 1996.1266
4	Anastasius I	Constantinople	Au	*solidus*	*MIBE* 3a (491–2)	Sussex (East)	Stray find	B&L 845

No.	Emperor	Mint	Metal	Denomination	Coin ref	Find location	Find details	Find references
5	Anastasius I	Constantinople	Au	*tremissis*	*MIBE* 12	Coddenham, Suffolk	Detector find in Anglo-Saxon cemetery; grave good	B&L 837; EMC 2001.0014
6	Anastasius I	unknown	Au	unknown		Canterbury, Kent	Stray find	B&L 790
7	Anastasius I	Constantinople	Ae	*follis*		Ilchester, Somerset	Stray find; deep digging in garden; pierced coin	Moorhead 2009, 6; Boon 1991, p. 44
8	Anastasius I	Constantinople	Ae	*follis*		University of Exeter, Devon	Stray find, early 1960s during building work	Boon 1991, 22
9	Anastasius I	unknown	Ae	*follis*		Exmouth, Devon	Stray find, c.1970 on beach	Boon 1991, 9 from Pearce 1970,29
10	Justin I	Constantinople	Au	*solidus*	*MIBE* 3	Colchester (near), Essex	Stray find; No evidence for local provenance except museum location	B&L 775; Laf-M p. 93 (err. as Justinian); Boon 1991, p. 43
11	Justin I	Constantinople	Au	*solidus*	*MIBE* 3	Wiveton, Norfolk	Detector find	B&L 832

No.	Emperor	Mint	Metal	Denomination	Coin ref	Find location	Find details	Find references
12	Justin I	Constantinople	Au	*tremissis*		Yorkshire	Stray find	B&L 849
13	Justin I	Constantinople	Au	*tremissis*	*MIBE* 5	Ash, Gilton, Kent	Detector find; grave good in Anglo-Saxon cemetery; on same site, balances, touchstone, and two Byzantine weights and two *solidi* (Avitus and Julius Nepos) both w loops	B&L 787
14	Justin I	Constantinople	Au	*tremissis*		Coombe, Kent	Stray find	B&L 794
15	Justin I	Constantinople	Au	*tremissis*	*MIBE* 5	Uncertain, Yorkshire	Detector find *c.*2003	B&L 850
16	Justin I	Constantinople ?	Au	*tremissis*	*MIBE* 5 (518–27)	Uncertain, Essex	Stray find	B&L 779
17	Justin I	Constantinople	Ae	*follis*		Dodworth, South Yorkshire	Detector find	Moorhead 2009, 31; A&W 83

No.	Emperor	Mint	Metal	Denomination	Coin ref	Find location	Find details	Find references
18	Justin I	Constantinople	Ae	*follis*		Meols, Cheshire	Detector find; found with a follis of Maurice (below, no. 64)	Moorhead 2009, 9; Harris 2003, fig. 47
19	Justin I	Constantinople	Ae	*follis*		Otterton, Devon	Casual find in riverbed (four coins or more)	Moorhead 2009, 14–17; PAS DEV-467426 (1–4)
20	Justin I	Constantinople	Ae	*follis*		Caerwent, Monmouthshire, Wales	Stray find 1920s; considered modern loss	Boon 1958, 1; Metcalf 1995
21	Justin I	Nicomedia	Ae	*follis*		Littlehampton, West Sussex	Garden find; considered modern loss (Moorhead)	Moorhead 2009, 22; PAS SWYOY-34B356
22	Justin I	Nicomedia	Ae	unknown		Glasgow (Knightswood), Lanarkshire, Scotland	Stray find	A&W 82; Boon 1991, p. 45; Robertson 1949–50, 145

No.	Emperor	Mint	Metal	Denomination	Coin ref	Find location	Find details	Find references
23	Justin I	unknown	Ae	unknown		Glasgow (Bishopbriggs), Lanarkshire, Scotland	Stray find	A&W 84; Robertson 1983, 438
24	Justin I	unknown	Ae	unknown		Kirkcaldy, Fife, Scotland	Stray find	A&W 85; Robertson 1983, 438
25	Justinian I	Constantinople	Au	solidus	MIBE 7 (538–65)	Riby, Lincolnshire	Detector find in field	B&L 823; PAS NLM-400892
26	Justinian I	Constantinople	Au	solidus	MIBE 6 (538–65)	Ozengell Grange, near Ramsgate, Kent	Stray find	B&L 808; Laf-M p. 94 (after Roach Smith 1848–80, pl. 5,13)
27	Justinian I	Constantinople	Au	solidus	MIBE 7	Tenby, Pembrokeshire, Wales	Detector find 1997 in the same area as a solidus of Tiberius III (below, no. 100); ?from a shipwreck	B&L 851

No.	Emperor	Mint	Metal	Denomination	Coin ref	Find location	Find details	Find references
28	Justinian I	Constantinople	Au	*tremissis*	*MIBE* 19	Kent (East), Kent	Stray find	B&L 817: Laf-M p. 94
29	Justinian I	Constantinople	Ae	*follis*		Gloucester, Gloucestershire	Detector find	Moorhead 2009, 19
30	Justinian I	Constantinople	Ae	*follis*	*MIBE* 84 (*c.* 527–37)	Preston Brook (near Meols), Cheshire	Detector find	A&W 95; Moorhead 2009, 29; EMC 2005.0028; PAS LVPL 1440
31	Justinian I	Constantinople	Ae	*follis*		Stonehouse, Lanarkshire, Scotland	Stray find on bank of river Avon	A&W 86; Bateson 1989, 170
32	Justinian I	Constantinople	Ae	*follis*	*BMC* 28 type (527–38)	Exeter, Foregate St, Devon	Excavations 1810 in a sewer	Boon 1991, 2
33	Justinian I	Constantinople	Ae	*follis*	Profile type before 538	Exeter, Foregate St, Devon	Excavations 1810 in a sewer (coin of Anastasius, Justin I or Justinian before 538)	Boon 1991, 1; after Shott

No.	Emperor	Mint	Metal	Denomination	Coin ref	Find location	Find details	Find references
34	Justinian I	Constantinople ?	Ae	half-*follis*	cf. *MIBE* 96	Langport, Somerset	Detector find	Moorhead 2009, 18; PAS SOM-3B55D0
35	Justinian I	Constantinople	Ae	half-*follis*	540–566 AD	Loch Sween, Argyllshire, Scotland	Stray find	A&W 87; Bateson & Holmes 1997, 535
36	Justinian I	Constantinople	Ae	*pentanoummion*		Fressingfield, Suffolk	Detector find in field	A&W 96; Moorhead 2009, 26; EMC 2005.0026
37	Justinian I	Constantinople	Ae	unknown		Shotts, Lanarkshire, Scotland	Stray find	A&W 88; Robertson 1960–1, 145
38	Justinian I	Thessalonica	Ae	16 *noummia*	*MIBE* N169a (*c.*538–52)	Isle of Wight	Detector find	Moorhead 2009, 20; PAS IOW-0FD7D6

No.	Emperor	Mint	Metal	Denomination	Coin ref	Find location	Find details	Find references
39	Justinian I	Nicomedia	Ae	*follis*		Keele Hall, Staffordshire	Stray find	*NC* 1953, 144; Boon 1991, p. 44; Laf-M p.94
40	Justinian I	Nicomedia	Ae	*follis*	*MIBE* 107 (527–37)	Silchester, Hampshire	Stray find	A&W 90; not in Moorhead 2009; Boon 1959, 84
41	Justinian I	Cyzicus ?	Ae	*dekanoummion*	cf. *MIBE* 123a (560/1)	Padstow, Cornwall	Detector find	Moorhead 2009, 13; PAS CORN-72D1D7; *CR* 2007, 59
42	Justinian I	Antioch	Ae	*follis*	*MIBE*145a	Seacombe, Merseyside	Detector find	Moorhead 2009, 30; PAS LVPL-874C64
43	Justinian I	Antioch	Ae	*dekanoummion*	*BMC* 327 type 550/1	Exeter, Broadgate, Devon	Stray find 1823	Boon 1991, 14

No.	Emperor	Mint	Metal	Denomination	Coin ref	Find location	Find details	Find references
44	Justinian I	Antioch	Ae	unknown		Kirkintilloch, Dunbartonshire, Scotland	Stray find	A&W 91; Boon 1991, p. 45; Robertson 1949–50, 140
45	Justinian I	Carthage	Ae	*dekanoummion*	*MIBE* 199 (539/40)	Hamwih (Southampton), Hampshire	Excavation find	A&W 92; Moorhead 2009, 2; Boon 1991, 44; Metcalf 187 (pp. 25 and 56); Harris 2003, fig. 46
46	Justinian I	Carthage	Ae	*dekanoummion*	*MIBE* 199 (539/40)	Meols (Moreton in the Wirral), Cheshire	Stray find in a garden	A&W 92; Moorhead 2009, 8; Boon 1991, 43; Harris 2003, fig. 46
47	Justinian I	unknown mint	Au	*tremissis*		Temple Newsam, Yorkshire	Stray find 1774; not certain whether imperial coin, no details nor ill.	B&L 849; Laf-M p. 94 (after VCH 1912)

No.	Emperor	Mint	Metal	Denomination	Coin ref	Find location	Find details	Find references
48	Justinian I	unknown	Au	unknown		Osmundthorpe Hall, Yorkshire	Stray find	Sutherland 1948, p. 24 (no. 1); Laf-M p. 94
49	Justinian I	unknown	Ae	*follis*	pre-538 issue	Ilchester, Somerset	Casual find from spoil excavated from a water trench	Moorhead 2009, 7; Boon 1991, p. 44
50	Justin II	Constantinople	Au	*tremissis*	*BNC* 11–12	Southwold, Suffolk	Detector find	B&L 840; EMC 1983.0001; Laf-M p. 93 (from *BNJ* 1983, 176)
51	Justin II	Constantinople	Ae	*follis*	*DOC* 26c	Winchester, Hampshire	Stopher coll, found late 19th century	Georganteli 2012, 1
52	Justin II	Thessalonica	Ae	half-*follis*	*BMC* 110 or 114 type, 571/2	Poltimore, Devon	Stray find 1838	Boon 1991, 16

No.	Emperor	Mint	Metal	Denomination	Coin ref	Find location	Find details	Find references
53	Justin II	Ravenna	Au	*tremissis*	*MIBEC* 26	Canterbury, Kent	Grave good; Saint Martin's cemetery	B&L 789; Laf-M p.93 (from Sutherland 1948, p. 23, n. 6, Rigold 1975, p. 665,16)
54	Justin II	Cyzicus	Ae	*follis*	*MIBEC* 50b (574/575)	Caerwent, Monmouthshire, Wales	Stray find; considered modern loss	A&W 98; Boon 1958, 2
55	Justin II	unknown	Ae	unknown		Froxfield, Wiltshire	Uncertain	Boon 1991, p. 44; Laf-M p.93
56	Justin II	unknown	Ae	unknown		London (City, Throgmorton Ave.)	Stray find, during building work of Carpenters' Hall with Byzantine coins from 6th–7th (below, no. 85) to 14th centuries	A&W 99; Boon 1991, p. 44
57	Tiberius II	Constantinople	Au	*solidus*	*MIBEC* 4	Shalfleet, Isle of Wight	Detector find in field	B&L 783; PAS IOW-5B4395

No.	Emperor	Mint	Metal	Denomination	Coin ref	Find location	Find details	Find references
58	Tiberius II	Constantinople	Au	*solidus*		Northwold, Norfolk	Detector find near river Wissey; coin in beaded wire mount	B&L 830
59	Tiberius II	Constantinople	Ae	*follis*	*BMC* 35 type (581/2)	Princetown, Devon	Casual find in drainage trench	Moorhead 2009, 4 = Boon 1991, 20; Rowe 1885, 69–70
60	Maurice	Constantinople	Au	*solidus*	*MIBEC* 6	Selling, Kent	Detector find; coin with loop attachment	B&L 812; PAS KENT EF4810
61	Maurice	Constantinople	Au	lightweight *solidus* (OBXX)	*MIBEC* 14	Dorchester-on-Thames, Oxfordshire	Stray find; not *MIBE* 6 as in Bland (did not recognize the lightweight exergue)	B&L 836; LafM p. 93 (from Sutherland 1948, p. 24, n. 3; Rigold 1975, p. 665, 17)
62	Maurice	Constantinople	Au	*tremissis*	*MIBEC* 20	Fenton, Lincolnshire	Detector find	B&L 821; EMC 2005.0025; PAS LVPL-9C93A2

No.	Emperor	Mint	Metal	Denomination	Coin ref	Find location	Find details	Find references
63	Maurice	Constantinople	Au	*tremissis*	*MIBEC* 49–50	Salehurst & Robertsbridge, Sussex	Detector find; coin with loop attachment	B&L 844; PAS KENT8 before 1998
64	Maurice	Constantinople	Ae	*follis*	*MIBEC* 67D (600/1)	Meols, Cheshire	Detector find, found with *follis* of Justin I (above no. 18)	A&W 100; Moorhead 2009, 10; Harris 2003, fig. 48
65	Maurice	Cyzicus	Ae	*follis*	*MIBEC* 84D (583/4)	Norfolk uncertain/unknown/imprecise, Norfolk	Detector find	A&W 103; Moorhead 2009, 27, EMC 2005.0024; PAS BH-781624
66	Maurice	Antioch	Ae	unknown		Falkirk, Stirlingshire, Scotland	Stray find	A&W 102; Robertson 1983, 416
67	Maurice	Alexandria	Ae	*dodekanoummion*	cf *MIBEC* 106/7	Chysauster, near Penzance, Cornwall	Stray find	Moorhead 2009, 12; *CR* 2004, 44

No.	Emperor	Mint	Metal	Denomination	Coin ref	Find location	Find details	Find references
68	Maurice	Carthage	Au	*solidus*		Aylesbury, Buckinghamshire	Casual find in a garden; wrongly as Cple in B&L (debatable find according to B&L, p. 116)	B&L 773
69	Maurice	Catania	Ae	*dekanoummion*	cf. *MIBEC* 136/7 (597/8)	Thelnetham, Suffolk	Stray find; context unknown	A&W 101; Moorhead 2009, 25; EMC 1993.0135
70	Phocas	Constantinople	Au	*solidus*	*MIBEC* 9 (607)	Bossall, Yorkshire	Detector find	B&L 848; PAS NCL-6A6EF5
71	Phocas	Constantinople	Au	*tremissis*	*MIBEC* 26 (603–7)	Suffolk, Suffolk	Detector find	B&L 842
72	Phocas	Nicomedia	Ae	*follis*	*MIBEC* 69a (602–4)	Leominster, Herefordshire	Casual find, digging in garden; modern loss (Moorhead n. 9)	Moorhead 2009, 23

No.	Emperor	Mint	Metal	Denomination	Coin ref	Find location	Find details	Find references
73	Phocas or uncertain emperor	Alexandria	Ae	*dodekanoummion*		Woburn, Buckinghamshire	'Modern loss' (Moorhead n. 8)	A&W 97; Moorhead 2009, 21; EMC 2005.0027; PAS BUC-4840C3
74	Phocas or Heraclius	Carthage	Ae	*follis*	*MIBEC* 98 (Phocas) or *MIBEC* 235 (Heraclius)	Bedford, Bedfordshire	Detector find	Moorhead 2009, 28; EMC 1997.0001
75	Phocas	Ravenna	Au	*solidus*		Crondall, Hampshire	From hoard; wrongly considered an imitation by Sutherland	B&L 858; Laf-M p. 93 (from *MEC* 1, pp. 126–7)
76	Heraclius	Constantinople	Au	*solidus*	*MIB* 9a (613–16)	Ingham, Suffolk	Detector find before 2007	B&L 883
77	Heraclius	Constantinople	Au	lightweight *solidus* (BOXX)	*MIB* 65 (616–25)	Hockwold cum Wilton, Norfolk	Stray find; set in cloisonné cross pendant	B&L 861; Laf-M p. 93 (from Rigold 1975, p. 665, 18); Archibald 2013

No.	Emperor	Mint	Metal	Denomination	Coin ref	Find location	Find details	Find references
78	Heraclius	Constantinople	Au	lightweight *solidus* (BOXX)	*MIB* 65 (616–25)	Kent (east)	Stray find	B&L 862; EMC 1982.9015; Laf-M p. 94 (from Adelson 129 and Rigold 1975, p. 665, 19)
79	Heraclius	Constantinople	Ae	*follis*	*BMC* 197 type 639–40	Exeter Devon	Excavations 1810, in a sewer	Boon 1991, 3
80	Heraclius	Constantinople	Ae	half-*follis*	*MIB* 171a (629/30)	Caerwent, Monmouthshire, Wales	Stray find; considered modern loss	A&W 104; Boon 1958, no. 3
81	Heraclius	Nicomedia	Ae	*follis*	*MIB* 174	Middleton, Warwickshire	Detector find	Moorhead 2009, 24
82	Heraclius	Carthage	Ae	half-*follis*	*MIB* 234	Cosmeston, Glamorgan, Wales	Stray find in excavation	Moorhead 2009, 11
83	Heraclius	Carthage	Ae	*dekanoummion*	*MIB* 237b	Fordham Place, near Colchester	Casual find	Fitzwilliam Museum, Cambridge, don. M. Blackburn, CM.655-2010

No.	Emperor	Mint	Metal	Denomination	Coin ref	Find location	Find details	Find references
84	Heraclius	Sicily	Ae	*follis*	*DOC* 243	Winchester, Hampshire	Stopher coll., found late 19th century, countermarked type, clipped	Georganteli 2012, 2
85	Heraclius	unknown	Ae	unknown		London (City, Throgmorton Ave.)	Stray find during building work in/ at Carpenters' Hall with Byzantine coins from 6th (above no. 56) to 14th century	A&W 105; Boon 1991, p. 44

No.	Emperor	Mint	Metal	Denomination	Coin ref	Find location	Find details	Find references
86	Constans II	Constantinople	Au	*solidus*	*MIB* 31 (*c*.662–7)	Horndean, Hampshire	Detector find with *solidi* of Honorius, Anastasius I (above no. 1) and Constantine IV (below no. 97); Anglo-Saxon cemetery on the site; debatable (cf B&L, p. 331)	B&L 859.3; *NC* 1998, 298
87	Constans II	Constantinople	Ae	*follis*	*BMC* 102? type	Exeter, Foregate St, Devon	Excavations 1810, in a sewer	Boon 1991, 4; after Shott
88	Constans II	Constantinople	Ae	*follis*	*BMC* 133 type	Exeter, Foregate St, Devon	Excavations 1810, in a sewer	Boon 1991, 5; after Shott
89	Constans II	Carthage	Ae	half-*follis*	*MIB* 196b	Richborough, Kent	Excavation find site of a Roman fort	A&W 106; Moorhead 2009, 5; Boon 1991, 44; Laf-M p. 94 (mistakenly as *dekanoummion*)

No.	Emperor	Mint	Metal	Denomination	Coin ref	Find location	Find details	Find references
90	Constans II	Carthage	Ae	*follis*	*DOC* 144–5	Winchester, Hampshire	Stopher coll., found late 19th century, clipped	Georganteli 2012, 3
91	Constans II	Carthage	Ae	unknown		Banff, Banffshire, Scotland	Stray find in a garden in the 1950s	A&W 109; Robertson 1960–1, 131
92	Constans II	Carthage	Ae	unknown		Aberdour, Fife, Scotland	Casual find, during house building 1950s	A&W 110; Robertson 1983, 412
93	Constans II	Syracuse	Ae	*follis*	*MIB* 210 (662–8)	Caerwent, Monmouthshire, Wales	Casual find, considered modern loss	A&W 111; Boon 1958
94	Constans II	unknown	Ae	*follis*		Eldinhope Selkirkshire, Scotland	Stray find	A&W 107
95	Constans II	unknown	Ae	*follis*		Lauder, Berwickshire, Scotland	Stray find	A&W 108
96	Constans II	unknown	Ae	*follis*	Cf. *MIB* 170 (651–5)	Saint Anne's, Alderney, Channel Islands	Casual find, during excavations at Dolphin House, Oliver St	A&W 113; information from Alderney Museum RAA in *CR* 2003

No.	Emperor	Mint	Metal	Denomination	Coin ref	Find location	Find details	Find references
97	Constantine IV	Constantinople	Au	*solidus*		Horndean, Hampshire	Detector find; grave good? (cf. B&L, p. 331) found with *solidi* of Honorius, Anastasius, Constans II (above nos. 1 and 86); site of an Anglo-Saxon cemetery. Pierced.	B&L 866 (ill. 859.4); *NC* 1998, 298
98	Constantine IV	Constantinople	Ae	*dekanoummion*		Exeter, Foregate St, Devon	Excavations 1810, in a sewer	Boon 1991, 5
99	Justinian II	Syracuse	Ae	*follis*	*BMC* 47	Caerwent, Monmouthshire, Wales	Stray find 1920s; considered modern loss	Boon 1958, 5
100	Tiberius III	Constantinople	Au	*solidus*	*MIB* 1	Tenby, Pembrokeshire		B&L 867
101	Leo III	Syracuse	Au	*solidus*		Westerham, Kent	Casual find; details not recorded	B&L 868

Chapter 11

Thrymsas and *Sceattas* and the Balance of Payments

D.M. Metcalf

The original and famous hypothesis of Henri Pirenne regarding north-west Europe was that Flanders was the focal point of economic recovery after the Viking assaults, and the focus of the development (for the first time) of a 'normal' money economy, replacing the manorial, local self-sufficiency of the Dark Ages.[1] Pirenne's thesis relied, in a sense, upon a lack of information to the contrary. There is remarkably little in the surviving written sources which would alert one to the existence of a widespread network of exchanges and payments, and nothing from which one could gain any perspective on the relative scale of monetary activity regionally. Archaeological information about economic activity and about coin finds from Flanders, which could have underpinned his observation, and which would have needed to show, for example, that coin losses began only after the Viking assaults, was virtually non-existent, and indeed the information from Flanders is not very helpful even now.[2] But at least we have Jean Lafaurie's splendid inventory of finds, mostly single-finds, of Merovingian coins from well over 1,000 localities throughout France.[3] Yet even that is dwarfed by the corpus of information about single-finds from the Netherlands[4]

---

[1]   H. Pirenne, *Medieval Cities: their Origin and the Revival of Trade* (Princeton, NJ, 1925).

[2]   V. Zedelius, 'Eighth-century archaeology in the Meuse and Rhine valleys: a context for the sceatta finds', in *Coinage in Ninth-Century Northumbria. The Tenth Oxford Symposium on Coinage and Monetary History*, ed. D.M. Metcalf, BAR British Series, 180 (Oxford, 1987), 405–13 (this paper was read at the Seventh Oxford Symposium, but by an editorial oversight was not printed in the volume of proceedings of that meeting). For another alternative paradigm to Pirenne, based on pots rather than coins, see C. Wickham, *Framing the Early Middle Ages: Europe and the Mediterranean, 400–800* (Oxford, 2005), 1–10.

[3]   J. Lafaurie and J. Pilet-Lemière, *Monnaies du haut Moyen Âge découvertes en France (V^e– VIIIe siècle)*, Cahiers Ernest-Babelon, 8 (Paris, 2003).

[4]   W. Op. den Velde and C.J.F. Klaassen, *Sceattas and Merovingian Deniers from Domburg and Westenschouwen*, Koninklijk Zeeuwsch Genootschap der Wetenschappen: Werken, 15 (Middelburg, 2004). The NUMIS database is extensively utilised in two monographs published as volumes of the periodical *Jaarboek voor Munt- en Penningkunde*, namely W. Op. den Velde and D.M. Metcalf, *The Monetary Economy of the Netherlands, c.690–c.715 and the Trade with England:*

and from eastern England.[5] Because millions of silver deniers or *sceattas* were minted in the late seventh and eighth centuries, in France, in the Rhine mouths region, in Friesland, and especially at a dozen or more localities in England, we can construct a moving picture, so to speak, of the inter-regional circulation of coinage, based on comparing where the coins were minted, with where they were lost. If the volume of the inter-regional transfers is a measurable fraction of the total mint-output, it raises insistent historical questions about the uses of money. The first half of the eighth century is where the evidence is at its most elaborate and abundant, and where it is most amenable to analysis. In particular, *sceattas* minted in the Netherlands came to make up between a quarter and a third of the English currency, with very little in the way of counterflows of English coins in the other direction.[6] In short, England was running a massive balance-of-payments surplus with the Netherlands. That in itself implies that the economic activity of some regions of England was geared to exporting. What the Frisians were buying here is a matter for guesswork, and the list will no doubt have been varied, but the proportion of their coins is particularly high in certain wool-producing regions, e.g. the Cotswolds.[7] It seems from the numismatic evidence that merchants proceeded directly there, up the Thames valley, spending their Netherlandish money only when they got there. The proportion of foreign coins among the stray losses in those districts is higher than it is in the south-east of England, through which the merchants must have passed. The high point of this activity was from *c.*720 to *c.*750. In peripheral areas such as the Cotswolds[8] and the Yorkshire Wolds,[9] it seems that these foreign *sceattas* were what kick-started a regional money economy.

But even in the seventh century, in the age of gold coinage, England was already running a substantial balance-of-payments surplus with the Continent,

---

a Study of the Sceattas of Series D, Jaarboek voor Munt- en Penningkunde, 90 (Amsterdam, 2003); D.M. Metcalf and W. Op. den Velde, *The Monetary Economy of the Netherlands, c.690–c.760 and the Trade with England: a Study of the 'Porcupine' Sceattas of Series E*, Jaarboek voor Munt- en Penningkunde, 96–7 (2 vols., Amsterdam, 2009–10).

    [5]   The English evidence has been extensively published in the annual 'Coin Register' in the British Numismatic Journal, and on two web-sites, namely EMC and the PAS.

    [6]   D.M. Metcalf, *Thrymsas and Sceattas in the Ashmolean Museum, Oxford*, RNS Special Publication, 27A–C (3 vols., London, 1993–4), esp. 8.

    [7]   D.M. Metcalf, 'Variations in the composition of the currency at different places in England', in *Markets in Early Medieval Europe. Trading and 'Productive' Sites, 650–850*, ed. T. Pestell and K. Ulmschneider (Macclesfield, 2003), 37–47 (with maps).

    [8]   R.J. Laight and D.M. Metcalf, 'Fifty sceattas from South Warwickshire', *BNJ*, 82 (2012), 29–45.

    [9]   M.J. Bonser, 'The "North of England" productive site revisited', in *New Perspectives: Studies in Early Medieval Coinage 2*, ed. T. Abramson (Woodbridge, 2011), 159–80, including commentary by D.M. Metcalf.

mainly with Merovingian Gaul rather than with the Netherlands.[10] All this was happening well before the Viking assaults. Indeed, the conspicuous wealth of the North Sea and cross-Channel trade may have looked to the Vikings to be worth their plundering. In short, then, Pirenne got it badly wrong. A very large and vigorous monetary circulation existed in north-west Europe already in the first half of the eighth century, and even in the seventh century similar patterns of maritime trade and balance-of-payments surpluses between England and the Continent are visible. The upturn that Pirenne detected after the Viking assaults was not the beginning of monetisation in north-west Europe, but rather the recovery after an earlier downturn. It was the second half, that is to say, of a major recession. We can, I suppose, excuse Pirenne, or at least understand how he came to get it so wrong. The archaeological and numismatic information which would undoubtedly have changed his judgement did not yet exist. But an absence of evidence is not the same thing as negative evidence.

In 1982 Richard Hodges published his book, *Dark Age Economics: the Origins of Towns and Trade, 600–1000*. Coins in the Dark Age, he claimed, served an élite, and facilitated their purchase of luxury goods, which conferred or reinforced status. One feels that there is a hidden agenda here: it must have been so, because coins were few. I would say in rejoinder that this hypothesis is incompatible with the existence of millions of coins, tens of millions even, and incompatible with the ways in which they moved about, between regions. If you want to study the élite, study the élite. But do not construct a hypothesis backwards. Hodges' book has cast a long shadow, particularly among archaeologists, and it continues to do so, witness for example, an article by Gareth Davies in the 2010 issue of *Medieval Archaeology* discussing early medieval 'rural centres', where manufacturing took place, that had previously been supposed to have been confined to the *wic*.[11] This manufacturing was, however, still in response to demand led by the élite. Qualifications keep being added to the original hypothesis, which tend to make it unfalsifiable. Or, the original hypothesis morphs into a rather different one, without proof of the connection being offered. Let me give another example, saying very much the same. I picked up in a library a recent book by Francis Pryor, an archaeologist who has often taken part in television programmes, on the making of the British landscape, published by Allen Lane in 2010. I opened

---

[10] R. Abdy and G. Williams, 'A catalogue of hoards and single finds from the British Isles, *c*. AD 410–675', in *Coinage and History in the North Sea World c.500–1250. Essays in Honour of Marion Archibald*, ed. B. Cook and G. Williams (Leiden and Boston, 2006), 11–73; G. Williams, 'The circulation and function of coinage in conversion-period England', ibid., 145–92; D.M. Metcalf, 'Merovingian and Frisian gold in England. Was there a money economy in the sixth and seventh centuries?', in *Studies in Early Medieval Coinage 3*, ed. T. Abramson (forthcoming).

[11] G. Davies, 'Early medieval "rural centres" and west Norfolk: a growing picture of diversity, complexity, and changing lifestyles', *Medieval Archaeology, 54* (2010), 89–122.

the book (naturally) at the chapter on the early Middle Ages. It offers a widely informed, balanced, and hard-headed narrative, but I came across the following:

> It is widely accepted that early medieval (that is, 600–1000) trade was exchange centred on the wealth and influence of ruling élites. Recent metal detector finds would indicate that the central élite focus of exchange stimulated a series of less high-flown networks between individuals probably of lower status, and between middlemen or brokers too. Ultimately ordinary British farmers of the mid-Saxon period could use the system to acquire objects such as querns made from central European volcanic lava.[12]

How to construct a hypothesis backwards, while making a grudging and partial retreat from Hodges' idea of a coinless *hoi polloi*. I turned the page of Pryor's book, and was galvanised to see a map of 'productive' sites, which are quite *le dernier cri*. The map even includes Bidford-on-Avon, which was not then published.[13] How did he know about Bidford?[14]

What is needed is a new paradigm. There is a saying about not being able to see the wood for the trees. A more distressing affliction is not to be able to see the trees, when one is surrounded by thousands of them. Hodges' book was published in 1982, just before the first impetus to record metal detectorists' single-finds, given by Mark Blackburn and Mike Bonser in 1984. From their work there soon developed both the annual Coin Register of the British Numismatic Society, and also the Corpus of Early Medieval Coin finds (EMC) website. In 2010, for example, the Coin Register published and illustrated 100 separate coin finds of the sixth to eighth centuries, and in 2009 nearly 200. The finds continue into the first three-quarters of the ninth century. Pirenne, thou should'st be living at this hour! And it is not just the overall quantities: each of these finds is provenanced. In the Netherlands the story is similar. Our colleagues there, Arent Pol, Jan Pelsdonk and Bauke Jan van der Veen, have registered single-finds over the years and have gradually built up a corpus of material which is now accessible in the NUMIS database, and which permits the construction of distribution maps for different coin types. We can, I suppose, excuse Hodges in so far as he was writing just before all this wonderful accession of new material began to be reported. To describe it as a major step forward is an understatement.

We now have all these hundreds upon hundreds of finds, widely distributed, but we should take care to keep in mind that they are only a minute fraction of all the coins that once existed. We can estimate, by well-established statistical

---

[12]   F. Pryor, *The Making of the British Landscape* (London, 2010), p. 227.

[13]   M. Blackburn, '"Productive" sites and the pattern of coin loss in England, 600–1180', in *Markets in Early Medieval Europe*, ed. Pestell and Ulmschneider, 20–36.

[14]   Laight and Metcalf, 'Fifty sceattas'.

methods, how many different dies were used, by finding out how many die-duplicates occur in a random sample. To put the argument very simply, the more duplicates, the nearer we are to a complete tally. But then we have to think how many coins each die, on average, produced. We know for a fact, from official records, that in the thirteenth and fourteenth centuries the dies for English silver pennies produced on average around 15,000 coins, or even 20,000.[15] That refers to the upper or reverse dies, which wore out sooner than the lower or obverse dies. A conventional multiplier of 10,000 for the little *sceattas*, which were manufactured in exactly the same way, is therefore a reasonable or even a conservative guess, the force needed to strike a coin being proportional (*inter alia*) to the area of its flan. Those who are reluctant to believe that dark-age coinage was plentiful may try to argue that dies were under-used, below their technical capacity. That is special pleading. I knew of an American collector who specialised in Northumbrian *stycas*. Because he had never come across a die-duplicate he firmly believed that each different die was used to strike only one coin. That was carrying eccentricity out into the wilderness. To argue that dies were seriously under-used is a last-ditch defence, and the answer to it is that dies were high-tech and quite expensive to make.[16]

If statistical estimation shows, as it does beyond peradventure, that in many issues scores of dies of the same design were used, why would they have been discarded while still serviceable? Using the conventional multiplier of 10,000, a hundred dies means a million coins: it is easy to remember. That is a lot of coins, but to put the numbers into some sort of human context (which is what this essay is mainly about), see Figure 11.1.

It shows finds of seventh-century gold coins, minted up to *c*.675. Most are Merovingian or Frisian, the rest are Anglo-Saxon. There are approximately 300 single-finds or grave finds from the mapped area. The English *thrymsas* catalogued by Humphrey Sutherland were struck from some 70 known reverse dies.[17] Statistical estimation suggests that that total reflects about two-thirds of the original total, which was thus roughly 100, at a conservative estimate. Non-numismatists may need to be reminded how extremely scarce the surviving specimens of *thrymsas* are. Meanwhile, among the single-finds, Merovingian

---

[15]   B.H.I.H. Stewart, 'Medieval die-output: two calculations for English mints in the fourteenth century', *NC, 7th series, 3* (1963), 97–106; B.H.I.H. Stewart, 'Second thoughts on medieval die-output', *NC, 7th series, 4* (1964), 293–303; M. Mate, 'Coin dies under Edward I and II', *NC, 7th series, 9* (1969), 207–18; M.R. Allen, *Mints and Money in Medieval England* (Cambridge, 2012), 131–3; M.R. Allen, 'Medieval English die-output', *BNJ, 74* (2004), 39–49.

[16]   E.J.E. Pirie, 'The minting evidence', in *Post-Roman Coins from York Excavations, 1971–81*, ed. E.J.E. Pirie, Archaeology of York, 18.1 (York, 1986), 33–41 sets out the evidence for the use of two qualities of metal, *viz.* a specially hardened die-cap, in the time of Athelstan.

[17]   C.H.V. Sutherland, *Anglo-Saxon Gold Coinage in the Light of the Crondall Hoard* (Oxford, 1948).

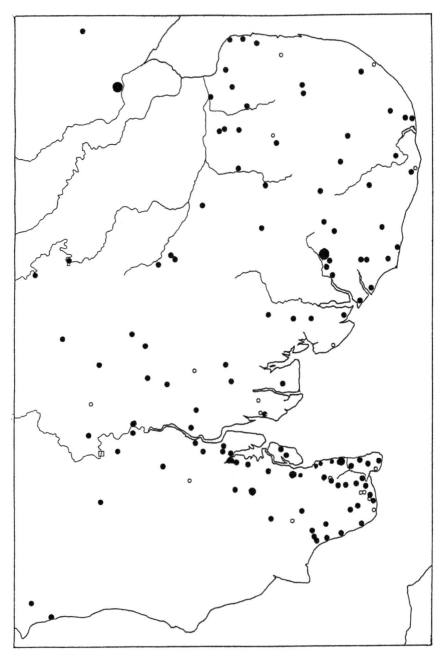

Figure 11.1   Finds of seventh-century gold coins (to *c.*675). Larger circles
             indicate multiple finds from the same locality. Empty circles refer
             to find-spots of sixth-century coins.

and Frisian *tremisses* are roughly three and a half to four times as plentiful as English *thrymsas*. We use the *thrymsas* as markers to estimate the size of the whole currency. And so we add another 350 or 400 equivalent reverse dies, and the total English currency would seem to have been roughly equal to the output of 450 to 500 reverse dies of *thrymsas*. We have to express it in those terms because there is no way of telling what proportion of the output of any particular Merovingian die ended up in England, and what proportion stayed at home. The *thrymsas* that have been discovered since Sutherland wrote his catalogue of the Crondall hoard have served to shift the statistical estimate upwards, especially for the post-Crondall phase.[18] That automatically pushes the other figures upwards, to somewhere more in the region of 600 dies. All these figures are very sketchy, but the shape of the argument is secure.

Next, let us say for the sake of compromise that dies were used to produce on average only 5,000 gold coins, not 10,000.[19] Even using the figure of 5,000, the estimated overall volume of the currency will have been roughly 600 times 5,000, or 3,000,000 gold coins. At any particular moment in the first three-quarters of the seventh century, not all these will have been present. Some will have fallen out of circulation, others will not yet have been minted. (Figure 11.1, however, records all the finds from *c.*600 to *c.*675.) So let us think of 1,000,000 coins above ground at any particular date, on the basis of a low figure for average die-output, and a low figure for availability. Now, in the area covered by the map, how many villages were there in the seventh century? An off-the-cuff guess based on the number of modern parishes in the mapped area would be 3,000. If the number of settlements was of the same order of magnitude in the seventh century, as place-name studies may suggest, the number of coins in existence per village will have been something resembling 1,000,000 over 3,000, which is 300 gold coins, above ground, per village. This is why we need a new paradigm, and this is what I mean by not being able to see the trees, when thickly surrounded by them. Now to speak of 300 gold coins per village is obviously an extremely artificial concept. But to put it another way, these are mostly foreign coins, and this is mostly money that the English had earned through exporting, over the decades. It may not all have been passing from hand to hand all the time. Some may have been stored as savings. But most of the dots on the map (Figure 11.1) refer to villages, and if we had ten times as many recorded single-finds, a great

---

[18]   B.H.I.H. Stewart, 'Anglo-Saxon gold coins', in *Scripta Nummaria Romana. Essays Presented to Humphrey Sutherland*, ed. R.A.G. Carson and C.M. Kraay (London, 1978), 143–72. Since then, stray finds have continued to come to light, and are usually recorded in the Coin Register of the *BNJ*, from 1986 onwards.

[19]   Although gold, and even gold-silver alloys, were softer than coinage silver. In the later Middle Ages English gold dies were less heavily used than the penny dies upon which calculations have been based. It may be that the batches of coins minted were smaller, and also it may be that they paid for themselves sooner.

many villages would have at least one. The accidental losses of coinage were not concentrated in *wic* or even at 'productive' sites. There cannot, by definition, have been a member of the élite in every one of 3,000 villages. And the map shows no obvious signs of clustering in or around what might have been the seats of an élite.

Moving on to the period of the *sceattas*, i.e. *c.*675 to 750-ish, gold disappears from circulation, but single-finds of silver are far more numerous – ten times more numerous – than finds of gold. They are equally widely distributed through the countryside. But before we jump to the conclusion that the *sceattas* exemplify all the same arguments that have been rehearsed above, but ten times more so, we should remember that the loss-rate of the silver coins could have been far higher. Whether mint-output was correspondingly greater remains to be demonstrated. We can assume that *sceattas* minted in England stayed in England, to the tune of 95 per cent or more of mint-output: they occur in only the most trivial proportions in the databases from the Netherlands and from France. For each of the two dozen major types, minted in different regions of the country, we could in principle construct a die-corpus, and derive an estimate of the original total of dies. A full survey of single-finds allows us to say what proportion of the total each series or type contributes. If a particular type made up, for example, 3.5 per cent of the single-finds from England as a whole, we could multiply the die-estimate by 100 over 3.5, to obtain a global estimate. We could do all that a dozen times, and in theory we ought to get roughly the same global answer each time – or if not, we should at least have uncovered some interesting anomalies to look into. In practice we might hope that most out of the dozen results would be in the same ball-park, and that we should get a cluster of values that would identify the area where the correct figure lay. Rigold in 1960 published catalogues for 20 coins of Pada and 12 of Vanimundus, which included only one die-duplicate.[20] These samples point the way, but they are too small to overcome the problem of margins of statistical variation. For Series A Rigold listed obverse dies, which is not ideal for the present exercise. For Series B he catalogued just over a hundred specimens, and this is clearly an attractive topic for an updated survey. Beyond that, rather surprisingly, we have got hardly anything as yet that can claim to be a useful corpus of reverse dies of *sceattas*, except for Types R1–2[21] and the scarce Series W,[22] and the equally scarce coins of Aldfrith,[23] but we have got a list of percentages for the share that each series contributed, nationwide, based on a large random sample from the 1980s. For

---

[20] S.E. Rigold, 'The two primary series of sceattas', *BNJ*, 30 (1960), 6–53.

[21] D.M. Metcalf, 'Runic sceattas reading EPA, Types R1 and R2', *BNJ*, 77 (2007), 49–70.

[22] D.M. Metcalf, 'The first series of sceattas minted in southern Wessex: Series W', *BNJ*, 75 (2005), 1–17.

[23] D.M. Metcalf, 'The coinage of King Aldfrith of Northumbria (685–704) and some contemporary imitations', *BNJ*, 76 (2006), 147–58.

the purposes of this exercise, randomness is essential. I remember one detectorist who came to me, with the best will in the world, and said, 'At last I've found something *interesting*. I think you'll be *interested* in this one'. Bless his kind heart, what could I reply? How could we measure the percentage that common-or-garden porcupines, originating in the Netherlands, contributed to the English currency, if finders didn't bother to report them because they thought them uninteresting? Randomness is all. The corpus of Types R1–2 includes 62 specimens, from 43 dies, with 30 die-duplicates, yielding an estimate of originally 89 dies. These account for 1.4 per cent of the overall sample (including foreign *sceattas*), which is approximately 1.4 per cent of the currency, yielding a global figure of 6,357 dies. A somewhat rough and out-of-date estimate for the primary Series B works out by similar arithmetical steps to 6,585 reverse dies, which should be taken as provisional, but which is encouraging, although the similar totals might be partly coincidence. Using a multiplier of 10,000 gives a global currency estimate of 60 to 65 million silver *sceattas*, again not all of which will have been above ground concurrently. Even so, compared with the number of villages, the size of the currency was prodigious. We shall have to wait and see whether other English series of *sceattas* point to a closely similar figure. Meanwhile, it is already obvious that the correct figure is going to be huge, significantly greater for example than for the broad pennies of King Offa – for which we now have highly reliable estimates. These indicate a probable total of 1,500 reverse dies for the whole coinage of Offa and his contemporaries up to 796, thus, let us say, 15 million pennies, or a quarter of what the *sceattas* had amounted to.[24] For the purposes of our historical argument, the principle of overkill applies: fine tuning is not going to change the general conclusion.

We also now have an up-to-date and very reliable corpus for both main kinds of Dutch *sceattas*, Series D and E respectively.[25] Series D, Types 8 and 2c, minted in Friesland in the primary phase, are estimated to be from 176 and 2,670 dies respectively, thus 25–30 million coins. By no means all of these accumulated in England, perhaps only about 15 per cent of the whole. We have to measure them *pro rata* against the English types. A corpus of Series E, the porcupines, comprises some 3,500 specimens, which have been very carefully checked for die-duplication, a labour of love. They yielded estimates of 900 primary-phase dies, 4,200 secondary-phase dies, and 350 of the tertiary phase. Roughly 5,500 dies, 55 million porcupines. They were exported to England in huge numbers, without corresponding counterflows of English coins to the Netherlands. Again, we have to estimate the inflows by the *pro rata* method. They made up 8.1 per cent of the primary-phase single-finds, and *c.*12.6 per cent of the secondary phase. If

[24]   D. Chick, *The Coinage of Offa and his Contemporaries*, ed. M. Blackburn and R. Naismith, BNS Special Publication, 6 (London, 2010), 182–4.

[25]   See n. 4 above.

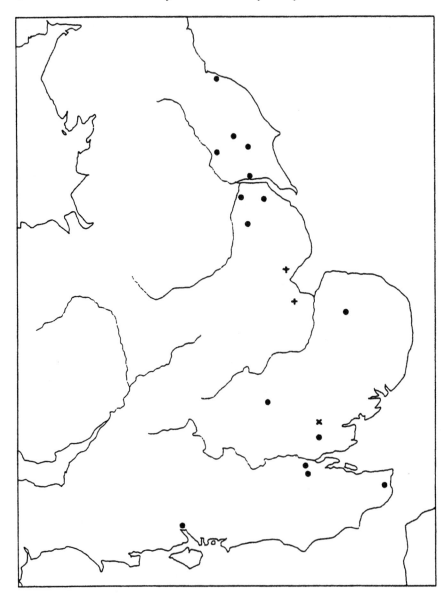

Figure 11.2   Finds of *sceattas* of King Aldfrith of Northumbria; crosses are
imitations; x is the Rodings hoard.

we want to know what proportion of the Dutch mint-output was exported to
England, we have to calculate it from an established total for the English *sceattas*,
not the other way round. Together, the Netherlands *sceattas* of Series D and E

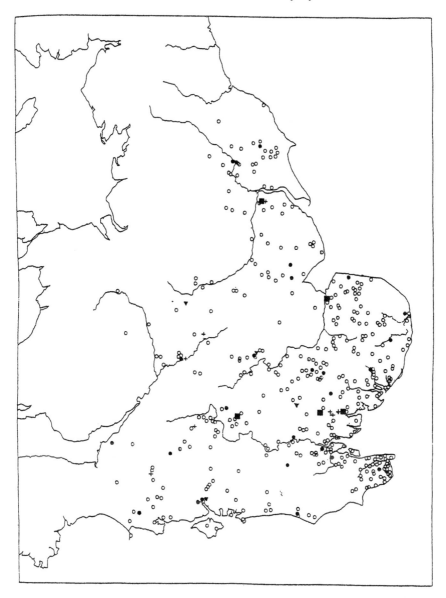

Figure 11.3   Finds of Types R1 and R2 (dots), imitations of same (triangles), R/C2 'mules' (crosslets), and hoards containing R1–2 (squares). Open circles are other *sceatta* types.

account for roughly a quarter of all single-finds in England. If our estimates of around 6,500 reverse dies for the whole of the English currency are in the right ball-park, finds of Series D and E represent the equivalent of 1,625 dies. Thus,

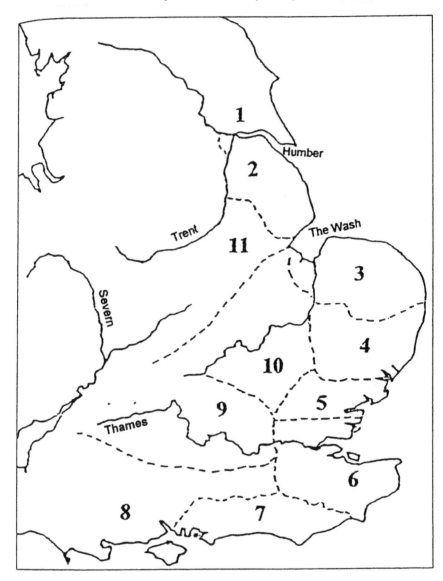

Figure 11.4   Eleven regions of England (for the purposes of calculating the regional occurrence of finds of *sceattas*).

most of the output of Series D and E stayed at home in the Netherlands (or was carried to Scandinavia) but 16 million coins silted up in England – our balance-of-payments surplus with the Low Countries. Pirenne, please note.

Another major aspect of the evidence for Anglo-Saxon monetary history is the extent to which all these millions of coins circulated within England, and in particular the degree of inter-regional circulation. This is something which Pirenne had no means of knowing about; nor was Hodges in a much better position. Only the mapping of hundreds of single-finds allows us to see what was going on.

Figure 11.2 shows finds of coins of King Aldfrith of Northumbria (685–704). They were undoubtedly minted in Yorkshire, and yet more than half the finds are from south of the Humber. The third map, Figure 11.3, shows finds of Types R1–2, which may perhaps have originated in East Anglia, but which are found so widely that any original concentration is hardly visible. The best way of presenting the evidence for diffusion of the currency – best because it summarises the totality of the evidence – is to divide eastern and southern England into a dozen regions (Figure 11.4), and for each region to prepare a pie-chart of the different types and series of *sceattas* found there. That can usefully be supplemented by pie-charts for Hamwic, London, Canterbury, and any other well-documented centres. And, of course, one could extend the comparison to the Netherlands, and in particular to Domburg. Inter-regional transfers within England took place on a considerable scale. If, for example, Aldfrith's *sceattas* were struck from roughly a hundred dies, and more than half the finds are south of the Humber, it might suggest that more than half a million coins were carried south. Arithmetically, the argument is not quite as secure as that, but the example may serve to make the general point. Money from Kent and London was being carried into the Midlands, and into Wessex, on a large scale. If money was moving about between regions, it was doubtless also changing hands within each region. That is, unfortunately, almost impossible to demonstrate from the distribution-patterns of single-finds.

Finally, a few words about 'productive' sites, of which Blackburn listed 31. The leading sites have each yielded 50 or even 100 *sceattas*. They were for the most part traditional trading sites in pre-urban England,[26] and were doubtless visited by merchants every year for many years, and a great deal of money will have changed hands. Now, 'productive' sites do not jump out of the ground fully recorded and bite you in the leg. They are known as a result of many hundreds of man-hours of skilled searching with metal detectors. A large field may yield perhaps two or three *sceattas* in a year. Because they are mostly located in what seems like the middle of nowhere in particular, there is no telling where a new 'productive' site may emerge. You are deep in the countryside, admiring the view: are you looking at a 20-acre field with a fine crop of potatoes, or are you looking at an undiscovered 'productive' site? Imagine asking a friend to conceal two or three *sceattas* in a 20-acre field, and then your trying to find them again with a metal detector. The number of finds from a site may be largely a function of the persistence or intensity of searching. There are plenty of sites where over

---

[26]   Blackburn, '"Productive" sites'.

the years just six or eight *sceattas* have been found. Are these second-order sites, or would prolonged searching, or deeper ploughing, or whatever, yield more? In short, the known tally of 31 sites, mapped by Blackburn and referred to by Francis Pryor, is in all probability incomplete, and the only scientifically sound way to compare one site with another is by pie-charts of the different types of *sceat* found at each, which at least shows you the extent to which coins were being transferred between regions.

Thrymsas and *sceattas* are survivors from a lost world. They speak of a monetised economy at an unexpectedly early date, and of a phase of intense activity in the second quarter of the eighth century. The estimated numbers of dies are subject to margins of statistical variation, but that does not create serious uncertainties, where the known dies are a large fraction of the estimated original total. As to the supposed average output of a die, each student will arrive at his or her own opinion, but the degree of overkill is such that the general tendency of the historical conclusions is hardly affected. Written records would not have led us to suspect that there were so many coins in existence, and even intensive archaeological excavations do not reveal the relativities of the economic perspectives. In the third quarter of the eighth century it all collapsed, and England sank into a recession, from which it emerged painfully, gaining momentum only late in the reign of King Offa.[27] There were other fluctuations still to come, and the ravages of the Viking armies in the last quarter of the ninth century resulted in economic dislocation, from which economic recovery came in the first quarter of the tenth century. For Pirenne, that was a sea-change; but the patient recording of single-finds has shown that what went before was far from being monetarily a blank.

---

[27]   D.M. Metcalf, 'Betwixt sceattas and Offa's pence: mint-attributions and the chronology of a recession', *BNJ*, 79 (2009), 1–33.

Chapter 12

The Use of Coin in the Carolingian Empire in the Ninth Century

Simon Coupland

Viking raids were a constant fear in Brittany in the mid-ninth century. According to the near contemporary *Life of St Malo* a peasant farmer in the region of Alet named Hetremaon heard that the invaders had torched the neighbouring settlements and were now approaching his village, Cherrueix in Ille-et-Vilaine. So he placed four *denarii* on the threshold of his cottage with a prayer to St Malo: 'Take this money and protect my home'. Other monastic tenants did the same, 'each according to his means' (*unusquisque secundum quod poterat*). Their secular neighbours, however, who owed their loyalties only to the Breton ruler Judicael, said to themselves, 'Why bother to give anything? Our houses are next to theirs, so St Malo will look after us, too'. The Northmen arrived at the village, burned down the houses of Judicael's half of the village and drove away their cattle, but spared those belonging to St Malo.[1] One modern reader with a hermeneutic of suspicion towards miracle texts[2] sees this as a tribute of four deniers per house which has been disguised by the hagiographical author,[3] but this surely misses the whole point of the story, namely that the money ended up with the Church, not the invaders. For the numismatist and economic historian the tale has a very different significance, however, in that it implies that an ordinary Breton peasant could have owned at least four *denarii* during the period in question in order for the miracle to have had any plausibility. This is particularly interesting, because as will become clear below, minting in Brittany at this time was limited, and if any region of the Frankish west might be expected to have had little access to coin, it would be Brittany. This incident – whether legendary or based on a genuine event – thus offers an invaluable insight into the contemporary perceptions of the use of coin in the Carolingian empire in the ninth century.

---

[1]   Bili, *Vita sancti Machutis*, ch. 15–16: *Vie de Saint-Malo, évêque d'Alet*, ed. G. le Duc (Saint-Malo, 1979), 250–51.

[2]   An expression of Paul Ricœur commonly used in Biblical criticism: see e.g. D. Stewart, 'The hermeneutics of suspicion', *Journal of Literature and Theology*, 3 (1989), 296–307.

[3]   J.C. Cassard, *Le Siècle des Vikings en Bretagne* (Paris, 1996), 37.

Numerous other contemporary sources (generally hagiographical texts) mention in passing the use of coinage, props in the drama of the everyday life they describe. Thus at the annual fair near the monastery at Fleury two friends who had come to trade (*mercandi gratia*) had an argument over 12 deniers which one of them had in his bag.[4] In a tavern at Saint-Philibert-de-Grand-Lieu a pilgrim ordered half a penny's worth of wine and paid with a penny, but was mistakenly given a penny's measure of wine and an obole (halfpenny) in change.[5] On the 'British Sea' the various monastic fishing fleets banded together to catch whales, paying what was essentially a guild fee (*solidos contubernii*), but in 875 the St Vaast fishermen fell out with them, were blessed with a great catch, and gave the money to the monastery instead: two *solidi*, or 24 pennies.[6] In the 830s in Fulda (another region where there was probably little minting) a father is said to have placed three *denarii* on the withered hand of his daughter, who was healed as the coins fell on the altar.[7] At a similar time in Mulinheim, also in the coin-poor east, a young man in Louis the German's retinue named Drogus who had been ill for months reportedly spent four deniers on candles as an offering to St Marcellinus.[8] Other texts mention similar sums: three *denarii* stolen by a monk of the abbey of la Croix-Saint-Ouen in Normandy and hidden in his clothing,[9] four *denarii* paid for wine in Dorestad,[10] two *denarii* belonging to a poor woman in Hochfelden in Alsace, dropped by her neighbour on his way to market but then found thanks to divine intervention.[11]

All these anecdotal references paint a vivid picture of the everyday use of coin in the ninth century, but do not by themselves provide a sound historical basis on which to determine the extent to which coin was used in the lands which made up the Carolingian empire in the ninth century. For one thing, hagiographical texts are viewed with considerable scepticism as historical

---

[4]   Adrevald of Fleury, *Miracula sancti Benedicti*, ch. 35: MGH, SS, XV.1, ed. O. Holder-Egger (Hanover, 1887), 496.

[5]   Ermentarius, *De translationibus et miraculis sancti Filiberti*, I.71: *Monuments de l'histoire des abbayes de Saint-Philibert*, ed. R. Poupardin (Paris, 1905), 49–50.

[6]   *Miracula sancti Vedasti*, ch. 6: MGH, SS, XV.1, ed. Holder-Egger, 400.

[7]   Rudolf, *Miracula sanctorum in Fuldenses ecclesias translatorum*, ch. 12: MGH, SS, XV.1, ed. G. Waitz, 338.

[8]   Einhard, *Translatio et miracula sanctorum Marcellini et Petri*, IV.1: MGH, SS, XV.1, ed. Waitz, 256.

[9]   *Vita S. Leutfredi*, ch. 26: *AASS IV Iunii 21*, 110. Most of the above are also cited in O. Bruand, *Voyageurs et marchandises aux temps carolingiens. Les réseaux de communication entre Loire et Meuse aux VIIIe et IXe siècles* (Brussels, 2002), 160–61.

[10]   *Vita Anskarii*, ch. 20: MGH, SSRG, 55, ed. G. Waitz (Hanover, 1884), 66.

[11]   *Translatio et Miracula sancti Adelphi Mettensis*, ch. 12, reproduced and translated in R. Naismith, *Money and Power in Anglo-Saxon England: the Southern English Kingdoms 757–865* (Cambridge, 2012), 281.

documents: they were written not to record contemporary events but to glorify the saint, and could be influenced by biblical or other earlier model accounts. In this context, however, such suspicion is unjustified. Many ninth-century authors were notably circumspect in their accounts, with a clear emphasis on establishing the veracity of the miracles they reported.[12] What is more, where these miracles display similarities to biblical episodes, the obvious differences in the ninth-century texts actually support their veracity. Thus although there are two stories in the gospels of a miraculous catch of fish (Luke 5:6, John 21:6) the St Vaast account bears no similarity to either, and no money is offered by Jesus' disciples. Or again, in a parable of Jesus a woman loses and then finds a coin (Luke 15:8–9), but it is one of ten, not both of two as at Hochfelden. Where the text is contemporary in its origin (and all the above date from the ninth century), the point made earlier merits reiteration: for the story to have had any impact on a contemporary audience it must have described what was usual at that time and in that locality in order to have been plausible. For example, it must have been possible to buy wine for half a penny in the Loire region, and two pennies must have been a significant sum for a poor villager in Alsace, or the tales lose all impact. Yet these few texts cannot offer an adequate answer to the questions this chapter seeks to address, namely: did everyone in the Frankish lands really have access to coinage? Was coin used for everyday purchases, or primarily for taxation and long-distance trade, with barter being the order of the day for everything else? Is it possible to estimate, even broadly, how much coin was in circulation?

The remarkable thing is that for more than a century scholars have looked at the evidence – both historical and numismatic – and come up with diametrically opposing conclusions. A debate has raged between proponents of two very different views of the Carolingian economy, represented on the one side by those who draw the same conclusions as Alfons Dopsch and on the other by those who share the outlook of Henri Pirenne.[13] Put simply, Dopsch saw the Carolingian period as one of economic development: rejecting the then prevailing view of a closed economy based on barter, he argued that contemporary sources revealed the increasing use of coin in trade and other everyday transactions.[14] In contrast, Pirenne saw the Carolingian era as an age of economic stagnation, with the closure of the Mediterranean and the Viking invasions leading to localised

---

[12]   See several papers in P. Riché and E. Patlagean (ed.), *Hagiographie, cultures et sociétés, IVe–XIIe siècles* (Paris, 1981), notably those by M. van Utyfanghe (205–31), M. Heinzelmann (235–57) and M. Rouche (319–37).

[13]   For a brief recent discussion see M. Costambeys, M. Innes and S. MacLean, *The Carolingian World* (Cambridge, 2011), 326–8, though there is minimal consideration of the use of coin.

[14]   A. Dopsch, *Die Wirtschaftsentwicklung der Karolingerzeit*, 2nd ed. (2 vols, Darmstadt, 1962).

economies, the collapse of commerce, and the reduction of monetary circulation to a minimum.[15]

Similarly opposing views were held by Philip Grierson and Michael Metcalf in their sometimes heated debate over the use of coin in the Carolingian period in the latter part of the twentieth century. Grierson's view is summed up by the last few lines of his article on the coinage of Charlemagne: 'Carolingian coins seem to have circulated surprisingly little; their use in commerce was in fact of a marginal character'.[16] By contrast, Metcalf believed that coins were minted in huge numbers, circulated widely and were extensively used as a means of exchange.[17] In a case study examining the reign of Charles the Bald, he concluded that at 'a very conservative estimate' upwards of 50 million coins were struck, meaning that 'we cannot be viewing an essentially non-monetary economy'.[18]

Two recent books surveying the Carolingian economy show that two scholars can still make equally contrasting judgements. Jean-Pierre Devroey, drawing upon his extensive studies of Carolingian polyptychs, argued in 2003 that throughout the late eighth and ninth centuries the coin stock remained limited in size, and even in the heart of the empire, between the Loire and the Rhine, coinage never enjoyed general use or circulation.[19] Published a year earlier, Olivier Bruand's book on Carolingian travellers and trade drew completely the opposite conclusion, that coinage was known and used everywhere ('la monnaie est connue et utilisée partout'), especially along the great river valleys, and that this was a monetary economy ('le monde carolingien est monétaire'), even if coinage was less common for the poorest and in more remote areas.[20]

Other scholars, both numismatists and historians, have contributed to the debate. In 1981 Suchodolski concluded that the truth lay somewhere between

---

[15]   H. Pirenne, *Mahomet et Charlemagne* (Paris, 1937), 219: 'la circulation monétaire est réduite au minimum'.

[16]   P. Grierson, 'Commerce in the Dark Ages: a critique of the evidence', in *TRHS, 5th series*, 5 (1959), 123–40; P. Grierson, 'Money and coinage under Charlemagne', in *Karl der Grosse, Lebenswerk und Nachleben*, ed. W. Braunfels (4 vols, Düsseldorf, 1965), 1, 501–36; both reproduced in his *Dark Age Numismatics* (London, 1979), nos. II and XVIII. The quotation is from Grierson, 'Money and coinage under Charlemagne', 536.

[17]   D.M. Metcalf, 'The prosperity of north-western Europe in the eighth and ninth centuries', *EcHR, 2nd series, 20* (1967), 344–57.

[18]   D.M. Metcalf, 'A sketch of the currency in the time of Charles the Bald', in *Charles the Bald: Court and Kingdom*, ed. M. Gibson and J.L. Nelson, 2nd ed. (Aldershot, 1990), 65–97, quotations from 92 and 69 respectively.

[19]   'Dans le cœur même de l'Empire, entre Loire et Rhin, où il a été frappé plus abondamment, il [le denier carolingien] n'a jamais connu de circulation et d'usage généralisés': J.-P. Devroey, *Économie rurale et société dans l'Europe franque (VI–IX siècles), vol. 1: Fondements matériels, échanges et lien social* (Paris, 2003), quotation from 166.

[20]   Bruand, *Voyageurs et marchandises*, 155–84, quotations from 183 and 184 respectively.

the positions adopted by Grierson and Metcalf,[21] with coin undoubtedly available to the whole population, but to a widely differing extent, with the rich using coins to buy luxury goods, and merchants, buyers and sellers using them at markets, but with smaller purchases still relying on barter.[22] Doehaerd revealed how she regarded the topic of the use of coin in her book on the Frankish economy by including it in her section, 'Problèmes et directions de recherche'.[23] In general she saw coinage as used increasingly in everyday exchanges, ironically citing Grierson as a proponent of the view that the adoption of the silver denier was evidence of growth of commerce in the Carolingian era.[24] McCormick was equally positive but even briefer in his survey of the economy of the Mediterranean world, citing my own study of the coinage of Louis the Pious as evidence that 'the advanced regions of the Frankish economy were more monetized than almost anyone dreamed three decades ago'.[25] Verhulst's survey of the Carolingian economy emphasised the important differences between the more economically developed region between the Loire and the Rhine and the less monetised territories east of the Rhine and in Italy. Beyond this, he surmised, 'Much more cannot be said'.[26] Most recently, Rory Naismith's analysis of coinage and currency in southern England in the late eighth and early ninth centuries included a lengthy discussion of the use of coinage.[27] Despite the wealth of English single-finds now available for study, Naismith had to draw on the Continental written sources because of the paucity of comparable Anglo-Saxon texts.[28] His conclusion applies equally to the Carolingian realms as to England: 'Although Anglo-Saxon England may not have been a monetized economy, there was a substantial monetary component to the economy'.[29]

Despite Verhulst's comment that 'Much more cannot be said', the present article will draw upon the most recent numismatic discoveries to offer a fresh assessment of the use of coin by the Frankish populace in the Carolingian period. Many more coin hoards are known, and there is a much greater appreciation (and significantly larger number) of single-finds, which, as Mark Blackburn's

---

[21]   S. Suchodolski, 'Der Geldumlauf in der karolingischen Epoche', in *Deutscher Numismatikertag München 1981: Vorträge* (Augsburg, 1983), 43–53.

[22]   Suchodolski, 'Geldumlauf', 51–2.

[23]   R. Doehaerd, *Le Haut Moyen Age Occidental: économies et sociétés* (Paris, 1971), 297–332, esp. 323–6.

[24]   Ibid., 318–19.

[25]   M. McCormick, *Origins of the European economy. Communications and commerce AD 300–900* (Cambridge, 2001), 9, 670–71, 681–6 (quotation from 681).

[26]   A. Verhulst, *The Carolingian Economy* (Cambridge, 2002), 122–3.

[27]   Naismith, *Money and Power*, 252–92.

[28]   Ibid., 244–5.

[29]   Ibid., 291; on its application to Francia cf. 244–6, 278.

pioneering work has demonstrated, offer invaluable economic insights.[30] It is important, too, to relate the numismatic material to the written evidence: Carolingian polyptychs, charters and wills, as well as the miracle texts cited earlier, which shed significant light on the use of coin. The evidence will be considered under four headings: coin hoards, single-finds, mints and minting, and contemporary texts, before a conclusion draws these strands of evidence together.

Coin Hoards

The number of known hoards continues to rise all the time, as Table 12.1 shows. In order to compare like with like, only those discovered in France have been included, comparing the figures recorded in 1967, 1985 and 2011.[31]

Table 12.1   French coin hoards (of 3 or more coins).

Date of deposition*	Morrison & Grunthal 1967	Duplessy 1985	Coupland 2011
751–800	2	4	5
800–50	14	21	41
850–900	30	44	73
900–50	10	15	23
950–87	3	3	4
Total	*59*	*87*	*146*

*Where the date of deposition could be in one 50-year period or the next, the hoards have been allocated proportionately to the number of years falling within each period.

New hoards keep turning up: in the three years since publishing my Checklist I have become aware of no fewer than 23 further Carolingian hoards, most of them discovered in the intervening period, as well as two new parcels to add to previously published hoards.[32] 16 of these were found in France, two in

---

[30]   S. Coupland, 'Carolingian single-finds and the economy of the early ninth century', *NC, 170* (2010), 287–319.

[31]   MG; J. Duplessy, *Les trésors monétaires médiévaux et modernes découverts en France, vol. 1: 751–1223* (Paris, 1985–); S. Coupland, 'A checklist of Carolingian coin hoards, 751–987', *NC, 171* (2011), 203–56.

[32]   S. Coupland: 'A Supplement to the Checklist of Carolingian Coin Hoards', *NC*, 174 (2014, forthcoming). A 24th hoard in the Supplement replaces two previously listed and so is not a new find.

the Netherlands, and one apiece in Belgium, England, Germany, Hungary and Switzerland.

It is crucial not to misinterpret the table: a rise in the number of hoards (or in the total number of coins they contain) does not necessarily indicate a rise in the amount of coin in circulation at the time, still less an increase in the use of coinage.[33] On the one hand, it may reflect a rise in modern detection and discovery, or even improved reporting of finds, factors which vary from region to region. The figures would thus undoubtedly be higher were it not for the laws restricting metal detecting in France, which mean that significant numbers of hoards are being dispersed without any record. On the other hand, the concealment of numerous hoards may reflect a change in circumstances at the time of deposition, perhaps increased prosperity but more likely increased danger, since many hoards were buried – and some not recovered – because of war or invasion or the threat of these. Simon Armstrong's survey of ninth-century hoards from France showed that a number of factors were influential, including a rise in the amount of coin in circulation, but also civil war and Viking incursions.[34] An examination of hoarding in Carolingian Frisia (which was significantly larger than the modern province of Friesland) revealed a subtly different picture, with a closer correlation between the level of hoard deposition and the intensity of Viking incursions in the region.[35] To underline the point made above about the interpretation of Table 12.1, here in the north a rise in the number of hoards occurs at a time when silver appears to have been increasingly scarce.

Despite these caveats, coin hoards can shed some light on the use of coin. For instance, the fact that someone – or arguably a group of people – in Friesland in the early 850s could amass a sum as large as the 2,789 *denarii* found at Tzummarum is highly significant.[36] This represents the not negligible sum of over 11 pounds in cash, and the hoard comes from a region where there were few large settlements and very few monasteries, but where trade is assumed to have been a significant occupation. Other ninth-century hoards may well have been larger, but unfortunately there is uncertainty about the original composition, either because the contents were lost, as in the case of the Wiesbaden-Biebrich hoard from the beginning of the century, said to have weighed 8–10 kilos, but sealed in

---

[33]   An error unfortunately committed by Bruand, *Voyageurs et marchandises*, 169–70, following G. Depeyrot, *Le numéraire carolingien: corpus des monnaies*, 3rd ed. (Wetteren, 2008), 83–101.

[34]   S. Armstrong, 'Carolingian Coin Hoards and the Impact of the Viking Raids in the Ninth Century', *NC,* 158 (1998), 131–64.

[35]   S. Coupland, 'Between the devil and the deep blue sea: hoards in ninth-century Frisia', in *Coinage and History in the North Sea World c.500–1250. Essays in Honour of Marion Archibald*, ed. B. Cook and G. Williams (Leiden and Boston, 2006), 241–66.

[36]   Tzummarum II 1991: Coupland, 'Checklist', no. 121.

a block of concrete,[37] or the Montrieux-Courbanton hoard from the 890s, over which confusion reigns as to just how many pots it comprised, though the most likely guess is that there were three, each containing 1,200–1,500 coins.[38] These hoards are exceptional, however: as Table 12.2 shows, most Carolingian hoards were small, with nearly half containing fewer than two dozen coins.[39]

Table 12.2   Sizes of Carolingian coin hoards.

Date of deposition	3–9 coins	10–24	25–49	50–99	100–199	200–399	400–799	800+	Total
751–800	6	6	3	1	1	-	-	-	*17*
800–50	22	10	12	10	5	5	3	3	*70*
850–900	20	12	5	12	10	8	8	9	*84*
900–50	6	11	2	4	2	5	3	2	*35*
950–87	3	-	-	1	-	1	1	1	*7*
Total	57	39	22	28	18	19	15	15	213

One surprising feature among Carolingian hoards is that a significant number were found concealed in graves, even though grave goods no longer accompanied burials in the Christian Frankish west at this late period. The phenomenon is markedly more prevalent than in Anglo-Saxon England.[40] Some if not all of the larger hoards were probably buried with the intention of later recovery, concealed in graveyards because these were seen as places of greater security – and sanctity – than other locations, while others were most likely the small change carried by the deceased at the time of their death.[41] Both types of hoard can be taken as representing the coinage owned by a particular individual in the given location at the time, though the smaller 'clothing' hoards from the Frankish heartlands are of particular interest in the present context. Dating from the 820s to the 880s, some consisted of just three or four coins, consistent with the reference in the *Life* of St Leutfred cited earlier, while others included six,

---

[37]   Ibid., no. 22.

[38]   Ibid., nos. 192–4 and discussion in nn. 104–6. Of the six supposedly large Carolingian hoards listed by Suchodolski in 1981, only Pilligerheck is properly recorded and available for study: 'Geldumlauf', 46.

[39]   The figures are based on Coupland, 'Checklist'; subsequent finds do not alter the picture. Only Carolingian hoards from within Frankish territory have been included, and only the number of Carolingian coins is taken into account.

[40]   M. Blackburn, 'Coinage in its archaeological context', in *The Oxford Handbook of Anglo-Saxon Archaeology*, ed. H. Hamerow, D.A. Hinton and S. Crawford (Oxford, 2011), 580–99.

[41]   Coupland, 'Checklist', 207–9. See also M. Schulze-Dörrlamm, 'Gräber mit Münzebeigabe im Karolingerreich', *Jahrbuch des Römisch-Germanischen Zentralmuseums* 57 (2010), 339–88.

eight, or, at Catillon, 18 coins, almost certainly the contents of a purse, as they were found 'on the middle of the right femur of one of the skeletons'.[42] This not only reveals the kind of sum that an individual might have been carrying when they died (though of course we know nothing about that individual's station in life) but also arguably suggests that at these times in these places such a sum was thought too trivial to take from the deceased (other grave goods were not recorded as present, nor would be expected at this date).

Hoards reveal that foreign coin was effectively excluded from the economy, with hardly any non-Frankish coinage in even the largest of ninth-century deposits. Just two Anglo-Saxon coins have turned up among the tens of thousands contained in ninth-century Frankish hoards.[43] Arabic dirhams are found in a growing number of hoards, but in very specific local contexts: three from the Rhine valley at the turn of the ninth century, five in Viking contexts in the Netherlands and Normandy, and two exciting new finds from south-west France, the result of contacts with Arab Spain.[44] For the sake of completeness papal coins should perhaps also be mentioned, most of which bore the name of a Frankish ruler and could thus be seen as quasi-Carolingian coinage. Yet even these have only turned up in three ninth-century hoards outside Italy (five papal coins in total) and three from Italy itself (containing 21 papal coins).[45] All this indicates that when people in the ninth century did use coin, it was Carolingian coinage that was changing hands, and that it was being used in a rigorously controlled economy.

Hoards also disclose how quickly coins from right across the empire could mingle with one another. Louis the Pious replaced all previous coinage types in empire-wide recoinages in 816 and 822/3, and the hoards from Apremont-sur-Allier in Berry and Belvézet in Languedoc-Roussillon demonstrate not only how effectively the previous types were excluded from circulation (among 1,048 coins there were just five earlier issues), but also how freely and rapidly the new currency circulated. Both finds contained coins from a wide range of mints, from Dorestad in the north to Barcelona in the south, Nantes in the west to Venice

---

[42]   For the *Life* of St Leutfred, see n. 9 above. For Catillon see A. Leroy, 'Notice sur une découverte de monnaies carlovingiennes (commencement du IXe siècle), faite à la ferme de Morvillers', *Bulletin de la Société des antiquaires de Picardie, 1* (1841–3), 131–2.

[43]   S. Coupland, 'The Roermond coins reconsidered', *Medieval and Modern Matters, 2* (2011), 25–50, at 41.

[44]   L. Ilisch, 'Der Steckborner Schatzfund von 1830 und andere Funde nordafrikanischer Dirhams im Bereich des Karlsreiches', in *Simposio Simone Assemani Sulla Monetazione Islamica*, ed. G. Gorini (Padua, 2005), 67-91; Coupland, 'Roermond coins', 41, n. 132; Matha (Charente-Maritime) and Prats-de-Mollo (Pyrénées-Orientales): M. Parvérie, 'Questions sur l'importation de dirhams d'al-Andalus dans l'Empire carolingien', *BCEN* 49 (2012), 14-23 and Coupland, 'Supplement' (forthcoming).

[45]   Coupland, 'Roermond coins', 42–3.

and Treviso in the east.[46] This is not of course necessarily evidence of trade, as the coins could have served other purposes, including as alms, gifts, fines, taxes or tolls, but it clearly contradicts Grierson's statement, cited earlier, that 'Carolingian coins seem to have circulated surprisingly little', and consequently also undermines his deduction from that premise that 'their use in commerce was of a marginal character; they provided a standard of value and a means of storing wealth'.[47]

The composition of one mixed hoard (that is, containing both numismatic and non-numismatic silver) does indicate that it was most likely the property of a merchant. The Roermond hoard, deposited in 853–54 beside the river Maas (Meuse) consisted of at least 1,130 and perhaps as many as 1,650 coins as well as a number of silver belt buckles and mounts.[48] A few recent, locally minted coins in the hoard demonstrate that it definitely belongs in its geographical context, but unusually for this period the find also includes significant parcels of coins from Italy, Aquitaine and Neustria, which other contemporary hoards reveal to have had little economic interaction with one another or with the Maas region at this time. This suggests that the owner of the Roermond hoard was engaged in inter-regional trade, though not necessarily that he himself had visited those regions. He may have been selling the kind of decorative military equipment found in the hoard, or may perhaps have been a silversmith producing the items for others to sell. Either way, the hoard offers a rare glimpse into what was surely mercantile activity in the mid-ninth century.

Single-Finds

As has already been mentioned, single-finds offer a much more reliable indication than hoards of the amount of coin in circulation, and it was of course Mark Blackburn who first made this point widely understood and then used the data provided by single-finds to demonstrate their value as evidence. Our understanding of Anglo-Saxon coinage and currency has been transformed in recent years thanks to the willingness of metal-detectorists to record and report their finds; as Mark commented to me not many months before his untimely death, there is now scarcely a parish in South-East England which has not witnessed the discovery of at least one Anglo-Saxon coin, and in some

---

[46] S. Coupland, 'Money and coinage under Louis the Pious', *Francia*, *17* (1990), 23–54, at 30–31, repr. in S. Coupland, *Carolingian Coinage and the Vikings: Studies on Power and Trade in the 9th Century* (Aldershot, 2007). The dating of Louis's recoinages is revised in Coupland, 'Carolingian single-finds', 298–300.

[47] As n. 16 above.

[48] J. Zuyderwyk and J. Besteman, 'The Roermond hoard: a Carolingian mixed silver hoard from the ninth century', *Medieval and Modern Matters*, *1* (2010), 73–154; Coupland, 'Roermond coins'.

parishes it is many more. This means that it is now possible to make die studies of even short-lived coinages and study circulation patterns in ways that would have been unthinkable even a decade ago.[49] On the Continent a list of single-finds is gradually building up,[50] but the very different attitudes on the part of the authorities in France in particular mean that large numbers of finds go unreported and there is a massive disparity compared with the situation across the Channel. The Netherlands has a marvellous research tool in the form of the NUMIS project,[51] and archaeologists are continuing to register their finds on the database, but the recent closure of the Geldmuseum and the savage cuts to the number of staff working in the field of numismatics means that the identification, study and publication of finds will be drastically cut back for the foreseeable future.

The work of collating the information is still very much in its infancy: Figure 12.1 shows the fruit of my attempts to date to track down single-finds of Louis the Pious's second coin-type (struck 816–22/3), trawling published works, internet detector sites, and requesting information from a range of contacts across the Continent.[52] As was noted above, this type was minted for at most seven years, between 816 and 823, and very effectively removed from circulation by 825. The map may be prone to some distortion by locality, in that finds tend to cluster close to where they were minted, and a number of 'productive sites' (see below) are responsible for multiple finds: 39 at Wijk bij Duurstede (Dorestad), 8 at Mainz, 7 at Domburg, 4 at Nord-Isère and 4 at Schouwen. Even so, the map represents 237 single-finds from over 160 locations, which is a large enough sample to offer a reliable impression of the size of the various mints, particularly since it is largely paralleled by the evidence of contemporary hoards.[53]

One remarkable feature of the discovery of single-finds is their concentration in so-called 'productive' sites, another area where Mark Blackburn made a significant contribution.[54] These are sites which were neither towns nor emporia

---

[49]   *Pers. comm.* Mark Blackburn, June 2011. See e.g. Naismith, *Money and Power*, 199–202.

[50]   The fullest published list to date is in C.M. Haertle, *Karolingische Münzfunde aus dem 9 Jahrhundert* (2 vols, Cologne, Weimar and Vienna, 1997), nos. 500–876, although I would classify some of these as small hoards. Jean-Luc Dengis is also compiling a very useful list of all known finds in Belgium province by province (*Trouvailles et trésors monétaires en Belgique* (10 vols, Wetteren, 2009–), and Ermano Arslan is compiling an invaluable online list of all Italian finds known to him: <www.ermannoarslan.eu/Repertorio/RepertorioAMAggiornamento>.

[51]   www.geldmuseum.nl/museum/content/zoeken-numis.

[52]   Because of the uncertainty over their location, *Alaboteshain*, *Aldunheim* and *Stottenburg* have been omitted from Figure 12.1.

[53]   Coupland, 'Louis the Pious', 32–4. Only coins have been included for which a definite find-spot is known, in some cases a French département or Dutch province.

[54]   M.A.S. Blackburn, '"Productive" sites and the pattern of coin loss in England, 600–1180', in *Markets in Early Medieval Europe. Trading and 'Productive' Sites, 650–850*, ed. T. Pestell and K.

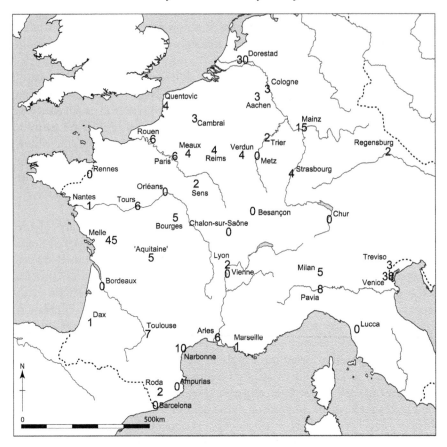

Figure 12.1　Map of mints producing Louis the Pious's Class 2 coinage (struck 816–22/3), with number of single-finds from each.

but at which unusually large numbers of coins and sometimes metalwork have been found, as single-finds rather than the dispersed content of a hoard.[55] In the words of Ulmschneider and Pestell, these are most likely 'smaller, less well-documented trading-places', and their discovery has 'started to challenge the notion that such rural sites were of little importance to the economic system as a whole'.[56] By far the largest number of single-finds on the Continent come from Wijk bij Duurstede, the great trading centre of Dorestad (over 430 Carolingian coins), significant parts of which have been excavated and which is a favoured

---

Ulmschneider (Macclesfield, 2003), 20–36.

[55]　K. Ulmschneider and T. Pestell, 'Introduction: early medieval markets and "productive" sites', in *Markets in Early Medieval Europe*, ed. Pestell and Ulmschneider, 1–10.

[56]　Ibid., 1.

haunt of Dutch metal-detectorists. Another significant concentration (220 Carolingian coins) comes from Domburg, which is widely assumed to have been an emporium on the basis of the mass of finds, especially coins, despite the lack of archaeological or written evidence.[57] There are in addition two other locations in the Netherlands which might be termed 'productive' sites, both on the coast: Wijnaldum in Friesland, where 15 Carolingian coins were found during excavation, and Schouwen in Zeeland, where no fewer than 70 stray finds have turned up, more than twice the number found at either of the important urban sites of Mainz or Trier.[58] An examination of Hubregtse's collection at the Zeeuws Museum in Middelburg has revealed significant errors in the figures on which previous publications (by Mark Blackburn and myself) relied. This is not the place for full details but a summary is provided in Table 12.3.

Table 12.3   Finds of Carolingian coins from Schouwen.

Pippin the Short (751–68)	2
Charlemagne Pre-reform (768–93/4)	6
Charlemagne Monogram (793/4–813)	11 (+ 1 obole?)
Louis the Pious Portrait (814–16)	2
Louis the Pious Class 2 (816–22/3)	4
Louis the Pious *Christiana religio* (822/3–40)	38 deniers + 1 obole
Charles the Bald (840–64)	2
Lothar I (840–55)	2
Pippin II of Aquitaine (845–8)	1 obole

Note: The figure for Charlemagne's monogram coinage includes an obole of Melle which could possibly belong to the period 840–64.

I am also aware of a 'productive' site somewhere in the north of the département of Isère, where over a hundred Carolingian coins have been unearthed[59] (including six further finds since the publication of my article on Carolingian single-finds: a coin of Carloman (768–771) minted in Lyon; and five more *Christiana religio* coins of Louis the Pious: four deniers and an obole). Regrettably the lack of a precise location, historical context or even

---

[57]   Coupland, 'Carolingian single-finds', 288–9, to which should be added 18 further finds of which I have become aware. On Domburg see S. Lebecq, 'L'emporium proto-médiéval de Walcheren Domburg: une mise en perspective', in *Peasants and Townsmen in Early Medieval Europe: Studia in honorem Adriaan Verhulst*, ed. J.-M. Duvosquel and E. Thoen (Ghent, 1995), 73–89.

[58]   Coupland, 'Carolingian single-finds', 290–95. I am very grateful to the Middelburg Museum staff for their help.

[59]   Coupland, 'Carolingian single-finds', 291.

accurate descriptions of all the coins means that very little can be said about this specific site and its significance. What it does reveal nonetheless is that there are 'productive' sites in France similar to those known from England and the Netherlands. Unfortunately they are not being properly studied or the finds adequately recorded, and more are undoubtedly awaiting discovery. I have for instance seen internet reports by detectorists mentioning rural sites where intriguing groups of coins have been found: one in Deux-Sèvres where the range includes coins of Charlemagne (pre-reform and monogram), Charles the Bald, Pippin II and Raoul, another in Eure where Merovingian and Carolingian brooches and buckles have been found alongside a *sceat* and at least seven coins of Louis the Pious (two mint-signed and five *Christiana religio*), and a third in Seine-et-Marne where the list of finds apparently runs from Merovingian through pre-reform coinage to coins of Pippin II and Charles the Bald before 864 and the *Gratia Dei rex* (GDR) type. In none of these cases are the precise find-spots reported, in none of them can I be sure that this is a complete list (indeed, I suspect the contrary) and in none of them has the finder (or finders) published proper descriptions of the coins for reference and study. All this is deeply frustrating, yet even these few facts suggest that these are 'productive' sites: neither towns, emporia, nor ecclesiastical establishments, but rural locations where significant numbers of coins were evidently circulating. Without further details it is impossible to say what role these coins were playing, whether for instance for rent, taxes or in commerce, but they are unquestionably evidence of the use of coin outside urban centres and emporia. It is important to emphasise that this is equally true of Domburg/Walcheren, Schouwen and Wijnaldum, for although they are now referred to as an 'emporium', a 'coastal wic' and a 'production centre engaged in trade' respectively,[60] there is no reference to any of them as trading places in any ninth-century document: the inference has been drawn from the archaeological and numismatic finds.

Although strictly speaking outside the scope of this article, a recently discovered Danish site is of particular interest in this context. At Havsmarken on Ærø, Arabic coins, silver objects and now some 40 Carolingian coins (the vast majority of them *Christiana religio* deniers of Louis the Pious) have been found by metal-detectorists, in a context which indicates that they were almost certainly being used for buying and selling. The finds from this site have done more than anything else to convince Danish numismatists and archaeologists

---

[60]   Domburg: see n. 57 above; Schouwen: M. Blackburn, 'Coin circulation in Germany during the early Middle Ages. The evidence of single-finds', in *Fernhandel und Geldwirtschaft. Beiträge zum deutschen Münzwesen in sächsischer und salischer Zeit*, ed. B. Kluge (Sigmaringen, 1993), 37–54, at 48; Wijnaldum: C. Tulp, 'Tijtsma, Wijnaldum: an early medieval production site in the Netherlands', in *Markets in Early Medieval Europe*, ed. Pestell and Ulmschneider, 221–33, at 232.

that in the early ninth century coins were being used for trade in Denmark at market sites outside the international emporia of Hedeby and Ribe.[61]

Another particularly significant contribution of single-finds to the debate over the use of coin relates to the Italian economy in the early ninth century. The dearth of finds of Carolingian coins in numerous Italian excavations has led Alessia Rovelli to conclude that the production and circulation of coin in Italy was extremely limited at this time. She has argued that the presence of significant numbers of Italian coins in a small number of well-documented hoards is anomalous, and provides insufficient evidence to demonstrate that Italian mints played a leading role in the Carolingian economy.[62] However, an ever increasing number of single-finds of mint-signed coins of Louis's second coinage type, with the mint-name in field, and of Italianate issues of Louis's third type, the *Christiana religio* coinage, leads to the indisputable conclusion that Milan, Pavia and particularly Venice were among the leading mints of Louis the Pious and that the coins which they minted circulated widely in very large numbers. Figure 12.1 reveals that there are more single-finds of Louis's Class 2 coinage from Venice than from any other mint except Melle, and that Pavia is the sixth-best represented mint, a remarkable statistic given that none of those finds come from archaeological contexts in Italy whereas many of the finds at Dorestad (12/29) and Mainz (6/13) are from local excavations (the Appendix lists the find-spots of the Italian coins). Figure 12.2 shows the single-finds of *Christiana religio* issues attributable to Milan and Venice (my Groups F and G respectively): in south-eastern France these two groups are by far the most commonly found among Louis's *Christiana religio* coins, both in hoards and among single-finds, with new specimens being discovered all the time.[63] It is essential to appreciate that the map offers a very incomplete picture, since it includes only those coins whose provenances are recorded and whose photographs I have been able to study. Many more *Christiana religio* coins – including several of those found in Italy – may well belong to one or other group but have not been illustrated; others have been pictured on detector sites but without a reported find-spot. Even so, these figures indicate both that significant amounts of Italian coin were being minted in the early ninth century and that they were circulating widely, even if that circulation began to break down in the 830s and was then drastically

---

[61]   J.C. Moesgaard, 'Sensationelt fund af karolingiske mønter på Ærø', *NNUM* 2009, 170–71. More finds have come to light since that article was written; for an up-to-date account see <http://www.historieinfo.dk/Karolingere.html>.

[62]   A. Rovelli, 'Some considerations on the coinage of Lombard and Carolingian Italy', in *The Long Eighth Century*, ed. I.L. Hansen and C. Wickham (Leiden, 2000), 195–223, at 214–16; A. Rovelli, 'Coins and trade in early medieval Italy', *EME, 17* (2009), 45–76, at 69–71 (both repr. in her *Coinage and Coin Use in Medieval Italy* (Farnham, 2012), nos. VI and VII).

[63]   Coupland, 'Carolingian single-finds', 310–14; Coupland, 'Roermond coins', 46, n. 65, and new finds are constantly turning up.

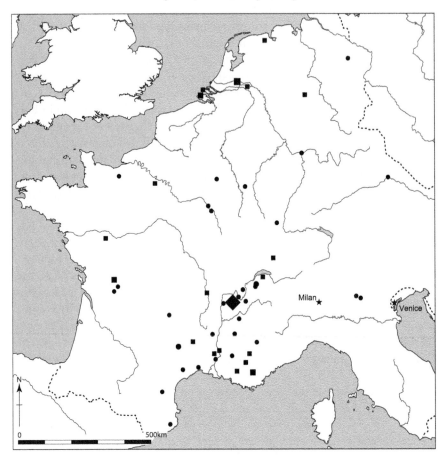

Figure 12.2   Map of single-finds of *Christiana religio* coins of Louis the Pious
               attributable to Milan (square) or Venice (round). The size of the
               symbol reflects the number of coins; the diamond represents finds
               of both mints together.

curtailed from the 840s onwards.[64] It is consequently hard to account for the
paucity of finds described by Rovelli; even though it is a well-established fact
that urban excavations often turn up few coins, particularly if the spoil is not
double-washed, the extremely low numbers she reports are still far lower than
would be expected given the number of finds elsewhere. There is no satisfactory
explanation for this discrepancy: the best working hypothesis is that advanced by
Rovelli, namely that there was less coin use in Italy than elsewhere in the empire

---

[64]   Coupland, 'Roermond coins', 31–2.

at this time, and that the majority of the coins were used in long-distance trade rather than in local markets, as was obviously the case in independent Venice.[65]

This finding in turn underlines the crucial importance of recognising regional differences when writing about the Carolingian economy, and holding together the written, archaeological and numismatic evidence region by region. We cannot make general statements such as 'in Francia ... some 80 per cent of coins are found inside a 100-kilometre radius of their mints':[66] of the 54 finds of Italian coins struck between 816 and 823 (see Appendix), just 5 coins (9 percent) were found within 100 km of where they were minted.[67] Circulation patterns varied widely both between regions and over time, making any such generalisations both misleading and, in this case, highly inaccurate.

Figures 12.1 and 12.2 also underline how on the Continent as in England the ever increasing number of single-finds offers an invaluable resource for the study of the economy of the time. It is a source of immense frustration that only a small proportion of finds are being properly recorded. Table 12.4 shows the number of single-finds known to me at the end of June 2014, including emporia, urban settlements and productive sites, and grave and church finds: if the aim is to assess the availability and use of coin across the empire, rather than to compare circulation at individual sites, then all such data can and should be included.

Table 12.4 Single-finds from all known sites, 751–864.

Pippin the Short	124
Carloman	4
Charlemagne Pre-reform	190
Charlemagne Monogram	230 + 137 (see below)
Charlemagne Portrait	15
Louis the Pious Portrait	47
Louis the Pious Class 2	237
Louis the Pious *Christiana religio*	722
Lothar I	119
Charles the Bald before 864	68 + 40 (see below)
Pippin II of Aquitaine	48
Louis the German before 864	6
Total:	*1987*

---

[65]   Rovelli, 'Some considerations', 220–21.

[66]   C. Wickham, *The Inheritance of Rome. A History of Europe from 400 to 1000* (London, 2009), 547.

[67]   Comparable figures for the reigns of Pippin the Short and Charlemagne can be found in S. Coupland, 'Charlemagne and his coinage', in *Charlemagne : les temps, les espaces, les hommes. Construction et déconstruction d'un règne*, ed. R. Große (forthcoming).

It should be emphasised that these figures are constantly changing and potentially skewed by the fact that some regions are better covered than others, and some coinage types better studied than others. Nevertheless, the sheer size of the corpus, the randomness of the data and the inclusion of material from all regions make these usable figures, as long as they are treated with caution. The table includes only finds from within the former Frankish empire, and the Monogram coins of Melle from the reigns of Charlemagne and Charles the Bald have had to be estimated because the types were identical and cannot be distinguished. However, because of the significance of the Melle mint, it is important to include a figure for the likely numbers, and these have been calculated using the ratio of the other single finds which can definitely be attributed to one ruler or the other, as listed in the table. Other factors support the general reliability of the resulting figures.[68]

Table 12.4 is misleading, however, as raw data because some coinage types were minted for longer periods than others, and recoinages removed some types from circulation quickly, while others remained in the coin stock for years. For example, Louis's Class 2 was minted for seven years and circulated for just nine; the *Christiana religio* type was minted for 17 years but remained in circulation for over 40. Again bearing in mind the caveats expressed above, if these factors are taken into account and the finds plotted over time, a surprising and remarkable picture emerges, as shown in the upper chart in Figure 12.3.

Here recoinages and wastage rates have been factored in, and the number of finds averaged out over the length of time they were circulating. Quite unexpectedly, the figures reveal a steady growth of the amount of coin in circulation type by type until the reign of Louis the Pious. Unfortunately, single-finds of GDR coins can rarely be attributed to Charles the Bald or Charles the Simple, meaning that the timeline cannot be extended beyond 864. The chart reveals a significantly different picture from that offered by the charts plotting individual sites published in 2010, which unsurprisingly display marked regional variations.[69] This graph provides cautious support to the notion that the amount of coin in circulation in the Carolingian territories rose steadily over time from the reign of Pippin III to *c.*840, with a significant peak during the reign of Louis the Pious. Then the chaos of internecine feuding, political instability and Viking incursions caused an evident decline – but to levels still above those of the late eighth century. More data needs to be collected to consolidate this finding, and it is very important to emphasise again that although it may have been a general phenomenon across the empire, there were very different levels of coin availability and coin use in different regions, as the finds at individual sites demonstrate and as further evidence will underline below.

---

[68] Ibid.

[69] Coupland, 'Carolingian single-finds', 302–4. Those figures are all included in this data.

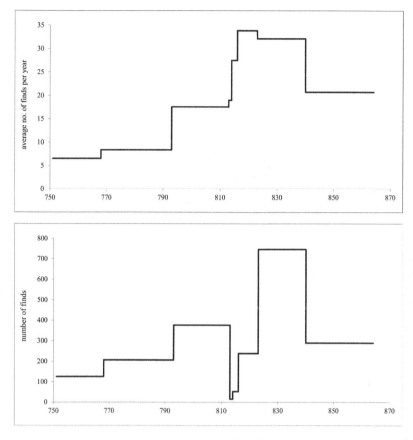

Figure 12.3   Above: Average number of Carolingian single-finds per year. Below: Unadjusted number of finds (as Table 12.4)

Mints and Minting

Combining the insights offered by coin hoards, single-finds and the many unprovenanced coins in public and private collections and auction catalogues allows us to draw further conclusions about the use of coinage in the ninth century which cannot be obtained from the study of any one of these on their own. These include the distribution of mints, the possible number of dies used by those mints and thus, by extrapolation, the potential size of the coinages produced, and the significance of individual coinages, in particular the use of oboles, or halfpennies, in the Carolingian economy.

Looking first at the location and size of mints during the period under discussion, certain major differences can be observed over time, as well as certain consistent features. One factor which varies significantly not only between reigns but also within them is the number of mints in operation. During the eighth century, prior to the reform of 793/4, a large number of often small mints were striking coinage. New types of Pippin III and Charlemagne are being discovered all the time, frequently when a new coinage type is offered for sale, generally without a provenance. The location of a number of these mints is uncertain. To give one remarkable recent example, at the end of 2011 a hitherto unknown type of pre-reform penny of Pippin with the reverse legend XPI (for *Christi*) was found 6 kilometres from Wijk bij Duurstede (Figure 12.4a),[70] and in January 2012, a parallel type for Charlemagne appeared, although this coin was reportedly discovered a few kilometres from Laon in the 1970s (Figure 12.4b).[71] There is no reason to suspect that either coin is other than genuine, and the two finds were made and reported in very different circumstances: their publication a month apart appears to be no more than a remarkable coincidence.

By contrast, the discovery of new mints striking the heavy deniers produced by Charlemagne and then Louis the Pious is extremely rare. Thus only one new mint of Charlemagne's monogram type has been identified since the publication of Morrison and Grunthal's survey of Carolingian coinage in 1965, Roda in

Figure 12.4   a–b Coins of Pippin III (left) and Charlemagne (right) with the reverse legend XPI (Guido Cornelissens).

Spain, and that from a single coin,[72] while no new mints of Louis the Pious's second coinage type have been discovered since Gariel and Prou were writing in the late nineteenth century.[73] Indeed, in the past 50 years just one name has been added to the list of mints active during Louis's reign, Maastricht, which produced what was undoubtedly a small and short-lived coinage bearing the

[70]   *Pers. comm.* Guido Cornelissens.

[71]   <http://www.numismaticom.com/t3770-demande-d-identification-denier>.

[72]   M. Crusafont i Sabater, 'Tipo inédito de Carlomagno de la ceca de Roda', *Acta numismatica, 13* (1983), 125–35.

[73]   E. Gariel, *Les monnaies royales de France sous la race carolingienne* (2 vols, Strasbourg, 1883–4), 2, 164–88; M. Prou, *Catalogue des monnaies françaises de la Bibliothèque Nationale: les monnaies carolingiennes* (Paris, 1892), LXXIX.

mint-name around a temple at the very end of the emperor's life.[74] From the reign of Charles the Bald the picture has been complicated by uncertainty over the attribution of both his monogram coinage (also struck by Charlemagne) and the GDR type (also minted under Charles the Simple). Even so, I am not aware of any new mints of Charles the Bald from either before or after the reform of 864 whose issues have been discovered in the past 50 years. By contrast, in the case of Lothar I, three new mints have turned up since 1965: Dinant, Maubeuge and Namur, each represented by a single coin, while Pippin II is now known to have struck deniers as well as oboles at Cahors.[75] Despite the large number of new hoards and single-finds made in the last half century, no new mints of Louis the German have come to light, and it is evident that minting in the east of the former empire remained very limited.[76] One new mint can however be added to the number striking coinage under Odo: Beauvais.[77]

Turning now to consider where coin was produced across the Frankish regions in the course of the ninth century, Figure 12.5 shows the mints striking Charlemagne's Monogram coinage, Figure 12.1 those producing Louis the Pious's second type, and Figure 12.6 all those known to have been active between 840 and 864. The mints of the two short-lived Portrait coinages have not been mapped, nor is it possible to plot the mints striking Louis the Pious's *Christiana religio* coinage, since it is not known how many there were, let alone where they were all located. A comparison of Figures 12.1, 12.5 and 12.6 shows a measure of continuity over the 70 years between 794 and 864, in terms of both the most prolific mints and the regions where coinage must have been scarce. Dorestad and Melle remained by far the most important mints throughout the period, and the Italian mints of Milan and Pavia also maintained significant economic roles. In the west, Bourges, Tours and Toulouse all appear to have been consistently productive, albeit on a considerably smaller scale than Dorestad and Melle. Louis the Pious clearly sought to expand the empire-wide network of mints, and very probably did so further when minting the *Christiana religio* type, but several regions evidently remained poorly monetised throughout: Brittany and Lower Normandy in the west; Frisia north and east of Dorestad (although the emporium's massive output may well have made up for that); and the area east of the Rhine and north of Italy (even if the unidentified *Alaboteshain*, *Aldunheim* and *Stottenburg* were located in this region, they are all characterised by an absence of provenanced finds). As for significant developments, there appears

---

[74]   The most recent survey can be found in J.C. Besteman, 'Westerklief II, a second Viking silver hoard from the former island of Wieringen', *JMP, 93–94* (2006–2007), 5–80, at 49–50.

[75]   P. Crinon and B. Chwartz, 'Deux exemples de soulèvements aquitains illustrés par des monnaies inédites, l'une de Marseille, l'autre de Cahors', *BSFN, 65* (2010), 138–43.

[76]   The most recent survey of finds is in Coupland, 'Roermond coins', 39–40.

[77]   T. Cardon, J.C. Moesgaard, R. Prot and P. Schiesser, 'Le premier trésor monétaire de type viking en France. Denier inédit d'Eudes pour Beauvais', *RN, 164* (2008), 21–40.

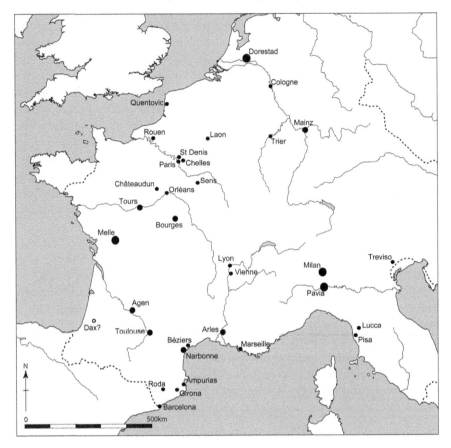

Figure 12.5   Known mints producing the Monogram coinage of Charlemagne
(793/4–812). (Size of dot in this and Figure 12.6 corresponds to
the likely significance of the mint.)

to have been a marked increase in the production and thus availability of coin
between the Seine and the Rhine, with not only more mints appearing, but several
of those mints increasing their output over the period in question. Meanwhile
in the south a string of mints in Tuscany and along the Mediterranean seem to
have disappeared; the larger mints of Narbonne and Arles may have been active
between 840 and 864, but if so there is no evidence of this.

If we then compare a map of mints striking after 864 these trends continue,
with the contrast between the economically thriving west and the monetarily

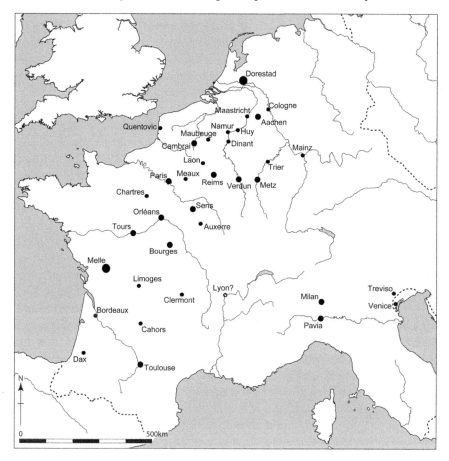

Figure 12.6   Known Carolingian mints active 840–64.

impoverished south and east becoming even more pronounced.[78] A plethora of mints sprang up between the Loire and the Rhine, first in the West Frankish kingdom and then in Lotharingia as well, while in the eastern kingdom and Provence only a few coins were struck at a very limited number of mints.[79] At this time the dislocation of Italy from the Carolingian west and the scarcity of Italian finds make it difficult to judge the level of production there,[80] but suggest a likely decline in the second half of the ninth century. The disappearance of Dorestad

---

[78]   Metcalf, 'Sketch of the currency', 87; *MEC* 1, 234, to which should be added the southern mints of Bourges, Melle, Clermont, Toulouse, Agen and Dax, and after 875 Arles, Nîmes, Uzès and Béziers: 232, 235.

[79]   *MEC* 1, 225–7.

[80]   D.M. Metcalf, 'North Italian coinage carried across the Alps. The Ostrogothic and Carolingian evidence compared', *Rivista Italiana di Numismatica e Scienze Affini, 90* (1988),

in the north caused a dramatic drop in the amount of coinage circulating in Carolingian Frisia,[81] but at the same time appears to have led to a significant rise in the fortunes of the Channel ports of Quentovic[82] and Rouen. Another area to benefit from the West Frankish expansion was the far west, with Nantes and Rennes both striking coinage again, and a number of mints established in Lower Normandy, including the new and productive mint of *Curtisasonien*, whose precise location is still uncertain. Other mints which evidently played a significant role in the late ninth-century economy without having produced mint-signed coinage earlier in the century are Amiens, Le Mans, St Quentin and Soissons. Meanwhile at the very end of the century Cologne and Strasbourg re-emerged as mints, striking coin on a much larger scale than ever before.

One interesting point from the 860s is that there are no known coins from two places which are sometimes cited as new mints established to stimulate commercial activity, Prüm and Châlons-en-Champagne.[83] Although royal charters granted minting rights at Rommersheim for Prüm in 861 and at Châlons in 864,[84] there is no numismatic evidence that coinage was actually produced at either location, despite what is now a large corpus of finds. The likely explanation in the case of Châlons is that the charter is a forgery,[85] and certainly the absence of any coins bearing its name means that the charter cannot be relied upon as evidence of contemporary minting practice.[86] In the case of Lothar II and Prüm it could be argued that the Rommersheim/Prüm mint produced coins bearing the anonymous *Christiana religio* legend, but given the fact that only two specimens of this coinage are known, both attributable to Verdun on stylistic grounds, this is implausible as well as clutching at straws.[87] If the charter is genuine then the mint it permitted appears never to have been established. By contrast, another Carolingian charter granting minting rights

---

449–56, at 454–6; S. Coupland, 'The coinage of Lothar I (840–855)', *NC, 161* (2001), 157–98, at 176–8, 192, repr. in Coupland, *Carolingian Coinage and the Vikings*, no. VII.

[81]   Coupland, 'Between the devil and the deep blue sea', 252–63.

[82]   S. Coupland, 'Trading places: Quentovic and Dorestad reassessed', *EME, 11* (2002), 209–32, repr. in Coupland, *Carolingian Coinage and the Vikings*, no. XIII.

[83]   A point noted by Devroey, *Économie rurale*, 164.

[84]   *Hlotharii II Diplomata*, 16: MGH, DD Kar., III, ed. T. Schieffer (Berlin and Zurich, 1966), 408–9; *Recueil des actes de Charles II le Chauve roi de France*, ed. G. Tessier (3 vols, Paris, 1943–55), 2, 120–21 (no. 277).

[85]   Bruand, *Voyageurs et marchandises*, 170–71.

[86]   *Contra* P. Grierson, 'The *Gratia Dei Rex* coinage of Charles the Bald', in *Charles the Bald: Court and Kingdom*, ed. Gibson and Nelson, 52–64, at 54–5; *MEC* 1, 233.

[87]   MG 1190: Gariel, *Monnaies royales*, LX.6 is the coin in Berlin; 'The Hague' (now Geldmuseum) 17736 is the Wagenborgen coin; none was found at York.

to the abbey of Corvey in 833[88] may indeed have led to the creation of a local mint, as there was evidently an expansion of minting at this time, when Louis's *Christiana religio* coinage was being produced,[89] and there was almost certainly a rise in the number of mints, even in what was, as we have seen, an area with few ateliers during the rest of the century.

Taken together, this cumulative evidence suggests that coinage was potentially increasingly available across much of the West Frankish kingdom as the ninth century went on, even if this was not the case in the east. An increase in the number of mints might imply a rise in circulation and an increase in the coin stock, as during the reign of Louis the Pious, but could equally reflect a breakdown in the circulation and availability of coinage, as in Aquitaine under Pippin II, whose minting at Limoges and Cahors was essentially a political gesture, representing neither an economic upturn nor an increased use of coin.[90] Other factors must thus be taken into account before conclusions can be drawn about a proliferation of mints, and in the case of the West Frankish realm in the 860s and 870s, the dramatic rise in the number of ateliers striking GDR coinage has been interpreted in contrasting ways. Grierson proposed that it was a result of the need to provide coins for the tribute payment of 866,[91] but there is no reason to believe that the Vikings preferred their silver coined, and indeed contemporary sources explicitly reported that the tribute was paid by bullion weight, rather than in coin.[92] What is more, the comparable proliferation of mints in the 870s in Lotharingia, from which no tribute was taken, shows that this expansion was a deliberate policy of Charles the Bald, despite the limitation of the list of the initial mints in 864 to just ten.[93] The increase in the number of mints – striking coinage of a good weight and silver content, unlike much of the coinage before 864[94] – thus appears to be a sign of an increasing use of coin across the West Frankish kingdom. Ironically, the very tributes cited by Grierson are evidence that every man in the West Frankish kingdom had access to coinage

---

[88] Prou, *Monnaies carolingiennes*, lviii, n. 2; see now H. Bartel, 'Das Münzprivileg Ludwigs des Frommen für Corvey (BM2 922)', *Archiv für Diplomatik, Schriftgeschichte, Siegel- und Wappenkunde, 58* (2012), 147–68.

[89] Coupland, 'Carolingian single-finds', esp. 305–16.

[90] S. Coupland, 'The coinages of Pippin I and II of Aquitaine', *RN, 6th series, 31* (1989), 194–222, at 217–19, repr. in Coupland, *Carolingian Coinage and the Vikings*, no. VIII.

[91] Grierson, '*Gratia Dei Rex* coinage', 60, 63–4; *MEC* 1, 233, repeated by Devroey, *Économie rurale*, 163.

[92] S. Coupland, 'The Frankish tribute payments to the Vikings and their consequences', *Francia, 26* (1999), 57–75, at 62–3, repr. in Coupland, *Carolingian Coinage and the Vikings*, no. XIV.

[93] Metcalf, 'Sketch of the currency', 88.

[94] S. Coupland, 'The early coinage of Charles the Bald, 840–864', *NC, 151* (1991), 121–58, at 155, repr. in Coupland, *Carolingian Coinage and the Vikings*, no. IX.

in order to be able to contribute. In 866 the wealthy paid between 60 and 720 *denarii*, merchants a tenth of what they owned, poorer tenant farmers two, four or seven pence, and even the very poorest were apparently able to contribute one and a half deniers.[95]

As for the absolute level of production and the size of the coin stock in circulation, it has been argued that the small amount of silver given to the mints to launch the GDR coinage in 864 indicates that the latter must have been small,[96] yet die studies of a few ninth-century coinages suggest the opposite. Much more work remains to be done in this area, and the lack of fully published hoards from the period or hoards available for study is frustrating, but the studies which have been carried out suggest large numbers of dies striking very large numbers of coins. For instance, with the help of Jean-Paul Bailleul I have recently surveyed the 63 illustrated specimens of the Portrait deniers struck by Louis the Pious at Melle between 814 and 816 and found five obverse die pairs.[97] Warren Esty's formulae for the calculation of the original number of dies used to strike a series suggest nearly six hundred obverse dies being used over this three-year period, although there is a large margin of error.[98] Too few specimens of Louis's Class 2 coinage are currently available to undertake any comparable study, but certain groups of *Christiana religio* coinage are sufficiently large to permit die studies. For example, the 90 Group B (Dorestad) coins in the Roermond hoard were struck from 82 obverse dies; the 76 Group D (Trier) coins found at Pilligerheck from 66 obverse dies,[99] and among Group E *denarii* from Orléans the 80 coins which I have been able to study were struck from 70 obverse dies. For Group F, Milan, the figures are significantly higher: remarkably, among the 141 coins of this group at Hermenches I found only one obverse die pair. Esty's formulae suggest some 400 dies for the Orléans coinage, 500 for that of Trier, 600–700 for the Dorestad coinage, and many thousands for that of Milan.[100] These estimates should be treated with considerable caution, but they nonetheless give

---

[95]   Coupland, 'Frankish tribute payments', 62–4.

[96]   Devroey, *Économie rurale*, 163.

[97]   S. Coupland, 'Great David's greater son? The portrait coinage of Louis the Pious', in *La productivité d'une crise: Le règne de Louis le Pieux (814–840) et la transformation de l'Empire carolingien*, ed. P. Depreux and S. Esders (forthcoming).

[98]   W. Esty, 'How to estimate the original number of dies and the coverage of a sample', *NC*, *166* (2006), 359–64. Coverage is just 0.16; the estimated number of dies 574, and the confidence interval between 289 and 1523.

[99]   Coupland, 'Louis the Pious', 41; S. Coupland, 'The Trier mint 822–840', *Trierer Zeitschrift*, *54* (1991), 287–9, at 289, repr. in Coupland, *Carolingian Coinage and the Vikings*.

[100]   Orléans: coverage 0.26, estimated dies 383, confidence interval 210–740; Trier: coverage 0.18, estimated dies 516, confidence interval 264–1136; Dorestad: coverage 0.18, estimated dies 661, confidence interval 343–1411; Milan: coverage 0.02, estimated dies 10,475, confidence interval 11,045–34,057!

an idea of the ballpark figures, and suggest that, even if the dies struck fewer than the 10,000 coins apiece that is often quoted, very large numbers of coins were entering circulation during the reign of Louis the Pious.

Another element of the Frankish economy which deserves consideration in the context of the use of coin is the existence of oboles, or half-deniers. These were previously underestimated or even disregarded: Suchodolski referred to 'den selten vorkommenden Obol' which had little place in the economy.[101] Because these coins are smaller than deniers, few were found in the past, but now with the discovery of many new hoards, metal detecting and archaeological excavation, significantly more finds are turning up. Cut halfpennies are hardly ever found on the Continent, since the obole served that purpose. There have been some recent discoveries of the centres of monogram deniers,[102] with the suggestion that these perhaps served the role of oboles, but their size and appearance are sufficiently different from the official half-deniers to make this unlikely, while the cracks on some whole deniers indicate that this was a spot prone to structural weakness.

Grierson and Blackburn stated in 1986 that Charlemagne did not strike oboles, which were introduced by Louis the Pious, but this was an unfortunate slip: Grierson himself wrote about oboles of Charlemagne in 1965, and drew my attention to an even earlier half-denier, struck by Pippin III.[103] Pre-reform oboles are still rare, but the bracteate oboles of Melle minted by Charlemagne are starting to appear on the market in increasing numbers, even if the provenance is rarely reported.[104] After the reform of 793/4, many more mints produced oboles: Agen, Arles, Bourges,[105] Dorestad, Lyon, Melle, Narbonne, Toulouse, Tours and the mint producing coinage with a Greek monogram,[106] implying a wider use of this lower-denomination currency across the empire. This trend continued apace under Louis the Pious, with Portrait oboles struck by seven mints and Class 2 oboles produced in at least 16, a list which is still growing.[107]

---

[101]   Suchodolski, 'Geldumlauf', 51–2.

[102]   See e.g. <http://detect53.forumactif.org/t1154-obole-de-charles-le-chauves-et-denier-charles-le-chauves> [*sic*].

[103]   *MEC* 1, 206, 213; compare Grierson, 'Money and coinage under Charlemagne', 518; Coupland, 'Louis the Pious', 26, n. 15.

[104]   Prou, *Monnaies carolingiennes*, nos. 678–80; Gariel, *Monnaies royales*, 2, pl. VIII.92–3; P. Schiesser, 'Les oboles unifaces de Charlemagne de Melle', in *Numismatique et archéologie en Poitou-Charentes, Actes du colloque de Niort 7–8 décembre 2007, Musée Bernard d'Agesci*, ed. A. Clairand and D. Hollard (Paris, 2009), 49–62. See Coupland, 'Charlemagne and his coinage' (forthcoming) for further pre-reform oboles.

[105]   G. Sarah, 'Charlemagne, Charles the Bald and the *Karolus* monogram coinage. A multi-disciplinary study', *NC, 170* (2010), 227–86, at 251–4.

[106]   Coupland, 'Charlemagne and his coinage' (forthcoming).

[107]   Coupland, 'Louis the Pious', 26–7, 28, plus Roda: <http://www.la-detection.com/dp/message-95322.htm>.

Sixteen per cent of the single-finds of this type plotted on Figure 12.1 are oboles: 38 of the 237 coins. This is a significant proportion of the coinage in circulation, and as is illustrated by the passage in the Miracles of St Philibert quoted earlier,[108] it indicates that more people were using coinage for smaller scale transactions.

This was not, however, an empire-wide phenomenon, and the partition of Verdun threw the regional differences into sharp focus. The largest number of oboles bearing mint-names were struck at Aquitanian mints,[109] and the Aquitanian hoards of Brioux-sur-Boutonne and Limoux contained significant numbers (48 out of 145 coins and 25–30 of 170 respectively).[110] They are also found in hoards from the heart of Charles the Bald's kingdom such as Luzancy (31), Fontaines (5), Méréville (5) and Thoiry (not specified).[111] In contrast, only two Lotharingian mints ever produced oboles, and then in very small numbers: Cologne (under Louis the Pious) and the Palace, most likely Aachen,[112] while Lotharingian hoards such as Tzummarum II (2,787 recorded coins), Emmen (337), Wagenborgen (170) and Yde (112) contained none, and Pilligerheck just three out of 2,111 coins. The exceptional nature of the Roermond hoard was noted above; here the presence of oboles matches the broader character of the hoard as an inter-regional collection of coinage, almost certainly linked with trade.[113] No Italian oboles are known at all, a further indication of the limited use of coin within Carolingian Italy. After 864 the number of mints producing oboles increased significantly, and this is reflected in the hoards composed of GDR coinage. There were thus over 30 at Glisy (the inventory records 'deniers and oboles' from several mints, without specifying numbers), 33 at Longjumeau (21 per cent of the hoard), and 35 at Cauroir (fully 40 per cent of the hoard).[114] All this suggests that oboles were becoming more widely available in the West Frankish kingdom for smaller scale transactions, and playing an increasing part in the everyday economy.

Contemporary Texts

We cited earlier a number of references to the use of coin in ninth-century miracle texts which described how ordinary people carried, gave or spent small sums of money in their everyday lives. At the other end of the economic

---

[108] See n. 5 above.

[109] Coupland, 'Coinages of Pippin I and II', 216–17; Coupland, 'Early coinage of Charles the Bald', 141–3.

[110] Coupland, 'Checklist', nos. 99, 132.

[111] Coupland, 'Checklist', nos. 85, 98, 111, 128.

[112] Coupland, 'Coinage of Lothar I', 188.

[113] See above, at n. 48.

[114] Coupland, 'Checklist', nos. 170, 173, 169 respectively.

spectrum, a range of contemporary texts refer to very large amounts of capital held in coin by the wealthy Frankish elite. For example, in May 840 Abbot Rodulf of Beaulieu-en-Dordogne paid 75 pounds of silver for a piece of property (*in argento convalescentes solidos mille quingentos*: 'in silver to the value of 1500 *solidi*'), and in the 880s Count Odo of Toulouse sold an estate to Archbishop Frotarius of Bourges for *argenti XXX libras*, that is, 7,200 *denarii*. The smaller but still significant sum of *de argento libras XVIII* (equivalent to 4,320 deniers) was left by Walgarius, the chaplain to Eberhard of Friuli, in his will.[115]

These sums could of course have included uncoined silver, such as silver objects or silver ingots, but three factors should be taken into account. The first is that certain sources recording the wealth of contemporary magnates specifically noted that the silver in question was coined. Thus a letter of Archbishop Hincmar of Reims recorded a gift of *ducentos scilicet solidos de meris denariis* ('200 *solidi* in pure *denarii*') to the monks of St Denis, that is to say, no fewer than 2,400 coins (ten pounds).[116] Moreover, this was evidently only a fraction of Hincmar's assets. Towards the end of his life Bishop Herifrid of Auxerre (d. 909) gave 50 pounds which he had collected in coin (*denariorum*) for furnishings for the church.[117] Secondly, silver bars or ingots are extremely rare in Carolingian contexts, both in contemporary texts and as finds. The only written reference of which I am aware is the report that a peasant who had lost his ox placed a silver ingot weighing 20 *denarii* on the tomb of St Philibert, cited by Olivier Jeanne-Rose in his valuable survey of the insights into economic life offered by hagiographical texts from the west of France.[118] As for the few specimens that have been discovered on Frankish soil, virtually all can be linked to the Scandinavian incursions.[119] A third significant factor is that mixed hoards, containing coins and silver objects, are uncommon in Carolingian contexts. The small number which are known tend to occur in marginal areas, particularly

---

[115] *Cartulaire de l'abbaye de Beaulieu (en Limousin)*, ed. M. Deloche (Paris, 1859), 25, 47; *Cartulaire de l'abbaye de Cysoing et de ses dépendances*, ed. J. de Coussemaker (Lille, 1845–6), 6.

[116] Flodoard, *Historia Remensis ecclesiae*, III.25 : MGH, SS, XIII, ed. J. Heller and G. Waitz (Hanover, 1881), 538.

[117] 'Summam denariorum, quam ad hoc collegerat, dispertivit, triginta scilicet libras ad faciendam ante altare sancti Stephani tabulam, viginti quoque ad ornanda beatae Mariae beatique Joannis altaria': *De gestis episcoporum Antissiodorensium*: *PL* 138, col. 258.

[118] O. Jeanne-Rose, 'L'histoire économique du Centre-Ouest Atlantique d'après la littérature hagiographique (VIIIe–XIIe siècle)', *Revue historique du Centre-Ouest*, 6 (2007), 137–64, at 149, n. 91: 'cuneum argenti fusilem pondo viginti denariorum' (Ermentarius, *De translationibus et miraculis sancti Filiberti*, I.76: *Monuments*, ed. Poupardin, 52).

[119] Cardon, Moesgaard, Prot and Schiesser, 'Premier trésor monétaire', esp. 25; Besteman, 'Westerklief II', 13–17; S. Coupland, 'Raiders, traders, worshippers and settlers: the Continental perspective', in *Silver Economies, Monetisation and Society in Scandinavia, AD 800–1100*, ed. J. Graham-Campbell, S.M. Sindbæk and G. Williams (Aarhus, 2011), 113–31, at 121–2.

Carolingian Frisia: the overwhelming majority of hoards consist solely of coin.[120] These factors all militate in favour of these large sums consisting primarily if not exclusively of silver coins.

Is it reasonable to cite such large sums owned by Frankish magnates as evidence of the use of coin, given that the coins in question were apparently being thesaurised within the narrow confines of the Church and wealthy lay elite, rather than used as everyday currency? I believe that it is, on the one hand because the references given above show these sums being used in commercial transactions, and on the other because the regular recoinages of much of the ninth century, demonetising old coin types and necessitating their replacement with the new coinage, meant that silver coins could not be put away for lengthy periods without losing their value. A few hoards are known which contain two or more groups of coins which cannot have been in circulation together, but these are rare and again found predominantly in Carolingian Frisia, which evidently operated in a different way to the central Frankish economy.[121] The overwhelming majority of hoards contain only the type(s) currently in circulation, indicating that the coins were serving a monetary function at the time of their deposition.

One very important function of coinage in the ninth century which these texts – and those cited at the beginning of the chapter – highlight is that of almsgiving. This promoted the use of coin in two directions. On the one hand, rich and poor alike gave to the Church, sometimes in kind, no doubt, but also definitely in coin, such as Hetremaon's four deniers in Brittany, the Arras fishermen's two *solidi*, the father's three *denarii* at Fulda and Drogus's four pence at Mulinheim. It is not insignificant that three of these four episodes took place in areas where the distribution of contemporary mints shows that coin was scarce, suggesting that in other regions people may have had the potential to make larger gifts of coin than these. On the other hand, the Church also gave to the poor, and several passages in contemporary texts reveal that these gifts were in coin. Thus Rimbert reported in his *Life* of Anskar that a young Scandinavian woman took plenty of coins to give to the poor in Dorestad, and that Anskar always carried a purse with coins in it to give to the poor.[122] These are unquestionably idealised portrayals of sanctity, but there is no reason to doubt that they reflected contemporary practice. A non-hagiographical text, Adalard's *Statutes*, record that in the early ninth century Corbie abbey expected to give at least four deniers daily to the poor, and in 851 Charles the Bald endowed the monastery of St Denis with a gift to enable, among other things, a penny to be given to each of the 12 paupers

---

[120] The Checklist contains 169 ninth-century Frankish hoards, of which just 13 were mixed hoards: Coupland, 'Checklist', nos. 18–197, excluding non-Carolingian hoards. On the disproportionate number of mixed hoards in Frisia, see Coupland, 'Between the devil and the deep blue sea', 256–60.

[121] Coupland, 'Between the devil and the deep blue sea', 260–62.

[122] *Vita Anskarii*, ch. 20, 35: ed. Waitz, 66, 112.

whose feet were washed at the Maundy Thursday mass.[123] This is incidentally an important counterargument to those who suggest that a single penny had too high a purchasing power to be used in everyday commerce by ordinary people;[124] it was deemed sufficiently small a sum to be given away to the poorest of the poor. Likewise we saw earlier that a drink at the Grand-Lieu tavern could cost an obole, and the Edict of Pîtres of 864 referred to 'those who sell baked bread or meat by the *denarius* in towns, villages and markets'.[125] These and other texts show that coinage was in daily use for giving, buying and selling, not just for taxation and trade in high-status goods.

Two final aspect of the use of coin which have been studied in some detail are the role of money in land sales and the financial contributions of the tenants of the great Carolingian estates, both the monetary dues which they were required to provide each year and the sums they could pay instead of performing labour services. In both cases it is vital to take into account the regional and chronological variations in the availability of coin over the course of the century. Evidence for the use of coin in land sales and exchanges is cited by Devroey with reference to the south of France and Italy between the ninth and eleventh centuries,[126] while Wendy Davies has studied the transactions recorded in the Cartulary of Redon, which offers invaluable insights into economic life in ninth-century Brittany.[127] As was noted above, both Brittany and Italy are areas where the circulation of coin appears to have been extremely limited for significant periods: in Brittany until the 860s, in Italy after the 850s. It is consequently not surprising that Devroey finds barter playing a significant part in transactions in Italy after 850, or that Davies concludes, 'Much combines to suggest that money was hard to come by in the villages and that the volume of transactions was limited'.[128] Neither region offers any indication of the use of coin across those Frankish lands where active mints were near enough to provide a regular money supply, that is, as Figures 12.1, 12.3, 12.5 and 12.6 show, the vast majority of the West Frankish kingdom and Lotharingia. Davies's further comments are also worth citing: 'This was an economy in which there *was* money, which was used by peasants, but it was not in any sense a monetized economy: money was used for very specific things but not for everyday purposes'.[129] Even in Brittany money was available, even to peasants (as we saw in the case of Hetremaon), and the likelihood is that in the latter part of the century this became more and more the case.

---

[123] *Consuetudines Corbeienses*, II: *Corpus consuetudinum monasticarum*, ed. J. Semmler (Siegburg, 1963–), 1, 374; *Recueil des actes de Charles II le Chauve*, ed. Tessier, 1, 359 (no. 135).

[124] E.g. Devroey, *Économie rurale*, 161.

[125] *Edictum Pistense* (864), ch. 20: MGH, Capit., II, ed. A. Boretius and V. Krause (Hanover, 1897), 319.

[126] Devroey, *Économie rurale*, 165–6.

[127] W. Davies, *Small Worlds: the Village Community in Early Medieval Brittany* (London, 1988), 56–60.

[128] Ibid., 57.

[129] Ibid., 58.

As for the use of coin on the great monastic estates as detailed in the ninth-century polyptychs, this is tabulated in slightly different ways by Bruand and Devroey, the former maximising the figures cited by giving the annual sums taken in by the monasteries each year (between 1,100 and 30,000 deniers), the latter minimising the ones he quotes by listing the average amount paid per head by the tenants (between 'practically nothing' and 18 deniers per year). For Bruand, the figures demonstrate the everyday use of coinage, while Devroey draws precisely the opposite conclusion, that the small sums paid in some regions show that the coin stock was limited and unequally distributed.[130] One estate that Devroey oddly omits from his chart is Reims, whose polyptych he himself edited; it is typical of the others in including a wide range of annual dues, with some *mansi* paying just four deniers and others up to two *solidi*.[131] The polyptych also mentions numerous types of estate work which could be redeemed for cash: transporting half a cart of wine or paying 6 *denarii*, providing a cart of wood or paying 4 *denarii*, working 15 days at harvest time or paying 2 *denarii*, and so forth.[132] This brings out the point which Devroey has made elsewhere, that the polyptychs show clearly that in the ninth century 'peasants regularly manage to accumulate small sums of money' which they can 'draw on when they feel the need'.[133] Yet what is small? More than 400 tenant farmers on the estates of St Germain-des-Prés were each paying over 20 *denarii* per year; more than 200 over 30: are these really 'small sums'?[134] To summarise, the polyptychs parallel the numismatic evidence in showing that certain areas were less monetised than others, with Italy being the clearest example. Nevertheless, even in those regions tenants could pay small amounts per year in coin. Between the Rhine and the Loire, however, at monasteries such as Prüm, Reims, St Germain-des-Prés or Montier-en-Der, peasants were able to pay not insignificant annual sums in cash, raised presumably either through the sale of surpluses at market or through doing additional labour service on the estate.

---

[130]   Bruand, *Voyageurs et marchandises*, 163–4; Devroey, *Économie rurale*, 166–7.

[131]   J.-P. Devroey, *Le polyptyque et les listes de cens de l'abbaye de Saint-Remi de Reims (IXe–XIe siècles)* (Reims, 1986), 4, 27.

[132]   Devroey, *Polyptyque de Saint- Remi*, 8–9.

[133]   J.-P. Devroey, 'Réflexions sur l'économie des premiers temps carolingiens 768–877: grands domaines et action politique entre Seine et Rhin', *Francia, 13* (1986), 475–88, at 486; J.-P. Devroey, 'Les services de transport à l'abbaye de Prüm au IXe siècle', *Revue du Nord, 61* (1979), 543–69, at 554 (both repr. in his *Études sur le grand domaine carolingien* (Aldershot, 1993), nos. X and XIV).

[134]   K. Elmshäuser and A. Hedwig, *Studien zum Polyptychon von Saint-Germain-des-Prés* (Böhlau, Cologne, Weimar and Vienna, 1993), 496.

Conclusion

This chapter set out to establish to what extent coin was accessible and used in everyday life in the Carolingian realms in the ninth century. The distribution of mints shows that there were wide variations across time and space: some regions, in particular those at the eastern, western, northern and southern fringes of the empire, would have had little access to coin for much of the period, although this probably improved during the reign of Louis the Pious, especially during the minting of the *Christiana religio* type between 823 and 840, and in some areas developed significantly at the end of the ninth century. Contemporary texts indicate that even in these marginal regions everyone had access to small amounts of coinage, but in no way could these areas be described as having a monetised economy. The evidence of single-finds, grave hoards, written sources and mint output consistently paint a very different picture for the great swathe of territory which constituted the Frankish heartlands, however. Here coin was available to and used by the whole range of the population, in very large amounts by the wealthy magnates and in small sums even by the poorest. People would carry a purse containing *denarii* on their person, spend them in markets and taverns, give a number of them to their lord every year, and donate them to the Church and to the poor. When the Vikings threatened the kingdom they could manage to give some to pay a tribute to the invaders, the amount varying according to their wealth. The amount of coin in circulation was apparently rising steadily over the latter half of the eighth century and into the ninth, and projections suggest that by the 830s hundreds of thousands if not millions of coins were being produced each year, though this varied markedly from region to region and mint to mint, and fell back a little during the conflicts of the 840s and 850s. There was thus unquestionably a strong monetary component to the Carolingian economy, significantly more than Grierson allowed in 1965. Coin was not just used by the rich and powerful, but permeated all levels of society, and while not only used for trade, did have an important commercial role. Whether the ninth century can be described as having 'a monetary economy' is, however, more debatable. Devroey is justified in emphasising the regional variations – to which we would add the temporal fluctuations – as signs of underlying weakness. Ultimately it is a semantic question, dependent on how the term 'monetary economy' is defined. But what the evidence makes clear is that the ever increasing number of single-finds is steadily strengthening the case for the role of coin in the economy, and in the rural economy as well as the towns, in the villages as well as the emporia. This was undoubtedly an economy on its way towards monetisation, whether or not it is adjudged to have reached that stage in the ninth century.

Appendix

Single-Finds of Italian Coins of Louis the Pious's Class 2 Coinage

Mint	Find-spot	Country	Reference
Milan	Merxheim	France	unpublished
[Milan]	Rimini?	Italy	Arslan no. 1978 (*see note*)
Milan	Rossfeld	France	unpublished
Milan	Verona province	Italy	unpublished
Milan	Wijk bij Duurstede	Netherlands	van Gelder 1980, no. 15
Pavia	Aveyron	France	Haertle 1997, no. 512
Pavia	l'Épine, Marne	France	unpublished
Pavia	Les Andelys	France	unpublished
Pavia	Saint-Marcel	France	*RN* 2008, 364
Pavia	Wijk bij Duurstede	Netherlands	van Gelder 1980, no. 16
Pavia	Wijk bij Duurstede	Netherlands	Janssen 1842–5, vol. 2, 124–5 = Völckers 1965, III.111?
Pavia	Wijk bij Duurstede	Netherlands	Janssen 1842–5, vol. 2, 124–5
Pavia	Wijk bij Duurstede	Netherlands	Dolley & Sárkány 1971/2, no. 2
Treviso	Hatten	France	unpublished
Treviso	Mantua	Italy	unpublished
Treviso	Wijk bij Duurstede	Netherlands	Völckers 1965, III.118
Venice	Alphen aan den Rijn	Netherlands	<http://www.muntenbodemvondsten.nl/index.php?topic=70823.0>
Venice	Alsace	France	<http://numisalsace.forumactif.org/t316-20-denier-de-louis-1er-dit-le-pieux-814-840-type-venecias-venise>
Venice	Ampass	Austria	Emmerig 2004, B2
Venice	Aquileia	Italy	Arslan no. 2230

Mint	Find-spot	Country	Reference
Venice	Asolo	Italy	unpublished
Venice	Asolo	Italy	unpublished
Venice	Asolo	Italy	unpublished
Venice	Bas-Rhin	France	unpublished
Venice	Bédarieux	France	unpublished
Venice	Boppard	Germany	Haertle 1997, no. 532
Venice	Commachio	Italy	Arslan nos. 1853–4
Venice	Couffé	France	unpublished
Venice	Domburg	Netherlands	Völckers 1965, II.67
Venice	Ferwerderadeel	Netherlands	NUMIS 1015204
Venice	Gundolsheim	France	unpublished
Venice	Harlingen	Netherlands	Haertle 1997, no. 616 = NUMIS 1013616
Venice	Havsmarken, Ærø	Denmark	<www.historieinfo.dk/Karolingere.html>
Venice	Het Bildt	Netherlands	NUMIS 1020637
Venice	Hüttenberg	Germany	Emmerig 2004, B24
Venice	Isère	France	<http://detectomania38.info/forum/viewtopic.php?t=2732>
Venice	Karlburg	Germany	Emmerig 2004, B28
Venice	Krogstrup	Denmark	*pers. comm.*, Jens Christian Moesgaard
Venice	Nr. Leeuwarden	Netherlands	unpublished
Venice	Lejre	Denmark	Galster 1935
Venice	Loir-et-Cher	France	<www.la-detection.com/dp/message-101004.htm>
Venice	Mantua	Italy	unpublished
Venice	Mantua	Italy	unpublished
Venice	Neumünster-Grotenkamp	Germany	Haertle 1997, no. 687

Mint	Find-spot	Country	Reference
Venice	Nord-Isère	France	unpublished
Venice	Regensburg	Germany	Haertle 1997, no. 725 = Emmerig 2004, B35
Venice	Schouwen	Netherlands	Völckers 1965, XIX.14
Venice	Tiel	Netherlands	unpublished
Venice	Tietjerksteradeel	Netherlands	NUMIS 1006376
Venice	Valais	Switzerland	unpublished
Venice	Venzone	Italy	Arslan no. 2490
Venice	Wijk bij Duurstede	Netherlands	Janssen 1842–5, vol. 2, 123
Venice	Wijk bij Duurstede	Netherlands	Völckers 1965, III.119
Venice	Wijk bij Duurstede	Netherlands	van Gelder 1980, no. 17
Venice	Wijk bij Duurstede	Netherlands	Haertle 1997, no. 846 = NUMIS 1033497

Note: this may well be a coin of the *Christiana religio* type, which is often erroneously attributed to Milan. This is also true of similar coins from Buja (Arslan 2275), the four coins found at Lurate Abbate (3745), and one from Venzone (2490).

References

Arslan: <www.ermannoarslan.eu/Repertorio/RepertorioAMAggiornamento>.

Dolley and Sárkány 1971–2: M. Dolley and T. Sárkány, 'Four Carolingian Coins Found at Wijk-bij-Duurstede and now in the Royal Coin Cabinet at Stockholm', *JMP, 58–9*, 5–9.

Emmerig 2004: H. Emmerig, 'Der Freisinger Münzschatz und das Geldwesen in Bayern zur Karolingerzeit', in *38. Sammelblatt des Historischen Vereins Freising*, 11–75.

Galster 1935: G. Galster, 'Møntfundet fra Lejre (før) 1643', *Numismatisk Forenings Medlemsblad, 14*, 193–7.

Haertle 1997: C.M. Haertle, *Karolingische Münzfunde aus dem 9 Jahrhundert* (2 vols, Cologne, Weimar and Vienna).

Janssen 1842–5: L.J.F. Janssen, *Oudheidkundige Mededeelingen* (4 vols, Leiden).

NUMIS: <www.numis.geldmuseum.nl/nl/zoek/numis>

van Gelder 1980: H.E. van Gelder, 'Coins from Dorestad, Hoogstraat 1', in W.A. van Es and W.J.H. Verwers, *Excavations at Dorestad 1: The Harbour, Hoogstraat I* (Amersfoort), 215–23.

Völckers 1965: H.H. Völckers, *Karolingische Münzfunde der Frühzeit (751–800)*, Abhandlungen der Akademie der Wissenschaften in Göttingen, philologisch-historische Klasse, III.61 (Göttingen).

Chapter 13

Monetary Activity in Viking-Age Ireland: The Evidence of the Single-Finds

Andrew R. Woods*

Introduction

The study of single-finds – where one coin is found in isolation, not as a part of a hoard – has helped to reshape views regarding coinage in the early medieval period. In England, this process has largely rested upon the enormous number of new finds that have accrued with the extensive use of metal-detectors since the early 1980s. Mark Blackburn was at the forefront of this development, collating and analysing this new data. Initially this involved recording the finds in a series of *BNJ* articles which evolved into the yearly Coin Register and eventually culminated in the online database, the EMC.[1] He was also among the first to present systematic analyses of the material, offering new methodologies and interpretations across a range of subjects.[2] The legacy of this work can be seen today with research, using these tools, which continues to break new ground.[3]

*   I would like to thank a large number of people for their help in the preparation of this chapter. Far too many to name have provided details of individual finds and I am very grateful to all of them. In particular, Michael Kenny has been incredibly helpful, making the National Museum of Ireland's collection open to me and providing details of new finds, often in advance of their publication. Kristin Bornholdt Collins has also made her notes on the Dublin collection freely available, without which this chapter could not have been written.

[1]   M.A.S. Blackburn and M.J. Bonser, 'Single finds of Anglo-Saxon and Norman Coins I', *BNJ*, 54 (1984), 63–73; *Early Medieval Corpus of Coin Finds* <www.medievalcoins.org>.

[2]   M.A.S. Blackburn, 'Znaleziska Pojedyncze Jako Miara Aktywnosci Monetarnej We Wczesnym Sredniowieczu (Single-finds as a Measure of Monetary Activity in the Early Middle Ages)', *Prace i Materialy, Muzeum Archeologicznego i Etnograficznego w Lodzi. Seria numizmatyczna i konserwatorska*, 9 (1989), 67–85; M.A.S. Blackburn, '"Productive" sites and the pattern of coin loss in England, 600–1180', in *Markets in Early Medieval Europe: Trading and 'Productive' Sites, 650–850*, ed. T. Pestell and K. Ulmschneider (Macclesfield, 2003), 20–36.

[3]   R. Naismith, 'The English monetary economy, c. 973–1100: the contribution of single-finds', *Economic History Review*, 66 (2013), 198–225; M. Allen, 'The volume of the English currency, c.973–1158', in *Coinage and history in the North Sea world, c. AD 500–1200*, ed. G. Williams and B. Cook, (Leiden, 2006), 487–523, at 498–502.

Single-finds are usually connected to chance loss and can be contrasted to hoards where a number of factors may have influenced the make-up of the hoard and the circumstances of its deposition. The chance loss element of single-finds is of particular importance as they should, with recovery circumstances being equal, provide a random sample from the circulating currency. This means that single-finds can be used as a proxy for 'monetary activity'. They allow for both geographical and chronological comparison; areas or periods where there was significant monetary activity should produce a greater number of single-finds than areas or periods where there was little or none. The term 'monetary activity' is favoured as single-finds can represent one or both of two factors: the number of coins in circulation and the frequency of exchange.[4]

Viking-Age Coinage in Ireland

The study of the silver economies of Viking-Age Ireland has been well served by a relatively extensive hoard record. There are over 80 hoards containing coins from the period 900–1170 to which can be added another 50 entirely non-numismatic silver hoards, although these probably date from the mid-ninth century onwards.[5] This study of hoards has allowed for a chronological framework of coin usage in Ireland to be constructed. Dolley and Blackburn were in the vanguard of this process. These two scholars arrived at the conclusion that, in contrast to the nearly coinless eighth and ninth centuries, during the tenth century coins became more common, with relatively significant numbers of Anglo-Saxon coins appearing to circulate in Ireland.[6] Around 995, the Hiberno-Scandinavian ruler of Dublin, Sitric Silkenbeard (*c.*989/95–1036), had coinage struck in his own name and effectively demonetised the older, English coinage.[7] The Hiberno-Scandinavian coinage, in various guises, continued to be struck up until the Anglo-Norman invasion of Ireland, and sack of Dublin, in 1170.[8]

The evidence from hoards has also been deployed to discuss questions concerning who was using coinage. A traditional view saw the argument advanced that coinage was exclusively the preserve of Hiberno-Scandinavians in

---

[4]   Blackburn, 'Single-finds'.

[5]   M.A.S. Blackburn, 'Currency under the Vikings, Part 3. Ireland, Wales, Man and Scotland', *BNJ*, 77 (2007), 119–49, at 126 (*VCCBI*, 59–90, at 66).

[6]   R.H.M. Dolley, *SCBI 8: Hiberno-Norse Coins in the British Museum*, (London, 1966), 27–37; Blackburn, 'Currency under the Vikings, Part 3'.

[7]   Dolley, *SCBI 8*, 119–45; M.A.S. Blackburn, 'Currency under the Vikings. Part 4: the Dublin coinage *c.* 995–1050', *BNJ*, 78 (2008), 111–37 (*VCCBI*, 91–117).

[8]   *Contra* Dolley, *SCBI 8*. Dolley subsequently revised this view, in an unpublished note, in light of new excavation evidence. Dating the bracteate production up to 1170 is highly likely based upon evidence from Dublin city and Trim Castle excavations.

Ireland with inland hoards representing isolated raiding activity.[9] This view has been comprehensively overturned by Kenny and Gerriets with an appreciation that decisions to use coinage, or not, cannot be split along simplistic 'ethnic' lines.[10] Kenny's work in particular pursued a spatial analysis, noting how the distribution of hoards was focused in certain polities beyond the boundaries of the kingdom of Dublin.[11]

Scholarly discourse has gravitated towards the early part of the period, the ninth and tenth centuries. This period witnessed enormous economic change and the beginning of a coin-using economy in Ireland. It is also at this time that evidence is strongest, with about 65 per cent of coin hoards dating to the period before AD 1000.[12] There has been relatively little discussion of the monetary economy of Ireland in the eleventh century onwards. This, and the fact that Michael Dolley in classifying and dating the series described some coins in a somewhat negative manner, has – quite probably against his wishes – created an unfavourable view of the later coinage.[13] It is tempting to think of a simple and inevitable decline after a high watermark of AD 1000.

Single-finds have rarely been a part of discussion in Ireland, and this is primarily due to their low numbers. Laws making most metal-detecting illegal and liable to penalise any detectorist with a sizeable fine mean that Ireland has only produced a small number of single-finds.[14] These are collated in the Appendix to this chapter and number 206 for the period 600–1170. This appendix represents all specimens that are known to the author at present, although it is likely that further specimens exist, either unidentified or unpublished.[15] Because of the illegality of metal-detecting, the finds are heavily biased towards excavations. Around 80 per cent of single-finds are from excavation contexts with the remainder representing a mixture of chance finds and illicit detecting. Given the dominance of excavation finds, particularly since the rise of rescue archaeology

---

[9] R.H.M. Dolley and J. Ingold, 'Viking-Age coin-hoards from Ireland and their relevance to Anglo-Saxon studies', in *Anglo-Saxon Coins: Studies Presented to F. M. Stenton on the Occasion of his 80th Birthday*, ed. R.H.M. Dolley (London, 1961), 241–65, at 260.

[10] M. Gerriets, 'Money among the Irish: coin hoards in Viking Age Ireland', *Journal of the Royal Society of Antiquaries of Ireland*, 115 (1985), 121–39; M. Kenny, 'The geographical distribution of Irish Viking-Age coin hoards', *Proceedings of the Royal Irish Academy. Section C: Archaeology, Celtic Studies, History, Linguistics, Literature*, 87 (1987), 507–25.

[11] Kenny, 'Geographical Distribution', 512–13.

[12] Cf. Figure 13.2.

[13] Cf. Blackburn, 'Currency under the Vikings. Part 4', 116.

[14] E.P. Kelly, 'Protecting Ireland's archaeological heritage' in *International Journal of Cultural Property*, 3 (1994), 213–26.

[15] A card catalogue of Irish single-finds compiled by W. Seaby and maintained by R. Heslip in the Ulster Museum cannot currently be traced but will probably include further unknown specimens.

in the 1970s, it is not surprising that the overwhelming majority of finds have also been discovered in the past 50 years. The relative increase in the number of finds is most stark when the number of finds (22) recorded in Hall's 1973 checklist is compared with the appendix where nearly ten times that number are recorded.[16]

Whilst over 200 finds is a significant improvement upon the data available to Dolley it does not represent a large sample and thus must be used somewhat cautiously. It certainly does not stand up to comparison with the English dataset where Rory Naismith has been able to analyse nearly 2,000 coins for a similar period.[17] However, even small samples can yield useful results. Gareth Williams has demonstrated that it is possible to offer meaningful analysis from even smaller numbers of finds.[18] Similarly, the relatively small number of single-finds analysed by Blackburn in the late 1980s exhibited a pattern that has been broadly confirmed by the much large number of finds that have been found subsequently.[19] The number of tenth- to fifteenth-century English finds considered in 1989 is comparable to the numbers that are currently available from Ireland. Thus, whilst the small number of coins would urge caution, it is hoped that the tentative conclusions drawn below may hold up as more finds emerge.

Despite the small number of finds, the newly acquired data from single-finds has the potential to move discussion forward in an Irish context. Although hoards can be, and have been, instructive when it comes to considering when and where coinage was available for deposition, they are far less useful for appreciating where it was actually in use. Single-finds, acting as a proxy for monetary activity, are much more appropriate for this kind of analysis and are considered below in terms of their chronological and geographical distribution. The entire period, 900–1170, will be considered as the evidence from the single-finds is far more balanced than that of the hoards and suggests that the latter part of that period is at least as important for understanding the silver economy of Ireland as the period before AD 1000.

The Chronological Distribution of Single-Finds

The chronological distribution of the single-finds is visible in Figure 13.1 and can be contrasted with hoards in Figure 13.2. Figure 13.1 is a chronological

---

[16]   R. Hall, 'A check-list of Viking-Age coin finds from Ireland', *Ulster Journal of Archaeology*, *36–37* (1973), 71–86.

[17]   Naismith, 'English Monetary Economy'.

[18]   G. Williams, 'Monetary economy in Viking-Age Scotland in the light of single finds', *Nordisk Numismatisk Årsskrift, 2000–2002* (2006), 163–72.

[19]   Blackburn, 'Single-finds', 73; Naismith, 'English Monetary Economy'.

distribution of single-finds modelled according to their probable date of loss rather than their date of striking. This is based upon the residuality of old coins in hoards of various periods. The main effect of this is in the tenth century, when coins remained in circulation for far longer than during the following 200 years. The first point to note is that the single-finds would suggest that the tenth century witnessed the beginnings of coin usage in Ireland. Before this period there had been only a smattering of coins in Ireland: seven English coins datable to the ninth-century, to which can be added a further seven dirham finds. The steadily increasing numbers of single-finds would suggest an expansion of monetary activity in Ireland during this period. It is likely that this permeated outwards from Dublin with coin finds in the town suggesting that from the 930s coins were being used there. This view would accord well with that offered by the hoards which suggest that coinage became an increasingly important element within hoards during the mid- to late-tenth century.[20]

There is a divergence in the hoard and single-find evidence after the year 1000. Comparing Figures 13.1 and 13.2, it is notable that there is a significant peak in hoarding activity during the mid-tenth century with the number of hoards deposited *c.*970 outnumbering the combined twelfth-century total. In contrast, the single-finds give a quite different impression and are far more consistent across the period. At no point is there the same dramatic spike visible in the hoard record. Indeed, the period around *c.*970 does not appear particularly remarkable in the single-find record. The reasons behind this divergence can only be interpreted within the context of differing deposition circumstances. It seems likely that the single-finds represent the underlying monetary trends with unusual peaks in hoarding attributable to political circumstances. The disruptive effects of the 'Great Army' in England are one example of this. These are clearly visible in an intense period of coin hoarding and it seems possible that the Irish peak might be similarly connected to political instability or warfare.[21] This point is emphasised as Kenny has suggested that Midland hoards were geographically limited to areas where significant kings were based, and which may have attracted raiding activity.[22] This point is difficult to prove beyond doubt, especially as there is no disruptive force on the scale of the Great Army visible in Irish written sources around 970.[23] At a more general level, the evidence of the single-finds suggests that any simple equation of the availability of coinage and numbers of hoards is patently false. Where spikes occur in the single-finds they do not

---

[20]   Blackburn, 'Currency under the Vikings. Part 3', 130; K. Bornholdt-Collins, 'The Dunmore Cave [2] hoard and the role of coins in the tenth-century Hiberno-Scandinavian economy', in *The Viking Age: Ireland and the West Proceedings of the Fifteenth Viking Congress, Cork, 2005*, ed. J. Sheehan and D. Ó Corráin (Dublin, 2010), 19–46.

[21]   Blackburn, '"Productive" sites', 24–5.

[22]   Kenny, 'Geographic distribution', 512–13.

[23]   Cf. D. Ó'Corráin, *Ireland before the Normans* (Dublin, 1972).

match the size, or chronology, of the peak in hoards. The single-find evidence shows that across much of the period 940–1080 there was a reasonably stable amount of coinage being lost, suggesting broadly similar levels of monetary activity during the period.

Continuation of the use of coinage into the eleventh century and beyond is a point worthy of emphasis. Significant monetary activity in the eleventh century is what would be expected as Dublin produced its own coinage from *c.*995 onwards. The Hiberno-Scandinavian coinage, as it is often known, is a complicated phenomenon which began with coins closely modelled upon Anglo-Saxon exemplars, with subsequent designs which moved further away from these prototypes. The stylised imagery might make these later coins easy to dismiss but the single-finds are quite unequivocal in showing that the coinage, particularly of the early eleventh century, was of some importance. For example, the coinage of Dolley Phase II (*c.*1020–40) is the most common among Irish Viking-Age single-finds. Blackburn described this phase as a 'coinage of national identity', representing the first currency produced in a uniquely Dublin style.[24] The importance of coinage in this period is certainly emphasised in the single-finds record. The early eleventh century appears to represent a period in which coinage was at its most plentiful, or was used most intensively, in Viking-Age Ireland. It would certainly appear to represent a high point, with coin finds growing during the tenth century and peaking in the first half of the eleventh century.

In the hundred-year period after this peak there is a decline in single-finds, reaching a nadir in the early years of the twelfth century. This decline is probably an indication of a shrinking currency. It is certainly mirrored in a decline in the metrology of the coins. Their weight gradually, if sporadically, decreases from around 1.0g in 1020 to around half of this value by the early twelfth century. A lighter coinage, probably produced on a smaller scale, can be interpreted in the context of European parallels. Coinage across a number of regions showed a similar decline, probably in relation to a growing scarcity of silver. The increasing scarcity of silver can be seen in the coinages of Norway, Poland and Saxony.[25] It suggests that Ireland was not insulated from wider European trends with a currency that must have gradually suffered, along with the rest of Europe, from significant silver wastage.

In contrast, the sudden explosion of finds in the mid-twelfth century is remarkable and it is one of the most important aspects of the single-finds evidence. Hoards are almost non-existent for the period after the opening years of the twelfth century. This is the point at which bracteate coins were struck in Dublin and their absence from hoards can perhaps be connected to their extreme

---

[24]   Blackburn, 'Currency under the Vikings. Part 4', 127.

[25]   P. Spufford, *Money and its Use in Medieval Europe* (Cambridge, 1988), 96.

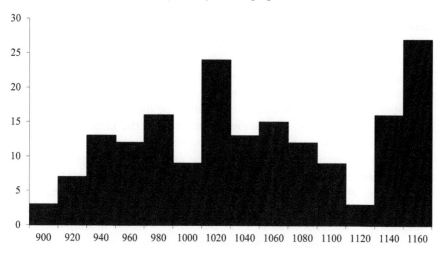

Figure 13.1   The number of single-finds, by modelled date of deposition.

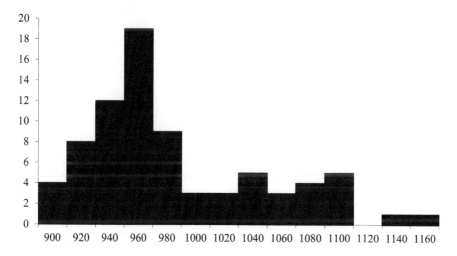

Figure 13.2   The number of coin hoards, by deposition date.

fragility as well as to the fact that they may not have been deemed worthy of hoarding. Recent archaeological excavation has transformed knowledge of the bracteates with only one of over fifty bracteates found before the archaeological revolution of the past half-century. The bracteate coinage was the last struck in Ireland before the Anglo-Norman invasion of 1169 and recent metallurgical work has shown that the late types, struck from the *c.*1140 onwards, were of increasingly base silver.[26] This is in contrast with earlier types, through to at least *c.*1120, the alloy of which has been found to be of reasonably high silver content.[27]

The single-find evidence completely alters perceptions of the end of the Hiberno-Scandinavian coinage. The view that the coinage gradually peters out, with poor quality and light-weight coins, must be dismissed as the bracteate coins are among the most common single-finds of the entire period. This is despite their extreme fragility, suggesting that the surviving numbers are probably an underestimate compared with the more robust silver pennies.[28] The recovered numbers rival the early eleventh-century peak, but interpreting this large number of single-finds is not simple. It is tempting to suggest that their production – as light-weight pieces of very low silver – might well have been a reaction to a shortage of silver in Ireland. After a period of declining finds and metrology, the sudden explosion of single-finds would suggest the debased, and presumably lower value, bracteates were a very active part of the monetary economy. They may either have been struck on a far larger scale than has previously been envisaged or perhaps, due to their lower value, used for a greater number or range of transactions. It is tempting to draw parallels with the ninth-century styca coinage of Northumbria where copper-alloy coins replaced silver and appear to have been struck on a far greater scale, presumably to compensate for their lower value.[29]

The Geographical Distribution of Single-Finds

The relatively limited number of Irish single-finds complicates analysis of their geographical distribution. Single-finds have been found almost exclusively during the course of archaeological investigation, with over 80 per cent found in this manner. This means that areas which have seen quite extensive excavation

---

[26]   M. Kenny, 'Coins, Tokens and Related Numismatic Material from Knowth', in *Excavations at Knowth 5: The Archaeology of Knowth in the First and Second Millennia AD*, ed. G. Eogan (Dublin, 2012).

[27]   R. Heslip and P. Northover, 'The alloy of the Hiberno-Norse coinage', in *Sigtuna Papers: proceedings of the Sigtuna Symposium on Viking-Age Coinage, 1–4 June 1989*, ed. K. Jonsson and B. Malmer (London, 1990), 103–111.

[28]   Late bracteate coinages are very fragile due to their high copper content. At the High Street excavation in Dublin one coin disintegrated before it could be conserved. Another coin, from the Fishamble Street excavations, was conserved alongside sediment as it was deemed too fragile to remove it.

[29]   Cf. D.M. Metcalf, 'Introduction', in *Coinage in Ninth-Century Northumbria: the Tenth Oxford Symposium on Coinage and Monetary History*, ed. D.M. Metcalf, BAR British series, 180 (Oxford, 1987), 1–10.

are more likely to have produced single-finds. Some attempt to address these problems is presented in Table 13.1 where counties are ranked by the number of single-finds in addition to their number of excavations and hoards.[30] Whilst merely considering the number of excavations is quite a crude control – it would be better also to consider size, type and excavation technique – it can nonetheless help to add nuance to an analysis of single-finds. For example, Armagh has produced a fairly significant number of coins, making it the third highest ranked county in Ireland despite being subject to a relatively small number of archaeological investigations. If it were as extensively excavated as other counties then an even greater number of finds might be expected. Conversely, the counties of Kildare, Galway and Tipperary have been relatively extensively excavated but have only limited evidence for single-finds. The table would suggest that the distribution of single-finds is not merely a product of recovery circumstances. If it were, a closer correspondence would be expected between the number of single-finds and the amount of excavation. I would be reasonably confident that the single-finds distribution probably represents the genuine geographical distribution of monetary activity even if, in some cases, areas are slightly under- or over-represented due to the number of excavations in each.

Table 13.1   Summary of single-finds, hoards and excavations, divided by county.

County	*Number*			*Rank*		
	Single-finds	Hoards	Excavations	Single-finds	Hoards	Excavations
Dublin	123	14	2300	1	1	1
Meath	17	8	2064	2	4	2
Armagh	5	3	218	3	7	27
Westmeath	4	12	617	4	3	13
Roscommon	3	0	468	=5	=21	18
Clare	3	0	699	=5	=21	11
Limerick	3	3	1003	=5	12	6
Cork	3	3	1549	=5	17	3

---

[30]   The numbers of single-finds are drawn from the Appendix. Hoards are those noted on the online listing, the Checklist with some additions. Excavations are those listed in I. Bennett, *Excavations* bulletin from 1970 to 2009 <www.excavations.ie.>. Rank is decided, in the first instance, by the number of single-finds, hoards or excavations. Where these are the same, counties are divided by area, with the smallest county ranked the highest.

County	Number			Rank		
	Single-finds	Hoards	Excavations	Single-finds	Hoards	Excavations
Longford	2	0	154	=9	=21	30
Offaly	2	5	397	=9	6	21
Down	2	4	402	=9	9	20
Kerry	2	0	736	=9	=21	10
Waterford	2	1	542	=9	15	17
Wicklow	1	4	417	=14	8	19
Londonderry	1	1	273	=14	16	24
Kildare	1	5	1043	=14	5	5
Sligo	1	0	560	=14	=21	16
Louth	1	7	960	=14	2	7
Antrim	1	2	642	=14	14	12
Leitrim	0	0	198	=20	=21	29
Cavan	0	0	205	=20	=21	28
Carlow	0	0	236	=20	=21	25
Monaghan	0	0	152	=20	=21	31
Laois	0	2	339	=20	11	23
Wexford	0	2	579	=20	13	14
Donegal	0	1	390	=20	20	22
Fermanagh	0	0	110	=20	=21	32
Tyrone	0	1	228	=20	18	26
Kilkenny	0	3	837	=20	10	9
Tipperary	0	1	1239	=20	19	4
Mayo	0	0	569	=20	=21	15
Galway	0	0	842	=20	=21	8

All of the coin finds from 900 to 1170 are mapped in Figure 13.3. The map conflates the whole period but does allow some general conclusions to be drawn. The first point to emphasise is the absolute pre-eminence of Dublin. Whilst Co. Dublin is the most heavily excavated area in Ireland, this alone cannot explain its disproportionately large number of finds. Over half of all single-finds come from the town. This is unsurprising because, as discussed above, it is likely that Dublin was the first place to use coinage, from the early tenth century, and it was the only major pre-Norman mint.

The importance of Dublin is also visible in the distribution of finds in the Irish interior. As has been noted by a number of authors the hoards are arrayed in an arc around the town leading to the suggestion that Dublin acted as the conduit of silver into Ireland.[31] The single-finds would certainly suggest that Dublin represented the centre of Ireland's monetary activity. Beyond the town, the single-finds suggest that monetary activity was most prevalent in Mide and Brega with Northern Leinster, to the south of Dublin, less engaged with monetary activity. What might be termed a 'zone of monetary activity' forms a *c.*7,500 sq. kilometre area around Dublin, largely to its north and west, and has been noted on Figure 13.3. At the edge of this to the west is Clonmacnoise with most finds contained within the modern counties of Dublin, Westmeath, Meath and Longford. The area which appears to be indicative of significant monetary activity is quite small, representing around 10 per cent of the total area of Ireland. There are isolated finds beyond this but the point can be made that most monetary activity is likely to have occurred at a maximum of 120km from Dublin.

Contact between the town and inland areas may well have been mediated through ecclesiastical settlements as there is a concentration of finds around religious houses. Armagh (six single-finds and two hoards, *c.*780–1110), Glendalough (three hoards, *c.*940–1100), Clonmacnoise (two single-finds and one hoard of the tenth and eleventh century), Inish Cealtra (two single-finds and one hoard, *c.*1030–1100) have all produced a series of coins. Other ecclesiastical settlements, including Ardfert, Derrykeighan, Rahan and Ardagh, have also produced evidence for the use of coinage. The consistency of finds at ecclesiastical sites is in contrast to most sites outside Dublin where few can claim any more than either a single-find or a hoard. The presence of numerous finds means that it can be argued that there was a consistent level of coin loss over relatively significant periods of time at ecclesiastical sites. The numbers of coins found at ecclesiastical settlements and their loss over a period of time is suggestive of at least semi-regular coin use, although not on a scale to rival Dublin. This should not be surprising as, certainly by the eleventh century and possibly earlier, some ecclesiastical sites had fairly extensive economic functions including some evidence of market activity.[32]

The presence of coinage in Dublin and at ecclesiastical settlements can be contrasted with the almost complete absence of coin finds from the north and west of Ireland. Connacht and Ulster have virtually no coin finds, either single-

---

[31] Dolley and Ingold, 'Viking-Age coin hoards'; Gerriets, 'Money amongst the Irish'; Kenny, 'Geographical distribution'; J. Sheehan, 'Ireland's early Viking-Age silver hoards: components, structure, and classification', *Acta Archaeologica*, 71 (2000); Blackburn 'Currency under the Vikings, Part 3', 66

[32] C. Doherty, 'Exchange and trade in early medieval Ireland', *Journal of the Royal Society of Antiquaries of Ireland*, 110 (1980), 67–89, at 82–3.

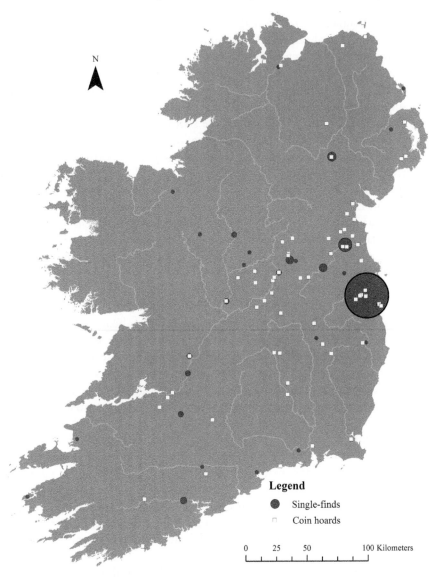

Figure 13.3   The distribution of coins, 900–1170.

finds or hoards, between the tenth and twelfth centuries. It is unlikely that this distribution is anything other than a reflection of the economic reality of the Viking Age. It can be contrasted with the high medieval period – when coins are known across both areas – suggesting the distribution is not one of find circumstance.[33] It can be more comfortably compared to the distribution of the handful of pre-Viking Age coins which display a similar eastern and coastal bias. Counties such as Galway or Mayo have been subject to a reasonable degree of archaeological investigation and have produced no finds of Viking-Age coins.[34] It seems likely that these were areas where the economy was largely coinless throughout the Viking Age. The distribution highlights the fact that, as Kenny has previously noted, Ireland had quite a regionalised economy, with enormous variety between different areas.[35]

To emphasise this point, there is notable variation in distribution within the period 900–1170. Figures 13.4–13.6 represent coin finds from Ireland in the tenth, eleventh and twelfth centuries respectively. Figure 13.4 shows that the tenth century is dominated by single-finds from the Irish midlands to the west and north of Dublin. The number of finds in this area, especially in comparison to other areas of Ireland in the tenth century, suggests that monetary activity was being conducted in Mide. The greatest concentration of hoards is also located in this area. Kenny has explored the relationship between the hoards of the tenth century, the kingdom of Dublin and the dominant kings of the Irish Midlands, the Clann Cholmáin.[36] The overlap of coin hoards and single-finds in this area would suggest coinage was being actively used in these areas, with the coin hoards representing deposits of wealth that had circulated in the area near to its deposition. The connection to Dublin is frequently emphasised when considering these hoards. It is, of course, important as it is likely that the town represented the entry point for silver into the Midlands and close economic connections may have encouraged coin use in this area. However, the single-finds would suggest that coinage was not only used for exchange with the town, but that it also formed a valid means of exchange within some areas of inland Ireland.

In the eleventh century, monetary activity continued to be dominated by Dublin. The town remained the most common place to find coins during this period. Figure 13.5 also highlights that there was, broadly speaking, a continuity of finds in the Irish midlands between the tenth and eleventh centuries. There are fewer hoards but a general similarity in the number of single-finds. Finds from Ardagh, Tipper, Clonmacnoise and two imprecise 'Irish Midlands' coins show that coinage was being used into the 1080s. To these single-finds can be added the hoards of Mullingar (*c.*1025–50), Tonyowen (*c.*1040) and Clonmancoise (*c.*1070) which show monetary activity continued into the latter half of the century. This point highlights the fact that coinage remained important for

---

[33] R.H.M. Dolley, *Medieval Anglo-Irish Coins* (London, 1972), 61.

[34] Cf. Table 13.1.

[35] Kenny, 'Geographic distribution', 519–20.

[36] Ibid., 513–19.

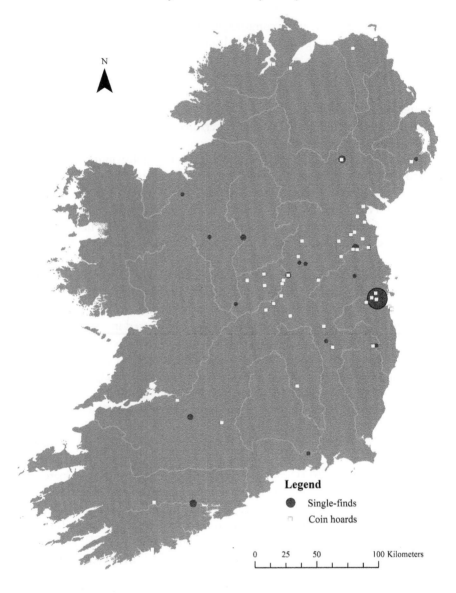

Figure 13.4   The distribution of coins, 900–1000.

the Irish midlands from the tenth, into and throughout the eleventh century. The late chronology of these coins is of importance as it would suggest that the connection between Dublin and Mide was not only at an elite or royal level. The political landscape of Ireland altered substantially between the mid-tenth and mid-eleventh centuries, with the waning of the power of Mide and

Dublin increasingly pulled into the political orbit of Leinster, but the economic connection between Dublin and the Midlands persisted in spite of this.[37] The stable rate of coin loss in Mide points to continued, regular and peaceable contact with Dublin during the eleventh century which is likely to have fostered a coin-using mentality.

The geographical scope of monetary activity appears to expand somewhat during the course of the eleventh century. The average distance of single-finds from Dublin increases from 111km in the tenth century to 150km in the eleventh. This expansion is reflected in a slight increase in the number of coin finds from south-west Ireland. This was an area with a small number of silver finds from the tenth century. In the eleventh, single-finds from Beal Boru and Inish Cealtra can be added to hoards at Limerick and Adare. All of the finds from this area can be placed within a relatively defined chronology stretching from *c.*1020 to *c.*1070. These finds are clustered around Limerick and up the River Shannon, an area which would appear to have been the economic, as well as the political, heartland of Munster in the eleventh century. Whilst the evidence should not be overstated, the relatively small, but concentrated, number of finds in Munster is suggestive of some monetary activity. This was not particularly widespread and appears focused around Limerick. The increase in the number of finds certainly suggests that the area was becoming more familiar with coinage, and the absolute number of finds compares favourably with most other parts of contemporary Ireland. A political or dynastic link to explain the presence of this coinage would be tempting as the coin finds are focused in areas controlled by the kings of Munster, the Uí Bríain. However the period when coin finds are common coincided with the control of Dublin by Diarmait mac Máel na mBó, the king of Leinster (d. 1072), who frequently led raids into Munster.[38] There were much closer political connections between the south-west and Dublin from 1070, when Uí Bríain kings intermittently exerted authority over Dublin for a 45-year period, but no coin finds are known to match this political link. Again, as with Mide above, a gradual acceptance of coinage as a viable medium of exchange rather than overt political links with Dublin must probably be interpreted as the reason behind an increase in monetary activity.

The distribution of twelfth-century finds is quite different from the preceding period. As discussed above, the twelfth-century coins are among the most common as site finds despite the fact that they are struck in a fragile form and, from around 1140, in quite base metal. However, this large total quantity comes from a very small number of sites. To illustrate the point, single-finds of the twelfth century have been found at five sites with Dublin (43), Knowth (8)

---

[37]   Ó Corráin, *Ireland before the Normans*, 120.

[38]   M. Valante, *The Vikings in Ireland: Settlement, Trade and Urbanization,* (Dublin, 2008), 154–6.

Figure 13.5   The distribution of coins, 1000–1100.

and Trim Castle (4) producing numbers of single-finds that make them among
the most productive in the whole period. The sites with single-finds are also quite
geographically constricted, with only the shadowy and uncertain Drumbo coin
being found at a distance greater than 50km from Dublin. In this regard there
is a contrast between hoards, all but one found over 100km from Dublin, and

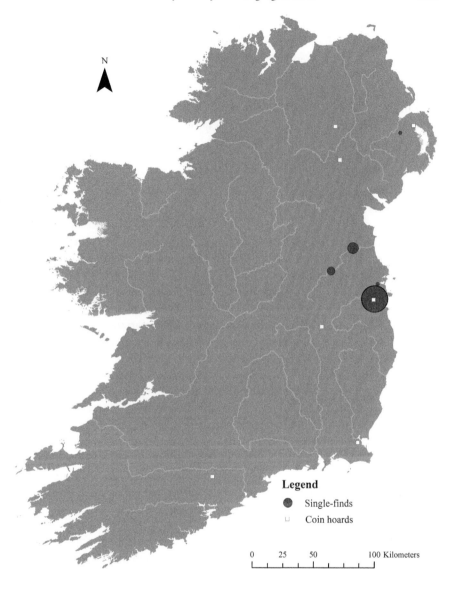

Figure 13.6 The distribution of coins, 1100–1170.

single-finds, nearly all found within 50km. The geographical constriction can
be interpreted in a chronological manner. The area characterised by monetary
activity shrank over the course of the twelfth century. The reason behind this can
probably be found in the worsening alloy of the coins themselves. The distant
hoards are mostly from the early part of the twelfth century, and contain coins

struck in good silver, whereas the single-finds are later, and struck in debased silver. In the area with the longest history of coin usage, Dublin and its environs, an essentially copper, token currency may have been viable. Across much of the rest of Ireland, where coinage was a more recent or ephemeral phenomenon in the early periods, the decision to cease striking in good silver may have destroyed trust in the value of coinage. Without a link to the inherent value of silver, and with no long-term commitment to coin usage on either a political or mercantile level, it is perhaps unsurprising that areas beyond the immediate vicinity of Dublin ceased to use coinage in the twelfth century.

Conclusions

There have been two purposes to this chapter. The first has been to put the single-find evidence on record and the second has been to offer some initial thoughts on its interpretation. With regard to the first of these points, it is hoped that the Appendix will act as a reference and may spur the reporting or publication of further finds. In my interpretation I have sketched a model of monetary activity in Viking-Age Ireland. Across the whole period, the importance of Dublin is the most striking element of the finds. They show that it was not only the conduit of silver to the interior but also the place where it was most likely to have been used. In chronological terms, Dublin appears to be the first area to use coinage, in the early tenth century, with the midlands and possibly the south-west following its lead. This gradual expansion is probably reflected in an increased number of finds, which peak in the eleventh century. Monetary activity in these areas may have been replacing other types of silver exchange, such as weight-adjusted arm-rings, and thus we should not view coin use as a revolutionary step. Coinage certainly was not a prerequisite for the Viking-Age economy as can be seen from an absence of finds across most of the north and west.

Coinage did not prove to be a long-term part of the economy in many areas. A probable decline in silver availability, with a matching decline in finds from the mid-eleventh century, ultimately led to a very base bracteate coinage in the mid-twelfth century. This provoked two parallel reactions. Across much of Ireland, in areas where monetary activity had occurred but not intensively, the reaction to a base, light coin was to seek other means of exchange, leading to a lapse into coinlessness. In Dublin and areas close to it, where coinage had been a more important element in the economy, the response was quite different. Here, the numbers of finds indicate either a larger or substantially more active coinage in the mid-twelfth century. Coin use, at least for a small and urban minority, had become a well-embedded part of the economy.

Appendix

Single-Finds from Ireland *c.*600–1170

	Find-spot	Type	Date	Reference
1	Trim, co. Meath, 1860	Merovingian *tremissis*, Beaufay	600–75	Blackburn, no. 1.
2	Maryborough, co. Laois, pre-1863	Merovingian *tremissis*, Le Mans	600–75	Blackburn, no. 2.
3	Bawnaughragh TD, co. Laois, 1867	Offa, Type 208, London, Ibba	780–92	Blackburn, no. 3.
4	Site B, near Dublin, co. Dublin, 1990s	Offa, *Portrait* (Light), Ethilwald	780–92	Blackburn, no. 4.
5	Armagh (near site of a religious house), co. Armagh, 1849	Offa	780–96	Blackburn, no. 5.
6	Londonderry (near), co. Londonderry, 1847	Offa	780–96	Blackburn, no. 6.
7	Dundalk, co. Louth, 1848	Offa	780–96	Blackburn, no. 7a.
8	Dundalk, co. Louth, 1848	Offa	780–96	Blackburn, no. 7b.
9	Dunamase, co. Laois, 1990s	Ecgbert of Wessex	825–39	Blackburn, no. 8.
10	Kilclief, co. Down, uncertain	Dirham	C9th/10th	(*Pers. comm.*) Cormac Bourke.
11	Woodstown, co. Waterford, 2003/4	Dirham	C9th/10th	Blackburn, no. 9.
12	Woodstown, co. Waterford, 2003/4	Dirham	C9th/10th	(*Pers. comm.*) excavator.
13	Site A or C, near Dublin, co. Dublin, 1990s	Dirham	C9th/10th	Blackburn, no. 10a.
14	Site A or C, near Dublin, co. Dublin, 1990s	Dirham	C9th/10th	Blackburn, no. 10b.
15	Site A or C, near Dublin, co. Dublin, 1990s	Dirham	C9th/10th	Blackburn, no. 10c.

	Find-spot	Type	Date	Reference
16	'Irish Midlands', 1980s	Continental, Louis the German, Trier	855–75	NMI, ex Rice Collection.
17	Ireland, pre-1990	Burgred, Lunettes (A), Dealinc	866–74	Blackburn, no. 11.
18	Ireland, pre-1990	Alfred, Lunettes, Sigeric	871–5	Blackburn, no. 12.
19	Shanmullagh, co. Armagh, 1990s	Alfred, Lunettes, Canterbury, Bernred	871–5	(*Pers. comm.*) Cormac Bourke.
20	High Street, Dublin, co. Dublin, 1967–72	Alfred, *London Monogram*	880–5	Blackburn, no. 13; NMI, Wallace, p. 210, no. 1 (E71:19687).
21	Carrowreilly, co. Sligo, 1988	Dirham, Volga imitation	900–10	Blackburn, no. 14.
22	Lough Gur, co. Limerick, 1940	Archbishop Plegmund, *Horizontal Trefoil* 1, Canterbury, Wilric	910–23	Ó Ríordáin.
23	Lagore, co. Meath, 1934–6	Edward the Elder, *Horizontal Trefoil* 1, Wulfeard	899–924	Blackburn, no. 15.
24	Lough Gur, co. Limerick, 1940	Edward the Elder, *Horizontal Trefoil* 1, Grimwald?	899–924	Ó Ríordáin.
25	Rathcrogan, co. Roscommon, pre-1950	Edward the Elder, *Bust Crowned*, East Anglian	920–4	Blackburn, no. 16.
26	Drogheda, co. Louth, 1810	Athelstan, London, Beahred	924–39	Hall, i.
27	Fishamble Street, Dublin, co. Dublin, 1978–81	Athelstan, *Horizontal Trefoil* 1, Oxford?, Sigeland	924–39	Blackburn, no. 17; NMI, Wallace, p. 211, no. 1 (E172:14391).

	Find-spot	Type	Date	Reference
28	Fishamble Street, Dublin, co. Dublin, 1978–81	Athelstan, *Circumscription Cross*, Derby, Ma [ ]	924–39	Blackburn, no. 18; NMI, Wallace, p. 211, no. 2 (E172:14306).
29	Christchurch Place, Dublin, co. Dublin, 1972–6	Athelstan, *Circumscription Cross*?	924–39	NMI, not in Wallace (E122:16563).
30	Fishamble Street, Dublin, co. Dublin, 1978–81	Athelstan, *Circumscription Cross*, Chester, Paules	924–39	Blackburn, no. 20; NMI, not in Wallace (E141:3232).
31	Fishamble Street, Dublin, co. Dublin, 1978–81	Athelstan, *Bust Crowned*, Canterbury, Aelfric	924–39	Blackburn, no. 19; NMI, Wallace, p. 211, no. 3 (E172:13845).
32	(near) Cork, co. Cork, 1810	Anlaf Guthfrithsson, *Raven*, York, Aethelferth	939–41	Blackburn, no. 26.
33	High Street, Dublin, co. Dublin, 1967–72	Anlaf Guthfrithsson or Sihtricsson, *Horizontal Trefoil* 1, Stamford, Bleseret	940–2	Blackburn, no. 27; NMI, Wallace, p. 210, no. (E71:13083).
34	Christchurch Place, Dublin, co. Dublin, 1972–6	Edmund, *Horizontal Trefoil* 1, Eferulf	939–46	Blackburn, no. 21; NMI, Wallace, p. 210, no. 1 (E122:18652).
35	Knowth, co. Meath, 1962–80	Edmund, *Horizontal Rosette* 1, Frard	939–46	Kenny 2012.
36	Co. Westmeath (Mullingar?), co. Westmeath, 1988	Edmund, *Horizontal Rosette* 1, Cenberht	939–46	Blackburn, no. 22.
37	Knowth, co. Meath, 1962–80	Edmund, *Horizontal Rosette* 1	939–46	Kenny 2012.
38	Temple Bar West Excavations, co. Dublin, 1996–8	Edmund, *Horizontal Rosette* 2?	939–46	Blackburn, no. 23.

	Find-spot	Type	Date	Reference
39	Ireland, pre-1990	Edmund, *Bust Crowned*	939–46	Blackburn, no. 25.
40	Knowth, co. Meath, 1962–80	Edmund, *Bust Crowned*	939–46	Kenny 2012.
41	Wood Quay, co. Dublin, 1974–81	Eadred, *Horizontal Rosette* 1, Raegtheres	946–55	Blackburn, no. 29; NMI, Wallace, p. 211, no. 5 (E172:14276).
42	Wood Quay, co. Dublin, 1974–81	Eadred, *Horizontal Rosette* 1, Agtardes	946–55	Blackburn, no. 28; NMI, Wallace, p. 211, no. 4.
43	Fishamble Street, Dublin, co. Dublin, 1978–81	Eadred, *Bust Crowned*, Norwich?, Hrodgar	946–55	Blackburn, no. 30; NMI, Wallace, p. 211, no. 6 (E172:11222).
44	Cork (in), co. Cork, 1833	Eric Bloodaxe, *Horizonal Trefoil* 1, York, Ingelgar	948–50	Blackburn, no. 31.
45	Waterford, co. Waterford, pre-1837	Anlaf Sihtricsson, *Floral* A, York, Padter	948–52	Lewis; probably *SCBI* 2, no. 521.
46	Abbey St., Armagh, co. Armagh, 1977	Eadwig, *Horizonal Trefoil* 1, Baldwin	955–9	Blackburn, no. 32.
47	Cloonart Beg, co. Roscommon, 1986	Eadwig, *Horizontal Trefoil* 1, Her[ ]	955–9	Blackburn, no. 33.
48	Cloonart Beg, co. Roscommon, 1986	Edgar, *Horizontal Trefoil* 1, [ ]s	959–73	Blackburn, no. 40.
49	'Ireland', pre-1990	Edgar, *Horizontal Trefoil* 1, Farman	959–73	Blackburn, no. 34.
50	Fishamble Street, Dublin, co. Dublin, 1978–81	Edgar, *Horizontal Trefoil* 1, Ive	959–73	Blackburn, no. 35; NMI, Wallace, p. 211, no. 8 (E172:11683).
51	Fishamble Street, Dublin, co. Dublin, 1978–81	Edgar, *Horizontal Trefoil* 1?, Cnapa?	959–73	Blackburn, no. 36; NMI, Wallace, p. 211, no. 9 (E190:7396).

	Find-spot	Type	Date	Reference
52	Dublin, co. Dublin, 1695	Edgar, *Circumscription Rosette*	959–73	Blackburn, no. 38.
53	Fishamble Street, Dublin, co. Dublin, 1978–81	Edgar, *Circumscription Rosette*, Siferth	959–73	Blackburn, no. 39; NMI, Wallace, p. 211, no. 7 (E172:3005).
54	Christchurch Place, Dublin, co. Dublin, 1972–6	Edgar, *Circumscription Cross*, O(swerd?)	959–73	Blackburn, no. 37; NMI, Wallace, p. 210, no. 2 (E122:18563).
55	Disert, co. Westmeath, 1988	Edgar, *Reform Small Cross*, Winchester, Raegenulf	973–5	Blackburn, no. 41.
56	Armagh (in or near), co. Armagh, pre-1839	Edgar	959–75	Blackburn, no. 42.
57	Fishamble Street, Dublin, co. Dublin, 1978–81	Æthelred II, *First Hand*, Barnstaple, Aelfelm	979–85	Blackburn, no. 43; NMI, Wallace, p. 211, no. 10 (E172:13397).
58	Fishamble Street, Dublin, co. Dublin, 1978–81	Æthelred II, *First Hand*, London, Aelfgar	979–85	Blackburn, no. 44; NMI, Wallace, p. 211, no. 11 (E190:3832).
59	Fishamble Street, Dublin, co. Dublin, 1978–81	Æthelred II, *First Hand*, London, Aelfgar	979–85	Blackburn, no. 45; NMI, Wallace, p. 211, no. 12 (E190:3102).
60	Fishamble Street, Dublin, co. Dublin, 1978–81	Æthelred II, *Second Hand*, London, Cynsige	985–91	Blackburn, no. 46; NMI, Wallace, p. 211, no. 13 (E190:6104).
61	Central co. Westmeath (Mullingar?), co. Westmeath, 1988	Æthelred II, *Second Hand*, London, Aelfnoth	985–91	NMI, ex Rice Collection. CR 1988, no. 171.
62	Central co. Westmeath (Mullingar?), co. Westmeath, 1988	Æthelred II, *Second Hand*, London, Aelget	985–91	NMI, ex Rice Collection. CR 1988, no. 172.

	Find-spot	Type	Date	Reference
63	High Street, Dublin, co. Dublin, 1967–72	Æthelred II, *Crux*, Barnstaple, Aelfsige	991–7	Blackburn, no. 47; NMI, Wallace, p. 210, no. (E71:9726).
64	Fishamble Street, Dublin, co. Dublin, 1978–81	Æthelred II, *Crux*, London, Aegnulf	991–7	NMI, Wallace, p. 211, no. 14 (E190:361).
65	High Street, Dublin, co. Dublin, 1967–72	Æthelred II, *Crux*, London, Byrhtlaf	991–7	Blackburn, no. 48; NMI, Wallace, p. 210, no. (E71:9760).
66	Fishamble Street, Dublin, co. Dublin, 1978–81	Æthelred II, *Crux*, London, Swetinc	991–7	NMI, O'Meara 1981.
67	'Convent Field', Wicklow Town, co. Wicklow, pre-1991	Æthelred II, *Crux*, Winchester, Leofpold	991–7	NMI.
68	Fontstown, co. Kildare, 1830s	Æthelred II	978–1016	Blackburn, no. 49.
69	Werburgh St., co. Dublin, 1994	Sitric Silkenbeard?, Phase Ia	995–7	NMI, Hayden 2002.
70	Werburgh St., co. Dublin, 1994	Sitric Silkenbeard?, Phase Ia	995–7	NMI, Hayden 2002.
71	Castle Street, Armagh, co. Armagh, 1968	Sitric Silkenbeard, Phase Ia	995–7	Blackburn, no. 50.
72	Fishamble Street, Dublin, co. Dublin, 1978–81	Æthelred II, *Long Cross*, Exeter, Wynsige	997–1003	NMI, Wallace, p. 211, no. 15 (E172:9352).
73	Christchurch Place, Dublin, co. Dublin, 1972–6	Æthelred II, *Long Cross?*, Osmund?	997–1003	NMI, not in Wallace (E122:13656).
74	'Londonderry', co. Londonderry, pre-1835	Sitric Silkenbeard, Phase Ib	997–1003	Hall, o.
75	Fishamble Street, Dublin, co. Dublin, 1978–81	Sitric Silkenbeard, Phase Ib, 'Winchester', 'Godman'	997–1003	NMI, Wallace, p. 211 (E172:7816).

	Find-spot	Type	Date	Reference
76	Cathedral Hill, Downpatrick, co. Down, 1992	Sitric Silkenbeard, Phase Ib?	997–1003	Reported in Bennett 1992 (E34).
77	'Irish Midlands', 1980s	Insular Imitation, Long Cross, 'Chester', 'Aescman'	997–1003	NMI, ex Rice Collection.
78	Christchurch Place, Dublin, co. Dublin, 1972–6	Continental	C10/11th	NMI, not in Wallace (E122:12683).
79	Fishamble Street, Dublin, co. Dublin, 1978–81	Æthelred II, *Helmet*, Exeter, Wulfsige	1003–9	NMI, Wallace, p. 211, no. 16 (E172:9817).
80	Christchurch Place, Dublin, co. Dublin, 1972–6	Æthelred II, *Helmet*	1003–9	NMI, not in Wallace (Coin untraceable).
81	Christchurch Place, Dublin, co. Dublin, 1972–6	Æthelred II, *Last Small Cross*, Shaftesbury	1009–18	NMI, Wallace, p. 210, no. 3 (E122:10800).
82	Fishamble Street, Dublin, co. Dublin, 1978–81	Cnut, *Pointed Helmet*, Gloucester, Godric	1023–9	NMI, Wallace, p. 211, no. 17 (E190:4294).
83	Christchurch Place, Dublin, co. Dublin, 1972–6	Cnut, *Pointed Helmet*, Gloucester, Sigered	1023–9	NMI, Wallace, p. 210, no. 4 (E122:10910).
84	Knowth, co. Meath, 1962–80	Cnut, *Pointed Helmet*	1023–9	Kenny 2012.
85	Limerick, co. Limerick, 1999	Cnut, *Short Cross*, London, Edwine	1029–36	O'Donovan.
86	Inish Cealtra, co. Clare, 1970–80	Cnut, *Short Cross*, London, Goda(ma)n?	1029–36	NMI.
87	'Irish Midlands', pre-1990	Hiberno-Scandinavian, Phase II	1020–40	NMI, ex Clarke Collection.
88	Fishamble Street, Dublin, co. Dublin, 1978–81	Hiberno-Scandinavian, Phase II	1020–40	NMI, Wallace, p. 211 (E172:4056).

	Find-spot	Type	Date	Reference
89	Christchurch Place, Dublin, co. Dublin, 1972–6	Hiberno-Scandinavian, Phase II	1020–40	NMI, Wallace, p. 210 (E122:8971).
90	Christchurch Place, Dublin, co. Dublin, 1972–6	Hiberno-Scandinavian, Phase II	1020–40	NMI, Wallace, p. 210 (E122:11050).
91	Christchurch Place, Dublin, co. Dublin, 1972–6	Hiberno-Scandinavian, Phase II	1020–40	NMI, Wallace, p. 210 (E122:8435).
92	Christchurch Place, Dublin, co. Dublin, 1972–6	Hiberno-Scandinavian, Phase II	1020–40	NMI, Wallace, p. 210 (E122:16526).
93	Christchurch Place, Dublin, co. Dublin, 1972–6	Hiberno-Scandinavian, Phase II	1020–40	NMI, Wallace, p. 210 (E122:11302).
94	Christchurch Place, Dublin, co. Dublin, 1972–6	Hiberno-Scandinavian, Phase II	1020–40	NMI, Wallace, p. 210 (E122:16708).
95	Christchurch Place, Dublin, co. Dublin, 1972–6	Hiberno-Scandinavian, Phase II	1020–40	NMI, Wallace, p. 210 (E122:16355).
96	Christchurch Place, Dublin, co. Dublin, 1972–6	Hiberno-Scandinavian, Phase II	1020–40	NMI, Wallace, p. 210 (E122:16547).
97	Fishamble Street, Dublin, co. Dublin, 1978–81	Hiberno-Scandinavian, Phase II	1020–40	NMI, Wallace, p. 211 (E172:9202).
98	Fishamble Street, Dublin, co. Dublin, 1978–81	Hiberno-Scandinavian, Phase II	1020–40	NMI, Wallace, p. 211 (E172:908).
99	Fishamble Street, Dublin, co. Dublin, 1978–81	Hiberno-Scandinavian, Phase II	1020–40	NMI, Wallace, p. 211 (E172:9205).
100	Fishamble Street, Dublin, co. Dublin, 1978–81	Hiberno-Scandinavian, Phase II	1020–40	NMI, not in Wallace (E148:1312).
101	High Street, Dublin, co. Dublin, 1967–72	Hiberno-Scandinavian, Phase II	1020–40	NMI, Wallace, p. 210 (E71:16598).

	Find-spot	Type	Date	Reference
102	Christchurch Place, Dublin, co. Dublin, 1972–6	Hiberno-Scandinavian, Phase II	1020–40	NMI, Wallace, p. 210 (E122:14131).
103	Islandmagee Area?, co. Antrim, pre-2002	Hiberno-Scandinavian, Phase II	1020–40	(*Pers. comm.*) R. Heslip and N. Marsden.
104	Illaunloughan, co. Kerry, 1992–5	Hiberno-Scandinavian, Phase II	1020–40	Marshall and Walsh, p. 108.
105	St. Brendan's Cathedral, Ardfert, co. Kerry, 1990	Hiberno-Scandinavian, Phase II	1020–40	Moore, p. 57.
106	'Ireland', 1820	Harthcnut	1035–42	Hall, r.
107	Christchurch Place, Dublin, co. Dublin, 1972–6	Hiberno-Scandinavian, Phase III	1040–60	NMI, Wallace, p. 210 (E122:13411).
108	Christchurch Place, Dublin, co. Dublin, 1972–6	Hiberno-Scandinavian, Phase III	1040–60	NMI, Wallace, p. 210 (E122:11051).
109	Christchurch Place, Dublin, co. Dublin, 1972–6	Hiberno-Scandinavian, Phase III	1040–60	NMI, Wallace, p. 210 (E122:9870).
110	Christchurch Place, Dublin, co. Dublin, 1972–6	Hiberno-Scandinavian, Phase III	1040–60	NMI, Wallace, p. 210 (E122:9871).
111	Christchurch Place, Dublin, co. Dublin, 1972–6	Hiberno-Scandinavian, Phase III	1040–60	NMI, Wallace, p. 210 (E122:6857).
112	Christchurch Place, Dublin, co. Dublin, 1972–6	Hiberno-Scandinavian, Phase III	1040–60	NMI, Wallace, p. 210 (E122:9550).
113	Christchurch Place, Dublin, co. Dublin, 1972–6	Hiberno-Scandinavian, Phase III	1040–60	NMI, Wallace, p. 210 (E122:11707).
114	High Street, Dublin, co. Dublin, 1967–72	Hiberno-Scandinavian, Phase III	1040–60	NMI, Wallace, p. 210 (E71:4110).
115	High Street, Dublin, co. Dublin, 1967–72	Hiberno-Scandinavian, Phase III	1040–60	NMI, Wallace, p. 210 (E71:16518?).

	Find-spot	Type	Date	Reference
116	Abbey St., Armagh, co. Armagh, 1977	Hiberno-Scandinavian, Phase III	1040–60	Dolley 1977.
117	Beal Boru Fort, co. Clare, 1961	Hiberno-Scandinavian, Phase III	1040–60	Hall, q.
118	Inish Cealtra, 1970–80	Hiberno-Scandinavian, Phase III	1040–60	NMI.
119	Dalkey, co. Dublin, 1956–9	Continental denier	C11th	Liversage.
120	'Ireland', pre-1839	Hiberno-Scandinavian, Phase V	1060/70s	Dolley 1973.
121	Christchurch Place, Dublin, co. Dublin, 1992	Hiberno-Scandinavian, Phase V	1060/70s	NMI, Wallace, p. 210 (E92:30210).
122	Christchurch Place, Dublin, co. Dublin, 1972–6	Hiberno-Scandinavian, Phase V	1060/70s	NMI, Wallace, p. 210 (E122:435).
123	Christchurch Place, Dublin, co. Dublin, 1972–6	Hiberno-Scandinavian, Phase V	1060/70s	NMI, Wallace, p. 210 (E122:12074).
124	Christchurch Place, Dublin, co. Dublin, 1972–6	Hiberno-Scandinavian, Phase V	1060/70s	NMI, Wallace, p. 210 (E122:9571).
125	Christchurch Place, Dublin, co. Dublin, 1972–6	Hiberno-Scandinavian, Phase V	1060/70s	NMI, Wallace, p. 210 (E122:187).
126	Fishamble Street, Dublin, co. Dublin, 1978–81	Hiberno-Scandinavian, Phase V	1060/70s	NMI, not in Wallace (E141:2071).
127	Fishamble Street, Dublin, co. Dublin, 1978–81	Hiberno-Scandinavian, Phase V	1060/70s	NMI, Wallace, p. 211 (E190:6018).
128	Fishamble Street, Dublin, co. Dublin, 1978–81	Hiberno-Scandinavian, Phase V	1060/70s	NMI, not in Wallace (E141:3381).

	Find-spot	Type	Date	Reference
129	Winetavern Street, Dublin, co. Dublin, 1969–73	Hiberno-Scandinavian, Phase V	1060/70s	NMI, Wallace, p. 210 (E81:3951).
130	Winetavern Street, Dublin, co. Dublin, 1969–73	Hiberno-Scandinavian, Phase V	1060/70s	NMI, Wallace, p. 210 (E81:2300).
131	Tipper, co. Longford, 1986	Hiberno-Scandinavian, Phase V	1060/70s	*(Pers. comm.)* M. Kenny.
132	Beal Boru Fort, co. Clare, 1961	Hiberno-Scandinavian, Phase V	1060/70s	Hall, s.
133	Christchurch Place, Dublin, co. Dublin, 1972–6	Hiberno-Scandinavian, Phase V	1070s	NMI, Wallace, p. 210 (E122:12669).
134	Christchurch Place, Dublin, co. Dublin, 1972–6	Hiberno-Scandinavian, Phase V	1070s	NMI, Wallace, p. 210 (E122:9836).
135	Winetavern Street, Dublin, co. Dublin, 1969–73	Hiberno-Scandinavian, Phase V	1070s	NMI, Wallace, p. 210 (E81:4334).
136	Abbey St., Armagh, co. Armagh, 1992	Hiberno-Scandinavian, Phase V	1080s	Hurl.
137	'Irish Midlands', pre-1990	Hiberno-Scandinavian, Phase V	1080s	NMI, ex Clarke Collection.
138	Christchurch Place, Dublin, co. Dublin, 1972–6	Hiberno-Scandinavian, Phase V	1080s	NMI, (E122:9880).
139	Christchurch Place, Dublin, co. Dublin, 1972–6	Hiberno-Scandinavian, Phase V	1080s	NMI, (E122:5818).
140	Christchurch Place, Dublin, co. Dublin, 1972–6	Hiberno-Scandinavian, Phase V	1080s	NMI, (E122:1656).
141	Winetavern Street, Dublin, co. Dublin, 1969–73	Hiberno-Scandinavian, Phase V	1080s	NMI, Wallace, p. 210 (E81:1814).

	Find-spot	Type	Date	Reference
142	Shandon, Dungarvan, co. Waterford, 2002	Hiberno-Scandinavian, Phase V	1080s	(*Pers. comm.*) J. Tierney.
143	Fermoy, co. Cork, 1820	Hiberno-Scandinavian, Phase V	1090s	Hall, u.
144	Christchurch Place, Dublin, co. Dublin, 1972–6	Hiberno-Scandinavian, Phase V	1090s	NMI, Wallace, p. 210 (E122:317).
145	Fishamble Street, Dublin, co. Dublin, 1978–81	Hiberno-Scandinavian, Phase V?	1060–1100	NMI, not in Wallace (E141:1325).
146	Fishamble Street, Dublin, co. Dublin, 1978–81	Hiberno-Scandinavian, Phase V?	1060–1100	NMI, not in Wallace (E141:1375).
147	Winetavern Street, Dublin, co. Dublin, 1969–73	Hiberno-Scandinavian, Phase VI?	1100s?	NMI, Wallace, p. 210? (E81:788).
148	Winetavern Street, Dublin, co. Dublin, 1969–73	Hiberno-Scandinavian, Phase VI?	1100s?	NMI, not in Wallace? (E81:1805).
149	Wood Quay, co. Dublin, 1974–81	Hiberno-Scandinavian, Phase VII	1110s	NMI, Wallace, p. 210 (E132:16285).
150	Christchurch Place, Dublin, co. Dublin, 1972–6	Hiberno-Scandinavian, Phase VII	1110s	NMI, Wallace, p. 210 (E122:1920).
151	Christchurch Place, Dublin, co. Dublin, 1972–6	Hiberno-Scandinavian, Phase VII	1110s	NMI, Wallace, p. 210 (E122:1145).
152	High Street, Dublin, co. Dublin, 1967–72	Hiberno-Scandinavian, Phase VII	1110s	NMI, Wallace, p. 210 (E71:1843).
153	Knowth, co. Meath, 1962–80	Hiberno-Scandinavian, Phase VII	1110s	Kenny 2012.
154	Christchurch Place, Dublin, co. Dublin, 1972–6	Hiberno-Scandinavian, Phase VII	1110s	NMI, Wallace, p. 210 (E122:6753).

	Find-spot	Type	Date	Reference
155	Wood Quay, co. Dublin, 1974–81	Hiberno-Scandinavian, Phase VII	1110s	NMI, Wallace, p. 210 (E132:302741).
156	Christchurch Place, Dublin, co. Dublin, 1972–6	Hiberno-Scandinavian, Phase VII	1120/30s	NMI, Wallace, p. 210 (E122:6963).
157	Christchurch Place, Dublin, co. Dublin, 1972–6	Hiberno-Scandinavian, Phase VII	1120/30s	NMI, Wallace, p. 210 (E122:6747).
158	Knowth, co. Meath, 1962–80	Hiberno-Scandinavian, Phase VII	1120/30s	Kenny 2012.
159	High Street, Dublin, co. Dublin, 1967–72	Stephen	1136–54	NMI, not in Wallace (E71:5923).
160	Christchurch Place, Dublin, co. Dublin, 1972–6	Hiberno-Scandinavian, Phase VII	1130–50s	NMI, Wallace, p. 210 (E122:1191).
161	Fishamble Street, Dublin, co. Dublin, 1978–81	Hiberno-Scandinavian, Phase VII	1130–50s	NMI, not in Wallace (E141:4119).
162	Patrick Street Excavation, co. Dublin, 1991–2	Hiberno-Scandinavian, Phase VII	1130–50s	Walsh.
163	High Street, Dublin, co. Dublin, 1967–72	Hiberno-Scandinavian, Phase VII	1130–50s	NMI, Wallace, p. 210 (E71:15766).
164	High Street, Dublin, co. Dublin, 1967–72	Hiberno-Scandinavian, Phase VII	1130–50s	NMI, Wallace, p. 210 (E71:3429).
165	High Street, Dublin, co. Dublin, 1967–72	Hiberno-Scandinavian, Phase VII	1130–50s	NMI, Wallace, p. 210 (E71:2393).
166	High Street, Dublin, co. Dublin, 1967–72	Hiberno-Scandinavian, Phase VII	1130–50s	NMI, Wallace, p. 210 (E71:3331).
167	High Street, Dublin, co. Dublin, 1967–72	Hiberno-Scandinavian, Phase VII	1130–50s	NMI, Wallace, p. 210 (E71:3128).

	Find-spot	Type	Date	Reference
168	High Street, Dublin, co. Dublin, 1967–72	Hiberno-Scandinavian, Phase VII	1130–50s	NMI, Wallace, p. 210 (E71:2963).
169	Patrick Street Excavation, co. Dublin, 1991–2	Hiberno-Scandinavian, Phase VII	1130–50s	Walsh.
170	High Street, Dublin, co. Dublin, 1967–72	Hiberno-Scandinavian, Phase VII	1130–50s	NMI, Wallace, p. 210 (E71:1116).
171	Winetavern Street, Dublin, co. Dublin, 1969–73	Hiberno-Scandinavian, Phase VII	1130–50s	NMI, not in Wallace (E81:9043).
172	Winetavern Street, Dublin, co. Dublin, 1993	Hiberno-Scandinavian, Phase VII	1130–50s	Halpin.
173	Trim Castle, co. Meath, 1971–4	Hiberno-Scandinavian, Phase VII	1130–50s	Sweetman.
174	High Street, Dublin, co. Dublin, 1967–72	Hiberno-Scandinavian, Phase VII	1150–60s	NMI, Wallace, p. 210 (E71:1514).
175	Christchurch Place, Dublin, co. Dublin, 1972–6	Hiberno-Scandinavian, Phase VII	1150–60s	NMI, Wallace, p. 210 (E122:1810).
176	Christchurch Place, Dublin, co. Dublin, 1972–6	Hiberno-Scandinavian, Phase VII	1150–60s	NMI, Wallace, p. 210 (E122:1155).
177	Winetavern Street, Dublin, co. Dublin, 1969–73	Hiberno-Scandinavian, Phase VII	1150–60s	NMI, not in Wallace (E81:7910).
178	High Street, Dublin, co. Dublin, 1967–72	Hiberno-Scandinavian, Phase VII	1150–60s	NMI, Wallace, p. 210 (E71:1791).
179	Patrick Street Excavation, co. Dublin, 1991–2	Hiberno-Scandinavian, Phase VII	1150–60s	Walsh.
180	High Street, Dublin, co. Dublin, 1967–72	Hiberno-Scandinavian, Phase VII	1150–60s	NMI, Wallace, p. 210 (E71:757).

	Find-spot	Type	Date	Reference
181	High Street, Dublin, co. Dublin, 1967–72	Hiberno-Scandinavian, Phase VII	1150–60s	NMI, Wallace, p. 210 (E71:1117).
182	High Street, Dublin, co. Dublin, 1967–72	Hiberno-Scandinavian, Phase VII	1150–60s	NMI, Wallace, p. 210 (E71:1092).
183	High Street, Dublin, co. Dublin, 1967–72	Hiberno-Scandinavian, Phase VII	1150–60s	NMI, Wallace, p. 210 (E71:1402).
184	High Street, Dublin, co. Dublin, 1962–3	Hiberno-Scandinavian, Phase VII	1150–60s	NMI, Wallace, p. 210 (E43:44).
185	High Street, Dublin, co. Dublin, 1967–72	Hiberno-Scandinavian, Phase VII	1150–60s	NMI, Wallace, p. 210 (E71:3144).
186	High Street, Dublin, co. Dublin, 1967–72	Hiberno-Scandinavian, Phase VII	1150–60s	NMI, Wallace, p. 210 (E71:1211).
187	High Street, Dublin, co. Dublin, 1967–72	Hiberno-Scandinavian, Phase VII	1150–60s	NMI, Wallace, p. 210 (E71:3682).
188	High Street, Dublin, co. Dublin, 1967–72	Hiberno-Scandinavian, Phase VII	1150–60s	NMI, Wallace, p. 210 (E71:5410).
189	High Street, Dublin, co. Dublin, 1967–72	Hiberno-Scandinavian, Phase VII	1150–60s	NMI, Wallace, p. 210 (E71:3145).
190	Back Lane, co. Dublin, 1996	Hiberno-Scandinavian, Phase VII	1150–60s	NMI.
191	Knowth, co. Meath, 1962–80	Hiberno-Scandinavian, Phase VII	1150–60s	Kenny 2012.
192	Knowth, co. Meath, 1962–80	Hiberno-Scandinavian, Phase VII	1150–60s	Kenny 2012.
193	Knowth, co. Meath, 1962–80	Hiberno-Scandinavian, Phase VII	1150–60s	Kenny 2012.

	Find-spot	Type	Date	Reference
194	Knowth, co. Meath, 1962–80	Hiberno-Scandinavian, Phase VII	1150–60s	Kenny 2012.
195	Knowth, co. Meath, 1962–80	Hiberno-Scandinavian, Phase VII	1150–60s	Kenny 2012.
196	Trim Castle, co. Meath, 1995	Hiberno-Scandinavian, Phase VII	1150–60s	Kenny 2011.
197	Trim Castle, co. Meath, 1995	Hiberno-Scandinavian, Phase VII	1150–60s	Kenny 2011.
198	Trim Castle, co. Meath, 1995	Hiberno-Scandinavian, Phase VII	1150–60s	Kenny 2011.
199	Fishamble Street, Dublin, co. Dublin, 1978–81	Continental	C12th	NMI, not in Wallace (E141:1574).
200	High Street, Dublin, co. Dublin, 1967–72	Continental, Poitiers?	C12th	NMI, not in Wallace (E71:7615).
201	Swords Castle, co. Dublin, 1971	Continental	C12th	NMI.
202	Knowth, co. Meath, 1962–80	Hiberno-Scandinavian, Phase VII (uncertain type)	1120–70	Kenny 2012.
203	Drumbo, co. Down, 1841	Hiberno-Scandinavian, Phase VII (uncertain type)	1120–70	Getty.
204	Clonmacnoise, co. Offaly, 1994	Uncertain Anglo-Saxon coin	C10th	Bennett 1994 (E197).
205	Clonmacnoise, co. Offaly, 1997	Uncertain Hiberno-Scandinavian coin	C11/12th	Bennett 1997 (E448).

	Find-spot	Type	Date	Reference
206	Ardagh, co. Longford,	Uncertain Hiberno-Scandinavian coin	C11/12th	Hall, v.

Notes: Several of the coins may be part of small, two-coin hoards. This is uncertain in each case and thus they have been left within the list of single-finds. These are as follows:

1. Dundalk, nos. 7 and 8.
2. Lough Gur, nos. 22 and 24.
3. Cloonart Beg, nos. 47 and 48.
4. Christchurch Place, Dublin, nos. 90 and 108.
5. Christchurch Place (2), Dublin, nos. 109 and 110.
6. High Street, Dublin, nos. 170 and 181.
7. Knowth, nos. 192–4 and 202.

Find-Spot References:

Blackburn   M. Blackburn, 'Currency under the Vikings. Part 4. The Dublin coinage *c.* 995–1050', *BNJ, 78* (2008), 111–37.

Bennett   I. Bennett (ed.), *Excavation Bulletin* (Dublin), published annually since 1986.

Dolley 1973   M. Dolley, 'A Hiberno-Norse penny misattributed to the 1834 hoard from Kirk Michael', *NCirc, 81* (1973), 2.

Dolley 1977   M. Dolley, 'The two Viking-Age coins recently found at Abbey Street, Armagh', *Seanchas Ardmhacha: Journal of the Armagh Diocesan Historical Society, 8* (1977), 281–3.

Getty   E. Getty, 'Notices of the round towers of Ulster', *Ulster Journal of Archaeology, 3* (1855), 110–16.

Hall   R. Hall, 'A check-list of Viking-Age coin finds from Ireland', *Ulster Journal of Archaeology, 36–7* (1973), 71–86.

Halpin   A. Halpin, *The Port of Medieval Dublin: Archaeological Excavations at the Civic Offices, Winetavern Street, Dublin 1993* (Dublin, 2000).

Hayden   A. Hayden, 'The excavation of pre-Norman defences and houses at Werburgh Street', in *Medieval Dublin III*, ed. S. Duffy (Dublin, 2002), 44–68.

Hurl   D.P. Hurl, 'Excavations in Abbey Street, Armagh', *Ulster Journal of Archaeology, 62* (2003), 97–115.

Kenny 2011   M. Kenny, 'Coins and tokens', in *Trim Castle, Co. Meath: Excavations 1995–8*, ed. A. Hayden (Dublin, 2011), 320–21.

Kenny 2012 M. Kenny, 'Coins, tokens and related numismatic material from Knowth', in *Excavations at Knowth 5: The Archaeology of Knowth in the First and Second Millennia AD*, ed. G. Eogan (Dublin, 2012).

Lewis S. Lewis, *A Topographical Dictionary of Ireland* (London, 1837).

Liversage G.D. Liversage, 'Excavations at Dalkey Island, Co. Dublin, 1956–1959', *Proceedings of the Royal Irish Academy. Section C: Archaeology, Celtic Studies, History, Linguistics, Literature*, 66 (1967), 53–233.

Marshall and Walsh J.W. Marshall and C. Walsh, *Illaunloughan Island: an Early Medieval Monastery in County Kerry* (Dublin, 2005).

Moore F. Moore, *Ardfert Cathedral: Summary of Excavation Results* (Dublin, 2007).

Ó Ríordáin S.P. Ó Ríordáin, 'Lough Gur excavations: Neolithic and Bronze Age houses on Knockadoon', *Proceedings of the Royal Irish Academy. Section C: Archaeology, Celtic Studies, History, Linguistics, Literature*, 56 (1953), 297–459.

O'Donovan E. O'Donovan, 'Limerick: new discoveries in an old city', *History Ireland*, 11 (2003).

O'Meara P. O'Meara, 'Further finds of numismatic items from Wood Quay', *Irish Numismatics*, 14 (1981), 147–8.

SCBI 2 A.S. Robertson, *SCBI 2: Hunterian and Coats Collections, University of Glasgow. Part I: Anglo-Saxon Coins* (London, 1961).

Sweetman P.D. Sweetman, 'Archæological excavations at Trim Castle, Co. Meath, 1971–74', *Proceedings of the Royal Irish Academy. Section C: Archaeology, Celtic Studies, History, Linguistics, Literature*, 78 (1978), 127–98.

Wallace P.F. Wallace, 'The English presence in Viking Dublin', in *ASMH*, 202–22.

Walsh C. Walsh, *Archaeological Excavations at Patrick, Nicholas and Winetavern Streets, Dublin* (Dingle, 1997).

Chapter 14

Vestfold: A Monetary Perspective on the Viking Age[*]

Svein H. Gullbekk

Vestfold is particularly rich in Viking Age heritage. Striking examples are the Gokstad and Oseberg grave mounds with the famous ships that are on display in Oslo today; the Borre burial complex, within the vicinity of the Viken area (Oslofjord area); the Hon-treasure, the largest Viking Age gold hoard; and the *Skiringssalskaupang*, Norway's oldest town-like settlement established c.800.[1] During the last couple of years another significant site has emerged in Vestfold, making the region even more outstanding in the context of the Viking Age.[2] The number of Viking-Age hoards, grave finds with equipment for metal production, imported beads and amber and weights provide evidence for Vestfold being a centre of exchange.[3] And, from a monetary persepective, the largest coin hoard from ninth- and tenth-century Norway was found in the area between the Gokstad and Oseberg ship burials, at Grimestad in Stokke.[4]

In recent years coin finds from Vestfold have increased radically, and thus provide a laboratory for further studies of the use of coins and money in the Viking Age. While coin finds from ninth- and tenth-century Norway in general are rather modest compared to their equivalents from Denmark and Sweden, and especially Gotland, Öland and Bornholm, the stray finds from Vestfold have

---

[*]   I am grateful to Professor Jan Bill for his generosity in making the coin material from Heimdalsjordet available for discussion at an early stage and to Houshang Khazaei for his attributions of the dirham material found in Norway.

[1]   Vestfold is also famous for Stone Age settlements sites like Auve in Sandefjord, see for example E. Østmo, *Auve. En fangstboplass fra yngre steinalder på Vesterøya i Sandefjord. I. Den arkeologiske del*, Norske Oldfunn, 28 (Oslo, 2008).

[2]   For a general survey of coin finds from Viking and medieval Vestfold, see K. Skaare, *Coins and Coinage in Viking-Age Norway* (Oslo, 1976); K. Skaare, 'Utmyntningen i det gamle Tunsberg', *Vestfold-minne* 1971, 86–102.

[3]   Frans-Arne Stylegard, Kaupangs omland og urbaniseringstendenser i norsk vikingtid, in J. Brendalsmo, F.-E. Eliassen and T. Gansum (eds), *Den urbane underskog. Strandsteder, utvekslingssteder og småbyer i vikingtid, middelalder og tidlig nytid* (Oslo, 2009), 81–9.

[4]   Skaare, *Coins and Coinage*, 138 (no. 43).

during the last decade become more prolific than most other regions in Viking Scandinavia.

The first new stray finds of coins from Vestfold were associated with the Kaupang project.[5] By utilising new methods and asking different questions, a large-scale project was initiated on the site where Norway's first town was situated, at Kaupang in Vestfold, a site mentioned in the geographical account of Ohthere, written down in an expanded Old English translation of Orosius' *Historia adversus paganos* at the court of Alfred the Great in the late ninth century. The Kaupang project has produced three large volumes interpreting the results from archaeological excavations and metal-detector searches in the settlement area during the years from 2003 to 2005. The number of stray coins from the ninth and tenth century surpasses all previous site finds in the Norwegian context. As a consequence coins and money became important features in the second volume, entitled *The Means of Exchange*. Mark Blackburn was responsible for the numismatic material in this volume and also delivered important contributions to the discussions of the project through his participation in workshops, seminars and conferences. He placed the coin finds from Kaupang into their local, national and Scandinavian contexts, and combined meticulous numismatic research with innovative ideas and interpretations.[6] Mark's approach to interpretation and dating of the deposition dates for the stray finds of coins has provided a very interesting insight into the import of coins to Kaupang, where Western coinage seems to have dominated before *c.*840/50, when the Islamic dirhams started to take over. Comparisons made by Mark between coin finds from sites of similar nature in Scandinavia and northern Europe, clearly show that the number of coins lost at Kaupang was significant, and that this is presumably best interpreted as a reflection of coins and silver being used quite extensively.[7]

---

[5]　　For a general survey of the economy of Kaupang, see D. Skre, 'Post-substantivist towns and trade AD 600–1000', in *The Means of Exchange: Dealing with Silver in the Viking Age*, ed. D. Skre, Kaupang Excavation Project Publication Series, 2, Norske Oldfunn, 23 (Aarhus, 2008), 327–41; D. Skre, 'Dealing with silver: economic agency in south-western Scandinavia AD 600–1000', in *Means of Exchange*, ed. Skre, 343–55.

[6]　　M. Blackburn, 'The coin-finds', in *Means of Exchange*, ed. Skre, 29–74. This is also acknowledged in a review of the volume by S. Sindbæk in *Fornvännen, 106* (2011), 261–2; see also M. Blackburn, 'Coin finds from Kaupang: a Viking emporium on the North Sea', in *XIII Congreso Internacional de Numismática, Madrid 2003: Actas*, ed. C. Alfaro, C. Marcos and P. Otero (2 vols, Milan, 2005), 1, 1143–9.

[7]　　Blackburn, 'Coin-finds', 73. A few years previously, Blackburn made valuable contributions to another Norwegian research group working on reinterpretations of the largest gold hoard from the Viking Age, the Hon hoard in new contexts. For an extensive discussion of the Hon-hoard, see S.H. Fuglesang and D. Wilson (eds), *The Hon Hoard. A Viking Gold Treasure of the Ninth Century*, Norske Oldfunn, 20 (Oslo, 2006). During his participation with the Hon-

East and West in Coin Finds from Ninth-Century Kaupang

In this chapter I will build on Mark's contributions and introduce new evidence to the discussion of money and its use in Vestfold and the Viken area in the ninth and tenth century. The Viken area comprises the coastland of the Oslofjord and its surrounding hinterland. In medieval literature the area is referred to as Viken, and is often believed to be the etymological origin for the term *Viking* as it appears in contemporary Carolingian and Anglo-Saxon sources.[8] The western side of the Viken has an etymological reference related to the old Norse *fold* which means 'plain' and *Vest* refers to the west side of the fjord, and the two words put together in Vestfold became the term for the broad open landscape along Viken's western edge. The people living there are mentioned in ninth-century Frankish sources as *Westfaldinga*. The men from 'Westfold' are reported to have been raiding Frankish territory in the year 842: the *Westfaldingi*, according to Frankish sources, set sail up the Seine with 67 ships. Afterwards they set up a winter-camp on the island Noirmoutier in the estuary of the Loire. The island was already at that time an established centre of trade where large quantities of salt and wine passed from south to north. In contemporary Frankish sources the activity of the *Westfaldingi* was portrayed as an example of violent ravaging.[9] Numismatic evidence of four Carolingian deniers and a gold *tremissis* link Vestfold with the Frankish realm: the *tremissis* from Dorestadt and three of the deniers were found at Kaupang; and the fourth denier was discovered during the investigations of the Heimdalsjordet in Sandefjord, in the vicinity of the Gokstad ship-burial. In addition three Carolingian deniers have been found in the Viken area since 1999.[10] These seven deniers, all of the well-known *Christiana religio* type struck *c.*822/3–840 in the name of Louis the Pious (814–840), fit

---

project Blackburn's interest in gold as a feature in Viking society developed, and one of the lasting impacts of this fascination was his study of gold coins in Anglo-Saxon England: M. Blackburn, 'Gold in England during the age of silver (eighth–eleventh centuries)', in *The Silver Economy in the Viking Age*, ed. J. Graham-Campbell and G. Williams (Walnut Creek, CA, 2007), 55–98.

8   For exploration of this point see F. Askeberg, *Norden och kontinenten i gammal tid. Studier i forngermansk kulturhistoria* (Uppsala, 1942), 114–83; S. Hellberg, 'Vikingatidens vikingar', *Arkiv for nordisk filologi, 95* (1980), 25–88; C.E. Fell, 'Old English *wicing*: a question of semantics', *Proceedings of the British Academy, 72* (1986), 295–316; C.E. Fell, 'Modern English "Viking"', *Leeds Studies in English, 18* (1987), 111–23.

9   *Annales Engolismenses* s.a. 843: MGH, SS XVI, ed. G.H. Pertz (Hannover, 1859), 486; G. Jones, *A History of the Vikings* (Oxford, 1968), 210. For a discussion of how these Viking attacks had consequences for Carolingian minting, see S. Coupland, 'The coinages of Pippin I and II of Aquitaine', *RN, 6th series, 31* (1989), 194–222; S. Coupland, The Frankish tribute payments to the Vikings and their consequences, *Francia 26, 1* (1999), 57–75.

10   UMK find nos. 2100 (1999), 2165 (2003) and 2265 (2012).

in remarkably well with the records of the *Westfaldingi* and other Viking raiding towns like Dorestad and Paris in the 830s and 840s.[11]

The fact that only two of seven deniers from Viken were perforated (and hence had been transformed into jewellery), suggests that the remainder had not been in circulation for a long period within the northern lands before they ended up in Vestfold. Studies of Carolingian coins of the *Christiana religio* type provides evidence for these coins often being transformed into jewellery, and thus removed from the monetary scene as such.[12] Interestingly, the Carolingian coins from Kaupang are without traces of secondary functions and must presumably have been used as money. Comparison between the stray finds of Carolingian deniers from Kaupang and stray finds from different sites in the Viken area suggests that the Carolingian deniers were more common in the hinterland of Kaupang. While the *Christiana religio* deniers represent 3 out of 107 coins from Kaupang in the period c.800–950, they account for 3 of 14 coins outside known market contexts elsewhere in Viken. The comparison is based on a small number of finds, and should be considered with caution, but reveal close links between Vestfold and Carolingian society, in the same way as finds from modern Denmark.

Yet, considering the extensive evidence for contacts between Carolingian Francia and Anglo-Saxon England and Scandinavia, the relevant coin finds are remarkably few: in total 107 Frankish deniers from the period 754–840 and 15 Anglo-Saxon pennies from the period c.750–875.[13] Records of substantial tribute payments to Vikings and extensive Viking raiding activity in both the Frankish realm and on the British Isles are described in contemporary sources, and suggest large riches becoming Viking property. In addition archaeological sources provide material evidence for trade and other direct and indirect contact in the same period.[14]

The overall lack of Western European coins in Scandinavian ninth and tenth century contexts is therefore remarkable and surprising. Coins and silver were not strange objects in the Viking world. On the contrary, more than 170,000

---

[11] For a survey of Viking references in Frankish sources, see E. Albrectsen, *Vikingerne i Franken: skriftlig kilder fra det 9. århundrede* (Odense, 1981).

[12] J.C. Moesgaard, 'Christiana Religio', *Skalk*, 6 (2004), 12–17.

[13] I.H. Garipzanov, 'Carolingian coins in ninth-century Scandinavia: a Norwegian perspective', *Viking and Medieval Scandinavia, 1* (2005), 43–71, at 68 (table 1); E. Screen, 'The Norwegian coin finds of the early Viking Age', *Nordisk Numismatisk Årsskrift 2003–5* (2009), 93–121, at 94–5; M. Blackburn and K. Jonsson, 'The Anglo-Saxon and Anglo-Norman element of north European coin finds', in *Viking-Age Coinage in the Northern Lands. The sixth Oxford symposium on Coinage and Monetary History*, ed. M. Blackburn and M. Metcalf, BAR International Series, 122 (2 vols, Oxford, 1981), 1, 147–255, at 150, table 2.

[14] For a survey of archaeological evidence for contact between the British Isles and Vestfold in the Viking Age, see H. Aannestad, *Import, identitet og materiell kultur i vikingtid* (forthcoming).

Islamic silver dirhams from the ninth and tenth centuries have been found within Scandinavia. Subsequently Anglo-Saxon pennies and German Pfennige from the Ottonian and Salian dynasties have been found in even greater numbers in hoards from the period *c.*950–1100.

In his studies of the coin imports to Kaupang in particular and Scandinavia in general,[15] Mark Blackburn pointed out that the western European coins dominated the imports to Scandinavia in the beginning of the ninth century, albeit still in small numbers.[16] His argument indicated – rather surprisingly, but convincingly – that Western coins dominated the scene at Kaupang in its very first phase, from *c.*820 to 840/50, before Islamic coins seem to have been present in any great quantity.[17] In the past Islamic dirhams have been viewed as the first Viking currency to have penetrated Scandinavia. Instead, it seems the Islamic silver arrived in Scandinavia within the period *c.*840 to *c.*940; that is, within a single century. In longer-term perspective, Roman coins had previously appeared in Norwegian finds from the Roman Iron Age, but the use of western currency in Norway in the first half of the ninth century represents the beginning of the continuous use of coined money in Norway that eventually developed into a money economy.

The first arrivals of Islamic dirhams coincide with the introduction of the hack-silver economy in Norway. Hack-silver became part of the monetary scene at Kaupang sometime in the period *c.*840–860.[18] The arrival of hack-silver is, of course, also reflected in the adoption of precious metal standard weights of universal acceptability. This must be considered a major step in the history of the

---

[15] When Kaupang was excavated from 1956 to 1974 the excavations produced 27 coins and fragments of coins: 1 late Roman bronze, 2 Carolingian deniers, 2 Anglo-Saxon pennies, 1 Danish penny and 21 Islamic dirhams. At that point these constituted an unprecedented number of stray finds of Viking coins from a Norwegian site. Archaeological excavations and surveys from 1998 to 2003 produced an additional 76 coins, bringing the total to 103 coins: 1 Late-Roman bronze coin; 2 Byzantine bronze coins of the eighth/ninth and ninth/tenth centuries respectively; 1 Merovingian gold *tremissis*; 1 Carolingian denier; and 71 Islamic dirhams. In addition a crucible melt in the form of a partially molten cake was found which contained another 12 identifiable Islamic coins and at least two pieces of hack-silver (Skaare, *Coins and Coinage*, 139, no. 48; Blackburn, 'Coin-finds', 30; M. Blackburn, K. Jonsson and G. Rispling, 'Catalogue of the coins', in *Means of Exchange*, ed. Skre, 75–93).

[16] Blackburn, 'Coin finds', 57, 70.

[17] Ibid., 70. These findings have been discussed and some reservations expressed due to the limited number of coins used as the basis for the conclusion in a review of this volume by Søren Sindbæk (see above, n. 6).

[18] B. Hårdh, 'Hacksilver and ingots', in *Means of Exchange*, ed. Skre, 95–118, at 118; U. Pedersen, 'Weights and balances', in *Means of Exchange*, ed. Skre, 119–78, at 162; C. Kilger, 'Kaupang from afar: aspects of the interpretation of dirham finds in northern and eastern Europe between the late 8th and early 10th centuries', in *Means of Exchange*, ed. Skre, 199–252, at 228–35; Skre, 'Dealing with silver', 347–49.

Viking-Age economy, and it most certainly took effect at Kaupang in Skiringssal before anywhere else in Norway. However, a second site in the Vestfold region now shows that Kaupang's close involvement with the emerging monetary economy was not an isolated phenomenon. The finds from Kaupang provide a 'profile' of coin finds from the ninth century that can in future be tested against finds of similar volume and context from just some 15 kilometres further north along the Oslofjord coastline.

Heimdalsjordet and the Context of Kaupang

A town-like settlement has recently been discovered close to the Gokstad burial mound where the famous Viking ship was excavated by Nicolaysen in 1880.[19] The site is called the Heimdalsjordet after the local place-name. This new excavation is part of the project 'Gokstad Revitalized' headed by Professor Jan Bill at the Museum of Cultural History in Oslo.[20] For some years archaeologists have made geophysical surveys of the landscape surrounding Gokstad, and in 2012 they were able to detect traces of a settlement around 500 metres south of the burial mound, alongside the Viking-Age waterfront. At least 15 smaller houses have been detected on each side of a street. Nearby is an area with several small burial mounds. According to the preliminary reports from the first season of excavations, this seems to have been a settlement which supported production activities.

One of the most interesting questions concerning the new site will, of course, be whether it was a permanent or seasonal settlement. Whatever the conclusion, the number of coins and weights suggests a place where trade and production of precious metal was an important feature of the inhabitants' lives. Through a systematic archaeological approach and extensive use of metal detectors, the total number of coin finds now stands at 183, all but one of them Islamic dirhams. This is the largest number of stray coin finds from any Norwegian Viking site: it surpasses Kaupang in the number of coins found. The dirhams from the new site are very fragmented, which is a common feature of dirhams from similar sites all over Scandinavia. The preliminary work that has been carried out attributes a large share of the dirhams to the Abbasid and Samanid dynasties; the latest coin dates to *c.*905. The coins are undergoing conservation, and more detailed attributions and dating will be made available in future publications. The only non-Islamic coin identified so far is a Carolingian denier of the *Christiano religio*

---

[19]   N. Nicolaysen, *Langskibet fra Gokstad ved Sandefjord* (Christiania, 1882).

[20]   The project is presented online at <http://www.khm.uio.no/english/research/projects/gokstad/index.html>. Finds from this site have recently been discussed by U. Pedersen and C.L. Rødsrud, 'Nye vektlodd fra Vestfold', *Nicolai, 119* (2013), 53–9.

type, struck *c*.822–840. The number of weights from Heimdalsjordet is 147, compared to 420 weights from Kaupang. Vestfold now contains the two sites with most finds of Viking-Age weights anywhere in Scandinavia, in the same way as for single-finds of coins.

The link between this settlement and the grave burial at Gokstad is, of course, of pivotal interest given the closeness of the two sites. In spite of the remarkable nature of the Viking ship burials from Gokstad and Oseberg, not a single artefact of precious metal was found in either of them. The reason is simply that both were targeted by grave robbers. The break-in at Oseberg took place in between 953 and 990, according to dendrochronological dating of wooden spades that the robbers left behind.[21] The date for the robbery of the Gokstad burial assembly is more difficult to establish with precision, but has been dated to between 939 and 1050, again on the basis of dendrochronologically dated wooden spades.[22] In both cases the burial chambers were plundered, and this is most likely the answer to the lack of precious metal items among the finds. The closest one can get to a coin find at Gokstad or Oseberg is a note in the find registry at the Coin Cabinet in Oslo that refers to a find reportedly made in or around the Gokstad burial mound before 1878. The coin is a Roman orichalcum *sestertius* struck in the reign of Claudius (AD 41–54). The coin is undoubtedly genuine, and has been interpreted as an amulet. However, there is no conclusive evidence that can place it with certainty within the Gokstad mound.[23]

The missing link between the ship burial at Gokstad and monetary history has now seemingly been found. Since the coins from the Heimdalsjordet provide solid evidence for the settlement being active when the burial was made *c*.900, further connections between trade, values and the use of money in the area associated with this and similar burials can be discussed. Indeed, recently a Byzantine *miliaresion* in the name of Emperor John I (969–76) was found by a metal detectorist at the farm Basberg Nordre in Tønsberg, approximately 800 metres south-east of the Oseberg burial mound.[24] This provides suggestive evidence for coins being in circulation in the immediate vicinity of the Oseberg burial as well.

Another site in the region which may be compared with Heimdalsjordet and Kaupang is Manvik in Brunlanes, in the south of Vestfold, some 20 kilometres south of Kaupang along the coast. Manvik was a manor first mentioned in 1184 when its owner, the *lendmann* Lodin of Manvik was slain in the battle

---

[21]   J. Bill and A. Daly, 'The plundering of the ship graves from Oseberg and Gokstad: an example of power politics?', *Antiquity, 86* (2012), 808–24.

[22]   Ibid.

[23]   S.H. Gullbekk, 'Keiser Claudius i Gokstadhaugen', *Viking*, 2009, 169–73.

[24]   The farm Basberg Nordre (farm registration no. 90/10) in Tønsberg (UMK find no. 2275).

of Fimreite.[25] The area around the medieval church (Berg church was built in the first half of the twelfth century) has produced several stray finds in recent years: two Abbasid dirhams issued by Harun al Rashid in AD 796/7 and AD 806/7 and an Anglo-Saxon penny issued by Edward the Confessor c.1050.[26] Two English sterlings from the late thirteenth and early fourteenth century have been found in the same area.[27] Within Berg church itself (a medieval stone church dating from c.1100) some 203 stray finds of coins from the period c.1170 to c.1320 have been found as a result of archaeological excavations under the floors.[28] Taken as a whole, these stray finds provide strong evidence for use of money in relation to the church in particular, but also for permanent or seasonal market activity from the Viking Age to the late Middle Age, and presumably also into the early modern period.

Table 14.1   The recent excavation finds and stray finds from Viken, Norway.

Heimsdalsjordet

Carolingian, *Christiana religio* denier	1	Publication forthcoming
Islamic dirhams (latest coin: c.905)	182	(see n. 21)

Huseby Vestre site, Rygge kommune, Østfold

Islamic dirhams (latest coin: 813/14)	7	UMK Find no. 2187

Metal-detector finds

Carolingian, *Christiana religio* deniers	3	UMK Find nos. 2100, 2165 and 2265
Islamic dirhams (latest coin: 860/61)	7	UMK Find nos. 2114, 2146, 2192, 2193, 2197, 2199, 2206
Byzantium, John Tzimisces (976–96), *miliaresion*	1	UMK Find no. 2275
Anglo-Saxon, Edward the Confessor *Expanding Cross* penny	1	UMK Find no. 2235

Note. For a summary of the Kaupang coin finds, see n. 15.

---

[25]   *Store Norske Leksikon*: Manvik (http://snl.no/Manvik).

[26]   The dirhams: UMK find nos. 2114 and 2206; E. Screen, *SCBI 65: Norwegian Collections. Part I: Anglo-Saxon Coins to 1016* (Oxford, 2013), no. 76.

[27]   UMK find nos. 2273 and 2292.

[28]   Archaeological excavations in 1962, 1964 and 1968: see K. Skaare, 'Norske funn av svenske mynter preget før 1319. Festskrift i anledning Brita Malmers 60-års dag', *Hikuin, 11* (1985), 237–48, (no. 9); Oslo, Coin Cabinet, Museum of Cultural History, University of Oslo (UMK) find archive.

In sum, nearly 300 stray finds of Viking-Age coins have now been recorded from Vestfold (Table 14.1). A major part of these come from the sites of Kaupang (107) and Heimdalsjordet (183) and other places (7). A survey of the stray finds of coins from the Viken area provides evidence for silver dirhams and some Anglo-Saxon and Carolingian coins being used not only in Vestfold, but presumably also all around Viken. It is difficult to estimate the scale and pattern of inflows of silver from abroad, but at Kaupang and Heimdalsjordet they apparently remained available for a sustained period, and had the potential to support both daily transactions and the development of trade institutions and standards that became important beyond these places in Viking society more widely.

This question of how people used silver and money in the dirham period is an intriguing one. The concept of hack-silver was long ago demonstrated by Professor Birgitta Hårdh.[29] It seems clear that a so-called 'hack-silver' economy was prevalent at Kaupang from the mid-ninth century onwards, and if anything the degree of fragmentation seems to be even more significant at Heimdalsjordet than at the Kaupang site. The evidence from Kaupang suggests that fragmentation of coins was the rule rather than the exception among stray finds. Fragmentation seems to have been a common feature at many places in Viking Norway. It is reflected in hoards as far apart as Teisen in Oslo and Rønnvik in the north of Norway (*tpq* 932 and 949 respectively). Both contain a high proportion of dirham fragments, 71 and 97 per cent of the coins respectively.[30] These two hoards, from the 930s and 940s, confirm the hack-silver-economy prevailed not only in the Abbasid period in the ninth century, but also during the Samanid period in the tenth century. They (and others like them) also illustrate that hack-silver was used all over Norway, not only at the marketplace in Kaupang. The finds from Vestfold have in recent years been complemented with finds from other parts of the Viken area, in the vicinity of Vestfold. While the west side of the fjord is rich in spectacular Viking heritage, the Viking-Age finds from the east side are, however, less remarkable. This is true for coins and hoards, and, indeed, also for the saga references. But finds are not completely lacking. Excavations in 2007–8 resulted in finds of seven dirhams from the site Huseby Vestre, in Rygge in Østfold together with three fragments of silver artefacts, a fragment of a copper key, a glass bead, lead weights, a lead ingot, lead waste from metal production and the remains of a house structure, all scattered within a

---

[29]   B. Hårdh, *Wikingerzeitliche Depotfunde aus Südschweden: Katalog und Tafeln*, Acta Archaeologica Lundensia, Series in 4o, 9 (Lund, 1976); Hårdh, 'Hacksilver and ingots'.

[30]   Skaare, *Coins and Coinage*, nos. 130 and 173. The Islamic dirhams found in towns and productive sites in the Viking world are often heavily fragmented, as for example at Hedeby, Schleswig-Holstein, Germany: V. Hilberg, 'Silver economies of the ninth and tenth centuries AD in Hedeby', in *Silver Economies, Monetisation and Society in Scandinavia, AD 800–1100*, ed. J. Graham-Campbell, S.M. Sindbæk and G. Williams (Aarhus, 2011), 203–25, at 219–20.

single field.[31] The dirhams, the hack-silver and the weights provide evidence that trade was conducted at this site in the ninth century with dirhams being used as money.

The finds from Huseby Vestre provide evidence that points in the direction of a settlement or small 'productive site'. The finds of Viking Age artefacts are similar in nature to those that have been discovered at Kaupang, albeit in much smaller quantity – although Kaupang has been the object of extensive archaeological investigations, while the site at Huseby Vestre has as yet only been superficially investigated. Further excavations will probably not produce finds on the same scale as Kaupang, but might very well reveal more about the site.

The six dirham fragments from Huseby Vestre that it has been possible to date were all minted between 784/5 and 813/14.[32] These seven stray finds date to the same period as a major part of the dirham finds from Kaupang. The date of production of the latest coin being 813/14 does, however, suggest that the activity on the site diminished in the ninth century rather than the tenth century, and thus earlier than at both Kaupang and Heimdalsjordet.[33]

Broader analysis of Scandinavian hoards provides overwhelming evidence for the influx of Islamic silver being much more modest in Norway in the ninth and tenth centuries than in Sweden and Denmark. The largest hoard of Islamic coins in Norway contained 77 dirhams: the Grimestad hoard from Stokke in Vestfold, *TPQ* 921/2.[34] In comparison with the many large hoards from elsewhere in Scandinavia this is minute. The striking hoard found at Slemmedal near Grimstad in Aust-Agder (*c.*150 kilometres south along the coast from Kaupang) dated *TPQ* 921 contained nearly three kilos of precious metal, gold (*c.*400 g) and silver (*c.*2,500 g), but only five coins: four Samanid dirhams and one Anglo-Viking penny of the *Sword St Peter* type, dated *c.*921–7.[35] Finds of early Anglo-Saxon coins from the Viking Age are more numerous in Norway than the rest of Scandinavia, although still scarce in comparison to Islamic coins.[36] The Islamic dominance among finds of Norway of this period is less prominent than other

---

[31]   C. Kilger, *Vikingatida dirhamsspor & bosättningsspår. Huseby Vestre, 87/12, Rygge, Østfold, Rapport arkeologisk utgravning*, Oslo (unpublished; Oslo, 2009), 13–14. An area of 50×50 metres was investigated, and seven trenches were opened. The use of metal detectors was instrumental in the search for metal objects. The investigations were conducted under the leadership of Dr Christoph Kilger on behalf of the Museum of Cultural History, 6–9 October 2008.

[32]   Kilger, *Vikingatida dirhamsspor*, 20–21.

[33]   A Carolingian denier of the *Christiana religio* type was found at Kure Nordre in Rygge, in the vicinity of the Huseby Vestre site, UMK find no. 2165.

[34]   Skaare, *Coins and Coinage*, 138 (no. 43).

[35]   K. Skaare, 'Myntene i Slemmedal-skatten', *Viking* 1981, 32–43; see Screen, *SCBI 65*, no. 57 for the Anglo-Scandinavian *Sword St Peter* penny of York (*c.*921–7).

[36]   Screen, 'Norwegian coin finds'.

parts of Scandinavia, for example Sweden where Islamic dirhams (including the Volga-Bulgar issues) make up more than 99 per cent of all coins found.[37]

However, the total of 76 dirhams found as strays at the Kaupang settlement in Vestfold is a high number compared to other similar settlements in Scandinavia.[38] The 182 dirhams from Heimdalsjordet and five additional finds of dirhams from different sites in Vestfold provide strong support for Blackburn's observations; the relation between the limited overall number of finds from Norway in ninth- and tenth-century contexts compared to those from the eleventh century, and the fact that the finds from Kaupang provide excellent and exceptional evidence for intense economic activity.[39]

Other Single-Finds from Viken

In addition to the finds mentioned above, from Kaupang, Heimdalsjordet, Manvik and Rygge, another ten stray finds have been found in Viken: six Abbasid dirhams dated from AD 796/7 to 860/61, three Carolingian deniers in the name of Louis the Pious and the previously mentioned Byzantine *miliaresion* struck for John I Tzimisces (969–76). The finds are distributed unevenly between the east and the west sides of the fjord: four dirhams on the west side, six dirhams and one denier on the east side, while Oslo accounts for one dirham and two deniers. In sum, these finds suggest that dirhams and deniers were distributed into the hinterland, and into the purses and belongings of people living as farmers outside the markets and productive sites.[40]

The chronology of the dirhams found as stray finds harmonises well with that of the dirhams from Kaupang and Rygge, and also the preliminary results of attributions of the dirhams from Heimdalsjordet. In this way these new finds correspond well with Blackburn's model for coin import in which the influx of dirhams to Scandinavia and Norway commenced in the period *c.*825–60 and lasted until the 890s. After this came a shift from Abbasid to Samanid dirhams in the find material. This was governed by political factors in the Caliphate rather than Viking society. In total the Samanid dirhams from Scandinavia

---

[37]   K. Jonsson, 'Sweden in the tenth century: a monetary economy?', in *Silver Economies*, ed. Graham-Campbell, Sindbæk and Williams, 245–57, at 248.

[38]   Blackburn, 'Coin finds', 48–51.

[39]   Ibid., 72.

[40]   In the vicinity of the Oslofjord area some finds further support this picture: an Abbasid dirham find (found *c.*1985) from Svinholt, Porsgrunn in Telemark, some 30 kilometres north of the outer Oslofjord (UMK find no. 2146); a Samanid dirham (found 2012) from Ringsaker in Hedmark, some 50 kilometres north of the inner Oslofjord (UMK find no. 2272); a *Christiana religio* denier (found 2012) struck for Louis the Pious in Quentovic *c.*822/3–840, from Vetten, Jessnes, Ringsaker, Hedmark (UMK find no. 2256).

substantially outnumber those of the Abbasids: in Sweden 38,523 (69 per cent) of dirham finds belong to the Samanids as opposed to 14,201 (25 per cent) for the Abbasids; in Norway the totals are 309 (58 per cent) and 179 (33 per cent) respectively.[41] Even though the inflow of Abbasid dirhams went on for several decades longer in the ninth century than the import of Samanid dirhams in the tenth, the Samanid dirhams were much more numerous. However, this was not the case at Kaupang, where the Abbasid dirhams account for 81.8 per cent, and the ratio might be even higher in favour of Abbasid dirhams.[42] In other words, Vestfold saw outstandingly rich importation and circulation of silver coins in the ninth century, but played a relatively small part in the heyday of the Scandinavian silver economy during the tenth. This should be interpreted in context of both the sites Kaupang and Heimdalsjordet being abandoned before mid-tenth century.

Currency and Kingship in Ninth-Century Vestfold

In many studies the Viking world is described as a homogeneous area when it comes to the use of money. This is in many respects correct, but when we consider the finds of coins from individual regions, towns and productive sites, it becomes evident that there were significant differences.

In the ninth century Vestfold was a kingdom that incorporated Lier and Eiker (in modern Buskerud). The first mention of Vestfold in documentary sources is a reference to the Danish kings Harald and Reginfred raising an army to suppress an uprising in *Westarfolda* in 813, in the north-western part of their kingdom.[43] Dagfinn Skre has suggested the Danish king was the founder of Kaupang around AD 800, and linked this with the adoption of a new continental concept of lordship, one that was territorially defined.[44] Danish influence both

---

[41]   Kilger, 'Kaupang from afar', 204.

[42]   Houshang Khazaei, Museum of Cultural History, University of Oslo, *pers. comm.*

[43]   *Sed ad Westarfoldam cum exercitu profecti, quae regio ultima regni eorum inter septentrionem et occidentem sita ... cuius principes eis subici recusabant* ('but they set out with an army for Vestfold, the furthest region of their realm, situated between north and west ... whose chieftains were refusing to be subjected to them') *Annales regni Francorum* s.a. 813: MGH SS rer. Germ. 6, ed. G.H. Pertz and F. Kurze (Hannover, 1895), 130 and 138.

[44]   D. Skre, 'Towns and markets, kings and central places in south-western Scandinavia *c.* AD 800–950', in *Kaupang in Skiringssal*, ed. D. Skre, Kaupang Excavation Project Publication Series, 1, Norske Oldfunn, 22 (Aarhus, 2007), 445–69, at 461–3. The Yngliga dynasty was based in Vestfold and was recognised in the *Beowulf* and the *Ynglingatal* as part of Snorre Sturlungson's *Heimskringla*. For a discussion of the validity of *Beowulf*'s reference to *Ynglingatal*, see G. Rausing, '*Beowulf, Ynglingatal* and the *Ynglingasaga*. Fiction or history?', *Fornvännen, 80* (1985), 163–78; and D. Skre, 'The dating of *Ynglingatal*', in *Kaupang in Skiringssal*, ed. Skre, 407–29.

politically and economically seems to have been significant at Kaupang. Danish overlordship did not, however, necessarily mean strict Danish control of trade at Kaupang. From a monetary perspective it is clear that Danish kings never took control of the circulation of coins and silver in any way that resembles the situation in Ribe or Hedeby. The one Danish penny struck at Ribe *c.*825–40 and found at Kaupang confirms Danish connections,[45] but cannot in any way be used as evidence for a controlled Danish currency in either Kaupang or Vestfold.

In his study of the conditions for trade at Kaupang, Skre has dismissed Richard Hodges' views on kingship and control of trade.[46] Instead he argues that 'production and trade grow out of natural conditions, social relationships, cultural norms and an economic agency – all of which lay well beyond the range of control of the earliest kings'.[47] Danish influence would, however, mean that Kaupang presumably was easily accessible and much used by Danish merchants. In this way Kaupang and Viken were closer to Europe through Denmark than by other routes. It is often difficult to make direct links between political history and coinage in regions that had not established coinage of their own, but there are certain points to be made in the case of Vestfold and its Danish connections.

Their many Viking expeditions made the *Westarfolda* well known from the eighth century onwards in Anglo-Saxon England, Carolingian Francia, and presumably also in the *Austerweg*. Vikings from Vestfold sailed out from Viken and many returned with valuable experience from foreign lands. With regard to coinage, it is evident that minting was never adopted in Vestfold or anywhere else within the Norwegian realm in the tenth century. And this in spite of Norway becoming one unified kingdom during the reign of king Harald Hårfagre (*c.*872–*c.*930). However fragile their kingdom may have been, there were several strong kings that ruled the country for long periods. In particular there were two important reigns: the first that of Harald Hårfagre, the second of his son Håkon the Good, Adelstainsfostre (*c.*933–961), who spent his entire adolescence in England at King Athelstan's court where he must have had first-hand experience of the English monetary system. Harald was a descent of the Ynglinga dynasty on his father's side. As he rose to power over Norway, the most common view today is that he ruled from western Norway from *c.*872 to his death in *c.*931.[48] How Vestfold was ruled at this time is uncertain, but from a numismatic point of view, evidence for a local coinage or local monetary economy has not been

---

[45]   Blackburn, Jonsson and Rispling, 'Catalogue of the coins', 77 (no. 11).

[46]   R. Hodges, *Dark Age Economics: the Origins of Towns and Trade, AD 600–1000* (London, 1982); for new edition of this book, see R. Hodges, *Dark Age Economics: a New Audit* (London, 2012).

[47]   Skre, 'Post-substantivist towns ', 340.

[48]   P.S. Andersen, *Samlingen av Norge og kristningen av landet 800–1130* (Bergen, Oslo and Tromsø, 1977), 41–7.

detected in any part of the early Norwegian kingdom nor has any central control over the use of money been observed.

In this context the career of Eirik Bloodaxe provides an example of how a Norwegian could adopt minting in his own name at the middle of the tenth century under the right circumstances. After Eirik Haraldsson (son of Harald Hårfagre), better known as Eirik Bloodaxe, was driven out of Norway (having been king there from *c.*933 to *c.*935), he established himself as king of Northumbria in the year 948 and again 952–54.[49] In this position he issued coinage in his own name, ERIC REX, distinguished by the use of a sword as its main symbol across several issues. When Norwegians settled in places with monetary traditions, like Northumbria, they picked up and exploited local traditions of coinage and minting. That King Eirik did not establish a Norwegian coinage is obviously connected to the fact that he never returned to Norway.

To the south, the Danish king Harald Bluetooth (*c.*958–*c.*987) established Christianity as the dominant religion in a unified Denmark. During his long reign he introduced many measures and institutions of state-like character: the ring-forts at Trelleborg on Sjælland, Nonnebakken at Fyn, Fyrkat in central Jutland, Aggersborg alongside the Limfjord in Jutland and a second Trelleborg in Skåne. He also made an effort to establish a national coinage, which seems to have been only a partial success.[50] King Harald also made serious claims on Norway, and he *de facto* ruled Norway for some years in the beginning of the 970s.

This coincided with the import of silver dirhams from the Caliphate coming to a halt some decades before the large-scale influx of silver from Western Europe commenced. In this window that lasted for a few decades from around the 940s to the 980s, silver would have become a scarce commodity, at least in many parts of the Viking world. Empirically this is backed up by an overall trend in the hoard material, with fewer and smaller hoards being recorded within Norway from the decades 950s, 960s and 970s.[51] The Norwegian material is rather limited; a much larger sample of material from Viking-Age Scandinavia provides evidence for this trend, but also for regional variations within southern Scandinavia.[52]

---

[49]   For a general account of Eirik Bloodaxe's history, see G. Williams, *Eirik Blodøks* (Hafrsfjord, 2010). Recently it has been argued that this Northumbrian Eric was not the Norwegian Eirik Bloodaxe, but another largely unknown Eric (C. Downham, 'Eric Bloodaxe – axed? The mystery of the last Scandinavian king of York', *Mediaeval Scandinavia, 14* (2004), 51–77).

[50]   J.C. Moesgaard, *King Harold's Cross Coinage* (forthcoming).

[51]   Skaare, 'Coins and coinage', 22–3, at table 9. The Norwegian material is rather limited; a much larger sample of material from Viking Scandinavia provides evidence for this trend, but also for regional variations within southern Scandinavia: C. von Heijne, *Särpräglat. Vikingatida och tidigmedeltida myntfynd från Danmark, Skåne, Blekinge och Halland (ca 800–1130)*, Stockholm Studies in Archaeology, 31 (Stockholm, 2004), 376–81.

[52]   C. von Heijne, *Särpräglat. Vikingatida och tidigmedeltida myntfynd från Danmark, Skåne, Blekinge och Halland (ca 800–1130)*, Stockholm Studies in Archaeology, 31 (Stockholm, 2004),

When silver became a scarce commodity within the Viking world, it was drawn out of areas on the periphery, like Norway, towards centres of economic and political power such as those associated with king Harald's rule in Denmark. The evidence for a drain of silver from a peripheral north, in this case Vestfold and Viken in Norway southwards to Denmark, is difficult to provide in the form of direct references in documentary sources or conclusive archaeological evidence. If a local coinage had been produced, it would have been possible to follow the distribution of local coins in the finds, and thereby establish a pattern of distribution. If Norway had natural silver resources, these could also have provided an excellent starting point for analyses of metallurgical trace elements in silver objects. But without any sources of this kind one must turn to slightly later material, from the 990s onwards, that can be appraised for a study of silver distribution taking Norway as a starting point.

The first Norwegian coinage struck in the name of the Viking king Olaf Tryggveson (995–1000) provides evidence for the distribution of Norwegian silver.[53] Altogether only five specimens have been found, all of them outside Norway: one has been discovered in each of Gotland, Skåne, Fyn, Pomerania and possibly Uppland.[54] This means that two of the five specimens were hoarded within the Danish realm, and one most probably travelled through Danish territory on its way to Pomerania. This example indicates that silver minted in Norway was being drawn out of the Norwegian realm towards the south. After the 990s minting was not taken up again in Norway until after 1015, when Olaf Haraldsson (later Saint Olaf) gained power (r. 1015–28, d.1030). The coinage minted during Olaf's reign was also limited in scope, with only thirteen pennies recorded. Seven of these have been found outside Norway: three in Gotland and one each in Skåne, Finland, Öland, Poland and Schleswig-Holstein. In comparison only four have been found in Norway, three in Buskerud and one in Møre og Romsdal.[55]

The next coinage produced in Norway was that of Harald Hardrade (1047–66) who returned from the Byzantine Empire and established a national currency.[56] After only a brief period at the start of his reign Harald's coins began to be heavily debased. A large share of his overall coinage was thus debased, but

---

376–81.

[53] For a discussion of the coinage in the name of Olaf Tryggvason, see Brita Malmer, 'Numismatiken, Olof Skötkonung och slaget vid Svolder', *Scandia* 2008, 7–9.

[54] For a summary of the finds of Olaf Tryggveson's pennies, see K. Skaare and J.S. Jensen, 'Olav Tryggvasons mønt', *Nordisk Numismatisk Unions Medlemsblad*, 4 (1993), 50–51.

[55] Skaare, 'Coins and coinage', 191–2.

[56] For general surveys of Harald Hardrade's coinage and monetary regime, see Skaare, 'Coins and coinage', 65–107; S.H. Gullbekk, 'Myntvesenet som kilde til statsutvikling i Norge ca.1050–1080', in *Statsutvikling i Skandinavia i middelalderen*, ed. S. Bagge, M.H. Gelting, F. Hervik, T. Lindkvist and B. Poulsen (Oslo, 2012), 76–100.

his very first issue was struck in good quality silver, and these pennies seem to have been drawn out of Norway in the same way. In total 21 pennies are known which have both a silver content of above 75 per cent and a find provenance: 11 of these have been found in Norway and ten outside Norway, in Gotland (4), Denmark (2), Sweden (2), the Faeroe Islands (1) and Russia (1).[57] It was only after the national currency was heavily debased that the export seems to have been interrupted. The evidence from export of coins from Norway in the period *c.*995 to *c.*1050 suggests that Norwegian coins of sterling quality soon became part of the silver flow and coin circulation within the northern lands. In this period one presumes that silver in other forms was also being drawn from Norway in the direction of Denmark, Skåne, Gotland. There are good reasons to believe that Norwegian coins also travelled towards Anglo-Saxon England even though the evidence for this appears slightly later, from the 1050s onwards.[58] The missing evidence is presumably explained by England's effective monetary regime, which guaranteed that imported coins were for the most part directed to the mints and reissued as local English pennies.[59]

Conclusion

The many single-finds discovered in Vestfold and its surroundings during recent decades provide strong evidence for silver and coins being widely used and playing an important part in society in this part of the Viking world in the ninth, tenth and eleventh centuries. Whatever perspective one takes on numismatics, coinage and monetary history, the Viking Age represents a bridge between Iron Age and medieval Scandinavia, and a decisive period in the early phases of coinage and monetary history.

Vestfold most certainly played an important role in this development within the Norwegian part of the northern world. The existence of two sites with high numbers of Viking stray coin finds less than 20 kilometres from each other opens up new questions in both a Norwegian and a broader northern European context. As single-finds reflect accidental losses from circulation, they indicate

---

57   Skaare, 'Coins and Coinage', 192–206.

58   The Portable Antiquities Scheme Database records finds of two Harald Hardråde pennies: EMC 1997.0029 (Doncaster), 2001.1252 (Gainsborough); and seven pennies of Olaf Kyrre are recorded: EMC 1980.0033 (Thetford), 1983.9937 (Lincoln), 1991.0336 (London), 2007.0263 (Wimbotsham, Norfolk), 2012.0322 (Wordwell, Suffolk), 1987.0168 (Lincoln), 1989.0090 (Raunds, Northamptonshire).

59   For a general discussion of wastage rates and re-export of Anglo-Saxon coins from Scandinavia back to England in the decades around the year 1000, see D.M. Metcalf, 'Some twentieth-century runes. Statistical analysis of the Viking-age hoards and the interpretation of wastage rates', in *Viking-Age coinage in the Northern Lands*, ed. Blackburn and Metcalf, 329–81.

the impressive scale of the Viking-Age silver currency in the area of Vestfold county, and suggest that it was among the wealthiest, not only in the Norwegian realm, but also within the Viking world. Hardly any region within the northern part of Viking-Age Scandinavia has a more striking assemblage of stray coin finds from ninth and tenth century than Vestfold. In this way new finds from recent years have only served to confirm Blackburn's conclusion that the coin finds from Kaupang provide evidence for intense use of coinage, on the same scale as at similar places elsewhere in Scandinavia.[60]

The many new finds from Vestfold and its vicinity will probably be supplemented by more additions in the years to come, especially after further archaeological investigations of the Heimdalsjordet. In this way, the Kaupang material has become even more important, thanks to the comparative perspective supplied by single-finds, especially those from a nearby settlement that may have been of comparable size and function to Kaupang in the ninth and tenth centuries. This development would surely have fascinated Mark. I know he would have appreciated the new evidence, and been truly enthusiastic about the possibilities for new interpretations. With his immense knowledge of Viking-Age numismatics and the Norwegian Viking Age, including its archaeology and history (especially of the Vestfold and the Viken area), he would certainly have produced original insights and interpretations, and been enthusiastic and encouraging to others (such as myself) that shared his interest in these issues.

---

[60] Blackburn, 'The coin-finds', 72.

Chapter 15

Currency Conversion: Coins, Christianity and Norwegian Society in the Late Tenth and Eleventh Centuries

Elina Screen*

Mark Blackburn's many projects and insights included his work on the coins from the Hoen hoard, in the course of which he developed a classification for the different types of loops on coins, and revealed the contrasting practices used in different times and places.[1] His work on the iconography of the Anglo-Scandinavian coinages demonstrated the potential of the religious imagery on the coins to open up the ideas and aims of the Anglo-Scandinavian rulers of York.[2] Ildar Garipzanov has also worked on the Carolingian coins found in Scandinavia, with particular attention to their use in Norway, showing the potential role of coins as status symbols and considering their changing use over the course of the ninth century.[3] Consideration of the iconography and meaning of the coins

*   An earlier version of this chapter was delivered in Bergen at the conference Material Markers of Christian Identity in Northern Europe (c.820–c.1200), 26–28 April 2010, by the kind invitation of Ildar Garipzanov, as part of the project The 'Forging' of Christian Identity in the Northern Periphery (c.820–c.1200). I am very grateful to the members of the audience on that occasion for their acute comments; to Alex Woolf for discussing Viking-age Norway with me; and to Kristin Bornholdt Collins, Svein H. Gullbekk and Rory Naismith for commenting on drafts of the chapter. Finally, without Mark Blackburn's encouragement, I would never have entered numismatics; my work in this field is owed entirely to him.

[1]   M.A.S. Blackburn, 'The loops as a guide to how and when the coins were acquired', in The Hoen Hoard. A Viking Gold Treasure of the Ninth Century, ed. S.H. Fuglesang and D. Wilson, Acta ad archaeologiam et artium historiam pertinentia, 14 and Norske Oldfunn, 20 (Rome and Oslo, 2006), 181–99.

[2]   M.A.S. Blackburn, 'Crosses and conversion: the iconography of the coinage of Viking York ca.900', in Cross and Culture in Anglo-Saxon England: Studies in Honor of George Hardin Brown, ed. K.L. Jolly, C.E. Karkov and S.L. Keefer, Medieval European Studies, IX (Morgantown, WV, 2007), 172–200 (VCCBI, 308–36).

[3]   Ildar H. Garipzanov, 'Carolingian Coins in Early Viking Age Scandinavia (c.754–c.900): Chronological Distribution and Regional Patterns', NNÅ, 2003–5, 65–92; Ildar H. Garipzanov, 'Carolingian Coins in Ninth-Century Scandinavia: a Norwegian Perspective', Viking and Medieval Scandinavia, 1 (2005), 43–71.

to their users in Norway thus has hitherto focused on the earlier part of the Viking Age, prior to the main import of Western coins, which started in around 980 and ended around 1050, with imports peaking in the period *c.*1010–30.[4] In 980–1050, Norway was undergoing an important period of change, with major political, economic and religious developments underway. Compared with the period after 1050, when the activities of the kings of Norway, the emergence of a controlled royal coinage and the process of Christianisation become more visible, this period is a shadowy time.[5] Recovering the lived experience of Norwegians in this time of change is therefore a challenge, given the limited available evidence. Extending the analysis of coins used as ornaments to the period *c.*980–1050, therefore, focusing particularly on the Anglo-Saxon coins, may add to our understanding of this important time of change in Norway.

Coins in Viking-Age Norway underwent various forms of secondary treatment, including the addition of graffiti, fragmentation, and testing through edge-nicking, pecking and bending, in addition to their occasional use as ornaments. There are many possible reasons to pierce a coin, from acting as a symbol of status or wealth, to use as amulets or religious symbols, to simply finding it attractive, to some combination of these. While some coins were transformed into elaborate pendants or made into brooches, in the Viking Age most seem to have been looped or pierced to be worn as necklaces either alone or as part of a larger assemblage. But to be able to interpret the Norwegian evidence, first we must consider how Anglo-Saxon coins were used in their English context before their arrival in Norway.

Coins as Ornaments in Anglo-Saxon England

The single finds recorded in the Early Medieval Corpus and by the Portable Antiquities Scheme provide extensive data for coin use in England, while Gareth Williams has studied the later eleventh-century phenomenon of coin brooches,

---

[4]   Kolbjørn Skaare, *Coins and Coinage in Viking-Age Norway. The Establishment of a National Coinage in Norway in the XI Century, with a Survey of the Preceding Currency History* (Oslo, Bergen and Tromsø, 1976), 33–57, the essential overview of the period, includes some important observations on coin use and iconography, but focuses on the coin history.

[5]   For the political history, see Claus Krag, 'The early unification of Norway', in *The Cambridge History of Scandinavia, vol. 1: Prehistory to 1520*, ed. K. Helle (Cambridge, 2003), 184–201; on kingship and Christianisation in general, see S. Bagge and S. Walaker Nordeide, 'The kingdom of Norway', in *Christianization and the Rise of Christian Monarchy. Scandinavia, Central Europe and the Rus' c. 900–1200*, ed. N. Berend, (Cambridge, 2007), 121–66; Sæbjørg Walaker Nordeide, *The Viking Age as a Period of Religious Transformation. The Christianization of Norway from AD 560–1150/1200*. For economic developments, see Svein H. Gullbekk, *Pengevesenets fremvekst og fall i Norge i middelalderen* (Copenhagen, 2009), 29–65.

registering a group of 21 related brooches (Table 15.1).[6] The 72 pierced or looped coins in the EMC database form 0.8 per cent of the 8,983 coins recorded from *c*.400–1100. Including the 23 finds from other sources would raise the percentage slightly to approximately 1.1 per cent of total finds; however, since it has not been possible for me to review all the PAS data, the following calculations use the EMC data alone, to offer a secure but potentially under-reported total.

Table 15.1   Single-finds of coin ornaments from England, by data source.

	Pre–750	750–900	900–73	973–1050	1050–1100	Total
EMC	26	12 [(a)]	7 [(b)]	6 [(c)]	21	72
PAS	8	2	0 [(d)]	0	2	12
Williams 2001, 2006					11	11
TOTAL	34	14	7	6	34	95

Notes: (a) Including two Scottish finds of centrally pierced stycas (EMC 1006.0022 and 1006.0043); (b) A Burgred (852–74) *Lunettes* penny converted into a coin weight (EMC 1998.0019) has been omitted; (c) Including a coin of Æthelred II, *Crux* type, pierced twice, found in the Brough of Birsay, Orkney (EMC 2001.1193). A seventh coin of Otto III (983–1002), *Sancta Colonia* type (EMC 1986.0127), has been omitted as the two piercings appear to be modern plough damage; (d) One coin of this period found abroad appears on the PAS database and has been omitted.

---

[6]   See <www.fitzmuseum.cam.ac.uk/emc>, consulted 27 May 2013; <www.finds.org.uk>, consulted 27 May 2013; G. Williams, 'Coin brooches of Edward the Confessor and William I', *BNJ*, 71 (2001), 60–70; G. Williams, 'More Late Anglo-Saxon and Norman Coin Jewellery', *BNJ*, 76 (2006), 337–9. Williams also notes a brooch made from an imitation of Edward the Confessor's *Expanding Cross* type, 'Lincoln' mint, from the London Vintry site ('Coin brooches', 66). 11 of these 22 coin brooches (including the Vintry find) do not seem to appear on the EMC or PAS databases. The PAS coins have been cross-checked against the EMC database, though some accidental duplication for the pre-750 material in particular cannot be ruled out. Some additional coin brooches have been found since 2006 (G. Williams, *pers. comm.*).

Table 15.2   Percentage of pierced coins in the EMC, by period.

	Pierced coins (EMC)	Total finds (EMC)	%
Up to 680	26	508	5.1
791–900	12	2633	0.5
901–73	7	591	1.0
973–1050	6	1242	0.5
1050–1100	21	1174	1.8

Note: Given the very high numbers of *sceattas* from the period *c.*680–720 especially, and that no pierced coins struck in the period *c.*680 to 790 are known, the figures have been calculated using these narrower date ranges. The totals per period given here therefore do not equate to the total number of EMC finds.

Over the period, the numbers of pierced coins fall from a relatively high proportion of coins used as ornaments in the post-Roman and Christianisation period, to a low level thereafter, with a rise in the second half of the eleventh century. Plotting the methods of suspension, looped coins are no longer attested in the eighth century (Table 15.3).[7] Indeed, no pierced coins at all are known from *c.*680–750, the period of the so-called *sceattas*.[8] The ninth century saw a small number of coins pierced centrally (a method not met in Norway), and from the tenth century, a clear preference for mounting coins as brooches emerges. Gareth Williams has published a group of 21 coin brooches, characterised by a tendency to gild the coin, and to display the cross face of the coin. The style was introduced during or shortly after the inception of the *Expanding Cross* type (*c.*1050–52), and – given the display of the cross face – he interprets the brooches as 'some form of religious badge'.[9] These brooches form 68 per cent of all known coin ornaments from the period 1050–1100. With the spread of these brooches, the use of coins as ornaments increased in the later eleventh century in England.

The English finds indicate that any loops on coins from the Viking Age are likely to have been added within Scandinavia or the Baltic, as this was no longer a contemporary practice within Anglo-Saxon England. We can also assume that pierced coins struck between 973 and 1042 were pierced in Scandinavia, or within Scandinavian-influenced contexts, rather than in England.[10] The English

---

7   Noted by Blackburn, 'Loops', 190.

8   Tony Abramson, James Booth and Keith Chapman, *pers. comm.* James Booth kindly drew my attention to a pair of *sceattas* of Series B soldered together, with a fragment of a third coin attached, for an uncertain but possibly decorative purpose.

9   Williams, 'More Late Anglo-Saxon and Norman Coin Jewellery', 338, 339.

10   The two pierced coins from 973–1050 are a *Crux* penny of Æthelred II, from the Scandinavian-influenced context of the Brough of Birsay (EMC 2001.1193), and a *Short Cross*

evidence nevertheless suggests that even in a controlled coin economy and in times when coins were widely available, we may expect to find some coins used as ornaments for their specific iconographic properties. Contemporary trends such as the prevalence of the religious badges or brooches in England after 1050 could clearly influence the pattern too.

Table 15.3   Secondary treatment of coins found in Anglo-Saxon England, by period and type (including EMC, PAS and Williams's data).

	Pre–750	750–900	900–73	973–1050	1050–1100
Border or frame and loop	3				
Looped	13				
Pierced	14	9	5	2	8
Pierced and looped or trace of loop	1				
Traces of loop	1				
Central piercing		4			
Brooch		1	2	3	23
Mounted or traces of mount	2			1	3
TOTAL	34	14	7	6	34

The Norwegian Evidence

Before focusing on the Anglo-Saxon coins found in Norway from the 980s to 1050s, it is important to establish the incidence of piercing in the body of Norwegian finds overall, and to place the practice in the wider context of coin use in Norway. Kolbjørn Skaare's exemplary catalogue of the Viking-Age Norwegian finds included details of the piercing of coins whenever the information was available, allowing the incidence of piercing to be analysed by period and coin type. Skaare's complete list of finds included 187 entries (up to 1100), for which the available information varies from the excellent and fully published, to ambiguous and uncertain references to finds discovered

---

coin of Edward the Confessor (*c*.1048–50, EMC 1998.0185), a harbinger of the rising trend to pierce and use coins as ornaments in the middle of the eleventh century.

in the eighteenth and nineteenth centuries.[11] Forty-eight finds for which the information is incomplete have been omitted.[12] I have based this analysis on the 139 finds listed by Skaare for which there is better information, and a further nine selected finds made since 1976 (those for which I have been able to check the secondary treatment of all the material), bringing the total of finds analysed to 148.[13] The finds include hoards, stray finds and grave finds (both categories including a number of older finds, for which there are incomplete data), and excavation finds (including the finds from Kaupang, as well as Kjøpmannsgate in Trondheim and the smaller sites Hjelle and Vesle Hjerkinn).

There are also church finds: in Norway as elsewhere in Scandinavia, the excavation or renovation of medieval churches (including Mære, Ringebu, Lom and Trondheim, among others) has led to the recovery of very large accumulations of coins from beneath the floors. Svein Harald Gullbekk has examined the 9,639 coins minted before 1319 in the church finds as part of his study of the medieval Norwegian coin economy.[14] The coins in the church finds are overwhelmingly Norwegian; only 10 foreign coins from before 1050 are known. All were deposited after 1050, when the Norwegian royal coinage made rapid headway, and foreign coins were no longer current, though it is difficult to assess when precisely after 1050 these coins were deposited.[15]

Tables 15.4–15.7 present the pierced and looped coins in the 148 Norwegian finds, first giving the overall totals by period, and then broken down by find context. The quality of the data available for the 148 finds varies, and therefore data from the less well-attested finds have not been included in every table.[16]

---

[11]   Skaare, *Coins and Coinage*, 127–76 ('I. A catalogue of Norwegian finds of coins and some related objects earlier than *c*.1100'), nos. 1–12a, 13–90a, 91–148a, 149–84, hereafter cited as Skaare nos. 1–184.

[12]   Skaare nos. 2, 14, 32, 75, 97, 101, 152 (dispersed Roman coin finds); 41, 53, 85–6, 158, 164, 181, 183 (750–900); 7, 17, 29, 51, 57, 89, 138, 149, 174 (probably before 980); 9, 21, 44, 71, 99, 124, 156, 167 (probably after 980); 15, 22, 25–6, 28, 46, 52, 54, 60, 80, 98, 136, 155, 166, 168, 170, 182 (after 980). Two additional probable finds mentioned on coin tickets only, and identified in the preparation of the list of finds for Elina Screen, *SCBI 65: Norwegian Collections. Part I. Anglo-Saxon Coins to 1016* (Oxford, 2013) (hereafter *SCBI 65*), 12–68, nos. 63 and 74, have also been omitted. The later coins appear in E. Screen, *SCBI 66: Norwegian Collections. Part II. Anglo-Saxon and later British Coins, 1016–1279* (Oxford, 2014) (hereafter *SCBI 66*).

[13]   *SCBI 65*, nos. 3 (Slemmedal); 55 (Hjelle); 61 (Kvamme); 65 (Vesle Hjerkinn), 68 (nr Molde); 69 (nr Skrudshuset, Trondheim), 75 (Domkirkeodden, Hamar), 76 (Manvik), 77 (Nedre Holter). For the recent significant material discovered in Viken, which it has not been possible to incorporate here, see Gullbekk, Chapter 14, this volume.

[14]   Gullbekk, *Pengevesenets fremvekst og fall*, 50–56, at 55.

[15]   Ibid., 55. Gullbekk's analysis of the hoards, ibid., 44–7, indicates that hoards deposited after 1067 effectively contained only Norwegian coins.

[16]   In particular, coins with less certain find provenances have been excluded from the counts of grave finds and stray finds, to give secure (if under-reported) figures.

Table 15.4   Pierced and looped coins in Norwegian finds, by period.

	No. of finds	No. of coins	No. pierced/ looped	% pierced
Roman coins [a]	28	30	16	53.3%
750–900 [b]	30	175 (74 excl. Kaupang)	43 (40 excl. Kaupang)	24.6% (54.1% excl. Kaupang)
900–60 [c]	19	290	25	8.6%
980–1050 [d]	35	5733	79	1.4%
1050–1100 [e]	36	4347	29	0.7%
Incomplete data (all periods)	48	230 + x	x	–

Notes: (a) Skaare nos. 1, 8, 11, 13, 18, 37, 40, 55, 59, 63, 73–4, 76, 81, 100, 105, 107–8, 112, 114, 116, 120–21, 130–32, 154, 161.

(b) Skaare nos. 5, 12a, 30, 33, 45, 47–8, 50, 64, 66–7, 72, 84, 90a, 93, 96, 103, 106, 111, 113, 118, 122, 125, 133, 142, 153, 160, 162, 165 and *SCBI 65*, no. 55 (Hjelle).

(c) Skaare nos. 4, 12, 43, 61–2, 77, 109, 126, 140, 144–5, 150–51, 169, 171, 173, 174, 184 and *SCBI 65*, no. 3 (Slemmedal)

(d) Skaare nos. 3, 6, 10, 20, 24, 34, 36, 39, 42, 56, 65, 68, 78–9, 82, 88, 91, 95, 110, 117, 123, 127, 128 (first, earlier coin), 134–5, 137, 141, 146–7, 157, 159, 179 and *SCBI 65*, nos. 61 (Kvamme); 68 (nr Molde); 69 (nr Skrudhuset, Trondheim).

(e) Skaare nos. 16, 19, 23, 27, 31, 35, 38, 49, 58, 69–70, 83, 87, 90, 92, 94, 102, 104, 115, 119, 128 (second, later coin), 129, 139, 143, 148–8a, 163, 172, 176–8, 180 and *SCBI 65*, nos. 65 (Vesle Hjerkinn; see also Table 15.6, (c)), 75 (Domkirkeodden, Hamar), 76 (Manvik), 77 (Nedre Holter). The two grave finds from Borgund are entered individually under 980–1050 and 1050–1100, giving a total of 188 here.

Table 15.5   Proportion of pierced coins in Norwegian grave finds.

	No. of grave finds	Total coins in graves	No. of pierced coins	%
Roman coins	19	21	15	71
750–900	13	28	12	43
900–60	2	2	0	0
980–1050	4	6	2	33
1050–1100	2	6	0	0
Incomplete data (all periods)	9	46+x	x	–

Table 15.6   Proportion of pierced coins in stray finds and excavation finds (in italics).

	Stray finds	Total coins	No. pierced	%
Roman coins	9	9	1	11.1%
750–900	9	9	3	33%
Kaupang[a]		*101*	*3*	*3.0%*
Hjelle[b]		*1*	*0*	*0%*
900–60	6	6	0	0
980–1050	7	7	0	0
1050–1100	11	15	1	6.6%
Vesle Hjerkinn[c]		*19*	*1*	*5.3%*
Kjøpmannsgate[d]		*16*	*0*	*0%*
Incomplete data (750–1100)	17	19	x	–

Notes: (a) Skaare no. 48; for a full catalogue of the coins, see G. Rispling, M.A.S. Blackburn and K. Jonsson, 'The coin finds from Kaupang', in *The Means of Exchange: Dealing with Silver in the Viking Age*, ed. D. Skre, Kaupang Excavation Project Publication Series, 2, Norske Oldfunn, 23 (Aarhus and Oslo, 2008), 75–93.

(b) SCBI 65, find no. 55.

(c) See K. Skaare, 'Myntfunnene fra Vesle Hjerkinn', in *Vesle Hjerkinn – Kongens gård og sælehus*, ed. B. Weber et al., Norske Oldfunn, 21 (Oslo, 2007), 71–5.

(d) Skaare no. 148a; see the updated analysis by Jon Anders Risvaag and Axel Christophersen, 'Early medieval coinage and urban development: a Norwegian experience', in *Land, Sea and Home*, ed. J. Hines, A. Lane and M. Redknap, The Society for Medieval Archaeology Monograph, 20 (Leeds, 2004), 75–91. I have been unable to consult the full catalogue in K. Skaare, *Mynt*, Fortiden i Trondheim Bygrunn: Folkebibliotekstomten. Meddelelser, 22 (Trondheim, 1989).

Table 15.7 Proportion of pierced coins in the hoards.

	No. of hoards	Total coins in hoards	No. of pierced coins	%
750–900	6	36	25	69.4
900–60	11	282	25	8.9
980–1050	21	5706	77	1.4
1050–1100	15	4184 (2253 Gresli)	27 (2 Gresli)	0.7 (1.3% excl. Gresli)
Incomplete data (750–900)	14	153+x	x	–

Note: There are no hoards of Roman coins, if two uncertain finds (Skaare nos. 32 and 152) are excluded.

Coins as Ornaments before 900

The earliest coins found in Norway are Roman coins, struck from Roman Republican times to the early fifth century. Their date of deposition is particularly hard to establish, but many of these coins seem to have been in circulation for a long time: for example, a Roman denarius struck AD 119–22 was found in a burial mound in Aust-Agder dated to *c.*400, and the Hoen hoard, from the later ninth century, included a fourth-century coin.[17] The high proportion of looped Roman coins (just over half, rising to 71 per cent of the grave finds) suggests the importance of coins as ornaments and precious items in early Iron-Age Norway (Tables 15.1–15.2). For instance, as Kolbjørn Skaare noted, all but one of the securely attested gold *solidi*, *solidus* multiples and imitations of Roman gold coins were looped, or framed and looped, revealing that they were used and valued as jewellery.[18] A similar pattern continues in the finds from the early Viking Age (750–900). The high proportion of pierced and looped coins in all types of find – stray finds, grave finds and hoards – indicates that coins continued to be prized principally as ornaments, and potentially 'markers of social status', as Ildar Garipzanov has suggested for the Carolingian coin finds.[19] The trading place at Kaupang, where coins were circulating as means of exchange, is an exception to this picture: here only three of the 101 coins were pierced.[20]

Table 15.8 points to interesting changes in the numbers of looped coins present relative to pierced coins. Whereas the Roman coins were almost all equipped with frames or borders and loops, in the early Viking Age there was a preference for loops only: all the carefully selected coins in the Hoen hoard are looped, for example. In his analysis of the coins from the Hoen hoard, Mark Blackburn examined the different loops used to suspend the coins. He established that the types of loop used changed over time, such as the preference for Blackburn's Type III, the 'sandwiched' loop, in the Viking Age.[21] Analysing the types of loop on all the Norwegian finds is beyond the scope of this chapter. However, a striking feature emerging from the data is that increasing numbers of coins in the early Viking Age are pierced, without surviving loops: a similar trend

---

[17]   Skaare nos. 73, near Lyngdal church, Vest Agder, and 33, Hoen, Buskerud; see Skaare, *Coins and Coinage*, 33–9, on the Roman coins in general.

[18]   Skaare, *Coins and Coinage*, 34–6.

[19]   Garipzanov, 'Carolingian coins in early Viking-age Scandinavia', 81.

[20]   Rispling, Blackburn and Jonsson, 'Coin finds from Kaupang', nos. 11, 44 and 63. A fourth coin (no. 37) had a narrow slot, perhaps to allow an additional strip of silver to be added, to increase its weight. On coin use in Kaupang and Viken, see Gullbekk (Chapter 14, this volume); J.K. Øhre Askjem, 'The Viking-Age silver hoards from eastern Norway', in *Silver Economies, Monetisation and Society in Scandinavia AD 800–1100*, ed. J. Graham-Campbell, S.M. Sindbæk and G. Williams (Aarhus, 2011), 173–84, at 180–82.

[21]   Blackburn, 'Loops', 184.

to that already seen in the English data at an earlier date. It is hard to interpret the data, which might either indicate that more coins in the early Viking Age were suspended using simple wire loops (Blackburn's Type VI), or merely that many riveted loops were lost or removed over time as the coins circulated.[22]

Breaking down the number of coins used as ornaments by type, the less common coin types are more often pierced or looped than the Islamic dirhams, which were the most widely available coins at this time (Table 15.9). As the Roman coin finds reveal, imported coins had long been seen as valuable and high-status objects, which were therefore appropriate for inclusion in furnished burials. Roman coins also strongly influenced Scandinavian gold bracteates.[23] Ildar Garipzanov has argued that as increased numbers of Carolingian coins found their way to Scandinavia, they lost their scarcity value and thus their potential to act as status symbols.[24] The choice of a simpler and less costly method of suspending coins might reflect this gradual increase in the availability of coins in the course of the ninth century. Other factors besides scarcity or prestige seem to have played a part in determining how coins were treated, however. The relatively rare Byzantine, Roman, Frankish and Anglo-Saxon coins found at Kaupang were all unpierced, reflecting a different and possibly more exchange-focused use of the coins.[25] Not all coins in the grave finds were suspended, suggesting that sometimes these coins too had significance as means of exchange (also reflected in the regular inclusion of weights and balances in the graves), as well as ornaments conveying wealth and status.[26] The clustering of means of exchange in a handful of the areas examined by Nordeide (for example Rauma, Møre og Romsdal, and Valle and Grimstad, Aust-Agder), with the Viken evidence, suggests regional factors may also have come into play.[27]

The finds of coins from *c.*750–900, therefore, perhaps hint that the preferred method of suspension was changing, possibly in response to the greater availability of coins. The apparent loss or removal of loops thus might

---

[22]   Ibid., 188. For surviving wire loops from the early eleventh century, see e.g. I. Leimus and A. Molvõgin, *SCBI 51: Estonian Collections. Anglo-Saxon, Anglo-Norman and later British Coins* (Oxford, 2001), 11, Figure 1: the Paunküla hoard, *t.p.q. c.*1009, includes a necklace from which six coins are suspended, four with riveted loops and two with wire loops.

[23]   Especially bracteates types A and C, and M, the imitations of imperial multiples: see *Die Goldbrakteaten der Völkerwanderungszeit*, ed. K. Hauck et al., Münstersche Mittelalter-Schriften, 24, 3 vols in 7 parts (Munich, 1985), for an illustrated catalogue.

[24]   Garipzanov, 'Carolingian Coins in Early Viking Age Scandinavia'; Garipzanov, 'Carolingian Coins in Ninth-Century Scandinavia'.

[25]   See Gullbekk, Chapter 14, this volume.

[26]   E.g. Nordeide, *Viking Age as a Period of Religious Transformation*, groups coins with other means of exchange such as balances, weights and purses, in her catalogue of grave finds from her 21 case-study municipalities: 327–63, at 330.

[27]   Ibid., 246–7.

also indicate that some of these coins were returning from use as ornaments to circulation in a more monetary context. Overall, however, the pierced coins of the earlier Viking Age largely reflect the continuity of earlier traditions of coin use as ornaments, and as stores of value.

Table 15.8   Methods of suspension of the Norwegian pierced coins.

	Roman	750–900	900–60	980–1050	1050–1100	Total
frame or border and looped	11	0	0	0	0	11
looped	2	23	2	1	2	30
pierced	1	15	23	77	26	142
loop or traces of loop and pierced	1	3	0	0	0	4
traces of loop	0	2	0	1	1	4
TOTAL	**15**	**43**	**25**	**79**	**29**	**191**

Table 15.9   Pierced coins deposited in finds from the four periods, by coin type.

		*c.*750–900		*c.*900–60		*c.*980–1050		*c.* 1050–1100	
		No.	Pierced	No.	Pierced	No.	Pierced	No.	Pierced
Dirhams	Coins	132	21	252	25	62	9	3	1
	% pierced		*15.9%*		*10.1%*		*14.5%*		*33%*
Byzantine and Roman	Coins	8	4	14	0	6	2	1	0
	% pierced		*50%*		*0%*		*33%*		*0%*
Frankish	Coins	22*	13	0	0	6	0	0	0
	% pierced		*59.1%*		*0%*		*0%*		*0%*
Anglo-Saxon	Coins	12	3	8	0	3012	49	231	10
	% pierced		*25%*		*0%*		*1.6%*		*4.3%*
German	Coins	0	0	15	0	2281	16	941	13
	% pierced		*0%*		*0%*		*0. 7%*		*1.4%*
Scandinavian	Coins	5	2	0	0	7	0	0	0
	% pierced		*40%*		*0%*		*0%*		*0%*

		c.750–900		c.900–60		c.980–1050		c. 1050–1100	
		No.	Pierced	No.	Pierced	No.	Pierced	No.	Pierced
Anglo-Scandina-vian	Coins	0	0	0	0	143	3	13	0
	% pierced		*0%*		*0%*		*2.1%*		*0%*
Denmark	Coins	0	0	0	0	97	0	205	2
	% pierced		*0%*		*0%*		*0%*		*1.0%*
Sweden	Coins	0	0	0	0	23	0	0	0
	% pierced		*0%*		*0%*		*0%*		*0%*
Norway	Coins	0	0	0	0	9	0	2936	3
	% pierced		*0%*		*0%*		*0%*		*0.1%*
Other (inc. Hiberno-Scandina-vian)	Coins	0	0	0	0	51	0	5	0
	% pierced		*0%*		*0%*		*0%*		*0%*
Uncertain type and condition	Coins	0		0	0	32		12	

Note: * Including 1 Merovingian *tremissis* and 3 imitative Frankish *solidi*.

Pierced Coins in the Emerging Coin Economy, 900–1100

After 900, more Islamic dirhams became available in Norway with the import of Samanid coins from the east, and dominate the finds from the period (252, or 87 per cent of the 290 coins). Overall, only 9 per cent of the coins in finds from *c.*900–960 are pierced, all of them dirhams (Table 15.9). Just two Samanid dirhams retain loops, again hinting that other methods of suspension were preferred, or that coins may have lost their loops in circulation. It is striking that none of the Byzantine and Western coins (including 14 Byzantine *solidi* in the Nedre Strømshaug hoard)[28] were pierced or looped, as one might expect given their relative scarcity, and therefore their potential prestige. The pierced dirhams from this period appear in hoards, particularly the two larger hoards of Grimestad (Vestfold) and Holtan (Sør-Trøndelag).[29] The absence of pierced coins from the few stray finds recorded from the period after *c.*900 suggests that pierced coins were not apparently circulating in transactions. The two certain grave finds from the period also included unpierced coins.[30] The declining

---

28   Skaare no. 4; the *solidi* are dated 921/7–945/59.
29   Skaare nos. 43 and 140.
30   Skaare nos. 77 (Kjørmo, Rogaland), 173 (Børøya, Nordland).

incidence of piercing and looping seems to support other evidence indicating that this period was important in the development of the monetary use of coin, with the fragmented coins necessary for use in smaller transactions in a bullion economy (first seen at Kaupang and now Heimdalsjordet) becoming more common in the hoards at this time.[31]

Table 15.10   Proportions of coins and non-numismatic silver in Norwegian hoards, by weight.

	% coin	% other silver
Before 900	2	98
900–50	9	91
950–1000	29	71
1000–50	81	19
1050–1100	84	16

Note: after Gullbekk, *Pengevesenets fremvekst og fall* (see n. 5), 32.

As Svein H. Gullbekk has demonstrated, the period around the year 1000 saw a significant shift in the composition of hoards, as the relative proportion of non-numismatic silver declined in relation to the coins (Table 15.10).[32] Coins were becoming more readily available, and people's preference for hoarding coined silver as opposed to other forms of silver was increasing.[33] The downward trend in coin piercing continues in the much larger body of coins deposited in 980–1050, where only 1.4 per cent (79 coins of 5,733) are pierced. Of the 79, 77 are pierced and only two looped: a German coin of Otto II, and an Islamic dirham bearing traces of a loop, from the Jøsen and Årstad hoards respectively. While the two pierced Byzantine coins in the Tråen and Slethei hoards had clearly lingered long in circulation, and some of the dirhams probably also formed part of an older stock of pierced coins, the dates of striking of the coins and the deposition dates of the hoards reveal that most of the coins must have been pierced within the period (see Table 15.12 for the age structure of the Anglo-Saxon pierced coins). Strikingly, Anglo-Saxon coins and imitations of Anglo-Saxon types were two or three times more likely to be pierced than

---

[31]   S.H. Gullbekk, 'Norway: commodity money, silver and coins', in *Silver Economies, Monetisation and Society*, ed. Graham-Campbell, Sindbæk and Williams, 93–111, at 98–9; finds containing fragmented dirhams include Teisen (Oslo) and Rønnvik (Nordland), Skaare nos. 12 and 171. See also Gullbekk, Chapter 14, this volume, on the Heimdalsjordet finds.

[32]   Gullbekk, *Pengevesenets fremvekst og fall*, 32, Diagram 1.

[33]   Ibid., 32; Askjem, 'Viking-age silver hoards', 180.

German coins (Table 15.9).[34] This might reflect their generally superior striking and clearly defined types.

Attempting to interpret the piercing data from 980–1050 hoard by hoard, or region by region, is more complicated, however. As earlier analysis of pecking in the Norwegian hoards also revealed, the incidence of piercing does not follow any easily discernible patterns.[35] The Tråen hoard, dominated by German coins, stands out for its high incidence of piercing (8 coins out of 128), but other hoards deposited in the period 990–1000 such as Fuglevik include no pierced coins. The unusually high proportion of Anglo-Saxon coins in the Fuglevik hoard suggests that this had a different composition history and may have been deposited soon after the arrival of the coins in Norway.[36] While it is unsurprising that the two hoards with the longest chronological spread of Anglo-Saxon coin types, Brøholt and Foldøy (*t.p.q.* 1050 and 1051), have relatively high numbers of pierced coins (nine and ten respectively), other hoards which share very similar chronological distributions differ markedly in the numbers of pierced coins they contain: for example, the Årstad hoard (*c.*1,849 coins, *t.p.q. c.*1029) has 13 pierced coins compared with 29 in the Dronningensgate 10 hoard from Trondheim, which is half its size (*c.*964 coins, *t.p.q. c.*1035).[37] The Jøsen and Slethei hoards (both from Rogaland, with a similar age structure, and *t.p.q.* of *c.*1014 and *c.*1018 respectively), contain no pierced coins and three pierced coins respectively, with the smaller hoard, Jøsen, again containing more pierced coins.[38] Thus no obvious chronological or geographical explanation stands out from the evidence; the pool of coins available to those who assembled hoards, and potentially also individual preferences and the purposes behind hoards, may have played a part.

At first sight, the trend to use coins as ornaments further declined in the period after 1050, which saw the introduction of a large and controlled Norwegian currency for the first time (Tables 15.4–15.7). Only 0.7 per cent of 4,347 coins are pierced. However, the picture is perhaps distorted by the very large Gresli hoard, and if this is omitted, the other hoards and stray finds suggest that the use of coin ornaments continued at similar levels to the preceding period, or possibly even increased slightly. Two out of the total of 50 single-finds and excavation finds are pierced (4 per cent), as are 1.3 per cent of coins in the other hoards (see Tables 15.6–15.7). The small number of looped coins that

---

[34]   See below, pp. 364–6, on variation in the piercing of different Anglo-Saxon coin types.

[35]   S.H. Gullbekk, 'Some aspects of coin import to Norway and coin circulation in the late Viking Age', *NNÅ, 1991*, 63–87.

[36]   Skaare nos. 3 (Fuglevik) and 36 (Tråen). On Fuglevik, see Gullbekk, 'Some aspects of coin import', 70–71.

[37]   Skaare nos. 35 (Brøholt, Buskerud), 90 (Foldøy, Rogaland), 95 (Årstad, Rogaland) and 147 (Dronningensgate 10, Trondheim).

[38]   Skaare nos. 82 (Slethei) and 91 (Jøsen).

appear in this period, all of contemporary types, hint that the manufacture of coin ornaments remained a small-scale trend in the context of the increasingly monetised economy, a trend also seen in England.[39] The 47 coins from the church finds struck before 1100 include one pierced coin (2.1 per cent). Rather than reflecting contemporary practice, the church finds (which were deposited in the period after 1050) may give a better indication of the numbers of pierced coins in the residual stock of foreign coins surviving after 1050.

Overall, the Norwegian finds and English single-find data reveal that the incidence of piercing followed a similar chronological trajectory in both countries. Coins were less likely to be turned into ornaments at times when they were widely available. The comparative data suggests we might tentatively expect approximately 1 per cent of recovered finds in such periods to have been used as ornaments.

Chronological Distribution of Pierced Anglo-Saxon Coins in Norway, *c*.980–1050

The recent completion of *SCBI* 65 and 66 allows the Anglo-Saxon coins and the chronological distribution of the pierced coins to be assessed more closely. The Norwegian collections include 74 pierced Anglo-Saxon coins out of a total of 3,913 coins and 317 fragments under 0.20 g (Table 15.11).[40] Of the 74, eight coins derive from hoards deposited outside Norway, and a further nine coins now in the Oslo and Bergen collections probably or possibly derive from Norwegian finds, but have no detailed provenance information.[41] A further three coins belong to the period before 973. This analysis has been based on the 54 coins with secure find provenances, struck *c*.973–1066. The face from which the coins were pierced has not been assessed, and holed coins have not been considered, because of the difficulty in establishing whether these were pierced by accident or design.

---

[39]   Skaare no. 163 (Mære church: a Norwegian penny, *c*.1055/65–65/80); *SCBI 65* nos. 65 (Vesle Hjerkinn: Denmark, Sven Estrithsen, 1047–74) and 76 (Manvik: Anglo-Saxon, Edward the Confessor *Expanding Cross* (*c*.1050–2); the rivet indicates the coin was originally mounted or looped).

[40]   *SCBI 66* includes appendices listing 449 further fragments, mainly under 0.10 g, and tabulates the weights of 901 minute fragments.

[41]   Probably: *SCBI 65*, cat. nos. 225, 389, 690 (acquired before 1875); *SCBI 66*, 2938 (ex Schive collection); possibly: *SCBI 65*, cat. no. 92; *SCBI 66*, cat. nos. 3467, 3535 (ex Bjørnstad collection), 3545, 3607.

Table 15.11 Pierced   Anglo-Saxon   coins   in   *SCBI*   65   and   66,
Norwegian collections.

	Pierced coins in Norwegian finds	Pierced coins from other finds
Pre-Reform coins	3	1 (Lough Lene hoard, Ireland)
973–1066	40	0
Anglo-Scandinavian and Hiberno-Scandinavian imitative coins	21	7 (Lodejnoje Pole hoard, Russia)
Coins in the collections without secure find provenances	9	0
TOTAL	66	8

Table 15.12 Pierced Anglo-Saxon coins in Norwegian collections, by type.

Ruler and coin type	Pierced coins (from finds)	Pierced coins (unprovenanced)	Total no. of coins of the type	% of total (incl. unprovenanced)	% of total pierced (imitations incl.)
Edgar (958–75), Edward (975–8) and Æthelred II (978–1016)					
Reform Small Cross/ First Small Cross type (*c*.973–9)		1	8	*(12.5%)*	*(12.5%)*
Æthelred II (978–1016)					
Hand types (*c*.979–91)	3		57	*5.3%*	*5.3%*
Crux type (*c*.991–97)	6	2	339	*1.8% (2.4%)*	*2.0% (2.6%)*
'Crux' imitations	1		10	*10%*	
Long Cross type (*c*.997–1003)	3	1	353	*0.90% (1.1%)*	*1.5% (1.7%)*
'Long Cross' imitations	5		172	*2.9%*	
Helmet type (*c*.1003–09)	4	1	192	*2.1% (2.6%)*	*3% (3.5%)*
'Helmet' imitations	2		6	*30%*	
Agnus Dei type (*c*.1009)	0		1	*0*	*0*
Last Small Cross type (*c*.1009–17)	6		576	*1.0%*	*1.3%*
'Last Small Cross' imitations	2		55	*3.6%*	

Ruler and coin type	Pierced coins (from finds)	Pierced coins (unprove-nanced)	Total no. of coins of the type	% of total (incl. unprove-nanced)	% of total pierced (imitations incl.)
Cnut (1017–35)					
Quatrefoil type (c.1017–23)	9		742	1.2%	1.2%
'Quatrefoil' imitations	0		12	0%	
Pointed Helmet type (c.1023–29)	3		761	0.4%	0.5%
'Pointed Helmet' imitations	1		44	2.3%	
Short Cross type (c.1029–35)	1	1	65	1.5% (3.1%)	1.5% (3.1%)
Harold I (1035–40)		2	34	(5.9%)	(5.9%)
Harthacnut (1036–37, 1040–42)	1		25	4.0%	4.0%
Edward the Confessor (1042–66)	4	1	163	2.5% (3.1%)	4.0% (4.6%)
'Edward the Confessor' imitations	3		11	27.3%	

Note: Figures in brackets give the percentages including the unprovenanced pierced coins in the collection. Coins struck after 1066 and small fragments have been omitted.

Table 15.12 presents the chronological distribution of the pierced Anglo-Saxon coins, giving the percentage of pierced coins by type, calculated both with and without the coins of less certain provenance. The numbers for Anglo-Saxon and the Hiberno-Scandinavian and Anglo-Scandinavian imitative coins together are given in the final column, as users would surely have found it hard to distinguish between the 'best' unofficial products and real Anglo-Saxon coins.[42] In general, the Anglo-Saxon coins and the smaller sample of imitative coins largely follow the same trajectory as the finds as a whole. A larger proportion of coins struck before 1000 are pierced, and fewer are pierced once coins become more common in the first quarter of the eleventh century, though the numbers are low throughout. The highest proportion of pierced coins is in the *Hand* types (5.3 per cent), falling to 0.4 per cent in the *Pointed Helmet* type. This agrees with the overall trend visible in other types of secondary treatment such as test marks, which also decline in number over this period, as Svein H. Gullbekk has demonstrated. The increasing rarity of secondary treatment suggests that

---

[42] See e.g. *SCBI 66*, cat. no. 4120, a pierced imitation of Æthelred II's *Helmet* type with a literate obverse die cut by the 'Helmet-master' – given away by its square flan.

Norwegians were becoming more familiar with coins and treating them more casually.[43]

Æthelred II's *Helmet* type, which perhaps has a more attractive reverse design, and is also rather rarer in the Scandinavian finds than the preceding and following types, is pierced slightly more often (2.1 per cent). Although the *Agnus Dei* penny from the Nesbø hoard was not pierced, in Scandinavia and the Baltic, this exceptional type was singled out for suspension and imitation in particular, reflecting its clearly unusual and resonant design. Eight of the 13 *Agnus Dei* coins from Scandinavian and Baltic finds are pierced (61.5 per cent).[44] This suggests that some Scandinavian users were likely to pay attention to the coin design in selecting which coins to pierce. Some evidence for the careful placement of the pierced holes in the coins also suggests thoughtful choices could be involved in the process. For example, four of the coins in the Årstad hoard are pierced through a letter such as an O or wynn (æ).[45] The later types of Harthacnut and Edward the Confessor also have a higher number of pierced coins, perhaps reflecting the relative scarcity value of these coins as more and more Norwegian coins came into circulation, or (given the English data) a wider eleventh-century trend. Overall, therefore, the piercing of coins in the Norwegian finds seems to correlate with the changing use of coins, and their developing monetary function, across the Viking Age. Within this picture, some types attracted more attention than others, most probably because of their particular scarcity or design.

Anglo-Saxon Coins in Norway: Christian Symbols?

Within England, the political and religious meanings carried by the Anglo-Saxon coinage were clear. In the later tenth century, Anglo-Saxon kings such as Edgar (959–75) developed a sophisticated ideology of Christian kingship. Under the influence of the Ottonian Empire, where the emperor's sacrality was emphasised, the English king was increasingly associated with Christ. King Edgar was crowned in 973, and both the prayers of his coronation rite and the manuscript illuminations from his reign such as the charter for New Minster reflect this ideology.[46] From the mid-tenth century, Anglo-Saxon laws also

---

[43]   Gullbekk, 'Some aspects of coin import to Norway', pointing also to the complications of evaluating the pecking data.

[44]   See S. Keynes and R. Naismith, 'The *Agnus Dei* pennies of King Æthelred the Unready', *ASE, 40* (2011), 175–223, noting that 10 of the 21 known coins are pierced (206) and discussing brooches and coin types responding to the design (203–8).

[45]   *SCBI 65*, cat. nos. 1135, 1257, 1383; *SCBI 66*, 2030.

[46]   See R. Deshman, *The Benedictional of St Æthelwold* (Princeton, NJ, 1995), 192–214, on the royal programme of imagery; and *Charters of the New Minster, Winchester*, ed. S. Miller,

increasingly emphasised the duty of the king to oversee a Christian society.[47] It is not surprising, then, to find that the iconography of the Anglo-Saxon coinage reinforced the connection with the king and Christianity. After 973, with the sole exception of the *Agnus Dei* penny, all Anglo-Saxon coins depicted the ruler on the obverse, often with designs influenced by Roman coinage, while the reverse type was always a cross, of varying design.[48] Ildar Garipzanov has discussed the importance of coinage as a medium for spreading ideological messages to a wider audience, beyond the world of the court and the Church.[49] Late Anglo-Saxon silver pennies in England were thus part of a well-controlled coin economy, closely associated with the king, and used iconography which emphasised both his regality and Christianity.

But what happened when these coins moved outside England and reached Scandinavia? Members of the Scandinavian elite, who had experience of Anglo-Saxon England and the royal court, seem to have been a receptive audience alert to the message of Christian kingship carried by the Anglo-Saxon coins. For example, King Olaf Haraldsson of Norway had been baptised at the court of King Æthelred II (978–1016), and went on to adopt Anglo-Saxon coin designs on his own coinage, including the *Long Cross* and *Agnus Dei* types.[50] The influence of Anglo-Saxon and post-Conquest coin types upon the design of royal Scandinavian coinages into the twelfth century is well known. For example, the *Agnus Dei* type was widely copied in eleventh-century Denmark under rulers from Cnut (1017–35) to Erik Ejegod (1095–1103).[51] In Norway, Olaf Kyrre's (1066–93) coin types drew on Anglo-Saxon, Danish and Byzantine designs.[52] Anglo-Saxon coins also provided the models for the large-scale imitative coinages struck at Sigtuna and Lund, and in the Hiberno-Scandinavian world, where the *Long Cross* design was especially important. It is striking that, despite the wealth

---

Anglo-Saxon Charters, IX (Oxford, 2001), no. 23, 95–111 (S 745); C.E. Karkov, *The Ruler Portraits of Anglo-Saxon England* (Woodbridge, 2004), 85–93, on the image in the New Minster charter.

[47] See E. Screen, 'Anglo-Saxon law and numismatics: a reassessment in the light of Patrick Wormald's *The Making of English Law*', *BNJ, 77* (2007), 150–72, at 155–7.

[48] On the *Agnus Dei* type, see Keynes and Naismith, '*Agnus Dei* pennies'. For the types and their models, see D.M. Metcalf, *An Atlas of Anglo-Saxon and Norman Coin Finds 973–1086* (Oxford, 1988).

[49] I.H. Garipzanov, *The Symbolic Language of Authority in the Carolingian World (c.751–877)* (Leiden and Boston, 2008), 157 and 207.

[50] For example, he issued coins using the *Agnus Dei* type in 1015–28 and 1030. See Skaare, *Coins and Coinage*, 60–4. Gullbekk, Chapter 14, this volume, discusses the earlier adoption of Anglo-Saxon style coinage by Eirik Bloodaxe.

[51] On the *Agnus Dei* types issued at Lund, see Keynes and Naismith, '*Agnus Dei* pennies', 208.

[52] See the illustrations in Gullbekk, *Pengevesenets fremvekst og fall*, 39.

and prestige of the German emperors of the day, German coins were rarely used as models in the same way.[53] Familiarity with Anglo-Saxon coin types, their iconographic uniformity, and awareness of their Christian, royal resonances seem to have played a part in this process of adaptation and imitation.

Those issuing coins in Scandinavia, therefore, responded actively to the iconography of the Anglo-Saxon coinage. Assessing the impact of the coinage upon other coin users in Norway, however, is more challenging. How did people respond to Anglo-Saxon coins in the very different world of Viking-Age Scandinavia, with its bullion economy, and variegated religious practices, in the period 980–1050? Were the coins understood as Christian, given their prominent imagery of the cross? The handling and use of the Anglo-Saxon coins may reveal more about Norwegian society in the Christianisation period.

The Christianisation of Norway was a long process, which made particular progress in the later tenth century and first half of the eleventh century, as successive kings of Norway promoted and enforced the new religion with increasing success. Sæbjørg Walaker Nordeide's recent analysis of the archaeological evidence indicates this was a period of co-existence between Christians and pagans, as initially small Christian communities lived, probably sometimes uncomfortably, alongside neighbours practising traditional religion in all its variety.[54] For many Norwegians their first sustained encounters with Christianity would have come in the period from 980 to 1030, through contacts with Christian kings such as Olaf Tryggveson and Olaf Haraldsson, or with the missionary bishops the later saga evidence suggests were at work in Norway in this period.[55] Nordeide has emphasised the importance of centres of Christian influence such as the newly established town of Trondheim, and other small Christian communities at sites such as Veøy and Borgund in Møre og Romsdal in the Christianisation process.[56]

---

[53]   Skaare, *Coins and Coinage*, 57.

[54]   See Nordeide, *Viking Age as a Period of Religious Transformation*, 279–83, esp. tables 13–14, 280, 28, for the latest and earliest evidence for paganism and Christianity, and e.g. her discussion of the Trøndelag, 123–7, at 126, for the 'struggles and setbacks [that] may have been involved in the Christianisation process' at sites such as Hove, Mære, Rol and Hustad.

[55]   For kings and Christianisation, see Bagge and Nordeide, 'Kingdom of Norway' (n. 4). On Grímkell, Anglo-Saxon missionary bishop under Olaf Haraldsson and later promoter of his cult, see M. Townend, 'Knútr and the cult of St Óláfr: poetry and patronage in eleventh-century Norway and England', *Viking and Medieval Scandinavia*, 1 (2005), 251–79, at 265.

[56]   Nordeide, *Viking Age as a Period of Religious Transformation*, 116–23 (Trondheim) and 147 (Borgund). On Veøy, see ibid., 141–6, and B. Solli, *Narratives of Veøy. An investigation into the Poetics and Scientifics of Archaeology* (Oslo, 1996). Nordeide, *Viking Age as a Period of Religious Transformation*, 287–316, emphasises the role of early cult centres such as Veøy, towns, royal estates and the activities of kings in the process of Christianisation.

Previous studies of pierced and looped coins in the earlier Viking Age by Mark Blackburn indicated a preference to mount coins in order to display the bust, correctly oriented (with all but one of the 20 coins in the Hoen hoard so presented).[57] Of the other two Anglo-Saxons coins from this period, the Veka find of a coin of Offa (757–96), moneyer Osmod, with its text in three lines, conforms with Mark Blackburn's finding for the looped Islamic dirhams in the Hoen hoard, that these were generally displayed horizontally or vertically relative to the piercing.[58] The Søndre Bø grave find, a coin of Coenwulf (796–821), however, is pierced to display the geometric reverse design rather than the bust, which was pierced at its base.[59] Ildar Garipzanov's detailed analysis of the looping and piercing of the Carolingian coin finds pointed to regional variation, with finds in some areas such as North Jutland generally respecting the design of the cross and sometimes also the temple, while those in the Norwegian and Birka graves he analysed in the main did not respond to the Christian imagery of the coins.[60] Practices in the earlier Viking Age therefore seem to have varied, with a few people apparently responding to the Christian imagery of the Frankish deniers, but more not respecting elements such as the initial cross on coins, or preferring to display the portrait bust, rather than the cross on coins.

The orientation of the pierced Anglo-Saxon coins has been assessed, in order to cast light on whether these coins were perhaps used as Christian ornaments, given their prominent Christian iconography. Was the piercing located so as to display a cross, or the bust of the king, when the coin was suspended? The regular striking of Anglo-Saxon coins meant that in some cases both of these could be achieved with a single hole, displaying both the king and the cross, dependent on the user's preference; it is harder therefore to work out what the user intended, and therefore these coins are noted as a separate category. Table 15.13 first records coins pierced to display both the portrait bust and the cross correctly (with a tolerance of up to 20° clockwise or counter-clockwise); then those where the cross would display correctly, but with the bust suspended at an angle (usually within ±20° of 90°, 180° or 270°, given the regular die axis of Anglo-Saxon coins); and finally, coins pierced at other angles, generally so that the cross appears as a saltire or X. Overall, as Figure 15.1 reveals, just over half the coins in the hoards orient the cross (52 per cent), with 26 per cent of coins preferring to orient the bust (or bust and cross), and 22 per cent not orienting

---

[57] It is possible that the exceptional character of the hoard, comprising gold or gilded coins, affects their orientation, influenced by older Roman coins and the gold bracteates. I am grateful to Svein H. Gullbekk for drawing this point to my attention.

[58] Blackburn, 'Loops', 192–3.

[59] *SCBI 65*, cat. nos. 23 (Veka), 24 (Søndre Bø).

[60] Garipzanov, 'Carolingian Coins in early Viking-Age Scandinavia', 72–80; Garipzanov, 'Carolingian coins in ninth-century Scandinavia', 51–2.

either.[61] This represents a change from the earlier Viking Age preference to orient the bust noted for the Hoen hoard. Either users were no longer responding to the design as a bust, or the cross type was increasingly the focus of their attention when deciding how to suspend the coin.

Table 15.13   Orientation of 50 pierced Anglo-Saxon coins.

Orient- ation:	Dronning- ensgate	Årstad	Foldøy	Brøholt	Other hoards	Total: all hoards	Uncertain prove- nance	Lodej- noje Pole
Bust and cross	4	3	2	0	4	13	3	0
Cross oriented only	9	5	3	2	7	26	4	6
Other orient- ation	4	2	2	1	2	11	2	1

Note: Of the 54 pierced coins, two specimens of uncertain provenance pierced multiple times have been omitted (neither seemed to prefer the bust, but both could have been suspended either to display a cross or an X). Two coins of *First Hand* type from other hoards have also been omitted, one oriented to display either the bust or the hand, the other to display the hand. The coins of uncertain provenance in the Norwegian collections, and those from the Lodejnoje Pole are included for comparative purposes, the latter suggesting that Norwegian practice differed slightly from that in north-west Russia.

However, it is uncertain how far this preference reflects a Christian interpretation of the symbol; while all objects clearly had meaning and value to those who used them, it is notoriously difficult to establish what exactly this was, and especially to identify religious significance, or reconstruct the ideas or memories objects may have embodied.[62] Certainly some explicitly religious objects appear in hoards, and seem to have been treated differently from jewellery and hack-silver. Anne Pedersen has noted that 'very few of these

---

[61]   Thirty out of the 39 coins in the bust-cross and cross groups are oriented to 0°, 5 to within 10° and 3 to within 20°. For a necklace including two coins with the bust suspended at 270°, see T. Berga, *SCBI 45: Latvian Collections. Anglo-Saxon and Later British Coins* (Oxford, 1996), 17, Figure 3, necklace from grave 161, Lauskola burial field.

[62]   See e.g. Askjem, 'Viking-Age silver hoards', 177–8, on value and the re-contextualisation of objects; and P. Purhonen, *Kristinuskon saapumisesta Suomeen. Uskontoarkeologinen tutkimus* [On the arrival of Christianity in Finland. A Study in the Archaeology of Religion], Suomen muinaismuistoyhdistyksen aikakauskirja, 106 (Helsinki, 1998), 45–58 (English summary, 189), on the earliest objects with Christian imagery in the Finnish finds, and the challenges in interpreting them, 57.

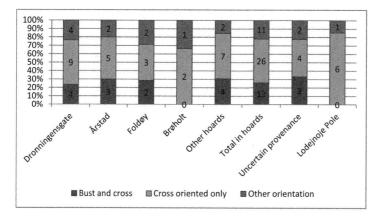

Figure 15.1   Orientation of pierced coins (as per cent, by hoard).

symbols or amulets (and Christian crosses) were subjected to fragmentation' in South Scandinavia.[63] Some such objects may have been included in the hoards in order to protect the contents.[64] Contemporaries could also have exploited the potential ambiguity between crosses and Thor's hammers, although perhaps less so in the Trøndelag, since Nordeide's recent analysis of the cult of Thor indicates that this was largely a South Scandinavian phenomenon, with the two most northerly finds a stray find from the Trøndelag, and a grave find from Stryn, Sogn og Fjordane.[65] Grave goods would also have been carefully chosen to convey status and reputation, and perhaps also for their cultic significance.[66] The presence of comparative material and information on the context thus becomes especially important in determining religious symbolism. In the final part of this study, I shall consider whether the evidence from Trondheim allows us to say anything more about the use and meaning of the pierced coins in a specific context.

---

[63]   See A. Pedersen, 'Jewellery in hoards in southern Scandinavia', in *Silver Economies, Monetisation and Society*, ed. Graham-Campbell, Sindbæk and Williams, 153–72, at 164.

[64]   Objects with a potential apotropaic function include the crucifix from the Horr, Rogaland, hoard (Skaare no. 78), and the Thor's hammers in the hoards from Bråtveit, Rogaland, and Tråen, Buskerud (Skaare nos. 36, 88). It is striking that these, like the Dronningensgate 10, Trondheim, and Haukøy, Troms hoards which included crucifixes and a figure of Christ respectively (Skaare nos. 147, 179), were all deposited away from the settled area.

[65]   On the cult of Thor, see Nordeide, *Viking Age as a Period of Religious Transformation*, 235–44, at 237–8 (ambiguity between crosses and Thor's hammers), and 240–2 (southern focus of the cult).

[66]   See e.g. Garipzanov, 'Carolingian coins in ninth-century Scandinavia', 53–5, for analysis of some of the grave finds. Compare also the two unpierced coins found in Christian burials at Borgund (Skaare no. 128; their placement within the grave is not noted).

Trondheim was established as a Christian town from the outset, although the surrounding region has strong evidence for pagan traditions too.[67] The sagas link the town's foundation with Olaf Tryggveson (995–1000), and the archaeological evidence supports a date 'towards the end of the tenth century'.[68] The town was also a key royal centre for Olaf Haraldsson (1015–28), and the residence of Cnut's son and regent, Svein, and his mother Ælfgifu of Northampton, in 1029/30–35. During Svein's reign, the cult of Olaf Haraldsson was promoted, and Olaf's bishop Grímkell seems to have returned from exile.[69] By the later eleventh century, the cult of Olaf was well established, with evidence for local production of encolpions (reliquary pendants with a sacred image or containing a relic).[70] The archaeological excavations of the Folkebibliotekstomten (the Library Site) revealed a growing and thriving trading centre, where coins were increasingly in use in the second half of the eleventh century.[71]

The Dronningensgate 10 hoard was probably deposited in the early years of King Magnus's reign (1035–47), in a farming area outside Trondheim itself.[72] The hoard included two silver crucifixes, chains and hack-silver and a few coin blanks, as well as at least 964 coins. It also stands out for the very high number of pierced coins in the hoard, 29 overall, including 17 Anglo-Saxon and Anglo-Scandinavian imitative coins. The higher incidence of pierced coins in the hoard suggests that more pierced coins than usual were available in the local coin supply. Two of the Anglo-Saxon and imitative coins have four and three piercings (the latter coin is chipped, meaning the probable fourth piercing is lost), suggesting that the coins were mounted or sewn onto something.[73] Fifty-three per cent of the pierced coins are oriented to the cross, and 76 per cent of the coins could have been used as Christian symbols. Overall, taken with the

---

[67]   E.g. the cult site at Mære, active until *c*.1050–1100: Nordeide, *Viking Age as a Period of Religious Transformation*, 107–13.

[68]   Ibid., 116–23, at 116.

[69]   See Townend, 'Knútr and the Cult of St Óláfr', 265 (Grímkell), and T. Bolton, *The Empire of Cnut the Great. Conquest and Consolidation of Power in Northern Europe in the Early Eleventh Century* (Leiden and Boston, 2009), 269–87, on Svein and Ælfgifu's rule in general.

[70]   Nordeide, *Viking Age as a Period of Religious Transformation*, 121–2.

[71]   Risvaag and Christophersen, 'Early medieval coinage and urban development'.

[72]   Ibid., 87. *T.p.q.* Denmark, Harthacnut (1035–42). See O.A. Digre, 'Myntfunnet fra Dronningensgate 10, Trondheim. En foreløbig meddelse', *Det Kongelige Norske Videnskabers Selskabs Museet Årsbok*, 1950, 1–6, at 5–6; J.A. Risvaag, *Mynt og by. Myntens rolle i Trondheim by i perioden ca. 1000–1630, belyst gjennom myntfunn og utmynting*, Doctoravhandlinger ved Norges teknisknaturvitenskapelige universitet 2006, 200 (Trondheim, 2006), 346–8, for a listing of the hoard.

[73]   *SCBI 66*, cat. nos 2061 (Cnut, *Quatrefoil*), 3954 (Anglo-Scandinavian 'Crux' imitation). Both are oriented to display the bust and cross correctly.

finds of the crucifixes, might this hoard reflect links to a Christian context, and Christian use of the pierced coins?

Sæbjørg Walaker Nordeide has examined the finds from Trondheim from the late tenth to the mid-twelfth century for religious symbols.[74] No pagan symbols were present, but 20 objects used signs of the cross, ranging from crucifixes, cross pendants and crucibles for the manufacture of encolpions, to crosses and designs such as ankhs incised into the bases of wooden vessels or on to wooden shafts. Of the seven finds dated before 1050, only the two crucifixes in the Dronningens gate 10 hoard were clearly and explicitly Christian (excluding a cross pendant datable only to between *c*.1000 and the early twelfth century). The incised crosses and symbols on the wooden objects might have had other meanings, perhaps production marks or decoration, and their meaning cannot be interpreted at present.[75] Certainly Christian objects become more common in the Trondheim finds after 1050. This evidence does, however, confirm that the cross was a symbol in regular use in Trondheim by 1050, and – whether interpreted as a Christian symbol by its wearers or not – the pierced coins fit into a context of more general use and display of the cross. The increased spread of the cross, and crucifixes, seems to be a characteristic feature of the Christianisation period.[76]

As Mark Blackburn noted for the Hoen hoard, the methods of suspension can assist in identifying groups of coins within hoards.[77] The pierced coins from Trondheim might also help identify a group of coins within the hoard. As noted above, the regular die axis of the Anglo-Saxon coins means that the coin piercings cluster around 0° (the bust-cross group in Table 15.13), and 90°, 180° and 270° (where the cross is oriented, but the bust is at an angle; noted in the second row of Table 15.13). In all the other Norwegian finds, the coins in this second group divide evenly between the four angles. For example the ten pierced coins in the Årstad hoard divide as follows: 3 coins (0°), 2 (90°), 1 (180°), 2 (270°) and 2 (other, irregular angles). In the Dronningens gate 10 hoard, however, there is a distinct preference for coins pierced with the bust at 180°: of the 17 coins, 4 are pierced at 0°, 1 at 90°, 7 at 180°, 1 at 270° and 4 at other, irregular angles. This might imply that the coins derived from the same source, perhaps a necklace, designed to display the cross side of the coins, although a sample of four Viking-Age coin necklaces suggests a less consistent approach to mounting coins.[78]

---

[74] Nordeide, *Viking Age as a Period of Religious Transformation*, 121–2; table 5, 120, lists the 20 objects and their datings.

[75] Nordeide, *Viking Age as a Period of Religious Transformation*, 121.

[76] See e.g. Purhonen, *Kristinuskon saapumisesta Suomeen*, on the Finnish evidence.

[77] Blackburn, 'Loops', 191–2.

[78] See *SCBI 51*, 11, Figure 1, Paunküla necklace, *c*.1009, with 3 Byzantine and 2 Islamic coins, all but one horizontally or vertically aligned, and 1 *Last Small Cross* coin, irregularly oriented (bust and cross at 120°); *SCBI 45*, 17, Figure 3, Lauskola necklace, with 3 German coins, 2 not regularly oriented and the third too worn to tell, and 3 Anglo-Saxon coins, two with the

Figure 15.2   Pierced *Transitional Crux* coin from the Horr hoard (Totnes, moneyer Ælfstan), *SCBI* 65, cat. no. 490. Nicked, bent and with 20 peck marks on the obverse and 12 on the reverse; pierced to orient the cross.

Conclusions

Coins and other objects of value circulated for long periods of time in Viking-Age Norway. For example the crucifix from the Horr hoard, with its broken loop and test marks, had circulated as silver bullion, and perhaps had no, or only residual, numinous power to its last owner.[79] Coins too probably were used differently by different owners, and moved in and out of use as ornaments, as the pierced and much-tested *Crux* coin from the Horr hoard suggests (Figure 15.2). The low incidence of looped coins relative to pierced coins after 900 might in part be explained by coins losing their loops in the course of circulation, as they returned from use as ornaments into the sphere of hoarding. The long period of circulation of the coins complicates analysis of the material,[80] but this survey of the

bust at 270° (Cnut and Harold I), and one *Last Small Cross* coin, oriented to show the bust and cross; T. Talvio, *Coins and Coin Finds in Finland*, ISKOS, 12 (Vammala, 2002), Figure 11, 71 and 180–81, Luistari, Eura, grave 56, necklace *c.*1017, with 2 silver-sheet pendants, 9 Islamic, 1 Volga-Bulgar, 1 German and 1 Anglo-Saxon coin of Cnut, *Quatrefoil* type. The last is oriented to show the cross, but the design of the German coin and the horizontal/vertical epigraphy of 5 of the remaining coins are not respected. The Södvik, Öland, Sweden find includes two chains of 5 and 7 coins, pierced twice and linked edge to edge. Of 3 Anglo-Saxon coins displaying a bust, two are correctly oriented, and one is at 270°; 3 more Anglo-Saxon coins display a cross: illustrated in A. Forsgren, *Sköna smycken i silverne skattfynd. Smycken och smyckesfragment i depåer av tidigmedeltida gotländska mynt (ca 1140–1220)*, C-uppsats i arkeologi, Stockholm universitet (Stockholm, 2004), 15.

[79]   G. Gustafson, 'Sølvfundet fra Horr samt tillæg og rettelser til et par tidligere indkomne myntfund', *Bergens Museums Aarbog, 15* (1896), 3–36, at 27–8.

[80]   The evidence presented above suggests coin piercing was an ongoing phenomenon, but one wonders what the wastage rates were for pierced coins. See D.M. Metcalf, 'Some twentieth-century runes. Statistical analysis of the Viking-age hoards and the interpretation of wastage rates', in *Viking-Age Coinage in the Northern Lands. The Sixth Oxford Symposium on Coinage and*

pierced coins in the Norwegian finds suggests or confirms certain trends in the use of coins in Viking-Age Norway. Though the piercing of coins was an ongoing practice, the use of coins as ornaments seems to have declined over the period, to a level similar to that seen in the single finds from Anglo-Saxon England, reflecting wider changes in coin use, brought about by the increased availability of coins and the emergent monetised economy in Norway. After 1050 in particular, the finds of all types attest to the rapid increase in the use of coins in Norway. When coins were readily available, they were less likely to be singled out for use as ornaments in both Anglo-Saxon England and Norway.

The period also saw continuity in the use of coins: some coins went on being included in grave finds across the period, by Christians and pagans alike, although in the latter case, to judge by the decline in the deposition of pierced coins, they were perhaps increasingly included as stores of value rather than valuable ornaments.[81] No pierced coins were apparently lost in use in Norway between *c.*900 and 1050, though the evidence is too slender to assess whether this reflects owners of ornaments being more careful, or that pierced coins could not return into the world of more monetary circulation. The Anglo-Saxon coinage exerted a striking influence on the iconography of Scandinavian coins, suggesting that Viking-Age rulers responded to the religious and regal messages of the Anglo-Saxon coin types. When Norwegians chose coins to pierce, they were more likely to single out Anglo-Saxon coins than German coins, though it is unclear whether they were preferred for their designs, their quality of striking or religious or royal resonances. However, the small sample size and the methodological challenges involved in assessing and interpreting the evidence make it hard to draw more than tentative conclusions from the orientation of the pierced Anglo-Saxon coins. In the ninth century, the cross design on Carolingian coins had sometimes already been favoured, though only rarely in enough numbers to suggest a specifically Christian use. Examination of the pierced Anglo-Saxon coins struck after 980 nevertheless gives some interesting hints at a slight but apparent preference for the cross design, and a move towards displaying the cross instead of the bust when using coins as ornaments. This may not always have been intended as a religious statement, but does hint that the cross was becoming an increasingly visible symbol as the Christianisation of Norway intensified around the year 1000.

Monetary History, ed. M.A.S. Blackburn and D.M. Metcalf, BAR International Series, 122 (2 vols., Oxford, 1981), 2, 329–82, for a study of wastage rates of coins.

[81]   For example, the famous 'last' pagan grave from Nomeland, Aust-Agder, deposited after 1065 (Skaare no. 70; Nordeide, *Viking Age as a Period of Religious Transformation*, 189–90, 279), included 5 coins, all unpierced, and 21 weights, emphasising the link with exchange.

Overall, perhaps the strongest message from the coin evidence is that the same object was very probably perceived in several ways, with Christian symbolism one of the meanings that Viking-Age Norwegians read into the Anglo-Saxon coins they used.

Chapter 16

Islamic and Christian Gold Coins from Spanish Mints Found in England, Mid-Eleventh to Mid-Thirteenth Centuries[*]

Marion M. Archibald

In a masterly study published a few years before his untimely death Mark Blackburn discussed 'Gold in England during the Age of Silver'.[1] He dealt with gold coins found in England from all sources, both home and overseas, dating from the eighth to twelfth centuries, when locally produced coinage was at first almost entirely, and latterly exclusively, in silver. The present chapter dedicated to the memory of my distinguished colleague and good friend is also concerned with foreign gold coins in England but over a narrower period. Still in the local Age of Silver, it overlaps with the later part of Mark's survey from the late eleventh century but extends to the appearance of Henry III's gold penny in 1257. It is based on the increased number of gold coins, all from Spain and all but one Islamic, now recorded from England, and other material confirmation of the presence of Islamic gold issues in the earlier part of that period. The absence of finds during its later years is also discussed. The resulting pattern is set against the documentary evidence for Islamic coins in England and trading connections with Spain. Islamic coins of the period found elsewhere in north-west Europe, particularly in the adjacent territories of France and the Netherlands, are noted for comparison.

[*] I am indebted to Barrie Cook, British Museum, for reading a draft of this chapter and giving valuable advice; any remaining errors and misinterpretations are my own. My grateful thanks are also owed to the editors, Martin Allen, Rory Naismith and Elina Screen; the private owner of the brooch Catalogue no. 6; Arent Pol, formerly of the Geldmuseum, Utrecht, and Kenneth Jonsson, Numismatic Institute, University of Stockholm, for information on Netherlands and Swedish finds respectively; and Robert Bracey, British Museum, for preparing the map; also for other help and advice to: Edward Besly, National Museum of Wales; Nicholas Holmes, National Museums of Scotland; Fernando Lopez-Sanchez, University Jaume I, Castellón, Spain; Nicholas Mayhew, Ashmolean Museum, Oxford; and Luke Treadwell, Institute for Asian Studies, Oxford.

[1] M. Blackburn, 'Gold in England during the Age of Silver (eighth to eleventh centuries)', in *Silver economy in the Viking Age*, ed. J. Graham-Campbell and G. Williams (Walton Creek, CA, 2007), 55–98.

Historical Context

The historical context in Spain may be briefly outlined.[2] Most of the Iberian Peninsula, except the north-west, had been overrun by Islamic invaders from North Africa in and just after AH 92 (AD 711). At the start of the period covered by this review, an increasing area of the north was back in the hands of Christian states but the rest of Spain was still ruled by Islamic dynasties, initially by the Almoravids, who were in control in North Africa from AH 454 (AD 1062) and in Spain AH 479–537 (AD 1086–1142). During their later years, the Almoravids' power declined and a number of breakaway Islamic states were formed, mainly small and unstable associations, like the *taifas* of the previous century, but including the longer-lived kingdom of Murcia in the south-east. At the same time, Christian rulers took the opportunity to recover more territory. Meanwhile, the Almohads had quickly gained control in North Africa from AH 524 (AD 1130), and in AH 537 (AD 1142) extended their rule into Islamic southern Spain, capturing Murcia in AH 566 (AD 1172). In AH 609 (AD 1212) they were defeated by an alliance of Christian princes and left the Peninsula just over a decade later. They lost control in North Africa in AH 668 (AD 1269). By this time, the Christian re-conquest of the Peninsula had progressed until only Granada remained in Islamic hands as an independent Nasrid Emirate.

Islamic and Christian Gold Coins from Spanish Mints Found in England

Blackburn's study, covering more than four hundred years, listed 28 native and overseas gold coins with English provenances of which eight were Islamic. Four of these, from just three find-spots, fall within the period of the present review, all Almoravid dinars produced in Islamic Spain and dated between AH 479–500 (AD 1086–1106) and AH 524 (AD 1130) (Blackburn nos A25–8, here nos 2–5). No coins of the later Almohad dynasty or the contemporary Spanish Christian states had been found. Also absent were bezants (Byzantine *hyperpera*) which documentary sources show were present in England in significant numbers from the mid to late twelfth century.[3] Rory Naismith, writing around the same time on 'Islamic coins from Early Medieval England', limited his entries

---

[2]   Principal authorities consulted: A.M. Gómez, *Monedas Hispano-Musulmanas* (Toledo, 1992); and C.E. Bosworth, *The New Islamic Dynasties. A Chronological and Genealogical Manual* (Edinburgh, 1996).

[3]   B. Cook, 'The Besant in Angevin England', *NC, 159* (1999), 255–75, at 256. As the bezants are comprehensively covered in this paper, they will be mentioned only incidentally here.

to finds dating before *c.*1100 and therefore included only the earliest Almoravid piece (his Table 4, 'Gold single finds', no. 7; Blackburn A25; here no. 2).[4]

The Islamic gold coins found in England for the period under present review now number seven (including one counterfeit mounted as a brooch). A Christian derivative raises the total number of gold coins from Spain to eight, thus doubling the total available to Blackburn in 2007. They are listed in the Catalogue below, where numismatic details and current locations are recorded, while this section outlines the English background to each find, particularly those found since the previous listing.

Islamic gold coins began to be struck in Spain in 967 but no English finds have been recorded as yet from issues of the later tenth to mid-eleventh centuries. In the Anglo-Saxon era before 1066, England had probably been involved in some stages of the slave trade with Islamic Spain but there is no evidence of direct contact.[5] The gold coins from that period found in England are still confined to the two Fatimid quarter-dinars (*tari*) of baser gold from Sicily, one dated AH 358 (AD 969) and the other AH 442–62 (AD 1050–70), listed by Blackburn (A21 and A24).[6]

Figure 16.1   Barcelona   *mancus*,   1069–75.   Present   owner   unknown (Photograph, British Museum) (Cat. no. 1).

The earliest English gold find from Spain is in fact a Christian coin, a *mancus* from the county of Barcelona in north-east Spain, found at Denham, Buckinghamshire, in 1994.[7] Struck for Raymond Berengar I (1035–75) in the

---

[4]   R. Naismith, 'Islamic coins from early medieval England', *NC, 165* (2005), 193–222, at 218.

[5]   P. Nightingale, *A Medieval Mercantile Community. The Grocers' Company and the Politics and Trade of London 1000–1485* (New Haven, CT, and London, 1995), 9. For English involvement in the slave trade in the Anglo-Saxon period see D. Pelteret, 'Slave raiding and slave trading in early England', *ASE, 9* (1981), 99–114.

[6]   The context of the *taris* is discussed in M. Blackburn and M. Bonser, 'Single-finds of Anglo-Saxon and Norman coins – 3', *BNJ, 56* (1986), 64–101.

[7]   Some Gallic pseudo-Imperial *solidi* copied from fifth-century Roman prototypes found in England are possibly to be attributed to the Visigoths (R. Abdy and G. Williams, 'A catalogue of hoards and single finds from the British Isles, *c.* AD 410–675', in *Coinage and History in the North Sea World, c. AD 500–1250: Essays in Honour of Marion Archibald*, ed. B. Cook and G.

period 1069–75 (no. 1, Fig 16.1), it is one of the type known to numismatists as 'bilingual', as it copies a dinar with Arabic inscriptions of the Hammudid ruler Yahya-al-Murali AH 412–26 (AD 1021–35), from the mint of Ceuta on the African side of the Straits of Gibraltar, with the count of Barcelona's name and title in Latin letters inserted into the outer circle of the reverse text.[8] Coins of this bilingual series are rare, having been produced in smaller numbers than previous Barcelona issues which had commenced in 1017/19. Much of the gold for the Barcelona series was derived from the *parias*, more or less fixed tributes exacted regularly from the neighbouring petty Islamic states, and also from hiring out mercenaries to take part in the warfare of these *taifas* among themselves. The Christian soldiers were allowed to share in the booty, so some Islamic gold was dispersed among the population as well as reaching the count's own coffers and his mint.[9] The rest of the gold for the Barcelona coinage was accessed in Ceuta in the form of both local dinars (such as the prototype of the Denham *mancus*) and uncoined metal.[10] It was ultimately derived, like the gold for the other North African and Spanish Islamic coinages, from sources in trans-Saharan Africa.[11]

Denham is recorded in the nearly contemporary Domesday Book (1086) as a manor belonging to the abbot of St Peter's of Westminster (now Westminster Abbey), London. Located about 25 kilometres west-north-west of London, it was situated on an important route to Oxford and further west.

No coins of the Barcelona series appear among the west European finds listed by Duplessy in 1956 and over 20 years later Balaguer could still write that 'Andalusian *mancusos* did not penetrate Europe'.[12] Pilgrimages to the shrine of St James at Santiago de Compostela in north-west Spain are recorded from the mid-tenth century and English pilgrims can be associated with a small hoard of six silver pennies of Æthelred II, the latest of the *Second Hand* type, currently dated

---

Williams (Leiden and Boston, 2006), 11–73, at 38–9), but there are no representatives of the regal series of Visigothic gold tremisses produced in Spain *c*.AD 580–714 (*MEC* 1; R. Pliego Vázquez, *La moneda visigoda*, 2 vols. (Seville, 2009).

[8]   A.M. Balaguer, *Del Mancús a la Dobla. Or i Paries d'Hispánia* (Barcelona, 1993), 144–9, esp. 146. This coin was the subject of a paper given by the present writer at the International Numismatic Congress in Glasgow, 2008, which was not published in the subsequent proceedings.

[9]   A.M. Balaguer, '"Parias" and the myth of the "Mancus"', in *Problems of Medieval Coinage in the Iberian Area 3*, ed. M. Gomes Marques and D. M. Metcalf (Santarém, 1988), 499–545, at 500.

[10]   Balaguer, '"Parias"' sets out the documentary evidence and discusses the historical and numismatic context; Balaguer, *Del Mancús* is concerned with the detailed classification of the series.

[11]   P. Spufford, *Money and its Use in Medieval Europe* (Cambridge, 1988), 184.

[12]   Balaguer, '"Parias"', 500.

*c.*AD 985–91, found at the site of a ruined hospice on the pass of Roncesvalles.[13] Merchants and pilgrims generally followed the same routes and English traders were operating in Compostela by 1130.[14] Since the second half of the eleventh century, around the date of the Denham coin, Barcelona was established as a specialist market for spices,[15] and Nightingale has explored the connections between the London pepperer and moneyer dynasty, the Deormans, and their church named in honour of St Antolin, some of whose relics had been translated from Pamiers in southern France to the cathedral of Palencia near Burgos in the early eleventh century.[16]

Although exceptions must always be allowed for, representatives of coin-issues produced in small numbers do not normally survive long in circulation in significant quantities. The Denham *mancus* is therefore likely to have been brought to England and deposited relatively soon after it was struck. It is not possible to establish the route which it took between Barcelona and England, whether overland or by sea, but sea trade was often favoured and the Bay of Biscay was already referred to in the early twelfth century as 'the Sea of the English' by the Arab geographer Edrisi.[17] The coin might have been brought all the way by an English merchant, but it could have passed through the hands of traders of different nationalities and therefore does not necessarily establish a direct link. While the Barcelona *mancus* found at Denham may not quite provide the 'cogent evidence of commercial links between London and northern Spain in the eleventh century' required by Nightingale,[18] it is a valuable indicator of such a connection.

The earliest Spanish Islamic find, from near York in 1752, is an Almoravid dinar probably of Yusuf b. Tashufin AH 480–500 (AD 1087–1106) of uncertain mint and date, known only from an incomplete drawing included in the minutes of the Society of Antiquaries of London for 7 May of that year (Blackburn A25 (drawing illustrated), here no. 2).[19] The next three dinars listed in Blackburn's corpus all belong to the following long reign of Ali. b. Yusuf AH 500–37 (AD

---

[13]   F. Mateu y Llopis and R.H.M. Dolley, 'A small find of Anglo-Saxon pennies from Roncesvalles', *BNJ, 27* (1952–4), 89–91.

[14]   Nightingale, *Mercantile Community*, 39.

[15]   Nightingale, *Mercantile Community*, 36–8.

[16]   Nightingale, *Mercantile Community*, 23–42. For early trade with Spain generally see C. Verlinden, 'Studies in sources and bibliography VII: the rise of Spanish trade in the Middle Ages', *EcHR, 10* (1940), 44–59; and P. Nightingale, 'The London pepperers' guild and some twelfth-century trading links with Spain', *Bulletin of the Institute of Historical Research, 58* (1985), 123–32.

[17]   Nightingale, *Mercantile Community*, 39.

[18]   Nightingale, *Mercantile Community*, 37.

[19]   D.M. Metcalf, 'Eighteenth-century finds of medieval coins from the records of the Society of Antiquaries', *NC, 6th series, 18* (1958), 73–96, at 95.

1106–42). Two, struck at Almeria in AH 527 (AD 1130), which have never been illustrated (Blackburn nos A27–8; here nos 4–5), were found 'within sight of St Paul's', London. The cathedral lay to the west of the commercial heart of the city in the twelfth century but the goldsmiths' quarter was located immediately to its east.[20] Helen Mitchell Brown suggests that the third, a perfect coin, found at St Aldates, Oxford, struck at Denia in AH 500 (AD 1106/07 (Blackburn no A26, here cat. no. 3, Colour Plate 16.1a), may have been presented there as an oblation.[21]

The reign of Ali b. Yusuf is now further represented by a gold-plated base-metal counterfeit of an Almoravid dinar mounted as a brooch, found near Winchester in 2011 (cat. no. 6, Colour Plate 16.1b).[22] The front of the brooch shows the reverse of the prototype. Riveted to the back is a rather rough strap which held the pin (now missing), and a hole and a surviving rivet where the catch plate (now missing) was attached. The inscriptions on both sides are sufficiently close copies of the prototype that the reign and mint (Valencia) can be identified, and the gilding is not just a thin dusting of gold but a more substantial plating on both sides. These points suggest that it was not, like many pseudo-coins mounted as brooches, made expressly as jewellery, but was a struck forgery created with the intent to deceive for monetary purposes.[23] It would have been highly deceptive when new. Only subsequently, possibly when its false status had been recognised, was it made into a brooch. It is therefore in a different category from the uniface brooches in repoussé bronze with devolved Islamic inscriptions discussed below. It is not certain whether it was made abroad or in England, but probably the latter, although not necessarily in Winchester where it was found. This piece provides the first example of a counterfeit Islamic gold coin found in England. Cook quotes several cases from the early thirteenth-century *Curia regis* Rolls involving forgeries of the then more plentiful bezants but none of these counterfeits has so far been found in England. Cook's remark about false bezants is equally apposite for false dinars: 'There seems little point in forging something unless it is both familiar and functional'.[24]

---

[20] C.N.L. Brooke with G. Keir, *London 800–1216: the Shaping of a City* (London, 1975), 277.

[21] H. Brown, 'A dinar for St Frideswide?', *The Ashmolean*, 18 (1990), 9–10.

[22] This brooch is included here and illustrated with the generous permission of its private owner.

[23] It may be contrasted with the imitations of Islamic dinars which Stephen Album has suggested were made specifically as jewellery, probably in Muslim regions or in the southern parts of Christian Europe, which are almost always found holed or pierced for wearing as pendants (S. Album, *A Checklist of Islamic Coins*, 3rd edn (Santa Rosa, CA, 2011), 79). The customers for coin- or pseudo-coin jewellery in England and the Netherlands at this time preferred brooches although pendants were also favoured in Sweden.

[24] Cook, 'Besant', 248.

Plate 2.1   Two recent major hoards from Viking England: (a) The Vale of
             York hoard, buried *c.*927–8, discovered 2007 (above). (b) The
             Silverdale hoard, buried *c.*900–10, discovered 2011 (below) (both
             Trustees of the British Museum).

Plate 2.2   Part of the assemblage of coins, bullion and weights from the riverine site in North Yorkshire, deposited in the mid-870s (Trustees of the British Museum).

Plate 16.1 Illustrations of gold coins from the catalogue and related objects. Above: (a) Almoravid dinar, AH 500 (AD 1106/7) (Ashmolean Museum, Oxford) (cat. no. 3); (b) Almoravid false dinar, AH 500–37 (AD 1106–42), mounted as a brooch (private owner) (Photograph, Fitzwilliam Museum, Cambridge) (cat. no. 6). Below: (c) Murcia dinar, AH 565? (AD 1169/70?), large fragment (British Museum) (cat. no. 7); (d) Almohad dinar, AH 563–80 (AD 1168–84) (Fitzwilliam Museum, Cambridge) (cat. no. 8); (e) Repoussé brooch front, excavated in Winchester, from the courtyard of the bishop's Wolvesey Palace (Winchester Excavations Committee, included and illustrated with its permission).

Plate 17.1   (a) *Solidus* from the Fitzwilliam Museum, Cambridge; (b) *Solidus* from author's collection.

Plate 17.2   (a) *Lucinius* shilling (T&S 37; Ashmolean Museum, Oxford); (b) Pada shilling (MEC 1, 669; Fitzwilliam Museum, Cambridge)

Plate 22.1   Part of the 2003 Glenfaba hoard (c.1030) (reproduced courtesy of
                Manx National Heritage).

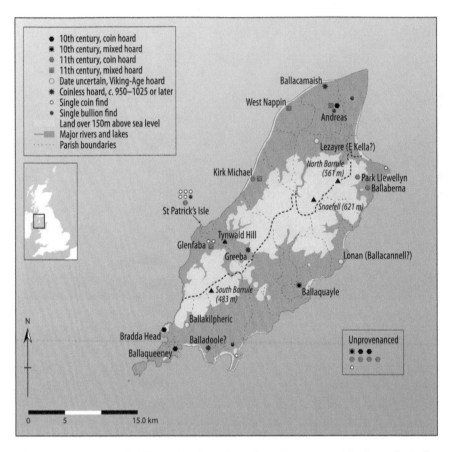

Legend:
- 10th century, coin hoard
- 10th century, mixed hoard
- 11th century, coin hoard
- 11th century, mixed hoard
- Date uncertain, Viking-Age hoard
- Coinless hoard, *c.* 950–1025 or later
- Single coin find
- Single bullion find
- Land over 150m above sea level
- Major rivers and lakes
- Parish boundaries

Map labels: Ballacamaish, West Nappin, Andreas, Lezayre (E Kella?), North Barrule (561 m), Park Llewellyn, Ballaberna, Kirk Michael, St Patrick's Isle, Snaefell (621 m), Tynwald Hill, Glenfaba, Greeba, Lonan (Ballacannell?), South Barrule (483 m), Ballaquayle, Ballakilpheric, Bradda Head, Balladoole?, Ballaqueeney

Unprovenanced

N

0   5   15.0 km

Plate 22.2   Map of Viking-Age hoards and single coin and bullion finds from the Isle of Man.

Plate 22.3   Three views of the arm-ring from the Glenfaba hoard (diameter 57.0 mm, wt 53.68 g; reproduced courtesy of Manx National Heritage): actual size and enlarged (top left).

Plate 25.1   The Linnakse hoard, Anija county, Estonia (Institute of History, Tallinn University).

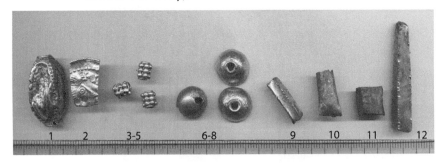

Plate 25.2   The non-numismatic silver from the Linnakse hoard. Note the numerous peck-marks on the silver bars, nos. 9 and 12 (Institute of History, Tallinn University).

A third additional find is the fragmentary Murcia dinar of Muhammad b. Si'd AH 542–67 (AD 1147–72), probably of AH 565 (AD 1169/70), found at Standon, Herefordshire, in 1995 (cat. no. 7, Colour Plate 16.1, c). It belongs to the series produced in this south-east Spanish Islamic kingdom after its breakaway from Almoravid rule and before its capture by the Almohads in AH 567 (AD 1172).The issues of the revived kingdom of Murcia in the thirteenth century have not been found in England. Several Murcian dinars occur among French finds, and one mounted as a pendant was included in the Duneslatten hoard found in 1881 at Dune on the island of Gotland, Sweden.[25] The issues of Murcia were one of the main sources of the gold used in the production of coins by the Christian states of the *Reconquista* as Islamic control in Spain retreated.[26]

The final addition to the corpus is the first recorded find of a gold coin of the Almohad dynasty in England and the latest Islamic coin represented here. It is a damaged dinar of Abu Ya'qub Yusf I, AH 558–80 (AD 1163–84) of the period AH 563–80 (AD 1168–84), found at Wattisham, Suffolk, in 2006 (cat. no. 8, Colour Plate 16.1, d).The list might possibly be extended by one more find. John Kent drew numismatic attention to a 'strange piece of gold' sent by the abbot of Hailes to Thomas Cromwell in 1538 and, discussing it in the context of the evidence for Almoravid and Almohad dinars in England, he suggested that it was perhaps one of them.[27] Theoretically, a gold coin with an Arabic inscription could belong to any of the series of Islamic gold coins known to have reached England since the eighth century, but the four known English find-spots of the five eighth-century examples (one possibly a plated counterfeit), are located in the eastern and south-eastern parts of the country, in East Anglia and Sussex.[28] If the Hailes coin were a local discovery, as seems likely, it was found in Gloucestershire in the middle west of England, which would not fit the distribution of these earlier coins. It would be more comfortably placed, as Kent suggested, within the later period being discussed here when finds of Islamic gold coins are slightly more plentiful and their distribution more widely spread throughout the country radiating from London (Figure 16.2). As there is no

---

[25] J. Duplessy, 'La circulation des monnaies arabes en Europe occidentale du VIIIe au XIIIe siècle', *RN, 5th series, 18* (1956), 101–63; M. Golabiewski Lannby and G. Rispling, 'Duneskattens mynt, myntsmycken och besvärjelser', *Svensk numismatisk tidskrift, 1* (2006), 60–3, at 61–2, Figure 2a–b.

[26] Balaguer, *Del Mancús*, 76, 129–30 and 150.

[27] J.P.C. Kent, *Coinage and Currency in London from the London and Middlesex Records and Other Sources from Roman Times to the Victorians* (London, 2005), 11, citing G.H. Cook, *Letters to Cromwell and Others on the Suppression of the Monasteries* (London, 1965), 206 (no. CXXXI).

[28] Naismith, 'Islamic coins', 218 (Table 4. *Single gold finds*). To the three eighth-century dinars listed there may now be added a fourth, an Abbasid dinar of Al-mahdi AH 168 (AD 784/5) (identified by Lutz Ilisch) found at Brandon, Suffolk, in 2007, EMC 2007.0235.

Figure 16.2   Find-spots of coins numbered as in the Catalogue.

detail available about this coin it has not been added to the Catalogue of finds below.

The later Islamic gold finds in England are thus concentrated in the narrow period from the mid-eleventh century to around the third quarter of the twelfth century. No gold coins from the North African mints of the Islamic dynasties have been found in England although they are present among French, Dutch and Swedish finds. Later Islamic and Iberian Christian gold coins are also unrepresented in England, as indeed are any other foreign gold coins for the rest of the period under review.[29] There are, as yet, no comparable finds recorded from Wales or Scotland.

Copies of Islamic Gold Coins as Brooches

The total number of Islamic gold coins found in England is still low, so it is useful to augment it by taking account of cheap locally made jewellery in bronze whose designs were copied from Islamic gold coins and thus bear witness to the presence of the prototypes in England. So far, no jewels made from genuine Islamic gold coins have been found in England, although they are known on the continent, for example plentifully in the Netherlands and also in Sweden.[30] All six known examples of English pseudo-dinar brooches of this period are incomplete, surviving only in the form of repoussé stamped bronze discs which have been identified as brooch-fronts on the basis of better-preserved examples of other nummular and non-nummular brooches dating between the early eleventh and early twelfth centuries displaying similar craft techniques.[31] The Arabic inscriptions on the examples on record are all so far devolved from the originals that, while the prototypes can be recognised as dinars of the Almoravid dynasty, AH 255–536 (AD 1063–1142), it is not possible to identify individual rulers, mints or dates. The difficulty is increased as extant examples are all uniface, providing only half the potential pseudo-Arabic inscriptions on which to base identifications. There are at present no English brooches of this kind yet known to have been copied from the later Almohad dinars, although nine related examples modelled on coins of this period are among finds from

---

[29]   B. Cook, 'Foreign coins in medieval England', in *Moneta locale, moneta straniera: Italia ed Europa XI–XV secolo*, ed. L. Travaini (Milan, 1999), 231–84. I am indebted to Dr Barrie Cook for details of a Byzantine gold coin reported found in the Bedale area of Yorkshire. It is a *histamenon trachy* of Emperor Michael VII Ducas (1071–78) and is pierced for wearing as a pendant (*Treasure Report* 2010, no. T298).

[30]   I am indebted for advice and literature on the Netherlands finds to Arent Pol, formerly of the Geldmuseum, Utrecht; and on the Swedish finds to Kenneth Jonsson of the Numismatic Institute, Stockholm.

[31]   M. Archibald, 'Pseudo-Kufic base-metal coin brooches from England', in *Magister Monetae: Studies in Honour of Jørgen Steen Jensen*, ed. M. Andersen, H.W. Horsnæs and J.C. Moesgaard, Publications of the National Museum Series in Archaeology and History, 13 (Copenhagen, 2007), 127–38, at 132–3; and T. Pestell and A. Marsden, 'Three repoussée foils imitating Arabic coins', in *The Winchester Mint, and Coins and Related Finds from the Excavations of 1961–71*, ed. M. Biddle (Oxford, 2012), 653–7, at 655.

the Netherlands.[32] The evocation of gold and wealth no doubt explains their attraction, but also involved were the magic and amuletic associations of exotic scripts.[33]

One of these repoussé brooch-fronts was excavated in a post-medieval context on the top of the south-western motte at Lewes Castle in Sussex.[34] Three were excavated in Winchester: two, produced by the same stamp, from the courtyard of the bishop's Wolvesey Palace (one is illustrated as Colour Plate 16.e) and a third more devolved example from a house in Brook Street.[35] The other examples were metal-detector finds from Norfolk: one from Burnham Market, and another from West Rudham produced from the same stamp as the pair from Wolvesey Castle. These six brooches thus establish the presence of four further Almoravid dinars in England.

The brooches are less useful in providing evidence for the places where the prototypes were available, because their places of manufacture were not necessarily the same as their find-spots. Unlike the early tenth-century brooches in lead, based on earlier Islamic silver dirhams of the Umayyad and Samanid dynasties which arrived from the east, and whose manufacture seems to be focused on London,[36] the production of the later dinar copies is less securely localised. No example has hitherto been found in London, but with the strong documentary evidence for the presence of Islamic gold coins in the capital, it remains a possibility. Winchester, with its three finds, is another candidate as it was a wealthy city where Islamic gold coins were also available. The accounts of the Bishop of Winchester show that in 1255/6 he purchased 12 marks *auri de musc* (Islamic gold coins) of unspecified denomination.[37] If they were

[32] J.P. Koers, J.N. Lanting and J. Molema, 'De muntfibula van een Almohadische dobla uit Scheemda: vondstomstandigheden, parallellen en historiche context', *Palaeohistoria: Acta et Communicationes Instituti Bio-Archaeologici Universitatis Groninganae*, 32 (1990), 331–8.

[33] A.L. Meaney, *Anglo-Saxon Amulets and Curing Stones*, BAR British Series, 96 (Oxford, 1981); and H. Maguire, 'Magic and money in the early Middle Ages', *Speculum*, 72 (1997), 1037–54 have much that is generally relevant for the magic and talismanic role of coins although they do not mention Islamic pieces specifically. See also K. Scarfe Beckett, *Anglo-Saxon Perceptions of the Islamic World*, Cambridge Studies in Anglo-Saxon England, 33 (Cambridge, 2003).

[34] Archibald, 'Pseudo-Kufic', 132–4 (no. 11).

[35] Pestell and Marsden, 'Three repoussée foils'. Neither of the two foils from the palace courtyard has visible remains of mounts so they are from two different brooches. There are no finds from England of brooches of the type found in the Netherlands where pairs of foils struck from the same stamp based on Almohad coins are mounted back to back (Koers *et al.*, 'De mintfibula').

[36] Archibald, 'Pseudo-Kufic', 128–32 and nos 1–10.

[37] P. Grierson, 'Muslim coins in thirteenth-century England', in *Near-Eastern Numismatics, Iconography, Epigraphy and History: Studies in Honor of George C. Miles*, ed. D.K. Kouymjian (Beirut, 1974), 387–91 (repr. in his *Later Medieval Numismatics (11th–16th Centuries)* (London, 1979), no. VIII), at 391, calculated that this represented about 1,200 obols (Almohad dinars).

contemporary coins they would have been Almohad but the coin stock of his supplier may still have included some earlier Almoravid dinars (see below).

Brooches thus increase the evidence for the presence of Islamic dinars to eleven which, with the Christian *mancus* from Barcelona, makes a total of 12 gold coins from Spain known to have been in England, and the number of places where they were available at some point is raised to at least seven. The incidence of pseudo-coin brooches is perhaps as dependent on fashion as it is on the availability of prototypes, but the English brooches are all in fact copied from issues of the Almoravid period, which also produces most of the coin finds. Thus there is currently evidence for nine Almoravid dinars (five with issue dates between AH 480/500 and 480/500 (AD 1087/1106 and 1106/42), and four from the brooches with unknown dates), one Murcian dinar of AH 565 (AD 1169/70) and one Almohad dinar of AH 558–80 (AD 1163–84).

Single finds do not reflect the presence of the different series of coins in circulation precisely but, as numbers rise, they provide an increasingly accurate indicator. Here, the numbers are still small and new discoveries could alter the exact proportions, but the corpus is now large enough to have established a pattern: one of clear preponderance of Almoravid over Almohad issues and the absence of anything later. As the Almohads enjoyed a longer period of power than the Almoravids, the difference in their representation is not the result of the duration of production. The reasons for this pattern will be discussed below after the documentary evidence has been explored.

Denominations, Weights and Names[38]

The Almoravids issued just one gold denomination, the dinar, the standard issue weight of which was 4.1 g. It was known in England, and widely throughout Europe, as the *marabitino* (varied spellings). In general, weights of Islamic gold coins from circulation are usually just below the standard: extant Almoravid dinars weigh mainly within the range 3.92–3.96g. The Almohads issued three gold denominations. The largest, the double dinar, which at first was set at a weight standard of 4.7g (later stabilising at 4.6g), was known, in England only, as the *denier de musc*. The dinar, standard issue weight 2.30g, was known (also in England only) as the *obol de musc*. There was also a half dinar, with a standard issue weight of 1.15g. The half dinar, effectively a farthing of *musc*, does not appear to have featured separately by name in the English accounts and none has been found in England. The Spanish name for the Almohad double dinar, the *dobla*, applied also to Christian Spanish derivatives. It is not found referring to the original Islamic coins in English sources, although the term is found

---

[38] P. Grierson, '*Oboli de musc*", *EHR, 66* (1951), 75–81.

elsewhere in Europe. The name of the ruler appears on all these coins and while the mint and date of issue are found on Almoravid coins, they are absent from Almohad ones. Few people in medieval England could read Arabic and English sources do not take note of individual rulers' names and mints, referring to Islamic coins only by these generic names. Almoravid coins could, then as now, be distinguished easily from Almohad ones because the former have the central area of inscription on both sides enclosed within a circle, and the latter within a square. Islamic gold coins are sometimes recorded by tale.[39] A particular price may have been agreed on occasion when gold coins were being exchanged, but official records do not appear to have taken account of individual differences in the weights of specimens. Standard values in terms of marks of gold no doubt allowed for normal variations in individual weights, and bulk weighings could result in the slight differences in valuations recorded. Changes in the silver to gold conversion rate also affected valuations.

The English Documentary Evidence

The documentary evidence for Islamic gold in England at this time has been discussed by Philip Grierson, David Carpenter and Barrie Cook.[40] It is almost entirely concentrated on the later part of the period under review since it is mainly sourced from the Pipe Rolls and other official records not extant for the earlier period. Detailed ecclesiastical and lay financial records are still scarce during this period, particularly in the earlier years, but mention of Islamic gold coins in the accounts of the Bishop of Winchester for 1255/56 has been noted above and those of the manor of Taunton, Somerset (held by the Bishop of Winchester), record the sum of 1529 *denari auri musc'* a year later.[41]

Mentions of gold in the earlier narrative sources are often regarded as conventional descriptions of cupidity or wealth, for example when the *Anglo-Saxon Chronicle* says that William I (1066–1087) 'seized from his subject men many a mark of gold' and that Henry I (1100–1135) had gathered 'a great amount [in] gold and silver',[42] but the finds, few as they are, show that gold coins were in fact available at those times in England, particularly in the reign of Henry

---

[39]   For example, in the earlier entries of Peter Chaceporc's Wardrobe accounts for 1242–53 (D.A. Carpenter, 'The gold treasure of Henry III', *Thirteenth Century England, 1* (1986), 61–88, at 81–8).

[40]   Grierson, '*Oboli de musc'*, and 'Muslim coins'; D.A. Carpenter, 'Gold treasure', and 'Gold and gold coins in England in the mid-thirteenth century', *NC, 147* (1987), 106–13; Cook 'Besant', and 'Foreign coins'.

[41]   Grierson, 'Muslim coins', 391.

[42]   *The Anglo-Saxon Chronicles*, ed. and trans. M. Swanton, rev. ed. (London, 2001), 220–21, 263.

I, and uncoined gold is mentioned in financial records as soon as they become available. The earliest isolated Pipe Roll for 1129/30 (in the Almoravid period) refers to sums in gold but no Islamic coins are mentioned. Although Almoravid *marabitinos* account for a majority of the English finds, there appears to be only a single mention of one by name in the English written sources. An Inventory of St Paul's cathedral, London, compiled in 1295, records a *marabitino* fixed to the altar of St Lawrence there.[43]

The main series of Pipe Rolls begins in 1155/6, by which time the Almohads were dominant in Islamic Spain. These rolls are concerned only with transactions which involved the court and do not include all royal financial business, some of which was channelled by different routes. Almohad gold coins do not feature in the Pipe Rolls until 1189/90 when it is recorded that *obol' de Muscze* had been purchased for Richard I (1189–99). Other similar entries are to be found in 1191/2, 1192/3 and 1210/11, and an *obolum musc'* is mentioned in the Patent Rolls in 1216.[44] It is notable, however, that every one of the Islamic coins so far known to have been found in England was issued before even the earliest of these entries. The possibility of extended survival of gold coins will be considered below. Between 1238 and 1240 there are many entries in the growing number of official financial rolls recording *ad hoc* purchases of both *obols* and *deniers de musc*, mainly for royal alms and to further Henry III's personal interests. They increased massively from 1242 to 1253 as a consequence of his demand that all payments be made in gold in order to build up treasures intended to finance major projects overseas. Another treasure which began to be accumulated in 1254 was used to produce his gold penny, launched in 1257.[45] A major part of Henry III's gold came from the Jewish community as gifts and fines, the rest from ecclesiastical sources and laypeople as gifts, fines and payments for favours or concessions. The king eventually accepted some payments in silver which he had converted into gold by his agents. The larger part of the gold received overall was, however, in the form of ingots, dust or leaves rather than coins.[46]

Apart from royal officials and Jewish sources, the agents named in Peter Chaceporc's Wardrobe accounts for 1242–53 are Henry Frowick, John Hardel and William Hardel.[47] Both families had longstanding connections with the

---

[43]   Grierson, 'Muslim coins', 391.

[44]   Grierson, '*Oboli de musc*", 75–7. Cook has pointed out that Henry III may have obtained more Islamic gold coins because the supply of new bezants dried up for 30 years as production ceased in Constantinople in 1204 following the Fourth Crusade, and was only recommenced by the Nicene emperors under John III Ducas-Vatatzes (1221–1254) (Cook, 'Besant', 273).

[45]   Carpenter, 'Gold treasure', and 'Gold and gold coins'.

[46]   Carpenter, 'Gold treasure'.

[47]   The Frowicks were identified as pepperers (G.A. Williams, *Medieval London: from Commune to Capital* (London, 1963), 144), but Nightingale warns against identifying families with one exclusive trading interest before the fourteenth century, when Walter Frowick was one of

London mint. Henry Frowick and John Hardel had experience as moneyers and the former was presented as an assayer at London in 1247.[48] William Hardel served as Warden with control of the mint and the exchanges of London and Canterbury from 1234 to 1248.[49] All three thus had expertise in dealing with the business of coins, exchanges and the bullion markets. In 1244–45 the Wardrobe received 510 *ob musc* from William Hardel: the largest number of Islamic coins accounted for in any one year throughout the entire period of these Wardrobe accounts.[50]

Sources of the Uncoined Gold and Gold Coins

The old idea that Islamic gold coins found in England were 'souvenirs of the Crusades', while not impossible in the odd case, may be generally discounted. Crusaders occasionally acquired large amounts of booty, for example the English, Flemings and men of Cologne at the capture of Lisbon in 1147.[51] In that instance, what outlasted their onward journey to the Levant, the Crusaders' defeat there and the return of survivors, is likely to have been negligible. The Crusades do not account for the considerable presence of uncoined gold and Islamic gold coins in England represented by the current corpus of finds and documentary evidence. Verlinden and Nightingale have demonstrated the trade connection between western Europe, London and Spain. Nightingale in particular has followed the Deorman family of moneyers and city merchants specialising in the spice trade known as the 'pepperers'.[52] London merchants in

---

the two wardens of the Grocers' Company (successors of the pepperers), or projecting known later specialisations back to an earlier period (Nightingale, *Mercantile Community*, 43–8, 215, 237). The Hardels were identified as vintners but had also other interests (Williams, *Medieval London*, 54 and 64).

[48]   Mayhew, 'From regional to central minting, 1158–1464', in *A New History of the Royal Mint*, ed. C.E. Challis (Cambridge, 1992), 83–178, at 115n; R. Churchill, *Mints and Moneyers in the Reign of Henry III* (London, 2012), 41–9, 57–65.

[49]   Mayhew, 'From regional to central minting, 1158–1464', 103 and 114; Churchill, *Mints and Moneyers*, 57–65.

[50]   Carpenter, 'Gold treasure', 84.

[51]   *De expugnatione Lyxbonensi. The Conquest of Lisbon*, ed. and trans. C.W. David, with foreword and bibliography by J.P. Phillips (New York, 2001), esp. 110–15, the contract between the crusaders and the king of Portugal under which they were allowed to keep all the wealth found in the town and the money obtained from ransoms.

[52]   Verlinden, 'Spanish trade'; P. Nightingale, 'Pepperers' guild', and 'The evolution of weight standards and the creation of new monetary and commercial links in northern Europe from the tenth to the twelfth century', *EcHR, 2nd series, 38* (1985), 192–209, also *Mercantile Community*, 23–42.

northern Spain would have had access there to local Christian gold coins and more numerous Islamic issues, as well as to gold in other forms. The acquisition of gold was not confined to balances from normal trade, but would have been derived from silver in coin or bullion brought to Spain by English merchants and financiers specifically to take advantage of the fluctuating but favourable exchange rate.[53] Gold purchased there could be brought back to England and sold at a profit.

Role of the Islamic and Other Gold Coins from Spain

Uncoined gold in England at this time had primarily a craft and bullion function and gold coins did not circulate to the same extent as silver pennies, but they were not merely a commodity employed by goldsmiths and hoarded as treasure. Some people no doubt needed to purchase gold in non-monetary form from goldsmiths or in coin from financiers expressly for the purpose of making payments in Henry III's medium of choice,[54] but the distribution of the finds shows that Islamic gold coins were in fact widely available, and lost, throughout the provinces, and this points to a monetary role. The seven gold coin finds from England are all apparently un-mounted coins,[55] again confirming their use as money in the conduct of normal, if high level, commercial and personal business. The gilded base-metal counterfeit mounted as a brooch probably also represents an original monetary use. French finds are comparable to English in that all are apparently un-mounted coins.[56] In contrast, the eleven single finds from the Netherlands all survive as brooches, with no recorded losses of un-mounted coins, suggesting a stronger emphasis there on the coins' bullion function.[57] In Sweden both mounted and un-mounted coins have been found.[58]

---

[53] Nightingale, *Mercantile Community*, 40–41.

[54] Carpenter, 'Gold treasure', 68 and 80.

[55] Of the seven gold coins, the four extant were certainly never mounted (nos 1, 3, 7 and 8); the other three (nos 2 (recorded from a drawing), 4 and 5 (recorded from a description) cannot now be checked but they were said to be coins not brooches and no mounts are shown or mentioned.

[56] J. Duplessy, 'Circulation des monnaies', *Les trésors monétaires médiévaux et modernes découverts en France*, 2 vols (Paris, 1985–95).

[57] Details of the Netherlands finds here and below are based on information provided by Arent Pol, formerly of the Geldmuseum, Utrecht.

[58] Details of the Swedish finds here and below are based on information provided by Kenneth Jonsson, Numismatic Institute, University of Stockholm.

Comparison of the Pattern of Finds and the Documentary Evidence

The documentary evidence just outlined, showing large numbers of Almohad gold coins available in England in the 1240s and into the 1250s, appears at variance with the eight English finds which close somewhere between 1163 and 1184, with only one Almohad piece. By contrast, among the Dutch finds (all brooches), there is just one Almoravid dinar, but ten Almohad gold coins from both Spain and North Africa ending with a dinar of Abd Allah I, AH 621–24 (AD 1224–27) and one Portuguese *morabitino* of Pedro I (1185–1211). The French evidence is more plentiful but is sometimes equivocal because only one or two coins are identified in each of several large groups. Making use of Duplessy's lists,[59] there are five finds of, or including, Almoravid dinars, four with coins of Murcia and five with Almohad coins. Almoravid and Murcian gold coins are found together but no hoard is said to have included both Almoravid and Almohad issues, although again the evidence is not conclusive in some cases. Almoravid and Almohad coins (mounted as pendants) were found together in the Duneskatten bullion hoard of gold and silver artefacts and coins from Gotland, Sweden, deposited in the fourteenth century, and thus hardly valid evidence on this point.[60] The European finds thus bear out the English documentary sources that early Almohad gold coins were present in north-west Europe in considerable numbers. Later Almohad coins and the issues of their successors in North Africa are not clearly present in the French hoards, and the Islamic coins are replaced by more limited numbers of gold coins from Christian Spain. Later in time Italian issues are more plentiful, particularly the florins of Florence, issued from 1252. Coins of none of these groups have been found so far in England, although the Italian coins are mentioned in documentary sources.

Longevity of Gold Coins

Medieval gold coins often had a long life, even in such a highly managed coinage as the English,[61] and good quality gold coins – in a context where they were not subject to regulation – probably remained indefinitely in circulation until

---

[59] Duplessy, 'Circulation des monnaies', *Trésors monétaires*. The paper given by Monsieur Duplessy at the International Numismatic Congress at Madrid in 2003 on a related subject did not appear in the *Proceedings*.

[60] Golabiewski Lannby and Rispling, 'Duneskattens mynt', 62 (no. 3).

[61] The Fishpool, Nottinghamshire, hoard deposited in *c*.1463/4 included 27 coins of Edward III (1327–77) struck from 1351, and a total of 40 nobles and half nobles issued prior to 1411 when the weights were lowered. This represents about 4 per cent of the English coins present. (M. Archibald, 'Fishpool, Blidworth (Notts.), 1966 hoard', *NC*, 7th series, 7 (1967), 133–46, at 134)

they disappeared through natural wastage. While it is more likely that the majority of the English finds were deposited a relatively short time after they were struck, some Almoravid *marabitinos* must certainly have remained in the available English coin stock in the early days of the Almohad issues. They may well have survived even later to be swept up into Henry III's treasures, some perhaps returning to circulation from long dormant reserves to meet the king's demands. The Almoravid dinar (*marabitino*) at 4.1 g issue weight was somewhat lighter than the Almohad double dinar (*denier de musc*) at 4.6 g issue weight but the two denominations had distinctive types and might have circulated together like the pre-decimal British two shilling piece and the half-crown.

Ideally, gold hoards of appropriate dates would demonstrate if, and to what extent, earlier Almoravid coins had survived, but no English hoard of gold coins is known from this time. There is one piece of evidence for the contemporaneous use of these two coinages, provided by the Almoravid *marabitino* and the two Almohad *obols of musc* which the 1295 Inventory records were fixed, with four rings, to the altar of St Lawrence in St Paul's cathedral, London.[62] These coins had not been mentioned in the previous Inventory of 1245, which had noted a ring fixed to another altar, so it would appear that they had been added to St Lawrence's altar either separately or together at some time between 1245 and 1295. In other words, the Almoravid and Almohad coins had both been available at some time between those years and the writer in 1295 was familiar enough with the two denominations to recognise and name them.

The other documentary evidence, including Chaceporc's Wardrobe accounts of 1242–53, ostensibly includes Almohad issues alone among the Islamic gold coins, as only *deniers de musc* and *obols de musc* are named. If any Almoravid *marabitinos* had been offered in payment to the king, they could have been distinguished by sight but perhaps the accountants did not want to complicate matters by creating another category and simply counted and recorded them with the slightly heavier, Almohad *deniers de musc*, relying on differences in bulk weighings to provide an accurate valuation. A possible example of the less than strict identification of individual denominations in the accounts is the problem of the valuation of a group of *augustales* which might possibly have included a half denomination.[63] The half dinar denomination is apparently completely absent from the accounts, but perhaps examples were grouped with obols (possibly in pairs) or other gold issues.

---

[62]   Grierson, 'Muslim coins', 391.

[63]   Carpenter, 'Gold and gold coins', 109.

Decline in the Presence of Gold

It would be natural to conclude that the low representation of Almohad gold coins and the absence of later issues among the English finds were the result of Henry III bleeding the country of its gold in order to build up his treasure.[64] Carpenter has calculated that, by the end of 1253, Henry III had accumulated 650 kilograms of gold worth some 28,390 marks of silver.[65] Much of the earlier treasure was expended outside England and the latest, which began to be accumulated from 1254 and was originally intended for another overseas venture, was converted into the king's new gold pennies issued from 1257, leaving fewer Islamic gold coins around to be lost locally. The effect of Henry III's activities was undoubtedly a factor in the later period, but it cannot be the whole story. The king began collecting in earnest only in 1242, but the issue date of the latest of the English finds is AH 563–80 (AD 1168–84), in the days of his grandfather. Even allowing that a number of the coins may have been deposited some years after they were issued, an explanation is still required to account for the absence of survivors from issues between these dates and of any later finds.

The most straightforward explanation is that gold coins of that period were simply not present in sufficiently large numbers in England to ensure their representation among the finds. Considering the low total of English finds, the *marabitinos* struck during the later Almoravid period (which came into the country around the time the king's great-great-grandfather Henry I (1100–35) was building up his own treasure) are well represented, accounting for up to five out of the total of eight, and four out of seven find-spots. This suggests that they had been available in larger numbers in England than the following Almohad coins, although the absence of financial records for the earlier period does not allow this to be tested or compared with the scale of the documented presence of the later Almohad issues. The second half of the twelfth century is represented among the finds by only two coins: one dinar of Murcia dated AH 565? (AD 1169/70?) and one Almohad dinar of AH 563–80 (AD 1168–84), with nothing later. Numbers are small and some coins can be dated only within wide brackets, but the scenario they suggest is clear: the amount of gold entering England peaked in the first half of the twelfth century, declined in the second half and still further by its end and into the thirteenth century. The cumulative evidence of the English coin-finds thus supports Nightingale's observation, based on the interrupted Pipe Rolls, that the availability of gold in the late twelfth century had declined from what it had been earlier.[66]

---

[64] Carpenter, 'Gold treasure', 'Gold and gold coins'.

[65] Carpenter, 'Gold and gold coins', 106.

[66] Nightingale notes that payments in gold are not uncommon in the isolated Pipe Roll of 1129/30 but that, when they resume in 1155/6, the early Pipe Rolls of Henry II indicate that they

By the end of the twelfth century, the routes by which trans-Saharan gold was reaching Europe were changing.[67] The gradual expulsion of the Moors from almost all of Spain reduced the amount of gold arriving there from Africa. Gold coins continued to be produced by the Nasrids in Granada and the Islamic mints in North Africa, and the expanding Christian kingdoms in Spain and Portugal produced successful gold coinages of their own, but not on a scale to compare with the previous Islamic issues. More gold was already reaching Italy in the late twelfth century and, alongside the on-going *taris*, increasing supplies were used to produce new gold coinages: the *augustales* of Frederick II of Sicily from 1231; the numerous gold florins produced in Florence from 1252; and other Italian issues. These soon took the place of the earlier Islamic issues of Spain and North Africa in providing fresh supplies of gold coin for the rest of Europe but in the later thirteenth century the gold coins of Florence and Genoa both initially circulated more in the Levant than in the west.[68] They are present in French hoards and, although they feature in the English written sources, were apparently not reaching the country in sufficient quantities to be represented as yet among finds. As more coins are found, they may be expected to appear, but the present pattern suggests that they will continue to be outnumbered by earlier twelfth-century issues, particularly Islamic ones, and especially those from Spain. After the failure within a few years of Henry III's gold penny, 'The Age of Silver' resumed in England for close on another century. Edward III's experiments with gold coins from 1344, followed in 1351 by the launch of his successful and enduring gold coinage, finally brought it to an end.

---

were becoming rarer (Nightingale, 'Evolution of weight standards', 204).

[67] Spufford, *Money*, 176–7.

[68] Spufford, *Money*, 177.

Catalogue

1. Barcelona, bilingual *mancus*, Raymond Berengar I (1036–94), period 1069–75. Wt: 1.90g. Balaguer type 19 except the obverse legend is retrograde as on type 18. Found at Denham, Buckinghamshire, in 1995 and shown at the British Museum (Figure 16.1; photograph from British Museum). Present location unknown.

2. Almoravid dinar, probably Yusuf b. Tashuf in AH 480–500 (AD 1087–1106), mint, date and weight not known. Found near York, 1752. Recorded with an incomplete drawing in the minutes of the Society of Antiquaries of London. Blackburn, 'Gold in England', 84–5 (no. A25) (drawing illustrated). Present location unknown.

3. Almoravid dinar, 'Ali b. Yusuf (AH 500–37; AD 1106–42), dated AH 500 (AD 1106/7) mint of Denia. Found at St Aldates, Oxford, 1825. Wt: 4.1g. Christ Church collection no. 364. Brown, 'Dinar'; Blackburn, 'Gold in England', 84–55 (no. A26). Ashmolean Museum, Oxford; included and illustrated here by permission of the Trustees.

4 and 5. Two Almoravid dinars, Ali b. Yusuf (AH 500–37; AD 1106–42), Almeria mint, dated AH 525 (AD 1130/1). Weight not known. Found near St Paul's, London, before 1879. Anonymous, 'Old coins exhumed in London', unillustrated note in *American Journal of Numismatics, 13* (1878/9), 92–93. Cited by Duplessy, 'Circulation des monnaies', 133 (no. 36); Blackburn, 'Gold in England', 84–5 (nos A27–8). Present location unknown.

6. Gilded base-metal counterfeit of an Almoravid dinar of Ali b. Yusuf (AH 500–37; AD 1106–42) mounted as a brooch, Valencia mint. Found near Winchester in 2011. Width of coin at widest point, 22.5 mm. Identification by Vladimir Nastich. Private collection; included and illustrated here with by permission of the owner.

7. Murcian dinar, Muhammad b. Si'd (AH 542–67; AD 1147–72), AH 565? (AD 1169/70?). Wt: 2.10g (fragment). Found at Standon, Hertfordshire, 1995. Identification by Venetia Porter. British Museum; included and illustrated here by permission of the Trustees.

8. Almohad dinar, Ya'qub Yusuf I (AH 558–80; AD 1163–84), AH 563–80 (AD 1168–84). Wt: 2.01g (incomplete). Found at Wattisham, Suffolk, 2006. PAS SF-9EB484; EMC 2006.0231; CR 2007, no. 420. Fitzwilliam Museum, Cambridge; included and illustrated here by permission of the Fitzwilliam Museum.

PART IV
Coins and Coin Hoards in Context

Chapter 17

A Seventh-Century Anglo-Saxon *Solidus* Pendant of the *Cross-on-Steps* Type Found in Kent

Stewart Lyon,* with an Appendix by Michael Cowell

Sixty years ago Professor Philip Grierson brought together and illustrated three specimens of a type of imitative *solidus* that had not been included in C.H.V. Sutherland's *Anglo-Saxon Gold Coinage in the Light of the Crondall Hoard*.[1] The obverse was based on a *solidus* of the late fourth century with diademed bust, while the reverse copied the cross-on-steps design of seventh-century Byzantine *solidi*. One of the three specimens was in the Germanisches National-Museum in Nuremberg (Figure 17.1a), with a die-duplicate in the Bibliothèque Nationale in Paris (Figure 17.1b), while the third – a cast, subsequently replaced by the original specimen (Colour Plate 17.1) – was in the Fitzwilliam Museum and from different dies; it is now catalogued as *MEC* 1, 665 (*SCBI* 1, 217). Grierson endorsed the opinion of Le Gentilhomme that the type is Anglo-Saxon.[2]

No recorded provenance exists of any of the three specimens, though Grierson thought the Cambridge specimen had probably been found locally. Ian Stewart (now Lord Stewartby) agreed that an English origin for these *solidi* was likely and commented that the area most familiar with gold in the form of *tremisses* was south-east England.[3] It is satisfying, therefore, that an entire pendant with a

* Acknowledgements: The writer gratefully acknowledges the kindness of the Trustees of the British Museum and subsequently the Syndics of the Fitzwilliam Museum, and their respective Keepers of Coins and Medals, in accepting on loan and taking care of the *solidus* pendant, which is now due to remain at the Fitzwilliam Museum for his lifetime. Special thanks are due to Dr Gareth Williams for enabling Mr Cowell's report on its composition to be included in this publication.

[1]   P. Grierson, 'A new Anglo-Saxon *solidus*', *NC, 6th series, 13* (1953), 88–91; C.H.V. Sutherland, *Anglo-Saxon Gold Coinage in the Light of the Crondall Hoard* (Oxford, 1948).

[2]   P. Le Gentilhomme, 'Le monnayage et la circulation monétaire dans les royaumes barbares en Occident (Ve–VIIIe siècle)', *RN, 5th series, 8* (1944–5), 45–112, at 62 and pl. II, 4.

[3]   I. Stewart, 'Anglo-Saxon gold coins', in *Scripta Nummaria Romana: Essays Presented to Humphrey Sutherland*, ed. R.A.G. Carson and C.M. Kraay (London, 1978), 143–72, at 154. For more recent finds see G. Williams, 'Anglo-Saxon gold coinage. Part 1: the transition from Roman to Anglo-Saxon coinage', *BNJ, 80* (2010), 51–75.

Figure 17.1   (a) *Solidus* from the Germanisches National-Museum, Nuremberg
(left); (b) *Solidus* from the Bibliothèque Nationale (right) (both
reproduced from P. Grierson, 'A new Anglo-Saxon *solidus*', *NC, 6th
series, 13* (1953), 88–91, by kind permission of the RNS).

Kentish find-spot is now known (Colour Plate 17.1b). It was found in December
1984 at Bell Farm, Minster, Isle of Sheppey, by metal detectorist Vincent Cato
while searching a recently ploughed field. A Coroner's Court at Gillingham
decided that the pendant was not Treasure Trove. It was acquired by the present
writer shortly afterwards from Spink and placed initially on lifetime loan with
the Department of Coins and Medals at the British Museum. By arrangement
between the respective keepers the loan was transferred to the Fitzwilliam
Museum in 2008, and the pendant was given a public viewing through its
inclusion later that year in the Museum's travelling exhibition *Anglo-Saxon Art
in the Round*, organised by Mark Blackburn.

The three previous specimens all have fragments of a mount still adhering,
but the fourth is complete with suspension loop and is mounted in a beaded
band. It weighs 4.67g, which is, not surprisingly, significantly heavier than
the others (3.65, 3.96 and 4.14g respectively). The reverse, with a jumbled
inscription and, in exergue, o w o, is from the same die used for the Nuremberg
and Paris specimens (Stewart A.92),[4] while the obverse, reading k3ãi TĩVC,
is from the same die as the Cambridge specimen (Stewart A.93), so the Sheppey
pendant may be classified as Stewart A.93/92. The detail of the obverse, which
is now fully visible (the Cambridge specimen being holed), shows that the die
was engraved more finely than that used to strike A.92 – for example, the ear
is depicted by a curve rather than a large pellet and the hair at the back of the
head and neck is moulded rather than pelleted – but the general impression of
similarity is such that the cruder die is probably to be construed as the finer one
recut.

While the pendant was at the British Museum it was examined for the
Department of Coins and Medals by Mr M.R. Cowell, a synopsis of whose
report is as follows:[5]

---

4   Stewart, 'Anglo-Saxon gold coins', 162.
5   See the Appendix for his detailed report.

The coin was examined by optical and scanning electron microscopy (SEM) and analysed by x-ray fluorescence. The coin, which seems to have been die struck, has been mounted with a small suspension loop and beading has been attached around the edge. The beading and loop are of similar composition with about 68 per cent gold, 30 per cent silver and 2 per cent copper. The coin is of different composition with about 56 per cent gold, 42 per cent silver and 2 per cent copper. Possible areas of solder attaching to the loop and beading were analysed and gave compositions similar to the adjacent components. No metals indicating modern manufacture (e.g. cadmium) were detected in the solder areas. The SEM examination showed features characteristic of ancient gold, such as stress-corrosion cracking. The composition of the coin is similar to equivalent gold objects of the Anglo-Saxon period. The coin is not inconsistent with the purported [sixth–seventh century] origin.

For comparison, the Fitzwilliam specimen *MEC* 1, 665 was recently analysed by XRF in connection with the forthcoming BM Sylloge volume and yielded 62.2 per cent gold, 36.7 per cent silver and 1.1 per cent copper, with <0.1 per cent of lead.[6]

The fact that all four surviving *solidi* of this type were mounted for use as pendants is in keeping with the view that such pieces may only have been produced for medallic purposes or as articles of jewellery.[7] However, the explanation could be that pendants had a better chance of survival than unmounted coins, if such there were. Mr Cowell's conclusion that the loop and band of the Kentish pendant are of finer gold than the central *solidus* – a discrepancy which he observes is paralleled by other Anglo-Saxon and Merovingian specimens – suggests that the mounting may have been undertaken at a different place and time than the minting.

As to the dating, the gold content of the *solidus* is within the 51–59 per cent range of the *Lucinius tremisses* (most probably *scillingas*, or shillings) present in the Crondall hoard (Colour Plate 17.2a).[8] There are also some common stylistic features, notably the use of large pellets in the treatment of hair or diadem or both, as Le Gentilhomme remarked. The closest comparative facial portrait is to be found on an example of the *Pada* series, Stewart A.113 (*MEC* 1, 669, *SCBI* 1, 220) (Colour Plate 17.2b), which also has a similar if more lengthy obverse

---

[6]   G. Williams and D. Hook, 'Analysis of gold content and its implications for the chronology of the early Anglo-Saxon coinage', in A. Gannon, *SCBI 63: British Museum, Anglo-Saxon Coins. Part I: Early Anglo-Saxon Gold and Anglo-Saxon and Continental Silver Coinage of the North Sea Area, c. 600–760* (London, 2013), 55–70, at 58–9.

[7]   Sutherland, *Anglo-Saxon Gold Coinage*, 38.

[8]   D.M. Metcalf, *Thrymsas and Sceattas in the Ashmolean Museum Oxford* (3 vols, London, 1993–4), 1, 62.

inscription. However, although the engraver may perhaps be the same, the gold content is recorded in *MEC* as 10 per cent, which suggests a significant time lag.

Unless *solidi* and shillings were minted to different gold standards, the *solidus* in the pendant is likely to have been broadly contemporary with the *Lucinius* shillings. They are among the less fine coins in Crondall; are all from the same obverse die; and may therefore have been struck close to the date of the hoard's deposit, put by Metcalf at *c*.635–45.[9] Grierson and Blackburn, confirming Grierson's original impression, describe the obverse of the Cambridge *solidus* as copied from an imperial *solidus* of the late fourth century, and the reverse from a *solidus* of Heraclius (610–41).[10] Grierson had suggested a date 'towards the middle of the century' on the reasoning that the O W O in the exergue of the reverse was derived from a CONOB in which the C and B had tended to separate from the ONO and fuse with the rest of the legend, as on the Sicilian *solidi* of Constans II (641–68) and his successors.[11] The new *solidus* pendant does nothing to detract from that perception.

[9] Ibid., 1, 31 and pl. 2.

[10] *MEC* 1, 665.

[11] Grierson, 'New Anglo-Saxon *solidus*', 90.

Appendix: Report on the Examination of a Mounted Gold Coin Purported to be a Sixth- to Seventh-Century Anglo-Saxon Copy of a Roman *Solidus* by M.R. Cowell

Introduction

The mounted coin, a rare early Anglo-Saxon type which copies the style of a Roman gold *solidus*, has been on loan to the Department of Coins and Medals for some years. The coin is numismatically acceptable and was submitted for confirmation that it is technically consistent with its purported origin.

Microscopy

The coin was examined by optical and scanning electron microscopy (SEM). The coin has been mounted with a suspension loop and the initial microscopic examination showed that a beaded wire has also been attached round the edge of the coin. Both of these components appear to have been fused to the coin using only small amounts of solder, if any. The beads on the beaded wire are not regularly spaced and seem to have been formed individually; this could have been done by filing or rolling using a v-shaped single-edged tool.[12] The suspension loop has a grooved surface which is very similar to that observed on Anglo-Saxon mounted coins.[13]

All components of the artefact show similar amounts of wear. Thus, on the coin proper, the high points of the design are worn smooth but there are also numerous cuts and abrasions. The outer edge of the beaded wire has lost most of the grooves separating the beads whereas they are visible adjacent to the recessed join with the coin. The loop shows wear on its exposed surfaces and slight wear inside where it could have been attached to a suspension wire, cord or chain.

The expected method of manufacture of the coin would be by die-striking. Unfortunately, the clearest evidence of this technique, namely surface flow lines indicating metal movement under the dies, are not visible here. However, these features are readily obliterated by wear and are often only seen on freshly minted coins. The sharpness of the edge of some of the lettering and punch-mark flaws on some letters are indications that the coin was die-struck. Nevertheless, there are also some other features present that seem to be casting defects.

---

[12]   N. Whitfield, 'The manufacture of ancient beaded wire: experiments and observations', *Jewellery Studies*, 8 (1998), 57–86.

[13]   S.C. Hawkes, J.M. Merrick and D.M. Metcalf, 'X-ray fluorescent analysis of some Dark-Age coins and jewellery', *Archaeometry*, 9 (1966), 98–138.

Other surface characteristics observed include small raised granular features, cracks, and raised lines. The granular features are generally in the range 50–100μm across and are present mainly in the recessed areas of the coin; none were observed on the raised areas although occasionally they are present on the side of the raised areas. They are visible on both faces of the coin although they are more frequent on the obverse (head side) and a few are also evident on the inner edge of the beading where it joins the coin. These granular features are similar in appearance to certain casting flaws which can arise from defects in a moulding material; they are however rather different from features associated with electro-forming.

The cracks are present on both faces of the coin and have an irregular zig-zag format. They traverse both the recessed and raised areas of the design and continue from the coin face into the beaded edge showing that they formed after the components were joined. Where they occur near the granular features they generally track along the edge of these rather than through them.

A further feature observed on some areas of the obverse, in recesses and not on parts of the design and inscription, is a network of raised lines about 1μm in thickness and enclosing areas about 50μm across. As with the cracks, they skirt the edge of the granular features and seem to form a linked network around the granules.

The coin was also examined for the presence of platinum group element (PGE) inclusions, material which may be characteristic of alluvial gold, but none were found.

Traces of a silicaceous material were found in the recesses on parts of the coin and particularly under the suspension loop. This material includes quartz grains and a finer grained component with some black inclusions that were not identified. (There was much sand in the gulleys between the coin and the beading when the object was acquired, and most of it was subsequently removed.)

Analysis

The components were analysed non-destructively by x-ray fluorescence XRF with the following semi-quantitative (approximate) results (see Table 17.1 below which also shows comparative analyses):

Table 17.1   XRF analysis for the coin components and comparative analyses
from other sources.

	% gold	% silver	% copper
Coin	56	42	1.9
Beaded wire	68	30	2.0
Suspension loop	67	31	2.0
Merovingian coins (6th–7th century)[a]	49–70	30–50	2–4
Anglo-Saxon jewellery[b]	50–90	10–50	1–5

(a) W.A. Oddy, 'The analysis of four hoards of Merovingian gold coins', in *Methods of Chemical and Metallurgical Investigation of Ancient Coinage*, ed. E.T. Hall and D.M. Metcalf (London, 1972), 111–25.

(b) Hawkes, Merrick and Metcalf, 'X-ray fluorescent analysis'.

The precision (reproducibility) of the above XRF results is about ±1–2 per cent for gold and silver and about ±10–20 per cent relative for copper. The accuracy cannot be defined as the analysis is predominantly of the surface and this may not be fully representative of the bulk composition. However, the gold content is likely to be overestimated due to surface depletion of the silver and particularly the copper. The respective publications should be consulted for errors associated with the comparative analyses.

In addition to the above, areas which appeared to be solder, joining the beading or loop to the coin, were also analysed using XRF and energy dispersive spectrometry in the SEM (EDS-SEM). However, the results were very similar to that of the adjacent areas of the respective components of the artefact; no additional metals were detected in these areas and no exclusively modern materials, such as cadmium, were identified.

Some of the granular features were also analysed by EDS-SEM and compared with other raised areas on the coin to examine the possibility that they may be particles of solder. No significant differences in composition were found between these features and the body of the coin.

Discussion and Summary

The microscopic examination of the coin shows features that are consistent with manufacture by die-striking, the expected method of production. These features are the relative sharpness of edges in the design and several instances of punch-mark faults in the lettering. For example, on the reverse, the letter 'n' is shown with part of the letter doubled; this defect on the die would arise from double hammering the letter punch used to mark the die and moving slightly between blows. However, there are other features that seem to be consistent with manufacture by casting, which could account for some or all of these features:

1. The coin was produced by casting from an original which had been die-struck.
2. The coin is die-struck and the surface grains are residues from the soldering operations to fix the beading and the loop.
3. The coin is die-struck and the imperfections arise from the cast blank.
4. The coin is die-struck and the casting features are imperfections transferred from the dies.

These processes, and the likelihood of them accounting for the manufacture of the coin, are discussed below:

1. If two-piece moulds were taken from a die-struck coin, using fine clay, then most of the struck features could be reproduced in the moulds. Then, during the firing of the mould prior to casting, particles can spall off the mould surface leaving voids. These voids would then appear as raised granulations on a cast taken from the moulds. However, this process would not account for the network of raised lines which seems to be associated with the granulations. Also, the spalling would be expected to occur over the whole surface, including those areas which are raised on the coin (recessed on the mould), when in fact no granulations are visible in these areas. Wear could have removed these but some residual traces might be expected and significantly none are present on the lower surface of the doubled letters where there would be some protection from wear. Additionally, other evidence of casting such as a dendritic structure would be expected on the surface of the coin but this seems to be absent.

2. If the surface granulation on the otherwise struck coin was due to particles of solder then they would be expected to be different in composition from the body of the coin. In practice, as noted above, the granulations are not significantly different which indicates that this is unlikely to be the origin of the grains. Furthermore, this would also not explain the network of lines. It also seems unlikely that particles of solder would be so frequent on both faces of the coin, particularly as the joints seem to show minimal quantities of solder. Arguments similar to those above about the absence of granulations on the raised areas would also apply to this mechanism.

3. Most coin blanks are at least initially manufactured by casting but they would then usually be worked by hammering to the required size and shape for coining. Any surface features associated with the original casting operation would be obliterated either at that stage or when the coin was struck. Hence the surviving features on the coin in question are unlikely to have derived from the original blank.

4. The working face of a die should be perfectly flat and smooth prior to the addition of the incuse design by punching or engraving. However, during the initial stages of die manufacture the face will be far from smooth. For example, with dies made of high tin bronze (the likely material used during the period in question) the basic shape would be formed by casting and the working face would then have an irregular surface. The latter would include imperfections from the mould surface, cast features such as dendritic and grain structure, and porosity due to dissolved gases in the melt; some of these features (e.g. grain structure) may be accentuated by pickling processes to clean up the die. Normally these imperfections would be removed by filing or abrading the working face to achieve a smooth plane surface prior to adding the design. However, if this process was incomplete or omitted altogether, then some or all of these defects would remain on the working face. The porosity could be particularly difficult to remove as it would be present within the body of the die. Although these defects may be present over most of the die face they would tend to be obliterated by the operations of punching or engraving the design and lettering. Thus, when a letter was punched into the die, the end of the punch would compress the metal and eliminate any surface features or internal porosity although porosity adjacent to the side of the punch may be retained. Other features on the cast surface of the die, such as grain boundary defects, could be reproduced on a coin struck from the die; this may account for the linear network features. Some of the features observed on the coin in question have also been observed occasionally on other gold coins. An example which also happened to be available for analysis, an Iron Age coin (1854–06–28,1) of the BOII type from central Europe probably dating to the second century BC, shows the granular features but it is clearly die-struck as it exhibits the characteristic surface striations. The granular features on the Iron Age coin were therefore almost certainly present on the die for the reasons outlined above.

Although the possibility that the Anglo-Saxon coin was cast cannot be entirely ruled out, it is much more likely that it was struck and that the unusual surface features are due to imperfections on the die as described above in option 4. Even if a cast copy, other features such as wear and stress cracking would indicate an ancient rather than a modern copy.

The coin has been mounted with a beaded wire edge, probably hand formed, and a suspension attachment. The wear traces are similar across the whole object and consistent with normal handling over a long period of time; wear on the suspension loop is specific to areas where an attachment would have been located.

The irregular cracks in the surface must have formed after the individual components were joined and their morphology is consistent with stress-corrosion cracking, a phenomenon which develops at the grain boundaries. Such cracking follows the equiaxed (annealed) grain boundaries. This is a feature that is generally considered to develop mainly over comparatively long periods of time for high gold and silver content alloys. However, for base alloys (generally those with high copper contents), it can develop over shorter periods of time and can be accelerated by acid pickling; there is no supporting evidence for pickling in this case. Cracking across the joined components, as observed here, is perhaps indicative of long-term formation and presumably resulted from relieving stresses generated in the joining process.

The compositions of the beading and suspension loop are similar, and could have a common origin, but they are different from the coin itself. All the components are gold-silver alloys with small amounts of copper. They do not correspond with any modern standard carat alloys, in particular the proportions of copper to silver are much lower than usually found in modern gold alloys. Comparisons with near-contemporary gold jewellery and coins show similarities (see Table 17.1, above) but it should be noted that the composition of gold alloys in antiquity covers a very wide range with no systematic chronological pattern.

The analytical evidence does not show clear signs of solder being used as the compositions at the joins are similar to that of the individual components but this is common to many ancient gold objects. The meniscus form of the joined areas is strongly suggestive of a joining alloy being used, but this may have been of a similar composition to the components, or (as has often been observed on ancient jewellery) diffusion between the components and solder has resulted in a uniform composition. Certainly, no modern metals, such as cadmium, were found in the join areas.

In summary, the mounted coin appears to have been die-struck. The wear and surface features on the artefact, such as cracking, are characteristic of ancient gold artefacts. The composition is similar to comparable gold objects of the Anglo-Saxon period and no modern metals were found in the coin or in areas which may have been soldered. Other, similar, mounted coins are known from the early medieval period, using Merovingian coins for example; note that the analyses of these quoted by Hawkes, Merrick and Metcalf often show that the attachments are of slightly different composition to the coin.[14] The evidence of wear, composition and construction, suggests that the coin under investigation here was mounted in antiquity. The object is therefore consistent with its purported origins.

---

[14]   Hawkes, Merrick and Metcalf, 'X-ray fluorescent analysis'.

Chapter 18

A Small Hoard of Burgred Pennies from Banbury Castle, Oxfordshire

David Symons

Although the group described here is small, hoards of Burgred coins are not common,[1] and this particular find is of some interest on two grounds. First, it includes only the eighth known example of the rarest variety of the Lunettes pennies, and second, it appears to add a new name to the corpus of Burgred's moneyers. It therefore seems an appropriate offering to Mark's memory and a small token of gratitude for all the advice, help and encouragement that he gave me over so many years. I know that he would have been interested to hear of this find.

The hoard was discovered during excavations on the site of the later Banbury Castle carried out by the then Birmingham University Field Archaeology Unit in 1998. The final report on these excavations, which will include a discussion of all the coin finds, is now in preparation by a team based at the University of Birmingham. This separate note on the hoard is published here by their kind permission. The images of the coins were generously taken by my former colleague Dr Tom Brindle.[2]

---

[1]   While single finds of Burgred's coins continue to accumulate steadily, the same cannot be said of hoards. In his *Inventory*, J.D.A. Thompson recorded only 13 finds containing coins of Burgred (Inventory), while none at all appear in the seven volumes of *Coin Hoards* (Royal Numismatic Society, 1975–85). The latest version of the Checklist prepared by Mark Blackburn and Hugh Pagan lists 26 finds from the UK and Ireland probably or certainly including coins of Burgred.

[2]   The discussion of this hoard has benefited greatly from comments made by Adrian Lyons and William MacKay, who are in the process of completing a major study of Burgred's Lunettes coinage. They very kindly read an initial draft and suggested a number of improvements which I have been happy to adopt, although any errors which remain are naturally my responsibility. The suggestion that the moneyer's name might be read as Biled(?) is MacKay's. I am also grateful to the editors of this volume, Martin Allen, Rory Naismith and Elina Screen, for their help and advice with this chapter.

The Hoard

The hoard comprises a fused group of three coins. The two outer coins of the stack (Coins A and C) are both Lunettes type pennies of Burgred, King of Mercia (852–74). The middle coin (Coin B) is heavily corroded, largely obscured by the other two and unidentifiable in its current condition, but is also likely to be a Lunettes penny. Of the two outer coins, one obverse face (Coin A) and one reverse face (Coin C) are visible. Coin A has cracked and about 40 per cent of the coin has broken off, but is preserved and fits neatly back into position. The reverse of this loose fragment is completely illegible. Two smaller fragments have detached from Coin C. The larger of these, representing one eighth of the coin, also fits back neatly in place; the smaller fragment, a very tiny sliver, comes from the rim of the coin. Once again, the other faces of these two fragments are completely illegible. The diameter of Coin A is 20 mm and of Coin C 21 mm. The weight of the group as preserved is 2.58g (not including the very small fragment of Coin C). This is considerably lighter than one would normally expect for three coins,[3] but is probably the result of the corrosion the coins have experienced rather than wear.

Figure 18.1 Burgred pennies from Banbury Castle, Oxfordshire. (a) Coin A, obverse (left); (b) Coin C, reverse (right).

Coin A, the Obverse Face (Figure 18.1a):

BVRGRED REX– (with a suspension mark above the X).
Diademed bust right, breaking the inner circle.
The legend begins at 7 o'clock and there is no cross before the king's name. Despite its corroded state, the coin appears to be relatively sharp and unworn.

---

[3] Typically one would expect a coin of Burgred to weigh somewhere in the range 1.15–39g, so (very approximately) a group of three should weigh *c.*3.5–4.0g.

Coin C, the Reverse Face (Figure 18.1b):

Legend in three lines across the flan. In the centre line, possibly [B?]IL·ED followed by two of an original trefoil of pellets; above, MO/H; below, ET/A. The upper and lower legends are divided by long-stemmed M motifs.

The Coin A obverse is typical of Burgred's later coinage, with the king's bust and the legend BVRGRED REX, sometimes with the addition of M (for *Merciorum*, 'of the Mercians'). The last major published account of Burgred's coinage was produced by Hugh Pagan in 1965, although this should be read in conjunction with a clarification and discussion by Stewart Lyon in 1968.[4] Coin A is of Pagan's 'vertical' type, a name derived from the style of the headband of the king's diadem. Lyon rechristened this Series V and conveniently summarized the features which distinguish the type. Pagan, as interpreted by Lyon, saw the Series V obverse type as introduced during what Pagan called the Middle Phase of the coinage and remaining in use throughout the Late Phase, i.e. from *c.*866 to 874.[5] However, Adrian Lyons and William MacKay, building on Lyon's proposals, would now classify this coin as Series Vb and would date it to the period *c.*870–74 because of the simple design interpretation.[6]

The Coin C reverse is altogether more unusual. The reverses of Burgred's Lunettes coins all have the moneyer's name in the central line, with MONETA divided between the upper and lower lines. They are classified into five varieties, based on the form of the 'lunettes' above and below the moneyer's name.[7] By far the rarest of these varieties is Type E, which was first published by Christopher Blunt in 1958 and reviewed by Gareth Williams in 2008.[8] It is characterized by having 'lunettes' formed of horizontal lines with a crook at each end together with long M-shaped ornaments which divide the legends in the top and bottom lines. Williams identified two sub-varieties of Type E: Ei, where the elongated M motif has a single stalk; and Eii, where the stalk is doubled. The Banbury coin belongs to sub-variety Ei. Type E is exceptionally rare. Williams listed six examples and Adrian Lyons kindly advises that there is a seventh in the Museum of Haderslev in Denmark. The Banbury specimen is thus only the eighth one recorded. Pagan suggested that Type E was struck in parallel with the much

---

[4]   H.E. Pagan, 'Coinage in the age of Burgred', *BNJ, 34* (1965), 11–27; C.S.S. Lyon, 'Historical problems of Anglo-Saxon coinage (2): the Ninth century – Offa to Alfred', *BNJ, 37* (1968), 216–38, at 230–34. Pagan subsequently revisited the subject in H.E. Pagan, 'Coinage in southern England, 796–874', in *ASMH*, 45–65.

[5]   Pagan, 'Age of Burgred', 18; Lyon, 'Historical problems', 232–3.

[6]   Lyons and MacKay, *pers. comm.*

[7]   J.J. North, *English Hammered Coinage, vol. 1: Early Anglo-Saxon Coinage to Henry III c. 600–1272*, 3rd ed. (London, 1994), 72.

[8]   C.E. Blunt, 'Some new Mercian coins', *BNJ, 29* (1958–9), 8–11, at 10–11, pl. XV.16; G. Williams, 'Burgred "Lunette" type E reconsidered', *BNJ, 78* (2008), 222–7.

more common variety Type D in the Middle Phase of the coinage, c.866–68, being largely replaced in the Late Phase, c.868–74, by a late version of Type A.[9] Williams has, however, challenged this interpretation, suggesting that Type E should be seen as distinctly separate from Type D and dating it to c.874, at the very end of Burgred's reign, although he does admit that the dating evidence is still somewhat ambiguous.[10]

The evidence of Coin A and Coin C thus combines to suggest that this group is likely to have been lost/deposited c.871 at the earliest, and quite possibly as late as 874. (We do not know what variety the completely illegible Coin B, the central coin of the stack, is, but even if it was of an earlier type it would not affect this dating.) During the third quarter of the ninth century the coins of both Wessex and Mercia suffered from major debasement. The stages of this are reflected in the Lunettes coins, which were the sole type issued by Burgred from his accession in 852. (From c.865, the Lunettes type was also issued by successive rulers of Wessex, so that there was effectively a common currency in the two kingdoms.)[11] From an initial fineness of c.92.5 per cent silver in Burgred's first issues, they seem to have declined in steps to c.75 per cent fine, c.50 per cent, c.25 per cent and finally as low as c.18 per cent by 874. However, from the late 870s, new-style *Cross and Lozenge* coins, of a better weight and fineness than the Lunettes series, were struck by Alfred in Wessex and Ceolwulf II in Mercia.[12] These swept the debased, late Lunettes coins from circulation. How quickly this change was achieved is unclear from the existing hoard evidence, but it was certainly complete by c.880.[13] In the circumstances, therefore, we are probably best dating the deposition of this group of coins c.871/4–c.880.

The moneyer's name on the reverse of Coin C is very difficult to make out, but MacKay's suggestion of Biled(?) does seem the most likely reading. However, this presents something of a problem since this name is completely unparalleled on any other Anglo-Saxon coin and it is difficult to see what the derivation might be. This makes one wonder whether it could have been blundered by the die cutter. In the circumstances it is probably therefore best to record Coin C as issued by 'an uncertain moneyer (Biled?)'.

---

[9]   Pagan, 'Age of Burgred', 14, 'Southern England', 61–2. Lyon agreed with this interpretation: Lyon, 'Historical problems', 232–3.

[10]   Williams, 'Burgred', 223–5.

[11]   See A. Lyons and W. MacKay, 'The coinage of Æthelred I (865–71)', *BNJ*, 77 (2007), 71–118 for a study of the coins of Æthelred I of Wessex, the first West Saxon ruler to adopt the Mercian Lunettes type for his coinage.

[12]   Pagan, 'Southern England', 62–3; M. Blackburn, 'The London mint in the reign of Alfred', in *Kings, Currency and Alliances: History and Coinage of Southern England in the Ninth Century*, ed. M. Blackburn and D.N. Dumville (Woodbridge, 1998), 105–24, at 106.

[13]   See Lyons and MacKay, 'Coinage of Æthelred', 74, 76 for the speed with which the Lunettes coins disappeared from the hoard record.

Chapter 19

The 1699 Port Glasgow Hoard[*]

Hugh Pagan

The surviving manuscript catalogue of the coin collection formed by James Sutherland (*c.*1638–1719), Intendant of the Edinburgh Physic Garden and Professor of Botany at Edinburgh University, records that Sutherland also possessed two silver pennanular arm-rings, both deriving from the same discovery made near Port Glasgow, Renfrewshire.[1] The entry in Sutherland's catalogue for the first of these reads: 'a silver Fibula in shape of a half Moon which was found with a great number of Saxon Coyns near New-Port-Glasgow'. The entry for the second arm-ring reads similarly.

Sutherland's collection was sold by him to the Faculty of Advocates in Edinburgh in 1705, and was acquired by the National Museum of Antiquities of Scotland (now National Museum of Scotland), along with the rest of the Advocates' coin collection, in 1873. Although some of Sutherland's coins were among actual or supposed duplicates disposed of by the Museum at a Dowell's auction in Edinburgh on 6 June 1874, the late Robert Stevenson, when putting together his 1966 *SCBI* volume devoted to the Anglo-Saxon coins in the Museum, was able to identify the majority of Sutherland's Anglo-Saxon coins among the Museum's then holdings, and Stevenson's sensible decision to include in his volume a transcript of the relevant part of Sutherland's manuscript catalogue provides the student with a reliable means of cross-checking the accuracy of Stevenson's identifications, some definite, others explicitly conjectural.[2]

Regrettably, the only references in Sutherland's catalogue to the coins found with the pennanular arm-rings are in these entries, which offer no clues even to the century in which the coins in question were struck. Stevenson offered a tentative suggestion that the hoard might have been the source of Sutherland's holdings of coins of Edgar of *Horizontal Rosette* types, but he did so with appropriate caution,[3] and in the absence of any proof that Sutherland acquired coins as well as arm-rings from the Port Glasgow hoard, scholars have been

---

[*] My thanks are due to James Graham-Campbell, who has kindly read, and commented on, a draft version of these remarks.

[1] For Sutherland's career see now the entry on him by Anita Guerrini in the *ODNB*.

[2] The transcript is printed in R.B.K. Stevenson, *National Museum of Antiquities of Scotland. Part 1, Anglo-Saxon Coins (with associated foreign coins)*, SCBI, 6 (London, 1966), xxv–xxvii.

[3] Stevenson, *National Museum of Antiquities of Scotland*, xv.

reluctant to commit themselves to any definite view as to the hoard's numismatic content. In his excellent and wide-ranging introduction to his catalogue of the Hiberno-Norse coins in the British Museum, also published in 1966, the late Michael Dolley referred to the Port Glasgow hoard as being 'lost', but suggested, following Stevenson, that it might well have ended with coins of Edgar.[4] In his accompanying provisional listing of Viking-Age coin hoards from the British Isles he dated its deposit *c.*975 and dated its discovery to before 1705.[5] Mark Blackburn and the present writer, updating Dolley's listing in the mid 1980s, were not at that time aware of any further evidence relating to the hoard, but moved the proposed date of deposit both of this hoard and of a group of other hoards back from *c.*975 to *c.*970, reflecting our view that hoards certainly or probably ending with pre-Reform coins of Edgar are not likely to have been deposited after Edgar's reform of the coinage in *c.*973.[6] Not long afterwards the present writer noticed the letter written by William Nicolson to Ralph Thoresby in September 1699, from which an extract is given below (no. 6 on p. 416), which indicated that James Sutherland visited Glasgow in 1699 specifically in search of Anglo-Saxon coins. He drew the conclusion that since Glasgow is not at all a likely place to come by such coins, Sutherland's motivation was likely to have been the fact that the Port Glasgow hoard had then recently been discovered.[7] As a result, a date of 1699 for the hoard's discovery has been accepted by Graham-Campbell and by other scholars interested in Viking-age metalwork.[8]

What had not previously been realised by numismatists or other interested scholars, least of all by the present writer, is that there are quite a number of direct and indirect references to the discovery of the Port Glasgow hoard in letters which have long been available in print, mostly written by or addressed to the Rev. Robert Wodrow (1679–1734).[9] Wodrow, in 1699 the very youthful and

---

    [4]   R.H.M. Dolley, *The Hiberno-Norse Coins in the British Museum*, SCBI, 8 (London, 1966), 33.

    [5]   Dolley, *Hiberno-Norse Coins*, 51, hoard no. 115.

    [6]   Checklist, at 297, hoard no. 169.

    [7]   Personal communication from the present writer to James Graham-Campbell, 14 August 1989, as quoted in J. Graham-Campbell, *The Viking-Age Gold and Silver of Scotland (AD 850–1100)* (Edinburgh, 1995), 9. Graham-Campbell's summary also suggests that the present writer had found evidence that Sutherland had gone to Glasgow to look specifically for coins of Edgar, but that suggestion arose from a misunderstanding of the communication from the present writer to Graham-Campbell at that time.

    [8]   Graham-Campbell, *Viking-Age Gold and Silver*, 9, 95. The two pennanular arm-rings preserved in the National Museum of Scotland were illustrated as Figure a on pl. 1.

    [9]   Wodrow's outgoing letters for the period 1698–1709, preserved in copies made by him at the time, are printed in L.W. Sharp (ed.), *Early Letters of Robert Wodrow 1698–1709*, Scottish History Society, 3rd series, 24 (Edinburgh, 1937). Subsequent outgoing letters had already been printed from Wodrow's copies in Rev. T. McCrie (ed.), *The Correspondence of the Rev. Robert*

newly appointed Librarian of the University of Glasgow but shortly to become a minister in the Church of Scotland, is best known for his well-researched book *The History of the Sufferings of the Church of Scotland*, published in two volumes in 1721–22 and describing the Church of Scotland's struggle against persecution in the period between 1660 and 1688, but he had cultivated wide scholarly interests from early in life, and was on correspondence terms with the leading antiquaries of the time both in Scotland and further afield. Here then are the relevant passages in contemporary correspondence, all previously published but brought together for the first time. As will emerge, the information that they collectively provide could well be more helpful, but the hoard that they describe is, as far as the present writer is aware, the only coin hoard of the post-Roman period to be found in the seventeenth century anywhere in the British Isles of which the discovery is documented in contemporary correspondence that still survives, and the evidence should be judged with that fact in mind. The extracts are arranged in date order.

1. Extract from a letter from Robert Wodrow to William Nicolson, dated 3 July 1699:[10]

> I have lately received accompt from Neuport Glasgou, about 18 miles from this, there have been descovred there by the falling doun of some earth a great deal of old coins and other things that have [been] hid there. I have received no clear account of them yet, and only one of the coines quhich (according to my small insight in to that study) seems not be very antient. Perhaps I may goe shortly to the place; however I am promised some of them. I am informed they are of different metals, some of pure silver, some of tine or other mixed matter; some in the forms of this [curved line], some like Indian nose rings, &. I shall give you a fuller accompt of them & shall, if it be possible, send you one at least of evry kind.

2. Extract from a letter from William Nicolson to Robert Wodrow, dated Great Salkeld, Cumberland 26 August 1699:[11]

> Mr Sutherland, as he told me, intended to be with you very lately; in quest (as I imagine,) of those very coins which you mention to have been lately found at Newport-Glasgow. I presume you are now able to give some farther account of that treasure; the history whereof would be very acceptable to, Sir, your affectionate humble servant, Will. Nicolson.

Wodrow, vol. 1 (Edinburgh, 1842). The texts of some relevant incoming letters to Wodrow from various correspondents are to be found in *The New Scots Magazine* for 1829, and in J. Maidment (ed.), *Analecta Scotica: Collections ... Chiefly from Original MSS., Second Series* (Edinburgh, 1837).

[10] Sharp, *Early Letters*, 11. William Nicolson (1655–1727: see *ODNB*), at that time archdeacon of Carlisle, had first met Wodrow on a visit to Glasgow in the early summer of 1699.

[11] As printed in *The New Scots Magazine* (1829), 442.

3. Extract from a letter from William Nicolson to Robert Wodrow, dated Carlisle 28 August 1699:[12]

> If any of the rarities from Newport-Glasgow be in your possession, I hope you will communicate some samples of them to, Sir, your humble servant, Will. Nicolson.

4. Extracts from a letter from Sir Robert Sibbald to Robert Wodrow, dated Edinburgh 29 August 1699:[13]

> I take the occasion of the bearer, Mr. James Sutherland, to write to yow and thank you for the civilities yow did me at Glasgow ... Yow will show Mr. James where he may sie a collection of Saxon coines, if yow know of any.

5. Extracts from a letter from Robert Wodrow to Sir Robert Sibbald, 8 September 1699:[14]

> I received yours by Mr Sutherland whom I heartily wish I could have better enterteaned both upon your recommendation and his oun worth. I count my self happy that I have any acquaintance of soe learned and curiouse a gentleman ... I am much straitned in time, Mr Sutherland being just going away.

6. Extract from a letter from William Nicolson to Ralph Thoresby, undated, but endorsed by Thoresby as having been received on 17 September 1699:[15]

> Mr Sutherland (of Edinb:) will be a special benefactor in this particular [in the provision of Anglo-Saxon coins for illustration in 'the new edition of Dr. Hickes's Grammars', i.e. for Hickes's *Thesaurus*]. He tells me he has (in his own possession) no less than 44 pieces omitted in Camden. He lately went to Glasgow in quest of others; and he is now in Fife, whence he resolves to bring what Aberdene & St Andrews will afford him. He has sent me a specimen of some of 'em; which are taken by a curious and fine hand.

---

[12] *The New Scots Magazine* (1829), 442.

[13] Maidment, *Analecta Scotica*, 133.

[14] Sharp, *Early Letters*, 21–2. This extract is included as evidence that Sutherland's visit to Glasgow in search of Anglo-Saxon coins took place early in September 1699, rather than at the end of August.

[15] W.T. Lancaster (ed.), *Letters addressed to Ralph Thoresby FRS*, Thoresby Society Publications, 21 (Leeds, 1912), 77–8.

7. Extract from a letter from William Nicolson to Edward Thwaites, 13 September 1699:[16]

> I am in weekly expectance of having a good collection of Saxon coins (in a fair cut) from Scotland. Mr Sutherland has been lately at Glasgow on this single errand; and he is now in Fife, whence he promises to bring all the treasure (in this kind) that either Aberdene or S.Andrews will afford us.

8. Extract from a letter from Robert Wodrow to William Nicolson, 28 September 1699:[17]

> The reason in part of this omission [in failing to reply to the letters written to him by Nicolson on 26 and 28 August] was my oft being out of toun in the time of our vacancy, & in part I deferred this till I hoped to be in case to give you some farther accompt and some specimina of these Saxon coins I spoke of. But things not succeeding as I could heartily have wished, I could defer noe longer my writing to you. As to the coins, I have as yet got none of them for myself, but the Principle has got 5 or 6 for the Library quiche Mr Sutherland has att present to take the inscriptions of. I hope ere this time he has given you a better accompt of them then I am in case to doe. I assure you, Sir, that any of them I can fall upon that are doubles to quhat we have already, shall be sent to you.

9. Extract from a letter from Robert Wodrow to James Sutherland, 23 September 1700:[18]

> I was at Portglasgou and at the place quher the Saxon coins wer found; the place I need not describe, for I suppose you wer there. I found none there tho I was at some pains to search it. I had a bit of silver from ane acquaintance there was gote among the coins, of the fibula kind, like quhat you gote ther.

10. Extract from a letter from Robert Wodrow to Sir Robert Sibbald, 23 November 1710:[19]

> I send you likewise part of a fibula of silver or mixed mettall. This was gote within a mile of Port Glasgow, by the falling of a brae; and with it a considerable number of Saxon coins, severall of which I have.

---

[16] R.L. Harris, *A Chorus of Grammars. The Correspondence of George Hickes and his Collaborators on the Thesaurus Linguarum Septentrionalium* (Toronto, 1992), 303.

[17] Sharp, *Early Letters*, 24.

[18] Sharp, *Early Letters*, 113.

[19] Maidment, *Analecta Scotica*, 151 (a more accurate transcript than that printed by McCrie, *Correspondence*, 172).

Putting all this information together, it can now be seen that the hoard was found 'within a mile of Port Glasgow' and on a 'brae', i.e. not within what was at the time the urban centre of the newly created town of Port Glasgow;[20] that its discovery presumably took place around the end of June 1699; that it contained a 'considerable' number of Anglo-Saxon coins; that it contained at least two pennanular arm-rings and part of a third, adding the fragment given by Wodrow to Sibbald in 1710 to the two whole arm-rings that James Sutherland had acquired and had sold to the Faculty of Advocates in 1705; and that it may also have contained some further items of Viking-age metalwork, presumably in the form of hack-silver. More tellingly, Wodrow's supposition that Sutherland had visited the hoard's actual find-spot, coupled with his statement to Nicolson that Sutherland had temporarily been entrusted with the coins from the hoard that had been acquired for Glasgow University Library by Wodrow's 'Principle' (Rev. William Dunlop, the University's Principal), points to Sutherland's close involvement with the hoard very soon after its discovery, and thus to what must be certainty that he would have acquired coins as well as arm-rings from the hoard.[21]

What then were the coins? Sutherland's catalogue records that at the time of its compilation he possessed 63 Anglo-Saxon pennies and seven Northumbrian *stycas*. Of the pennies, 2 were of ninth-century date; 39 were struck between the beginning of the tenth century and Edgar's monetary reform of *c.*973; and 22 were struck in the reigns of subsequent Anglo-Saxon kings down to 1066. It will be helpful to turn first to those struck after *c.*973. These divide into 7 coins of Æthelred II, 9 coins of Cnut, 5 coins of Edward the Confessor and 1 coin of Harold II:

---

[20]   The town of Port Glasgow (or New Port Glasgow, as it was originally styled), just up river from Greenock on the Renfrewshire bank of the River Clyde, owed its name and its urban character to the construction there from the late 1660s onwards of a harbour and breakwater that made it Glasgow's first proper deep water port.

[21]   William Dunlop (1654–1700), described by Wodrow in a letter to William Nicolson of 29 March 1700 as 'one of the greatest antiquaries this nation ever produced', may also have had a personal collection which included Scottish coins (letter from Wodrow to Nicolson, 23 Oct. 1699, printed Sharp, *Early Letters*, 26–7).

Æthelred II

First Hand or Second Hand type	1	(a broken coin, mint and moneyer not stated, not now in the Museum's collection)
Benediction Hand type	1	*SCBI* 6, 659, London, Godwine
Small Crux type	1	*SCBI* 6, 662, London, Æscman
Long Cross type	3	*SCBI* 6, 665, Canterbury, Leofric; *SCBI* 6, 666, Totnes, Godwine; *SCBI* 6, 667, York, Cetel
Last Small Cross type	1	*SCBI* 6, 668, Lincoln, Leofwi

Cnut

Quatrefoil type	3	*SCBI* 6, 669, London, Leofwold; *SCBI* 6, 671, York, Selecol; *SCBI* 6, 672, York, Tocaa
Pointed Helmet type	4	*SCBI* 6, 673, Exeter, Leofwine; *SCBI* 6, 674, London, Ælfgeat; *SCBI* 6, 675, Shrewsbury, Etsige; *SCBI* 6, 676, York, Ire
Short Cross type	2	*SCBI* 6, 680, London, Godere; and another, 'the same double Crosse, but the inscription not legible', not now in the Museum's collection

Edward the Confessor

Trefoil Quadrilateral type	1	*SCBI* 6, 684, Colchester, Brihtric
Expanding Cross type	1	*SCBI* 6, 686, London, Bricsie
Sovereign/Eagles type	1	*SCBI* 6, 688, Chester, Bruninc
Hammer Cross type	1	*SCBI* 6, 690, Chester, Bruninc
Pyramids type	1	*SCBI* 6, 692, York, Aleof

Harold II

Pax type	1	(a coin said to have had the reverse reading WIL-LEM ON OXENF, not now in the Museum's collection)

Note: The reverse of the coin of Harold II is evidently that illustrated in Sir A. Fountaine, *Numismata Anglo-Saxonica & Anglo-Danica illustrata* (Oxford, 1705), pl. viii, Harold 6.

These coins of post-*c.*973 date include no significant grouping of coins of closely adjacent date and struck at geographically adjacent mints that is at all likely to derive from a hoard, and they can safely be dismissed from further consideration as possible components of the Port Glasgow hoard.

By contrast, the tenth-century coins pre-dating Edgar's monetary reform divide into reigns and types as follows:

Edward the Elder

Horizontal Trefoil 1 type	1
Athelstan	
Circumscription Cross type	1
Edmund	
Horizontal Trefoil 1 type	2
Horizontal Rosette 1 type	2
Eadred	
Horizontal Trefoil 1 type	3
Eadwig	
Horizontal Trefoil 1 type	1
Horizontal Rosette 2 type	1
Edgar	
Horizontal Trefoil 1 type	14
Horizontal Rosette 2 type	3
Horizontal Rosette 3 type	1
Circumscription Cross type	7
Circumscription Rosette type	1
Anlaf Cuaran	
Flower type	1
Eric Bloodaxe	
Sword type	1

It is not difficult to come to the conclusion that if a parcel from the Port Glasgow hoard passed into Sutherland's possession, its principal ingredient must have been pre-reform coins of Edgar. As it happens, all significant hoards from the British Isles ending with pre-reform coins of Edgar also contain a longish tail of earlier issues, since no organised demonetisation of older coins had taken place in the reigns of Edgar's tenth-century predecessors, and it is a reasonable presumption that at least some, and possibly rather more, of the other pre-reform coins in Sutherland's collection also derive from the Port Glasgow hoard.

Robert Stevenson's efforts at identifying which of James Sutherland's coins of Edgar remain in the National Museum of Scotland's collection were significantly hampered both by the 1874 sale of duplicates and by the fact that the National Museum of Scotland also possesses coins of Edgar from the 1782 Tiree hoard (from the Inner Hebrides), the 1850 Machrie hoard (from Islay) and the 1830 Inch Kenneth hoard (from a small island west of Mull), very similar to those recorded as having been in Sutherland's collection.[22] His efforts at resolving the provenances of the numerous coins concerned that are still in the Museum, guided by their patination, were admirable by any standard, and they remain central to determining which coins in the Museum's collection today might be from the Port Glasgow hoard.

Happily, though, as pointed out in general terms by the late Christopher Blunt,[23] many of Sutherland's Anglo-Saxon coins are illustrated on the plates of Sir Andrew Fountaine's *Numismata Anglo-Saxonica & Anglo-Danica breviter illustrata*, 1705, published as part of Hickes's *Thesaurus*, and Fountaine's plates provide some unlooked-for aid. Although Fountaine does not record which coins on his plates derive from specific individuals' collections, an analysis of the illustrations that he provides of coins of Edmund, Eadred, Eadwig and Edgar, other than those which his engraver was copying from Speed or from the plates of the 1695 edition of Camden's *Britannia*, reveals so close a correspondence with the content of Sutherland's collection that it can reasonably be presumed that Sutherland's collection was Fountaine's principal new source for illustrations of coins of these rulers. It is especially relevant that of the 21 coins of Edgar which are illustrated in Fountaine's book, leaving out the three for which Fountaine's engraver was merely reproducing illustrations from the plates of the 1695 edition of Camden's *Britannia*, and also one further coin divinably from the collection of Ralph Thoresby, 16 of the 17 remaining are coins which accord with descriptions of coins of Edgar in Sutherland's manuscript catalogue, and this can scarcely be a coincidence.[24] One remaining difficulty in this connection is that James Sutherland is not mentioned as a source for Anglo-Saxon coins either in George Hickes's general introduction to the *Thesaurus* or in the text of Fountaine's *Numismata Anglo-Saxonica*, while a diary entry by William Nicolson for 11 November 1704 records that 'Sir A. Fountain saies he never had any notice of Mr Sutherland's draughts of Saxon coins'.[25] The evidence nonetheless

---

[22]   Stevenson, *National Museum of Antiquities of Scotland*, viii–xii.

[23]   As quoted by Stevenson, *National Museum of Antiquities of Scotland*, x.

[24]   The probable ex Thoresby coin is that illustrated by Fountaine, *Numismata Anglo-Saxonica*, pl. v, Eadgar 5.

[25]   C. Jones and G. Holmes (eds), *The London Diaries of William Nicolson, Bishop of Carlisle, 1702–1718* (Oxford, 1985), 224. It had been Nicolson who had initially forwarded Sutherland's drawings to (presumably) Hickes (see Nicolson to Thwaites, 14 March 1700: 'I sent Mr Sutherland's draughts of the Saxon coins', Harris, *Chorus of Grammars*, 320). It is pertinent in this context that of the three individuals who Hickes does thank in his introduction to the *Thesaurus* for lending coins for illustration in it, only one, Hon. Heneage Finch (subsequently 6th Earl of Winchilsea), is also thanked by Fountaine, so there was obviously a certain lack of communication over matters of this nature between Hickes and Fountaine. For the record, the two other individuals thanked by Hickes were Charles Fanshawe, 4th Viscount Fanshawe (I) (1643–1710), who Hickes records as lending 20 silver Anglo-Saxon coins, and Robert Cotton

points clearly to drawings of Sutherland's coins being available to Fountaine and his engraver. The most plausible interpretation of Fountaine's remark, if it was truthful and if it is relayed accurately by Nicolson, is that Hickes had passed to Fountaine the drawings of Sutherland's Anglo-Saxon coins without telling Fountaine that the coins belonged to Sutherland.

With this assistance it is possible to provide a list of the tenth-century coins of pre-reform date in James Sutherland's collection which is a little less conjectural as regards those of Edgar than that which can be extracted from Stevenson's *SCBI* volume, and which may also serve as an approximate guide to the content of the Port Glasgow hoard. It remains however important to stress that the attribution of any individual coin to the Port Glasgow hoard remains a matter of conjecture, and that the attribution to the hoard of the coins of Edward the Elder, of Athelstan and of the two Norse rulers is particularly uncertain. The list is as follows:

Edward the Elder

1. *Horizontal Trefoil* 1 type, Kentish style, Biorhtred, *SCBI* 6, 86 (reverse ill. Fountaine, pl. vii, Edgar 73).

Athelstan

2. *Circumscription Cross* type, Chester, Sigferth, *SCBI* 6, 149 (reverse ill. Fountaine, pl. ii, Athelstan 20).

Edmund

3. *Horizontal Trefoil I* type, Southern style (Winchester?), Æthelm, *SCBI* 6, 202.

4. *Horizontal Trefoil 1* type, Southern style (London?), Birneard, *SCBI* 6, 204 (reverse ill. Fountaine, pl. v, Eadmund 16).

5. *Horizontal Rosette 1* type, Chester style, Deorulf, *SCBI* 6, 212 (reverse ill. Fountaine, pl. v, Eadmund 15).

6. *Horizontal Rosette 1* type, Chester style, Thurmod, *SCBI* 6, 218.

Eadred

7. *Horizontal Trefoil 1* type, Southern style, Athelmund, *SCBI* 6, 223 (reverse ill. Fountaine, pl. vi, Eadred 16).

(*c*. 1670–1749), of Gidding, Huntingdonshire, who Hickes records as the lender of ten Anglo-Saxon coins. Fanshawe appears to have been the inheritor of a significant collection of coins formed by his grandfather Sir Henry Fanshawe (1569–1616), of Ware Park, Hertfordshire. The source of Robert Cotton's Anglo-Saxon coins is less clear, for although he was later to inherit the baronetcy awarded to his celebrated ancestor Sir Robert Cotton, the antiquary and numismatist, he does not seem likely as early as 1700 (or thereabouts) to have had the capacity to lend to Hickes coins from the family collection lodged in the Cottonian Library. Maybe the coins in question had been acquired by him from a locally found coin hoard, or else they were coins that had been acquired by the original Sir Robert Cotton but had become detached from the Cotton collection proper.

8. *Horizontal Trefoil 1* type, Southern style, Leofric, *SCBI* 6, 250 (reverse ill. Fountaine, pl. vi, Eadred 15).

9. *Horizontal Trefoil 1* type, York style, Heriger, *SCBI* 6, 226 (reverse ill. Fountaine pl. vi, Eadred 17).

Eadwig

10. *Horizontal Trefoil 1* type, York style, Heriger, *SCBI* 6, 323.

11. *Horizontal Rosette 2* type, Chester style, Wilsig, *SCBI* 6, 348 (reverse ill. Fountaine pl. viii, Eadwig 4).

Edgar

12. *Horizontal Trefoil 1* type, North-East Midlands style (NE V), Adelaver. Stevenson suggests that this coin may be *SCBI* 6, 350 or 360, but notes that the first of these coins may alternatively be from the Tiree hoard. Sutherland's coin is presumably that of which the reverse is ill. Fountaine, pl. v. Edgar 19, differing slightly from that of both of the coins just mentioned.

13. *Horizontal Trefoil I* type, North-East Midland style (NE V), Adelger. Stevenson records that this coin may be *SCBI* 6, 361 or 362, but notes that both of these coins may alternatively be from the Tiree hoard. Sutherland's coin is presumably that of which the reverse is ill. Fountaine, pl. v, Edgar 17, very close in appearance to the reverse dies of both National Museum coins.

14. *Horizontal Trefoil 1* type, North-East Midlands style (NE V), Albutc. Stevenson records that this and the following coin might be *SCBI* 6, 368 and 374, but notes that both of these coins may alternatively be from the Tiree hoard. If one of Sutherland's coins is that of which the reverse is ill. Fountaine, pl. v, Edgar 14, that coin is no longer in the National Museum.

15. *Horizontal Trefoil 1* type, North-East Midlands style (NE V), Albutc. See comment on previous coin.

16. *Horizontal Trefoil 1* type, North-East Midlands style (NE V), Cnape. Stevenson suggests that this may be *SCBI* 6, 383.

17. *Horizontal Trefoil 1* type, North-East Midlands style (NE V), Eanulf. Stevenson suggests that this may be *SCBI* 6, 397.

18. *Horizontal Trefoil 1* type, North-East Midlands style (NE V), Grid. Stevenson notes the possibility that the Sutherland coin may be *SCBI* 6, 420, but he clearly thought it more probable that the coin in question was from the Inch Kenneth hoard or from the Machrie hoard. If Sutherland's coin is that of which the reverse is ill. Fountaine, pl. v, Edgar 18, this is struck from a different die to *SCBI* 6, 420 and is therefore no longer in the National Museum.

19. *Horizontal Trefoil 1* type, North-East Midlands style (NE V), Ive (reading IVE MONET). Stevenson records that this coin may be *SCBI* 6, 466, but notes that *SCBI* 6, 466 may alternatively be from the Machrie hoard. Sutherland's coin is presumably that of which the reverse is ill. Fountaine pl. v, Edgar 13.

20. *Horizontal Trefoil 1* type, North-East Midlands style (NE V), Ive (reading IVE MONEN). Stevenson records that this coin may be *SCBI* 6, 464, but notes that *SCBI* 6, 464 may alternatively be from the Tiree hoard.

21. *Horizontal Trefoil 1* type, North-East Midlands style (NE V), Levig. Stevenson identifies this as *SCBI* 6, 470.

22. *Horizontal Trefoil 1* type, North-East Midlands style (NE V), Mana. Stevenson suggests that this may be *SCBI* 6, 481.

23. *Horizontal Trefoil 1* type, North-East Midlands style (NE V), Morne (reverse inscription transcribed by Sutherland as MOLME MO). Stevenson identifies this as *SCBI* 6, 498.

24. *Horizontal Trefoil 1* type, North-East Midlands style (NE V), Unbein. Stevenson records that this coin may be *SCBI* 6, 454, but notes that *SCBI* 6, 454 may alternatively be from the Tiree hoard. Sutherland's coin is presumably that of which the reverse is ill. Fountaine, pl. v, Edgar 15.

25. *Horizontal Trefoil 1* type, North-East Midlands style (NE V), Unbein (reverse inscription transcribed by Sutherland as H.VNDEI MO, but easily interpretable as HVNBEIN MO). Probably no longer in the Museum collection, for the Museum's specimen with this reading of the moneyer's name appears to be from the Tiree hoard.

26. *Horizontal Rosette 2* type, Chester style, Ealfsige, *SCBI* 6, 591 (reverse ill. Fountaine, pl. v, Edgar 20). Stevenson records that this coin carries 'traces of corrosion' similar to those on *SCBI* 6, 618 (*Horizontal Rosette 3* type, below).

27. *Horizontal Rosette 2* type, Chester style, Thurmod, *SCBI* 6, 611 (reverse ill. Fountaine, pl. v, Edgar 7).

28. *Horizontal Rosette 2* type, Chester style, Werstan. Stevenson records that this coin may be *SCBI* 6, 613, but notes that *SCBI* 6, 613 may alternatively be from the Tiree hoard. If the coin is that of which the reverse is ill. Fountaine, pl. v, Edgar 16, it is no longer in the National Museum.

29. *Horizontal Rosette 3* type, Chester, Aelfsig, *SCBI* 6, 618 (reverse ill. Fountaine, pl. v, Edgar 12). Stevenson records that this coin carries 'traces of corrosion' similar to those on *SCBI* 6, 591 (above).

30. *Circumscription Cross* type, Southern style, Bath, Æthelsige, *SCBI* 6, 512 (reverse ill. Fountaine, pl. v, Edgar 24). Although Sutherland does not transcribe the reverse legend, which he merely describes as 'ane obscure inscription', his transcription of the obverse legend agrees with that of *SCBI* 6, 512, and Fountaine's illustration corresponds exactly to the reverse of *SCBI* 6, 512.

31. *Circumscription Cross* type, Southern style, Winchester, Wihtsige, *SCBI* 6, 516. Although Sutherland does not transcribe the reverse legend, which he again describes as 'ane obscure inscription', his transcription of the obverse legend agrees with that of *SCBI* 6, 516, and the only other coin of this type in the Museum with a similar obverse legend, *SCBI* 6, 511, appears to be from the Tiree hoard (and has a more legible reverse legend).

32. *Circumscription Cross* type, North-East Midlands style, Asferth (reverse inscription transcribed by Sutherland as ASFCAD MON). Evidently the coin of this type ill. Fountaine, pl. v, Edgar 11, with identical reading to that transcribed by Sutherland. If so, no longer in the Museum, for *SCBI* 6, 518, the only coin in the collection of this moneyer and type, is likely to be from the Machrie hoard.

33. *Circumscription Cross* type, North-East Midlands style, Leofinc, *SCBI* 6, 567 (reverse ill. Fountaine, pl. v, Edgar 8). Stevenson records that *SCBI* 6, 568, a very similar coin of this type and moneyer, and without provenance, has similar wear and appearance to *SCBI* 6, 567, but *SCBI* 6, 568, is chipped and *SCBI* 6, 567 is likely therefore to be the Sutherland coin and the coin illustrated by Fountaine.

34. *Circumscription Cross* type, York style, Durand. Presumably the coin of which the reverse is ill. Fountaine, pl. v, Edgar 9. No longer in National Museum.

35. *Circumscription Cross* type, York style, Fastolf (reading FASTOLFES MO). Presumably the coin of which the reverse is ill. Fountaine, pl. v, Edgar 10. No longer in National Museum.

36. *Circumscription Cross* type, York style, Fastolf (reading FASTOLF MON). Stevenson records that this coin may be *SCBI* 6, 531, but notes that *SCBI* 6, 531 may alternatively be from the Tiree hoard.

37. *Circumscription Rosette* type, Derby, Boiga, *SCBI* 6, 572 (reverse ill. Fountaine, pl. v, Edgar 22).

Anlaf Cuaran

38. *Flower* type, York style, Radulf, *SCBI* 6, 75. It is not clear whether the illustration of the coin of this moneyer and type in Fountaine, pl. iii, Anlaf 1, is an illustration based on a drawing of Sutherland's specimen, or whether it is copied by Fountaine's engraver from the illustration in Camden, *Britannia*, 1695, pl. viii, 34.

Eric Bloodaxe

39. *Sword* type, York style, Ingelgar, *SCBI* 6, 79 (ill. Fountaine, pl. viii, Eric 1).

If all of Sutherland's coins of Edgar derive from the Port Glasgow hoard, the likely date of the hoard's deposit is governed by the presence in it of the coin of *Horizontal Rosette 3* type by the Chester moneyer Aelfsig. Chester was in fact the principal mint of the *Horizontal Rosette 3* type, otherwise struck only by moneyers at Derby, Tamworth and a possible unidentified mint using the signature 'NE', and the absence of any coin of this type from the very substantial Chester (1950) hoard, deposited *c.*965, makes it apparent that the issue of coins of this type only began after the mid 960s.[26] A date of deposit of *c.*970 for the Port Glasgow hoard would thus seem appropriate, and it is no surprise that a similar date of deposit is currently assigned to the Machrie and Tiree hoards, with their

---

[26] *CTCE*, 253–4.

very similar Edgar content.[27] A whole raft of hoards from Ireland seem also to have been deposited at this approximate date, leading to a suggestion long ago by Dolley that the deposit of these might have been connected with 'the great contest for Ireland which culminated in the battle of Tara, the real turning-point in the fortunes of the Vikings in Ireland'.[28] It must however remain uncertain whether the contemporary Scottish hoards, all from Scotland's west coast, owed their deposit to ripples from political turbulence in Ireland or to a wholly distinct cause or causes.[29]

---

[27] Although the general character of the Machrie hoard and of the Tiree hoard is well established, the content of neither hoard has as yet been set out in accordance with the classification by type and style developed by Blunt, Stewart and Lyon, *CTCE*. As regards the Machrie hoard, it is convenient to record here that a paragraph in the *Glasgow Herald* newspaper for 28 October 1850 states that this hoard 'was found by some labourers while excavating a drain on a farm ... deposited in a horn, which on being thrown on the ground, burst, and the coins were discovered'.

[28] Dolley, *Hiberno-Norse Coins*, 33.

[29] It should be noted that in a letter to Sutherland, dated 7 December 1700 (Sharp, *Early Letters*, 132–3), Wodrow writes 'I have the prospect of some [coins] latly dugg up in Galloway, of David, as is said'. This would appear to be a reference to an otherwise unrecorded Scots coin hoard of the medieval period.

Chapter 20

The Viking Invasions 885–889 and the Activity of the Mint of Rouen

Jens Christian Moesgaard
with the collaboration of Michel Dhénin

Introduction

When I spotted an important Carolingian penny in the characteristic Quentovic style, but with the Rouen mint name, and it became clear that no relevant French museum wished to acquire it, Mark Blackburn promptly raised money to buy it for the Fitzwilliam Museum and thus secure it for the discipline and for posterity.

The coin derives from a hoard discovered south of Paris in 1930/1, in the Gravigny-Balizy hamlet, commune of Longjumeau (dép. Essonne). This hoard was not published until 2008, and it was subsequently dispersed.[1] The initial publication dated its burial to c.900 or shortly after, but in my attempt to put the Rouen/Quentovic coin into its right setting, I came to the conclusion that it must have been concealed c.879/87.[2] Mark agreed with my arguments; however he pointed out a strange feature: the suspiciously low average weight of the coins in the hoard. A closer look at the figures revealed that although low weights were to be found for all mints, most of the very low-weight specimens were of the mint of Rouen. The median weight of the Rouen pennies was 1.40g and the mean weight was 1.44g, well below the 1.80–60g constituting the legal weight up until c.910/20.[3] This observation became the starting point of the reflections presented in this chapter. It is thus highly appropriate to dedicate this chapter to the memory of Mark.

What was special about Rouen in the 880s which could explain why this mint struck underweight coins, and not Paris, Quentovic, Sens, Soissons or the other

---

[1]   C.-A. Daillan, 'Le trésor de Gravigny-Balizy (Essonne, France): deniers et oboles d'époque carolingienne', *BCEN, 45.3* (2008), 80–95.

[2]   J.C. Moesgaard, 'Le "maillon manquant" entre Quentovic et Rouen?', *BSFN, 65.3* (2010), 57–61.

[3]   J. Lafaurie, 'Deux trésors monétaires carolingiens: Saumeray (Eure-et-Loir), Rennes (Ille-et-Vilaine)', *RN, 6th series, 7* (1965), 262–305. There was however a small drop in the 880s, see below.

mints also represented in the Longjumeau hoard? Tentatively, I pursued the possibility that it may be more intense Viking activity. Indeed, during the years 885–87, the Lower Seine Valley witnessed more or less permanent occupation by Vikings, who used it as a safe-haven and winter camp during their incessant campaigns of raiding further inland. In 889 they were back again.[4]

Until then, most ecclesiastical authorities of the region had remained in place, but now the Viking pressure became unbearable and they fled for good to their safe inland possessions. They had held very important political secular powers, landed possessions and commercial privileges. As suggested by Jacques Le Maho, the result was that the Vikings eventually left a power vacuum after their departure, to be filled in by the Frankish king.[5] Thus, the raids probably meant a shift in the balance of power, from the Church to the king.

The mint is a core public institution within the city. In the case of Rouen, it was probably royal. Coins are, if they are carefully studied, fairly closely datable. The study of coinage thus potentially provides solid evidence of what happened to public life if a city came under attack, as was the case when the Vikings raided north-western France in the 880s. The case of Amiens has already been noted by Lafaurie,[6] and Metcalf has demonstrated how the Viking raids brought an outright halt to coinage in Flanders.[7] The disorders in the mint activity of Rouen could be seen in this context: the sub-standard coins may have been struck during the short period of Viking rule, or maybe they were part of the difficult process of returning to normal after the departure of the Vikings.

Method

It is of course somewhat hazardous to make conclusions from one hoard only, as I did in the paper on the Rouen/Quentovic coin. At the very least, the evidence from this hoard should be compared to a wider corpus of coins from the mint. In principle, one ought to make a full-scale die-study of the coinage. In this way, the very distinct styles of the coinage would be assigned to their proper place in the chronology and the evolution in weight would become clear. This is, however, a huge task, and, as a more realistic course, I decided to examine the

---

[4]   E. Déniaux, C. Lorren, P. Bauduin, T. Jarry, *La Normandie avant les Normands* (Rennes 2002), 375.

[5]   J. Le Maho, 'Les Normands de la Seine à la fin du IXe siècle', in *Les fondations scandinaves en Occident et les débuts du duché de Normandie*, ed. P. Bauduin (Caen, 2005), 161–79, at 169.

[6]   J. Lafaurie, 'Les trouvailles de monnaies mérovingiennes et carolingiennes d'Amiens', *BSFN, 24.6* (1969), 404–7.

[7]   D.M. Metcalf, 'Coinage and the rise of the Flemish towns', in *Coinage in the Low Countries (880–1500). The Third Oxford Symposium on Coinage and Monetary History*, ed. N.J. Mayhew (Oxford, 1979), 1–23.

coins recorded from dated hoards in terms of weight and literacy. Once one has a succession of hoards, it will be possible to study the chronological evolution of the activity of the mint.

The assumption is that the coins in a hoard are recent strikings and thus reflect the phase of coinage immediately prior to the date of burial of the hoard. This is of course not true for every individual coin, as coins can remain in circulation for some time. Die-identities between coins from hoards of various dates demonstrate this point (Figure 20.1a–b).[8] On the other hand, the vast majority of the coins considered here show no or little signs of wear, suggesting that they had not been circulating for long before being buried in the ground.

Figure 20.1   Charles the Bald, penny, Rouen, GDR-type, two specimens of degenerated style, same reverse die. (a) From the Ablaincourt hoard, cat. 8.18 (left; see below); (b) From the Féchain hoard, cat. 16.8 (right) (photographs Michel Dhénin).

The Material

A major impediment to more detailed study of the history of the Rouen mint in the late ninth century is the scarcity of publications of well-studied hoards. Indeed, frequently no details are given about weight or legends in the often very summary hoard reports, and illustrations of the coins are rather the exception than the rule. Consequently, I am extremely grateful to Michel Dhénin for providing descriptions and photos of the highly important, but hitherto unpublished hoards of Ablaincourt (dép. Somme) and Féchain (dép. Nord), containing 47 and 23 Rouen coins respectively. As will be seen, the present work would not have been possible without this act of generosity. Michel thus joins me in the tribute to Mark – but he does not necessarily agree with the opinions on dating the hoards expressed here.

Indeed, the next problem is the dating of the hoards. Of course hoards only known to us from a poor summary report are difficult to date. But even well studied, fully documented hoards may be problematic. This is mainly due to

---

8   Or demonstrate that the dating of the hoards is wrong, cf. the discussion below about the dating of the hoards of Ablaincourt, Féchain and Glisy.

the difficulty of dating many coin types closely. To which Charles should one attribute a particular coin: Charlemagne, Charles the Bald, Charles the Fat or Charles the Simple? Or could it be an 'immobilisation'? The publication of volume one of *Medieval European Coinage* by Mark together with Philip Grierson was a tremendous step forward, but a great deal yet remains to be resolved about these coinages.[9] This is why the dating of particular hoards by Lafaurie, Duplessy, Haertle, Armstrong and Coupland may vary considerably (Table 20.1).[10]

For the present study, the major problem is the dating of the hoards of Glisy, Ablaincourt and Monchy. Along with the hoard Féchain, they are part of a group of hoards from the region of Amiens up to the Belgian border. Jean Lafaurie, followed by Michel Dhénin, saw this group as connected with the presence of the Vikings in 889–91. A key argument is the study of the coins of Amiens. The first letter in the monogram changes from a K to a C, and at the same time, there is a considerable weight reduction (which may also be linked to the Viking activity). This phase of the Amiens coinage is not yet represented in Glisy, traditionally dated after 887 by the presence of a coin of Odo (887–98), but it occurs in the three other hoards, which must then be slightly later. Moreover, Lafaurie and Dhénin argued that the many die-links between the coins from Glisy, Féchain and Ablaincourt (see for instance catalogue below for the coins of the mint of Rouen) tended to show a close chronological relation between them. Thus, they date Ablaincourt to the early phase of the reign of Odo, notwithstanding the absence of his coins in the hoard. Indeed, there were only a few Odo coins in Féchain, and many more in Monchy, which is the latest of this series of hoards.[11] The Longjumeau hoard is also die-linked to this group of hoards.

It will be noted that apart from the historical context (although it should be added that Vikings were also raiding and living off the land in Picardy and the north earlier, in 881 and 883), the key argument for this dating is the presence of a penny of Orléans in the name of Odo in the hoard of Glisy. The identification of this coin has however been challenged by Coupland.[12] It is one single coin

---

[9]   *MEC* 1.

[10]   'Lafaurie, 'Les trouvailles'; J. Duplessy, *Les trésors monétaires médiévaux et modernes découverts en France*, 1, *751–1223* (Paris, 1985); C.M. Haertle, *Karolingische Münzfunde aus dem 9. Jahrhundert* (Cologne, Weimar and Vienna, 1997); S. Armstrong, 'Carolingian coin hoards and the impact of the Viking raids in the ninth century', *NC*, *158* (1998), 131–64; S. Coupland, 'A checklist of Carolingian coin hoards 751–987', *NC*, *171* (2011), 203–56.

[11]   Lafaurie, 'Les trouvailles'. M. Dhénin 'Bijoux et trésor monétaire argent', in *La Neustrie, Les pays au nord de la Loire de Dagobert à Charles le Chauve (VIIe–IXe siècle)*, ed. P. Périn and L.-C. Feffer (Rouen 1985), 416–19. I am grateful to Michel Dhénin for complementary information and fruitful discussion on this topic.

[12]   Coupland, 'Checklist', 234, n. 91; cf. Haertle, *Karolingische Munzfunde*, 860, n. 851. A re-examination of the coins kept at the Museum of Amiens might cast light on the question of the

out of almost 600. No coin whatsoever of Odo was mentioned in the partial reports of Bazot[13] and Charvet;[14] it only appeared in the synthesis of Gariel in 1883 as one of the four coins of Orléans, the three others being of Charles the Bald.[15] However, in Gariel's previous reports in 1867 and 1877, these four coins of Orléans are all listed as belonging to Charles the Bald.[16] As there are several other inconsistencies and contradictions between the three reports, Coupland suggests that the identification of the Odo coin is a misunderstanding. This is plausible, but unfortunately cannot be proven – as the hoard had been retrieved and dispersed in several parcels, new coins may have appeared between 1877 and 1883; alternatively the Odo coin may have passed unnoticed in the first instance and only been recognised when Gariel wrote up his corpus. If however Coupland is right, the *t.p.q.* would then be fixed by the presence of coins in the name of Louis III to 879 (on Louis II and III, see below). Whether this hoard (and the one of Ablaincourt) should be dated before or after the ascension to the throne of Odo in 887 – and in the latter case, how far into the reign – depends on when one thinks Odo started to strike coins and at what point they were distributed on a considerable scale. It is possible that Odo as a non-Carolingian wished to mark his new status by striking coins quickly, but the question is in need of more research.

As already noted, Monchy is clearly the latest of the four hoards. Coupland, however, wishes to date it well after the three others, arguing that the GDR coins must be of Charles the Simple rather than Charles the Bald. Thus, he dates the concealment to the early tenth century.[17] However, Gariel seems to indicate that the GDRs were more worn (on the basis of a sample of 20 coins, he stated 'bonne condition, mais non à fleur de coin') than the coins of Odo (on a sample of nine coins, 'fleur de coin'),[18] suggesting they are older. But this difference could reflect poorer workmanship rather than wear.

One may have hoped that the proportion of coins of Louis III and Carloman in the hoards would give some indication of the date of burial: low proportion, early date; high proportion, late date. This may be so, for instance, in the Loire Valley, where coins of Louis were struck and circulated in large numbers (cf. the hoard of Savigné-sous-le-Lude), but coin circulation was relatively regionalised

---

presence of an Odo coin in the hoard.

[13]   A.-P.-M. Bazot, 'Trouvaille de monnaies à Glisy', *Bulletin de la Société des antiquaires de Picardie, IX* (1865–7), 130–46, at 141.

[14]   J. Charvet, 'Monnaies découvertes à Glisy', *RBN, 5th series, 2* (1870), 417–39, at 432.

[15]   E. Gariel, *Les monnaies royales de France sous la race carolingienne* (2 vols, Strasbourg, 1883–84), 1, 101.

[16]   E. Gariel, 'Glisy', *ASFN, 2* (1867), 349–58, at 354; E. Gariel, 'Notes sur la classification des monnaies carolingiennes au moyen des trouvailles', *ASFN, 5* (1877), 158–74, at 163.

[17]   Coupland, 'Checklist', 238, n. 116.

[18]   Gariel, *Les monnaies,* 107, n. 1.

with limited intermingling of the pools of currency,[19] and in the north, coins of Louis only count for a few per cent even in late hoards, whereas coins of Carloman are virtually non-existent.

The weight patterns may be another clue to the dating. Thus for the Glisy hoard the recorded weights vary from 1.20 to 1.90g, with a concentration around 1.60–65g,[20] which is rather low – but not inconceivable – for the 880s (Coupland's date), and more in line with a date in the 890s (dating by Lafaurie and Dhénin). Yet for the hoard of Chalo-Saint-Mars, buried during the 880s, Duhamel likewise quotes a range of low-weight pennies from various mints from 1.30 to 1.70g, with an average of 1.56g (based on 35 specimens).[21] Gariel gives the later Monchy hoard an average weight at 1.53g based on 20 GDR coins of fair condition from various mints.[22] All these figures point to a general instability in weight standards during the 880s and 890s before the restoration in the early tenth century as reflected in, for example, the Cuerdale hoard.[23]

Thus, these four hoards either constitute a tight chronological group (according to Lafaurie and Dhénin) or cover a span of several decades (according to Coupland). To conclude, much more work on regional differences in the makeup of the currency, on die-links between hoards, on stylistic evolution at particular mints and on weight patterns is needed to determine the dates of the hoards – and to grasp the true nature of the coinage. Unfortunately, it is not possible to do so in this chapter. In the catalogue below, I have tried to lay out the arguments behind my preliminary proposals for dating the hoards, with due recognition of the uncertainties, and accepting that several are subject to discussion.

Mark always encouraged coin lists and catalogues, which, as he said, made the articles useful beyond the analyses and conclusions they contained. So in his spirit, I publish a full catalogue of the relevant coins at the end of the present chapter (Appendix 2).

Analysis

The coins relevant to the present study are of the so-called GDR-type. This type is named after the obverse legend GRATIA DEI REX, which surrounds a monogram reading KAROLVS ('Charles, king by the grace of God'). The type

---

[19]   D.M. Metcalf, 'A sketch of the currency in the time of Charles the Bald', in *Charles the Bald: Court and Kingdom*, ed. M.T. Gibson and J.L. Nelson, 2nd ed. (Aldershot, 1990), 65–97.

[20]   Charvet, 'Monnaies découvertes'; Gariel, *Les monnaies*.

[21]   V. Duhamel, 'Considérations sur les monnaies Carlovingiennes découverts à Beaumont', *Société historique et archéologique du Gâtinais. Annales de la société, 6* (1888), 233–42, at 236–7.

[22]   Gariel, *Les monnaies,* 107, n. 1.

[23]   Lafaurie, 'Deux trésors'.

was introduced under the West Frankish king Charles the Bald (843–77) by the Edict of Pîtres in 864, and it was struck in many mints in the northern half of the realm. When Charles was proclaimed emperor in 875, a new type with the new title was introduced at a few mints, but most kept the old type. Even after the king's death in 877, coinage continued in his name (a so-called 'immobilisation') at many mints – indeed, at one extreme, the hoard of Fécamp deposited *c.*980/5 shows that this type was still being struck in substantial numbers at Le Mans and Quentovic as late as the last third of the tenth century.[24]

The history of the mint of Rouen is not well known for this period. Yet the number of surviving specimens of the GDR-type, as well as the proportion of Rouen coins in the hoards, tells us that this mint was an important one. Indeed, it was one of the mere ten mints mentioned in the Edict of Pîtres in 864. A single specimen in the name of Carloman (879–84) is recorded as a single find from Mouthier-Hautepierre (dép. Doubs).[25] However, the total absence of this variety in the hoards shows that this issue must have been marginal. Most likely, the mint carried on striking GDRs with the KAROLVS-monogram for some time after the death of Charles in 877. The next secure points in the history of the mint are the pennies in the name of Saint-Ouen struck *c.*940 at the latest,[26] and those of William Long-Sword (927/33–42).[27] Meanwhile there may have been an issue of imitative *Temple*-type coins from 920 on, but the mint of this issue is far from secure.[28] The period from 877 to the early tenth century, which is under consideration here, may thus be described as fairly obscure.

GDR coins from the Rouen mint are recorded in 18 hoards dating from 869/79 to 942/5. Unfortunately, weights have not been reported for several of these hoards, but the available figures show that the drop in weight standard in the Longjumeau hoard is indeed significant compared to other hoards (Table 20.2). It represents a drop of some 10 per cent compared to the weight standard of the previous hoards. In this connection, it is interesting to note that coins from the hoard of Ablaincourt seem to divide into two distinct weight standards of *c.*1.40g and *c.*1.60g (Table 20.3). The same tendency may be detected in Longjumeau, but the figures are too small to be conclusive on this point. This may reflect coins struck before and after the alleged weight decrease in the

---

[24] F. Dumas, *Le trésor de Fécamp* (Paris, 1971).

[25] H. Grut and J.-P. Mazimann, 'Découverte d'un bijou monétaire en or du haut Moyen-Age, de trois sceattas et d'un denier de Carloman II inédit pour l'atelier de Rouen sur un même site en Franche-Comté', *BSFN, 60.4* (2005), 76–8.

[26] J.C. Moesgaard, 'Les deniers de Saint-Ouen de Rouen (Xe siècle)', *BSFN, 64.10* (2009), 242–6.

[27] J.C. Moesgaard, 'A survey of coin production and currency in Normandy, 864–945', in *Silver Economy in the Viking Age*, ed. J. Graham-Campbell and G. Williams (Walnut Creek, CA, 2007), 99–121, at 111–13.

[28] Moesgaard, 'Survey', at 109–11.

Figure 20.2   Charles the Bald, penny, Rouen, GDR-type. Two specimens of
               very different literacy, both from the Féchain hoard. (a) cat. 16.1,
               good literacy (left); (b) cat. 16.16, blundered obverse legend
               (right) (photographs Michel Dhénin).

880s. The evidence for the subsequent period is scanty, but seems to point to
a restoration in the weight standard, although not fully to the pre-crisis level.

A look at the literacy of the coins of the mint of Rouen reveals that slight
blundering is the norm throughout the period, from the very beginning of the
issue (Figure 20.2a–b) (Table 20.4). Indeed, the retrograde monogram, a few
retrograde letters (in particular the S), a missing abbreviation mark in 'D-I' and
other features are very frequent and may be considered normal. More serious
blunders (several missing letters) also occur very early in the issue, and indeed
prior to the alleged crisis of the 880s. One may even ask whether illiteracy
was more marked at all in the 880s than before or after. The evidence is slight.
Longjumeau contains 18 coins with few or no faults against five with more faults
or outright blunders. These figures demonstrate that the breakdown in literacy
was far from being complete, even at the highest point of the crisis. On the other
hand, the (presumably) slightly earlier hoard of Ablaincourt shows considerably
better literacy: 29 coins with no or few faults as opposed to three with several
faults and none completely blundered. At the other end of the scale, the slightly
later Féchain hoard has the same distribution as Longjumeau (18 better as
opposed to five blundered), and Laxfield, Bligny and Monchy contain much-
blundered specimens. Somewhat surprisingly, the Evreux hoard of the 940s
contains two specimens which according to the nineteenth-century report were
as new, in perfect style, and with good literacy. Taken at face value, this would
imply that the GDR-type was still being struck at this late stage, when ducal
Norman coins ought to have been the sole product of the mint. One cannot but
regret the absence of illustrations and recorded weights for these coins!

Many of the coins in Longjumeau, Ablaincourt and Féchain are so light
and so blundered, that one would instinctively have labelled them degenerated
issues from the early tenth century rather than coins struck in the 880s. Weight
and literacy are thus not very useful as guides to singling out late specimens in
chronological sequence.

Conclusions

This leads us to the conclusion that the crisis of the 880s was indeed real. It meant a small fall in the weight standard at the mint of Rouen, and literacy faltered to a certain degree. The weight standard was partly restored afterwards, but literacy never recovered, even though illiteracy never became dominant; far from it.

The most likely explanation for these features is that they are linked to the presence of the Vikings. As mentioned above, the Vikings had established their quasi-permanent base in the Lower Seine Valley from 885 to 887 during the siege of Paris. It is hard to know whether the low-weight coins reflect an issue produced during the Viking occupation or rather the difficulty of restoring the coinage after their departure. The coins cannot be dated sufficiently precisely to decide between these two scenarios. It seems certain, however, that coinage continued after the Viking *intermezzo*. Secular power and organisation of civic life thus resumed, probably under the patronage of the king.

Similar instability in the coinage occurred in Amiens, which witnessed Viking attacks in 881, 883 and 889–91. It is possible that the general weight decrease in the 880s or the 890s outlined above is also linked to the Vikings, even if it was not as deep as at Rouen. But weight and quality of the coinage were eventually restored when peace returned.

The opposite happened in Flanders. There, coinage stopped completely as a consequence of the very severe Viking raids of the 880s, until their departure from the ruined land in 892. The power vacuum left by them was eventually filled by the counts of Flanders. This left an enduring mark on the power landscape of the region. When coinage resumed in Bruges, it was no longer under royal control, but conducted by the count.

The present case study of the mint of Rouen, compared to the well-known evidence from Flanders and Amiens, demonstrates the potential of numismatics to enrich knowledge of the impact on civic society of the Viking raids and the process of disintegration of royal power. It would indeed be interesting to conduct similar case studies for other mints, such as Arras, Quentovic, Saint-Quentin, etc. in order to gain an overall view of the impact of Viking activity.

Appendix 1: Peck-marks in France in the 880s

Four Rouen pennies from the hoard of Ablaincourt in Picardy each have a peck in one of the quarters of the cross on the reverse (8.1, 8.2, 8.10, 8.11) (Figure 20.3a–b). This hoard was, as mentioned above, buried 879/87 at the earliest, maybe a few years later in *c.*891. One Rouen penny of the northern Féchain hoard, buried after 887 is also pecked (16.22) (Figure 20.3c).

Figure 20.3   Charles the Bald, penny, Rouen, GDR-type, four specimens with pecks. Above: (a–b) both from the Ablaincourt hoard, cat. 8.1 and 8.2. Below: (c) From the Féchain hoard, cat. 16.22 (left); (d) Unknown provenance (Ablaincourt?), 1.23g, Musée départemental des Antiquités de la Seine-Maritime, inv. 94.5.2 (right) (a–c: photographs Michel Dhénin; d: © cg76 – Musée départemental des Antiquités – Rouen, clichés Samuel Havel). Images reproduced slightly reduced.

I have previously published an unprovenanced GDR penny of Rouen with one peck (Figure 20.3d).[29] Its low weight and degenerated style led me to believe that it could be a late derivative from the tenth century, but in reality this coin derives from the same monetary environment as the pecked coins from Ablaincourt and Féchain. In fact, its reverse is struck from the same die as Ablaincourt 8.18 and Féchain 16.8, and the style of the obverse is very similar, albeit not from the same dies (Figure 20.1). It is linked to a series of coins also comprising one from Glisy. Compiègne region 6.1 and Longjumeau 9.1 and 9.4 are also of the same style.

This is astonishing! First of all, pecking is not supposed to occur in France. The only evidence hitherto is the Norman hoard of Saint-Pierre-des-Fleurs (dép. Eure) buried in the 890s, but this hoard clearly constitutes a sum carried by a Viking from East Anglia to Normandy, and the pecking was probably conducted in England, not in France.[30] Carolingian coins were pecked by the Vikings as

---

[29]   Moesgaard, 'Survey', 107.

[30]   T. Cardon, J.C. Moesgaard, R. Prot and P. Schiesser, 'Le premier trésor de type viking en France. Denier inédit d'Eudes pour Beauvais', *RN, 164* (2008), 21–40.

shown by the hoard of Cuerdale in North-Western England. However, careful examination by Marion Archibald has recently shown that the pecking of the Carolingian coins in the Cuerdale hoard took place in England around 900, not in France.[31] Some pecking of Carolingian coins also occurred in England in the 890s and maybe the 880s, as shown by the hoards of Laxfield (12.1) and Ashdon (14.1).

The hoards of Ablaincourt and Féchain have no Viking features about them, and it is likely that their owners were Franks not Vikings. For the time being, only the coins from the mint of Rouen have been examined, but to judge from this limited evidence, the pecked coins are just a small part of the two hoards. The vast majority of the Rouen coins in the hoards are not pecked. Moreover, the four pecked Ablaincourt coins (but not the Féchain one) are bent in the Viking manner in order to check the metal. These coins have probably passed through the hands of a Viking at some stage. Indeed, coins are meant to circulate from hand to hand. Did the transactions implying Viking involvement take place in France, in England or in the Netherlands? It is impossible to say. But afterwards, the coins re-entered the general circulation before arriving in the possession of the last owner, who was presumably a Frank.

There is more. On the present evidence, pecking is first documented in Viking England in the 890s (one may however add the pecked Rouen coin in the collection of Tony Merson, 12.1. If this coin really derives from the Laxfield hoard buried after 875 or after 882, this would be the oldest occurrence in England). It has been suggested, convincingly, that pecking started in the late 870s as a means of checking the silver in the monetary confusion following Alfred's reforms, but the lack of hoards from the late 870s and the 880s in England prevents us from proving this hypothesis.[32] As we saw above, the precise dating of the burial of the Ablaincourt hoard is difficult to determine. If it is from the 880s, this evidence constitutes the earliest occurrence of pecking whatsoever! But even if Ablaincourt and Féchain are to be dated to the early 890s, they would be among the very earliest documented instances of pecking.[33] Did pecking begin in France?

Vikings moved back and forth between England and the Continent all the time. The most likely scenario on the present evidence is that pecking indeed is an Anglo-Viking phenomenon provoked by the monetary reforms by Alfred in the 870s; that the Viking(s) who pecked and bent the coins from Ablaincourt and Féchain had learned this habit in England; and that they transposed it to

---

[31]   M. Archibald, 'Testing', in J. Graham-Campbell, *The Cuerdale Hoard and Related Viking-Age Silver and Gold from Britain and Ireland in the British Museum* (London, 2011), 51–64, at 60.

[32]   M. Archibald, 'Testing', 64. Cf. Checklist of coin hoards <www-cm.fitzwilliam.cam. ac.uk/dept/coins/projects/hoards>.

[33]   M. Archibald, 'Testing', 62 quotes me for saying that 'pecking nowhere [on the Continent] antedates its appearance in English finds'. This was before I saw the Ablaincourt and Féchain files.

another monetary landscape across the Channel, where it was less needed, as almost all coins were of good silver since the reform of Charles the Bald in 864.[34] Were there nevertheless reasons to be suspicious? There is evidence, outlined above, that style and weight standard were faltering in the 880s under the pressure of the Viking raids. The Vikings might have suspected the alloy to have been altered as well, unless pecking was just a habit taken from England and applied without any particular motive.

---

[34] D.M. Metcalf and J.P. Northover, 'Carolingian and Viking coins from the Cuerdale hoard: an interpretation and comparison of their metal contents', *NC, 148* (1988), 97–116; G. Sarah, 'Analyse et spéculation. Quelques deniers carolingiens reconsidérés', *BSFN, 67.1* (2012), 17–24.

Table 20.1   Proposed dates of the pre-920 French hoards containing GDR coins of the mint of Rouen.

Hoard	Lafaurie 1969	Duplessy 1985	Haertle 1997	Armstrong 1998	Coupland 2011	Moesgaard 2012
1. St-Denis	c.875–85	864–75?	aft. 869	864–77	869–77	869–79
2. Imbleville	-	864–75	aft. 869	864–77	869–77	869–79
3. Pt-St-Pierre	-	-	-	869–77	869–77	869–79
4. Compiègne	c.875–85	877–9	aft. 877	877–9	877–9	879–87
5. Savigné	-	877–82	aft. 877–79	877–82	877–82	879–87
6. Compiègne?	-	-	-	-	877–82	879–87
7. Chalo	c.875–85	879–84	aft. 879	879–84	879–84	879–87
8. Ablaincourt	c.891	-	-	879–84	879–84	879–87 (or later)
9. Longjumeau	-	-	-	-	882–5	879–87
10. Glisy	c.891	c.890	aft. 888	887–98	c.880	879–87 (or later)
11. Cauroir	-	-	-	-	c.880	882–7
13. Bligny	-	c.900–10	aft. 881	881–7	882–7	882–7
15. Montrieux	-	887–98	aft. 888	887–98	c.892–97	887–c.920
16. Féchain	c.891	-	-	887–98	c.890	887–c.920
17. Monchy	c.891	895–8	aft. 897/98	-	900–10	c.890–c.920

References: Lafaurie: *BSFN* (1969), 404–7 (see n. 6). The remainder: see introduction to catalogue below.

Table 20.2 Weights of GDR coins of the mint of Rouen in hoards.

Hoard	Date	Number	Range	Mean	Median
2. Imbleville	869–79	12	1.22–1.80g	1.50g	1.48g
3. Pont-St-Pierre	869–79	1	1.61g	-	-
8. Ablaincourt	879–87 (or later)	41*	1.30–1.85g	1.58g	1.59g
9. Longjumeau	879–87	16	1.19–1.71g	1.44g	1.40g
10. Glisy	879–87 (or later)	(1 or av. of 15?)	1.60g	-	-
11. Cauroir	882–7	1	1.66g	-	-
12. Laxfield	882–7	1	1.63g (?)	-	-
16. Féchain	887–	23	1.21–1.71g	1.49g	1.48g

*43 specimens in all, but two excluded: one chipped and one not cleaned. Lafaurie gives 45 weights for the remaining 41 coins. There must be four coins weighed twice, but it is impossible to check today. *Source:* Catalogue below.

Table 20.3 Distribution of weight of GDR coins of the mint of Rouen in four hoards.

	1.10–19	1.20–9	1.30–9	1.40–9	1.50–9	1.60–9	1.70–9	1.80–9
2. Imbleville	0	1	2	4	2	1	1	1
8. Ablaincourt	0	0	9	8	6	10	9	3
9. Longjumeau	1	2	4	2	4	2	1	0
16. Féchain	0	2	2	9	5	4	1	0

Source: Catalogue below.

Table 20.4   Literacy of GDR coins of the mint of Rouen in hoards.

Hoard	Date	No faults	1–3 faults	Several faults	Blundered
1. St-Denis	869–79	1	0	0	0
2. Imbleville	869–79	Most?	?	At least 1	?
3. Pt-St-Pierre	869–79	0	1	0	0
4. Compiègne	879–87	?	?	?	?
5. Savigné	879–87	?	?	?	?
6. Compiègne?	879–87	0	1	0	0
7. Chalo	879–87	Most?	At least 2	?	?
8. Ablaincourt	879–87 (or later)	3	26	3	0
9. Longjumeau	879–87	5	13	2	3
10. Glisy	879–87 (or later)	At least 1	At least 6	?	?
11. Cauroir	882–7	1	1	0	1
12. Laxfield	882–7	0	0	0	1?
13. Bligny	882–7	Most?	?	?	At least 1
14. Ashdon	c.890–c.895	1?	0	0	0
15. Montrieux	887–c.920	x	x	?	?
16. Féchain	887–c.920	2	16	4	1
17. Monchy	c.890–c.920	x?	x?	?	At least 1
18. Evreux	942–5	0	2?	0	0

Not considered as faults: the form of M (H or N); missing final I on the reverse; P instead of R in the monogram; dots in the legends. Considered as faults: retrograde letters; misspellings; missing letters (the latter considered as a serious fault, if it blunders the legend).

Source: Catalogue below.

Appendix 2: Catalogue of Hoards Containing Obols and Pennies of the GDR-Type from the Mint of Rouen

The proposed dates of burial of the hoards are given as a bracket corresponding to the date of introduction of the most recent coin(s) represented in the hoard (*t.p.q.*) and the date of introduction of the next prolific coinage which is absent from the hoard (*t.a.q.*). The following dates have been retained:

- Introduction of the GDR/KAROLVS-monogram in Lotharingia: August 869, when Charles the Bald acquired that kingdom.[35]
- Introduction of coinage in the name of Louis and Carloman: According to the convincing hypothesis of Grierson and Blackburn, probably not before the autumn of 879, when the empire was divided between Louis III and Carloman.[36] This implies that no coins would have been struck in the name of Louis II during his short reign (October 877–April 879), except for an irregular issue in Toulouse (and in Lotharingia). Most mints probably just continued to strike in the name of Charles the Bald. The number of coins of Louis and Carloman varies greatly from one region to another, making their value to determine the *t.a.q.* dependent on the region.
- Coin of Charles the Fat: According to the hypothesis of Grierson and Blackburn, Charles the Fat did not strike coins in West Francia during his reign there (884–7). In Lotharingia he probably struck coins with his imperial title in Maastricht, Metz, Verdun and maybe Saint-Géry of Cambrai from 882 onwards.[37] Other coins of an Emperor Charles (for instance from the mints of Mons, Tournai and others) must have been struck 875–7 under Charles the Bald. Genuine coins of Charles the Fat are generally speaking very rare in hoards in West Francia. Consequently, their absence in a particular hoard (especially in small hoards) has not been retained as criteria for determining the *t.a.q.*
- Introduction of coins in the name of Odo: December 887/February 888. Coins of Odo are relatively abundant. Consequently, absence of these coins is a good clue to the hoard being concealed before 887/88 (cf. however discussion above, p. 431).
- Introduction of coins of Charles the Simple: Charles the Simple was crowned with the support of the opponents of Odo on 23 January 893 and was recognised sole king when Odo died on 1 January 898. It is not clear when he introduced coinage in his own name. He resumed the

---

[35] *MEC* 1, 233.

[36] *MEC* 1, 242.

[37] *MEC* 1, 235, cf. 227, 253.

GDR-type of Charles the Bald, and it is often difficult to distinguish coins of the two reigns, even more so as the immobilised type had been widely struck after the death of Charles the Bald in 877. In many mints, they were probably still being produced at the accession of Charles the Simple, so there would have been no need to change. The coins from the end of the reign, *c*.920, are easier to distinguish, as they are struck to a lower weight standard and in some mints, like Paris and Saint-Denis, with a new type.[38] All these features make it difficult to date precisely the hoards of the first part of the reign.

Abbreviations Used in the Catalogue:

G = E. Gariel, *Les monnaies royales de France sous la race carolingienne*, tome 1 (Strasbourg, 1883).

D = J. Duplessy, *Les trésors monétaires médiévaux et modernes découverts en France*, 1, 751–1223 (Paris, 1985).

H = C.M. Haertle, *Karolingische Münzfunde aus dem 9. Jahrhundert* (Cologne, Weimar and Vienna, 1997).

A = S. Armstrong, 'Carolingian coin hoards and the impact of the Viking raids in the ninth century', *NC, 158* (1998), 131–64.

C = S. Coupland, 'A checklist of Carolingian coin hoards 751–987', *NC, 171* (2011), 203–56.

BNF = Bibliothèque Nationale de France, Paris.

MDA = Musée départemental des Antiquités de la Seine-Maritime, Rouen.

MG = K.F. Morrison and H. Grunthal, *Carolingian Coinage* (New York, 1967)

h = the commencement of the legend is indicated using the clockface, e.g. 11h30 a legend reading from 11.30 on a clock, where this is other than the standard 12.00 position.

1. Saint-Denis (France, dép. Seine-Saint-Denis), before 1965.

D 298; A 50; H 63; C 147; *L'Ile-de-France de Clovis* à *Hugues Capet* (Guiry-en-Vexin, 1993), 62–3.
T.p.q.: Probably[39] August 869 (GDR coins of the Lotharingian mints of Cambrai, Valenciennes and Verdun).

---

[38] Lafaurie, 'Deux trésors'.

[39] The date of the hoard depends on the date of a rare Quentovic variety present in the hoard (BNF 1965–1100), see M. Dhénin and P. Leclercq, 'The coins of Quentovic from the Cuerdale hoard in the Museum of Boulogne-sur-Mer', *BNJ, 52* (1982), 104–7, at 105–6 (to Charles the

T.a.q.: Probably autumn 879, maybe October 877 (absence of coins in the name of Louis and Carloman).

16 coins recorded. One coin of Rouen (BNF 1965–1102), published with photo by Haertle (H 63/009, photo pl. 39, 342):

1.1. Obol. 0.62g. No wear. Monogram CPLS; +CRATIA D-I REX (starts at 10h30) / +ROTVNACVS CIVI (starts at 11h30). Same obverse die as Longjumeau 9.18.

2. Imbleville (France, dép. Seine-Maritime), 1840.

D 168; A 45; H 62; C 144.

T.p.q.: August 869 (GDR coins of the Lotharingian mints of Couvin/ Curange and Gembloux).

T.a.q.: Probably autumn 879, maybe October 877 (absence of coins in the name of Louis and Carloman).

66 coins in total. 18 coins of Rouen known thanks to description in (1) MDA, inventory of gifts, no. 254, and (2) draft list in the archives of the museum. No specimen can be identified with certainty in MDA today – several were exchanged with other museums or collectors, the remainder are mixed up in the general collection.

2.1–12. 12 pennies (or 14?). 1.80, 1.75, 1.64, 1.59, 1.54, 1.48 (2), 1.40 (2), 1.38, 1.33, 1.22 g [34, 33, 31, 30, 29, 28 (2), 26.5 (2), 26, 25, 23 grains à 0.053g]. No information on wear. / 'ROTVMACVS CIVIT [*sic*]'. It is not clear whether all had the same legend, but major varieties would probably have been noted.

2.13–18. 6 (or 4?) obols. 0.64 (3), 0.61, ? (2) [12 (3), 11.5 grains]. One obol is drawn: Monogram CPLS; +CRATIA D-I REX (starts at 6h) / +ROTVMACVS CIVI (starts at 11h30). The reverse die may be identical to Ablaincourt 8.30. This coin does not seem worn. Otherwise two reverse legends are quoted: 'ROTVMACVS' and 'ROTACVS'. No information on wear for the remaining obols.

3. Pont-Saint-Pierre (France, dép. Eure), before 1995.

A 56; C 146; J.C. Moesgaard, *NC, 157* (1997), 235–6.

T.p.q.: August 869 (GDR coins of the Lotharingian mints of Mouzon and Valenciennes).

T.a.q.: Probably autumn 879, maybe October 877 (absence of coins in the name of Louis and Carloman).

Simple); C.E. Blunt, 'The composition of the Cuerdale hoard', *BNJ, 53* (1983), 1–6, at 5–6 (uncertain); S. Coupland, 'Charlemagne's coinage: ideology and economy', in *Charlemagne: Empire and Society*, ed. J. Story (Manchester, 2005), 211–29, at 218 (to Charlemagne).

8 coins recorded. One coin of Rouen (MDA, inv. R.95.245.2), published with photo by Moesgaard (pl. 49, 5):

3.1. Penny. 1.61 g. No wear. Obv. die worn. Retrograde monogram CRLZ; +CRATIA D-I RE+ (starts at 3h) / +ROTVM.ACVS CIVII

4. Compiègne (France, dép. Oise), 1877.

G XVII; MG 62; D 104; A 63; H 73; C 158; E. Gariel, *ASFN, 2nd series, 1* (1877), 164–5; A. de Roucy, *Bulletin de la Société Historique de Compiègne*, VI (1884), 39–41.

T.p.q.: Probably autumn 879, maybe October 877 (a MDR coin in the name of Louis from Tours).

T.a.q.: December 887/February 888 (absence of coins of Odo).

288 coins in all. 39 coins of Rouen. Summary lists published by A. de Roucy, then owner of the coins:

4.1–36. 36 pennies. No information on weight, wear, legends or monogram.

4.37–9. 3 obols. No information on weight, wear, legends or monogram.

5. Savigné-sous-le-Lude (France, dép. Sarthe), 1899.

MG 81; D 341; A 66; H 74; C 160; H. de Castellane, *RN, 4th series, 4* (1900), 435–8; H. Roquet, *La Province du Maine, XIX* (1911), 153–63; A. Dieudonné, *RN, 4th series, 19* (1915), 211–42, nos. 18–23, 30–8, 40–58.

T.p.q.: Probably autumn 879, maybe October 877 (MDR coins in the name of Louis from Tours).

T.a.q.: December 887/February 888 (absence of coins of Odo).

A coin of Odo from Angers has wrongly been attributed to this hoard.[40]

360 coins in all, rapidly dispersed, among others to Castellane and Roquet. One coin of Rouen, mentioned summarily by Roquet:

5.1. Penny. No information on weight, legends or monogram; no wear ('tous très bien conservés').

Haertle 74/052 identifies with a question mark the Rouen penny as Gariel XXXIII, 209, which has a blundered reverse legend. I have found no justification for this very precise attribution, which is in contradiction to his n. 591, p. 676, that it was of the 'normal type' and not described in detail in the available sources.

6. Unknown find spot, maybe near Compiègne (France, dép. Oise), 2006.

C 162; *pers. comm.* S. Coupland 11.1.2006 and 1.2.2006.

---

[40]   Haertle, *Karolingische Münzfunde*, 687, n. 597.

T.p.q.: Probably autumn 879, maybe October 877 (coin in the name of Louis from Visé).

T.a.q.: December 887/February 888 (absence of coins of Odo).

Four coins in all, sold on eBay. One coin of Rouen, known from poor quality photo:

6.1. Penny. Weight? No wear. Retrograde monogram CRLS; +CRATI DI RE+ (starts at 3h) / +ROTV[MACV]S CIVII (difficult to read due to corrosion).

7. *Chalo-Saint-Mars (France, dép. Essonne), 1881 (also known as 'Beaumont' and 'Etampes').*

G XVI; MG 63–64; D 79; A 69; H 77; C 166; Duhamel, *Société historique et archéologique du Gâtinais. Annales de la société, VI* (1888), 233–42; M. Legrand, *RN, 4th series, 20* (1916), 173–80.

T.p.q.: 15 October 879 (coin in the name of Carloman from Auxerre, in Burgundy).

T.a.q.: December 887/February 888 (absence of coins of Odo).

300–400 coins in all. 19 coins of Rouen, one parcel of 11 coins described by Gariel after the notes of Barthélemy, another of 8 coins published by Duhamel and Legrand. These eight coins belonged to the authors, to a collector from Sens and to the Museum of Etampes (lost in the Second World War[41]).

7.1–9. 9 pennies. No information on weight, wear or monogram. '+CRATIA D-I REX' / '+ROTVMACVS CIVII' (Gariel).

7.10. Penny. No information on weight, wear or monogram. '+CRAITA D REX' / '+ROTVMACVS CIVII' (Gariel).

7.11–17. 7 pennies. No information on weight or wear. 'Les variantes ... de droit ... n'ont pas été consignées' / '+ROTVMAGVS CIVI ou CIVII' (Duhamel 27 and Legrand).

7.18. Obol. No information on weight, wear or monogram. '+CRTIA D-I REX' / '+POTVMACVS CIVII' (Gariel).

7.19. Obol. No information on weight or wear. 'Les variantes ... de droit ... n'ont pas été consignées' / '+ROTVMAGVS CIVI ou CIVII' (Duhamel 28 and Legrand).

8. *Ablaincourt (France, dép. Somme), 1957.*

MG 83–4; A 67; C 164; C. Meert, *RBN, 108* (1962), 167–8; J. Lafaurie, *RN, 6th series, 7* (1965), 271; *RN, 6th series, 9* (1967), 293; *BSFN, 23* (1968), 324–5; *BSFN, 24* (1969), 406; J. Lafaurie in *Lagom. Festschrift für Peter Berghaus zum*

---

[41]   Haertle, *Karolingische Münzfunde*, 163, n. 525.

60. Geburtstag am 20. November 1979, ed. T. Fischer and P. Ilisch (Münster, 1981), 115; *NC, 148* (1988), 116; Monnaies et Médailles, Basel, sale 39, 9–10 May 1969; publication in preparation by M. Dhénin.

T.p.q.: Autumn 879 (coins of Louis (II)/III and Carloman).

T.a.q.: 887/8 (absence of coins of Odo).

Note: dated by Lafaurie to *c*.891, see above.

898 coins. Partly in coll. ANS, partly dispersed. 47 coins from Rouen, unpublished study by Jean Lafaurie. Bending and pecking judged by the author from photos.

8.1. Penny. 1.60g (Figure 20.3a). No wear. Bent. Pecks: 0/1. Retrograde monogram K(R inverted)LZ. +CRATIA DI REX (starts at 4h) / +ROTVMACVS CIVII (JL1) (ANS).

8.2. Penny. 1.39g (Figure 20.3b). No wear. Bent. Pecks: 0/1. Monogram KRLS. xCRATIA (C inverted)I RE+ (starts at 11h) / +ROTVNACVS CIVII (JL2) (ANS). Same obverse die as Féchain 16.15.

8.3. Penny. 1.85g. No wear. Seems slightly bent. Retrograde monogram CPLS. xCRATIA D-I PE+ (starts at 4h) / +ROTVIIACVS CIVII (JL3; Monnaies et médailles, no. 461).

8.4. Penny. 1.64g. No wear. Die identical to the previous coin (JL4; no photo).

8.5. Penny. Weight? No wear. Monogram CPLS. +CRATIA DI REX / +ROTVHACVS CIVII (JL5/30a) (ANS).

8.6. Penny. Weight? No wear. Seems slightly bent. Minor die cracks. Monogram CPLZ. xCRATIA D-I RE+ (starts at 11h) / +ROTVMACVS CIVII (JL5/30b).

8.7. Penny. Weight? No wear. Monogram CPLS. +CRATIA D-I REX (starts at 6h) / +ROTVNACVS CIVII (JL5/30c).

8.8. Penny. Weight? No wear. Seems slightly bent. Monogram CPLS. +CRATIA (C inverted).I REX (starts at 1h) / +ROTVNACVS CIVII (JL5/30d) (ANS).

8.9. Penny. 1.54g. No wear. Monogram CRLS. +CRATIA D-I REX (starts at 5h30) / +ROTVNACVS CIVII (JL5/30e) (ANS).

8.10. Penny. 1.48g. No wear. Bent. Pecks: 0/1. Retrograde monogram CPLZ. +CRATIA D-I REX (starts at 1h30) / +ROTVHACVS CIVII (JL5/30f) (ANS).

8.11. Penny. 1.37g. No wear. Bent. Pecks: 0/1. Monogram CPLZ. +CRATIA DI REX (starts at 11h) / +ROTVMACVS CIVII (JL5/30g) (ANS).

8.12. Penny. 1.80g. No wear. Monogram CPLZ. xCPATIA (C inverted)I REX (starts at 10h) / +ROTVHACVS CIVII (JL5/30h) (ANS).

8.13. Penny. 1.68g. No wear. Monogram CPLS. +CRATIA D-I REX (starts at 7h) / +ROTV(N inverted)ACVS CIVI (JL5/30i) (Monnaies et Médailles, no. 459).

8.14. Penny. 1.71g. No wear. Slightly bent. Monogram CPLS. xCPATIA DI REX (starts at 10h) / +ROTVHACVS CIVII (JL5/30j) (Monnaies et Médailles, no. 463).

8.15. Penny. 1.66g. No wear. Monogram CPLZ. xCRAITA D REX (starts at 10h30) / +ROTVHACVS CIVII (JL5/30l) (ANS).

8.16. Penny. 1.48g. No wear. Bent. Retrograde monogram CRLZ. '+GRATIA D-I REX' / '+ROTVMACVS CIVII' (JL 31; no photo).

8.17. Penny. 1.49g. No wear. Retrograde monogram CRLS. xCRATIA DI RE+ (starts at 4h) / +ROTVMACVZ CIVII (starts at 11h) (JL 32) (ANS).

8.18. Penny. 1.48g (Figure 20.1a). No wear. Retrograde monogram CRLS. +CRATIA RI RE+ (starts at 3h30) / +ROTVMACVZ CIVII (starts at 11h30) (JL33) (ANS). Same obverse die as Longjumeau 9.11–12, Glisy no. G69 (Musée d'Amiens, doc. Michel Dhénin) and Gariel 1884, XXXIII, 207. Same reverse die as Féchain 16.8 (Figure 20.1b) and MDA, inv. 94.5.2, unprovenanced (Figure 20.3d).

8.19. Penny. 1.60g. No wear. Same obverse die as the previous coin / '+ROTVMACV.S CIVII' (JL34; no photo).

8.20. Penny. 1.37g (1.45?). No wear. Monogram CRLS. +CRATIA DI REIX (starts at 10h) / +ROTVNACVS CIVI (JL35; Monnaies et Médailles, vente 39, 458).

8.21. Penny. 1.37g. No wear. Monogram CRLS. +CRATIA.D.I REX / +ROTVMACVZ CIVII (JL36; Monnaies et Médailles, no. 462).

8.22. Penny. 1.48g. No wear. Bent. Monogram CPLS. +CRATIA D-I REX / +ROTVMACAS CIVIII (JL37) (ANS).

8.23. Penny. 1.49g. No wear. Bent. Retrograde monogram CRLZ. Retrograde legend +CRATIA D-I RE+ (starts at 3h) / Retrograde legend +ROTVMACVZ CIVI.I (JL38; Monnaies et Médailles, no. 464, BNF).

8.24. Penny. 1.47g. No wear. Monogram CPLZ. xCPATIA DI REI+ (starts at 10h30) / .+ROTVHACVS CIVII (JL39).

8.25. Penny. 1.54g. No wear. Bent. Monogram CPLZ. xCRATIA DI PEX (starts at 11h) / +ROTVIIACVS CIVII (starts at 11h) (JL40).

8.26. Penny. 1.54g? Chipped. No wear. Same obverse die as the previous coin / +R.TVIIA(CV?)S CIYII (starts at 11h30) (JL41; ANS).

8.27. Penny. 1.47g. No wear. Monogram CPLS. +CRATIA D-I REX (starts at 11h30) / +ROTVMAS CIVIII (JL42; Monnaies et Médailles, no. 460). Same dies as Féchain 16.22 and 23.

8.28. Penny. 1.57g. No wear. Seems slightly bent. Monogram CPLS. +CRATIA DI REX (starts at 10h30) / +ROTVMVCVS CIVII (dot under M) (starts at 0h30) (JL43; ANS).

8.29. Obol. 0.67 g. No wear. Monogram CRLS. +CRA'TIA DI REX (starts at 8h30) / +ROTVIIACVS CIVII (JL44; ANS).

8.30. Obol. 0.63 g. Retrograde monogram CRLZ. +CR.ATIA D-I REX (starts at 4h) / +ROTVMACVS CIVI (starts at 11h30) (JL45; Monnaies et Médailles, vente 39, 457). The reverse die may be identical to Imbleville 2.13.

8.31. Obol. 0.74 g. No wear. Monogram? '+CRATIA RI RE+' / '+ROTVMACVS CIVII'. Style as 8.16–21 (JL46, no photo).

8.32. Obol. 0.62 g. No wear. Double struck. Monogram CRLZ. Retrograde legend +CRATIA D-I RE+ (starts at 2h) / +ROTVMACVS CI (JL47; ANS).

8.33–47. 15 pennies, no photographs. No information on wear. Same stylistic group as the 11 coins 8.5–15. Lafaurie (JL 5/30) describes the entire group:

'Groupe varié, qui semble homogène malgré le nombre très restreint de combinaisons de coins. Variétés principales:

α – + CRATIA D-I REX CRLS (6 coins) β – do. CRLZ (4 coins) γ – +CRATIA DI REX [CRLS] (6 coins) – δ – do. [CRLZ] (8 coins).

Rv o – +ROTVHACVS CIVII (13 coins) π – +ROTVMACVS CIVII (7 coins) ρ – +ROTVHACVS CIVI (1 coin) σ – +ROTVMACVS CIVI (3 coins) τ – +ROTVMACVS CIVII (? double frappe ?)'

For the 19 specimens 8.5–8, 33–47 Lafaurie gives 23 weights: 1.84, 1.79 (2), 1.75 (2), 1.74, 1.71, 1.70 (2), 1.69, 1.67, 1.64, 1.62 (2), 1.59 (2), 1.50, 1.39, 1.38 (2), 1.33, 1.30, ? (uncleaned).

Note: in his notes, Jean Lafaurie identifies three main styles: (1) 8.5–15, 8.29–30, 8.33–47; (2) 8.16–21, 8.31; (3) 8.23, 8.32.

9. Longjumeau (France, dép. Essonne), 1930–31.

C 173; C. Daillan, *BCEN, 45.3* (2008), 80–95; J.C. Moesgaard, *BSFN, 65.3* (2010), 57–61.

T.p.q.: Autumn 879 (coins in the name of Carloman and Louis III).

T.a.q.: December 887/February 888 (absence of coins of Odo).

155 coins in total, dispersed 2008/10. 24 coins of Rouen, published with photo by C.A. Daillan:

9.1. Penny. 1.60g. No wear. Retrograde monogram CRLS. +CRATIA DI RE+ (starts at 3h) / +ROTVMACVZ CIVII (Daillan 72).

9.2. Penny. 1.27g. No wear. Monogram C(P or R?)LS. +CRAT(dot?)IA DI REX / +ROTVHACVS CIVI (Daillan 73).

9.3. Penny. 1.19g. No wear. Monogram CRLS. +CRATIA DI REX / +ROTVMACVZ CIVII (Daillan 74).

9.4. Penny. 1.71g. No wear. Retrograde monogram CPLS. +CRATIA RI RE+ (starts at 3h) / +ROTVMACVZ CIVII (starts at 11h30) (Daillan 75).

9.5. Penny. 1.24g. No wear. Obverse die worn. Monogram CPLS. +CRATIA D-I REX / +ROTVHACVS CIVI (Daillan 76).

9.6. Penny. 1.41g. No wear. Obverse die a bit worn. Monogram CRLS. +CRATIA D-I REX / +ROTVHACVS CIVI (Daillan 77).

9.7. Penny. 1.54g. No wear. Retrograde monogram CPLS. +CRATIA D-I RE+ (starts at 5h) / +ROTVMACVS CIVII (Daillan 78).

9.8. Penny. 1.37g. No photo (Daillan 79 with wrong photo = Daillan 77).

9.9. Penny. 1.36g. No wear. Monogram CPLS. +CPATIIIA I(C inverted) I I'E+ (starts at 10h) / +ROTVMACAZ CIAII (Daillan 80; Fitzwilliam Museum CM.122–2010).

9.10. Penny. 1.40g. No wear. Retrograde monogram CPLZ. +CRATIA D(-?)I REX (starts at 10h) / +ROTVMACVS CVI (Daillan 81).

9.11. Penny. 1.65g. No wear. Retrograde monogram CRLS. +CRATIA RI RE+ (starts at 3h30) / +ROTVMACV.S CIVII – (intended?) small dot in second angle of the cross (Daillan 82). Same obverse die as the next coin, Ablaincourt 8.18, Glisy no. G69 (Musée d'Amiens, doc. Michel Dhénin) and Gariel 1884, XXXIII,207.

9.12. Penny. 1.36g. No wear. Same obverse die as the previous coin / +ROTVMACV.S CIVII (starts at 11h) (Daillan 83).

9.13. Penny. 1.56g. No wear. Monogram CPLZ. xCRATIA D-I RE+ (starts at 11h30) / +ROTVMACVS CIVII (Daillan 84). Obverse die probably identical to Glisy, Gariel XIV,126.

9.14. Penny. 1.55g. No wear. Monogram CRLZ. +CRATIA DI REX / +ROTVNACVS CIVII (Daillan 85).

9.15. Penny. 1.50g. No wear. Monogram CPLZ. +CPATIA DI REX / +ROTVMACVS CIVII (Daillan 86).

9.16. Penny. 1.31g. No wear. Monogram HRLS. +CRATA D REX (starts at 0h30) / +ROTVM.ACVZ CIVI; pellets in the 2nd and 3rd cross angles (Daillan 87; Fitzwilliam Museum, CM.123-2010, cf. Cat. 9.9 above.

9.17. Obol. 0.65g. No wear. Obverse die worn. Monogram CPLS. +CRATIA D.I REX (starts at 1h) / +ROTVM.ACVS CIVI (Daillan 88).

9.18. Obol. 0.66g. No wear. Monogram CPLS. +CRATIA D-I REX (starts at 10h30) / +ROTVM.ACVS CIVI (Daillan 89). Same obverse die as St-Denis 1.1.

9.19. Obol. 0.56g. No wear. Retrograde monogram CPLZ. +CRATIA D-I RE+ (starts at 3h) / +ROTVMACVS CVII (Daillan 90).

9.20. Obol. 0.67g. No wear. Retrograde monogram CRLZ. +CRATI DI REX (starts at 3h30) / +ROTVHACVS ICII (Daillan 91).

9.21. Obol. 0.57g. No wear. Bent. Monogram CPLS. +CRATIA D-I REX (starts at 1h30) / +ROTVMACVS CIVI (Daillan 92).

9.22. Obol. 0.70g. No wear. Monogram CRLS. +CRATIA D-I REX (starts at 9h30) / +ROTVHACVZ CIVI (starts at 0h30) (Daillan 93).

9.23. Obol. 0.57g. No wear. Retrograde monogram CRLS. +CA(TIA?) (retrograde D)-I (retrograde R)EX (starts at 11h) / +ROTVIIACVS CVII (starts at 1h) (Daillan 94).

9.24. Obol. 0.50g. No wear. Retrograde monogram CRLS. +CIATA DI IEI+ (starts at 7h) / +AROTAIACOM (Daillan 153).

10. Glisy (France, dép. Somme), 1864 or 1865.[42]

G XX; MG 75; D 154; H 90; A 74; C 170; A.-P.-M. Bazot, *Bulletin de la Société des antiquaires de Picardie, IX* (1865–7), 130–46; E. Gariel, *ASFN,* 2 (1867), 349–58; A. de Longpérier, *RN, 2nd series, 13* (1868), 188–200; J. Charvet, *RBN, 5th series, 2* (1870), 417–39; E. Gariel, *ASFN, 5* (1877), 161–5, 367; E. Caron, *ASFN, 16* (1892), 121; R. Serrure, *Bulletin de Numismatique,* 2 (1893–4), 150–51; F. Vercauteren, *Revue Belge de philologie et d'histoire, 13* (1934), 750–58.

Note: As this chapter was almost completed, Michel Dhénin kindly told me that part of this hoard is still preserved at the Museum of Amiens, but unfortunately, it was too late to check these coins for the present study.

T.p.q.: Autumn 879 (Coins of Louis III. Hypothesis of Coupland, discarding the coin of Odo as a misreading by Gariel, cf. above[43]) or 887/88 (possible Orléans coin of Odo).

T.a.q.: December 887/February 888 (apparent absence of coins of Odo, according to Coupland) or *c.*920.

*c.*600–700 coins in total. 35 coins of Rouen, two distinct parcels published by Bazot and Charvet, partial synthesis by Gariel (3 successive, partially contradictory, versions; see discussion above, pp. 430–1).

10.1–35. Bazot, no 26, says that there were four varieties, but does not mention the total number of Rouen coin known to him and acquired by the Société des Antiquaires de Picardie. Charvet's parcel (no. 60) comprised 15 pennies and no obols. According to Gariel, the hoard in total contained 35 coins of Rouen. In 1867, no. 47 and 1877, he only quotes pennies, whereas in 1883, no. XLIV, he quotes pennies and obols without giving the number of each. The mention of obols is probably erroneous. Charvet gives the weight of 1.60g, but it is not clear whether it is just the weight of one single specimen or the average of the 15 pennies known to him. No other published weight indications exist. Bazot (no. 26) gives exact drawings of the inscriptions (but not the monograms) of four varieties: (1) +CRATIA D-I RE+ / +ROTVIIACVZ

---

[42]   All authors state April 1865, except for Bazot and Longpérier who say April 1864. Serrure erroneously says 1862.

[43]   The ascription by Haertle to Bruges and Odo of a series of coins (H 90/242–4) is not certain.

CIVII (= G XIV,124?); (2) +CPATIA DI REX / +ROTVHACVS CIVII; (3) +CRATIA RI RE+ / +ROTVMACVZ CIVII (= Glisy G69, Musée d'Amiens? Photograps in the files of Michel Dhénin, retrograde monogram CRLS); (4) +CRATIA D-I REX / +ROTVMACVS CVI – Charvet (no. 60) gives a seemingly standardised description (except for the missing stroke in 'D-I'): '+ GRATIA DI REX' / '+ ROTVMACVS CIVII'. Gariel 1867, no. 47, gives only one description for the 35 specimens: 'Monogramme dégénéré'; '+ CRATIA D-. REX' / '+ ROTVNACVS CIVI'. In 1877, he only describes the reverse: '+ ROTVNVCVS CIVI'. The second 'V' would be an error for 'A'? In 1883, he illustrates 4 specimens (pl. XIV): (123) Monogram CPLS; +CRATIA D-I REX (starts at 5h) / +ROTVM.ACVS CIVII; (124) Retrograde monogram CRLS; +CRATIA D-I RE+ (starts at 3h) / +ROTVIIACVZ CIVII (starts at 0h30); (125) Retrograde monogram CPLS; +CRATIA DI REX (starts at 6h) / +ROTVHACVS CIVII; (126) Monogram CPLZ; xCRATIA D-I RE+ (starts at 11h) (obverse die probably identical to Longjumeau 9.13) / +ROTVIIACVS CIVII – Judging from the drawings, these four coins are not worn. Indeed Bazot says in general terms that the coins from this hoard were uncirculated or very slightly worn.

11. Cauroir (France, dép. Nord), 2000–2009.

C 169; Comptoir général financier (CGF), Paris, Ventes sur offres, trésors II, 17 November 2005, nos. 300–44; Monnaies XXVIII, 8 February 2007, nos 1396–1428; Monnaies 33, 6 December 2007, nos. 1010–25; Monnaies 35, 19 June 2008, no. 31; Monnaies 42, 28 January 2010, nos. 28–49.

T.p.q.: probably 882,[44] maybe 876 (coins with imperial title from Maastricht and Saint-Géry of Cambrai, probably Charles the Fat, maybe Charles the Bald).

T.a.q.: December 887/February 888 (absence of coins of Odo).

88 coins in total. Three or four coins of Rouen, published with photographs in sale catalogues:

11.1. Penny. 1.66g. No wear. Die damage on obverse. Monogram CRLZ. xCRATIA D-I REX (starts at 11h) / +ROTVNACVS CIVII (starts at 11h) (CGF tr.2.330).

11.2. Penny. 1.36g (fragment). No wear, corrosion. Monogram KRLS. [+] CRATIA D-I[REX] (starts at 11h) / [+]ROTVHACVS CIV[II] (CGF 42.32).

11.3. Penny. Contemporary forgery in plated copper. No wear. 1.14g (fragment). Retrograde monogram CRLZ. +CRATIA[D-I RE]X / (+?)[R] OTVMACVS CIVII (CGF 28.1423).

---

[44]   Coupland accepts my redating of this hoard, *pers. comm.* August 2012.

11.4. Obol. 0.67g (large edge chips). No wear. Monogram CRLS. +CRATI D-I[R]EX (starts at 9h) / +A ... OTOCVSM (CGF 28.1422 = 35.31 = 42.43).

12. Laxfield (UK, Suffolk), 1819.

MG 65; C 152; Dolley and Morrison, *BNJ*, 32 (1963), 79, no. 11; J.C. Moesgaard in *Silver Economy in the Viking Age*, ed. J. Graham-Campbell and G. Williams (Walnut Creek, CA, 2007), 108.

T.p.q.: probably 882,[45] maybe 876 (penny with imperial title from Saint-Géry of Cambrai, probably Charles the Fat, maybe Charles the Bald).

T.a.q.: December 887/February 888 (absence of coins of Odo).

Note: The English coins in the hoard are not described in detail, but according to the interpretation of Dolley and Morrison, they seem to be *c*.865–75.

Coins, unknown number. One coin of Rouen, described in Banks MSS, Dept. of Coins and Medals of British Museum, used by Dolley and Morrison in 1963. The Banks MSS are longer available:[46]

12.1. Penny. In 1963 described as 'Charles the Bald – Rouen. Cf. Prou 378 var.: Morrison-Grunthal 878'. Circumstantial evidence suggests that a specimen from the collection of R.A. Merson is identical to this coin (R.A. Merson, *pers. comm.*): Penny. 1.63g. Pecks: 0/3. No wear. Monogram CPLZ. xCPATIA CIRV PEX (starts at 10h) / +ROTVIIACVS CIVII (photo published by Moesgaard). Die identical to Féchain 16.16.

13. Bligny (France, dép. Aube), 1855.

G XIV; MG 69; D 47; A 71; H 80; C 174; D'Arbois de Jubainville, *Bibliothèque de l'Ecole des Chartes*, 18 (1857), 203–4; Ledain, *Mémoires de la Société d'archéologie et d'histoire de la Moselle*, 15 (1879), 79–98.

T.p.q.: January 882 (Charles the Fat, Verdun).

T.a.q.: December 887/ February 888 (absence of coins of Odo).

More than 98 coins in total. 10, maybe 11 coins of Rouen, described by D'Arbois de Jubainville, Ledain and Gariel. One is illustrated:

13.1–9. 9 pennies. Weight? Wear? Monogram? '+GRATIA D-I REX' / '+ ROTVMACVS CIVII' (Gariel). D'Arbois de Jubainville 19 ('ROTUMAGUS CIVIT[AS]') and Ledain III.11 ('ROTVMAGVS CIVII') only quote three pennies.

13.10. Obol. Weight? Wear? Monogram? '+GRATIA D-I REX' / '+ ROTVMACVS CIVII' (Gariel). Not quoted by D'Arbois de Jubainville nor by Ledain.

---

[45] Coupland accepts my redating of this hoard, *pers. comm.* August 2012.

[46] Checklist, hoard no. 77 <www-cm.fitzwilliam.cam.ac.uk/dept/coins/projects/hoards>.

13.11. Obol, maybe Rouen? Weight? Quoted as impossible to attribute by Gariel and Ledain (III.25). Engraved by Gariel: Apparently no wear. Monogram CR(retrograde L)S. +C D-I IAVCIVEX (starts at 3h) / AOCIAIVIVIIVCIVI (starts at 11h30) (Gariel, vol. 2, pl. XXXVII, 296).

14. Ashdon (UK, Essex), 1984.

C 188; Blackburn, *BNJ*, 59 (1989), 13–38.

T.p.q.: December 887/February 888 (coin of Odo); *c.*890 (Alfred two-line of middle style)

T.a.q.: *c.*895 (absence of St Edmund Memorial coins).

71 coins in all. One coin from Rouen (Fitzwilliam Museum, Cambridge), published with photograph by Blackburn.

14.1. Penny. 1.16g (fragment). Pecks: 0/1. Bent. Monogram not distinguishable on photo. +CRATIA D-I REX (starts at 9h) / +ROTVNACVS CIVII

15. Montrieux-en-Sologne (France, dép. Loir-et-Cher), c.1840 or 1857 (also known as 'Courbanton II' or 'III').

It is a subject of debate whether the coins described here are from the hoard found *c.*1840 or the one found 1857, cf. Duplessy, Haertle and Coupland quoted below.

G XIX; MG 89–90, 122; D 230–1; H 88; A 76; C 193–4; J. Charvet, *RBN*, 5th series, 2 (1870), 424; E. Gariel, *ASFN*, 5 (1877), 168–70; E. Besnard, *Bulletin de la société archéologique et historique de l'Orléannais*, VIII (1883–6), 284–7.

T.p.q.: December 887/February 888 (Coins of Odo).

T.a.q.: *c.*920 (absence of late coins of Charles the Simple).

*c.*1,200 or 1,500 coins in all. 8 coins of Rouen, described by Gariel:

15.1–8. 8 pennies. Weight? Wear? Monogram? '+ GRATIA D-I REX' / '+ ROTVNACVS CIVII' (Gariel 1877). '+ CRATIA DI REX' / '+ ROTVMACVZ (C inverted)IVII'. 'Il y avait 6 variétés de coins' (Gariel 1883, no. 27).

16. Féchain (France, dép. Nord), 1967.

A 72; C 186; M. Dhénin, in *La Neustrie. Les pays au nord de la Loire de Dagobert à Charles le Chauve (VIIe–IXe siècle)*, ed. P. Périn and L.-C. Feffer (Rouen, 1985), 416–19. Publication in preparation by M. Dhénin.

T.p.q.: 887/88 (Coins of Odo and Arnulf).

T.a.q.: *c.*920 (absence of late coins of Charles the Simple).

Note: the small number of coins of Odo indicates a date early in the bracket.

441 coins in total. Musée de la Chartreuse, Douai. It includes 23 coins of Rouen.

16.1. Penny. 1.42g (Figure 20.2a). No wear. Monogram KRLS. xCRATIA D-I REX (starts at 11h) / xROTVMACVS CIVII (starts at 0h30) (ill. *Neustrie*, 418).

16.2. Penny. 1.42g. No wear. Retrograde monogram CPLZ. +CRATIA D-I REX / +ROTVMACVS CIVII

16.3. Penny. 1.47g. Worn. Retrograde monogram CPLS. +CRATIA D-I RE+ (starts at 3h30) / +ROTVMACVS CIVII (starts at 11h30).

16.4. Penny. 1.30g. No wear. Same dies as the previous coin.

16.5. Penny. 1.61g. No wear. Monogram CRLZ. +CPATIA DI REX / +ROTVHACVS CIVII

16.6. Penny. 1.57g. A bit worn. Monogram CRLS. xCRATIA DI RE+ (starts at 10h) / +ROTVMACVS CIVII – Same obverse die as Prou 386. Same reverse die as the next coin.

16.7. Penny. 1.52g. No wear. Monogram CRLS. xCRATIA DI RE+ (starts at 10h) / Same reverse die as the previous coin.

16.8. Penny. 1.57g (Figure 20.1b). No wear. Retrograde monogram CRLS. xCRATIA DI RE+ (starts at 3h30) / +ROTVMACVZ CIVII (starts at 11h30). Same reverse die as Ablaincourt 8.18 and MDA, Rouen, inv. 94.5.2, unprovenanced.

16.9. Penny. 1.47g. No wear. Retrograde monogram CPLS. +CRATIA DI RE+ (starts at 3h) / +ROTVMACVZ CIVII (starts at 11h30).

16.10. Penny. 1.71g. No wear. Monogram CPLS. +CRATIA DI REX (starts at 11h30) / +ROTVHACVS CIVII (starts at 11h30).

16.11. Penny. 1.56g. No wear. Corroded. Monogram CPLS. +CRATIA C[inverted]I REX (starts at 11h) / +ROTVHACVS CIVII

16.12. Penny. 1.69g. No wear. Monogram CPLZ. x:CPATIA DI REX. (starts at 11h) / +ROTVHACVS CIVII

16.13. Penny. 1.69g. No wear. Weak striking. Monogram CPLZ. +CRATIA D-I REX (starts at 11h) / +ROTVHACVS CIVII – reverse die crack.

16.14. Penny. 1.46g. No wear. Monogram CPLZ. xCPATIA D-I REX (starts at 11h) / +ROTVNACVS CIVII (starts at 11h30). Same obverse die as Prou 380.

16.15. Penny. 1.44g; slightly chipped. No wear. Monogram KRLS. xCRATIA (C inverted)I RE+ (starts at 11h) / +ROTVNACVS CIVII – Same obverse die as Ablaincourt 8.2.

16.16. Penny. 1.48g (Figure 20.2b). No wear. Monogram CPLZ. xCPATIA CIRV PEX (starts at 10h) / +ROTVIIACVS CIVII – Die identical to Laxfield 12.1.

16.17. Penny. 1.49g. No wear. Monogram CRLZ. Retrograde legend +(CR inverted)ATIA D-I (RE inverted)X (starts at 7h30) / +ROTVNACVS CIVII

16.18. Penny. 1.61g. Some wear. Bent. Monogram CPLS. +CRATIA D-I RE.X. / +ROTVHACVS CIVI – Reverse die damaged.

16.19. Penny. 1.21g. No wear. Monogram CPLS. +CRATIA DI RE+ (starts at 9h) / +ROTVHACVS CIVI

16.20. Penny. 1.56g. No wear. Monogram CRLZ. +CRATIA DI REX (starts at 11h) / +ROTVMACVS CVII

16.21. Penny. 1.31g. No wear. Worn dies. Monogram CRLS. +CRATIA D-. REX (starts at 4h) / +ROTVNACVS CI

16.22. Penny. 1.47g (Figure 20.3c). No wear. Pecks: 1/1? Monogram CPLS. +CRATIA D-I REX (starts at 11h30) / +ROTVMAS CIVIII – Same dies as the next coin and Ablaincourt 8.27.

16.23. Penny. 1.24g. No wear. Obverse die worn. Same dies as the previous coin and Ablaincourt 8.27.

17. Monchy-au-Bois (France, dép. Pas de Calais), 1869 (also known as 'Arras').

G XXI; MG 67; D 217; H 101; C 207; L. Dancoisne, *Bulletin de la commission des antiquités du département du Pas de Calais,* 3 (1868–74), 172; E. Gariel, *ASFN,* 5 (1877), 165–7, 368.

T.p.q.:[47] *c.*890 (coins of Abbot Franco of Corbie[48])

*T.a.q.: c.*920 (absence of late coin types of Charles the Simple).

More than 475 coins in all. 7 coins of Rouen. Short partially self-contradictory description by Gariel. One coin illustrated:

17.1–6. 6 pennies. No information on weight or monogram; somewhat worn? '+ GRATIAD-IREX' / + ROTVNACVSCI [*sic* !]' (Gariel 1877); 'au type ordinaire' (Gariel 1883, no. 31).

17.7. Penny. No information on weight; apparently no wear. Monogram KRLS. +GRATIA D-I REX (starts at 11h30) / +ROTVI(C inverted) V(horizontal Z) CIVI (Gariel 1883, pl. XVII, 31; Gariel 1884, pl. XXXIII, 209).

---

[47] The coins of Clermont (type MG 1078) cannot be attributed to Charles the Simple with certainty (as does Haertle, following J. Lafaurie, review of MG in *RN,* 6.9 (1967), 291–5, at p. 294).

[48] M. Bompaire, A. Clairand, R. Prot, 'La monnaie de Corbie (XIe–XIIe siècles)', *RN, 153* (1998), 297–325, at 298.

18. Evreux/Saint-Taurin Church (France, dép. Eure), 1869.

G XXXIV; MG 104; D 136; C 260; A. Chassant, *Le progrès de l'Eure*, March 24 1869; A. de Longpérier, *RN, 2nd series, 14* (1869–70), 71–85; Moesgaard, *Cahiers numismatiques, 158* (2003), 23–40 (with additional references).

T.p.q.: 942 (pennies of King Louis IV struck in Rouen).

T.a.q.: 945 (absence of coins of Richard I, duke of Normandy).

More than 67 coins. Two coins of Rouen, described by Chassant:

18.1–2. Pennies, two or more. Weight not reported. ' ... sortis de cet atelier [Rouen], les beaux deniers de Charles le Chauve, aux reliefs si bien accentués, aux légendes si régulières, au monogramme si correct ... des exemplaires à fleur de coin. ... CAROLVS (en monogramme) GRATIA DI REX – *Revers* : ROTVMACVS CIVII'.

Chapter 21

The *Swordless St Peter* Coinage of York, c.905–c.919

Megan Gooch

The present study of the *Swordless St Peter* coins, based on a complete corpus of surviving specimens, was undertaken at the suggestion of Mark Blackburn and formed the basis of my PhD research into coins made in the Viking kingdom of York. This coin type was suggested as it was the only remaining Viking coinage that had not yet been the subject of a full die study, which was needed in order to gain a more complete understanding of the coins issued by the Viking kings of York during their rule between c.895 and 954. These kings began to strike coins in their own name in the late ninth century, resulting in what is known as the regal series of Viking coins.[1] The last coin issued by an independent Viking king was the *Sword* type of Eric, who was killed in 954.[2] The coin types of the intervening years have been the subject of much study and deliberation, and the *Anonymous St Peter* types, both with and without sword, have also been the focus of several papers.[3] The *St Peter* types, both with and without sword, have no king's name or title upon them, and what the dedication to the saint associated with York Minster means in terms of the rulership of York in the early tenth century is a matter of debate. The coins have been attributed both to Viking kings whose names and deeds are missing from the historical sources for this period, and to the archbishops or leading churchmen of York.[4]

---

[1]   M.A.S. Blackburn, 'Presidential Address 2005, Currency under the Vikings, Part 2: The two Scandinavian kingdoms of the Danelaw, c.895–954', *BNJ*, 76 (2006), 204–26, at 205 (*VCCBI*, 33).

[2]   R.H.M. Dolley, 'The post-Brunanburh coinage of York: with some remarks on the Viking coinages which preceded the same', *Nordisk Numismatisk Årsskrift*, 1957–8, 13–85, at 79.

[3]   Best summarised in B.H.I.H. Stewart, and C.S.S. Lyon, 'Chronology of the St Peter coinage', *Yorkshire Numismatist*, 2 (1992), 45–73.

[4]   M.A.S. Blackburn, 'The coinage of Scandinavian York', in *Aspects of Anglo-Scandinavian York*, by R.A. Hall, D.W. Rollason, M. Blackburn et al., The Archaeology of York, 8.4 (London, 2004), 325–49, at 333 (*VCCBI*, 281–307, at 289); D.W. Rollason, 'Anglo-Saxon York: the evidence of historical sources', in *Aspects of Anglo-Scandinavian York*, by Hall et al., 305–24, at 313–14.

The Viking kingdom of York was one of several geographical areas in tenth-century England which were under the control of Viking rulers and were collectively known as the Danelaw. The kingdom of York is the best known of these, with a strong output of coins, the majority of which name the kings who issued them. The rest of Viking England is generally called the Southern Danelaw or Southumbria, and an area centred on the Five Boroughs of Derby, Leicester, Lincoln, Nottingham and Stamford also features in the literature on the Vikings.[5] It is still a matter of debate what these kingdoms were called in the tenth century and which precise geographical areas they covered. In particular, there has been discussion over how far the power of the Viking kings of York extended, and whether their authority was recognised west of the Pennines, north of the Tees or south of the Humber.[6] There is some numismatic and historical evidence that the kings of York at various times held some power within the Five Boroughs, but there is no direct evidence that Danelaw areas south of these towns and in East Anglia were ever under the direct rule of the Viking kings of York.[7]

The *Swordless St Peter* coins are known from several hoards, some better documented than others, and it is this hoard evidence which has dated the coinage to between *c.*905 and *c.*919.[8] There are differing interpretations of many hoards and historical events between these dates and it is possible that the coinage was in production for only a portion of this period. The recent suggestion that the Cuerdale hoard was buried *c.*905–10 rather than *c.*905 may mean that the *St Peter* coins were not issued until slightly later than *c.*905 as no *Swordless St Peter* coins were found in the Cuerdale hoard itself.[9] At the later end of the date range, there has also been some debate among historians over the chronology of Regnald's rule in York; however the current consensus appears to be to date Regnald's reign from *c.*919 to *c.*920/1.[10]

---

[5]   M.A.S. Blackburn, 'Presidential Address 2004, Currency under the Vikings, Part 1: Guthrum and the earliest Danelaw coinages', *BNJ*, 75 (2005), 2–27, at 18–19 (*VCCBI*, 2–27, at 2–3); Blackburn, 'Scandinavian Kingdoms', 209–17 (*VCCBI*, 37–45); *ASC*, s.a. 942.

[6]   D. Rollason, *Northumbria, 500–1100: Creation and Destruction of a Kingdom* (Cambridge, 2003), 215–20.

[7]   Blackburn, 'Scandinavian Kingdoms', 215 (*VCCBI*, 43).

[8]   Dolley, 'Post-Brunanburh', 40–41; see the gazetteer of tenth-century coin hoards in M. Gooch, 'Money and power in the Viking kingdom of York' (PhD thesis, University of Durham, 2012), 271–315 for summaries of the details of relevant coin hoards.

[9]   G. Williams, 'The Cuerdale coins', in *The Cuerdale Hoard*, ed. J. Graham-Campbell (British Museum Research Publications, 185, London, 2011), 39–71, at 64. See also Williams's chapter in this volume (Chapter 2).

[10]   F.T. Wainwright, 'The battles at Corbridge', *Saga-Book of the Viking Society*, 13 (1946–53), 156–73; C. Downham, *Viking Kings of Britain and Ireland: the Dynasty of Ívarr to AD 1044*

The *Swordless St Peter* coins have until now not been the subject of a die study, the results of which are presented here. While studies of other Viking coinages may need to be updated in the light of new single-finds or hoards, such as the *Sword* coinages of the 920s in light of the Vale of York hoard, the conclusions drawn from them are in most cases still sound.[11] Until now there have been unanswered questions about the way the *Swordless St Peter* coins were produced, the scale of production and their chronology. These are the questions which the present study aims to answer.

The obverse and reverse dies of the *Swordless St Peter* type have been identified incorrectly in many numismatic catalogues, even though the correct arrangement was suspected some time ago.[12] The face reading +EBORACE CIV was made by the obverse die, and that reading SCI PETRI MO by the reverse. As the upper reverse die, bearing the brunt of each hammer blow, is more likely to wear out faster than the lower obverse, it is to be expected that there will be more reverse dies in any coinage. The present die analysis has shown that there are indeed far more of the SCI PETRI MO dies linked to noticeably fewer EBORACE dies. The use of the traditional reverse inscription on the obverse die raises the question of whether the dedication to St Peter was relegated to the reverse die as an acknowledgement that the king was the only individual whose name belonged on the obverse. Although this line of reasoning owes perhaps more to modern conceptions of 'heads' and 'tails' than it does to the medieval mind set, it is an interesting suggestion but does not form a compelling argument.

The second key issue concerning this coinage is that many numismatic catalogues list two types of the issue based upon weight: a heavy (early) type and a light (late) type.[13] Again, it has long been suspected that there was no sudden or substantial drop in weight standard during this coinage, and that this assumption was probably based upon the study of the British Museum specimens, of which a large number are black in colour, chipped and friable at the edges and therefore much lighter than other coins with a normal patina.[14] The coins in this British Museum group have no hoard provenance, although it has been suggested they are from a lost hoard found in Lancashire in the nineteenth century, or were part of the dispersed Walmgate hoard.[15]

(Edinburgh, 2007), 93; D.W. Rollason, *Sources for York History to AD 1000*, The Archaeology of York, 1 (York, 1998), 66.

[11] See Blackburn, 'Scandinavian kingdoms'.

[12] See e.g. N 553; queried by Stewart and Lyon, 'Chronology', 60.

[13] R.H.M. Dolley, 'The Anglo-Danish and Anglo-Norse coinages of York', in *Viking Age York and the North*, ed. by R.A. Hall, CBA Research Report, 27 (London, 1978), 26–31, at 27.

[14] Stewart and Lyon, 'Chronology', 46; M. Gooch, 'Notes on the Swordless St Peter coinage', *NCirc*, 115 (2007), 208.

[15] Stewart and Lyon, 'Chronology', 48; Gooch, 'Notes', 208.

The graph below (Figure 21.1) illustrates weight distribution and uses data from only 85 of the 181 known examples of the *Swordless St Peter* coins, as all chipped, pierced or cracked specimens, including the British Museum group, have been excluded. The graph shows that there was only one weight standard, as the weights are grouped around 1.15–1.45g, probably nearer the mean weight of 1.22g. A cluster of heavier or lighter coins in a particular hoard might give a clue, yet the majority of *Swordless St Peter* coins are not from known hoards. The best evidence for weight distribution from within a hoard comes from the Morley St Peter hoard which contained 12 *Swordless St Peter* coins, one of which was damaged and is therefore excluded from any weight calculations. The weight distribution of the Morley St Peter coins is very similar to that of the coinage as a whole, with a mean of 1.22g but a slightly higher median of 1.29g. The fact that the sample of 85 coins is small, and that many have no find-spot information, means that there is no way to tell whether the anomaly lies in the fewer coins weighing between 1.26–1.30g or the heavier coins weighing 1.31–1.35g. There are two outliers in terms of weights, the incredibly light 0.65g and one at 0.92g, although both are probably the result of a coin which appears sound but is damaged in some way that is neither visible from the photograph nor recorded in the published material.

The scale of production of Viking coins in York has been a subject of debate, and with most Viking coin types having been the subject of die studies, there has been some material to work with.[16] Most studies have employed methods of estimating the number of dies used to produce a coinage, and not gone on to make further estimates of the total number of coins which constituted that issue. This is because the number of coins a die could produce could vary so significantly that the results would be meaningless; a range of about 22,000 to 90,000 coins struck per obverse die is attested in later medieval records.[17] Another factor which has made some wary of using and interpreting die estimates is that the scarcity of coins for many, if not most of the Viking coin types, means that the estimated numbers of dies must be treated with some caution. However, the statistical models developed to estimate the numbers of dies are not intended to be used uncritically. There are two main approaches to estimating the accuracy of the die data. The first, advocated by Warren Esty, builds into the die estimation formula a value called the coverage. This is intended to give some indication of the completeness of the sample of extant coins being studied, and is expressed

[16]   Blackburn, 'Scandinavian kingdoms', 216 (*VCCBI*, 44).

[17]   M. Allen, *Mints and Money in Medieval England* (Cambridge, 2012), 131–3. A lively debate on the subject of coin production estimates took place between Buttrey and de Callataÿ in the *NC*; see the concluding part of the debate: F. De Callataÿ, 'Calculating ancient coin production: seeking a balance', *NC, 155* (1995), 289–311.

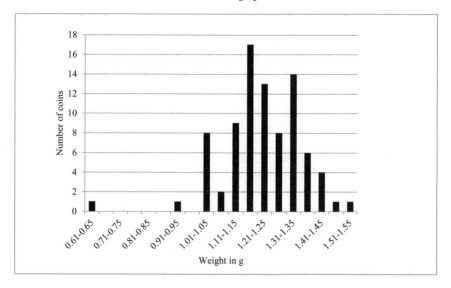

Figure 21.1   Graph showing the weight distribution of the *Swordless St Peter* coins (N = 85). Mean = 1.22g; Median = 1.22g; Mode = 1.17g; Lightest = 0.68g; Heaviest = 1.51g.

as a percentage.[18] The second method uses the number of coins per die (n/d), to compare data across coin types. An n/d figure of over two is generally an indication that the completeness of the sample is high enough that the results are statistically significant, and a lower figure should encourage more caution in the interpretation of the data. Unfortunately, as for so many Viking coin types, both the measure of coverage for the *Swordless St Peter* type at 57 per cent and the n/d of 1.5 are indications that the sample of extant coins is not really large enough to draw firm conclusions as to the exact number of dies produced to make the coinage. Yet they are large enough to attempt to draw some preliminary conclusions if these are used thoughtfully, and, until new hoards containing more of these coins are discovered, it is the best information available at this time.

Four formulae were used to estimate the number of obverse (Do) and reverse (Dr) dies, and the results are shown in Table 21.1 below. In further discussion, only the figure for the number of estimated obverse dies (Do) is used: as the lower, obverse, die is generally replaced less often than the reverse die it gives a more accurate reflection of the level of production, although some scholars do prefer to use the reverse die as the basis for calculations; both figures are included

---

[18]   W.W. Esty, 'Estimation of the size of a coinage: a survey and comparison of methods', *NC, 146* (1986), 185–215.

in Table 21.1. In estimating the number of dies, four different formulae have been employed in preference to relying on one method of calculation. This is because each method of estimation relies on several assumptions about both the nature of die production, and also regarding the number of coins now extant and used in the sample. By combining several methods, the effects of any erroneous assumptions in any particular formula can be mitigated, and the comparison of results will highlight any method with abnormal results.[19]

Table 21.1　Table comparing different estimates for obverse (Do) and reverse (Dr) dies, the ratio of the estimated number dies to each other (Dr:Do), and the estimated number of obverse dies per year (Do/t) for the *Swordless St Peter* coinage.

Formula	Do	Dr	Dr:Do	Do/t
Good	210.9	433.2	2.1	15.1
Esty 1986	279.4	611.2	2.2	20.0
Carter	285.4	587.6	2.1	20.4
Esty 2011	356.1	755.0	2.1	25.4

Note: The number of dies per year (n/do) = 1.5 is a good indicator of the reliability of the statistical data, the number of coins (n) = 181, the number of obverse dies (do) = 120, and number of reverse dies (dr) = 145. The number of obverse dies in the sample represented by one coin (F1o) = 78, and reverse coins represented by one coin (F1r) = 120, the number of years the coinage was thought to be issued (t) = 14. Using Esty's 1986 formula, coverage is: Do 57%, Dr 34%.

Source formulae: Good: $D = nd/n\text{-}F1$; Esty 1986: Coverage $= 1\text{-}(F1/n)$, $D = (d/\text{Coverage})^*(1+F1/2^*d)$, 95% Confidence intervals $= D + (2^*D/n)^2 \pm (2^*D/n)^* \sqrt{2}^*D$; Carter: If $n/d = <2$, $D = nd/(1.214n - 1.197d)$, if $n/d = >2$ and <3, $D = nd/(1.0124n - 1.016d)$, if $n/d = >3$, $D = nd/(1.069n - 0.843d)$, if $n/d > 4$, $D = 0.95nd/(n\text{-}d)$; Esty 2011: $D = nd/n\text{-}d$.

The estimates of die production range from between 211 and 356 obverse dies and between 433 and 755 reverse dies. The differences in these figures are expected given the n/do is only 1.5. The ratio of reverse to obverse dies is 2:1; a figure which is also to be expected given that the attrition rate of reverse dies is higher, from receiving the full force of each hammer blow in striking a coin. A rate of obverse dies per year (Do/t) has also been estimated, and ranges from

---

[19]　I.J. Good, 'The population frequencies of species and the estimation of population parameters', *Biometrika*, 40 (1953), 237–64; Esty, 'Estimation'; G.F. Carter, 'New methods for calculating the original number of dies in a given series', *NCirc*, *115* (June 2007), 151–3; W.W. Esty, 'The geometric model for estimating the number of dies', in *Quantifying Monetary Supplies in Greco-Roman Times*, ed. by F. De Callataÿ (Bari, 2011), 43–58.

15 to 25 per year, based on the *Swordless St Peter* type being issued for about 14 years between *c.*905 and *c.*919.

If these estimates are compared to other coin types as in Table 21.2 below, the numbers are unsurprising. The regal coinages, consisting of coins of Cnut and Siefred, the bulk of which were discovered in the Cuerdale hoard, seem to have had a slightly higher production of dies than the subsequent *Swordless St Peter*. The n/do figure is above 2 and should give some statistical assurance over the accuracy of the estimate, but the fact that most of the extant coins are derived from one hoard will undoubtedly have skewed the data, and make the sample appear more complete than it actually is. The data for Regnald's coinage are as unhelpful as would be expected for a small sample of 23 coins with an n/do of 1.1, and the range of estimates is so wide that very little in the way of a conclusion can be drawn. The *Sword St Peter* data appear to be better, with an n/do over 2, and a tight range of estimates. However, since the data on the *Sword St Peter* pennies were published, there have been some significant new finds of *Sword St Peter* coins in hoards, notably the Vale of York hoard, so these data need some revision.[20] Taking into account all these considerations about the credibility of the statistical data, it can tentatively be said that the *Swordless St Peter* coins may have been produced on a slightly smaller scale than the earlier regal coins, and that later coinages in Viking York may have been produced on a similar scale. The *Sword St Peter* coinages of the 920s were only one of several *Sword* types in production, so the output of these *Sword* coin types combined, even if some were made outside York, may not have meant a decline in the volume of coinage in circulation in the Viking-controlled area surrounding York.[21]

---

[20]   G. Williams, 'Hoards from the northern Danelaw from Cuerdale to the Vale of York', in *Vikings in the North-West*, ed. J. Graham-Campbell and R. Philpott (Liverpool, 2009), 73–83.

[21]   Blackburn, 'Scandinavian York', 335 (*VCCBI*, 291).

Table 21.2   Comparison of die estimates with other Viking and Anglo-Saxon coin types using the Good, Carter and Esty 2011 formulae expressed as a range of Do estimates for each coin type.

Coin type	t	n	Do	n/Do	Do/t
Regal	10	598	358–429	2.4	36–43
Swordless St Peter	14	181	211–356	1.5	15–25
Regnald	3	23	121–242	1.1	40–121
Sword St Peter	6	83	58–70	2.2	10–12
Æthelstan *Circumscription Cross*	15	16	18–35	1.5	1–2
Æthelstan *Bust Crowned*	15	23	18–30	1.8	1–2

Note: The Esty 1986 formula is not used as it requires data that is not published for the regal coins.

Source: C.S.S. Lyon and B.H.I.H. Stewart, 'The classification of Northumbrian Viking coins in the Cuerdale hoard', *NC, 7th series, 4* (1964), 281–2; C.E. Blunt and B.H.I.H. Stewart, 'The coinage of Regnald I of York and the Bossall hoard', *NC, 143* (1983), 146–63, at 147–9; Blackburn, 'Scandinavian kingdoms', 216; S. Lyon, 'Minting in Winchester: An introduction and statistical analysis', in M. Biddle (ed.), *The Winchester Mint, and Coins and Related Finds from the Exacavations of 1961–71* (Oxford, 2012), 3–54, at 46–7.

There has been some debate in recent years as to the issuing authority behind the *Swordless St Peter* type and the later *Sword St Peter* issue. One argument, advocated strongly by Blackburn, is that once kings gained control of minting and the valuable profits found in the production of coins, they were highly unlikely to forfeit that source of revenue.[22] However, the fact that the *St Peter* coins are anonymous, in that they name a saint rather than king, has been the central strand to arguments which counter that these coins were made by another authority, probably under the ecclesiastical authority of the archbishop of York.[23] The results from this die study show that York was a major mint in tenth-century England in which dies, and therefore coins, were being produced in vast numbers which are in some cases comparable to the York die output during the reigns of Æthelred II and Cnut, although it must be remembered that by the late tenth and early eleventh century there were significantly more mints producing coins under the late Anglo-Saxon kings than there were for the early Viking kings of York.[24]

It is difficult to compare this York data to other contemporary mints, as there are few published studies of the major Anglo-Saxon mints in the tenth century.

---

[22] Ibid., 333 (VCCBI, 289).

[23] Rollason, 'Anglo-Saxon York: the evidence of historical sources', 313–14.

[24] Gooch, 'Money and Power', 146–56.

However, the recent volume on the Winchester mint provides some data for the coinage of Athelstan's *Circumscription Cross* and *Bust Cross* types.[25] It can be seen in Table 21.2 above that the sample for both types is small, and the number of obverse dies per coin (n/do) is only 1.5 and 1.8, which means that the data must be used with caution. Revealingly, these results show that the *Swordless St Peter* type at York may have been a larger issue than the slightly later issues of Athelstan at Winchester. Although again it must be borne in mind that Winchester was one of several mints issuing theis coin type yet York was probably the sole source of *Swordless St Peter* coins. Notwithstanding these notes of caution, it is still possible to conclude that the mint of York in the early tenth century was a major one which would have had an impressive output of coins.

The success, and presumably profits, of the York mint during the *Swordless St Peter* issue would suggest that the Viking kings would have a lot to lose in surrendering their accustomed rights to mint coins, and a lot to gain by ensuring that the designs on those coins promoted and legitimised their rule; yet the question of why they gave up their right to be named as kings on their coins persists. Research into the iconography of the Viking coins of York has revealed extremely close links between the Church at York and the design of the coins, not just in the *Swordless St Peter* issue, but in the regal coinages of Cnut and Siefred, and in the later *Sword* issues.[26] The dedication of the coinage to a saint is unusual, but given the similar overtly Christian symbolism on the preceding regal coins, the dedication to St Peter appears part of a consistent approach to coin design in which Christianity, and in all probability, the cooperation of the Church at York, was part of a strategy for ruling the kingdom which included issuing coins.

A recent die study of the *Swordless St Peter* type carried out by the author has been used to estimate the scale of die production for the coinage, and has confirmed that the obverse was the EBORACE inscription. However, it has revealed less about the chronology of coins within this issue. There are remarkably few die-links within the coinage, most of which are simple connections between a single obverse and two reverse dies, and the majority of dies are only represented by a single coin.[27] There are only six more complicated die chains, the longest of which involves only three obverses and four reverse dies, and there is very little from the dies themselves which suggested a chronology of the coins. If the data for this coin issue were larger, there would be scope to interpret the limited number of die-links and chains as an indicator of a number of separate workshops or as evidence that dies were handed out in pairs at the start of minting rather than

---

[25]   M. Biddle (ed.), *The Winchester Mint, and Coin and Related Finds from the Excavations of 1961–71*, Winchester Studies, 8 (Oxford, 2012).

[26]   Gooch, 'Money and Power', 34–111.

[27]   Ibid., 257–8.

being picked randomly from a box, which could account for the pattern of mainly obverse and reverse pairs with few complex links or chains. Yet the evidence of die production discussed above shows that this was undoubtedly a large coinage, and that the surviving corpus represents only a small proportion of the estimated total dies which were used to produce the *Swordless St Peter* issue. As such, the lack of die-links reinforces the shortcomings of the data rather than revealing anything significant or verifiable about the number or nature of the workshops in which these coins were produced. A published version of the corpus should therefore be laid out according to stylistic features, in the manner preferred by earlier authors, with the most literate coins first.[28] The weights of the coins, as discussed above, do not fall into two distinct groups, but there is a very gradual decline in weight for most of the coins, with a few exceptions to this.

Figure 21.2   The phases of the *Swordless St Peter* coinage. Above: (a) early literate coin with key of St Peter as a contraction mark (*SCBI* 9, 229) (left); (b) coin with 'branch' symbol (British Museum 1959,1210.4) (right). Below: (c) later coin with shortened legend (British Museum 1959,1210.12).

The earliest *Swordless St Peter* coins (Figure 21.2) have inscriptions reading +EBORACE CIV and SCI PETRI MO and have three pellets dividing the reverse legend, with crosses above and below, and a contraction mark above the SCI turned into a key, the symbol of St Peter. Both the obverse and reverse legends were gradually shortened, with legends becoming BRACE and SCIII TII II or similar. The decorations on the reverses were firstly uniform in design, followed by a proliferation of symbols about the field, such as the distinctive 'branch' design, letters such as C, S or D variously rotated, and wandering

---

28   Stewart and Lyon, 'Chronology', 52. A full corpus has been assembled by the author, and is being prepared for publication.

contraction marks. The reverse designs have been categorised using the system proposed in *CTCE*; however, the variety of designs of the *Swordless St Peter* coins has necessitated additional comments in the catalogue as in many cases, the symbols above and below the inscription are not identical.

Figure 21.3   Examples of the one-line reverse group of *Swordless St Peter* coins: (a) *SCBI* 20, 694=*SCBI* 65, 52 (left); (b) PAS, FAKL-167C47 (reverse only, right) (courtesy of the Portable Antiquities Scheme).

The end of the coinage poses something of a problem as there are two distinct groups of coins: illiterate one-line reverses (Figure 21.3); and Karolus monogram obverses (Figure 21.4). The earliest group (illustrated above, Figure 21.3) consists of coins with a one-line reverse inscription with illiterate obverse inscriptions beginning with I, the reverse symbols having been enlarged to fill the space left by the missing second line of the inscription. The second group (Figure 21.4) contains coins which remained fairly literate, the distinguishing feature being the Karolus monogram in the centre of the obverse. These coins have been linked to the Portrait coins of Regnald which have a Karolus obverse, and which dates them towards the end of the coinage.[29] The Karolus obverse coins are die-linked to some coins without the monogram and have a mean weight of 1.15g, while the one-line reverse coins are die-linked to each other but no other coins, and have a lighter mean weight of 0.96g. As such, there is the possibility that these one-line types are part of a small imitative issue.

Figure 21.4   Examples of the Karolus group of *Swordless St Peter* coins (left, *SCBI* 4, 599; right, *BMC* 1123 (1862,0926.1)).

---

[29]   Ibid., 47.

The evidence for where these one-line coins were minted is speculative at best. Work on later coinages, such as the *Sword* issues of the 920s and some of Olaf Guthfrithsson's coins of the 940s, has revealed that not all coins attributed to the Viking kings of York were made in that city.[30] In his work on the *Sword* coinages, Blackburn concluded that the *Anonymous Sword* and Sihtric *Sword* issues were made in a mint south of the Humber, based upon the finds evidence and the name of the moneyers who had links to known mints other than York.[31] In *CTCE* the authors identified three Southumbrian groups of coins in the name of Olaf: the first group was identified as being made in Derby due to similarities with mint-signed coins of Athelstan, and the other two groups were linked on stylistic grounds to some coins of Athelstan made at Lincoln and by their distinct dissimilarity to coins minted at York.[32]

It is therefore a tantalising prospect to attribute the coins of the one-line group to a mint south of the Humber, but one which is not supported by the evidence. The geographical distribution of this small group is interesting as the coins were found in York itself, at Malton and near Ulceby in North Yorkshire, and from further afield in the Geashill hoard, Ireland, and in a grave in Birka, Sweden. The first three finds were single-finds and perhaps give some indication that these coins were a York issue which were produced, used and lost locally, although the Geashill and Birka finds show that some of the coins travelled further afield before their deposition.

This study of the *Swordless St Peter* coins may appear to have revealed little that was not already known or suspected about the scale of production or the nature of Viking coins at York, yet it has confirmed much. The thorny issue of the relationship between the Viking rulers and leading York churchmen, and which among them was responsible for the issue of these coins, finds no decisive answer in this new data, but given the scale of production it is unlikely that Viking kings would have chosen to relinquish their control over such a lucrative mint. This does not mean there was no involvement from the Church at York; in fact the designs on these coins, and those of the earlier regal coins, are strongly suggestive of significant ecclesiastical involvement in the production of all the early coins of York, and not just the *Swordless St Peter* type. The knowledge gained from understanding the details of the production provides scope for comparisons with other numismatic and historical material and reveals York to have been a major mint in early tenth-century England.

---

[30]   Blackburn, 'Scandinavian kingdoms', 212 (*VCCBI*, 40); *CTCE*, 217–19.

[31]   Blackburn, 'Scandinavian kingdoms', 212 (*VCCBI*, 40).

[32]   *CTCE*, 219.

Chapter 22

The 2003 Glenfaba Hoard (*c*.1030), Isle of Man

Kristin Bornholdt Collins, Allison Fox and James Graham-Campbell

Introduction and Background *by Allison Fox*

On the afternoon of Wednesday 26 March 2003, a remarkable collection of Viking-Age artefacts was brought to the Manx Museum in the Isle of Man. A total of 464 silver pennies, 25 silver ingots and one plaited silver arm-ring had been discovered by a local metal-detector user. At just under 1.5 kg in weight, the collection which became known as the Glenfaba hoard represented one of the largest hoards of Viking-Age material ever found on the Isle of Man, and the first for over 20 years (Colour Plate 22.1).[1]

At almost the geographic centre of the British Isles, the Isle of Man is a self-governing British Crown dependency with a population of nearly 85,000.[2] The Manx Tynwald parliament and its traditions are a legacy of the Viking period, when the Isle of Man was a powerful trading and administrative centre for the Kingdom of Man and the Isles.[3] The prehistory and history of the Isle of Man are very much part of the national identity of the Manx people.

The earliest human settlement was in the Mesolithic period, around eight thousand years ago, with the transition to the Neolithic *c*.4000 BC.[4] The Bronze Age and Iron Age followed, but there is no evidence for large-scale Roman

---

[1]   A. Fox and K. Bornholdt Collins, 'The 2003 "TT": a Viking-Age silver hoard from Glenfaba, Isle of Man', *Viking Heritage Magazine*, 1 (2004), 3–5.

[2]   R.H. Kinvig, *The Isle of Man: A Social, Cultural and Political History*, 3rd ed. (Liverpool, 1975); statistics based on 2011 Census, see <http://www.gov.im/isleofman/facts.xml> consulted on 27 October 2012.

[3]   For a recent overview see D.M. Wilson, *The Vikings in the Isle of Man* (Aarhus, 2008); on Tynwald specifically see 122–7; see also A.M. Cubbon, 'The archaeology of the Vikings in the Isle of Man' in *The Viking Age in the Isle of Man*, ed. C. Fell, P. Foote, J. Graham-Campbell and R. Thomson (London, 1983), 13–26.

[4]   D. Freke 'History', in *The Isle of Man. Celebrating a Sense of Place*, ed. V. Robinson and D. McCarroll (Liverpool, 1990), 103–22. Also, on aspects of the history and geography of Man consult the relevant volume of the ambitious five-volume series, *The New History of the Isle of Man* (Liverpool, 2000–), produced under the auspices of the Centre for Manx Studies.

influence. After the early Christians made their mark on the landscape with the small chapels, or *keeills*, the Vikings arrived – sometime in the years around *c.*900, perhaps somewhat later than one might have expected considering their activity in the wider region[5] – with their trade and new forms of government. The years succeeding Scandinavian rule were turbulent in Man, with rule alternating between Scotland and England until a relatively stable few centuries when the Stanley family of Lancashire took over the lordship, until finally in 1736 the British Crown bought the rights to the Island. As a result of these wide-ranging influences, Man has a wealth of portable antiquities and because of its relative autonomy, the legislation governing archaeological artefacts differs from its near neighbours around the Irish Sea.

The organisation responsible for advising on the portable antiquities is the Manx Museum and National Trust – popularly known as Manx National Heritage (MNH).[6] MNH runs 12 heritage centres on the Island, and the core of the organisation is based within the Manx Museum (in Manx Gaelic *Thie Tashtee Vannin* – 'the house of treasure of Man') in the capital, Douglas.

Most of the roles, as well as the governance of MNH, are laid out in the Manx Museum and National Trust Act 1959 (MMNTA 1959) and within this there are a number of provisions directly relating to finds of antiquities. Firstly, there is a legal requirement to report *any* archaeological object within 14 days of its discovery to allow MNH to record the find. Secondly, there are licence requirements for export from the Isle of Man, to the UK and elsewhere, as well as for any alteration and/or destruction of archaeological objects. There are also restrictions in place on metal detecting in certain protected areas. The legislation applied to archaeological objects in the Isle of Man applies equally to any artefact that has been declared Treasure Trove.

---

[5]   As noted and discussed by Wilson, *Vikings in the Isle of Man*, 16, 52–4. J. Graham-Campbell favours a date 'not before 900' in 'The Irish Sea Vikings: raiders and settlers', in *The Middle Ages in the North-West*, ed. T. Scott and P. Starkey (Oxford, 1995), 59–83, at 78; also 'The early Viking Age in the Irish Sea area', in *Ireland and Scandinavia in the Early Viking Age*, ed. H.B. Clarke, R. Ó Floinn and M. Ní Mhaonaigh (Dublin, 1998), 104–30, at 116–20. The subject was also considered in K. Bornholdt Collins, 'Viking-Age coin finds from the Isle of Man: a study of coin circulation, production and concepts of wealth during the Viking Age' (unpublished PhD thesis, University of Cambridge, 2003), at 150 and 334–5 ('a significant presence' in Man only after 914, with a major intensification of Scandinavian settlement in the mid tenth century). More recently, the topic has also been considered in C. Downham, *Viking Kings of Britain and Ireland to AD 1014* (Edinburgh, 2007), 180–84, who examines the relevant historical evidence (in particular the context for an end to Brittonic control in Man after 918, which may have made Man more open to Scandinavian settlement); and in D. Griffiths, *Vikings of the Irish Sea* (Stroud, 2010), 21 and 39.

[6]   <http://www.manxnationalheritage.im/> consulted on 22 October 2012.

The Isle of Man has a thriving community of metal-detector users and most are members of the Manx Detectorists Society. During the calendar year 2011–12, there were 31 separate reports of archaeological finds and 21 of these came from metal-detector users. The metal-detector users of Man have a strong commitment to ensuring the preservation of important finds and work alongside MNH. They regularly offer to donate their finds to the national collections, with the landowner's consent.

On Tuesday 25 March 2003, Andy Whewell had been metal detecting in a small pasture field in the parish of Patrick in the west of the Isle of Man. He discovered what he first thought were lots of 'lead discs'. Andy had only recently taken up the hobby of metal detecting and had been under the guidance of Rob Middleton, an experienced metal-detector user. That evening, Andy took his finds to Rob, who immediately identified them as being silver coins of Viking-Age date, and the procedures for Manx Treasure Trove began the following day.

Manx Treasure Trove items mainly date from two periods in Manx history, the Viking Age (*c.*800–1266) and post-Viking (1267–*c.*1400), the dividing point here distinguished by the date of the Treaty of Perth, when Man and the Western Isles were ceded by Norway to Scotland.[7] The Vikings, as already mentioned, valued the Isle of Man as a trading centre and as a result secreted a large number of hoards in the ground for safekeeping, essentially an early form of 'banking', during their occupancy. The period after the Vikings saw the Island alternating between Scottish and English rule for a period of about 100 years and presumably the insecurity that this generated was a significant factor leading to the deposition of hoards around the Island. These range in size from a hoard from Ballayelse, Arbory with just five coins from the early 1300s to one from Kilkenny, Braddan with over 600 coins from the same period.[8] The majority of the coins in these finds were minted in England, although coins from Scotland and Ireland also occur, reflecting influence from, and trade with, near neighbours at this time.

The Isle of Man Treasure Trove legislation states that items of silver or gold with no traceable owner that have been deliberately buried may be declared as Treasure Trove by the High Bailiff in his/her capacity as Coroner of Inquests (with or without a jury at their discretion). In practice, the requirement of *animus revertendi*, the intention to recover the buried items, has also applied in past cases. Andy Whewell's discovery in the spring of 2003 led to a programme of archaeological excavation and research to provide the Coroner with information

---

[7]   The Viking-Age and medieval coin finds are catalogued and discussed in K. Bornholdt Collins, 'Coinage', in *A New History of the Isle of Man Volume 3: Medieval Period, 1000–1406*, ed. S. Duffy and H. Mytum, (Liverpool, forthcoming), 411–65.

[8]   A.M. Cubbon, 'A remarkable decade of Manx coin hoards, 1972–82', *Proceedings of the Isle of Man Natural History and Antiquarian Society, 11, no. 1* (1997–9), 29–50; at least 80 extra coins have since been added to the Kilkenny hoard through metal detecting.

to assist him in his decision as to whether or not the Glenfaba hoard was Treasure Trove.

The Recovery of the Glenfaba Hoard

The hoard was found 18 inches below the surface of a turf-covered field, used for grazing sheep and not ploughed in modern times, in loamy soil. Andy reported that the coins were found among fragments of a lead jar – mostly held in the vertical plane as opposed to being spread horizontally. There were no known archaeological sites in the vicinity of the Glenfaba hoard, with the nearest site being a keeill 860 m to the south-east, one 560 m to the west-north-west and a find of a carved cross-slab 520 m to the south. On-site discussions between representatives from MNH and the Centre for Manx Studies resulted in the decision to conduct targeted archaeological excavation and geophysical survey of the area around the find-spot to assess the site and to ensure that the recovery of the hoard was complete.

On Monday 31 March 2003, under the supervision of Dr Peter Davey, Director of the Centre for Manx Studies and Nick Johnson, Senior Research Associate at the Centre for Manx Studies, work began on the excavation of two trenches and the geophysical survey of three 20 m² grids. In the subsequent excavation report, Nick recorded that:

> The site lies on level ground at the foot of a shallow slope which gradually steepens as it rises southwards ... To the west of the site is a small stream cut down through layers of river gravels, which are visible in the stream bank sections. The banks rise approximately 1.2 m above the level of the stream itself. To the south of the site the stream course steepens and its valley becomes steeply sided. The bed of the stream consists of mixed river gravels and larger rounded stones.

> The topography is such as to suggest that the site itself is located on the uppermost of a series of river terraces ... it is likely that additional material will have accumulated upon it by solifluction from the north-facing slopes of the higher ground to the south.

> The stratigraphy encountered by the excavation indicates a period of stasis in soil movement, with a distinct bioturbation horizon. The ploughsoil is approximately 0.15 m deep and overlies a more clay-rich material, free of humus and slightly coloured by iron salts. It was evident that the tip of the plough had scored this surface, with ploughlines visible suggesting a direction approximately parallel

to the axis of the boundary hedge to the east. The interval of these ploughlines suggests a modern machine, i.e. nineteenth-century or later.[9]

The archaeological excavation confirmed that the hoard and surviving container had been recovered in their entirety. The hole that Andy had dug to recover the hoard did not fully destroy the cut of the original hole into which the hoard was deposited, but there were few finds apart from some unrelated pieces of prehistoric flint and modern pottery, including one sherd of unglazed Manx granite-tempered ware dating to the fifteenth or sixteenth century, at least three sherds dating to the eighteenth century and an unidentified and unusual fragment of unglazed red earthenware, rare for Man. No further finds were recovered from either of the archaeological trenches excavated although an area of iron oxide staining under the hoard gave the appearance of a hook-like artefact alongside some oval shapes. However, there was no substance to either of these features. To the east of one of the trenches there were traces of a stone structure with an earth matrix and a long axis north–south. The full extent of this feature was not excavated, and the trenches were backfilled and re-turfed at the end of the excavation, with a geotextile (a permeable synthetic cloth barrier) being positioned over the site of the coin find to retain the excavated archaeological horizon.

Despite the indeterminate remains at the hoard site, the items themselves yielded enough information, through the hard work of Mark Blackburn and Kristin Bornholdt Collins, for a recommendation to be made that the hoard was Treasure Trove. At an inquest held on Wednesday 6 August 2003, the Glenfaba hoard was declared Treasure Trove by the High Bailiff, Mr Michael Moyle (retired).

Since negotiations led in the 1970s by the late Marshall Cubbon, Treasure Trove items can be retained on the Isle of Man by MNH, rather than being offered in the first instance to the British Museum, as was previously the case. With the hoard being such an important collection of material, the decision was made by the Trustees of MNH to acquire the Glenfaba hoard for the Manx National collections and a reward based on the market value of the hoard was paid to the finder. In 2007, items from the hoard were put on permanent display in the new Viking Gallery at the Manx Museum, and the Glenfaba hoard continues to be a major attraction to visitors.

The discovery of the Glenfaba hoard also facilitated a review of Manx Treasure Trove, which is currently (summer 2012) ongoing. The finder of the hoard, Andy Whewell, died suddenly on Friday 16 March 2012. At his funeral, his family told of his initial astonishment and later pleasure that he had made a

---

[9]   N. Johnson, unpublished excavation report, Centre for Manx Studies (Douglas, 2003).

discovery which would contribute so much to the understanding of the history of the island he proudly called home.

Numismatic Interpretation *by Kristin Bornholdt Collins*

Context: *The Manx Hoards*

There are 22 tenth- and eleventh-century coin hoards on record for Man, eight of which date to the mid- to late tenth century and no less than 12 (and perhaps 13 or 14) from the eleventh and early twelfth century (Colour Plate 22.2 and Table 22.1).[10] There are also three coinless hoards, including a rare and important gold assemblage from Greeba that was first discovered by metal detecting in 1981 (from the first half of the eleventh century).[11] Single bullion finds include a cut plain silver arm-ring fragment from below Peel Castle and, among recent metal-detector finds, at least one stray hack-silver find of tenth- to mid-eleventh-century date and two whole single ingots. In addition, 13 single coin finds are recorded for this period, the majority of which are Anglo-Saxon pennies. The total also includes three dirham fragments found since 2010, the first Islamic coins from Man.[12] The Glenfaba hoard is only the third Viking-Age

---

[10]   Bornholdt Collins, 'Coinage'. I am sincerely grateful to Andy Woods for sharing the results of his current doctoral research into the later Hiberno-Scandinavian coinage, which has led to revised dates for two Manx hoards: Laxey? pre-1950 and Unprovenanced, Manx? (National Museum of Scotland) pre-1785.

[11]   D.M. Wilson, 'A ring from Greeba', *Proceedings of the Isle of Man Natural History and Antiquarian Society, 11, no. 3* (2004 for 2001–3), 437–9; Wilson, *Vikings in the Isle of Man*, 114–15 and Figure 54; J. Graham-Campbell, *The Cuerdale Hoard and Related Viking-Age Silver and Gold from Britain and Ireland in the British Museum*, British Museum Research Publications 185 (London, 2011), Figure 1.16. The other two coinless hoards comprise an assemblage of arm-rings, possibly from Balladoole, Arbory, as discussed in J. Graham-Campbell and J. Sheehan, 'A Viking-age silver hoard of "ring money" from the Isle of Man rediscovered', *Proceedings of the Isle of Man Natural History and Antiquarian Society, 11, no. 4* (2007 for 2003–5), 527–40, and the remains of two silver neck-rings and a whole silver arm-ring found in 1868 at Ballacamaish, Andreas: see for example Graham-Campbell, *Cuerdale Hoard*, 248–9, no. 12, pl. 71.

[12]   It is curious that prior to this no Islamic coins were known from Man, although they occur in limited numbers in Scottish, Irish and English finds (Checklist) and they are a classic manifestation of Scandinavian activity in Britain and Ireland. The Manx dirham fragments appear to be variously dated, comprising one of Abbasid and one of Samanid origin, while the third is not yet identified (sincere thanks are due to Lutz Ilisch for identifying the fragments and for his helpful comments). While these appear to represent comparatively early material for Viking-Age Man, it is important to consider that dirhams could remain in circulation long after they were minted (R. Naismith, 'Islamic coins from early medieval England', *NC, 165* (2005), 193–222, at 194–5; *pers. comm.* L. Ilisch). In England, hoards with Arabic dirhams date between *c.*870–*c.*930

coin hoard recovered in modern times, using modern methods, and it is now the largest complete sample available for study from Man. The other two coin hoards, from Kirk Michael [2] (1972/5)[13] and Peel Castle (1982),[14] are much smaller, but they are useful for comparison since they also date to the eleventh century and were similarly recovered in their entirety. The Glenfaba hoard is important for its diverse content and because it dates to a time when there are very few other hoards with Hiberno-Scandinavian (Dublin) material recorded: our knowledge of the chronology and coin types in the early Dublin coinage is therefore less certain than for the Anglo-Saxon series, but this hoard can help us unravel some of the mysteries of the Dublin group; furthermore, the material is in pristine condition thanks to its protective lead container. That the four Manx hoards (three with coins, one coinless) found in the last 40 years all date to the eleventh century attests to the great wealth of the Island at the start of the new millennium, a high point for economic activity and coin and precious metal use in Man.

(Naismith, 'Islamic coins', 208), while they appear in Scottish and Irish contexts until the 970s. Of particular interest for its small Islamic component, and for its close parallels with the Manx material generally, is the mixed hoard discovered in Furness, Cumbria in 2011 (deposited *c.*955) (B. Ager, D. Boughton and G.Williams, 'Viking hoards: buried wealth of the Norse North West', *Current Archaeology, 264* (March 2012), 26–31); future work promises to shed new light on the circulation of dirhams in this region.

[13]   A.M. Cubbon and M. Dolley, 'The 1972 Kirk Michael Viking treasure trove', *Journal of the Manx Museum, VIII, no. 89* (1980), 5–20; Cubbon, 'Remarkable decade'.

[14]   W. Seaby, 'The 1982 coin hoard 82.150/C (263)', in *Excavations on St Patrick's Isle, Isle of Man,* ed. D. Freke (Liverpool, 2002), 320–25.

Table 22.1   Checklist of Manx coin hoards from the Viking Age

Abbreviations: A/S. Anglo-Saxon; C. Continental; H/M. Hiberno-Manx; H/S. Hiberno-Scandinavian; V. Viking; K. Kufic

TENTH CENTURY (8 coin hoards)

Unprovenanced, 19th C.?   *c.*955-60
Size: fewer than 20? [11 known]. A/S.

Ballaqueeney (Port St Mary), Rushen, 1874.   *c.*960
Size: 9 total. A/S, V & C.

Unprovenanced, *c.*1880s.   *c.*965
Size: fewer than 20? [18 known]. A/S.

Unprovenanced, Manx? pre-1994.   *c.*970s?
Size: ? [1 known]. A/S. Bullion.

Ballakilpheric, Rushen, pre-1880s.   *c.*970s?
Size: ? A/S. [none known]

Andreas parish churchyard [1] ('Tower'), 1867.   *c.*970
Size: 'nearly 100 coins' [44 traced, 27 known]. A/S & V.

Douglas (Ballaquayle), Onchan, 1894.   *c.*970
Size: several hundred, possibly 1000 coins
[over 400 traced, 348 known]. A/S & V. Bullion. Stone-lined pit.

Bradda Head, Rushen, 1848.   *c.*995
Size: 'several hundreds...mostly broken'
[25 traced, 22 known]. A/S. Found 'in a sort of roll'.

ELEVENTH AND EARLY TWELFTH CENTURIES (12 coin hoards)

Glenfaba, 2003.   *c.*1030
Size: 464 total. A/S, H/S, H/M, 'Irish Sea', Scand. imit.
Bullion. Lead vessel.

Park Llewellyn, Maughold, 1835.   *c.*1030
Size: ? [10 known]. A/S, H/S & H/M. Contained in a horn.

Ballaberna, Maughold, 1833. *c.*1040
Size: 'a large quantity' [8 known]. H/S & HM?
One or two urn(s).

Unprovenanced, Manx? (Hunterian Museum), pre-1783. *c.*1040
Size: ? [7 + 4? known]. H/M & H/S?

Andreas parish churchyard [2], 1874. *c.*1045
Size: 'a great number' [42 known]. A/S, H/S & H/M. Bullion.

West Nappin, Jurby, pre-1900. *c.*1045
Size: fewer than 20 [8 known]. A/S, H/S & H/M. Bullion.

St Patrick's Isle (Peel Castle), German, 1982. *c.*1050
Size: 42 total. H/S. Found in a roll configuration.

Kirk Michael parish churchyard [2], 1972/5. *c.*1065
Size: 81 total. A/S, H/S, H/M & C. Bullion.
Wrapped in a linen bag or purse.

Unprovenanced, pre-1785. *c.*1065
Size: ? [16 plus fragments + 2? known]. A/S & H/S?

Kirk Michael parish churchyard [1], 1834. *c.*1075
Size: fewer than 100? [69 known]. H/S & H/M.

Unprovenanced (Laxey?), Lonan?, pre-1950. *c.*1095
Size: ? [7 known]. H/S.

Unprovenanced, Manx? (National Museum of Scotland),
pre-1785. Size: ? [4 known]. H/S *c.*1110

CONTENT UNCERTAIN (2 coin hoards, not traced)

Near Sulby (E. Kella?), Lezayre, 1750. 10th-11th C.?
Size: 39 total, 'only one of a larger size'.
A/S and/or H/S? H/M or K?

Near Laxey (Ballacannell?), Lonan, 1786. 11th C., first half?
Size: at least 237 'Danish', including one 'square coin'.
H/S and/or H/M? 'Irish Sea'? A/S? C?

The other Viking-Age Manx finds with a coin component (perhaps as many as 19)[15] were discovered mainly in the eighteenth and nineteenth centuries (see Table 22.1), and the finds are generally incomplete and poorly documented. Three, at most, may be known in their entirety[16] – the rest rely on careful reconstructions of representative samples. Despite the challenges of interpretation, there exists a substantial body of numismatic material from Man that may be approached with a fair measure of confidence. This is first and foremost thanks to Michael Dolley, who began preparing the Manx Museum's collection for publication in the *SCBI* series in the 1970s, producing a wave of important Manx-related articles in the process.[17] James Graham-Campbell has also been instrumental in documenting the material, having published a seminal overview of the then-known finds in the 1983 Viking Congress volume, and more recently several articles on important re-attributions.[18] W.A. Seaby, Marshall Cubbon, Sir David Wilson, John Sheehan and Mark Blackburn have also all made noteworthy contributions to the study of Manx finds. The Manx Museum's collection, which will soon be published in the British Academy's *SCBI* series,[19] is unusual in being almost exclusively made up of local finds, making it ripe for closer analysis. It was therefore suggested by Mark Blackburn that the collection, along with groups of coins elsewhere with a Manx association, might form the subject of a general reappraisal, resulting in the doctoral thesis of one

---

[15]   And even this represents a minimum, as there are oblique references to no fewer than 10 hoards (and six or seven single coins), some of which may date to the Viking Age, and that are presumably dispersed, as noted in Bornholdt Collins, 'Coinage', under 'Possible hoards and single finds'.

[16]   These are Ballaqueeney (Port St Mary), Rushen, 1874; Unprovenanced, *c*.1880s; and West Nappin, Jurby, pre-1900.

[17]   Some of Michael Dolley's main contributions to the study of the Manx collection include: 'The "forgotten" Viking-Age silver hoard from West Nappin, Jurby', *Proceedings of the Isle of Man Natural History and Antiquarian Society, 8, no. 1* (1974), 54–64; 'The pattern of Viking-Age coin hoards from the Isle of Man', *Seaby's Coin and Medal Bulletin* (1975), 296–302 and 337–40; 'A Hiberno-Manx coinage of the eleventh century', *NC, 136* (1976), 75–84; 'Some Irish dimensions to Manx history', Inaugural Lecture delivered before the Queen's University of Belfast (Belfast, 1976); 'The two near contemporary findings of Hiberno-Norse coins from Maughold', *Journal of the Manx Museum, VII, no. 88* (1976), 236–40; 'The palimpsest of Viking settlement on Man', in *Proceedings of the Eighth Viking Congress*, ed. H. Bekker-Nielsen, P. Foote and O. Olsen (Odense, 1981), 173–81.

[18]   J. Graham-Campbell 'The Viking-age silver hoards of the Isle of Man', in *Viking Age in the Isle of Man*, ed. C. Fell et al., 53–80; J. Graham-Campbell, 'The lost coin of Æthelred II from Rushen Abbey, Isle of Man', *BNJ, 75* (2005), 161–3; J. Graham-Campbell and J. Sheehan 'A Viking-age silver hoard of "ring money"'.

[19]   K. Bornholdt Collins, *Manx Museum, Douglas: Anglo-Saxon, Hiberno-Scandinavian, Hiberno-Manx and other Coins to 1280, SCBI* (Oxford, forthcoming).

of the authors at the University of Cambridge in 2003.[20] Informed by new or previously overlooked evidence, this detailed reassessment of the formation of the collection and of Dolley's hoard attributions found, among other things, that there were at least three distinct groups embedded in the museum's collection, and thus undoubtedly deriving from Man, representing previously unrecorded (unprovenanced) finds.[21] Distinct parcels(?) from what are most likely to be a further three (unprovenanced) Manx hoards have also been traced off Man, one each in the collection at the National Museum of Scotland, Edinburgh and the Hunterian Museum, Glasgow, and an assemblage that was sold at Christies (6 July 1994, lot 466). Two further hoards that positively contained Viking-Age material are documented in general terms only in early sources, but cannot be traced (and so the content is uncertain), yet in each case the hoard is apparently distinct from other recorded finds; these are listed separately in Table 22.1. The checklist in Table 22.1, then, gives a minimum number of Manx coin finds for which we may feel confident about the general, if not specific, content.

The total is remarkable considering the comparatively brief period during which hoarding was prevalent – from the 950s to the 1070s – and the Island's relatively small size (572 km²) and topography (Colour Plate 22.2). Indeed, Man's hilly interior, much of which is over 100 m (highest point Snaefell, 621 m), was generally avoided by hoarders making the actual area where hoards occur significantly smaller. For comparison, other islands in the region, such as Anglesey, Islay and Mull, all of which are marginally larger than Man and are likewise along Viking routes, have only one or two hoards on record each.[22] Inhabiting a central and advantageous location at the geographical heart of the Irish Sea, the Isle of Man stands out in the context of Viking-Age Britain and Ireland. The obvious conclusion is that much maritime traffic passed through the Island, and that it was a major hub for Viking-Age trade in the post-950 era.

Composition of Manx hoards and the dual economy
Viking-Age silver hoards in Man, as elsewhere around the Irish Sea, sometimes contain coins only, or bullion only (arm-rings, ingots or hack-silver), or they may be a mixture of the two. The coins that occur in Man are predominantly foreign, since minting on the Island only began in the 1020s.[23]

---

[20] Bornholdt Collins, 'Viking-Age Coin Finds from the Isle of Man'. The author remains profoundly grateful for the opportunity to conduct this research, which was supervised by Mark Blackburn and Catherine Hills and generously funded by Manx National Heritage.

[21] Bornholdt Collins, 'Viking-Age Coin Finds from the Isle of Man', 151–63.

[22] Ibid., 237–8 and Appendix i; also Checklist; on Scottish hoards see J. Graham-Campbell, *The Viking-Age Gold and Silver of Scotland (AD 850–1100)* (Edinburgh, 1995), 83–4.

[23] Dolley, 'Hiberno-Manx coinage'; K. Bornholdt, 'Myth or mint? The evidence for a Viking-Age coinage from the Isle of Man', in *Recent Archaeological Research on the Isle of Man*, ed. P.J. Davey, BAR British Series 278 (Oxford, 1999), 199–220. See further below, pp. 488–94.

The tenth-century hoards therefore primarily contain coins from Anglo-Saxon England, as one would expect since the penny was widely trusted and circulated as a reliable currency,[24] sometimes reckoned by weight and sometimes counted out by tale, in a fluid and unregulated dual economy – even outside its intended area of jurisdiction. A much smaller number of coins from Anglo-Scandinavian Northumbria and the Continent are also present in the tenth-century hoards. Homogeneous, single-type coin hoards are in fact atypical for eleventh-century Man (only three of the 12 for which details are known), and it is more usual to find a mixture of currencies drawn from two, three or even more distinct regions, reflecting the wider eleventh-century movement towards 'national coinages'. Hiberno-Scandinavian coins became available with the start of minting at Dublin at the end of the tenth century (*c*.995), and Manx hoards deposited after the millennium typically included coins from Dublin, Anglo-Saxon England and Man, and might also include those struck in the 'Irish Sea', the Continent and Scandinavia; there are also various imitative types for which a minting place has not yet been isolated due to the lack of find evidence, but which clearly signal the proliferation of the idea of coin use and production at this stage.

Bullion represents yet another form of currency, and is a common feature of hoards of Scandinavian character from Britain and Ireland. It occurs in the form of whole ornaments or ingots, or fragments of them (hack-silver) with some frequency in the Manx hoards, particularly in the form of plain silver arm-rings of the type associated with Scandinavian Scotland (see below, pp. 000–00). Not only would bullion have been more practical than coin for larger transactions, but it was a universally recognised medium, a common language and meeting ground for international traders. That bullion had an active role in the Manx economy even after the 1020s, when the local coinage was being produced, is now positively demonstrated by at least four eleventh-century hoards, ranging in date from *c*.1030 to the mid-1060s. These hoards cannot be regarded as indicative of a purely bullion-based economy, each having included a Manx coinage component, but instead suggest that coin was not suitable for all transactions. One could think, negotiate and trade in both terms in this flexible economy, and a shrewd trader would have been prepared with alternatives. The persistent use of bullion suggests that something quite large or valuable was being traded that necessitated higher-value currency, and it seems reasonable to surmise that this may have included slaves and/or livestock, which are well

---

[24] Mark Blackburn discusses this concept in 'Currency under the Vikings. Part 4: the Dublin coinage *c*.995–1050', *BNJ, 78* (2008), 111–37, at 118 and 122–3 (*VCCBI*, 91–117, at 98 and 102–3).

attested for the region in documentary sources.[25] Indeed, a role in the trade of such perishable (and thus otherwise archaeologically elusive) commodities could well account for the disproportionate accumulation of wealth in Man in the mid-tenth and eleventh centuries, and it seems reasonable to envision Man as something of a centre for trans-Irish Sea trade in this period. Furthermore, the prevalence of bullion may even have discouraged the full adoption of a coin economy, or prevented it from developing sooner,[26] since bullion was so much more practical in certain situations.

It is therefore the diverse mixed hoards, such as that from Glenfaba (which comprises coins struck by no less than five different minting authorities plus bullion), that are characteristically 'Manx', and it is these which we must look to for a representative sample of the currency that was circulating in Man in this period. Prior to the 2003 discovery of the Glenfaba hoard the best example of this eclectic economy was the 1970s find from Kirk Michael [2] (*c*.1065), a chronologically wide-ranging savings hoard of 81 coins which included five distinct currencies, including ring-money most likely from Scandinavian Scotland. In contrast, the 1982 hoard from St Patrick's Isle (*c*.1050) contained coins from Dublin only, struck from a limited number of dies. This, along with its west coast deposition, suggests that it was a recent import and had not circulated much, in Man or elsewhere. This assemblage is therefore instructive as an exception to the rule, and does not provide a representative view of the eleventh-century Manx currency pool.

Thus, even before the 2003 Glenfaba hoard came to light, the true character of the Manx economy was beginning to emerge; the new hoard confirmed this. In Man, precious metal and coins of diverse origins circulated side by side in

---

[25] On the slave trade in Ireland see P. Holm, 'The slave trade of Dublin, ninth to twelfth centuries', *Peritia*, 5 (1986), 317–45; M. Metcalf has also noted the possibility that the Irish Sea economy may have been at least partially driven by the long distance trade in slaves in 'The monetary history of England in the tenth century viewed in the perspective of the eleventh century' in *ASMH*, 133–57 at 143. The slave trade in Ireland was initially a dimension of warfare, but it became a profit-driven industry in the mid-tenth century, reaching a peak in the eleventh century (Holm, 'Slave trade of Dublin', 331); it seems worth observing that, in broad terms, these developments essentially mirror the advent and expansion of hoarding in Man, and a period of exceptional prosperity for the Island. Other commodities are likely to have been traded, too, such as horses from Wales, as discussed in B. Hudson, 'The changing economy of the Irish Sea province: AD 900–1300', in *Britain and Ireland 900–1300: Insular Response to Medieval European Change*, ed. B. Smith (Cambridge, 1999), 39–66.

[26] For example, Gareth Williams questions why a locally produced coinage was not introduced earlier in Dublin ('Kingship, Christianity and coinage: monetary and political perspectives on silver economy in the Viking Age', in *Silver Economy in the Viking Age*, ed. J. Graham-Campbell and G. Williams (Walnut Creek, CA, 2007), 177–214, at 202).

what is best described as an 'eclectic dual economy'.[27] The term indicates an economic mind-set somewhere between the traditional metal-weight system normally associated with Vikings and coin use proper. It is a concept that may seem more suited to ninth- or tenth-century contexts, prior to regular coin production in Scandinavian spheres, but the 'eclectic dual economy' persisted even once a substantial Viking coinage appeared in the Irish Sea around the turn of the millennium and thereafter. Finds such as those from Kirk Michael [2] and Glenfaba demonstrate that the two methods of reckoning were not just compatible, but might even be complementary.

One may conclude, then, that in this vibrant 'international' economy, it was the custom to carry several different currencies at once. This was a practical development reflecting a flexible approach to means of payment, even after local coin production began, and continued well into the eleventh century. This contrasts with the homogeneous nature of contemporary coin hoards from England and the Dublin vicinity, where a conscious effort was made to exclude foreign coinage.[28] While such a mixture was not the trend in contemporary urban centres, one can see why this might have been the case in Man, an island emporium where cultures met and currencies mixed and merged.

The Glenfaba hoard: numismatic content

Since the material remains largely unpublished at present, the following provides an overview of the content and selected highlights of the find (including a summary of the numismatic content in the Appendix); detailed analysis is an ongoing process, and the forthcoming publication of the Manx Museum sylloge will also advance our understanding and interpretation of the find, and enable others to access a complete catalogue of the numismatic material. In the meantime, a brief overview of the main components, including a comprehensive account and illustrated catalogue of the non-numismatic component of the hoard (see Graham-Campbell below and Appendix), provides a sense of the range and nature of material and what it contributes to our understanding of the eleventh-century Irish Sea economy.

---

[27]   The idea of a 'dual economy' was a significant theme in Mark Blackburn's work, e.g. in 'Expansion and control: aspects of Anglo-Scandinavian minting south of the Humber', in *Vikings and the Danelaw*, ed. J. Graham-Campbell, R. Hall, J. Jesch and D. Parsons (Oxford, 2001), 125–42 (*VCCBI*, 149–66); and 'Currency under the Vikings, Part 5: The Scandinavian achievement and legacy', *BNJ*, 79 (2009), 43–71 at 48–51 (*VCCBI*, 119–47). See also J. Graham-Campbell, 'The Dual Economy of the Danelaw', *BNJ*, 71 (2001), 49–59; and K. Bornholdt Collins, 'The Dunmore Cave [2] hoard and the role of coins in the tenth-century Hiberno-Scandinavian economy', in *The Viking Age. Ireland and the West*, ed. J. Sheehan and D. Ó Corráin (Dublin, 2010), 19–46, at 24–5.

[28]   Blackburn, 'Dublin coinage', 117 (*VCCBI*, 97).

The Glenfaba hoard dates to the very beginning of the second period of Viking-Age hoarding (Table 22.1), following a lengthy hiatus in the record. It therefore usefully broadens the range of the established record, in particular offering new material to shed light on the transition and interface between Phases I and II of the Dublin coinage (*c.*1015–*c.*1020), as well as the earliest stage of the Manx mint in the mid-1020s, while providing new clues as to the possible origin for the imitative 'Irish Sea' *Quatrefoil* series. The evidence for circulation in the form of secondary treatment is also considered, as is the contemporary value of the find.

Anglo-Saxon

The Anglo-Saxon component comprises 17 per cent of the hoard, with 79 pennies ranging in date from the 990s to the early 1020s, thus representing the older material in the assemblage (see Appendix, p. 509). The 70 coins of Æthelred II cover all four of his last major types (*Crux, Long Cross, Helmet, Last Small Cross*), and there are also nine of Cnut, all of the *Quatrefoil* type, which was produced *c.*1017–*c.*1023. These are exactly the types that were copied in close succession, following their introduction in England, to make up the initial phase of minting in Dublin, and it is perhaps interesting that the hoard encapsulates the complete gamut of prototypes for the Hiberno-Scandinavian coinage. While only one type at a time would have been current in the regulated economy of contemporary England, where the rules of *renovatio monetae* governed, this was not the case in the Irish Sea region, where different types circulated side by side, and could remain in the currency pool for decades. This mix of English types remained a standard feature in Manx finds into the eleventh century. The Anglo-Saxon coins may have arrived directly from England or, as a small number of more heavily peck-marked coins might suggest, may have first travelled to Ireland (outside Dublin) or even Scandinavia before ending up in Man. While more detailed analyses might prove interesting, one is struck by the very broad range of mints represented: London, Chester, Exeter and Winchester are especially well represented; there are four each of Lincoln, Stamford and Wallingford; three each of Canterbury, Dover and York; two each of Cambridge, Norwich and Worcester; and single examples of Barnstaple, Bath, Cricklade, Gloucester, Huntingdon, Lewes, Northampton(?), Salisbury, Thetford, Warwick, Watchet and Wilton. This assortment was not drawn directly from England, but is suggestive of the wide-ranging trading interests that entered the Irish Sea economy, and also gives a sense of the intensity of mixing that then took place through rapid circulation.

Hiberno-Scandinavian

The 326 Hiberno-Scandinavian coins from Dublin are by far the largest component (70 per cent) of the Glenfaba hoard. These include 20 Phase I (c.995–1020) coins and 306 of Phase II (c.1020–35).[29] While the earliest coins struck at Dublin, *Crux*, are absent, as are the very rare *Helmet* coins, the Phase I material comprises 14 imitations of *Long Cross* pennies, mainly in the name of Sihtric Silkbeard (989/94–1036), but also 'Æthelred' (Dublin and an 'English' mint, Northampton) and 'Thymn', five *Last Small Cross* pennies (both Dublin and 'English' mint signatures), and one *Quatrefoil* type.[30] The majority are struck from known dies. Die-linking of Phase I coins within the hoard is limited (but not absent),[31] showing that the earliest Dublin coins accumulated locally over several decades, and circulated long enough to become thoroughly mixed before being hoarded. Three separate *Long Cross* reverses (nos. 81, 86 and 93) include several small, irregularly placed pellets in the reverse quarters: a foreshadowing, perhaps, of the four-pellet reverse design that would distinguish Phase II *Long Cross* coins from their Phase I predecessors. The occurrence of Phase I coins with reverse pellets is interesting alongside a large group of 'transitional' Phase II examples in the hoard, which lack the usual pellets on their reverses, perhaps supporting the idea that production of Phase II coins may have coincided with the last types in Phase I rather than a clean break occurring between phases. However, based on die-linking patterns and other observations prompted by the new hoard, Blackburn concluded that they instead 'demonstrate how closely a die-cutter in Phase II could copy Phase I issues when he chose to';[32] in other words, the similarities that have raised the question about an overlap can essentially be put down to skilful, intensive and deliberate copying where both Phases I and II were used as models. These coins clearly date to an earlier stage of production in Phase II, and provide a rare glimpse of the interface between the first two phases of the Dublin coinage, but apparent similarities across the phases appear to be an illusion only.

The name of Dublin's primary moneyer, Færemin, is clearly rendered on most of the Phase I *Long Cross* coins, except where English coins were copied, for example ones imitating Asgautr (Osgut) at Lincoln (rendered as 'Osgun') or Godleof at Stamford ('Godleov'). However, Færemin is absent from the *Last Small Cross* coins, as is typical of this type, which sport 'Goheln' (a corruption of Colbrand, for instance as found on *SCBI* 8, 51 and *SCBI* 22, 43, where the Colbrand reverse is paired with the same obverse die as the 'Goheln' coin from

---

29   See Blackburn, 'Dublin Coinage' for an overview of the Dublin coinage, expanding on the work of Michael Dolley and others, including a chronology of the phases distilled in Table 1, 116. His preliminary considerations of the Hiberno-Scandinavian material in the Glenfaba hoard (specifically, the dating of the Phase II coinage and the question of overlap between Phases I and II) also appear in this article, 128–30.

30   This last coin demonstrated that Blackburn's IS21 is actually a Hiberno-Scandinavian coin (HN23); see supplement to article XV in *VCCBI*, 388–9.

31   *Contra* Blackburn, 'Dublin coinage', 131 (*VCCBI*, 111).

32   Ibid., 132 (*VCCBI*, 112).

Glenfaba), 'Elewiren' and 'Ngremion' of Dublin, as well as Wulfsige at Chester and 'Dgdoan' at London. This demonstrates how the dies were produced through close copying in an attempt to be as similar as possible to, and therefore as economically viable as, the much admired English coinage, an indication of its fundamentally economic rather than political function. Both a disregard for literacy and copy-cat behaviour are themes throughout the various phases of the Dublin coinage, apparently bringing no disadvantage for the coinage in circulation.[33]

As noted by Mark Blackburn, the Phase II coins mark a major reform in the Dublin coinage when it finally severed its ties with the English coinage and essentially became an independent 'national' coinage.[34] Andrew Woods has also shown that it is the Phase II coins which occur most frequently among the singlefinds in Ireland, a direct reflection of how coin use and production took off in Ireland in the 1020s.[35] The coins are still predominantly struck in the name of Færemin (or abbreviated forms of this) as well as for instance (as seen in the Glenfaba sample) Car, Godric, Leofwine, Siult, 'Smiren', Steng, and 'Zigares', or they sport blundered legends, although die-linking (with shared obverses) indicates that the names are probably just copied from older coins and do not represent actual moneyers.[36] They are remarkably uniform on the one hand, all based on the popular *Long Cross* type, but are distinguished by the replacement of the single pellet behind the head first with a cross pattée or 'pi' symbol,[37] and later other ornaments, which also occur before the face or in the neck, and notably by the addition of a single pellet in each quarter of the reverse. The Glenfaba assemblage is an excellent reminder of the great innovation and variation within the phase in terms of the array of symbols employed on the obverses (Figure 22.1a–n). A beautiful and unique coin with a three-pronged pinwheel motif behind the head is intriguingly reminiscent of the three-legged ancient symbol for Man, although this is thought to have been a thirteenth-century invention. Another coin for which no parallel has been found sports a 'key'-like symbol behind the head.

While an impressive variety of coins is represented in this large group, unique coins are actually a minority. The extensive die-linking both within the hoard and with other known collections and finds gives the general impression that we have knowledge of a high proportion of the dies used in producing Phase II. Further detailed work is required on die-linking and other parallels with the

---

[33] Ibid., 123–4 (*VCCBI*, 103–4).

[34] Ibid., 127–8 (*VCCBI*, 107–8).

[35] See Woods, this volume. And yet, not a single Phase II single find is recorded from Man.

[36] Ibid., 132 (*VCCBI*, 112).

[37] As attested by the only Phase II coin in the Everlöv hoard from Skåne, *t.p.q.* 1018 (CNS 3.4.59.6) or 1014–15 according to Blackburn ('Dublin coinage', 128 n. 89 (*VCCBI*, 108)); three die duplicates of this coin are in the Glenfaba hoard (one is ill. in Figure 22.3a).

few near-contemporary hoards, all less substantial, in Man itself and elsewhere (such as the Fourknocks and Tonyowen hoards from Ireland and a parcel from Dull, Perthshire in Scotland, as well as any relevant Scandinavian finds such as the Everlöv find) before the publication of conclusive results, which promise to shed light on the internal relative chronology and dating of the varieties within the phase.[38]

There are two large groups of Phase II die-duplicates within the hoard, a run of 15 coins and one of 33, which were added to the hoard *en masse*, shortly after minting, and without having had the chance to circulate and mix more thoroughly in the Manx currency pool. These appear to be fairly close to each other chronologically in terms of style, and are perhaps not among the earliest Phase II coins, but would have occurred fairly early on with their classic design and good epigraphy (the die-links fall into Seaby's 'generally earlier grouping' in *SCBI* 32). One might expect a larger cluster of the latest, most current coins, but other coins in the find appear to be stylistically later (e.g. those with a serpent behind the head (no. 314), and hand (nos. 331–3, same as *SCBI* 32, 103 and others), all of which fall into Seaby's 'generally later grouping'. Clusters such as these provide a clue to the character of the assemblage, which does not represent a single sweep of the currency available at a given time. Instead, this pattern has occurred because the lead container that held the assemblage was added to like a piggy bank. It was not a traditional savings hoard *per se*, accumulated over an extended period or even over more than one lifetime (such as Kirk Michael [2], which spans 125 years), for the coins fall into a *c.*30 year span (and even the older material would have been regarded as more or less 'current' in the Irish Sea context). While this does not necessarily diminish the value of the find, it may have implications for understanding the finer details of the chronology of Phase II, and it is necessary to be wary of a simplistic reading of the find.

The fact that the latest types within Phase II (e.g. the so-called 'E' type) are absent contributes to the suggested date of deposition, *c.*1030. Based on the Anglo-Saxon element alone the hoard would appear to have been deposited by *c.*1025, and perhaps a little earlier since *Quatrefoil* coins are present, but do not dominate. However, the large Hiberno-Scandinavian element, with its diversity of Phase II issues, suggests that the hoard was deposited slightly later, well into production of the 'reformed' Dublin coinage.

Hiberno-Manx

The Manx component in Glenfaba represents the most recent material in the hoard, and stands at the head of the series originally identified by Michael

---

[38]   Sincere thanks are due to Andrew Woods for extensive work on the die-linking of Phase II, incorporating the Glenfaba material with the known corpus, and for his reflections on this which I have drawn upon in part here.

Figure 22.1   Sample of the variety of symbols found on Hiberno-Scandinavian Phase II obverses (all from the Glenfaba hoard). (a) 'Pi' symbol behind head (b) Cross pommée behind head (c) Pellets on neck, cross pattée (d) 'Flower' on neck, cross pommé (e) Pellets before face, cross pattée (f) 'Wishbone' on neck, cross pommée and pellets (g) Cross pattée and pellets (h) Annulet behind head (i) Pellet on cheek, cross pommée and pellets (j) Hand behind head (k) 'Key' behind head (l) 'Pinwheel' behind head (m) 'Serpent' on neck, cross pattée and two pellets before face (n) 'Serpent' or 'J' symbol behind head.

Dolley.[39] It comprises not only 30 examples of the Hiberno-Scandinavian/Manx 'Transfer die' (TD),[40] of which previously only 13 examples were recorded, but also 12 coins that appear to be the work of a new and distinct die-cutter at the start of the Hiberno-Manx coinage (HM 1).

Like those of Dublin Phase II, the Hiberno-Manx coins are of the *Long Cross* type with a portrait obverse and a single pellet in each reverse quarter (Figure 22.2). The more familiar examples from the main series have three pellet-crosses incorporated in the obverse: two within the legend, in place of customary cross pattée, and another behind the head. Cross pommée and additional pellets are found by the head on some Phase II coins, and on TD and HM 1 coins, but never in the legend: this was a later innovation and one of the distinguishing features of the second Manx die-cutter (HM 2). Also distinctive is a line before the face (originally a crack in the Transfer die), which was religiously copied in all stages of the Hiberno-Manx series (TD, First, Second and Third states of wear, HM 1, and HM 2, Early, Middle and Late styles) (Figure 22.3a–c).

Prior to Dolley, and even following his ground-breaking paper on the Manx coinage in 1976, it was generally assumed that all non-Anglo-Saxon coins from this period and region were struck in Dublin. It is now understood that striking coins was essentially a portable operation and not inherently difficult if one had access to the basic materials, tools and dies, and there were indeed other noteworthy attempts – whether official or of dubious intent – to coin silver in and around the Irish Sea.[41] Most significant of these in terms of size and chronological scope was the series of coins introduced in Man shortly after the start of the second phase of the Dublin coinage (*c.*1025), running parallel with Dublin's Phases III, IV and possibly V, to *c.*1065, although the lack of hoard evidence for the later eleventh century makes the end-point uncertain. Their occurrence in different stages and states in no less than seven variously dated Manx hoards, together with a study of dies and epigraphy, a steady but controlled decrease in weight, and variations in the silver alloy over time, has made it possible to discern a relative internal chronology, with Early, Middle and Late styles during the main period of production.[42] Obviously, only the earliest coins of the Manx series are present in Glenfaba, which usefully provides a first glimpse at the earliest years in the life of this series.

Transfer die (TD)   The Transfer-die coins are struck from an official Dublin obverse which at some point in the mid-1020s was brought to an unknown location in Man and possibly used with 'hand-me-down' Dublin reverses, and then locally made reverses copied from previous dies or other Dublin coins in

---

[39]   Dolley, 'Hiberno-Manx coinage'.

[40]   See Bornholdt, 'Myth or Mint?'.

[41]   See below; see also Leighton and Woods, Chapter 23, this volume.

[42]   Bornholdt, 'Myth or Mint?'.

circulation. This Dublin obverse, the 'Transfer die', was used intensively, with three states of die degradation discernible, until it deteriorated beyond repair. The Manx die-cutters, in close succession or perhaps working concurrently for a time, then produced obverses copying the same Dublin prototype, each producing a distinctive reinterpretation.

Figure 22.2   Hiberno-Manx (HM 2), Early style (Glenfaba hoard).

The movement of valuable dies between mints and across political boundaries, whether bought, commissioned, stolen or presented as gifts, is well attested in English, Hiberno-Scandinavian and Scandinavian contexts in this period and the situation in Man is a natural extension of this trend. In the Glenfaba sample, the seven TD coins in the First State of wear (nos. 417–23) are produced from a single set of official Dublin dies, either in Man or perhaps prior to the dies leaving Dublin, but the 23 in the Second State (nos. 424–46), where the obverse is noticeably degrading, are Manx.[43] Remarkably, the dividing line appears to be encapsulated in this assemblage which has literally witnessed the birth of the Manx coinage. One clue is seen in a drop in average weight between the earlier coins (1.28 g) and those in the second state (1.15 g), another in the proportion of reversed letters and nonsense, retrograde legends, and yet another in a subtle, but discernible, increase in diameter, from 18 mm to 19 mm in most cases. With the new find we now have 43 coins struck from the TD, including five new reverses represented by 10 coins.

Hiberno-Manx 1 (HM 1)   The few previously recorded examples of HM 1 coins were generally regarded as belonging to Phase II,[44] though they do not fit neatly into the series, and have been noted elsewhere as oddities which must be related to, or inspired by, the Manx coins.[45] With so few examples to go on, it was not possible to suggest where they fit into the picture, although the two other provenanced examples derive from another Manx hoard (Andreas [2], 1874

---

[43]   For convenience all coins from the Transfer die are counted as 'Manx', although it may be that seven are technically products of the Dublin mint.

[44]   For example, *SCBI* 32, nos. 81–2.

[45]   Bornholdt Collins, 'Viking-Age Coin Finds from the Isle of Man', 309 and n. 27.

Figure 22.3   Stages in the Hiberno-Manx coinage (Transfer die, HM 1 and
HM 2), from left to right.

22.3a +ZIHTRI6RE+DYFL   +FÄ/REH/NMO/DYFL
TD, First state: Glenfaba (2003) hoard (1.31 g, 270°, 18 mm)

22.3b +I3MIRER[ ]DII   +F,Ä[ ]MI/NHÖ/DYFIF
HM 1: *SCBI* Belfast, 82 (0.85 g, 195°, chipped)

22.3c :: IIIIIIIIIII :: DII6   +FÄ/RE[ ]NHÖ/DYFIF
HM 2: Cambridge, ex Blunt, CM 1.810–1990. Chipped, 3 *rev.* and 1 *obv.* peck-
marks (0.69 g, 18–19 mm)

dep. *c.*1045), which also included one TD coin as well as a HM 2, Early style.[46]
The HM 1 coins bear several of the hallmark features of the Manx coinage: a
Phase II-style *Long Cross* type with a line before the face, a cross pommée behind
the neck, and two pellets behind the head, and an inscription that attempts, if
loosely, to name the ruler 'Sihtric' as on the TD coins, in contrast to HM 2 coins
(see Figure 22.4d–e and Figure 22.3b). They seem typical of the Dublin mint,
yet features like the slash before the face immediately and intentionally recall
the Manx series. The main difference is in the enclosed 'almond' eye and small
head, which are similar to the TD group, but unlike the substantive Manx series
where the eye is always a single pellet. Both Dublin and Manx coins appear to
have had a role in inspiring their design. However, the overall style is clearly the
work of another die-engraver, and this sets the group apart from the established,
hitherto satisfyingly linear, progression of dies associated with the Manx mint.
They are more akin to the Transfer die than the later coinage, but they are *not*
Dublin-Manx hybrids, indicating that the earliest stage of the Manx coinage is
more stylistically diverse than previously understood.

The known sample of HM 1 now comprises 19 coins, struck from 13 obverses
and 16 reverses. The average weight of the Glenfaba examples is 1.12 g, which
corresponds closely with that of the TD coins in the Second State (First State

[46]   Previously, only seven coins of this group had been traced: two from Man, one from a
Swedish hoard and the others unprovenanced, but apparently not from Scandinavian finds based
on the virtual absence of peck-marks.

average: 1.28 g; Second State: 1.15 g; Third State: 1.06 g). The diameters in the Glenfaba sample are almost exclusively 19 mm (just one is 18 mm and another 18.5 mm), which in itself draws a line between the TD group and the Dublin series (Dublin Phase II: 17–18 mm; Phase III: 16 mm). A large proportion of the reverse legends are retrograde or include retrograde or inverted letters (also found on the obverses), a feature occurring at a low level among the Dublin

Figure 22.4   Copying within the early Hiberno-Manx coinage (note reverse, fourth quarter). Above, (a)–(c); below (d)–(e).

22.4a +ZIHTRI6RE+DYFL +FIE/R,EIII/NIIO/DIHE
TD, Second state: Glenfaba (2003) hoard (1.13 g, 70°, 18.5 mm)

22.4b +ZIHTRI6RE+DYFL +FIM/REIN/RIRO/DIML
TD, Third state: Dublin, RIA 3092 (1.06 g, 170°, 19 mm)

22.4c +,I,I,MTR6RI+Di,INI +FIE/REIM/NHÖ/DIME
HM 1: Glenfaba (2003) hoard (0.96 g, 270°, 19 mm)

22.4d +IIMT.R6RI+DiI3I +EHI/REIH/ÖHMI/DIME
HM 1: Glenfaba (2003) hoard (1.19 g, 200°, 19 mm)

22.4e :: IIIIIIIIIII :: DII6 +FIM/REIN/RIRO/DIME
HM 2, Early style: Dublin, RIA 3140 (1.21 g, 330°, 19 mm) (rev. same as 22.4b, re-cut).

coinage, but which is the norm for Manx coins. About one-third attempt an approximation of the moneyer Færemin, but most of the legends are nonsense strings of well-formed letters.

There are several reverses to note, including the distinctive TD die that was re-cut to produce some of the first HM 2 coins, because of the way they echo each other (Figure 22.4a–e).[47] This is seen in the fourth quarter of the reverse where it reads DIME or similar, a residual rendering of 'Dublin' that is otherwise unrecorded in the Phase II coinage. Through close copying, a clear association is seen among the earliest Manx coins, giving the impression that we have a close and coherent group, and have most certainly left Dublin.

Chronologically speaking, the new group fits between the introduction of the series through a Dublin-cut die or set of dies and what has been considered the main series proper (now HM 2), where a new style is evident and additional characteristics were added to the standard form that continued over three decades or more. The difference in style in HM 1 coins, yet repetition of the principal features, appears to signal the presence of a previously unappreciated die-cutter at work in Man immediately prior to, or perhaps coinciding for a time with, the HM 2 die-cutter. One wonders if perhaps the need demanded two experts, or if they worked as a team and the second was apprenticed to the first in an effort to establish the mint. That the second die-cutter not only judiciously recycled at least one older die, but also took the work of the first die-engraver as a prototype, is seen in another example of very close copying of reverses where the fourth quarters both read DYFIF (again, an otherwise unique rendering for the part of the reverse that once recorded the mint); however, very slight differences and the omission of the pellet between the 'F' and 'Æ' in the first quarter demonstrates that this was a near perfect copy rather than struck from the same die (Figure 22.3b–c).

Our understanding of this new group is only beginning to take shape and will doubtless evolve as the material unlocks its secrets, and as new finds come to light. Nevertheless, its identification helps to bring the once hazy Manx mint into sharper focus, which would not have been possible without the discovery of the Glenfaba hoard.

Scandinavian-'Irish Sea' coinage
(Anglo-Manx?) imitations of Cnut's Quatrefoil type   Another distinct currency in the assemblage is represented by 11 'Irish Sea' imitations of Cnut's *Quatrefoil* type.[48] The type, first isolated by Stewart Lyon in the 1960s,[49] is distinct from the *Quatrefoil* imitations produced during the first phase of the Dublin coinage in terms of style, epigraphy and a lower weight, and in his authoritative 1996 study, Mark Blackburn demonstrated that they are the product of a separate mint,

---

[47]   This is the critical die-link, as first noted by W.A. Seaby (Cambridge, Fitzwilliam Museum, Michael Dolley archive, letter 418), that demonstrates the connection between the Dublin and Manx series – a reverse that is paired with both the old Dublin prototype ('Transfer die') obverse and the Manx-made copy of it.

[48]   M. Blackburn, 'Hiberno-Norse and Irish Sea imitations of Cnut's *Quatrefoil* type', *BNJ*, 66 (1996), 1–20 (*VCCBI*, 349–70, and supplement, 384–90).

[49]   Blackburn, 'Hiberno-Norse and Irish Sea imitations', 11 (*VCCBI*, 359).

active around 1020, somewhere in the Irish Sea region. Although they form a relatively minor component of the large assemblage, the discovery at Glenfaba in 2003 resulted in a 25 per cent increase in the corpus of this material, including four examples of an unrecorded set of dies and one further new reverse. The hoard has provided the invaluable opportunity to reassess the type in the light of a securely recorded and demonstrably complete hoard context.

While most examples derive from Scandinavian and southern Baltic finds, one coin derived from the Pant-yr-Eglwys find from North Wales, providing strong evidence that Britain was home to the series, since Scandinavian coins are unusual here and vast quantities of Anglo-Saxon coins entered the Scandinavian market in the first half of the eleventh century.[50] The overwhelming Chester influence, with 75 per cent of the known reverses attempting to name the Chester mint or a Chester moneyer, suggested to Mark that their 'home' must be somewhere on the east side of the Irish Sea, on the fringes of Anglo-Saxon England, for Dublin imitations generally copied a variety of Anglo-Saxon mints reflecting the broad mix available as prototypes to the Dublin moneyers. This, and their fundamentally commercial nature (which transported them to Scandinavia and the Baltic), led to the suggestion that one possible, logical origin for the group might be the Wirral, where there was both a Scandinavian enclave and a well-established beach market at Meols. The coin finds from Meols of the reign of Cnut are indeed Chester-dominated, but as yet there are no confirmed examples of the imitative *Quatrefoils* from this location (although one 'illegible' nineteenth-century find, now lost, hints at the possibility).[51] David Griffiths, elaborating upon Boon's suggestion of a Welsh origin, has since proposed an alternative source, pointing out that they could have been struck for use by a non-Scandinavian group, perhaps by a Welsh ruler.[52] In his view, Rhuddlan, also in North Wales and geographically closer to the Welsh find, is a prime candidate. While the strategic location (albeit inland and therefore problematic in being removed from Irish Sea trade) and historical situation appear ripe for such a development, the suggestion is in Griffiths' view further supported by the Cheshire Domesday, which names Rhuddlan as a mint in 1086 (referring to the division of rights between the Earl of Chester and Robert of Rhuddlan), but there is no indication here of an earlier coinage, and the reference can hardly be linked to the situation in the 1020s. At present no coins of this date are known to bear the mint signature or can be attributed to Rhuddlan, and there is no

---

[50] *VCCBI*, XV, 360; M.M. Archibald, 'Against the tide: coin movement from Scandinavia to the British Isles in the Viking Age', *NNF-Nytt, 1* (1991), 13–22.

[51] The known corpus of coin finds is listed and discussed by S.C. Bean, 'The coins', in *Meols. The Archaeology of the North Wirral Coast*, ed. D. Griffiths, R.A. Philpott and G. Egan (Oxford, 2007), 295–350, with a discussion of a possible Meols mint at 349.

[52] Griffiths, *Vikings of the Irish Sea*, 109.

concrete evidence for a mint in Wales before the last quarter of the eleventh century.[53]

With a large proportion of the recorded finds now having a Manx provenance, the possibility of a Manx origin presents itself, and was seriously entertained by Mark Blackburn in some of his latest work.[54] One conundrum he grappled with is: if the coins came from a mint in the Wirral they would have circulated with other local coins, so why were they not accompanied by English *Quatrefoils* dominated by coins of Chester? The composition suggests that the Glenfaba Irish Sea imitations would have arrived direct from the mint, without mixing, although the die-linking is not as extensive as one would expect from a mint-sourced parcel. The logical conclusion, then, based on sound numismatic reasoning, is that the group must be 'home grown' and drawn directly from local circulation; indeed, this *would* be the conclusion if not for the fact that we already have a well-attested mint in Man and its product in no way resembles the *Quatrefoil* imitations. Could these really be the precursor to the mint that, no more than a decade later, looked solely to Dublin for its inspiration? Not only does it seem highly improbable that these could be products of the same mint based on the stylistically different, homogeneous, Dublin-oriented character of the established Manx series, but Mark also delineated the enigmatic differences between this group and the Hiberno-Manx coins *vis-à-vis* their implementation and organisation in production as indicated in part by the dramatically different ratio of obverse to reverse dies used (information which, like a genetic marker, provides specific information relating to identity), demonstrating that they are in no way related. If the Manx mint produced *Quatrefoil* imitations we must imagine that the mint began in a completely different tradition, enjoyed a brief period of production followed by a curious gap – and then, experienced an abrupt change in organisation which adopted a higher weight standard as well as an entirely new design that remained virtually uniform for three decades or longer. The sequence is hard to comprehend, yet – thanks to Glenfaba – the find distribution and hoard evidence is so compelling that in his supplement to the 1996 study Mark came to favour a Manx origin for the group.

But what if the *Quatrefoil* imitations are the product of a different mint in Man? There is no need to assume the Island could only accommodate a single mint, and an entirely separate minting outlet elsewhere in Man could better account for the differences observed. This opens up the possibility that further 'orphaned' imitative coins might belong to this other mint, or indeed that other short-lived minting attempts could have sprouted in this flourishing hive of economic activity.

---

[53]   M. Allen, *Mints and Money in Medieval England* (Cambridge, 2012), 23–6.

[54]   *VCCBI*, supplement to article XV, 388.

One wonders if Man's unique north–south divide is relevant here, a physical division that essentially follows the natural contours diagonally across the main ridge, forming two primary 'Deemster divisions' (recognised from at least the fifteenth century), each with its own Deemster Court.[55] It is also a deeply rooted concept that extends into time immemorial, the 'north' (or Northside, in geographical terms the north-west) traditionally looking more to Ireland and the 'south' (Southside, essentially the south-east) to England. Whether or not the division, which is both administrative and cultural (for example marriage across the boundary has not always been possible), existed in the sense that it has in more recent history, and still does in vestigial ways today, the idea at least helps us to envision how two such different mints – clearly influenced from these two directions (i.e. one Hiberno-Manx and the other essentially Anglo-Manx) – could occupy the same space. Furthermore, if we accept the idea of a separate and slightly earlier Southside mint, could this even have been a driving force in the subsequent establishment of a Dublin-inspired Northside mint in a bout of healthy competition (both economic and political)?

Still, the appearance of non-Dublin imitative *Quatrefoils* – even an impressive number of them – in only one Manx hoard may not seem like particularly strong evidence when the provenanced Hiberno-Manx coins derive from no less than seven Manx hoards, and if they are to be regarded as a local product their apparent absence from other Manx contexts seems problematic. While this could be partially due to chance, with the recovery and distribution of finds having favoured the Northside, it might also be explained by the significantly longer duration of the Hiberno-Manx mint. Additionally, it is a straightforward function of the dating of the known finds, as at present there are no Manx hoards of the 1020s, and the only other immediately chronologically relevant find is the Park Llewellyn 1835 hoard (*c*.1030), which is unlikely to be known in its entirety. The Kirk Michael [2] (*c*.1065) hoard included tenth-century pennies as well as coins of Cnut (and later), including two *Quatrefoils* from the York mint, so we might have expected the imitations to have made it into this assemblage if they were locally available. However, as noted above, the character of this hoard is most peculiar, with its broad and uneven age structure, and the irregular formation process could easily have missed this component. Furthermore, the preponderance of Hiberno-Manx and Hiberno-Scandinavian coins and its decidedly north-western find-spot also suggests that the owner had stronger ties with the Dublin axis, and therefore had less interest in, or limited access to, coinage that may have derived from a mint on the opposite side of Man.

Approaching from a different angle, the presence of a group of several other hitherto unlocalised Cnut imitations (one *Pointed Helmet* and four *Short*

---

[55]   E. Davies, 'Treens and Quarterlands: a study of the land system of the Isle of Man', *The Institute of British Geographers*, 22 (1957), 97–116 at 100.

Cross) in the second Andreas parish churchyard hoard (*c*.1045) also hints that an English-influenced mint contemporary with the reign of Cnut could have continued beyond the *Quatrefoil* type, contemporaneously with the Manx mint, but no longer exclusively looked to Chester for inspiration. While at present there is too little material to take this further, the possibility of a Manx origin for the group, perhaps even the same mint as the *Quatrefoils*, is much more likely if we think in terms of a second Anglo-Manx mint that was distinct from the one producing the Hiberno-Manx coinage.

A final possibility should, perhaps, be revisited: could these *Quatrefoils* be a Scandinavian product? Though this was firmly ruled out in Mark's original paper due to the rarity of Scandinavian finds in Britain, this very hoard contains indications of influence from, and even direct links with, Scandinavia (see below), and the Glenfaba parcel could in theory have travelled this distance. The absence of any peck-marks in the 11 coins suggests this is improbable though, and once again a Scandinavian origin can be ruled out. While the origin for the 'Irish Sea' imitations of Cnut's *Quatrefoil* type is still uncertain, and the Wirral remains a possibility, the appearance of a significant parcel in the Glenfaba hoard has shifted the focus away from the eastern seaboard of the Irish Sea, to Man. If we envisage two separate mints in different parts of the Island functioning in close succession, or perhaps even simultaneously for a time, the idea becomes easier to reconcile with the evidence. The case for a Manx attribution is strong, but can only be resolved as new finds come to light. If only we could have a glimpse of the lost hoard from Ballacannell, Lonan (located on the Southside of the Island) which might well have included the type! In the meantime, it is at least apparent that the mint was in a location that was part of the far-reaching nexus for trade with Man, and whether they travelled across the Irish Sea or were sourced locally it is not too surprising that these are among the great variety of currencies found on the Island.

Other Imitative Coins

There are also some much more unusual elements in the hoard, including five coins which are at present unidentified or unclassifiable, and which one would normally be obliged to assign to the reformed Dublin mint (Phase II) based on the presence of a single pellet in each of the reverse quarters. However, the obverse portraits are both distinct and erratic in form, and they simply do not fit stylistically – either in terms of portrait design or epigraphy – into the now very well-established corpus of types. Again, a Scandinavian source seems possible, but no stylistic parallels or die-links have been traced, and the total absence of peck-marks militates against this. One of the obverses has a sceptre before the face (an elaboration of the Manx slash?) and another has a likeness to the Manx DIIIII6 at the end of the obverse legend. As is common among other imitative coinages where the dies have been created by less experienced die-cutters, there is a high degree of retrograde and nonsense legends and lettering (four out of the five coins have retrograde reverses), again indicating a non-official mint which is likely to have been located in the Irish Sea, where Hiberno-Scandinavian – and Hiberno-Manx – coins were readily available for copying. As has been noted above, and also explored by Woods and Leighton elsewhere in this volume with regard to yet another group of imitations (copying Æthelræd II's *Long Cross* type), the circumstances in the decades around and shortly after the millennium were somehow ripe for both official and unofficial attempts at minting coinage. There are numerous possible motivations for such minting activity, for example to boost a local market and facilitate trade and taxation; or it may have been a matter of fashion, to keep up with the neighbours; or, to assert a political claim, exert power and/or create a revenue stream; or, to turn a profit by dodging minting premiums – and we have to make room in this picture for smaller scale imitative mints that tried to carve out a place for themselves in and around the Irish Sea.

Scandinavian imitation

One of the oldest coins in the hoard, a single Scandinavian imitation of Æthelred's *Long Cross* type, moneyer 'Leofstan', is heavily peck-marked (eight pecks), scratched and bent, and would have made a significant journey to join this assemblage. As noted above, its presence is atypical in the context of the British Isles,[56] and therefore somewhat curious, but a good reminder of the far-flung ties, and particularly Scandinavian connections, of the inhabitants of the Irish Sea.

The dies were identified by Mark Blackburn as from an imitative workshop active in southern Scandinavia at the turn of the millennium, possibly located in Lund, Denmark.[57] Prior to the discovery of the Glenfaba hoard only four examples were known. The coin falls into Malmer's chain 112/Blackburn's chain 2, which has an official York phase, linked by transported dies to a Scandinavian phase, where the English dies were subsequently copied. This chain now also links to Malmer's chain 105/Blackburn chain 1, positively demonstrating that they were from the same imitative workshop, as suspected by Blackburn in 1981 and confirmed in recent work by Bo Gunnarsson.[58] Chain 105 is also interesting

---

[56]   Archibald, 'Against the tide'.

[57]   M. Blackburn, 'An imitative workshop', in *Studies in Northern Coinages of the Eleventh Century*, ed. C.J. Becker (Copenhagen, 1981), 29–88, at 44–5 and no. 205. Also, B. Malmer, *The Anglo-Scandinavian Coinage c.995–1020*, Comm. NS, 9 (Stockholm, 1997), no. 9.104.1158, chain 112.

[58]   I am grateful to Bo Gunnarsson for discussing his work on the extensive die chains with me, and for providing a copy of his important article which traces the development of die-chain 105, including its connection to die-chain 112 and with York, and its Hiberno-Scandinavian

in including imitative coins of Hiberno-Scandinavian style, copied from Irish prototypes. Further Hiberno-Scandinavian-inspired dies have recently been found linked to the chain (as identified by Gunnarsson), although a direct die-link into the Dublin series has not been traced. The style of one of the newly linked obverses suggests that it is most likely of Dublin origin. If it can be confirmed, this is yet another example of the movement of an official die, for use elsewhere, far from its intended area of jurisdiction.

Secondary Treatment and Circulation

One way of accessing further information from this hoard material is through assessing the extent of secondary treatment, which reveals clues about circulation through marketplace rituals in which the currency was tested for quality or forgeries.[59] The presence of cut bullion and coins that have been pecked (generally a rare phenomenon in Britain and Ireland), and bent, a much more common form of testing for good money which continued in England right down to the Norman Conquest (and beyond),[60] provides unambiguous evidence that the material in this hoard was drawn from the currency in active circulation in Man in the first decades of the second millennium.

Bending was less destructive than pecking, which was a blatant form of mutilation, and may have been more socially acceptable at this stage, reflecting a certain regard for the coin as coin (as demonstrated for example by the prevalence of the method of testing at such a late date in England). The Glenfaba hoard includes 245 coins with signs of bending (*c.*53 per cent), some multiple

---

influences: 'Den gäckande kedja 105 – spåret av en vikingatida myntunion?', *Samlad Glädje 2009*, ed. Curt Ekström, Numismatic Society in Uppsala (Uppsala, 2009), 71–89.

[59]   On secondary treatment in finds from Britain and Ireland see M. Archibald, 'Pecking and bending: the evidence of British finds', in K. Jonsson and B. Malmer (ed.), *Sigtuna Papers: Proceedings of the Sigtuna Symposium on Viking-Age Coinage 1–4 June 1989*, Comm. NS, 6 (Stockholm and London, 1990), 11–24; the situation as relevant to Man is discussed in Bornholdt Collins, 'Viking-Age Coin Finds from the Isle of Man', 320–29. Archibald observes that the practice of testing coins was never as widespread in Britain and Ireland as it was in Scandinavia in the later tenth and eleventh centuries, but low level testing spanned a much broader period. While pecking was at its height from the end of the ninth century until the 920s, when random samples and exotic coins were chosen for testing, a strong tendency for bending is apparent in finds of the mid-tenth century from Scandinavian spheres around Britain and Ireland, and a general increase in the practice is observed in English finds during the eleventh century; in other words, testing the quality of silver coins through bending was not incompatible with a coin-using mentality and monetary economy, but at times can be shown to be a feature of it. See now M. Archibald, 'Testing', in Graham-Campbell, *Cuerdale Hoard*, 51–64.

[60]   Archibald notes that the practice of bending is still evident in English finds, although less prevalent, as late as the first half of the twelfth century ('Pecking and bending', 20–21).

times. The total includes four with probable tooth- or clamp-marks, which is a convenient demonstration of the fact that the bending was intentional and not part of natural post-depositional processes. This is further reinforced by the fact that the assemblage was protected by its lead container, and so the coins were necessarily deposited here in their bent state. The rate of bending is fairly consistent across the different components of hoard: no one currency seems to have been treated as more suspect than another.

Figure 22.5   Scandinavian   imitation   of   Æthelred's   *Long   Cross*   type (Glenfaba hoard).

The practice of pecking coins shows a fundamental concern both for forgeries and for intrinsic value, which might be seen as more consistent with a bullion mentality, but its prevalence in eleventh-century Scandinavia demonstrates that it also accompanied movement towards a coin-using economy, and it is evidence in itself that pecked coins still circulated whole rather than being chopped into random fractions. In Glenfaba there are 31 coins with peck-marks (6–7 per cent), most with one or maybe two marks only, and the highest proportion of these are, as one would expect, among the coins that were in circulation the longest, the Anglo-Saxon pennies, with the oldest coin bearing the most pecks of all (11 in total). This is more than any other eleventh-century coin from a secure British or Irish context, and one wonders if perhaps the Anglo-Saxon coins with multiple peck-marks had travelled via Scandinavia and entered the hoard as a parcel. Interestingly, the coins struck closest to 'home', the Manx series and the *Quatrefoil* and other imitations, are entirely peck-mark free: a possible measure of their general acceptance unlike more suspect foreign coins? The Scandinavian imitation, by contrast, is riddled with peck-marks, but here one assumes it is from having previously circulated in Scandinavian markets, where pecking practices varied greatly,[61] but were in some cases so extensive that it is still used as a diagnostic feature for broadly distinguishing Scandinavian-provenanced finds from those discovered in Britain and Ireland. It is striking to see this much evidence of pecking in an Irish Sea hoard, even if it seems insignificant compared with some eleventh-century Scandinavian/Baltic hoards.

---

[61]   S.H. Gullbekk, 'Some aspects of coin import to Norway and coin circulation in the late Viking Age', *NNÅ* 1991, 63–87.

The evidence of Glenfaba does bring this method of provenancing into question somewhat, although the fact remains that where pecking occurs, in contrast to many (but not all) peck-marked coins from Scandinavian contexts, it is usually in the form of a single peck-mark only. Nevertheless, it seems that one must now acknowledge a greater level of ambiguity in attempting to provenance a coin that has undergone this form of secondary treatment.

It is interesting to compare the Glenfaba results with the rest of the collection at the Manx Museum in Douglas (approximately 500 coins), where there are only eight coins in total (from four hoards) with peck-marks, or less than 2 per cent of the Manx Museum collection.[62] The rate of bending is much higher, and is observed in about one-fifth of the collection. Both practices are observed in the Glenfaba hoard at a much higher rate than expected, providing a strong sense that the material was particularly well-circulated, comparatively speaking, before being deposited.

Does this mean that coins in the Irish Sea passed through fewer hands because there are fewer marks, i.e. they were circulating at a lower rate? This is easily answered in the negative by the extreme diversity of currencies, coin types, varieties and mints observed, which together demonstrate rapid circulation in the giant mixing bowl of the Irish Sea. Pecking coins was a natural extension of the practice in Scandinavia, and where Scandinavians travelled and traded we are likely to see at least occasional pecking. We may even go so far as to suggest that the compiler of the Glenfaba hoard had to have had a more direct connection with Scandinavia to have acquired both the Scandinavian imitation and subjected the material to this kind of treatment beyond the local norm. It is important to note, thanks to the evidence of this large new find, that low-level pecking appears also to have been practised by traders in the Irish Sea region, although bending was clearly the preferred method of assessing silver quality.

Importantly, a discrepancy is observed between the extent of treatment in the Glenfaba coins versus that of the bullion, which Professor James Graham-Campbell observes has undergone only minimal circulation (see below). Could this paradox be a clue as to the secondary role of bullion by the first decades of the eleventh century, a supplement to coinage, which was after all readily available for smaller transactions? It may in this case mark a natural step in a general move towards coin use and acceptance. If bullion was saved for particular kinds of transactions, especially larger and less common ones, it might make sense that it circulated at a lower rate and presumably changed hands less often, and therefore bears fewer physical signs of circulation.

---

[62]   Bornholdt Collins, 'Viking-Age Coin Finds from the Isle of Man', 324.

The Glenfaba Hoard: Non-Numismatic Content *by James Graham-Campbell*

The bullion component of the eleventh-century silver hoard from Glenfaba, Isle of Man, consists of one arm-ring and 25 complete or fragmentary ingots. The weight of this non-numismatic material amounts to *c*.830 g, representing some 60 per cent of the total weight of the hoard (1.39 kg). The rather low frequency of fragmentation of the ingots, combined with the limited extent of their testing (as described and discussed below), suggests that the owner of the hoard may, in this respect, have been as much concerned with silver storage as its circulation. In other words, it may be suggested that the bullion had a more limited role to play in the economy of the period than the coins, given their evidence for some degree of significant circulation, as described and discussed above by Bornholdt Collins.

The quantity of ingots in the Glenfaba hoard is notable in a Manx context, given that only one ingot was previously known for certain from a Viking-Age hoard: the single small example from Ballaquayle (Douglas), deposited *c*.970.[63] It has been suggested, however, that the Chester (1950) hoard, which has many similarities to the Ballaquayle hoard, might have been the property of a merchant from Man.[64] The hack-silver cut from ornaments in the Chester (1950) hoard relates closely to that in Ballaquayle, but the greater part of its non-numismatic silver was in the form of (at least) 98 ingots; it was, however, deposited *c*.965 – some 60 or more years before Glenfaba.

It has hitherto been supposed that most non-numismatic silver in Man, during the later tenth to mid-eleventh century, was stored in the form of the type of plain arm-ring, known as 'ring-money', as was current in Scandinavian

---

[63]   Graham-Campbell, 'The Viking-age silver hoards of the Isle of Man', 75, no. 5.4419, Figure 9; Graham-Campbell, *Cuerdale Hoard*, 251, no. 13.20, pl. 76. Two stray finds of silver ingots, most probably of Viking-age date, have been metal detected in recent years from different locations in Man, one in the north of the Island and the other in the south (*pers. comm.* Allison Fox).

[64]   Graham-Campbell, 'Viking-age silver hoards of the Isle of Man', 69–70; Graham-Campbell, *Cuerdale Hoard*, 11–13, Figure 1.12; Wilson, *The Vikings in the Isle of Man*, 110–11. On the other hand, there are also major differences between the near contemporary hoards, and Bornholdt Collins, 'Viking-Age Coin Finds from the Isle of Man', 271 and 294–5 and tables 5.10 and 6.5, shows that the mint structure of the numismatic element is unique, and not drawn directly from the contemporary Manx, Irish or Scottish currency pools, or from a well-circulated general 'Irish Sea' stock, but rather appears to have been a composite, gradual accumulation of a Chester-based 'Irish Sea' merchant who traded both locally and in and around the Irish Sea over an extended period (elements within the hoard are therefore likely to have been acquired in Man, but the hoard itself was not assembled there).

Scotland at this period.[65] 'Ring-money' not only features prominently in the Ballaquayle hoard,[66] but is also present in the coin-dated hoards from West Nappin (*c*.1045) and Kirk Michael [2] 1972/5 (*c*.1065), and it is probable that the lost 'silver bracelets' from the Kirk Andreas 1874 hoard, deposited *c*.1045, will have been further examples.[67] In addition, there is the nineteenth-century discovery of a coinless hoard of four such rings;[68] this is of unknown provenance, although it has tentatively been suggested that it might have been found at Balladoole.[69]

The Arm-Ring

The Glenfaba plaited (six-rod) silver arm-ring (IOMMM: 2004–0123/490), with its lozenge-shaped linking-plate simply decorated with punched dots (Appendix, cat. no. 1; Colour Plate 22.3a–c), is a fine example of its kind. The break, at one end adjacent to the terminal, does not appear to be the result of wear and tear and could therefore have been deliberate (see below). The ring itself is well paralleled by a pair of plaited (six-rod) silver arm-rings which together constitute a coinless hoard from Ireland, now in the British Museum. These likewise have their ends fused into lozenge-shaped linking-plates, one of which is decorated with a border of punched dots.[70] Plaited-rod silver arm-rings are otherwise rare in the Viking-Age silver hoards of Britain and Ireland.[71] An earlier version of a plaited silver arm-ring from the Cuerdale hoard, Lancashire (deposited *c*.905–10), is of simpler (four-rod) construction, with the ends of the rods fused together and closed with a simple twist.[72] On the other hand, a single find of a gold arm-ring from Oxna, Shetland, which is likewise a four-rod plait, has a plain lozenge-shaped linking-plate.[73]

The form of such plaited arm-rings was used on a reduced scale for the manufacture of finger-rings, particularly in gold, as demonstrated by the elaborate example in the Greeba hoard.[74] Gold finger-rings more akin to the

---

[65]   Graham-Campbell and Sheehan, 'Viking-age silver hoard of "ring money"'.

[66]   Graham-Campbell, 'Viking-Age silver hoards of the Isle of Man', 74–5, no. 5, figs. 8–9; Graham-Campbell, *Cuerdale Hoard*, 250–53, no. 13, pls. 73 and 75–6.

[67]   Graham-Campbell, 'Viking-age silver hoards of the Isle of Man', 76, nos. 9–10 and 14, Figure 4.

[68]   Ibid., 76, no. 18, Figure 6.

[69]   Graham-Campbell and Sheehan, 'Viking-age silver hoard of "ring money"'.

[70]   Graham-Campbell, *Cuerdale Hoard*, 247, no. 11, pl. 70.

[71]   Ibid., 100–101.

[72]   Ibid., 211, no. 1: 696, cat. Figure 3, pl. 35.

[73]   Graham-Campbell, *Viking-Age Gold and Silver of Scotland*, 158–9 [S11], pl. 72, a–b.

[74]   M. Cubbon, 'A Viking-age plaited gold finger-ring from Greeba, Isle of Man', *Proceedings of the Isle of Man Natural History and Antiquarian Society*, 11, no. 2 (2003 for 1999–2000), 249–

Glenfaba arm-ring, being plaited from six rods, include fine examples from Oxford and Waterford,[75] both of which are single finds, and one in the coin hoard from Soberton, Hampshire, deposited c.1068.[76] Closer still in form to the Glenfaba arm-ring, because of being six-rod plaits with lozenge-shaped linking-plates, are three gold finger-rings which formed part of coinless hoards found in Scandinavian Scotland: from the Hebrides;[77] Stenness, Orkney;[78] and Iona (St Ronan's Church), Argyll.[79] The linking-plates on the finger-rings from both the Hebrides (North Uist?) and Orkney are decorated with punched dots,[80] in the manner of the Glenfaba arm-ring.

The Ingots

The majority of the 25 Glenfaba ingots (IOMMM: 2004–0123/465–489; see Figure 22.6) are of standard Viking-Age type in their oblong form and rounded terminals, although they vary considerably in size (cat. nos. 2–26); however, one is of rectangular shape (no. 8) and another is distinctive in being a small ovoid disc, hammered flat from a 'pellet' (no. 7). This is the latest occurrence of this particular type of small ingot known from a hoard in Britain or Ireland, others forming part of several tenth-century hoards deposited up until the 980s.[81] It is notable that six of the Chester (1950) ingots are of this form.[82]

Secondary treatment in the manufacture of the Glenfaba ingots is confined to hammering,[83] but in only three examples, including the ovoid ingot discussed above.

Silver Content

The estimated silver content of the bullion is uniformly high (83–100 per cent), with the exception of one ingot terminal fragment which is of surprisingly low fineness, at only 39 per cent. Indeed, the great majority of the items (22 of 26)

57; Wilson, *Vikings in the Isle of Man*, 114–15, Figure 54; Graham-Campbell, *Cuerdale Hoard*, 14, Figure 1.16.

[75] Graham-Campbell, *Cuerdale Hoard*, 260, no. 29, 262, no. 35, cat. figs. 44–5, pls. 82–3.

[76] Ibid., 243, no. 7:1, pl. 82.

[77] Graham-Campbell, *Viking-Age Gold and Silver of Scotland*, 127–9 [25.3], pl. 50, a.

[78] Ibid., 130–31 [27.2], pl. 50, b.

[79] Ibid., 166–7 [U7], pl. 73, k.

[80] Ibid., figs. 52–3.

[81] S. Kruse and J. Graham-Campbell, 'Classification and discussion of the objects in the Cuerdale hoard, Part 1: Ingots', in Graham-Campbell, *Cuerdale Hoard*, 73–86, at 83–4.

[82] G. Webster, 'A Saxon treasure hoard found at Chester', *Antiquaries Journal, 33* (1953), 22–32, at 29, nos. 41–6, pl. IX, b.

[83] Kruse and Graham-Campbell, 'Classification and discussion', 79–80.

fall within the estimated range of 87–97 per cent silver, with just three below it (and one above). The piece with by far the lowest silver content (39 per cent) is one end of a hammered ingot (no. 17); this, despite having been cut through, has not been subjected to any nicking. It is worth noting that good quality silver (91 per cent) was, not surprisingly, selected for the manufacture of the arm-ring by means of plaiting.[84]

Testing

As already observed, the arm-ring has not been subjected to any testing, being in excellent condition, other than having been broken in one place – and thus not deliberately severed with a view to further fragmentation for circulation in the form of hack-silver. This breakage might just be damage, but it could well have been deliberate with the intention of reducing the size of the ring (by coiling) for the purpose of storage.

It is notable that only 4 of the 25 ingots have been tested, of which one is complete (no. 9). On the other hand, 3 of the 13 ingots which have been cut up – presumably for use in circulation – are nicked, demonstrating that testing still had a role to play in commercial transactions involving bullion (presumably in the Irish Sea region) during the early part of the eleventh century. This does, however, accord with the secondary treatment of about half the Glenfaba coins, as described above by Bornholdt Collins (pp. 500–502).

Two ingot fragments have a couple of nicks each (nos. 18 and 26) which, it has been suggested,[85] was a standard practice in a single transaction. The remaining ingot fragment to have been tested has just three nicks – in contrast to a couple of pieces of hack-silver deposited more than a century earlier, in the Cuerdale hoard, Lancashire (*c*.905–10), which both have over 30 nicks, although such intensity is exceptional.[86] On the other hand, the division and/or testing of the two ingots cut at both ends (nos. 25–6) gives the appearance of having been carried out not long before deposition.

Weights and Fragmentation

There does not appear to have been much regard for weight standardisation in the manufacture of the 12 complete ingots in the Glenfaba hoard, with only two of them perhaps targeting a weight of about 1 oz and one of 2 oz, if a Viking-Age silversmith's target of 1 oz in the Irish Sea region is taken to be in the region of

---

[84]   Graham-Campbell, *Cuerdale Hoard*, 101.

[85]   Kruse and Graham-Campbell, 'Classification and discussion', 79.

[86]   Ibid., 78–9, Figure 4.5.

25 to 26 g, with Patrick Wallace proposing a 'Dublin unit' of about 26.6 g:[87] 1 oz: 24.61 and 26.93 g (nos. 10 and 6); 2 oz: 51.37 g (no. 8).

As already noted, 13 of the 25 Glenfaba ingots have been cut (*c.*50 per cent), which is a lesser proportion than in the Chester (1950) hoard, in which over three-quarters of the ingots were divided.[88] This fragmentation reduced one of the Glenfaba ingots to a '1 oz' unit (no. 21: 25.84 g), another to about a half (no. 17: 12.33 g) and a third to approximately a quarter (no. 16: 6.55 g), but such seems unlikely to be of any real significance.

Concluding Remarks *by Kristin Bornholdt Collins*

Finally, it is perhaps instructive to contemplate what a treasure like that from Glenfaba might have been worth in its day, which is possible, at least as a very rough calculation, based upon a tenth-century lawcode of Athelstan, which states that the compensation price for a sheep was five pennies.[89] In terms of weight, the Glenfaba coins weigh *c.*558 g, which with the bullion, as noted above by Graham-Campbell, makes a total weight of 1.39 kg. This is equivalent to something in the region of 1,078 pennies if it had consisted solely of coins from the start of the Dublin coinage's Phase II.[90] If the tenth-century value of an English sheep was anything near that in the eleventh and in a non-English context, the silver would have bought somewhere between 200 and 250 sheep (and, for example, even a small ingot such as no. 9, Appendix, had the value of four or five sheep). If a sheep is worth about £50–£100 by today's standards, then one can regard the total value of the Glenfaba hoard as something over £10,000, and perhaps nearer £20,000. Obviously, this does not claim to be an

---

[87] The problems related to establishing Viking-Age weight-units for ingots and ornaments in Britain and Ireland have recently been reviewed in Kruse and Graham-Campbell, 'Classification and discussion', 75–8, and by J. Sheehan, 'The Huxley hoard and Hiberno-Scandinavian arm-rings', in *The Huxley Viking Hoard: Scandinavian Settlement in the North West*, ed. J. Graham-Campbell and R. Philpott (Liverpool, 2009), 58–69, at 67–8; but see now P.F. Wallace, 'Weights and weight systems in Viking Age Ireland', in *Early Medieval Art and Archaeology in the Northern World: Studies in Honour of James Graham-Campbell*, ed. A. Reynolds and L. Webster (Leiden, 2013), 301–16.

[88] A total of 23 of the 98 ingots known from the Chester (1950) hoard are complete, the exact number being somewhat uncertain because a second parcel of ingots from the find was only delivered up to the Grosvenor Museum in 1975 (Graham-Campbell, *Cuerdale Hoard*, 11–13).

[89] VI Athelstan 6.2 in *EHD* 1, 424 (no. 37).

[90] 1390 g divided by *c.*1.29 g (average weight of penny in Dublin at start of Phase II) = 1,078 pennies, divided by 5 pennies (cost of a sheep) = *c.*215 sheep; or, 1.06 g = average weight of Anglo-Saxon penny *c.*1020 = 1,311 pennies divided by 5 = 262 sheep; based on weights in Blackburn, 'Dublin Coinage', 125, table 4 (*VCCBI*, 105).

exact conversion, but it is helpful to remember that the hoard is not just a market purse, but a sizeable fortune.

The Glenfaba hoard represents a gradual accumulation of wealth, substantial savings that were added to at different points in time, albeit within a relatively short window of a decade or so. This helps to explain the extreme diversity of content and die-linking patterns. Still, it is generally representative of what was circulating in Man in the 1020s and up to *c.*1030, and is both a reflection of the far-flung mercantile interests of its owner and further evidence of the complex economy that thrived in this location. Indeed, if nothing else, the eclectic nature of the Glenfaba material – seen in the context of other finds – reveals that Man was a vibrant hub for Irish Sea trade, which arrived from every direction of the compass, beginning in the mid-tenth century and continuing throughout the eleventh century. That the hoard provides new evidence and insights into the earliest stages of the Hiberno-Manx coinage, and a possible new origin for the imitative 'Irish Sea' *Quatrefoil* series, are particular bonuses, and the rich material will continue to bear fruit and inspire for years to come. Its most promising area for future work will be the development of our understanding of Dublin's Phase II coinage, which flourished – as spectacularly demonstrated by this find – in the 1020s.

Appendix: Overview of the Find and Detailed Catalogue of the Non-Numismatic Silver in the Glenfaba (2003) Hoard, c.1030

A mixed hoard comprising 464 coins, 25 cut and whole ingots and a heavy plaited silver arm-ring with a decorated linking-plate, as well as fragments of the lead container in which the assemblage was deposited. Full details for the coins will be published in *Manx Museum, Douglas: Anglo-Saxon, Hiberno-Scandinavian, Hiberno-Manx and other Coins to 1280, SCBI*, for The British Academy (Oxford, forthcoming), and can be summarised as follows:

Coins *by Kristin Bornholdt Collins*

Accession nos.: IOMMM: 2004–0123/1 to 464

Anglo-Saxon	**79**
ÆTHELRED II (978–1016)	70
*Crux c.*991–7, Wallingford: Ælfric.	1
*Long Cross c.*997–1003, Canterbury: Eadwold, Leofric, Leofstan; Chester: Elfnoð, Swegen; Dover: Leofhyse; Exeter: Edric, God; Gloucester: Leofsige; Huntingdon: Osgut; Lewes: Leofwine; Lincoln: Colgrim, Osgut; London: Ælfwine, Eadwold, Godman, Godwine (2), Leofstan, Lyfinc, Swetinc, Wulfwine (2); Northampton: Æðelnoð; Norwich: Ælfric; Warwick: Aðestan; Stamford: Cristin, Godleof, Swertgar (2); Watchet: Hunewine; Wilton: Leofwine; Winchester: Byrhtwold, Godwine.	34
*Helmet c.*1003–9, Cambridge: Cnit; Chester: Ælfstan, Ælfnoð (2), Swegen; Lincoln: Ulfcetel; London: Ælfwine, Leofwine; Wallingford: Ælfwold; York: Wulfsige.	10
*Last Small Cross c.*1009–16, Barnstaple: Huniga; Chester: Ælfnoð, Swartinc (2), Ðurradi; Dover: Godmann; Exeter: Æðestan (2), Carla, Eatstan, Wulfsige; Lincoln: Oðgrim; London: Elfric, Ælfwerd; Norwich: Hwataman; Salisbury: Sæman; Thetford: Wælgist; Wallingford: Edwig, Leofestan; Winchester: Burhstan, Cina, Seolca; Worcester: Leofgod (2); York: Dahfin.	25
CNUT (1016–35)	9
*Quatrefoil c.*1017–23, Bath: Ælfric; Cambridge: Ceht; Chester: Leofwine, Trotan (or Twotan?); Cricklade: Æðelwine; Dover: Eadwine; London: Æðelsig; Winchester: Ælfstan; York: Gunhwat.	9

Hiberno-Scandinavian   **326**

Phase I   20

Phase II   306

Hiberno-Manx   **42**

TD ('Transfer die')   30

HM 1   12

Scandinavian-'Irish Sea'   **16**

'Irish Sea' *Quatrefoil* type   11

Imitative Phase II/*Long Cross* type, minting place(s) unknown   5

Scandinavian   **1**

Imitation of Æthelred's *Long Cross*, 'York': 'Leofstan', possibly struck at Lund.   1

Figure 22.6   Complete ingots (nos. 2–13) and fragments (nos. 14–26) from
the Glenfaba hoard, by row: 2–3; 4; 5; 6–8; 9–10; 11; 12–13;
14–17; 18–19; 20–22; 23–6 (for further details see the catalogue
on pp. 512–14).

Catalogue of the Non-Numismatic Silver in the Glenfaba Hoard *by James Graham-Campbell*

Accession nos: IOMMM: 2004–0123/465–490; illustrated in Figure 22.6 and Colour Plate 22.3

Abbreviations: D = diameter; H = height; L = length; W = width; Wt = weight.

Note: The estimated silver content was assessed by Kim Holland (Higher Scientific Officer, Isle of Man Government), using the Archimedes principle to establish specific gravity which, in turn, gave a range of silver concentration. All other measurements were kindly provided by Manx National Heritage staff.

1. *Annular arm-ring* (IOMMM: 2004–0123/490), formed from six plaited silver rods which taper (D 2.2–1.9 mm) to a lozenge-shaped linking-plate (L 7.6 mm), with a border of punched dots. The plate is broken across at one end so that the ring might be tightly coiled; it is otherwise in excellent condition, with no apparent nicking. Nicks: 0. D 57.0 mm. Wt 53.68 g. Estimated silver: 91 %

See Colour Plate 22.3.

2. *Ingot* (472); small oblong, of D-shaped section, with rounded ends. Nicks: 0. L 45.4; W 7.5; H 6.4 mm. Wt 16.86 g. Estimated silver: 89 %

3. *Ingot* (474); small oblong, of sub-triangular section, with rounded ends (slightly pointed). Nicks: 0. L 42.4; W 6.7; H 6.1 mm. Wt 9.85 g. Estimated silver: 90 %

4. *Ingot* (475); oblong, of sub-rectangular section, with one rounded and one misshapen (beaked) end. Nicks: 0. L 70.8; W 14.4; H 8.3 mm. Wt 61.02 g. Estimated silver: 91 %

5. *Ingot* (476); long narrow ('pencil' shaped), of sub-rectangular section, with rounded ends. Nicks: 0. L 120.8; W 9.1; H 8.8 mm. Wt 67.09 g. Estimated silver: 88 %

6. *Ingot* (479); oblong, of D-shaped section, with one rounded and one pointed/angled end. Nicks: 0. L 57.8; W 9.0; H 7.2 mm. Wt 26.93 g. Estimated silver: 89 %

7. *Ingot* (481); thick ovoid disc, hammered from a 'pellet' on both its main faces and some sides. Nicks: 0. D 12.0 x 10.0; H 4.7 mm. Wt 4.09 g. Estimated silver: 97 %

8. *Ingot* (483); rectangular, of rectangular section, with rectangular ends (one slightly rounded). Nicks: 0. L 49.3; W 15.5; H 9.3 mm. Wt 51.37 g. Estimated silver: 86 %

9. *Ingot* (485); oblong, of sub-triangular section, with rounded ends. There is one (substantial) nick/slice across one angle. Nicks: 1. L 56.5; W 9.9; H 8.4 mm. Wt 28.03 g. Estimated silver: 91 %

10. *Ingot* (486); oblong, of sub-rectangular section, with rounded ends. Nicks: 0. L 55.0; W 9.9; H 6.9 mm. Wt 24.61 g. Estimated silver: 88 %

11. *Ingot* (487); long narrow ('pencil' shaped), of D-shaped section, with rounded ends. Nicks: 0. L 106.1; W 11.7; H 8.8 mm. Wt 70.63 g. Estimated silver: 87 %

12. *Ingot* (488); long narrow, with parallel sides, of high triangular section, with rounded ends. Nicks: 0. L 75.9; W 8.0; H 13.2 mm. Wt 48.85 g. Estimated silver: 83 %

13. *Ingot* (489); oblong, of sub-triangular section, with rounded ends. Nicks: 0. L 58.2; W 11.0; H 8.6 mm. Wt 35.43 g. Estimated silver: 84 %

14. *Ingot terminal fragment* (465); rounded end, of ovoid section, cut and broken. Nicks: 0. L 17.0; W 10.9; H 9.7 mm. Wt 11.83 g. Estimated silver: 95 %

15. *Ingot terminal fragment* (467); rounded end, of lop-sided sub-rectangular section, cut and broken from a narrow oblong. Nicks: 0. L 38.0; W 8.4; H 6.0 mm. Wt 14.94 g. Estimated silver: 87 %

16. *Ingot terminal fragment* (468); rounded end, severed from a narrow oblong ingot of rectangular section, having been hammered on all four faces. Nicks: 0. L 26.7; W 6.3; H 5.0 mm. Wt 6.55 g. Estimated silver: 93 %

17. *Ingot terminal fragment* (469); rounded end, severed from a narrow oblong ingot of rectangular section, having been hammered on its two side faces. Nicks: 0. L 31.5; W 7.5; H 6.2 mm. Wt 12.33 g. Estimated silver: 39 %

18. *Ingot terminal fragment* (470); rounded end, of sub-rectangular section, cut and broken from an oblong. There are two fresh nicks, made from opposite directions on the opposite angles of the same side. Nicks: 2 (a pair). L 45.5; W 12.1; H 7.6 mm. Wt 32.31 g. Estimated silver: 90 %

19. *Ingot terminal fragment* (473); rounded end, of ovoid section, clean cut from an oblong. Nicks: 0. L 54.1; W 10.3; H 7.3 mm. Wt 30.57 g. Estimated silver: 87 %

20. *Ingot terminal fragment* (477); rounded end, of ovoid section, cut and broken from an oblong. Nicks: 0. L 49.8; W 10.7; H 6.0 mm. Wt 23.50 g. Estimated silver: 91 %

21. *Ingot terminal fragment* (478); rounded end, of sub-rectangular section, cut and broke from an oblong. Nicks: 0. L 32.9; W 11.1; H 9.9 mm. Wt 25.84 g. Estimated silver: 89 %

22. *Ingot terminal fragment* (480); tapered rounded end, of sub-rectangular section, cut and broken from what would have been a substantial ingot. A slice from one angle of the terminal has removed most traces of a pair of nicks. Nicks: 3. L 43.5; W 18.2; H 13.4 mm. Wt 58.63 g. Estimated silver: 90 %

23. *Ingot terminal fragment* (482); sub-rectangular end, of sub-rectangular section, clean cut. Nicks: 0. L 46.5; W 9.4; H 8.2 mm. Wt 27.74 g. Estimated silver: 93 %

24. *Ingot terminal fragment* (484); rounded end, of sub-rectangular section, cut and broken. Nicks: 0. L 54.3; W 17.4; H 10.4 mm. Wt 67.58 g. Estimated silver: 93 %

25. *Ingot fragment* (466); freshly cut and broken at both ends, from an oblong ingot of sub-rectangular section. In excellent condition, with no nicking. Nicks: 0. L 13.9; W 11.2; H 8.5 mm. Wt 11.83 g. Estimated silver: 87 %

26. *Ingot fragment* (471); cut and broken at both ends, from different directions, from an oblong ingot of flat ovoid section. There are two fresh nicks, on one side angle and one cut edge. Nicks: 2. L 15.2; W 14.5; H 6.8 mm. Wt 11.56 g. Estimated silver: 100 %

Chapter 23

Insular Imitations of Æthelred II's
Long Cross Coinage

Joe Leighton and Andrew R. Woods*

Æthelred II's (978–1016) *Long Cross* coinage was among the most influential across the northern world. Very large numbers of these coins survive, a testament to the numbers struck and transported to Scandinavia and beyond. The success of the coinage is also attested by its imitation; both Dublin and Scandinavia copied the *Long Cross* design soon after its inception. Discerning between the regular and various imitative series has often proved a challenge; style, mint and moneyer-name were all copied by skilful die-cutters. Indeed, *Long Cross* dies were occasionally transported between official and imitative mints.[1] Mark Blackburn made an important contribution to this subject, suggesting that style could not be the only determining factor in the attribution of coins to English, Irish or Scandinavian series. In 1981, he suggested that a number of 'Chester' coins which had been previously attributed to Dublin but had no die-link into the Hiberno-Scandinavian series should be reconsidered, citing their presence in the Shaftesbury hoard.[2] This chapter presents an interpretation of these pieces. It suggests that they should be viewed as 'Insular imitations' and can be investigated

  * The authors would like to thank a number of people for the help in the preparation of this article. Stewart Lyon, Bo Gunnarsson and William Lean have read and offered advice on drafts. They have improved it immensely, even if not all of them will agree with its conclusions. Kenneth Jonsson has provided details of a number of Swedish coins which have made the corpus much more complete. Dr. A.J.P. Campbell loaned coins from his collection at an early stage. Lastly, thanks are due to Mark Blackburn for providing advice and encouragement. He truly was the catalyst behind this study.

[1] M. Blackburn, 'An imitative workshop active during Æthelræd II's Long Cross issue', in *Studies in Northern Coinages of the 11th Century*, ed. C. J. Becker (Copenhagen, 1981), 29–88; B. Gunnarsson, 'Den gäckande kedja 105 – Spåret av en Vikingatida myntunion?', in *Samlad Glädje 2009*, ed. C. Ekström and K. Bengtsson (Uppsala, 2009), 71–90.

[2] Blackburn, 'Imitative Workshop', 59. A.J.H. Gunstone, *SCBI 17: Midland Museums. Ancient British, Anglo-Saxon and Norman Coins* (London, 1977), no. 517.

and analysed in many of the same ways as the 'Irish Sea' *Quatrefoil* imitations that were the subject of Blackburn's analysis in 1996 and which he revisited in 2011.[3]

The Imitative Group

It has been proposed that during the *Long Cross* coinage there existed die-cutting 'schools' or centres, which were probably located at the main political and commercial sites within England. Early dies are postulated to have been issued by two centres, Winchester and London, with the latter producing the 'National' style. Further development of styles would indicate that local die-cutting centres opened within a fairly short time of the institution of the issue.[4] That imitation occurred outside this system has long been recognised. Pirie, Dolley and Talvio all noted coins which name Chester but appear to be struck from unusual, or imitative, dies.[5] Blackburn crystallised this issue, arguing that whilst the coins were stylistically different from the English norm they could not be simply attributed to Scandinavia or Dublin as had been the case previously.[6] The authors have assembled a grouping of these stylistically related coins, which will be referred to as 'Insular imitations' for ease of description. This listing is probably not exhaustive; a thorough combing of the Swedish hoards may well uncover further coins and other related dies. The coins are listed in the Appendix below where they are divided into three groups. Coins of the first group are given a prefix G1, the second G2 and the third G3. The groups are classed according to their likelihood of belonging to the Insular imitative mint, Group 1 being the most likely and Group 3 the least. The following will focus primarily upon Group 1 where most coins name Chester as their place of striking but a minority name Bath. In the course of discussing Groups 2 and 3 coins from dies naming Lincoln, Dublin and Winchester are also identified. The coins within each group were struck by an array of different 'moneyers', but can be connected through a number of common stylistic features.

---

[3]   M. Blackburn, 'Hiberno-Norse and Irish Sea imitations of Cnut's Quatrefoil issue', *BNJ*, 66 (1996), 1–20, and 'Supplements to the articles 2011', in his *Viking Coinage and Currency in the British Isles* (London, 2011), 384–90.

[4]   Blackburn, 'Imitative workshop', 38. However see T. Talvio, 'Stylistic analyses in Anglo-Saxon numismatics: some observations on the Long Cross type of Æthelræd II', in *Sigtuna Papers: Proceedings of the Sigtuna Symposium on Viking-Age Coinage, 1–4 June 1989*, eds. K. Jonsson and B. Malmer (London, 1990), 327–30.

[5]   E.J.E. Pirie, *SCBI 5: Grosvenor Museum, Chester. Coins with the Chester Mint-Signature* (London, 1964); M. Dolley, *SCBI 8: Hiberno-Norse Coins in the British Museum* (London, 1966), no. 38; G. Galster, M. Dolley and J. Steen Jensen, *SCBI 22: Royal Collection of Coins and Medals National Museum Copenhagen. Part V: Hiberno-Norse and Anglo-Irish Coins* (London, 1975), no. 27.

[6]   Blackburn, 'Imitative workshop'.

Utilising style as a means of determining where coins were struck can be problematic, as there can be both enormous consistency and great variability of styles depending upon when and where a die was cut. In the following description of the style of the Insular pieces, it is important to note that not all coins have every stylistic feature and that some features may not be unique to Insular imitative dies. It is the combination of features, along with the evidence of die axes and metrology discussed below, which is key to their constitution as a coherent group.

Figure 23.1   Line drawing of Insular *Long Cross* Imitation.

The style of the coins, summarised in Table 23.1 and illustrated in Figure 23.1, is reasonably distinctive and has been used to differentiate the imitative series from other *Long Cross* coins. The alignment of the initial crosses in both obverse and reverse legends is an unusual feature. The vertical of the initial cross, in the obverse legend, is aligned with the foremost vertical fold of the king's drapery. On the reverse, the vertical limb of the initial cross is generally aligned with the long cross rather than with the verticals of the lettering. This gives the impression of misalignment of the legend in the first quarter.

Table 23.1   Stylistic features of Insular Imitations.

Obverse	Reverse
Initial cross aligned with drapery	Initial cross aligned with *Long Cross* rather than legend
Straight line connecting chin and brooch	Subtly misaligned *Long Cross*
Closely spaced hair	Legend in straight lines rather than as radii from centre

The legends themselves are generally rendered in a small, neat fashion whilst showing a slight blundering of the ethnic on the obverse. There are also occasional features, such as + in RE+[7] and the terminal letter in the

---

[7]   Visible on obverse dies *D* and *E*.

king's name is sometimes rendered 5, which would not be out of place on a Hiberno-Scandinavian coin.[8] The use of lO5 within the moneyers' names is also a common Hiberno-Scandinavian feature.[9] The reverse legends display a reasonable degree of literacy, but with occasional lapses that might indicate a lack of familiarity with Anglo-Saxon name-forms. The rendering of the mint-names also diverges from the abbreviations used by the regular English coinage. The unusual rendering of Chester – LG or LIE – is unknown from official English Chester dies.[10] The alignment of the letters is also unusual as they are not arranged with their verticals as if on the radii of a circle – as seen on the regular English and Dublin coinages – but rather as though the die-cutter had punched the letters in each quarter of his dies separately. The lower edge of the letters follows a relatively straight line, giving the lettering an appearance of unequal heights. The impression that the reverse dies were cut as individual quarters is reinforced by the subtle misalignment of the limbs of the long cross.

There is a greater degree of variation in the style of bust than with other elements of the obverse, but there are a number of common characteristics.[11] The front of the king's neck is represented by a rather prominent straight line connecting the cloak's brooch directly to the pellet at the point of the chin. With the English 'National' dies this line generally terminates just behind the chin pellet, making the point of the chin appear slightly forward of the neck. Furthermore, the curve of the nape of the King's neck and his back on the Insular imitations is straighter than is usually found on English 'National' dies.[12] This emphasises the folds of the cloak, which lack the natural appearance of the disappearing curve around the king's back, as visible on official English dies. It would seem that the die-cutter was imitating Winchester-style obverse dies. These differ from the norm found at Chester, where nearly all regular coins are struck from National dies.

There appears a degree of variability within the grouping: Dies *B* and *C* below have a similarity to 'Winchester' dies, with the king's head finely rendered and with a smaller, slightly taller bust. However, unlike true 'Winchester' obverse dies, the imitative series shows the ear as the centre point of the obverse die, whereas official dies usually have a point on the cheek as the central referent.[13] Other obverses show the king's features in a more angular fashion, more closely

---

[8]   Visible on obverse dies *A, D, F, G, H* and *I.*

[9]   M. Dolley, 'An unexpected "mint" in the Hiberno-Norse imitative series', *NCirc, 81* (1973), 44.

[10]   LIE is not recorded in J. Carrol and D.N. Parsons, *Anglo-Saxon Mint Names I. Axbridge to Hythe* (Nottingham, 2007). Lè is recorded but the coin is likely to be an Insular imitation.

[11]   Talvio, 'Stylistic analyses', 327–30.

[12]   For example, G. Galster, *SCBI 7: Royal Collection, Copenhagen. Part II* (London, 1966), no. 470. Cf. Talvio, 'Stylistic analyses', 328, Figure 2.

[13]   Talvio, 'Stylistic analyses', 329.

related to Hiberno-Scandinavian *Long Cross* obverses. Obverse die *E* is quite crude in comparison to others but still has the same angular features as other busts in the series. Die *F* also shows a slight variation in the treatment of the king's features, in that the nose is represented by a 'wedge', rather than line-drawn. This does not seem to be an insurmountable objection to including coins struck from these dies within the Insular series, as other obverse and reverse die details are consistent. Obverse *C* does not sit easily within the series if the drawing of the bust alone is considered, but its epigraphy and reverse die combinations suggest it should be placed within the current corpus. One example struck from this obverse was found in the Shaftesbury hoard and thus, on balance, coins from this obverse are included.

Coins copying those of the Chester mint stand out among the imitative coinage. Seven dies utilise a Chester reverse, and it therefore seems probable that the die-cutter copied genuine coins of Chester. Reverse dies *a* and *c* are likely to be copies of known Chester dies whilst *e* and *f* might similarly be so.[14] The 'Chester' reverses are struck in the names of the moneyers Æthelwine, Ælfstan and Æthelnoth. The two reverse dies that name Æthelnoth, *b* and *g*, are of interest, as there is no recorded moneyer of that name at Chester throughout the reign of Æthelred II. A mis-spelling of Ælfnoth, a known Chester moneyer, or an as yet unrecorded moneyer of this name striking at Chester, are both outside possibilities. It is perhaps more probable that the die-cutter was copying a reverse die of the prolific Lincoln moneyer Æthelnoth and translated the mint signature to that of Chester. There are certainly strong similarities between the ordering and positioning of the letters on reverse die *b* and a known Lincoln die.[15] Elements of reverse die *g* might also be copied from another Lincoln coin, particularly the stop after the letter L in the mint name.[16]

Group 1 also includes two sets of dies (G1.9 and G1.10), represented by four surviving coins, which name Bath and Ælfric as their mint and moneyer. They are of unusual style and share some of the same characteristics as the Chester imitations. Their weight (*c*.1.50g) is quite consistent with the Insular pieces and is significantly lower than nearly all other recorded Bath coins. The average weight among the 41 Bath coins published within the *SCBI* is 1.68g with only one coin struck at a weight comparable to those identified here as probably imitative. It can thus be asserted with reasonable confidence that these Bath

---

[14] Reverse die *c* (G1.3) is possibly copied from the reverse of Pirie, *SCBI* 5, no. 126 and reverse die *a* (G1.1) by nos. 120–24. Similarly, reverse dies *e* and *f* (G1.5–7) could be also have been copied from nos. 120–24.

[15] H.R. Mossop, *The Lincoln Mint: c.890–1279* (Newcastle, 1970), pl. IX, no. 25. This Lincoln reverse die appears to be slightly irregular, perhaps the product of a Lincoln die-cutting centre. It occurs in combination with three obverse dies and a large number of heavy examples are recorded.

[16] Mossop, *Lincoln Mint*, pl. X, no. 8.

coins form a part of the Insular imitative group. The coins definitely have an Insular provenance as one was part of the Shaftesbury hoard and another is a single-find from Kent.

Detecting Imitation: Metrology and Die Axes

Reliance upon analysis of the style of coins is difficult as it represents a subjective process. Mark Blackburn highlighted the fact that an analysis of weight could be a useful means of determining imitation, showing that *Quatrefoil* imitations were often lighter than the coins they copied.[17] Figures 23.2–23.4 show a comparison of the distribution of weights of undamaged coins in the imitative series with the Dublin and official Chester series.[18] These show a clustering of the weights at just under 1.50g for the imitative series. This is significantly different from the official Chester coins, which were struck to a standard far closer to 1.70g. It is also somewhat higher than the majority of the Dublin coinage (struck around 1.35g) but this is less clear as there is a second, smaller spike at a similar weight. The important point is that the Insular coins were struck consistently and significantly lighter than the coinage of Chester.

Metrology can also be utilised by studying the weight variation between undamaged die-duplicates. Table 23.2 places the weight variation among the Insular imitations alongside near-contemporary coinages.[19] It suggests that the mint that was responsible for striking the Insular imitations was either unable – presumably because of a lack of appropriate technology or oversight – or deemed it unnecessary to maintain a very precise weight. The comparison again highlights the difference from Anglo-Saxon England where control over weight was much more precisely maintained. Analysis of undamaged Chester *Long Cross* die-duplicates recorded in *SCBI* volumes show a maximum deviation of 0.06g from the average weight of the die chain. This can be contrasted to Insular imitations where the deviation from the average weight in each set of die-duplicates varies between 0.09 and 0.26g. This represents an acceptable margin of error of 10 per cent among die-duplicates in the Insular imitative mint. Of the series summarised, the imitative *Long Cross* coinage is most closely aligned with the later *Quatrefoil* imitations. However, even compared to this other imitative series, it still displays slightly less precision in the maintenance of weights.

---

[17] Blackburn, 'Quatrefoil imitations', 11–12.

[18] English data is taken from Pirie, *SCBI 5*; G. Galster, *SCBI 7*; Gunstone, *SCBI 17*; and V. M. Potin, *SCBI 50. Hermitage Museum, St. Petersburg. Part I. Anglo-Saxon Coins to 1016* (London, 1999). Irish data is from Dolley, *SCBI 8*; Galster et al., *SCBI 22*; and W. Seaby, *SCBI 32: Ulster Museum: Belfast. Part 2, Hiberno-Norse Coins* (London, 1984).

[19] M. Blackburn, 'Currency under the Vikings. Part 4. The Dublin coinage *c.* 995–1050', *BNJ*, 78 (2008), 111–37, at 126.

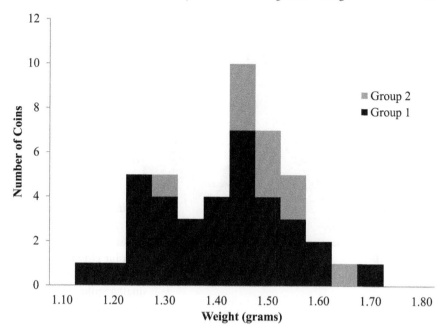

Figure 23.2   Distribution of weights of Imitative series.

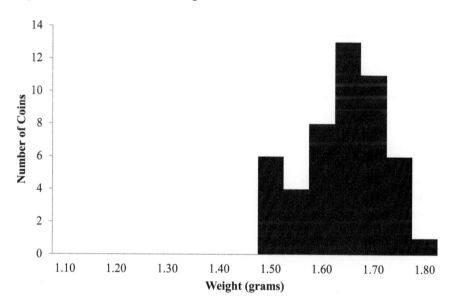

Figure 23.3   Distribution of weights of official Chester series.

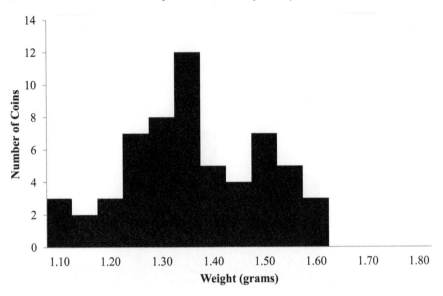

Figure 23.4   Distribution of weights of Hiberno-Scandinavian series.

Table 23.2   Weight difference among die-duplicates.

	Number of specimens	Within 0.03g	Within 0.06g	Within 0.09g
Anglo-Saxon				
Edgar–Harthacnut	389	42%	72%	83%
Hiberno-Scandinavian				
'Crux'	58	26%	41%	50%
'Long Cross'	139	26%	41%	63%
'Helmet'	18	17%	28%	39%
'Last Small Cross'	101	25%	37%	51%
'Quatrefoil'	8	25%	38%	50%
Other Insular Imitations				
'Irish Sea' Quatrefoils	54	15%	31%	54%
Insular Long Cross	105	19%	30%	40%

Die axes can also be used as a possible means of detecting different mints. Where axes vary significantly, it can suggest that there was a different minting practice. This was demonstrated in the Viking coinage of tenth-century York where irregular die axes suggested circular-shafted dies, a proposition confirmed by the discovery of intact dies.[20] This can be contrasted with contemporary Anglo-Saxon coinages where regular die axes, at 90° angles, suggest the use of square dies. Such a technological difference can also be suggested for the imitative series on the basis of its die axes. Table 23.3, illustrated graphically as Figure 23.5, summarises the die axes of the various *Long Cross* series.[21] In the figures, each segment represents the percentage of coins struck on that die-alignment with the arm of the axis being 30 per cent of the total. Black segments are 90° segments (0°, 90°, 180° and 270°), dark grey are 45° and light grey are all others. This highlights the difference between the official coins of Chester, almost exclusively struck with dies at 90° intervals, and the Insular imitative mint where this is far less common an occurrence.[22] Indeed, a majority of the imitative coins were struck at non-regular angles. This is also a contrast to the contemporary coinage of Dublin where, again, regularity is the norm.

Table 23.3   Summary of die axes of *Long Cross* and *Quatrefoil* series.

	Number of coins	Total at 90° angles	Total at 45° angles	Total at irregular angles
Long Cross				
Chester	83	76%	8%	16%
Hiberno-Scandi-navian	96	71%	7%	22%
Insular Imitations ('Chester')	32	31%	13%	56%
Quatrefoil				
Chester	160	64%	13%	23%
Hiberno-Scandinavian	29	76%	0%	24%
Irish Sea Imitations	38	34%	3%	63%

---

[20]   M. Blackburn, 'The coinage of Scandinavian York', in *Aspects of Anglo-Scandinavian York*, ed. R. A. Hall (York, 2004), 325–49, at 294–5. Reprinted in M. Blackburn, *Viking Coinage and Currency in the British Isles* (London, 2011).

[21]   The Insular *Long Cross* data is based upon the Appendix, that concerning *Quatrefoils* comes from Blackburn, 'Quatrefoil imitations'; and Blackburn, 'Supplements'. All other data is drawn from *SCBI* volumes. This method and English data draws upon the work of H.B.A. Petersson, *Anglo-Saxon Currency*, (Lund, 1969), table 491.

[22]   It would be tempting to attribute any difference of die-axis to the variety of sources of data. It is possible to imagine that the compilers of the various *SCBI* volumes 'rounded' figures to the nearest regular point. Careful checking of each volume has ensured that each author recognised non-regular die axes and thus it is possible to be reasonably confident that when a regular angle is recorded that is a genuine occurrence.

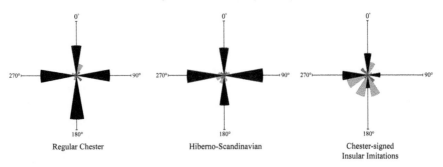

Figure 23.5   Die axes of *Long Cross* series.

The combination of the metrology and die axes of the coins suggests that the stylistically related group identified above is unlikely to be a product of the official English mint at Chester or the Hiberno-Scandinavian mint in Dublin. The style, die axes and weights suggest different die-engravers, techniques and issuing authorities to those of other mint-towns.

Associated Coins (Groups 2 and 3)

There is a series of similar dies (Group 2) which could also be interpreted as belonging to the Insular imitative group. The crucial die is *P* which provides an obverse link connecting reverses which name Lincoln, Winchester and Dublin as the mint.[23] The other dies are stylistically close to those within this small die chain; obverse dies *O* and *R* are very similar. Two of the 'Lincoln' reverses, *p* and *q*, are closely related in appearance and could have copied a Lincoln die which seems to show a 'kink' in the vertical of the squared C in the moneyer's name.[24]

The unusual style of the coins, the link between the three 'mints' and the Dublin mint signature suggests that these coins cannot have been struck in England. Their two Insular find-spots, Inch Kenneth and the 'Irish midlands', also rule out Scandinavia as their place of striking. However, whether they are to be associated with the other Insular imitations, as opposed to the regular Hiberno-Scandinavian series, is far from certain. As is visible in Figure 23.6, they are quite similar in bust style to the very early Hiberno-Scandinavian *Long Cross* dies, with their distinctive hair radiating out from the ear.[25] The early Dublin coins also name the Winchester moneyer Godwine on their reverse, which mirrors that of G2.7. The die-linking between the different 'mints' would also stand out from the rest of the Insular imitations, where a number of specimens are known

---

[23]   Dolley, 'An unexpected mint'.
[24]   Mossop, *Lincoln Mint,* pl. IX, no. 5.
[25]   See also Seaby, *SCBI 32,* no. 16.

for most die combinations with relatively little in the way of die-linking between them. Similarly, the die axes are markedly more regular although, admittedly, from only a small sample. In these respects, this small group of coins would sit more comfortably within the Hiberno-Scandinavian series.

Figure 23.6 Comparison of Early Dublin and Insular Imitative Group 2 obverse die (*SCBI* Stockholm).

However there are a number of features which would be highly anomalous in the Hiberno-Scandinavian coinage. The rendering of the obverse legend is quite distinct from the Dublin coinage. The use of X in REX is quite different to the normal Hiberno-Scandinavian + whilst the use of RE,X,A,IO is not repeated on any other Dublin die.[26] Indeed, the use of AIO is very unusual in itself, only occurring on one other known coin which is of quite regular Dublin style.[27] Perhaps more importantly the reverse die naming Dublin, die *r*, would also be unusual for that mint. As is illustrated in Figure 23.7, where the legend is FÆ REMI NM'O DYFLI on Dublin coins, there are only ever pellets in three of the terminals of the long cross. This can be contrasted to die *r* where pellets occur in all four. Thus whilst there are some similarities, the small details suggest that Dublin was not the mint for these coins. It is impossible to be certain about these coins but further die-links may help to determine whether they are to be regarded as Hiberno-Scandinavian or Insular imitative pieces.

Figure 23.7 Comparison of Dublin and Insular Imitative Group 2 reverse die (*SCBI* Dublin).

---

[26] Even on early Hiberno-Scandinavian dies the Rex is normally rendered with a + rather than an X. For example, see Dolley, *SCBI 8*, no. 40.

[27] The coin is from the Stora Sojdeby hoard.

A third group has been included in the corpus and serves to emphasise the difficulty in identifying an imitative coinage on style alone. This group was initially identified by Mark Blackburn and could be interpreted as Scandinavian.[28] There is a resemblance between obverse die *T* in this group with obverse die *C* from Group 1. In addition, reverse die *v* resembles dies *a, d* and *e* in details such as letter size and alignment. However, the obverse dies take the cheek as the centre point of the die and the alignment of initial crosses is also different from that of Group 1. The die-linking pattern of die *T* (one obverse with three different 'mints') is not typical but finds parallels in Group 2. G3.5 names Ælfheah of Shrewsbury, a moneyer who served as a model for imitations which link into Chain 105, a massive and probably international die chain largely struck in Scandinavia.[29] All of these factors would suggest a Scandinavian origin for Group 3.[30] However, G3.4 is very closely related in terms of its style to the other coins of Group 3 and derives from the Knockmaon hoard.[31] If the Irish find-spot is accepted, an Insular striking is perhaps more likely. However it is difficult to be certain about this, especially considering the unusual foreign nature of the Knockmaon hoard.

The Location of the Imitative Mint

Attempting to determine the location of the mint is difficult as the coins are known from only a handful of hoards, mostly from Scandinavia.[32] Imitation of *Long Cross* coinage was common, as was the movement of dies, and thus it is necessary to discuss the possibility of the mint being in England, Scandinavia, Ireland or at various sites within the 'Irish Sea Region'.

Table 23.4   Insular hoards and selected single-finds of *Long Cross* coins.

Checklist	*Hoard*	*Anglo-Saxon*	*Hiberno-Scandinavian*	*Imitative?*	*Scandinavian*
201f	Arreton	x			
189	Welbourn, Lincs.	x			
194	Inch Kenneth, Argyll		x	x (G2.1a)	

---

[28] M. Blackburn 'Some early imitations of Æthelræd II's Long Cross type', *Numismatic Circular*, 88 (1980), 130–32.

[29] Gunnarsson, 'Kedja 105'.

[30] B. Malmer, *The Anglo-Scandinavian Coinage, c.995–1020* (Stockholm, 1997), 133–4.

[31] J.R.B. Jennings, 'On some ancient coins found in west Waterford', *Journal of the Waterford Archaeology Society*, 15 (1912), 163–7, no. 2; Blackburn, 'Imitative workshop', 130–32.

[32] Cf. appendix for list of hoards.

Checklist	Hoard	Anglo-Saxon	Hiberno-Scandinavian	Imitative?	Scandinavian
195	Knockmaon, Co. Waterford			x? (G3.4a)	
196	Derrymore, Co. Westmeath	x	x		
197	Great Barton, Suffolk	x			
198	Harting Beacon, Sussex	x			
199	London (Honey Lane Market)	x			
200	Shaftesbury, Dorset	x		x (G1.3e, G1.5b, G1.10a)	x
201	York (Micklegate), Yorks.	x			
201a	Downham Parish, Cambs.	x			
201b	Barsham, Suffolk	x	x		
201c	Bramdean Common, Hants.	x			
201d	Cheriton, Hampshire	x			
201e	Hangleton, West Sussex	x			
202	Collinstown, Co. Westmeath	x	x		
217	Fourknocks, Co. Meath	x	x		
218a	Glenfaba sheading	x	x		x
219	Park Llewylln, Kirk Maughold	x	x		
261	London ('Walbrook')	x			
	Selected single-finds				
	'Irish Midlands'			x (G2.1b)	
	Newchurch, Kent			x (G1.10b)	
	Ickleton, Cambs.		x		
	Old Romney, Kent				x

Crucial to understanding where the coins were struck is an appreciation of where they have been found. Table 23.4 is a summary of Insular finds which included *Long Cross* coins.[33] The Shaftesbury hoard is very important because it is the only recorded Insular hoard containing coins from Group 1. It features, in parcel B, examples from three die combinations, representing both the 'Chester' and the 'Bath' mints. The number of die-duplicates between coins from parcels A and B may be fewer than Dolley suggested, meaning the coins of Bath in parcel A may have been struck from different regular or irregular dies. Unfortunately, neither the Teulon-Porter manuscript nor Michael Dolley's notes on parcel A can at present be located, so it is impossible to verify die-duplication between coins in parcel A and those in parcel B. The mints present in the hoard, together with three die-duplicates of the York moneyer Hundulf, would point to the Shaftesbury coins having been deposited by someone who had gathered his coins from northern trading centres at a fairly early stage within the official *Long Cross* period of circulation and carried them to the Shaftesbury area.

Assuming the 'Chester' pieces can be accepted as a stylistically related whole, their occurrence within the Shaftesbury hoard is very important for interpretation as it would suggest an Insular striking. Generally, finds of Scandinavian imitative coins are exceedingly rare in an Insular context.[34] Malmer records only two *Long Cross* imitations with Insular find-spots, to which might be added the coin from Knockmaon if a Scandinavian striking is deemed more likely.[35] If the expanded list, with associated coins, is accepted, then the number of find-spots in Britain and Ireland means that the mint is very unlikely to have been in Scandinavia. The fact that the majority of the specimens have been found in Scandinavian hoards simply serves to underline their success in entering the mainstream coin-economies of the time.

Accepting the likelihood of an Insular striking, there are a number of different possibilities for the site of the mint. If England is considered, accounting for the unusual style of the coins is difficult. Despite being a major die-cutting centre for much of the tenth century, Chester does not seem to have functioned separately after a very brief issue in Æthelred's *First Hand* type until re-emerging during the validity period of the *Last Small Cross* type.[36] Regular *Long Cross* pennies with Chester mint signatures appear to have been struck exclusively from London-

---

[33] Full references available via the Checklist. There are 105 single-finds of Long Cross coins recorded on EMC for England (as of 26 March 2012). Of these, 56 have images and can be confirmed as regular English coins.

[34] M. Archibald, 'Against the tide: coin-movement from Scandinavia to the British Isles in the Viking Age', *NNF-Nytt* 1991, 19–22.

[35] Malmer, *Anglo-Scandinavian Coinage*, no. 355.

[36] M. Blackburn and C.S.S. Lyon, 'Regional die-production in Cnut's *Quatrefoil* issue', in *Anglo-Saxon Monetary History: Essays in Memory of Michael Dolley*, ed. M. Blackburn (Leicester, 1986), 223–72, at 234–6; M. Dolley and T. Talvio, 'The regional pattern of die-cutting exhibited

cut dies.[37] Even if a local die-cutting centre had been set up officially at Chester during the validity period of the *Long Cross* coinage, it seems improbable that the coins produced would have had such different weights and die axes to other products of the same mint.

Moving across the Irish Sea, the relative consistency of the Hiberno-Scandinavian coinage has increasingly been recognised.[38] Hiberno-Scandinavian *Long Cross* coins generally have tightly spaced hair, seriffed lettering and a different alignment of the initial crosses when compared with English coins. The neat, well-centred appearance of coins struck from these dies is evidence of an organised, competent operation, the equal of many English mints. The imitative series is iconographically similar to the Hiberno-Scandinavian coinage in many respects: the rendering of the hair is closely spaced and the initial crosses are similarly aligned to those on the Hiberno-Scandinavian coins. However, Dublin emerges as an unlikely location for the mint striking the Insular imitations for many of the same reasons as Chester. It struck coins on a series of regular die axes and to a weight different from that of the imitations. The Insular imitations also lack the seriffed lettering of most Dublin coins. The mints named upon the coins differ substantially from those struck in Dublin. No definitively Irish *Long Cross* dies name Chester, normally preferring Dublin or Winchester. This is in marked contrast to the Insular imitations, where Chester dominates. Furthermore, the fact that the Group 1 coins are known from consistent die-duplicates rather than the longer, mixed die-chains of the Hiberno-Scandinavian coinage, suggests a different system of minting.

If Scandinavian imitations and the royal coinages of England and Ireland can be discounted, then the series is likely to have been an unofficial one. Negative evidence for the isolated, imitative nature of these coins lies in the lack of die-linking with genuine products of any English mints or with coins indisputably of Dublin. In this way it is similar to the Insular imitative series of *Quatrefoil* coins identified by Mark Blackburn. In 1996, he argued that Meols on the Wirral peninsula was the most likely site for the production of the later *Quatrefoil* imitations.[39] This was a view that he subsequently revisited in light of the 2003 Glenfaba hoard, again cautiously arguing for a north-western origin

---

by the *First Hand* pennies of Æthelræd II preserved in the British Museum', *BNJ*, 47 (1978), 53–65.

[37]   This even extends to the recently recorded specimen of a subsidiary issue penny by the moneyer Eadric recorded in I. Leimus and A. Molvõgin, *SCBI 51: Estonian Collections* (London, 2001), no. 149. A die-duplicate of this coin has been found in London (EMC 2006.0082). Note the similarity between the reverse die of this coin and that of a coin illustrated in Dolley, *SCBI 8*; Figure 5 on pl. E, which is apparently a coin of Dublin, moneyer Eadric, copying the Subsidiary Long Cross issue.

[38]   Blackburn, 'Imitative workshop', 60; Dolley, *SCBI 8*, 127.

[39]   Blackburn, 'Quatrefoil imitations', 14.

for the coins.[40] Bornholdt Collins et al. in this volume discuss the possibility of the series being from the Isle of Man. Accepting that a Manx mint is a possibility for the *Quatrefoil* imitations, a similar case is difficult to make for the *Long Cross* imitations. If the *Long Cross* imitations are compared with either the *Quatrefoil* imitations or the later Hiberno-Manx coinage the styles are quite distinct. Furthermore, the absence of the Insular imitations from the large Glenfaba (2003) hoard, despite the relatively large number of Dublin and English *Long Cross* pennies, suggests that they were not minted on Man.

Boon, and latterly Griffiths, have suggested a site in Wales for the striking of the Irish Sea *Quatrefoil* imitations, on the strength of a coin within the Pant-yr-Eglwys hoard.[41] Blackburn suggested that this was quite unlikely, with little in the way of evidence for minting in Wales until the later eleventh century.[42] For the *Long Cross* coins there is nothing to commend a northern Welsh mint; indeed coin finds are generally very scarce from this area. There is a similar lack of evidence to recommend any sites on the Lancashire or Cumbrian coasts.

Returning to Blackburn's original suggestion of Meols (or at least somewhere within the vicinity of Chester) as the origin of the *Quatrefoil* imitations, it is certainly possible to argue along similar lines for the Insular *Long Cross* imitations. Six dies copy regular Chester reverses, suggesting the imitative die-cutter had these coins to hand. If the coins naming 'Dublin' and found in Ireland are accepted as part of this imitative group then this need not change the interpretation. Nonetheless, it would seem more likely that the mint was on the eastern seaboard of the Irish Sea than the west. It was far easier for coins to pass from east to west, England to Ireland, than *vice versa*. To illustrate the point, fewer than 10 Hiberno-Scandinavian coins have been found in England which can be contrasted with the several hundred from Ireland.[43] The presence of the Insular imitations on both sides of the Irish Sea might suggest the mint was just outside the Anglo-Saxon monetary system, with coins passing into Ireland alongside legitimate Saxon coins.

Interpreting the Imitations

Returning to a comparison of the imitative *Long Cross* and *Quatrefoil* series, it seems that both series were struck in small but not completely insubstantial numbers. As described above, their die-linking patterns, die axes and

---

[40]   Blackburn, 'Supplements', 385–8.

[41]   G. Boon, *Welsh Hoards 1979–1981* (Cardiff, 1986); D. Griffiths, *Vikings of the Irish Sea* (Stroud, 2010), 109.

[42]   Blackburn, 'Supplements', 387–8.

[43]   Blackburn, 'Currency under the Vikings. Part 4', 134; Dolley *SCBI* 8, 55–69.

comparative metrology all find common ground. They were also both struck around periods of significant *geld* payments.[44] Perhaps the producers of imitative coinage viewed these periods as ideal times to conceal their operations within the increased official English minting activities, whose administration must have been stretched, even within a capable system. Chester's activity in the *Quatrefoil* period surged, for example: it was among the most active mints, probably functioned as a die-cutting centre, and had an expanded group of moneyers. The *geld* payments probably contributed to the fact that the Irish Sea was rich in silver around the millennium. This is attested to by the well over 100 known obverse dies used at Dublin during the *Long Cross* coinage. This coinage was an order of magnitude larger than other Phase I Dublin issues. This was not entirely mirrored on the English side of the Irish Sea, where the *Long Cross* coinage was a significant issue but one which was possibly smaller than the earlier *Crux* coinage.[45] There were, in short, particularly significant amounts of silver being minted and used in the Irish Sea region around the millennium. In such a context, a relatively small unofficial mint could be explained as a means of circumventing official mint charges that would have been associated with mints on either side of the Irish Sea. This would have been especially true as Chester *Long Cross* coins were among the heaviest struck across England and weighed in at 15 per cent more than the imitative pennies.[46] In practical terms, a similar amount of silver could produce about 20 regular Chester pennies or 24 pennies of the imitative series.

It is unlikely that either the *Long Cross* or *Quatrefoil* imitative series should be conceived of as overtly political statements. The absence of any other king's name and a similarity of style to official coins would militate against such a suggestion. In the case of the imitative *Long Cross* coinage, its purpose may in fact have been entirely the opposite. The relatively consistent literacy of the legends might indicate that these coins were intended to pass as official pieces of currency within the Anglo-Saxon monetary system. The English find provenances would indicate success if this was the aim.

The possibility of forgery is reflected in the official sensitivity to false coinage being issued within English territory that is present in several of Æthelred's

---

[44] Geld payments are recorded by the *Anglo-Saxon Chronicle* for the years 991, 997, 1002, 1007, 1012 and 1018.

[45] M. Allen, *Mints and Money in Medieval England* (Cambridge, 2012), 297–9.

[46] If the regular Chester *Long Cross* pennies in the Stockholm, Copenhagen and Grosvenor Museum collections are analysed they produce a median value of 1.70g with a quartile range of 0.09g. This compares favourably with the Insular imitations, for which the figures are 1.47g and 0.14g respectively. Similar figures can be obtained for coins in the Systematic Collection, Stockholm, but these do not exclude coins that may belong to the imitative series. C.S.S. Lyon, 'Variations in currency in Anglo-Saxon England', in *Mints, Dies and Currency. Essays in Memory of Albert Baldwin*, ed. R.A.G. Carson (London, 1971), 106–14.

laws.[47] It is visible in IV Æthelred, attributed to the mid-990s, which concerns the issue of base coin, use of dies bearing the name of another moneyer, traders who take good money to false coiners and those who make false dies and sell them to coiners for money.[48] Both III and IV Æthelred outlaw the striking of coinage 'in the woods', a direct allusion to those producing false currency.[49] These are restatements of earlier law codes, but would have been used to remind both those involved in coin-production and the coin-using population of the punishment that could be meted out to lawbreakers found within the English realm. The moneyers named on the imitative series do not seem to have been singled out for any sort of punishment or removal from office. Both the Chester moneyers, Æthelwine and Ælfstan, continued to strike throughout Æthelred's reign, as did Æthelnoth of Lincoln and Ælfric of Bath. Whilst it appears there was a chronological disjuncture between the striking of Insular imitations and promulgation of Æthelred's laws, they suggest that forgery was sufficiently prevalent, at a broadly comparable time, to warrant legislation.[50]

There are crucial differences between the *Long Cross* and *Quatrefoil* series which may help explain their existence. Firstly, it is very doubtful that they were both struck at the same, shadowy Irish Sea mint. The style of the *Quatrefoil* coins is much more distinctive and has noticeably poorer literacy. In comparison, the *Long Cross* imitations display a style and legend that could have been passed off as English more successfully. This is also reflected in their Insular find-spots, with a significant proportion of *Long Cross* imitations found within England whilst *Quatrefoil* coins have a more distinctly Irish Sea distribution. These differences might hint toward subtly different purposes in their production. *Quatrefoil* coins were struck imitating Chester, but perhaps for an Irish Sea context, whilst the *Long Cross* imitations might be justifiably termed forged English coins with the purpose being to penetrate the English economy. The Insular imitations may have represented an attempt to turn some of the undoubted wealth of the Irish Sea into usable 'English' currency without paying the full fee associated with doing so at the official mint at Chester.

Conclusions

This survey has identified a probably Insular, imitative issue copying coinage of a type current on both sides of the Irish Sea. It was convincing enough to enter local

---

[47]   E. Screen, 'Anglo-Saxon law and numismatics: a reassessment in the light of Patrick Wormald's *The Making of English Law I*', *BNJ*, *77* (2007), 150–72, at 160–63.

[48]   Ibid., 160; R.S. Kinsey, 'Anglo-Saxon law and practice relating to mints and moneyers', *BNJ*, *29* (1958), 12–50, at 17–23.

[49]   Screen, 'Anglo-Saxon law', 162–7.

[50]   Ibid., 160.

and wider currencies. With additional finds it may be possible further to refine the interpretation of it, particularly the extent to which other groups of unusual coins relate to it, and the location of the mint. Currently it appears reasonable to assert that the capacity existed to produce a well-organised imitative coinage in the Irish Sea area during the late Anglo-Saxon period, in spite of the relatively close proximity of official coinages and potentially hostile forces.

Figure 23.A   Die-combinations of insular imitations of Æthelred II's Long Cross coinage, reproduced at 80% of original size. (For further details, see pp. 535-42.)

Appendix: Corpus of Insular Imitations of Æthelred II's Long Cross Type

Group 1
Coins confidently associated with an 'Irish Sea' mint

With 'Chester' mint signatures:

G1.1 Aa   +ÆSELREЅ REX NLÖ +ÅL EPN EMÖ LEIè

= BEH 1480 = Malmer 9.137.[not recorded]

a) Chester (*SCBI* 5, no. 454); *ex* Willoughby Gardner, *ex* Bald-   1.35g   210°
win.

b) Copenhagen (*SCBI*7, no. 472); found Holsegaard.   1.47g   150°

c) Museum Narodowe in Cracow (*SCBI* 37, no. 71); *ex* Raciazek   1.38g   225°
hoard?

* d) Private collection; bt Baldwin.   1.40g   75°

e) British Museum; *ex* Morgan 1915, *ex* Evans.   1.52g   135°

f) Royal Coin Cabinet, Stockholm; *ex* Kännungs hoard.   1.41g

g) Royal Coin Cabinet, Stockholm; *ex* Kännungs hoard.   1.42g

G1.2 Ab   Same obv. die as G1.1 +ED ELN ÖDM ÖLè

= BEH 1508 = Malmer 9.137.1133

a) Chester (*SCBI* 5, no. 455); *ex* Willoughby Gardner, *ex* W. G.   1.37g   0°
Wells.

b) Chester (*SCBI* 5, no. 456); *ex* Willoughby Gardner.   1.50g   270°

c) Copenhagen (*SCBI* 7, no. 484); found Enner 1849.   1.50g   0°

d) Royal Coin Cabinet, Stockholm.   1.30g   260°

e) Royal Coin Cabinet, Stockholm (BEH 1508.1).   1.29g   260°

f) Royal Coin Cabinet, Stockholm (BEH 1508.2).   1.30g   260°

g) Royal Coin Cabinet, Stockholm; *ex* Myrande Hoard (CNS 1.1 19:1303).   1.16g   90°

* h) Gandarve hoard (to be acquired by Gotland Museum)   1.26g

i) Schleswig; *ex* List Hoard 186.   w.n.r.

G1.3 Bc   +ÆDELRED REX ALÖI +ELF çTāN MiÖ LEê6
= BEH 1522

a) Chester (*SCBI* 5, no. 460); *ex* Willoughby Gardner, *ex* Lincoln (dealer).   1.26g   30°

b) Chester (*SCBI* 5, no. 461); *ex* Willoughby Gardner, *ex* Lincoln (dealer).   1.43g   210°

c) Copenhagen (*SCBI* 7, no. 489); *ex* Siokrona.   1.72g   330°

d) Leicester (*SCBI* 17, no. 215), *ex* J. Young 1919.   1.42g   0°

e) Shaftesbury (*SCBI* 24, no. 517); *ex* Shaftesbury hoard.   1.52g   30°

f) Royal Coin Cabinet, Stockholm (BEH 1522).   1.55g

g) Schleswig; *ex* List hoard 188.   w.n.r.

h) Lund; *ex* Igelosa hoard.   w.n.r.

i) Lund; *ex* Igelosa hoard.   w.n.r.

* j) Private collection; bt Spink. — 1.60g — 315°

k) Hermitage Museum (*SCBI* 50, no. 640), Inv. 112410. — 1.24g — 210°

l) Royal Coin Cabinet, Stockholm; *ex* Kännungs hoard. — 1.50g

G1.4 Cd +EDELRED REX ONIÖ +ÂL EPN EMüO LEIè

= BEH 1479

a) Chester (*SCBI* 5, no. 125); *ex* Willoughby Gardner, *ex* Holmberg. — 1.57g — 150°

* b) Copenhagen (*SCBI* 7, no. 471); *ex* Stockholm 1856. — 1.32g — 210°

G1.5 Ce Same obverse die as G1.4 +EL EPN EMÖ LEIè

a) British Museum (BMC vol. II, no. 142). — 1.48g — 135°

* b) Shaftesbury (*SCBI* 24, no. 516); *ex* Shaftesbury hoard. — 1.48g — 180°

G1.6 Df +Â5ELRED RE+ NLÖ +EH EPN EMÖ LEIè

= BEH 1510 = Malmer 9.139.1136

a) British Museum (*SCBI* 8, no. 37); *ex* Morgan; *ex* Evans; *ex* Sweden. — 1.62g — 270°

b) Copenhagen (*SCBI* 7, no. 485); *ex* Hauberg 1937. — 1.48g — 30°

c) Royal Coin Cabinet, Stockholm (BEH 1510). — 1.60g — 140°

d) Leicester (*SCBI* 17, no. 211); *ex* J. Young, 1919. — 1.53g — 160°

* e) Private collection; *ex* S.N. Lane (Spink 21.9.1982, lot 8). — 1.59g — 160°

f) Lund; *ex* Igelosa hoard. — 1.43g — 180°

G1.7 Ef +ÄDELRED RE+ Aè Rev die as G1.6
= BEH 1509 = Malmer 9.176.1139
* a) Royal Coin Cabinet, Stockholm (BEH 1509). — 1.35g — 270°

G1.8 Fg XÄ5ELRED REX OÑILÖ +E5 ELN,J ÖDM ÖL,I.E.
a) Chester (*SCBI* 5, no. 462); *ex* Willoughby Gardner, *ex* Harris 1926, lot 193. — 1.48g — 270°
b) Chester (*SCBI* 5, no. 463); *ex* Willoughby Gardner, *ex* Seaby 1926. — 1.45g — 270°
* c) Fitzwilliam Museum; *ex* Blackburn; *ex* A.H. Baldwin collection. — 1.63g — 240°

With 'Bath' mint signature:
G1.9 Gh +Á5LRE5 REX NMLÖ +ÄL FR6 MiO B0D
* a) *ex* Baldwin 14.x.2002, lot 135. — 1.46g

G1.10 Hi +Ä5ELRED REX 0ILO +EL FRI6 MiÖ B05
a) Shaftesbury (*SCBI* 24, no. 498); *ex* Shaftesbury Hoard. — 1.52g — 90°
b) Yorkshire Museum (*SCBI* 21, no. 1035a); found Newchurch, Kent. — 1.13g (chipped) — 210°

* c) Estonian History Museum (*SCBI* 51, no. 136); *ex* Maidla 1.47g 315°
   hoard AM 21772/820.

Associated Coins

These coins may belong with the Insular imitations described above although this is not absolutely certain.

Group 2

With 'Lincoln' mint signature:

G2.1 Oo   +E5ELRE5 REX EI6Ö +CÖ LèRI MM,O ÖLI6

* a) Lincolnshire Museums (*SCBI* 27, no. 111); *ex* Hill; *ex* Argyll; 1.32g 0°
   ex Parsons; *ex* Lincoln (Dealer).

G2.2 Pp   +,Ä5LRED R,E,X, 0IÖ XÄ,ç 6Mä NMÖ L,H6

* a) British Museum (*SCBI* 8, no. 38); *ex* Inch Kenneth find. 1.56g 90°

   b) National Museum of Ireland, 'Irish Midlands' find. 0.76g
                                                           cut half

G2.3 Qq   XÄ5ELRED RE+ 0èLÖ +Äç 6Mä NMÖ LII6

* a) Fitzwilliam Museum, *ex* Studio coins 2009. 1.58g 270°

With 'Dublin' mint signature:

G2.4 Rr   XÄ5LRED REX 0IÖ +çIE LÖM DILI EèN

			1.53g	0°

* a) Copenhagen (*SCBI* 22, no. 26); Bruun 305.

G2.5 Ps   Same obverse die as G2.2 ҲFAEREMIN HO DYFLI

     a) Tystebols Find, Stenkyrka Parish, Gotland.   1.54g   180°

* b) National Museum of Ireland; *ex* Stacpoole collection.   1.67g   250°

G2.6 St   +Ã5ELRED REX 0IGLÖ +GÖI DçTEè MiÖ DYFLI

* a) Everlov hoard, Skåne (CNS 3.4 59:799).   1.28g   180°

With 'Winchester' mint signature

G2.7 Pu   Same obverse die as G2.2 +GOIDælNE MiO PIHT
     = BEH 4246

* a) Royal Coin Cabinet, Stockholm (BEH 4246).   1.48g

Group 3

With the 'Chester' mint signature

G3.1 Tv   +ÃDELRED REX AIGLOI +ÆLEPINE M'O LEIGI
     = BEH 1476 = Malmer 9.187.9168

a) Royal Coin Cabinet, Stockholm (BEH 1476). 1.45g 280°

* b) Chester (*SCBI* 5, no. 453); *ex* Willoughby Gardner, *ex* Bruun 1925. 1.48g 135°

With the 'Malmesbury' mint signature

G3.2 Tw   Same obverse die as G3.1 EALDRED M'O MLD+ (retrograde)

=Malmer 9.187.9104

a) Eskilstuna Museum; *ex* Thuleparken hoard. 1.52g 0°

* b) Schleswig; *ex* List Hoard. 1.45g 0°

With the 'Bath' mint signature

G3.3 Tx   Same obverse die as G3.1 +E5ZTāN MiO BaD

=Malmer 9.187.1148

* a) *ex* Digeråkra hoard, Barlingbo, Gotland. 1.34g 0°

G3.4 Uy   +ĂDELRED RE+ 0lèlO +EDçT0N MiO IB0D

* a) Knockmaon hoard (illus. Jennings 1912, no. 2). 0.71g (broken)

With the 'Shrewsbury' mint signature

G3.5 Vz +ÃDELRED REX AIGLOI +ÆLFHEH MiO SCRO

* a) Lund; *ex* Igelosa hoard. w.n.r.

Note: w.n.r. = 'weight not recorded.' * = coin illustrated in Figure 23A.

Image permissions: Kenneth Jonsson (G1.2), Committee of the Sylloge of Coins of the British Isles (G1.4, G1.5, G1.10, G2.1, G2.2, G2.4, G2.5 and G3.1), Fitzwilliam Museum, Cambridge (G1.8 and G2.3), Baldwin's (G1.9), editor of the CNS (G2.6), from *NCirc* by permission of Spink (G3.2, G3.3. and G3.5), from the Journal of County Kildare Archaeological Society by permission of the Society (G3.4).

Finds

Coin	Find	Details	*t.p.q.*
G3.3a	Digerika	Digeråkra hoard, Barlingbo, Gotland, 1928.	1002
G1.2c	Enner	Enner Hoard, Tamdrup sogn, Nim herred, Jylland, Denmark, 1849.	1035
G1.2h	Gandarve	Gandarve hoard, Alva, Gotland, Sweden, 2009.	uncertain
G1.1a	Holsegaard	Holsegaard hoard, Osterlarsker, Bornholm, Denmark, 1884.	1005
G1.3g G1.3h G1.6f G3.5a	Igelosa	Igelosa hoard, Skane, Sweden, 1924.	1005
G2.1a	Inch Kenneth	Inch Kenneth hoard, Hebrides, c.1830.	1002
G2.1b	Irish Midlands	Metal-detected single-find from Irish midlands.	-
G1.1f G1.1g G1.3l	Kännungs	Kännungs hoard, Hellvi, Gotland, 1934.	1018
G3.4a	Knockmaon	Knockmaon hoard, Co. Waterford, 1912.	997
G1.2i G1.3g G3.2b	List	List hoard, Sylt, Schleswig-Holstein, Germany, 1937.	1000
G1.10c	Maidla	Maidla hoard, Maidla, Kullamaa Parish, Estonia, 1974.	1066
G1.2g	Myrande	Myrande hoard, Myrande, Atlingbo, Gotland, Sweden, 1893.	1026
G1.10b	Newchurch	Single-find from Newchurch, Kent. Presented to Yorkshire Museum by Mr. Huddleston of Skelton, near York, 1944.	-
G1.1c	Raciazek	Raciazek hoard, Raciazek, woj. Wloclawek, Poland, 1940.	1035
G1.3e G1.5b G1.10a	Shaftesbury	Shaftesbury hoard, Shaftesbury, Dorset, c. 1941.	1003
G3.2a	Thuleparken	Thuleparken hoard, Södermanland, 1977.	1035
G2.5a	Tystebols	Tystebols find, Stenkyrka, Gotland, Sweden, two parcels, 1916 and 1920.	1035

Chapter 24

The English Element in the 2012 Övide Hoard, Eskelhelm par., Gotland

Kenneth Jonsson

Background

The Övide hoard was found on 21 July 2012 by Ingvar Nilsson on a pathway for cows. Two years earlier soil had been spread along the pathway. The original site from which the soil had been removed was probably destroyed when the soil was taken. The surrounding area will be excavated at a later date in order to determine if there are any undisturbed remains nearby which can throw light on the context, since Majvor Östergren has previously shown that most Viking-Age hoards on Gotland had been concealed inside houses.[1] The Övide hoard had been deposited in a bronze container, now much damaged. In addition to the coins a large number of silver objects were found, including cut ingots. It will take a long time before the entire hoard has been catalogued in detail. Here, only the English element in the hoard will be listed.

General Composition

It was immediately apparent that the hoard belonged to the large group of Viking-Age hoards found all over the island of Gotland. From a numismatic perspective the Viking-Age coin hoards can be defined as containing coins from a large number of countries and areas. The earliest hoards date to just after 800[2] and the latest is the Burge hoard, Lummelunda par., deposited after 1143.[3] In the early phase, c.800–990, the coins nearly all come from the Caliphate in the east, while in the latter phase, after c.990, nearly all coins come from Europe. A quick glance reveals that the Övide hoard belongs to the very end of the Viking-

---

[1] M. Östergren. *Mellan stengrund och stenhus. Gotlands vikingatida silverskatter som boplatsindikation* (Stockholm, 1989), 55–65.

[2] Hammars, Fårö par., *t.p.q.* 804/5, (*Corpus nummorum saeculorum IX–XI qui in Suecia reperti sunt. 1. Gotland. 4. Fardhem – Fröjel* (Stockholm, 1982), find 6) is the earliest.

[3] G. Hatz, *Die deutschen Münzen des Fundes von Burge I, Ksp. Lummelunda, Gotland (tpq 1143). Ein Beitrag zur ostfälischen Münzgeschichte*, Comm. N.S. 16 (Stockholm, 2001).

Age phase of coin importation. At present the latest coins which have been attributed are German (1131–7/1138–51), Hungarian (1116–31), and English (*c*.1121–3). Although many of the German coins have not yet been attributed, the present *t.p.q.* of the hoard (1131/8) will probably not change.

The oldest coin in the hoard is a Roman *denarius* from Emperor Trajan struck in Rome AD 103–11.[4] This coin belongs to a far earlier period of coin importation, probably dating back to the fourth century. One or more Roman *denarii* have been found in at least five late Viking-Age hoards on Gotland (including Övide) and probably represent coins found on the island and added to an already existing fortune in silver. The remaining coins all belong to the Viking Age.

Table 24.1   Preliminary composition by origin of the coins in the Övide hoard.

Roman Empire	1
Islamic	16
Byzantine	3
French	1
German	514
Bohemian	2
Hungarian	3
English	142
Hiberno-Scandinavian	1
Scandinavian	5
Danish	15
Norwegian	1
Swedish	8
Total	712

The English Element

Although only the English element in the hoard will be listed and analysed, comparisons will be made with the German component and the import of coins in general. The overall composition of the hoard is shown in Table 24.1. As usual in a late hoard the German coins are in a clear majority. It would have been even

---

    [4]   H. Mattingly and E.A. Sydenham, *The Roman Imperial Coinage, vol. II. Vespasian to Hadrian* (London, 1926), no. 190. The coin has been attributed by Lennart Lind.

greater if the hoard had not included a large early parcel which dates from a period when the share of the English coins was much higher than in the early twelfth century. The chronological composition of the English element is shown in Table 24.2. The number of coins peaks in the period *c*.991–1018 followed by a rapid decline and figures gradually lower until reaching a complete halt *c*.1056–80. A very small, and brief, increase occurred in the 1080s followed by another halt until the 1110s and early 1120s with a small number of coins. The age structure and its implications will be analysed in more detail below.

Table 24.2   Chronological composition of the English element in the Övide hoard.

King/type	BEH	Approximate date	No. of coins
Æthelred II 978–1016			
First Hand	B1	979–85	2
Second Hand	B2	985–91	2
Crux	C	991–97	12
Intermediate Small Cross	A(2)	997	1
Long Cross	D	997–1003	40
Helmet	E	1003–09	9
Last Small Cross	A(3)	1009–17	30
Cnut 1016–35			
Quatrefoil	E	1017–23	6
Pointed Helmet	G	1023–29	9
Short Cross	H	1029–35	5
Harold I 1035–40			
Jewel Cross	A	1035–37	5
Fleur-de-Lis	B	1037–40	2
Edward the Confessor 1042–66			
Pacx	D	1042–44	1
Radiate/Small Cross	A	1044–46	3
Expanding Cross	E	1050–53	1
Pointed Helmet	F	1053–56	1
King/type	***BMC***	**Approximate date**	**No. of coins**
William I 1066–87			
Profile/Cross and Trefoils	vii	1080–83	1
Paxs	viii	1083–86	6
Henry I 1100–35			

King/type	BMC	Approximate date	No. of coins
Full Face/Cross Fleury	x	1115–17	3
Smaller Profile/Cross and Annulets	xii	1119–21	1
Star in Lozenge Fleury	xiii	1121–23	2
Total			*142*

The English coins are listed in the Appendix below. The *Hand* types of Æthelred II are represented by two coins each of *First Hand* and *Second Hand*. The latter type was mainly struck in southern England. From the north a single coin is known from Torksey[5] and one or two from York,[6] while none is known from Lincoln. Chester was previously only known from five or six specimens struck by four moneyers.[7] The dies used for striking *Second Hand* are of a very uniform national style, which was also used at Chester, Torksey, and York. However, the style of the Chester coin in Övide is very crude with spelling errors. It is clear that it was struck from locally cut obverse and reverse dies. The average weight of *Second Hand* coins struck at Chester is high, 1.68g, compared to 1.32g for all mints;[8] and even this new specimen, which weighs 1.46g, is above the national average for the type. It is been debated whether both *First* and *Second Hand* were two types or if *Second Hand* was just a variety within the *Hand* series. The fact that *Second Hand* coins are extremely rare from northern mints suggests that *First Hand* continued to be struck in the north when *Second Hand* was struck in the south.[9] One of the *Second Hand* coins has been damaged by heating, but the first part of the name of the mint can be read, while the name of the moneyer is not intelligible except that he has a long name.

The 12 pennies of the *Crux* type show the strong presence of Maldon, Southwark, and Thetford which is a feature of late *Crux*. *Intermediate Small Cross* was the next type to be issued under Æthelred II.[10] It is a very rare type, which was aborted after a short time. Only 37 specimens are now known.[11] The Övide coin is struck at Hereford, a new mint for the type. Like the previously

---

[5]   *SCBI* 7 Copenhagen II, no. 1251.

[6]   *Corpus nummorum saeculorum IX–XI qui in Suecia reperti sunt. 1. Gotland. 2. Bäl–Buttle* (Stockholm, 1977), find 4, no. 999; BEH, no. 696.

[7]   K. Jonsson. *Viking-Age Hoards and Late Anglo-Saxon Coins* (Stockholm, 1987), 87.

[8]   H.B.A. Petersson, 'Coins and weights. Late Anglo-Saxon pennies and mints, *c.* 973–1066', in *Studies in Late Anglo-Saxon Coinage in memory of Bror Emil Hildebrand,* ed. K. Jonsson (Stockholm, 1990), 207–433, at 260 and 347.

[9]   I. Stewart. 'Coinage and recoinage after Edgar's reform', in *Studies in Late Anglo-Saxon Coinage,* ed. Jonsson, 455–85, at 471–4.

[10]   R.H.M. Dolley and F. Elmore Jones. 'An Intermediate Small Cross issue of Æthelræd II and some late varieties of the Crux type', *BNJ, 28* (1955), 75–87.

[11]   Jonsson, *Viking-Age Hoards,* 108.

known mints (except York) it is located in the western part of the country. With 40 coins, *Long Cross* is the best represented type in the hoard. This is in line with the general pattern on Gotland, where *Long Cross* is exceptionally prominent. The *Helmet* type is far less common with nine specimens. *Last Small Cross* is the second best represented type with 30 coins. Mints in the east – Cambridge, Huntingdon, Norwich and Thetford – are relatively well represented with eight specimens, while about three would normally have been expected.[12] One puzzle with the *Last Small Cross* type is that although it is usually common in the hoards, very few hoards end with this type. It suggests that many of the coins were imported when the type was no longer current in England.

The three types of Cnut (*Quatrefoil, Pointed Helmet,* and *Short Cross*) are comparatively poorly represented with just six, nine and five coins respectively. This suggests that they were added to the hoard at a late date, when the types were less common. Compared to Cnut, the coins of Harold I and Edward the Confessor are better represented than normal. This suggests that the majority of the coins of Cnut, Harold and Edward the Confessor may have been acquired in the mid-1050s. The proportion of each of these types approximates the quantity of English coins in circulation on Gotland in the mid-1050s or somewhat later. From the reign of Edward the Confessor only one type, *Radiate/Small Cross,* is represented by more than one coin. Godwine is a new Oxford moneyer for the *Pacx* type.

The remaining English coins belong to two isolated periods, one consisting of seven coins dating from the 1080s (all but one of the *Paxs* type), and six coins dating to *c*.1120. Each is likely to represent a small parcel forming part of a larger group of coins in which German coins were very dominant. The general composition of the Övide hoard reveals that it belongs to the large group of 'ancestral' hoards on Gotland (see below). In this case four generations seem to have contributed coins in varying proportions. The first generation (ending *c*.1020) represents a large share, the second a fairly small share (ending mid-1050s), the third a large share (ending *c*.1090) and the fourth a relatively small share (ending after 1131/38).

The Post-1050 Import of Coins

Since Övide is one of the latest Viking-Age hoards in Sweden, a comparison with the general process of coin importation is best confined to the period after about 1050. Throughout the Viking Age, Gotland is the province with the highest number of finds in Sweden. Thus, to be meaningful any comparison with Gotland must be with the remainder of Sweden. For the period of the 1050s to

---

[12]   Based on table IV in Petersson, 'Coins and weights'.

1140s Figure 24.1 shows the number of hoards with at least 100 coins deposited respectively on Gotland and the remainder of Sweden (excluding Skåne where the hoards contain almost only Danish coins). The number of hoards had been high up to the 1050s. After a sharp drop the Gotland figures pick up modestly followed by another deep decline until the hoards cease altogether in the 1140s. The drop in the number of non-Gotlandic hoards is very modest in the 1060s, but there follows a severe drop in the 1070s and 1080s and a very small rebound in the 1110s and early 1120s. The strong position of Gotland is also evident, save for the 1060s when the non-Gotlandic hoards are nearly twice as numerous as those on Gotland. The drop in the number of hoards is to some extent counterbalanced by the fact that the hoards become bigger both on Gotland and elsewhere.

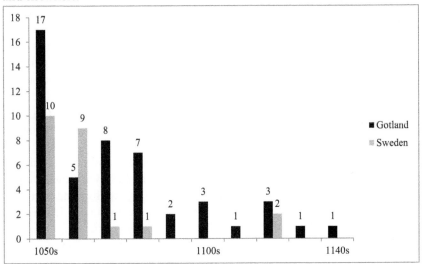

Figure 24.1   Number of hoards with at least 100 coins deposited between the 1050s and 1140s on Gotland and the remainder of Sweden.

The reason for the decreasing import from the late 1050s must be found in the debasement of the coinage in Germany, which had started at mints in Frisia at Jever, Emden and various others during the time of Count Bruno III (1038–57).[13] The practice, although not as extreme, also spread to other German mints.[14]

---

[13]   V. Potin. 'Funde westeuropäischer Denare im Norden der Sowjetunion', in *Sigtuna Papers. Proceedings of the Sigtuna Symposium on Viking-Age Coinage 1–4 June 1984,* ed. K. Jonsson and B. Malmer, Comm. N.S., 6 (1990), 265–73, at 271.

[14]   U. Zwicker, N. Gale and Z. Gale. 'Metallographische, analytische und technologische Untersuchungen sowie Messungen der Bleiisotope an Otto-Adelheid-Pfennigen und Vergleichsmünzen meist aus dem 9.–11. Jahrhundert', in G. Hatz et al., *Otto-Adelheid-Pfennige.*

This was evidently rapidly discovered on Gotland and no doubt made Gotlandic merchants hesitant to accept coined silver from virtually everywhere as payment in transactions. On the Swedish mainland merchants were apparently less aware of the development and imports continued. This is even more the case in Russia, where coin imports exploded and Frisian coins are abundant.[15] The reason must be that Frisian merchants came to Russia and brought their local, debased coins with them. The debasement, or at least the worst of it, came to an end in the 1070s, after which coin imports picked up again on Gotland, but now at a much lower level. At the same time it is evident that the level of trade involving other goods was not affected on Gotland or in Sweden, indicating that coins simply did not play the same role as before. This is evidenced by the expansion of trading sites such as Fröjel, where there was a large expansion of the settlement in the second half of the twelfth century.[16] At Köpingsvik on Öland, a trading site was established and saw a rapid expansion in the same period.[17] At Sigtuna in central Sweden contacts with the east are documented by pottery, for example.[18]

On Gotland ancestral hoards are very common throughout the Viking Age.[19] This means that a family treasure was handed over from one generation to another. In extreme cases, like the Ocksarve 1920 hoard,[20] no less than six generations might have built up the treasure. It is also probable, as in the case of the Stumle hoard, that the Gotlandic traders (*farmannabönder*) did not go on a trading expedition every year.[21] In this case two expeditions were undertaken about six years apart. The hoard also indicates that the family treasure was used to finance new expeditions. Thus, there was a repeated flow of coins in and out of the hoard. The continuous wastage rate caused by coins being hoarded,

---

Untersuchungen zu Münzen des 10./11. Jahrhunderts, Comm. N.S., 7 (Stockholm, 1991), 59–146, tables 3–4.

[15] V. Potin. 'Funde deutscher Münzen des 10.–17. Jahrhunderts aus dem europäischen Teil der Sowjetunion', *Hamburger Beiträge zur Numismatik, 21* (1967), 53–63.

[16] D. Carlsson, '*Ridanäs*'. *Vikingahamnen i Fröjel* (Visby, 1999), 69.

[17] H. Schulze, *Köpingvik på Öland – 30 undersökningar 1970–1994. Arkeologiska undersökningar i Köpingsvik, utförda av Riksantikvarieämbetet och Kalmar läns museum. RAÄ 215, 216 m fl, Köpings sn, Borgholms kn, Öland* (Kalmar, 2004), 47; K. Jonsson. 'Eastern contacts based on the coin finds', in *Situne Dei, 2009,* 57–67, at 64.

[18] M. Roslund. *Gäster i huset. Kulturell överföring mellan slaver och skandinaver 900 till 1300* (Lund, 2001), 216–17.

[19] K. Odebäck. 'Familje- och släktskatter under äldre vikingatid', *Myntstudier, 2009:2,* 9–25; C. Persson, 'Aktiv och passiv – klassificering av vikingatida skattfynd utifrån myntsammansättningen', in *Samlad Glädje. Numismatiska Klubben i Uppsala 1969–1999,* ed. K. Holmberg and H. Nilsson (Uppsala, 1999), 127–32.

[20] Jonsson, *Viking-Age Hoards,* 24, no. G215.

[21] K. Jonsson and M. Östergren. 'The Gotland hoard project and the Stumle hoard – an insight into the affairs of a Gotlandic farman', in *Sigtuna Papers,* ed. Jonsson and Malmer, 145–58, at 154–8.

melted down or exported meant that the composition was changing more or less rapidly.[22] It is only when a hoard has been recovered intact and a stratigraphy can be seen (as in the Stumle hoard), that we can get a glimpse of how a hoard was built up over a longer or shorter period of time. The average period of circulation for an imported coin in the Northern Lands can be estimated at *c.*30 years. That means that after *c.*30 years more than half of the coins once imported were no longer in circulation.

In the late Viking Age huge numbers of European coins were imported to Gotland.[23] Importation before *c.*990 was extremely small-scale. Coin imports from Europe were at their peak *c.*990–1030 and remained fairly high until the 1050s with German and English coins as the two main elements.[24] Thus, although new coins were acquired after this period, the pre-1050s coins would still be in the majority more or less to the end of the Viking-Age coin importation on Gotland *c.*1140. Although long-distance trade was important and brought in the more recently struck coins, we must assume that a lot of trading was regional and would probably have led to a mixture of old and new coins being acquired.

The Importation of English Coins in the Post-1050 Period

If we want to study the post-1050 period in more detail we have to rely on the English coins. Although the German coins are all dominant, they have the disadvantage that they can rarely be dated within short periods of time. Thus, the start and basis for any detailed analysis must be the (admittedly much smaller) English element, of which only one type was apparently current in England at any given time. Some old and new hoards have made scholars doubt whether this was true or not.[25] In any event the time of striking for each type can be dated within a few years. Before the Norman period the dates are more or less universally accepted, while nowadays for the Norman period the order and the dates show minor differences between scholars.[26] Coins from other countries are usually too few to allow an analysis.

---

[22]   M. Metcalf, 'Some twentieth-century runes. Statistical analysis of the Viking-age hoards and the interpretation of wastage rates', in *Viking-Age Coinage in the Northern Lands. The Sixth Oxford Symposium on Coinage and Monetary History*, ed. M.A.S. Blackburn and D.M. Metcalf, BAR International Series, 122 (2 vols, Oxford, 1980), 1, 329–82.

[23]   The present figure in the author's database is 172,000 excluding a new hoard with an estimated 5,000 coins waiting to be excavated.

[24]   The present figure in the author's database is 67,000 German and 26,900 English coins. Both figures exclude the new hoard.

[25]   Cf. the discussion in C.S.S. Lyon, 'Anglo-Saxon Numismatics', *BNJ*, 73 (2003), 58–73, at 70–71 (and references there cited).

[26]   Compare below n. 29 and Martin Allen elsewhere in this volume.

The majority of the English coins in the Swedish hoards have retained their provenance and these figures have been used here. The reason is that although the vast majority of the unprovenanced coins are likely to belong to Swedish finds, it is a fact that some do not, since they were found in other countries or bought.[27] Thus, although the figures presented here could also have included material without known provenance, the relative proportion between types would probably not change very much. The number of provenanced coins from the period 1042–66 is shown in Figure 24.2. Although the numbers testify to a continuous drop in the 1040s it is only during the *Expanding Cross* type that the number drops below 100 followed by much lower figures for the succeeding types. The *Expanding Cross* type was struck according to a light and a heavy standard with the former being considered the earlier, but the reverse order has also been suggested.[28] The higher weight standard has also been linked to the abolition of the *heregeld* in 1051, and a subsequent decrease in the export of English pennies. However, based on the Swedish figures, where a single hoard, Vanneberga,[29] accounts for more than a third of the total in the *Short Cross* type, it can be argued that the drop in the Swedish figures occurred already during the *Short Cross* type. The decrease would then not show a major drop with the *Expanding Cross* type, but rather a continuous long-term decrease starting in the 1040s. In fact this is suggested by the figures for the period *c*.1053–66, where each type is known from lower and lower numbers. Thus, the figures suggest a gradual decrease over an extended period of time, rather than sudden changes. In the latter part of the period before the Norman Conquest the figures are also so small that they must be used with caution. One hoard, Johannishus,[30] with a late *t.p.q.* of 1120 but in general extremely strong around the mid-eleventh century, accounts for nine of the 17 coins recorded for the last two types. The overall conclusion is that the decrease in the import of English coins *c*.1050–66 cannot be tied to events in England, but rather to debasement in Germany. For the reasons presented above it is sadly not possible to compare this conclusion with the German element.

---

[27]   Compare *SCBI* 54 for Harold II, where two (1283 and 1285) out of the five originally unprovenanced coins could be identified as having a non-Swedish provenance.

[28]   G. Williams. 'A hoard of "Expanding Cross" pennies from Appledore: preliminary report', *NCirc, 106* (1998), 152–3. 'A further parcel from the Appledore hoard', *BNJ, 68* (1998), 141; S. Lyon. 'The "Expanding Cross" type of Edward the Confessor and the Appledore (1997) hoard', *NCirc, 106* (1998), 426–8.

[29]   *SCBI* 54, p. 31.

[30]   *Corpus nummorum saeculorum IX–XI qui in Suecia reperti sunt 4. Blekinge. 1. Bräkne-Hoby–Sölvesborg* (Stockholm, 2010), find no. 5.

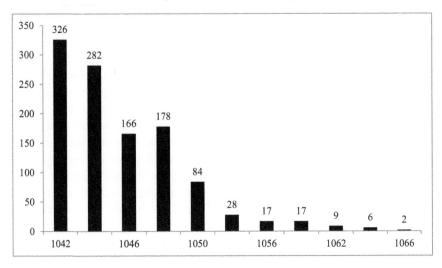

Figure 24.2   Number of hoard-provenanced English coins struck 1042–66 in Swedish finds (the total number of coins is 1,273).

Table 24.3   Number of provenanced English coins found from the period 1066–1135.

King/type	Brooke	Approximate date	No. of coins
William I			
Profile/Cross Fleury	i	1066–8	8
Bonnet	ii	1068–70	2
Canopy	iii	1070–72	4
Two Sceptres	iv	1072–74	3
Two Stars	v	1074–77	9
Sword	vi	1077–80	9
Profile/Cross and Trefoils	vii	1080–83	38
Paxs	viii	1083–86	61
William II			
Profile	i	1086–89	24
Cross in Quatrefoil	ii	1089–92	39
Cross Voided	iii	1092–95	14
Cross Pattée and Fleury	iv	1095–98	0

King/type	Brooke	Approximate date	No. of coins
Cross Fleury and Piles	v	1098–1100	3
Henry I			
Annulets	i	1100–02	1
Profile/Cross Fleury	ii	1102–03	2
Pax	iii	1103–05	0
Annulets and Piles	iv	1105–06	0
Voided Cross and Fleurs	v	1106–07	0
Pointing Bust and Stars	vi	1107–09	1
Cross in Quatrefoil	ix	1109–11	4
Larger Profile/Cross and Annulets	viii	1111–13	2
Quatrefoil and Stars	vii	1113–15	17
Double Inscription	xi	1115–17	5
Full Face/Cross Fleury	x	1117–19	3
Smaller Profile/Cross and Annulets	xii	1119–21	1
Star in Lozenge Fleury	xiii	1121–23	6
Pellets in Quatrefoil	xiv	1123–25	0
Quadrilateral on Cross Fleury	xv	1125–35	0

Note: The numbers for Henry I also include unprovenanced coins which have been pecked.

The number of find-provenanced Anglo-Norman coins is presented in Table 24.3.[31] Here, the figures are very small until the end of the reign of William I with a peak during the *Paxs* (*Brooke* viii) type followed by gradual drop until the William II, *Cross Voided* (*Brooke* iii) type. For the remaining period the figures

---

[31]   Coins of Henry I in the collection of the Royal Coin Cabinet which have been pecked are also included, since they no doubt have a Swedish find provenance. However, there was not enough time to check pecking among the unprovenanced coins of William I and William II. Unprovenanced Anglo-Norman coins are also included in the collections of museums in Karlskrona, Lund, and Uppsala. Some of these are pecked and thus likely to derive from Swedish finds. A few Anglo-Norman coins in private collections are also likely to belong to this group. The chronology is based on M. Blackburn, 'Coinage and currency under Henry I: a review', *Anglo-Norman Studies, 13* (1990), 49–81, but type VII and VIII have changed positions in accordance with W.J. Conte and M.A. Archibald, 'Five round halfpennies of Henry I: a further case for reappraisal of the chronology of types', *NCirc*, 98 (1990), 232–6, at 234. See also M. Allen, 'The mints and moneyers of England and Wales, 1066–1158', *BNJ, 82* (2012), 54–120.

are extremely low or non-existent with the exception of a few types struck in the 1110s and early 1120s. Half of the coins from the pre-*c.*1083 period come from only two hoards, Maspelösa and Johannishus.[32] The former accounts for four out of eight coins in the first Anglo-Norman type and another two coins (not included here) of this type could have the same provenance based on patination. It is interesting to note that a high proportion of the coins from the period *c.*1053–80 were struck in northern England or East Anglia, while London is poorly represented.

When did this renewed importation of coins commence? The composition of the hoards suggests *c.*1080–83 or later as the start, since two hoards end with more than one coin of the *Profile/Cross and Trefoils* (*Brooke* vii) type, while the following type as a rule is much better represented. Based on the English element, this small rebound in importation was, however, very short lived and ended already *c.*1092–95. For Henry I the figures are heavily dependent on two hoards: Burge and the new Övide hoard. The former is centred in the 1110s, and the latter *c.*1120.

How do these dates for the period compare with the English and German coins in the Övide hoard? The composition of the coins of Edward the Confessor suggests that his coins were not acquired on several occasions, but rather at one time in the mid-1050s. The German element consists of coins struck at a large number of mints and many coins have not yet been attributed. However, the general impression is that their chronological composition closely follows that of the English coins. During periods when the English coins are common, the German coins follow the same pattern. The best match is of course in the earliest component *c.*990–1020, when the German element is also very strong. This match between the English and German elements continues up to the very end, with German coins becoming more and more dominant and the English element becoming progressively smaller, which follows the general pattern for coin imports from the mid-eleventh century onwards.

There are many German coins contemporary with the last two issues of William I. The most notable are 31 coins of Verdun of two late issues of Bishop Dietrich (1051–89),[33] as well as 10 coins of a common type from Mainz, struck by the archbishops Siegfried (1060–84) and Wezilo (1084–88).[34] There are also numerous other mints represented from this period, such as Trier, Antwerp, Dinant, Liège, Huy, St. Trond, etc. It is also worth noting that there are just three late Danish coins in the Övide hoard (i.e. post mid-eleventh century). Two were struck under Olof Hunger (1086–95) and one under Erik Ejegod (1095–1103).

---

[32] Blackburn and Jonsson 'Supplement', table 3.

[33] Dbg, nos. 109–111, 1428.

[34] Dbg, nos. 812–13.

The English coins from the 1110s and 1120s can be compared with contemporary issues from eastern Germany: Quedlinburg, Abbess Agnes I (*c.*1110–25); Hildesheim, Bishop Udo (1079–1114 and probably later); Halberstadt, Bishop Reinhard (1107–23); and also a coin from Hungary, Stephan II (1116–31).[35] The latest German coin was (according to Hävernick) struck at Cologne by Archbishop Arnold I (1138–51),[36] but the legends are blundered and the type could just as well have been struck under Archbishop Bruno II (1131–37), which would agree better with the general composition of the latest elements in the hoard. In addition there are a number of late coins from Goslar, which have not yet been attributed in detail.

How can we explain these shifts in coin imports? The dip *c.*1055–80 can no doubt be explained by the debasement in Germany (above all in Frisia). The rebound in the 1080s and early 1090s is likely to be connected with the closure of the mints in Frisia. The minuscule figures for the English coins *c.*1095–1110 no doubt reflect a shift in coin imports in general. This can be seen in the German coins: issues from the Rhineland and the west more or less disappear and there is a concentration of coins from mints in the east, especially the Harz region. This shift could have been caused by either a change in the trade-routes used by the Gotlanders or a realignment in trade-routes within Germany. A detailed analysis would be required in order to see whether either of these explanations could be valid.

Concluding Interpretations

The Burge hoard, *t.p.q.* 1143, marks the end of the Viking Age in numismatic terms. The Övide hoard, *t.p.q.* 1131/8, is the second latest Viking-Age hoard found on Gotland. In the future a detailed analysis of the entire hoard can hopefully provide more answers to questions about trade involving coins in the final decades of the Viking Age.

The analysis made so far of the chronological structure of the Övide hoard suggests that the content of the hoard had been assembled during some four generations. The first of these starts in the last decade of the tenth century and continues into the first decades of the eleventh century; that is, more or less contemporary with the reign of Æthelred II. The following period, corresponding to the reign of Cnut, is much less well represented and it is likely that the family fortune lay more or less dormant until the 1050s, when new additions were made and the coins of Cnut, Harold I and Edward the Confessor

---

[35]   L. Huszár, *Münzkatalog Ungarn von 1000 bis heute* (Munich, 1979), no. 47.

[36]   W. Hävernick, *Die Münzen von Köln. Die Münzen und Medaillen von Köln* 1 (Cologne, 1935), no. 469.

were added. Although the numbers here are much smaller than during the reign of Æthelred II, it must be remembered that in the 1050s, the proportion of English coins in general circulation was considerably smaller than earlier. When the next generation took over, the debasement in Germany prevents us from seeing traces of trade until the 1080s, when coins again were imported. The coins suggest that the family was now again fairly active in trading transactions. The last generation's contribution was apparently more modest, but we also have to consider the possibilities of a more regional involvement, which would have resulted in comparatively fewer new coins. It is also possible that the prospects of acquiring silver from the west had become more difficult (perhaps due to a more localised German market). An eastern source for much of the ingot element of the hack-silver suggests Russia as a new market where silver could be acquired. This is even more true in the case of the slightly later Burge hoard, where Russian *grivnas* constitute an important part of the hoard. Thus, trading involving silver a few decades into the twelfth century would have continued at a higher level than the number of coins would suggest.

With the arrival of Christianity, which became dominant in the eleventh century, the need to build (wooden) churches must have consumed much capital. However, it was probably not until the twelfth century, when the churches were erected in stone, that the costs became very high. On Gotland it was usual that as few as 12–15 farms were responsible for building a church. The costs for building churches could have had an effect on hoarding silver already in the late eleventh century. In the twelfth century the impact must have been considerable, meaning that fewer silver (coins) were being hoarded. The basis for hoarding of imported coins on Gotland came to a complete end when the indigenous coinage started on Gotland in the early 1140s, and not a single English coin and just one German coin dating to the second half of the twelfth century have been found on Gotland.[37] From now on coins were spent on consumption and used for everyday transactions rather than being hoarded.

---

[37] K. Cassel et al., *Projekt Uppdragsarkeologi. Västergarnsstudier*, Rapport 1999:1 (Stockholm, 1999), 64, Figure 13.

Appendix

The English element in the Övide hoard. Coins marked with an asterisk are illustrated in Figure 24.3a–k.

Coin	King/type/mint	Moneyer (normalised)	Moneyer (on coin)	References/notes	Wt.
	Æthelred II 978–1016				
	First Hand type (BEH B1)				
1	Derby	Asulfr	Osulf	BEH 354	1.48
2	London	Wulfric	Wulfric	BEH 2976	1.49
	Second Hand type (BEH B2)				
3*	Chester	Ælfstan	Ælfstan	BEH 1491 (same dies); local style	1.46
4	Winchester?	?	WI/////?	Damaged by fire	1.42
	Crux type (BEH C)				
5	Canterbury	Gold[wine?]	Gol[?]	Cf. BEH 187–8	0.65 f
6	Ipswich	Leofsige	Leofsige	BEH 1064	1.35 o
7	London	Æthelred	Æthered	BEH 2207	1.69
8	London	Æthelred	Æthered	BEH 2206	1.63
9	Maldon	Leofwine	Leofwine	BEH 3077	1.24

Coin	King/type/mint	Moneyer (normalised)	Moneyer (on coin)	References/notes	Wt.
10	Shaftesbury	Goda	Goda	BEH 3343	1.60
11	Southwark	Beorhtlaf	Byrhtlaf	BEH 3599 var. obv. a10	1.60
12	Thetford	Osbern	Osbern	BEH 3784	1.42
13		Asfrith	Osfeth	BEH 3799	1.50
14	Totnes	Dodda	Doda	BEH 3840	1.34
15	Winchester	Eadnoth	Eadnoth	BEH 4205	1.63
16	York	Hundulfr	Hundulf	BEH 736	1.50

Intermediate Small Cross type (BEH A[2])

Coin	King/type/mint	Moneyer (normalised)	Moneyer (on coin)	References/notes	Wt.
17*	Hereford	Ælfgeat	Ælfget	BEH –; obv. a10 var. +ÆLFGET M~O HERE	1.77

Long Cross type (BEH D)

Coin	King/type/mint	Moneyer (normalised)	Moneyer (on coin)	References/notes	Wt.
18	Chester	Ælfnoth	Ælfnoth	BEH 1486	1.71
19		Leofwine	Leofwine	BEH 1550	1.67
20		Sveinn	Swegen	BEH 1568	1.73
21	Chichester	Æthelstan	Æthestan	BEH 270	1.77
22	Exeter	Ælfnoth	Ælfnoth	BEH 450	1.71
23		Dunstan	Dunstan	BEH 507	1.31 ooo
24		Manna	Manna	BEH 578	1.43

Coin	King/type/mint	Moneyer (normalised)	Moneyer (on coin)	References/notes	Wt.
25	Huntingdon	Ælfric	Ælfric	BEH 1370	1.74
26	Lewes	Merewine	Merewine	BEH 1462	1.41
27	Lincoln	Ælfsige	Ælfsige	BEH 1619	1.24
28		Ælfsige	Ælfsig	BEH 1622 var. obv. c, ir. 128	1.52
29		Asgautr	Osgut	BEH 1831 var. obv. a, ir. 107	1.77
30		Drengr	Dreng	BEH 1741–2	1.77
31		Grimr	Grim	BEH 1786	1.56
32	London	Beorhtlaf	Brihtlaf	BEH 2238	1.38 oo
33		Eadweald	Eadwold	BEH 2426–7	1.39
34		Eadwine	Edwine	BEH 2490 var. ir. 107	1.69
35		Godwine	Godwine	BEH 2633 var. no pellets on rev.	1.59
36		Godwine	Godwine	BEH 2638	1.58
37		Leofing	Lyfinc	BEH 2823 var. no pellets on rev.	1.76
38		Leofstan	Leofstan	BEH 2721–2	1.74
39		Leofstan	Leofstan	BEH 2723	1.66
40		Leofwine	Leofwine	BEH 2762	1.61
41		Wulfstan	Wulfstan	BEH 2991	1.33
42	Norwich	Hwætman	Hwateman	BEH 3138	1.42
43	Rochester	Eadweard	Eadwerd	BEH 3278	1.54
44	Romney	Leofwine	Leofwie	BEH 3315	1.39

Coin	King/type/mint	Moneyer (normalised)	Moneyer (on coin)	References/notes	Wt.
45	Shrewsbury	Wynsige	Wynsige	BEH 3386	1.76
46	Southampton	Æthelnoth	Æthelnoth	BEH 1236	1.52
47	Stamford	Cristin	Cristin	BEH 3460 var. STA	1.30
48		Goddag	Godag	BEH 3486	1.23 f
49	Thetford	Osbern	Osbern	BEH 3788–9	1.39
50	Warwick	Æthelstan	Æthestan	BEH 3868	1.73
51	Watchet	Hunewine	Hunewine	BEH 3883	1.55 o
52	Wilton	Godwine	Godwine	BEH 3995	1.68
53	Winchester	Ælfweald	Alfwold	BEH 4101	1.71
54	York	Eadric	Eadric	BEH 693–5	1.72
55		Oban	Oban	BEH 777	1.67
56	?	Æthelwi[?]	Æthelwi[?]		0.67 f
57	?	[?]inc	[?]inc		0.36 f
	Helmet type (BEH E)				
58	Cambridge	Cniht	Cnit	BEH 1153 var. GRANTE	1.06
59	Hertford	Leofstan	Leofstan	BEH 3862	1.18
60	London	Asulfr	Osulf	BEH 2890; obv. double struck	1.44
61		Brunstan	Brunstan	BEH 2267–8	1.45
62		Brunstan	Brunstan	BEH 2267–8	1.31

Coin	King/type/mint	Moneyer (normalised)	Moneyer (on coin)	References/notes	Wt.
63	Norwich	Ælfric	Ælfric	BEH 3102 var. MΩO	1.17
64	Winchester	Wulfnoth	Wulfnoth	BEH 4336	1.50
65	York	Kolgrimr	Colgrim	BEH 673 var. a5	1.36
66	?	[?]fsige	[?]fsig[?]		0.35 f
	Last Small Cross type (BEH A[3])				
67	Cambridge	Leofsige	Leowsige	BEH 1194	1.66
68	Chester	Ælfnoth	Ælfnoth	BEH 1482–3	1.71
69	Exeter	Æthelstan	Æthestan	BEH 461	1.81
70*	Huntingdon	Æthelweard	Æthelweard	BEH –; +Æ5ELæEARD M~O HV, obv. e3	1.40
71		Sæwine	Sæwine	BEH 1393; obv. double struck	1.70
72	Lincoln	Sumarlithr	Sumerleth	BEH 1905 var. LINC	1.25
73		Ulfketill	Ulfcitel	BEH 1962	1.66
74	London	Æthelwig	Æthelwi	BEH 2180 var. obv. ir 43, 5	1.15
75		Goldwine	Goldwine	BEH 2646	1.31
76		[?]	[?]		0.73 f
77	Norwich	Leofric	Leofric	BEH 3151	1.48
78		Leofric	Leofric	BEH 3149	1.28
79	Nottingham	Osweald	Oswold	BEH 3413	1.11
80	Rochester	Ælfheah	Ælfheh	BEH 3269	1.25

Coin	King/type/mint	Moneyer (normalised)	Moneyer (on coin)	References/notes	Wt.
81	Shaftesbury	Sæwine	Sæwine	BEH 3351	1.37
82		Sæwine	Sæwine	BEH 3351	1.34
83	Stamford	Godleof	Godeleof	BEH 3496	1.23
84	Thetford	Ælfwine	Ælfwine	BEH 3737	1.25
85		Eadwine	Edwine	BEH 3734	1.22
86		Valgestr	Walgizt	BEH 3823	1.33
87	Totnes	Goda	Goda	BEH 3845–6	1.72
88	Warwick	Hyse	Hyse	BEH 3871–2	1.64
89	W[inchester]	Beorhtric	[Brh]tric	BEH 4119; Biddle 736	0.55 f
90	Winchester	Cynna	Cina	BEH 4184	1.75
91		Scolca	Scolca	BEH 4298	1.16
92		Spileman	Spileman	BEH 4315	1.36
93	York	Asgautr	Osgot	BEH 819 var. M·O	1.28
94		Authgrimr	Outhgrim	BEH 850	1.47
95		Sumarlithr	Sumrlethe	BEH 897 var. SVMRLE5E	1.66
96	?	[?]dwi[?]	[?]dwi[?]		0.71 f
	Cnut 1016–35				
	Quatrefoil type (BEH E)				
97	Bath	Ælfweald	Alfwold	BEH 41	0.95 o

Coin	King/type/mint	Moneyer (normalised)	Moneyer (on coin)	References/notes	Wt.
98		Æthelstan	Æthestan	BEH 36	1.10
99	Ilchester	Oswig	Oswi	BEH 906–7 var. GIELC	0.78
100	Ipswich	Oda	Oda	BEH 957 var. MOΩ	1.38
101	Lydford	Sæwine	Sæwine	BEH 2865 var. HYD	0.88
102	Winchester	Ælfsige	Ælfsige	BEH 3667–8	1.10
	Pointed Helmet type (BEH G)				
103	Chester	Leofwine	Leofwine	BEH 1391	1.01
104	Dover	Leofwine	Leofwine	BEH 1096	0.96
105	Hastings	Ælfweard	Ælfwerd	BEH 1096	0.87
106	Lincoln	Crinan	Crina	BEH 1991–3	1.00
107		[?]	[?]		0.52 f
108	London	Æthelweard	Ælwerd	BEH 1991–3	1.02
109		Eadweald	Eadwold	BEH 2204	1.02
110	York	Iri	Ire	BEH 683	1.06
111		Sunnulfr	Sunolf	BEH 779	0.88 oo
	Short Cross type (BEH H)				
112	Lincoln	Aslakr	Oslac	BEH 1704	1.07
113*	Oxford	Colman	Colaman	BEH –; *SCBI* 15, 3254 (same rev. die)	1.22

Coin	King/type/mint	Moneyer (normalised)	Moneyer (on coin)	References/notes	Wt.
114	Shaftesbury	Goda	Goda	BEH 3113	1.15
115	Stamford	Thorsteinn	Thurstan	BEH 3356	1.11
116	York	Wulfnoth	Wulnoth	BEH 861–2	1.15
	Harold I 1035–40				
	Jewel Cross type (BEH A)				
117	Derby	Blacaman	Blacan	BEH 88	1.01
118	Hereford	Leofnoth	Leofnoth	BEH 300	1.10
119	Lincoln	Svartbrandr	Swertb[rand]	BEH 470; Mossop 24 (same dies)	0.80 f
120	London	Leofric	Leofric	BEH 674–5	0.99
121	Thetford	Ælfwine	Ælfwine	BEH 935 (same dies)	0.99
	Fleur-de-Lis type (BEH B)				
122	Hastings	Ælfweard	Ælfwerd	BEH 270	1.12
123	Stamford	Godric	Godric	BEH 885	0.91
	Edward the Confessor 1042–66				
	Pacx type (BEH D)				
124*	Oxford	Godwine	Godwine	BEH –; Pagan –; +GODæINE ON OCXA, obv. f k	1.15

Coin	King/type/mint	Moneyer (normalised)	Moneyer (on coin)	References/notes	Wt.
	Radiate/Small Cross type (BEH A)				
125	Colchester	Stanmaer	Standmyre	BEH –; *SCBI* 54, 394	0.96
126*	London	Wulfræd	Wuled	BEH –; +æVLED OON LVND, obv. h i	1.06
127	York	Æthelwine	Ælwine	BEH 97 var; ÆLæINE, EOF//, obv. f i	0.96
	Expanding Cross type (BEH E)				
128*	Wilton	Ælfweald	Alfwold	BEH –; *SCBI* 20, 1183 (different dies)	1.13
	Pointed Helmet type (BEH F)				
129*	Stamford	Wulfwine	Wulfwine	BEH –; +æVLFæINE ON STA, obv. h, ir. 71	1.26
	William I 1066–87				
	Profile/Cross and Trefoils type (Brooke vii)				
130	London	Eadwig	Edwi	Brooke 464	1.21
	Paxs type (Brooke viii)				
131	Gloucester	Sigelac	Silacwine	Brooke 683	1.39
132	Lincoln	Ulfr	Ulf	Brooke 752	1.39
133	London?	[?]	[?]	+[?]VN	0.32 f

Coin	King/type/mint	Moneyer (normalised)	Moneyer (on coin)	References/notes	Wt.
134	Norwich	Ulfketill	Ulf(citl?)e	Cf. Brooke 846–9	1.22
135	Romney	Winedæg	Windei	Brooke 875	1.43
136	Warwick	Leofric	Lifric	Brooke 1047; rivet	1.44
	Henry I 1100–35				
	Full Face/Cross Fleury type (Brooke x)				
137	Canterbury/Lincoln?	(Ag)mundr	(Ag)memund	Brooke –; ///MEMVND ON //////	1.42
138*	Northampton	Thorr	Thoor	Brooke –; +5OOR ON hAMTV	1.40
139	?	Ead////	Ed////	+ED//// ON [?]	0.97 f
	Smaller Profile/Cross and Annulets type (Brooke xii)				
140*	Chichester	Godwine	Godwine	Brooke –; +GODæINE ON CICE	1.39
	Star in Lozenge Fleury type (Brooke xiii)				
141*	Southwark	Leofwine	Lefwine	Brooke –; LEFæINE ON SVDæE	1.31
142*	Thetford	Godwine	Godwine	Brooke –; +GODæINE ON TETFOR	1.31

Note: Moneyers' names are given in column 3 in normalised form; where this differs from the form on the coin, this is given in the next column. The normalised form of the name follows *SCBI* 28, with amendments in *SCBI* 40. Fragments are denoted 'f' and holes 'ó'.

Figure 24.3   Select coins from the Övide hoard, listed in the Appendix.

Chapter 25

The Viking-Age Hoard of Linnakse: Some Observations

Ivar Leimus, Mauri Kiudsoo and Ülle Tamla

Introduction

On 17 August 2010 a Late Viking period hoard (*t.p.q.* 1059), consisting of silver coins, pieces of silver jewellery and fragments of hand-moulded ceramic vessel, was brought to the Institute of History, University of Tallinn (Colour Figs. 25.1 and 25.2(1–8). This remarkable discovery had been made a day earlier in a recently harvested field in the village of Linnakse (North-Estonia, county of Anija) using a metal detector. The finder of the hoard also handed over a number of bronze and iron artefacts from three different periods: the Roman, the Middle and the Late Iron Age. The artefacts, all of them with marks of intentional damage or fire deformation, had been found in the same field 20–50 m south of the find-spot of the hoard. The exact circumstances of the discovery remained unclear due to the urgent need to excavate the silver hoard. Therefore it was decided to proceed with archaeological investigation, including landscape survey and trial excavations, at the site.[1]

Results of the Archaeological Investigation

A burial site active over a long period and covering *c*.1.4 hectares was discovered on the basis of *c*.300 artefacts found with the help of metal detectors from the upper layer of the soil, and located more precisely by two stony patches in the field on the northern border of Linnakse village. The site consisted of two stone graves, the stone constructions and burials of which have been damaged by ploughing. Beneath the topsoil, at a depth of *c*.30 cm from the present surface, a thin burial layer is sporadically still preserved. On account of this the whole site was submitted for further protection to the National Heritage Board.

---

[1]   Ü. Tamla, M. Kiudsoo, K. Karro, and M. Ots, 'Archaeological investigations at Linnakse: stone graves and a Late Viking Age silver hoard', *Archaeological fieldwork in Estonia, 2010* (2011), 73–88.

Earlier burials were located on the moraine knoll, differing from the rest of the field in the concentration of burnt stones. Some large granite stones in a row, lumps of soil containing charcoal and artefacts of the Roman Iron Age suggest a *tarand*-grave. The artefacts found from the area are typical for *tarand*-graves and originate in the third and fourth centuries. *Tarand*-graves are a specific group of Estonian stone graves. *Tarands* are quadrangular stone enclosures for burials built on the ground, with the straight flat sides of the walls facing outwards. The number of *tarands* in a cemetery can vary from one to a few dozen, and if there is more than a single *tarand* they are joined together. Similar stone graves also occur in south-western Finland, the eastern part of central Sweden, and in the northern part of Latvia.

The other stony patch with darker soil was located *c.*15 m south of the *tarand*-grave and can be connected with the Migration-period and late Iron-Age burials. The artefacts dating back to the Migration period were concentrated at the northern edge of the patch, but were also uncovered from the area between the two patches. Therefore the question concerning the Migration period was whether the dead were buried in the border area of the *tarand*-grave, or whether a new burial construction was erected near the earlier grave.

The spread of the artefacts shows that the late-Iron-Age burial site must have been the largest, and the burial customs of the period were diverse. This can be deduced from streaks and larger patches of charcoal containing deliberately fragmented and whole pieces of artefacts, and also from burnt and unburnt fragments of human bones unearthed during ploughing. The concentration of weapons, especially specimens with rich silver decoration, raises the possibility that a certain part of the cemetery might have been reserved for the elite.

The late Viking-Age silver hoard of Linnakse was deposited outside the habitation area, but close to the burials, which represents a remarkable difference between Linnakse and other sites where late-Iron-Age silver hoards have previously been discovered in Estonia. A hand-moulded vase-shaped ceramic vessel with sides of uneven thickness and a small inward mouth – most probably specially designed as a container for keeping silver – had been buried in the immediate vicinity of the *tarand*-grave; therefore it can be interpreted as a grave hoard related to some ritual act other than burial. A number of silver coins, two fragments of silver bars (3.75g and 10.76g) and jewellery fragments found within a *c.*20 m span of the deposition spot of the hoard were evidently part of the hoard, and there was no hint of an ancient settlement site in the area nearby. Especially noticeable are the numerous peck-marks on some of the items (Colour Plate 25.2(9 and 12)), which clearly were made in testing the silver. The scattered finds also suggest that the hoard had been already partly destroyed by agricultural activities before it was found using a metal detector in 2010.

Coins

The number of coins still in the vessel was 1,311. The subsequent inspections of the find-spot revealed additional coins, bringing the total up to 1,357. The overwhelming majority of the coins (1,094) come from a large variety of German mints, followed by Anglo-Saxon (164), Danish (56), Islamic (15), Hungarian (10) and Anglo-Scandinavian (7) coins. A small number of specimens come from Ireland (4), Sweden (4) Bohemia (2) and Italy (1).

One of the first problems was to establish the *t.p.q.* of the find as precisely as possible. There are a number of German coins in the hoard that must have been struck in 1056 at the earliest (see Appendix). But there are some coins that may even be later. First, a penny of the Saxon Count Hermann (d.1086) from Jever must be mentioned,[2] the *t.p.q.* of which usually has been set at the last year of the reign of his father Duke Bernhard II of Saxony (d.1059).[3] The two pennies from Erfurt of the type Dbg 1837 were most probably struck by Siegfried, archbishop of Mainz (1060–84). So it seems that the *t.p.q.* of the German part of the hoard is quite likely *c.*1060.

As to the English part of the deposit, the latest coin is a *Pointed Helmet* penny of Edward the Confessor which probably was minted in *c.*1053–56. Also, none of the Swedish, Bohemian, Hungarian, Italian or Irish coins can be dated to the 1060s or later. Unexpectedly, the find contains four Danish coins of Sven Estridsen (1047–74/6) from Lund with runic inscriptions,[4] which Danish scholars date to the final part of the reign of Sven Estridsen, i.e. from *c.*1065 onwards.[5] Yet there are some finds from Estonia, Sweden and even Denmark that (leaving the runic coins aside) have a slightly earlier *t.p.q.*, mainly around 1060. Thus one cannot exclude the possibility that the runic type Hbg 30 commenced a little earlier than is generally assumed. If so, the *t.p.q.* of the Linnakse hoard could be set to *c.*1060 as indicated by the German coins.[6]

---

[2] Dbg 597.

[3] R. von Liliencron, F.X. von Wegele and A. Bettelheim (ed.), *Allgemeine deutsche Biographie* (56 vols., Leipzig, 1875–1912), 2, 437.

[4] P. Hauberg, *Myntforhold og Udmyntninger i Danmark indtil 1146* (Copenhagen, 1900), no. 30.

[5] Hauberg, *Myntforhold*, 52; E. Moltke, 'De danske runemønter og deres prægere', *Nordisk Numismatisk Årsskrift 1950*, 1–56, at 3; J. Steen Jensen, 'Runemønterne fra Lund', in *Tusindtallets Danske Mønter fra Den kongelige Mønt- og Medaillesamling*, ed. J. Steen Jensen (Copenhagen, 1995), 82–3; J. Steen Jensen, 'The introduction and use of runic letters on Danish coins around the year 1065', in *Runes and their Secrets. Studies in Runology*, ed. M. Stoklund (Copenhagen, 2006), 159–68.

[6] I. Leimus, 'Vikingetidsskatten fra Linnakse (Estland) og dateringen af de danske runemønter', *NNUM, 2* (2012), 54–6.

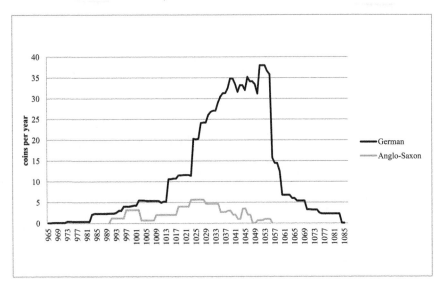

Figure 25.1   Distribution of German and Anglo-Saxon coins in the Linnakse hoard.

Another issue deserving our attention is the uneven chronological distribution of English and German coins in the hoard (Figure 25.1). While the main bulk of German pennies date to the period 1024–56, i.e. the reigns of Conrad II (1024–39) and Henry III (1039–56), the Anglo-Saxon coins mostly belong to the reign of Cnut (1016–35). A considerable proportion of them were also struck under Æthelred II (978–1016), which makes the percentage of Anglo-Saxon pennies in the older part of the hoard almost as high as that of German coins. In order to find out what significance might attach to this imbalance, we should view the Linnakse hoard against its broader background. The following analysis is based on finds from the Baltic area which all have a *t.p.q.* of 1035 or later; i.e. they were deposited after the reign of Cnut. They provide evidence for whether and how the older coins of Æthelred II and Cnut remained in use and if any particular features specific to individual coin types occur.

A strange point becomes apparent even at first glance. As is generally known, the total numbers of *Crux* and *Long Cross* pennies found in Sweden are approximately equal, with just a slight prevalence of *Long Cross.*[7] The same

        7   K. Jonsson, 'The routes for the importation of German and English coins to the Northern Lands in the Viking Age', in *Fernhandel und Geldwirtschaft. Beiträge zum deutschen Münzwesen in sächsischer und salischer Zeit. Ergebnisse des Danneberg-Kolloquiums 1990*, ed. B. Kluge (Sigmaringen, 1993), 205–32, at 214–15.

is largely true in other Nordic lands.[8] In Skåne the *Crux* type even surpasses *Long Cross*.[9] Only in hoards from the eastern Baltic (Estonia, Latvia and Russia) do numbers of *Long Cross* pennies seem to exceed *Crux* considerably.[10] In Estonian pre-Cnut finds the proportions between the two types are very close to those of other Nordic lands.[11] In finds deposited after 1035, however, we see an overwhelming prevalence of *Long Cross* pennies in comparison to the *Crux* type almost everywhere (cf. Figure 25.2–13).[12] In Sweden (except Skåne), Finland and on Bornholm, and also in Estonia and Latvia, the dominance of the *Long Cross* is very striking. This does not correspond at all to Michael Metcalf's theoretical model of the composition of the Anglo-Saxon component of the currency in the Northern Lands.[13]

In our opinion, this phenomenon can be explained in two ways. First, the pattern of hoarding could have changed radically during the influx of coins of these types. While the *Crux* pennies may have been deposited quite soon after their arrival in the Baltic and mostly remained buried, the *Long Cross* coins could have continued to be used to a much larger extent. Alternatively, importation of huge quantities of *Long Cross* pennies may have continued even later, after their

---

[8]   C. Persson, *Engelska mynt i svenska skatter – en studie av de vikingatida depåernas sammansättning med utgångspunkt från de engelska mynten*, C-uppsats i Arkeologi, Stockholms Universitet (Stockholm, 1992); A. Koronen, *Engelska mynt i nordiska fynd. En studie av de engelska myntens typsammansättningar i vikingatida fynd i Norden utom Sverige*, Uppsats i påbyggnadskurs i Arkeologi, Stockholms Universitet (Stockholm, 1996); cf. C. von Heijne, *Särpräglat. Vikingatida och tidigmedeltida myntfynd från Danmark, Skåne, Blekinge och Halland (ca 1130–800)*, Stockholm Studies in Archaeology, 31 (Stockholm 2004), 104.

[9]   Persson, *Engelska mynt*, 25–7.

[10]   Cf. T. Berga, *SCBI 45. Latvian Collections. Anglo-Saxon and later British Coins* (Oxford, 1996); V.M. Potin, *SCBI 50. Hermitage Museum, St Petersburg. Part I. Anglo-Saxon Coins to 1016* (Oxford, 1999); I. Leimus and A. Molvõgin, *SCBI 51. Estonian Collections. Anglo-Saxon, Anglo-Norman and later British Coins* (Oxford, 2001). Unfortunately, only a few finds from Russia are published satisfactorily enough in order to establish the typological composition of their Anglo-Saxon component. In addition, an overwhelming majority of coins have lost their provenance, which makes the use of the Russian material published in *SCBI* impossible. One can get only a very general picture, which, however, reveals a majority of *Long Cross* pennies compared with *Crux*.

[11]   A. Molvõgin, *Die Funde westeuropäischer Münzen des 10. bis 12. Jahrhunderts in Estland*, Numismatische Studien, 10 (Hamburg, 1994), nos. 6, 13, 14, 16, 18, taking the bigger or better documented hoards solely into account.

[12]   The graphs are based on the analyses of hoards; no single finds (which form just a minute fraction of the total material) are considered.

[13]   D.M. Metcalf, 'Some twentieth-century runes. Statistical analyses of the Viking-age hoards and the interpretation of wastage rates', in *Viking-Age Coinage in the Northern Lands. The Sixth Oxford Symposium on Coinage and Monetary History*, ed. M.A.S. Blackburn and D. M. Metcalf, BAR International Series, 122 (2 vols., Oxford, 1981), 2, 329–82, at 354–7.

production and general circulation in England had come to an end – although one wonders why just this type continued to be exported, in contrast to (for instance) the voluminous *Quatrefoil* type of Cnut.[14] In order to determine which of these two explanations should be preferred, we should look at some subsequent coin types of Æthelred II and whether they behave more like *Crux* or *Long Cross*.

The *Helmet* type is one of the less numerous coin types of Æthelred: specimens amount to only around 40 per cent of the number of *Crux* pennies and 33 per cent of the number of *Long Cross* pennies in Nordic finds.[15] Nonetheless, the proportion of *Helmet* is almost the same or even higher than that of *Crux* in post-1035 hoards from most areas. It roughly corresponds to the representation of the *Long Cross* type (Figure 25.2, 4–7, 10, 11).

The totals of *Last Small Cross* are high but in general also lower than those of *Crux*.[16] The line of *Last Small Cross* on the graphs, on the other hand, is as a rule higher or even much higher than that of *Crux* (Figures 25.3–25.8 and 25.10), the more so as one has to take into account the theory that *Last Small Cross* presumably was minted for an exceptional eight or nine years instead of six, which is considered to be normal for the time. In general, the totals of *Helmet* and *Last Small Cross* from Bornholm, Sweden, Finland and the Baltic lands seem to correspond to their appearance in the hoards deposited after 1035 and the types behave more like *Long Cross* than *Crux*, i.e. they remained available for users during the subsequent decades.

This may speak in favour of the first mentioned theory: that some changes in hoarding practice took place by the beginning of the eleventh century. In another context we have pointed out that the Islamic dirhams, which prevailed in Nordic hoards of the ninth and tenth centuries, almost totally disappeared from the use in the late tenth or (in the eastern Baltic) early eleventh century. Everywhere around the Baltic this change occurred very rapidly, in approximately 20 years; that is, during a single generation.[17] Consequently, the dirhams were generally deposited once and for all, and only in very few cases dug out and reused: their percentage in hoards of the eleventh century is, as a rule, extremely modest everywhere except Russia and it is limited even there. The same seems partly to be true in respect of the *Crux* pennies. Once having reached the Baltic, the *Long Cross* coins, on the contrary, as well as all the subsequent types of Anglo-

---

[14]   Cf. D.M. Metcalf, 'Can we believe the very large figure of £72,000 for the geld levied by Cnut in 1018?', in *Studies in late Anglo-Saxon coinage in memory of Bror Emil Hildebrand*, ed. K. Jonsson, Numismatiska Meddelanden, 35 (Stockholm, 1990), 165–76.

[15]   Jonsson, 'Routes', 215.

[16]   Jonsson, 'Routes', 215–16; Koronen, *Engelska mynt*, 12, 21, 25.

[17]   I. Leimus, 'How long did dirhams remain in use in the 10th century?', paper for the Oriental Numismatics Workshop, Wolfson College, Oxford 1–2 August 2011; publication forthcoming.

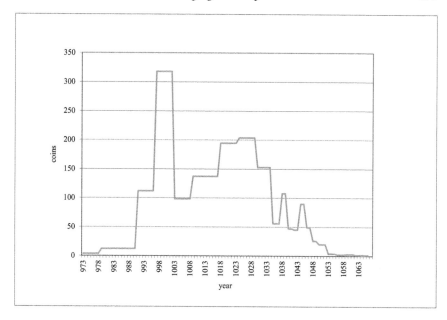

Figure 25.2   Anglo-Saxon coins in finds from Gotland, 1042–1143.

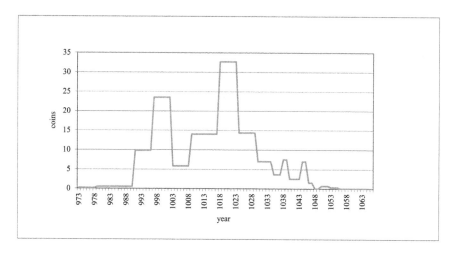

Figure 25.3   Anglo-Saxon coins in finds from mainland Sweden: 1. Svealand, 1034–60.

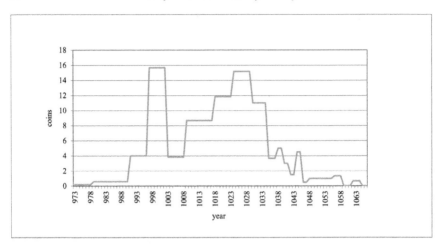

Figure 25.4   Anglo-Saxon coins in finds from mainland Sweden: 2. Götaland, 1035–1121.

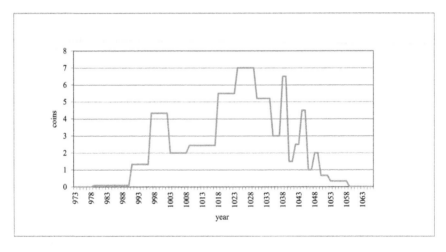

Figure 25.5   Anglo-Saxon coins in finds from Bornholm, 1038–1106.

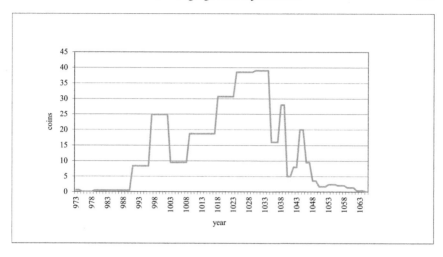

Figure 25.6   Anglo-Saxon coins in Estonian finds, 1038–1180.

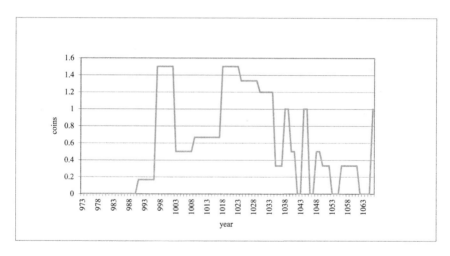

Figure 25.7   Anglo-Saxon coins in Latvian finds, 1046–68.

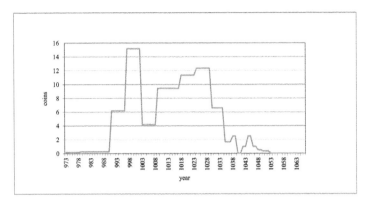

Figure 25.8   Anglo-Saxon coins in Finnish finds, 1035–1110.

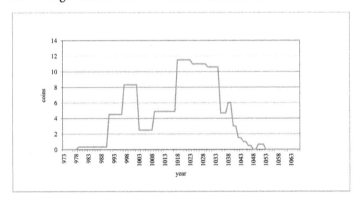

Figure 25.9   Anglo-Saxon coins in Polish finds, 1039–61.

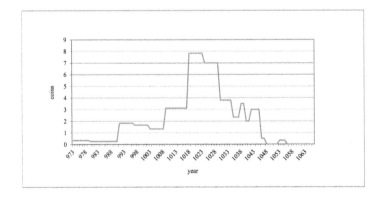

Figure 25.10 Anglo-Saxon coins in Russian finds, 1047–69.

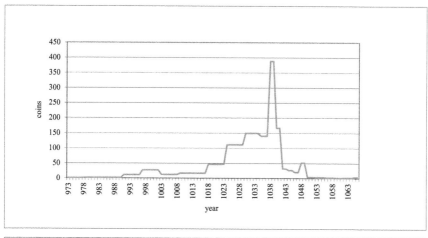

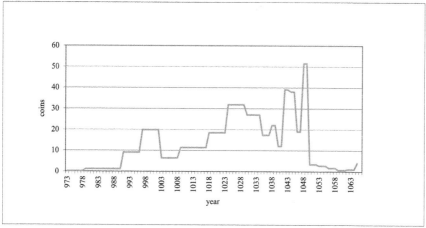

Figure 25.11 Anglo-Saxon coins in finds from Skåne, 1042–1120. (a) including the Äspinge hoard (above) (b) excluding the Äspinge hoard (below).

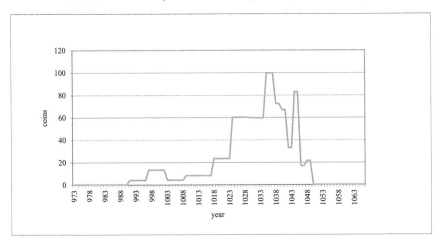

Figure 25.12 Anglo-Saxon coins in Danish finds, 1035–60.

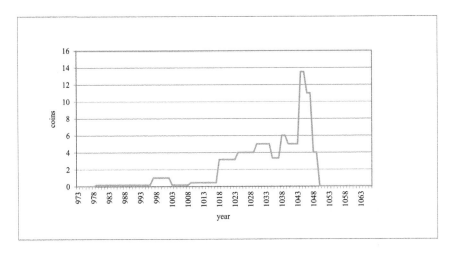

Figure 25.13 Anglo-Saxon coins in Norwegian finds, 1050–51 (Brøholt and
              Foldøy hoards only).

Saxon pennies, remained available during the whole eleventh and (in some
areas) the early twelfth centuries. That fact may be interpreted as an indication
of the increasing vibrancy of coin circulation, at least in most of the territories in
question, starting from around 1000.

Still, this explanation raises a problem in the context of Denmark, Norway
(judging on the basis of just two hoards) and, partly, Skåne. Although we can
observe the dominance of the *Long Cross* type among the pennies of Æthelred

II, the general percentage of his coins in post-1035 finds is remarkably low, even if we exclude the extraordinary and distorting hoard from Äspinge from the picture. Cecilia Persson (von Heijne) stresses the active character of hoards from Skåne,[18] which could explain this phenomenon. However, this is also the way she characterises most of the finds from Götaland and Svealand,[19] which otherwise have a totally different pattern, very close to that of Gotland. Thus, one could conclude that coin circulation in Denmark, Norway and Skåne was quite modest until the reign of Cnut – a suggestion that at least for Denmark seems to be disputable and needs further research. Michael Metcalf, faced with the same problem, tried to solve it by suggesting very high local wastage rates (due to reminting) and the re-export of coins from Denmark and Norway back to the west.[20]

To return to Estonia, the number of finds from there dating to the second quarter of the eleventh century is relatively low.[21] Taking into account the relatively high percentage of *Crux*-type pennies in the finds from the early eleventh century in Estonia, the scarcity of hoards from the intermediate period and the geographical location, one could assume that the Anglo-Saxon component of the later hoards (with a peak in the *Long Cross* type of Æthelred II) is of secondary character and reflects connections to Gotland. In other words, the pre-1035 Anglo-Saxon coins in Estonian post-1035 finds may have come mainly from Gotland. However, closer scrutiny reveals certain differences between Estonia and Gotland (cf. Figures 25.2 and 25.6). First, the percentage of *Long Cross* coins from Estonia is much lower than in Gotlandic finds. At the same time, the pennies of Cnut form a much larger part of Estonian hoards than of Gotlandic hoards. The relatively high curve of Cnut's last type, *Short Cross*, in Estonia is also unusual among Nordic finds. Thus, the Estonian pattern does not correspond completely to that of Gotland. The explanation here might lie in the late character of Estonian finds, which are particularly numerous starting from the 1060s. It seems that a selection of older Anglo-Saxon pennies in fact was obtained from Gotland but there must have been other sources, too, providing Estonia with fresher English currency.

It is widely presumed that the export of coins from England to Sweden and perhaps to other northern lands, too, had started to decrease already during Cnut's reign.[22] This seems to be true in the case of Sweden, indeed, but with

---

[18]   Persson, *Engelska mynt*, 26–7.

[19]   *Ibid.*, 29–31.

[20]   Metcalf 'Some twentieth-century runes', 357–8.

[21]   Cf. Molvõgin, *Die Funde*, nos. 22–33. A number of Estonian finds probably from that period were found in the early nineteenth century, and are poorly documented and therefore difficult to date. Some of them (for example the find of Kirumpää, which has been assigned a *t.p.q.* of 1056) may belong to the later part of the century.

[22]   K. Jonsson, 'The coinage of Cnut', in *The Reign of Cnut. King of England, Denmark and Norway*, ed. A.R. Rumble, (London/New York, 1994), 193–230, at 213.

the possible exception of Skåne. Also in Russia, the numbers of coins decrease remarkably during the reign of Cnut.[23] However, Denmark and Norway seem to have constantly received fresh bullion from England until the mid-eleventh century. Estonia in turn is somewhere in between. The influx of Anglo-Saxon coins to Estonia in Cnut's reign was, if not increasing, at least stable. Only afterwards did the obvious but still relatively slow downturn begin: the years 1035–40 brought half as many new Anglo-Saxon coins to Estonia as the years 1030–35. A decline in the number of English coins continues thereafter. However, there is one exception: the *Radiate/Small Cross* pennies of Edward the Confessor which are believed to have been struck *c.*1044–46. These are the most numerous among all the Edwardian coins found in Estonia.[24] Moreover, the same is true in almost all the other territories around the Baltic: on Gotland, in Svealand, Götaland, Bornholm, Norway, Denmark, Finland and Latvia (Figures 25.2–25.8 and 25.12–25.13).[25] The only exception is Skåne but the picture there may be distorted by a couple of finds of unusual composition (Figure 25.11).[26] And in Russia, too, the prevalence of this coin type is not so obvious (Figure 25.10).[27] It is difficult to explain why this particular coin type of Edward is so exceptionally numerous in most of the Nordic territories. The calculated numbers of dies for the *Radiate/Small Cross* and for the preceding and subsequent coin types (*Pacx* and *Trefoil Quadrilateral*) are, at least for a part of England, almost equal.[28] Thus, the prevalence of the *Radiate/Small Cross* pennies of Edward seems not to be directly related to their mint output. Peter Sawyer has pointed out that the export of Anglo-Saxon coins declined significantly after 1051, when the king disbanded his Scandinavian fleet.[29] He is right if one only considers coins of Edward's reign. More broadly, however, the graphs tell us that the export of Anglo-Saxon pennies to the Baltic started to decline much earlier, during the reign of Cnut and/or Harold I (1035–40). An apparent peak in Harold's *Jewel Cross* (again almost everywhere) may be a result of methodological error, caused by the theory of periodic type changes: it is not known for sure whether reforms were carried out every two or three years during Harold's reign.

Nevertheless, the import of Anglo-Saxon pennies to Estonia and also to other lands around the Baltic declined sooner than the influx of German *Denare* did.

---

[23] Cf. V.M. Potin, *SCBI 60. Hermitage Museum, St Petersburg. Part II. Anglo-Saxon Coins 1016–1066* (Oxford, 2008).

[24] Cf. Leimus and Molvõgin, *SCBI* 51.

[25] Jonsson, 'Routes', 229–30.

[26] Persson, *Engelska mynt*, 26.

[27] Cf. Potin, *SCBI* 60.

[28] Metcalf, 'Can we believe', 174.

[29] P. Sawyer, 'Anglo-Scandinavian trade in the Viking Age and after', in *ASMH*, 185–99, at 195–6, 198.

Kenneth Jonsson has put forward the theory that the Anglo-Saxon and German coins were already mixed before being imported to the Northern Lands, and proposed that this mixing occurred somewhere in the Rhine estuary. Based on the decline of the Anglo-Saxon coin imports, he suggested that the Rhine connections probably weakened from *c.*1030 and the centre of trade moved eastwards.[30] In the Linnakse hoard, however, the mints located along the Rhine route are well represented, including a considerable share of them among the later coins. Among these, coins from Speyer, Worms, Mainz, Cologne, Deventer and Tiel prevail. If one takes into account the many chronological reattributions of German coins that have been made during the last decades by various scholars, the same may also be true of some other Nordic hoards from the same period.

If Kenneth Jonsson is right (and even if he is not), the import of Anglo-Saxon pennies to the continent, for some reason or another, must have decreased markedly in the 1030s–1040s. At the same time, a few more or less direct contacts from England seem to have persisted, especially to Skåne, Denmark and Norway (and *vice versa*) but perhaps also to Estonia and other areas. Without these contacts it would be difficult to explain the differences in the composition of Anglo-Saxon parts of hoards from various territories located side by side around the Baltic. The export of the monetary silver from the Rhine mints, on the other hand, seems to have continued after 1030 on a large scale. If so, it speaks in favour of more or less direct contacts between the Northern Lands on one hand and England and Germany on the other, rather than for an international bullion market situated somewhere in the estuaries of German rivers. However, further detailed analyses of hoard composition from the mid-eleventh century are necessary to prove or reject this hypothesis.

Appendix: Catalogue of Coins in the Linnakse hoard

Coins marked with an * are illustrated on plates available on the website of the Eesti Ajaloomuuseum (www.ajaloomuuseum.ee/figures/plate1.jpg and www.ajaloomuuseum.ee/figures/plate2.jpg).
Abbreviations used:

Abp archbishop	Frg fragment
Abt abbot	K king
Bp bishop	per. period
Emp emperor	

For bibliographic abbreviations, see pp. 619–22 below.

---

[30] Jonsson, 'Routes', 227–8.

	Ruler	Mint	Year (AH)	Wt (g)
	ISLAMIC COINS			
	Umayyad caliphate			
1	'Abd al-Malik	al-Basra	80	2.86
2	uncertain ruler?	uncertain mint?	year?	0.39 (frg)
	'Abbasid caliphate			
3	Al-Mahdi	Madīnat as-Salām	161	2.75
	'Uqailid			
4	Husām ad-daula & Janāh al-Mawsil ad-daula		389	3.42 (frg, pierced)
5	Mu'tamid ad-daula & Nūr ad-daula	Nasibin	39x	2.42
	Abu Da'udid (Banijurid)			
6	Muhammad ibn Ahmad	Andaraba?	year?	4.54
	Samanid			
7	Nasr ibn Ahmad	Marw	302	3.60 (remains of silver suspension loop, rivet)
8	Nasr ibn Ahmad	aš-Šaš	325	4.65 (bronze suspension loop, pierced)
9	uncertain ruler?	uncertain mint?	year?	0.52 (frg)
	Governors of Khurasan			
10	Ahmad ibn Sahl	Andaraba	303	2.85 (bronze suspension loop, pierced)
11	Ahmad ibn Sahl	Andaraba	year?	2.16
	Volga-Bulgars			
12	'Nasr ibn Ahmad'	uncertain mint?	year?	2.76

Buyid

	Mint	Ruler	Date	Reference	Wt (g)
13		Rukn ad-daula & 'Adud ad-daula	[Sīrāf] Treadwell 2001, p. 68	339	2.84

Imitations

	Ruler	Mint	Date		Wt (g)
14	'Ismā'īl'	uncertain mint?	year?		3.04 (pierced twice)
15	Uncertain ruler?	uncertain mint?	year?		3.50 (bronze suspension loop, pierced 4 times)

	Mint	Ruler	Date	Reference	Wt (g)

GERMAN COINS

Upper Lorraine

	Mint	Ruler	Date	Reference	Wt (g)
16–17	Verdun	'Henry I'	c.983–1002	Dbg 92; CNG 3.3.	1.25, 1.20
18	Verdun	Bp Haimo	990–1024	Dbg 96; CNG 3.8.	1.20
19	Verdun	Bp Raimbert	1024–39	Dbg 102; CNG 3.11.	1.24
20	Toul	Bp Bruno	1026–51	Dbg 37; CNG 8.7.	1.31
21	Toul	Bp Bruno	1026–51	Var. Dbg 604; CNG 8.6.1.	1.16
22	Metz	Bp Dietrich I	965–84	Dbg 1400; CNG 9.11.	1.34
23	Metz	Bp Adalbero II	984–1005	Dbg 25, 25a; CNG 9.19.	0.88
24	Metz	Bp Adalbero III	1047–72	Dbg 36; CNG 9.22:3	0.60
25–9	Trier	Abp Poppo	1016–47	Dbg 466; CNG 17.14.	1.14, 1.13, 1.11, 1.06, 0.84
30–32	Trier	Abp Poppo	1016–47	Dbg 468; CNG 17.15.	1.17, 1.11, 1.10

	Mint	Ruler	Date	Reference	Wt (g)
33	Trier	Abp Poppo	1016–47	Var. Dbg 468; CNG 17.15. Obol	0.61
34	Echternach	Abt Humbert	1028–51	Dbg 494; CNG 19.1.	1.05
35	Prüm	Henry III	1039–56	Dbg 1189; CNG 20.5.2.	1.01
36	Prüm	anon		Dbg 1242/1225; CNG 20.7. (obv.)/ 20.8.(rev.)	1.01
37	Prüm	anon		Dbg 1242, 1242a (obv.)/ CNG 20.7. (obv.)	1.02
38–9	Andernach	Duke Dietrich	984–1027	Dbg 439/440; CNG 22.2.7:12	1.40, 1.17
40–2	Andernach		1024–	Dbg 433a–b; CNG 22.7	1.02, 0.91, 0.56 (cut halfpenny)
43	Andernach		1024–	Dbg 434; CNG 22.9.	1.32
44–50	Andernach		1027/30–1050/60	Dbg 449, 451; CNG 22.17.	1.24, 1.24, 1.20, 1.18, 1.13, 1.06, 0.87
51–70	Andernach		1027/30–1050/60	Dbg 449, 451; CNG 22.17. Var. with the 'mountain'	1.27, 1.25, 1.23, 1.22, 1.21, 1.20, 1.18, 1.14, 1.14, 1.13, 1.11, 1.11, 1.10, 1.10, 1.09, 1.08, 1.08, 1.07, 1.05, 0.93
71–2	Andernach?	Duke Dietrich?	984–1027	Var. Dbg 444, CNG 22.4. Head right	1.28, 1.16
73	Uncertain				1.18

LOWER LOTHARINGIA

Region of western Lower Lotharingia

	Mint	Ruler	Date	Reference	Wt (g)
74	Uncertain mint	Duke Gottfried I	1012–23	Dbg 1438	1.26
75–6	Uncertain mint	ducal		Dbg 1740; Albrecht 1959, Pl. 10	1.00, 0.82

	Mint	Ruler	Date	Reference	Wt (g)
77	Uncertain mint (Flanders)			Dbg 1366	0.75
78	St. Omer			Dbg 1389	0.69
79	Lens, Boulogne	Count Eustace	1046, 49	Dbg 1455	1.05
80–2	Brussels			Dbg 142, 142b	1.00, 0.99, 0.97
83	Nivelles	anon		Var. Dbg 143	0.98
84	Antwerp			Dbg 140	0.96
85	Bouillon	Duke Gottfried	c.1050	Dbg 188; Albrecht 1959, Pl. 7	1.21
86–8	Namur	Count Albert II	1018–64	Dbg 164	1.16, 1.16, 1.10
89–96	Namur	Count Albert II	1018–64	Dbg 165	1.18, 1.18, 1.10, 1.08, 1.07, 0.99, 0.98, 0.98
97–8	Dinant	Count Albert II	1018–64	Dbg 174	1.21, 1.16
99–102	Dinant	Count Albert II	1018–64	Dbg 176	1.10, 1.06, 1.01, 0.99
103	Dinant	Count Albert II	1018–64	Dbg 177	1.12
104	Liège	K. Henry II	1002–14	Dbg 194 (obv.)/ 197 (rev.)	1.12
105	Liège	K. Henry II	1002–14	Dbg 197	0.98
106	Liège	Emp. Henry II	1014–24	Dbg 195–196	1.08
107–8	Liège	anon		Dbg 200	1.49, 1.26
109–13	Liège	anon		Dbg 1228	1.13, 1.06, 1.02, 0.89, 0.85
114	Liège	anon		Dbg 1823	1.13
115–16	Liège?	Henry II	1002–24	Var. Dbg 286	1.31, 0.97

	Mint	Ruler	Date	Reference	Wt (g)
117	Liège?	anon		Dbg 1823?	1.21
118	Liège?	Conrad II	1024–39	Cf. Dbg 1849	1.31
119	Huy	K. Henry II	1002–14	Dbg 225	0.94
120	Huy	Henry II	1002–24	Dbg 226a	0.93
121	Huy	Emp. Henry II	1014–24	Dbg 228, 1492	1.23
122	Huy	Emp. Conrad II	1027–39	Dbg 230	1.11
123–4	Huy	Emp. Conrad II	1027–39	Var. Dbg 230	1.08, 0.83
125–7	Maastricht	Henry II	1002–24	Dbg 246a	1.14, 1.01, 0.91
128–30	Maastricht	Henry II	1002–24	Dbg 1500; Albrecht 1959, Pl. 3	1.22, 1.12, 1.03
131–3	Maastricht	Conrad II	1024–39	Dbg 249, 1370	1.11, 1.01, 0.97
134	Maastricht	anon		Dbg 252	1.00
135	Maastricht	anon		Dbg 253	1.13
136	Maastricht	anon		Dbg 254	1.12
137	Maastricht?	Henry II?	1002–24	Dbg 246a?	0.99
138–9	Ciney	anon		Dbg 1219a, b	1.23, 0.96
140–2	Visé	Henry II	1002–24	Dbg 541; Albrecht 1959, Table 4	1.15, 0.99, 0.96
143–4	St Trond			Dbg 340?, Ilisch 1987	1.35, 0.96
145	Celles	Emp. Henry II	1014–24	Dbg 186	1.15
146–7	Aachen	Henry III?	1039–56	Dbg 1192; Krumbach 1995, 4	1.16, 0.98

	Mint	Ruler	Date	Reference	Wt (g)
148	Aachen	anon		Dbg -; Krumbach 1995 -	1.07
149	Uncertain mint	Duke Friedrich		Dbg 1234a	0.97
150	Uncertain mint	royal?			1.42
151	Uncertain mint	ecclesiastical			1.17
152	Uncertain mint	ecclesiastical			1.24
153	Uncertain mint				1.08

Region of Cologne

	Mint	Ruler	Date	Reference	Wt (g)
154–67	Cologne	Otto III	983–1002	Häv. 34; Ilisch 1990, S. 128 ff.	1.95, 1.93, 1.58, 1.55, 1.37, 1.35, 1.33, 1.29, 1.25, 1.24, 1.24, 1.18, 1.16, 0.97
168	Cologne	K. Henry II	1002–14	Häv. 156	1.25
169–74	Cologne	Emp. Henry II	1014–24	Häv. 189	1.29, 1.28, 1.20, 1.18, 1.15, 1.06
175–84	Cologne	Emp. Conrad II & Abp Pilgrim	1027–36	Häv. 222	1.55, 1.48, 1.43, 1.42, 1.40, 1.31, 1.29, 1.29, 0.98, 0.71 (cut halfpenny)
185–8	Cologne	Emp. Conrad II & Abp Hermann	1036–39	Häv. 251a	1.59, 1.59, 1.44, 1.07
189–99	Cologne	Abp Hermann	1039–56	Häv. 278	1.55, 1.50, 1.35, 1.32, 1.28, 1.19, 1.14, 1.12, 0.62 (cut halfpenny), 0.59 (cut halfpenny), 0.54 (cut halfpenny)
200	Cologne	Abp Hermann	1039–56	Häv. 293	0.73 (cut halfpenny)
201–2	Cologne	Abp Anno	1056–75	Häv. 313f	1.05, 0.67 (cut halfpenny)

	Mint	Ruler	Date	Reference	Wt (g)
203	Cologne	Abp Anno	1056–75	Häv. 322	1.13
204–6	Cologne	Abp Anno	1056–75	Häv. 323, 323a	1.36, 1.15, 1.15
207	Cologne	Abp Anno	1056–75	Häv. 325	1.13
208–9	Imitations of Cologne	Frisian?		cf. Häv. 32	1.29, 1.20
210–12	Imitations of Cologne			Häv. 61	1.17, 1.09, 0.89
213–15	Imitations of Cologne	Rhenish		Häv. 78	1.27, 1.16, 0.91
216	Imitation of Cologne	Rhenish		Häv. 81–82	1.31
217–21	Imitations of Cologne	Slavic?		Häv. 135	1.28, 1.10, 1.07, 0.91 (frg), 0.87
222	Imitation of Cologne	Andernach? Conrad II & Abp Piligrim		Häv. 226	1.41
223	Imitation of Cologne	Count Palatine Henry I?	1045–60	Häv. 231d; Schulten 2011, type I	0.94
224	Imitation of Cologne	Orgerus?		Var. Häv. 263	0.76
225	Imitation of Cologne	Conrad II & Abp Hermann		Häv. 264	1.16
226	Imitation of Cologne	Conrad II & Abp Hermann		Häv. 265	1.19
227	Imitation of Cologne	Conrad II & Abp Hermann		Var. Häv. 270	1.32, 1.09
228	Imitation of Cologne	Abp Hermann II		Cf. Häv. 278	1.31
229	Imitation of Cologne	Slavic?			0.99
230–41	Imitations of Cologne	3 lines; uncertain			1.59, 1.48, 1.41, 1.33, 1.28, 1.26, 1.19, 1.04, 0.96, 0.92, 0.85, 0.72 (frg)

	Mint	Ruler	Date	Reference	Wt (g)
242-4	Xanten	Abp Hermann II	1036-56	Dbg 308; Häv. 772	1.14, 1.04, 0.94
245	Remagen	anon		Dbg 429	1.40
246-7	Remagen	anon		Dbg 430; Häv. 212; Petry 1995, p. 293	1.22, 0.67 (cut halfpenny)
248-52	Remagen	anon		Dbg 431; Häv. 214; Petry 1995, p. 293	1.59, 1.52, 1.37, 1.37, 1.31
253-4	Remagen or Andernach	Emp. Henry II	1014-24	Häv. 207	1.36, 1.24,
255	Remagen or Andernach	Emp. Henry II	1014-24	Häv. 208	1.42
256-60	Duisburg	Emp. Conrad II	1027-39	Dbg 311; Berghaus 1983 1:1	1.64, 1.37, 1.35, 1.29, 1.25
261	Duisburg	Emp. Conrad II	1027-39	Dbg 312; Berghaus 1983 1:7	1.42
262	Duisburg	Emp. Conrad II	1027-39	Dbg 311-313; Berghaus 1983 1:9	1.19
263	Duisburg	K. Henry III	1039-46	Dbg 315; Berghaus 1983 2:1a	1.24
264	Duisburg	Emp. Henry III	1046-56	Dbg 317; Berghaus 1983 5:1	0.64 (cut halfpenny)
265	Imitation of Duisburg	K. Henry IV	1056-84	Berghaus 1983 7:1cN	1.54
266	Duisburg or Minden	Emp. Henry III	1039-46	Ilisch 1977, 23; Häv. 299	1.10
267	'Minden'	K. Henry III	1046-56	Dbg 428; Ilisch 1977, 27	1.42
268-9	'Minden'	K. Henry III	1046-56	Dbg 727	1.27, 0.90

	Mint	Ruler	Date	Reference	Wt (g)
270	'Minden'	K. Henry III	1046–56	Dbg 728; Ilisch 1977, 17	1.17
271–2	'Minden'	K. Henry III	1046–56	Dbg 729; Ilisch 1977, 21	1.49, 1.45
273	Minden?	Uncertain issuer		CNS 8.1.3:30	1.14
	Region of Utrecht				
274	Utrecht	Conrad II or Bp Bernold		Dbg 540 or 543	0.75
275–6	Utrecht	Bp Bernold	1027–54	Dbg 544	0.78, 0.68
277	Utrecht	Bp Wilhelm de Ponte	1054–76	Dbg 545	0.65
278–90	Deventer	Emp. Henry II	1014–24	Dbg 563	1.25, 1.15, 1.14, 1.11, 1.10, 1.09, 1.06, 1.04, 1.03, 1.00, 0.95, 0.93, 0.56 (cut halfpenny)
291–3	Deventer	Emp. Henry II	1014–24	Dbg 564	1.12, 1.11, 0.54 (cut halfpenny)
294–8	Deventer	Emp. Conrad II	1027–39	Dbg 566	1.22, 1.21, 1.18, 1.14, 0.97
299–305	Deventer	Bp Bernold	1027–54 (1046–50)	Dbg 568; Watz 1992, p. 10–13	1.01, 1.01, 1.01, 1.00, 0.99, 0.97, 0.95
306	Deventer	Henry III & Bp Bernold	1039–54 (1050–60)	Dbg 571; Watz 1992, p. 10–13	1.06
307–8	Deventer	Bp Bernold	1027–54 (1050–60)	Dbg 572; Watz 1992, p. 10–13	1.10, 1.05
309–14	Deventer	Bp Bernold	1027–54 (1050–60)	Dbg 573; Watz 1992, p. 10–13	1.16, 1.14, 1.13, 1.04, 0.97, 0.95
315–18	Deventer	Bp Bernold	1027–54 (1050–60)	Dbg 570–573; Watz 1992, p. 10–13	1.11, 1.01, 1.01, 0.97
319–21	Groningen	Bp Bernold	1027–54 (1046–54)	Dbg 558; Johansson 1997, p. 7–8	0.85, 0.71, 0.65
322	Groningen	K. Henry IV & Bp Wilhelm	1056–76	Dbg 546	0.78

	Mint	Ruler	Date	Reference	Wt (g)
323–5	Tiel	Henry II– Conrad II	1014–39	Hatz 1968 D; Jonsson 2012, 2a–bo	1.40, 1.24, 1.24
326	Tiel	Conrad II	1024–39	Hatz 1968 D30; Jonsson 2012, 2b	1.31
327–9	Tiel	Conrad II– Henry III	1024–56	Hatz 1968 C; Jonsson 2012, 3a–c	1.38, 1.21, 1.12
330–3	Tiel	Henry III	1039–56	Hatz 1968 B2, Jonsson 2012, 4a	1.65, 1.64, 1.43, 1.21
334–44	Tiel	Henry III	1039–56	Hatz 1968 B; Jonsson 2012, 4a–b	1.34, 1.32, 1.31, 1.30, 1.29, 1.19, 1.14, 1.02, 0.96, 0.90, 0.64
345–7	Tiel	Henry IV	1056–84	Hatz 1968 D46 or 49; Jonsson 2012, 6c	1.01, 0.98, 0.87
348	Tiel? Subordinate mint?	Conrad II	1024–39	Hatz 1968 F31; Jonsson 2012, TN1	1.36
349–51	Tiel or Zaltbommel	episcopal	c.1056–70	Hatz 1968 D22; Jonsson 2012, E3a	1.33, 1.27, 1.23
352–4	Tiel or Zaltbommel	episcopal	c.1056–70	Hatz 1968 G68–69; Jonsson 2012, E3a	1.20, 1.02, 0.85
355	Tiel or Zaltbommel	episcopal	c.1056–70	Hatz 1968 G70; Jonsson 2012, E3a	1.40
356	Tiel or Zaltbommel	episcopal	c.1056–70	Hatz 1968 G72; Jonsson 2012, E3a	1.13
357	Tiel or Zaltbommel	episcopal	c.1056–70	Hatz 1968 G68–72; Jonsson 2012, E3a	1.18
358	Tiel or Zaltbommel	episcopal	c.1056–70	Hatz 1968 G74; Jonsson 2012, E3a	1.56
359	Imitation of Tiel?	episcopal	c.1055–70	Hatz 1968 G77; Jonsson 2012	0.93
360–1	Imitation of Tiel?	episcopal	c.1055–70	Hatz 1968 G79; Jonsson 2012	0.82, 0.77

	Mint	Ruler	Date	Reference	Wt (g)
362	Imitation of Tiel?	episcopal	c.1055–70	Hatz 1968 G79–80; Jonsson 2012	0.97
363	Imitation of Tiel?	episcopal	c.1055–70	Hatz 1968 88; Jonsson 2012	1.23
Frisian region					
364–8	Uncertain mint	Count Wichmann III	994–1016	Dbg 1229	0.87, 0.84, 0.82, 0.75, 0.73
369–70	Dokkum	K. Henry III & Count Bruno III	1034–45 (1045–57)	Dbg 499; Kjellgren 1993, pp. 9–11	0.73, 0.65
371	Dokkum?	K. Henry III & Count Bruno III	1034–45 (1045–57)	cf. Dbg 499; Kjellgren 1993, pp. 9–11	0.66
372	Stavoren	K. Henry III & Count Bruno III	1034–45 (1045–57)	Dbg 503; Kjellgren 1993, pp. 9–11	0.85
373–7	Emden?			Dbg 1299b; Kjellgren 1993, 16	0.92, 0.88, 0.85, 0.79, 0.76
378	Emden?			Dbg 1300; Kilger 2000, p. 176	0.84
379	Emden	Count Hermann von Kalvelage	1020–51 (1050–70)	Dbg 772–773; Kjellgren 1993, pp. 17–18	0.76
380	Jever	Duke Hermann	1059–86	Dbg 597	1.03
381–4	Uncertain mint	Duke Gottfried III	1044–57	Dbg 1311; Giesen 2008	0.84, 0.75, 0.71, 0.65
385	Uncertain mint	Emp. Henry III	1046–56	Dbg –; rev. +ESCH//EVVEGA	1.35
386	Uncertain mint	Emp. Henry III	1046–56	Dbg –	0.75

SAXONY

Westphalia

	Mint	Ruler	Date	Reference	Wt (g)
387	Dortmund	Emp. Otto III	996–1002	Berghaus 1978, 7	1.60
388	Dortmund	K. Henry II	1002–14	Berghaus 1978, 16	1.29
389	Dortmund	K. Henry II	1002–14	Berghaus 1978, 20	0.92
390	Dortmund	Henry II	1002–24		1.40
391	Dortmund	K. Conrad II	1024–27	Berghaus 1978, 23	1.24
392–5	Dortmund	K. Conrad II	1024–27	Berghaus 1978, 24	1.53, 1.38, 1.34, 0.76 (cut halfpenny)
396–432	Soest	Imitation of Cologne		Häv. 849–850; Ilisch 1990, pp. 142 f.	1.59, 1.57, 1.51, 1.44, 1.43, 1.42, 1.41, 1.39, 1.39, 1.38, 1.37, 1.37, 1.36, 1.36, 1.34, 1.34, 1.31, 1.30, 1.30, 1.29, 1.29, 1.28, 1.25, 1.23, 1.22, 1.19, 1.16, 1.14, 1.13, 1.12, 1.11, cut halves: 0.81, 0.81, 0.71, 0.57
433	Soest?	Copy of Cologne		Häv. 854	1.05
434–5	Soest?	Copy of Cologne		Leimus 2002	1.44, 1.39
436–9	Soest or Niederlothringen	Emp. Conrad II	1027–39	Häv. 852; Ilisch 1981, pp. 149 ff.	1.38, 1.23, 1.18, 1.12
440	Corvey	Emp. Henry III & Abt Ruthard	1046–50	Dbg 735	1.40
441–3	Corvey	Abt Arnold I	1051–55	Dbg 736	1.28, 1.25, 0.94
Lower Saxony					
444–50	Bremen?	Abp Adalbert?	1043–66	Dbg 1777; Ilisch & Jonsson 1993; Kilger 2000, BremD	1.05, 0.99, 0.99, 0.98, 0.85, 0.84, 0.75
451	Stade	Henry III	1039–56	Dbg 720	1.02
452–3	Bardowick?			Dbg 1278	1.15, 0.98

	Mint	Ruler	Date	Reference	Wt (g)
454	Bardowick?			Dbg 1289	1.00
455–6	Bardowick?			Dbg 1292	1.05, 0.85
457–9	Bardowick?			Häv. 309	1.11, 1.04, 0.37 (frg)
460–2	Bardowick?			Häv. 714, var.	1.06, 0.96, 0.84
463–4	Bardowick? Lüneburg?			Hatz 1967, 5–6; Kilger 2000, 3.2.6, IIIA	1.01
465	Hildesheim	Bp Bernward	993–1002	Dbg 710a; Mehl 1995, 3	1.04
466	Hildesheim	Bp Azelin	1044–54	Dbg 713; Mehl, 1995 12	1.34
467	Hildesheim?	Bp Azelin?	1044–54	Dbg 713 o. 717?	0.93
468–70	Goslar	Emp. Henry III	1046–56	Dbg 668	1.38, 1.31, 1.07
471–2	Goslar and others	Otto-Adelheid-Pfennige		Hatz 1961, III	1.66, 1.48
473–520	Goslar and others	Otto-Adelheid-Pfennige		Hatz 1961, IV	1.72, 1.69, 1.57, 1.52, 1.52, 1.51, 1.50, 1.48, 1.48, 1.48, 1.47, 1.46, 1.45, 1.45, 1.41, 1.34, 1.34, 1.33, 1.33, 1.33, 1.32, 1.32, 1.32, 1.31, 1.30, 1.29, 1.29, 1.28, 1.24, 1.23, 1.22, 1.22, 1.21, 1.20, 1.19, 1.18, 1.13, 1.11, 1.08, 1.08, 1.07, 1.07, 0.99 (frg), 0.96, 0.83, 0.63 (frg)
521–2	Goslar and others	Otto-Adelheid-Pfennige		Hatz 1961, IV, Obol; Giesen 2012, Group 2	0.73, 0.56

	Mint	Ruler	Date	Reference	Wt (g)
523–88	Gittelde?	imitations of Otto-Adelheid-Pfennige		Hatz 1961, V	1.58, 1.56, 1.46, 1.38, 1.32, 1.31, 1.31, 1.30, 1.29, 1.26, 1.25, 1.25, 1.24, 1.24, 1.24, 1.23, 1.22, 1.22, 1.22, 1.19, 1.19, 1.18, 1.18, 1.17, 1.17, 1.17, 1.16, 1.16, 1.15, 1.15, 1.14, 1.14, 1.13, 1.13, 1.12, 1.12, 1.12, 1.11, 1.11, 1.10, 1.10, 1.10, 1.09, 1.09, 1.07, 1.06, 1.05, 1.05, 1.05, 1.04, 1.04, 1.03, 1.03, 1.03, 1.02, 1.01, 0.96, 0.96, 0.96, 0.94, 0.88, 0.74
589	Uncertain mint	imitations of Otto-Adelheid-Pfennige		After Hatz 1961, V.4	0.76
590–604	Gittelde?	imitations of Otto-Adelheid-Pfennige		Hatz 1961, VI	1.57, 1.46, 1.46, 1.18, 1.13, 1.12, 1.12, 1.11, 1.11, 1.06, 1.00, 0.99, 0.98, 0.93, 0.68 (cut halfpenny)
605–11	Gittelde?	anon		Dbg 1310; Jammer 1952, pp. 67 ff.	1.36, 1.36, 1.30, 1.23, 1.16, 1.15, 1.04
612–14	Gittelde	anon		Dbg 1221; Jammer 1952, p. 67	1.26, 1.13, 0.95
615–17	Gittelde	anon		Dbg 1222; Jammer 1952, p. 67	1.14, 1.01, 0.98
618	Sachsen	Count Dietmar		Dbg 1559	0.97
619–21	Bursfelde?	Henry III	1046–56	Var. Dbg 1591; Jammer 1952, pl. 5	1.21, 1.21, 1.11
Eastphalia					
622–6	Magdeburg	anon	c.1035–50	Dbg 648; Mehl 2011, 42	1.44, 1.43, 1.39, 1.30, 1.29
627	Magdeburg	anon	c.1035–50	Dbg 648; Mehl 2011, 43	1.44
628–30	Magdeburg	anon	c.1035–50	Dbg 648; Mehl 2011, 44	1.44, 1.28, 1.18
631	Magdeburg	anon	c.1035–50	Dbg 648; Mehl 2011, 45	1.40

	Mint	Ruler	Date	Reference	Wt (g)
632	Magdeburg	anon	c.1035–50	Dbg 648; Mehl 2011, 42–46, imitations	1.12
633–4	Magdeburg	anon	c.1050–60	Dbg 647; Mehl 2011, 48	1.31, 1.27
635–40	Sachsenpfennige	Magdeburg?		Dbg 1330; Kilger 2000, 4.2.1; Mehl 2011, 30	1.42, 1.40, 1.30, 1.20, 1.15, 0.90
641	Sachsenpfennige	Merseburg?		Dbg 1333; Kilger 2000, 5.1.3A	1.37
642–3	Sachsenpfennige	Meissen?		Dbg 1335; Kilger 2000, 5.2.1A2	0.97, 0.89 (pierced twice)
644–6	Sachsenpfennige	south Saale region (Naumburg?)		Var. Dbg 1347; Kilger 2000, 5.1.4.AD2	1.12, 1.04, 1.00
647	Sachsenpfennige	south Saale region (Naumburg?)		Dbg 1347; Kilger 2000, 5.14.BD4	1.14
648	Halberstadt	Bp Burchard	1036–59	Dbg 628	1.22
649	Erfurt	Otto III and imitations		Dbg 778/9; Stoess 1989, 2	1.00
650	Erfurt	Otto III and imitations		Stoess 1989, 3	1.24
651–3	Erfurt	Otto III and imitations		Stoess 1989, 11	1.23, 1.10, 1.10
654–5	Erfurt	Otto III and imitations		Stoess 1989, 16	1.08, 1.03
656–62	Erfurt	Otto III and imitations		Stoess 1989, 17	1.24, 1.23, 1.20, 1.18, 1.14, 1.03, 0.95
663	Erfurt	Otto III and imitations		Stoess 1989, 21?	0.89
664	Erfurt	Otto III and imitations		Stoess 1989, 22	1.02
665	Erfurt	Otto III and imitations		Stoess 1989, 27	1.03
666–7	Erfurt	Otto III and imitations		Stoess 1989, 31	1.21, 0.93
668–9	Erfurt	Otto III and imitations		Stoess 1989, 32	1.14, 1.06

	Mint	Ruler	Date	Reference	Wt (g)
670	Erfurt	Otto III and imitations		Stoess 1989, 31–32	0.97
671–3	Erfurt	Otto III and imitations		Stoess 1989, ?	0.99, 0.95, 0.88
674–6	Erfurt	Abp Lupold	1051–59	Dbg 881	1.23, 1.12, 0.97
677–81	Erfurt	Abp Lupold	1051–59	Dbg 882	1.23, 1.21, 1.17, 1.17, 0.99
682–9	Erfurt	Emp. Henry III	1046–56	Dbg 883, a	1.28 (pierced), 1.25, 1.19, 1.15, 1.14, 1.06, 1.06, 0.91
690	Erfurt	Emp. Henry III	1046–56	Cf. Dbg 883, 1664	0.98
691–2	Erfurt	Abp Siegfried	1060–84	Dbg 1837; CNS 4.1.5:2245	1.02, 1.01
693	Erfurt or Hersfeld	Abp Lupold or Abt Rudhard		Cf. Dbg 1658, 1660	1.11
	FRANCONIA				
694–714	Fritzlar	Copies of Cologne		Ilisch 2004	1.30, 1.28, 1.27, 1.25, 1.21, 1.15, 1.13, 1.13, 1.13, 1.12, 1.09, 1.09, 1.08, 1.08, 1.06, 1.06, 1.06, 1.06, 1.04, 1.03, 1.02
715	Fritzlar	Conrad II	1024–39	Ilisch 2004, S. 15	1.58
716–17	Fulda	anon		Dbg 871	0.95, 0.93
718	Würzburg	Emp. Otto III	996–1002	Dbg 856	0.93
719–27	Würzburg	anon		Dbg 859	0.98, 0.96, 0.93, 0.90, 0.86, 0.82, 0.82
728	Würzburg	anon		Var. Dbg 859	0.68
729	Würzburg	anon		Dbg 862	1.25
730–1	Würzburg	Bp Bruno	1034–45	Dbg 863	1.04, 0.74

	Mint	Ruler	Date	Reference	Wt (g)
732–40	Würzburg	Bp Bruno	1034–45	Dbg 864	1.11, 1.04, 1.03, 0.86, 0.82, 0.80, 0.77, 0.72, 0.67
741	Würzburg	anon		Dbg 1845	1.00
742–3	Bamberg	anon		Dbg 1653b	0.97, 0.40 (cut halfpenny)
744–5	Mainz	K. Henry II & Abp Willigis	1002–11	Dbg 802	1.61, 1.59
746–52	Mainz	Henry II	1002–24	Dbg 785	1.15, 1.06, 1.04, 0.99, 0.94, 0.87, 0.71
753	Mainz	Emp. Henry II	1014–24	Dbg 788	1.49
754–7	Mainz	K. Conrad II	1024–27	Dbg 789	1.15, 1.10, 1.02, 0.92
758	Mainz	Henry II or Conrad II		Dbg 785 or 789	0.89
759–87	Mainz	K. Conrad II	1027–39	Dbg 790	1.38, 1.28, 1.20, 1.19, 1.16, 1.15, 1.14, 1.14, 1.13, 1.10, 1.08, 1.07, 1.06, 1.06, 1.05, 1.04, 1.04, 1.03, 1.02, 0.99, 0.99, 0.97, 0.97, 0.95, 0.89, 0.80, 0.79
788–800	Mainz	Henry III	1039–56	Dbg 793	1.25, 1.22, 1.17, 1.13, 1.11, 1.08, 1.04, 1.04, 1.03, 1.03, 1.03, 1.02, 0.92
801–2	Mainz	Henry III	1039–56	Dbg 793, Obol	0.66, 0.61
803–10	Mainz	Henry III & Abp Bardo	1031–51	Dbg 805	0.99, 0.98, 0.98, 0.98, 0.97, 0.97, 0.96
811–12	Mainz	Conrad II or Henry III & Abp Bardo		Dbg 804 or 805	0.90, 0.85
813–28	Mainz	Henry III & Abp Lupold	1051–56	Dbg 807	1.30, 1.26, 1.20, 1.17, 1.17, 1.17, 1.16, 1.16, 1.16, 1.16 (pierced), 1.14, 1.13, 1.12, 1.02, 0.97, 0.96
829	Worms	Otto II–III	973–1002	Dbg 842	1.15

	Mint	Ruler	Date	Reference	Wt (g)
830	Worms	Emp. Otto III	996–1002	Dbg 844	0.97
831–921	Worms	Henry II	c.1024–46	Dbg 845, var.; Leimus 1993	1.14, 1.12, 1.10, 1.10, 1.10, 1.09, 1.09, 1.09, 1.09, 1.09, 1.08 (pierced), 1.07, 1.07, 1.07, 1.07, 1.06, 1.06, 1.06, 1.05, 1.05, 1.05, 1.05, 1.05, 1.04, 1.04, 1.04, 1.03, 1.02, 1.02, 1.02, 1.01, 1.01, 1.01, 1.01, 1.00, 1.00, 1.00, 1.00, 1.00, 0.99, 0.99, 0.98, 0.97, 0.96, 0.95, 0.95, 0.95, 0.94, 0.94, 0.94, 0.93, 0.93, 0.93, 0.93, 0.93, 0.92, 0.92, 0.92, 0.92, 0.91, 0.91, 0.91, 0.89, 0.89, 0.87, 0.86, 0.86, 0.84, 0.84, 0.83, 0.82, 0.82, 0.79, 0.77, 0.75, 0.75, 0.75, 0.73, 0.73, 0.72, 0.72, 0.69, 0.67, 0.66, 0.66, 0.61, 0.40 (cut halfpenny), 0.31 (frg)
922–43	Worms	Henry III	1039–56	Dbg 847	1.21, 1.21, 1.20, 1.19, 1.18, 1.18, 1.18, 1.17, 1.17, 1.16, 1.15, 1.15, 1.14, 1.12, 1.11, 1.11, 1.10, 1.05, 1.03, 0.99, 0.98, 0.89, 0.60 (cut halfpenny)
944	Worms	Emp. Henry III	1046–56	Dbg 848	1.47
945–63	Worms	K. Henry IV	1056–84	Dbg 846; Leimus 2000	1.12, 1.12, 1.09, 1.08, 1.06, 1.04, 1.02, 1.02, 1.02, 1.01, 0.98, 0.98, 0.97, 0.96, 0.93, 0.86, 0.82, 0.49 (cut halfpenny), 0.42 (frg)
964–6	Speyer	Otto II–III	973–1002	Dbg 825	1.10, 1.05, 0.81
967–80	Speyer	anon	(1002–39)	Dbg 836; Berghaus 1954, p. 213	1.12, 1.09, 0.99, 0.94, 0.93, 0.93, 0.91, 0.90, 0.90, 0.88, 0.86, 0.84, 0.78, 0.73, 0.66 (frg)
981–93	Speyer	K. Henry III	1039–46	Dbg 830	1.13, 1.11, 1.04, 0.96, 0.89, 0.86, 0.83, 0.80, 0.77, 0.76, 0.67, 0.65

Mint	Ruler	Date	Reference	Wt (g)
994–1001 Speyer	Henry III	1039–56	Dbg 829; Berghaus 1954, p. 213	1.51, 1.45, 1.35, 1.03, 0.97, 0.96 (pierced), 0.75, 0.72,
1002 Speyer	anon	(1039–56)	Dbg 837; Ehrend 1976, 2/30	0.46 (frg)
1003–5 Speyer	Emp. Henry III	1046–56	Dbg 830c; Ehrend 1976, 2/19	1.21, 1.09, 0.89
1006–7 Speyer	Emp. Henry III	1046–56	Dbg 832; Berghaus 1954, p. 213	1.19 (rivet), 1.15
1008–10 Speyer	Emp. Henry III	1046–56	Dbg 833	1.24 (pierced), 1.06, 0.54 (frg)
1011–17 Speyer	Emp. Henry III	1046–56	Dbg 834–835; Ehrend 1976, 2/12–13	1.45, 1.19, 1.14, 1.04, 1.00, 0.95, 0.86
1018–21 Speyer	anon	(1046–56)	Dbg 838; Berghaus 1954, p. 213	1.31, 1.09, 1.00, 0.97
1022–5 Speyer	K. Henry IV	1056–84	Dbg 831	1.19, 1.17, 1.01, 1.01,
1026–8 Speyer	Bp Conrad	1056–60	Dbg 839	1.01, 0.99, 0.89
1029 Copies of Speyer			Cf. Dbg 827, 836	1.17
SWABIA				
1030 Strassburg	Emp. Henry II	1014–24	Dbg 920	1.15
1031–3 Strassburg	Conrad II	1024–39	Dbg 921	1.35 (pierced), 1.32, 1.18
1034–6 Strassburg	Conrad II	1024–39	Dbg 922	1.30, 0.87 (frg), 0.35 (frg, rivet)
1037 Strassburg	Conrad II	1024–39	Dbg 923	1.35
1038 Strassburg	Conrad II	1024–39	Dbg 707	1.27
1039–43 Strassburg	Henry III	1039–56	Dbg 709	1.44, 1.29, 1.26, 1.17, 1.09
1044–7 Strassburg	Conrad II or Henry III		Dbg 707 or 709	1.36, 1.29 (pierced), 1.20, 1.07

	Mint	Ruler	Date	Reference	Wt (g)
1048–51	Strassburg	anon		Dbg 715	1.11, 1.10, 0.95, 0.93,
1052	Strassburg	anon		Dbg 716	1.20
1053–4	Ulm	anon		Klein 1993, 50–55	0.97, 0.86
1055–7	Esslingen	Henry II	1002–24	Dbg 951–952; Klein & Raff 1997, 4	1.10, 0.82, 0.73,
1058	Esslingen	Henry II – Conrad II		Klein & Raff 1997, 8	1.10
1059	Esslingen	Henry II–III		Dbg 1272, 2; Klein & Raff 1997, 12	0.86
1060	Basel	Bp Adalbero	999–1025	Dbg 1281; Klein 2001, type 14	0.74
1061	Basel?	Bp Adalbero	999–1025	CNS 1.3.34,469; 3.4.59, 319–321	0.83
1062	Augsburg	Bp Bruno, 2nd per, 3rd type		Hahn 1976, III, 147b	1.12
1063	Augsburg	K. Conrad II	1024–27	Hahn 1976, 148	1.06
1064	Augsburg	Bp Eberhard I	1032–39	Hahn 1976, 151A1	1.22
1065	Augsburg	anon episcopal	1042–47	Hahn 1976, 155	1.04
BAVARIA					
1066	Regensburg	Duke Henry IV		Hahn 1976, IIIBd2	1.50
1067–8	Regensburg	Emp. Conrad II & K. Henry III	1027–39	Hahn 1976, 35B	1.49, 0.88
1069–70	Regensburg	K. Henry III, 2nd per.	1039–42	Hahn 1976, 38A	1.31 (pierced), 1.26
1071	Regensburg	K. Henry III, 2nd per.	1039–42	Hahn 1976, 42A, Obol	0.69

	Mint	Ruler	Date	Reference	Wt (g)
1072	Regensburg	K. Henry III, 2nd per.	1039–42	Hahn 1976, 43A	0.81
1073	Regensburg	K. Henry III, 3rd per.	1042–47	Hahn 1976, 44	0.99
1074	Regensburg	Emp. Henry III, 4th per.	1047–56	Hahn 1976, 48A	1.09
1075–7	Regensburg	Emp. Henry III	1046–56	Hahn 1976, 60	1.22, 0.69, 0.53 (frg)
1078–9	Regensburg	K. Henry IV	1056–84	Hahn 1976, 54	1.10, 0.93
1080	Regensburg	Bp Gebhard III, 2nd per.	1056–60	Hahn 1976, 57	1.29
1081	Eichstätt	Emp. Henry III	1046–56	Hahn 1976, 124	1.48

UNCERTAIN

	Mint	Ruler	Date	Reference	Wt (g)
1082	'Hevonacum'			Dbg 1194	1.10
1083	Uncertain mint			Dbg 1214	1.04
1084–9	Uncertain mint				1.49, 1.38, 1.17, 0.85, 0.79, 0.19 (frg)
1090–9	Uncertain mint	imitations			1.55, 1.35, 1.19, 1.13, 1.09, 1.02, 1.01, 0.95, 0.65, 0.32 (frg)
1100–9	Uncertain mint	completely worn			1.80, 1.58, 1.40, 1.37, 1.22, 1.20, 1.14, 0.84, 0.77, 0.50 (frg)

ITALIAN COINS

	Mint	Ruler	Date	Reference	Wt (g)
1110	Pavia	Emp. Henry II	1014–24	CNI 4:2	1.00

BOHEMIAN COINS

	Mint	Ruler	Date	Reference	Wt (g)
1111	Prague	Duke Boleslav II	967–99	Cach 1970, 122	1.31 (pierced)

Mint	Ruler	Date	Reference	Wt (g)
1112	Prague	Duke Oldřich	1012–34	Cach 1970, 296	0.87

HUNGARIAN COINS

1113–15	(Gran)	K. Stefan I	1000–38	Huszár 1979, 1	0.96, 0.85, 0.67
1116–17	(Gran)	K. Peter	1038–41	Huszár 1979, 6	0.63, 0.60
1118	(Gran)	K. Andreas	1046–60	Huszár 1979, 8	0.57
1119–22	(Gran)	K. Andreas	1046–60	Huszár 1979, 9	0.72, 0.69, 0.67, 0.55

Mint	Moneyer	Wt (g)

ANGLO-SAXON COINS

Æthelred II (978–1016)

Crux (BMC iiia, Hild. C)

1123	Hertford	Beornwulf (Beornulf)	1.58 (pierced)
1124	London	Leofstan	1.21
1125	London	unknown moneyer	0.68 (cut halfpenny)
1126	Rochester	Siduwine (Sidwine)	1.63
1127	Thetford	Godman	1.42
1128	Winchester	Beorhtnoth (Birhtnoth)	1.64
129	York	Asketill (Oscel)	1.85

Long Cross (BMC iva, Hild. D)

1130	Bath	Eadstan (Edstan)	1.70
1131	Bath	Hildsige	1.61 (pierced)
1132	Bedford	Leofnoth	1.65

	Mint	Moneyer	Wt (g)
1133	Dover	Cynsige (Cynsige)	1.64
1134	Exeter	Dunstan	1.44
1135–6	Huntingdon	Asgautr (Osgut)	1.71, 1.54 (pierced)
1137–8	Lincoln	Asgautr (Osgut)	1.65, 1.60
1139	London	Æthelweard (Æthelwerd)	1.67
1140	London	Brunstan	1.83 (pierced)
1141–2	Lydford	Goda	1.65, 0.87 (cut halfpenny)
1143	Northampton	Leofgod	1.48
1144	Rochester	Eadweard (Eadwerd)	1.72
1145	Southampton	Spilmann (Spileman)	1.52
1146–7	Wilton	Sæwine	1.72, 1.60 (pierced)
1148	York	Ulfketill (Ulfgitel)	1.37 (pierced)

Helmet (*BMC* viii, *Hild. E*)

	Mint	Moneyer	Wt (g)
1149	Lincoln	Sunegod	1.41
1150	Lincoln	Wulfwine	1.50
1151	London	Æthelmær	1.43
1152	Winchester	Æthelgar	1.46

Last Small Cross (*BMC* i, *Hild. A*)

	Mint	Moneyer	Wt (g)
1153	Exeter	Carla	1.39
1154	Lewes	Leofa	1.20
1155	Lincoln	Wulfric (Wulric)	0.90
1156	London	Ælfgeat (Elfget)	1.10
1157	London	Æthelwine (Æthelwne)	1.03

	Mint	Moneyer	Wt (g)
1158–9	London	Beorhtferth (Birhtferth)	1.39, 0.89
1160	London	Godman, ψ on the rev.	1.30
1161	London	Godwine	1.55
1162–3	London	Leofwine (Leofwine, Leofine)	1.15, 1.09
1164	Norwich	Eadwacer (Edwecær)	1.23
1165	Norwich	Wulfmær (Wulfmr)	1.24
1166	Salisbury	Sæmann (Sæman)	1.15
1167	Southwark	Ælfwine	1.28 (pierced)
1168	Wallingford	Æelfweard (Ælfwerd)	1.73 (double struck)
1169	Winchester	Ælfstan	1.40
1170	uncertain mint?	uncertain moneyer?	0.43 (cut centre of coin)

Cnut (1016–35)

Quatrefoil (BMC viii, Hild. E)

	Mint	Moneyer	Wt (g)
1171	Bath	Æthelstan (Æthestan)	1.08
1172	Cambridge	Orest (Oroeset)	0.96
1173	Colchester	Godric	0.95
1174	Exeter	Godwine (Gdwine)	0.94
1175	Exeter	Hunwine (Hunewine)	0.85
1176	Lewes	Leofnoth (Leofnod)	1.34
1177	Lincoln	Sumarlithr (Sumerlth)	1.08
1178	Lincoln	Wulfwine	1.28
1179	London	Eadweald (Eadwold)	0.99
1180	London	Wulfwine	1.12

	Mint	Moneyer	Wt (g)
1181–2	Maldon	Ælfwine (Ælwinei)	0.76, 0.75
1183	North/Southampton	Leofwine (Liofwine)	0.92
1184	Norwich	Æthelric	1.14
1185	Stamford	Capelin (Caplin)	1.00
1186	Sudbury	Sperling (Sprlinc)	0.83
1187	York	Authgrimr (Outhgrim)	0.96
1188	York	Frithkollr (Frithcol)	1.01
1189	York	Kolgrimr (Colgrim)	0.95
1190	York	Ulfgrimr (Ulfgrim)	1.04

Pointed Helmet (BMC xiv, Hild. G)

	Mint	Moneyer	Wt (g)
1191	Canterbury	Eadwine (Edwine)	1.13
1192	Canterbury	Leofnoth	0.86 (pierced)
1193	Dover	Leofwine	0.97
1194	Exeter	Eadmar (Edmar)	0.87
1195	Gloucester	Bolla	0.99
1196	Lincoln	Bruntat	1.15
1197	Lincoln	Iosteinn (Gustin)	1.02
1198	Lincoln	Leofwine	0.95
1199	Lincoln	Matathan	1.10
1200	London	Ælfweard (Ælfwerd)	1.04
1201–3	London	Ælfwine	1.11, 1.04, 0.97
1204	London	Bruning (Bruninc)	0.97
1205	London	Godhere (Godere)	1.02

	Mint	Moneyer	Wt (g)
1206	London	Godric (Gotric)	0.77
1207	London	Leofric (Lifric)	1.08
1208	London	Wulfric (Wulric)	0.92
1209	Norwich	Manna	1.08
1210	Oxford	Wulfwine	1.14
1211	Stamford	Thorulfr (Thurulf)	1.00
1212	Thetford	Leofing (Lifincc)	1.02
1213	Thetford	Wineman	1.03
1214	Wallingford	Eadweard (Edwerd)	1.11 (pierced)
1215	Winchester	Ælfstan	1.15
1216	York	Crinan	1.00
1217	York	Crucan	0.97
1218	York	Fargrimr (Fargrim)	0.99
1219	York	Grimulfr (Grimolf)	1.00
1220	York	Grurn (pellet in the 1st quarter of the cross)	1.03
1221	York	Hildulfr (Hildolf)	0.96
1222	York	Iri (Ire)	0.99
1223	York	Sunnulfr (Sunolf)	1.04
1224	uncertain mint?	(... werd)	0.54
Short Cross (BMC xvi, Hild. H)			
1225	Canterbury	Wynræd (Winred)	1.16
1226	Colchester	Wulfwine	1.15
1227	Dover	Leofwine	0.87

	Mint	Moneyer	Wt (g)
1228	Exeter	Huna (Hunni)	0.85
1229	Gloucester	Æthelric (Ægelric)	1.15
1230	Hastings	Ælfweard (Ælfwerd)	1.02
1231	Leicester	Wulfstan (Wulstan)	1.13
1232	Lincoln	Ælfnoth	1.05
1233	Lincoln	Harthknut (Harthcnut)	0.89
1234	Lincoln	Leofwine	1.20
1235	Lincoln	Svertingr (Swertinc)	0.89
1236	London	Ælfwig (Ælfwii)	1.06
1237	London	Brungar	1.18
1238	London	Æthelræd (Edred)	1.12
1239–40	London	Eadwulf (Eadulf)	1.05, 0.94
1241	London	Eadweard (Edwerd)	1.13
1242	London	Eadwine (Edwine)	1.15
1243	London	Goda (Godd)	0.92
1244	London	uncertain moneyer (…ic)	0.59 (frg)
1245	Shaftesbury	Æthelric (Æleric)	0.94
1246	Shrewsbury	Eadsige (Etsige)	1.15
1247	Stamford	Leofwine	1.03
1248	Thetford	Ælfwine	1.06
1249	Thetford	Brunstan	1.16
1250	Wallingford	Ælfwine	1.17
1251	York	Grimulfr (Grimulf)	1.12
1252	York	Authunn (Othin)	1.08

	Mint	Moneyer	Wt (g)
	Harold I (1035–40)		
	Jewel Cross (BMC i, Hild. A)		
1253	Canterbury	Beorhtræd (Brihtred)	0.99 (pierced)
1254	Chester	Æthelwine (Elewine)	1.12
1255	Gloucester	Æthelric (Ægelric)	1.13
1256–7	Hereford	Æthelwig (Elewig)	1.15, 1.12
1258	Lincoln	Asleikr (Oslac)	1.14
1259	Thetford	Ælfwine	1.01
	Fleur-de-Lis (BMC v, vi, Hild. B)		
1260	Ipswich	Leofing (Lifinc)	1.00
1261	Lincoln	Godric	0.99
1262	London	Brungar	1.13
1263	London	Eadric (Edric)	1.13
1264	London	Leofræd (Leofred)	1.14
1265	York	Srykollr (Stircol)	0.99
	Harthacnut (1035–37, 1040–2)		
	Jewel Cross (BMC i, Hild. A)		
1266	Warwick	Sigeweard (Siwerd), bust right	1.15
	Arm and Sceptre (BMC ii, xvii, Hild. B, I)		
1267	Lincoln	Matathan (Mathann)	1.16
1268	London	Godwine, with the name of Cnut on the *obv*.	0.85
1269	Oxford	Leofwing (Lifinc)	1.20
1270	Wallingford	Leofwine	1.09

	Mint	Moneyer	Wt (g)
	Edward the Confessor (1042–66)		
	Pacx (BMC iv, Hild. D)		
1271	Chester	Bruning (Brunin)	1.11
1272	London	uncertain moneyer	0.52 (cut halfpenny)
	Radiate/Small Cross (BMC i, Hild. A)		
1273	Lincoln	Ælfnoth	1.02
1274	Lincoln	Godric	1.03
1275	Lincoln	Udee (Udfe)	1.06
1276	London	Godman	1.08
1277	London	Wulfrad (Wulfred)	0.97
1278	London	uncertain moneyer (G ....)	0.47 (cut halfpenny)
1279	Shaftesbury	Ælwerd (Ælfweard)	1.12
	Trefoil Quadrilateral (BMC iii, Hild. C)		
1280	Colchester	Brunhyse	1.09
1281	London	Æthelwig (Æglwi)	0.86
1282	London	Leofing (Lyfincc)	0.96
1283	Norwich	Godwine	1.12
	Expanding Cross (BMC vi, Hild. E)		
1284	Bristol	Æthelstan (Æthestan)	0.85 (cut halfpenny)
1285	Wilton	Ælfweald (Ælfwald)	1.03
	Pointed Helmet (BMC vii, Hild. F)		
1286	Norwich	Thorfrithr (Thurfiorth)	1.13

HIBERNO-NORSE COINS

Sihtric (989–1036)

	Type	Mint		
1287	Crux	Dublin	Fastulfr (Fastolf)	1.70
1288–9	Long Cross	Dublin	Farmann (Færemin)	1.45, 1.32
1290	Long Cross, phase 3 (c.1035–55)	Dublin		0.85

Type   Mint

ANGLO-SCANDINAVIAN COINS

'Æthelred II'

	Type	Mint		
1291	Long Cross	mint?	Malmer 1997, 2252	0.99
1292	Long Cross/Last Small Cross	mint? ('South', 'Cambridge')	Malmer 1997, 378/1702	1.32
1293	Last Small Cross	mint?	Malmer 1997, 601/1791	1.29
1294	Last Small Cross	mint? ('South')	Malmer 1997, 604/1759	1.68

'Cnut'

	Type	Mint		
1295	Quatrefoil/Long Cross	mint? ('South' or 'North')	Malmer 1997, 739/1375	1.57
1296	Qatrefoil	mint?	+EO LÐO NOL ÐVS	1.46
1297	Pointed Helmet	mint?	Bust right, blundered legends	1.08

	Mint	Moneyer	Reference	Wt (g)
	DANISH COINS			
	Cnut (1018–35)			
1298–302	Lund	Alfnoth, Aslac, Alfward, Thorcetl, [As]lac	Hbg 1 (with the name of Hardeknud)	1.16, 1.00, 0.95, 0.91, 0.45 (cut halfpenny)
1303–5	Lund		Hbg 20 (Knud) or 1 (Hardeknud), blundered	1.01, 0.91, 0.89
1306	Slagelse		Var. Hbg 39/38	0.78
1307	Viborg		Hbg 49	0.88
1308–10	Ørbæk		Hbg 54	0.84, 0.82, 0.44 (cut halfpenny)
	Harthacnut (1035–42)			
1311	Lund	Asferth	Hbg 9; Becker 1981, H13/47	1.00
1312	Lund		Hbg 9, blundered	0.65
1313	Lund	'Rovec'	Var. Hbg 9, *rev.* ¤, +, – in the angles	1.05
1314	Lund	Tooci	Becker 1981, H35/226	0.91 (pierced)
1315	Aarhus		Hbg 44	0.69
1316	Hedeby		Var. Hbg 49, bust right	0.77
1317	Viborg		Hbg 43	0.80
	Magnus (1042–47)			
1318	Lund	Thursthn	Hbg 5; Becker 1981, M3/221	0.45 (cut halfpenny)
1319	Lund		Becker 1981, MX32/323	1.06
1320	Lund	Carl	Becker 1981, M15/65	1.05
1321	Lund		Hbg12	0.90
1322	Roskilde		Hbg 23	0.89

	Mint	Moneyer	Reference	Wt (g)
1323	Odense?		Var. Hbg 30?	0.42 (cut halfpenny)
1324	Hedeby		Hbg 36	0.73

Sven Estridsen (1047–75)

	Mint	Moneyer	Reference	Wt (g)
1325	Lund		Hbg 3	0.72
1326–9	Lund		Hbg 6	1.03, 0.99, 0.98, 0.50 (cut halfpenny)
1330	Lund		Hbg 6 var., rev. Short Cross	1.23
1331–2	Lund		Hbg 6/8	1.03, 0.45 (cut halfpenny)
1333–5	Lund		Hbg 8	1.08 (pierced), 0.97, 0.96,
1336	Lund		Var. Hbg 8, crescent in each angle	0.97
1337–8	Lund		Hbg 11	1.01, 0.94
1339	Lund		Hbg 21	1.05
1340–1	Lund	Sticar, Thorer	Var. Hbg 28, Jesus holding scales	0.96, 0.91
1342–5	Lund	Uoil, Styrkar, Thorkil, [Sa]ekrim	Hbg 30	1.07, 1.01, 0.97, 0.90
1346	Roskilde		Hbg 36	0.95
1347–8	Viborg		Hbg 56	0.69, 0.69 (pierced)
1349	Viborg		Hbg 56a	0.72
1350–2	Viborg		Hbg 57, var.	0.74, 0.74, 0.74
1353	Hedeby		Var. Hbg 70, rev. ¤ in the 1st quarter	0.80

	Type	Mint	Reference	Wt (g)
	SWEDISH COINS			
	Olaf Skötkonung			
1354	Crux	Sigtuna	Malmer 1989, 17/69	3.23
	'Æthelred II'			
1355	Long Cross	Sigtuna	Malmer 1989, 246/703	1.39
1356	Long Cross	Sigtuna	Malmer, 281/1286	1.77
1357	Helmet/Long Cross	Sigtuna	Malmer 1989, 301/601	1.36

Note: A few additional coins came to light through ploughing on the site of the hoard after the completion of this appendix. These included four German coins: Deventer, Henry IV and Bp Bernold, Dbg 571, 0.99g; Gittelde?, imitation of Otto-Adelheide-Pfennige, Hatz 1961, V, 0.98g; Speyer, anon., Dbg 836, 0. 95g; another as last, 0.86g. Also found were a fragment of an Anglo-Scandinavian Long Cross/Small Cross penny (0.53g) and a piece of sheet silver (2.56g).

Key to Bibliographic Abbreviations:

Albrecht 1959: G. Albrecht, *Das Münzwesen im niederlothringischen und friesischen Raum vom 10. bis zum beginnenden 12. Jahrhundert*, Numismatische Studien, 6 (Hamburg, 1959).

Becker 1981: C.J. Becker, 'The Coinage of Harthacnut and Magnus the Good at Lund *c.* 1040–*c.* 1046', in *Studies in Northern Coinages of the Eleventh Century*, ed. C. J. Becker, Det Kongelige Danske Videnskabernes Selskab. Historisk-filosofiske Skrifter, 9.4 (Copenhagen, 1981), 119–74.

Berghaus 1954: P. Berghaus, 'Beiträge zur deutschen Münzkunde des 11. Jahrhunderts', *Hamburger Beiträge zur Numismatik, 8* (1954), 207–23.

Berghaus 1978: P. Berghaus, *Die Münzen von Dortmund*, Dortmunder Münzgeschichte, 1(Dortmund, 1978).

Berghaus 1983: P. Berghaus, 'Duisburger Münzen', in *Duisburg im Mittelalter, 1100 Jahre Duisburg 883–1983, Begleitschrift zur Ausstellung*, ed. J. Milz and G. Krause (Duisburg, 1983), 89–113.

Cach 1970: F. Cach, *Nejstar i české mince* (4 vols, Prague, 1970).

CNG: B. Kluge, 'Conspectus Nummorum Germaniae Medii Aevi (CNG). Kommentierter Typenkatalog der deutschen Münzen des Mittelalters – von den Anfängen bis zur Ausbildung der regionalen Pfennigmünze, von 880 bis um 1140', *Geldgeschichtliche Nachrichten, 192–4* (1999), *197–200* (2000), *204* (2001).

CNI 4: *Corpus Nummorum Italicorum 4. Lombardia* (Rome, 1913).

CNS: *Corpus Nummorum Saeculorum IX–XI qui in Suecia reperti sunt* (Stockhom, 1975–).

Dbg: H. Dannenberg, *Die deutschen Münzen der sächsischen und fränkischen Kaiserzeit*, 4 vols (Berlin, 1876–1905).

Ehrend 1976: H. Ehrend, *Speyerer Münzgeschichte* (Speyer, 1976).

Giesen 2008: K. Giesen, 'Überlegungen zum Typ Dannenberg 1311', *Jaarboek voor Munt- en Penningkunde, 95* (Amsterdam 2008), 65–83.

Giesen 2012: K. Giesen, 'Die Hälblinge der Otto-Adelheid-Pfennige. Fundanalyse und Stempelvergleich', in *Nummi docent! Münzen – Schätze – Funde. Festschrift für Peter Ilisch zum 65. Geburtstag am 28. April 2012*, ed. G. Dethlefs, A. Pol and S. Wittenbrink (Osnabrück, 2012), 99–110.

Hahn 1976: W. Hahn, *Moneta Radasponensis, Bayerns Münzprägung im 9., 10. und 11. Jahrhundert* (Braunschweig, 1976).

Hatz 1961: V. Hatz, 'Zur Frage der Otto-Adelheide-Pfennige. Versuch einer Systematisierung aud Grund des schwedischen Fundmaterials', in *Comm. 1*, 107–51.

Hatz 1967: G. Hatz, 'Anmerkungen zu einigen deutschen Münzen des 11. Jahrhunderts (VI)', *Hamburger Beiträge zur Numismatik, 21* (1967), 39–52.

Hatz 1968: G. Hatz, 'Tieler Denare des 11. Jahrhunderts in den schwedischen Funden', in Comm. 2, 97–190.

Hbg: P. Hauberg, *Myntforhold og udmyntninger i Danmark indtil 1146*, Det Kongelige Danske Videnskabernes Selskaps Skrifter, 6. Række, histor.-filosof. Afd., 5, 1 (Copenhagen, 1906).

Huszár 1979: L. Huszár, *Münzkatalog Ungarn von 1000 bis heute* (Budapest and Munich, 1979).

Häv.: W. Hävernick, *Die Münzen von Köln. Die Münzen und Medaillen von Köln 1* (Cologne, 1935).

Ilisch 1977: P. Ilisch, 'Die Anfänge der Münzprägung in Minden', in *Zwischen Dom und Ratshaus, Beiträge zur Kunst- und Kulturgeschichte der Stadt Minden*, ed. H. Nordsiek (Minden, 1977), 37–59.

Ilisch 1981: P. Ilisch, 'Eine Gruppe niederlothringischer Pfennige Heinrichs II. und Konrads II', in *Lagom, Festschrift für Peter Berghaus zum 60. Geburtstag am 20. November 1979*, ed. T. Fischer, P. Ilisch and A. Betken (Münster, 1981), 149–64.

Ilisch 1987: P. Ilisch, 'À propos des imitations mosanes des deniers de Cologne du Xe siècle', *RBN, 133* (1987), 103–7.

Ilisch 1990: P. Ilisch, 'Zur datierung der in nordischen Funden vorkommenden ottonischen Münzen von Köln', *Nordisk Numismatisk Årsskrift, 1983/84* (1990), 123–144.

Ilisch 2004: P. Ilisch, *Die Fritzlarer Colonia-Prägung des 11. Jahrhunderts*, Beiträge zur Münzkunde in Hessen-Kassel, 21 (Kassel, 2004).

Ilisch & Jonsson 1993: P. Ilisch and K. Jonsson, 'En ärkebiskoplig mynttyp präglad i Bremen?', *Nordisk Numismatisk Unions Medlemsblad, 7* (1993), 120–5.

Jammer 1952: V. Jammer, *Die Anfänge der Münzprägung im Herzogtum Sachsen, 10. und 11. Jahrhundert*, Numismatische Studien, 3–4 (Hamburg, 1952).

Johansson 1997: M. Johansson, *Den vikingatida myntningen i Groningen*. B-uppsats i Arkeologi, Stockholms Universitet (Stockholm, 1997).

Jonsson 2012: K. Jonsson, 'The coinage of Tiel c. 980–1100', in *Nummi docent! Münzen – Schätze – Funde. Festschrift für Peter Ilisch zum 65. Geburtstag am 28. April 2012*, ed. G. Dethlefs, A. Pol and S. Wittenbrink (Osnabrück, 2012), 151–64.

Kilger 2000: C. Kilger, *Pfennigmärkte und Währungslandschaften. Monetarisierungen im sächsische-slawischen Grenzland ca. 965–1120*, Comm. n.s., 15 (Stockholm, 2000).

Kjellgren 1993: R. Kjellgren, *Myntningen i Friesland munder vikingatiden*, C-uppsats i arkeologi, Stockholms Universitet (Stockholm, 1993).

Klein 1993: U. Klein, 'Die Münzprägung im südwestlichen Schwaben. Stand und Aufgaben der Forschung', in *Fernhandel und Geldwirtschaft. Beiträge*

zum deutschen Münzwesen in sächsischer und salischer Zeit. Ergebnisse des
Dannenberg-Kolloquiums 1990, ed. B. Kluge (Sigmaringen, 1993), 89–109.

Klein 2001: U. Klein, 'Ein schwäbisch-alemannischer Münzschatz aus der Zeit
um 1050', *Schweizerische Numismatische Rundschau, 80* (2001), 139–70.

Klein & Raff 1997: U. Klein and A. Raff, *Die Münzen und Medaillen von
Esslingen. Süddeutsche Münzkataloge 7* (Stuttgart, 1997).

Krumbach 1995: K.G. Krumbach, *Aachener Münzen des Mittelalters* (Aachen,
1995).

Leimus 1993: I. Leimus, 'Einige Bemerkungen zu den Wormser Denaren
vom Typ Dannenberg 845', in *Fernhandel und Geldwirtschaft. Beiträge
zum deutschen Münzwesen in sächsischer und salischer Zeit. Ergebnisse des
Dannenberg-Kolloquiums 1990*, ed. B. Kluge (Sigmaringen, 1993), 119–24.

Leimus 2000: I. Leimus, 'Dbg. 846 – eine Prägung von Heinrich III. oder
Heinrich IV.?', *Geldgeschichtliche Nachrichten, 196* (2000), 57–61.

Leimus 2002: I. Leimus, 'Ein neuer westfälischer COLONIA-Münztyp des 11.
Jahrhunderts', in *Moneta mediaevalis. Studia numizmaticzne i historyczne
ofiarowane Profesorowi Stanisławowi Suchodolskiemu w 65. rocznicę urodzin*,
ed. R. Kiersnowski (Warsaw, 2002), 393–8.

Malmer 1989: B. Malmer, *The Sigtuna Coinage c. 995–1005*, Comm. n.s., 4
(Stockholm and London, 1989).

Malmer 1997: B. Malmer, *The Anglo-Scandinavian Coinage c. 995–1020*,
Comm. n.s., 9 (Stockholm and London, 1997).

Mehl 1995: M. Mehl, *Die Münzen des Bistums Hildesheim 1. Vom Beginn
der Prägung bis zum Jahre 1435*, Quellen und Dokumentationen zur
Stadtgeschichte Hildesheims, 5 (Hildesheim, 1995).

Mehl 2011: M. Mehl, *Münz- und Geldgeschichte des Erzbistums Magdeburg im
Mittelater*, 2 vols (Hamburg, 2011).

Petry 1995: K. Petry, 'Der Münzschatz von Remagen, Kreis Ahrweiler', in
Berichte zur Archäologie an Mittelrhein und Mosel, 4, Trierer Zeitschrift
für Geschichte und Kunst des Trierer Landes und seiner Nachbargebiete.
Beiheft, 20 (Trier, 1995), 277–304.

Schulten 2011: P. N. Schulten, 'Ezzonen (Erenfriede, Hezelinen)',
Geldgeschichtliche Nachrichten, 253 (2011), 13–20.

Stoess 1989: Ch. Stoess, 'Die frühesten Erfurter Münzen', in *Festschrift für Peter
Berghaus zum 70. Geburtstag*, ed. T. Albrecht and A. Sander-Berke (Münster,
1989), 1–10.

Treadwell 2001: L. Treadwell, *Buyid Coinage. A Die Corpus (322–445 A.H.)*
(Oxford, 2001).

Watz 1992: A. Watz, *Vikingatida tyska mynt. En analys av mynt präglade i
Deventer*. C-uppsats i Arkeologi, Stockholms Universitet (Stockholm,
1992).

Index

The letters ä, å, ö, ø are alphabetised as a and o, and æ as ae. The appendices to chapters 10, 24 and 25 have not been indexed.

For Product Safety Concerns and Information please contact our EU
representative GPSR@taylorandfrancis.com Taylor & Francis Verlag GmbH,
Kaufingerstraße 24, 80331 München, Germany

Printed and bound by CPI Group (UK) Ltd, Croydon, CR0 4YY
01/05/2025
01858417-0001